W9-ARQ-531

Political and Physical Map of the United States

Cape Flattery

Olympia ★
Mt. St. Helens
8,366 ft.
(2,550 m) ▲
Seattle •
Spokane •
WASHINGTON
RANGE
Columbia River

Portland •
Salem ★
Eugene •
OREGON
CASCADE RANGES

Cape Blanco

Cape Mendocino

COAST RANGES
Sacramento River
CENTRAL VALLEY
SIERRA NEVADA
Reno •
Carson City ★
Lake Tahoe
Sacramento ★
San Francisco Bay
San Francisco •
San Joaquin River

NEVADA

GREAT BASIN

GREAT SALT LAKE
Great Salt Lake
Ogden •
★ Salt Lake City
• Provo
UTAH
Green River

Mt. Whitney
14,500 ft.
(4,400 m) ▲
DEATH VALLEY
Las Vegas •
River
COLORADO PLATEAU

Los Angeles •
CALIFORNIA
RANGES
MOJAVE DESERT

San Diego •
Salton Sea
Colorado River

ARIZONA
Phoenix ★
• Mesa

Tucson •

Mt. Rainier
14,410 ft.
(4,300 m) ▲
Columbia River

ROCKY MOUNTAINS
COLUMBIA PLATEAU

Great Falls •
Helena ★
MONTANA
• Billings

IDAHO
Boise •
Idaho Falls •
Snake River
Pocatello •

WYOMING
Casper •

North Platte River
Laramie •
Cheyenne ★
ROCKY MOUNTAINS
Longs Peak
14,256 ft.
(4,344 m) ▲
South Platte River

Mt. Elbert
14,433 ft.
(4,400 m) ▲
Colorado River
★ Denver
COLORADO
• Colorado Springs
Pikes Peak
14,110 ft.
(4,300 m) ▲ • Pueblo
Arkansas River

COLORADO PLATEAU

Albuquerque •
★ Santa Fe
NEW MEXICO
Rio Grande
Las Cruces •
LLANO ESTACADO

NORTH DAKOTA
Bismarck ★

SOUTH DAKOTA
Rapid City •
BLACK HILLS
★ Pierre

GREAT PLAINS
NEBRASKA
Grand Island •
Platte River

KANSAS
Wichita •

OKLAHOMA
Oklahoma City •
• Lawto

TEXAS
Brazos River

Austin ★
San Antonio •
Rio Grande

MEXICO

ATLANTIC

PACIFIC OCEAN

Hawaii inset
KAUAI
OAHU
Honolulu ★
MOLOKAI
LANAI
HAWAII
MAUI
PACIFIC OCEAN
Hilo •
HAWAII
0   50 Miles
0   50 Kilometers
22°N
155°W
160°W
19°N

Alaska inset
SOVIET UNION
ARCTIC OCEAN
70°N
BROOKS RANGE
Arctic Circle
ALASKA
Yukon River
• Fairbanks
CANADA
ALASKA RANGE
Mt. McKinley
20,320 ft.
(6,194 m) ▲
• Anchorage
KENAI PENINSULA
Gulf of Alaska
Juneau ★
KODIAK I.
Bering Strait

BERING SEA
PACIFIC OCEAN
ALEUTIAN ISLANDS
0   250 Miles
0   250 Kilometers
60°N
140°W
150°W
160°W
170°W
170°E

Scott, Foresman and Company

Glenview, Illinois
London, England

VOLUME II: FROM 1865

America
PAST
AND PRESENT

Robert A. Divine
University of Texas

T. H. Breen
Northwestern University

George M. Fredrickson
Northwestern University

R. Hal Williams
Southern Methodist University

Library of Congress Cataloging in Publication Data
Main entry under title:
America, past and present.
  Includes bibliographies and index.
  1. United States—History. I. Divine, Robert A.
E178.1.A4894 1984   973   83-19146

ISBN 0-673-15420-3
ISBN 0-673-15882-9 (soft : v. 1)
ISBN 0-673-15883-7 (soft : v. 2)

About the Authors

Robert A. Divine

Robert A. Divine, the George W. Littlefield Professor in American History at the University of Texas at Austin, received his Ph.D. degree from Yale University in 1954. A specialist in American diplomatic history, he has taught at the University of Texas since 1954, where he has been honored by the Student Association for teaching excellence. His extensive published work includes *The Illusion of Neutrality* (1962), *Second Chance: The Triumph of Internationalism in America During World War II* (1967) and *Blowing on the Wind* (1978). His most recent book is *Eisenhower and the Cold War* (1981). In 1962–1963, he was a fellow at the Center for Advanced Study in the Behavioral Sciences and in 1968 he gave the Albert Shaw Lectures in Diplomatic History at Johns Hopkins University.

T. H. Breen

T. H. Breen received his Ph.D. from Yale University in 1968. Since 1975 he has been a Professor of History and American Culture at Northwestern University. Breen's major books include *The Character of the Good Ruler: A Study of Puritan Political Ideas in New England* (1970), *Puritans and Adventurers: Change and Persistence in Early America* (1980), and with S. Innes of the University of Virginia, *"Myne Owne Ground": Race and Freedom on Virginia's Eastern Shore* (1980). In addition to receiving an award for outstanding teaching at Northwestern, Breen has been the recipient of research grants from the American Council of Learned Societies, the Guggenheim Foundation, the Institute for Advanced Study (Princeton), and the National Humanities Center. He is currently preparing a volume for the Oxford University Press *History of the United States in Early America*.

George M. Fredrickson

George M. Fredrickson is William Smith Mason Professor of American History at Northwestern University. He is the author or editor of several books, including *The Inner Civil War* (1965), *The Black Image in the White Mind* (1971), and *A Nation Divided* (1975). His latest work, *White Supremacy: A Comparative Study in American and South African History* (1981) won both the Ralph Waldo Emerson Award from Phi Beta Kappa and the Merle Curti Award from the Organization of American Historians. He received both the A.B. and Ph.D. degrees from Harvard and has been the recipient of a Guggenheim Fellowship, a National Endowment for the Humanities Senior Fellowship, and a Fellowship from the Center for Advanced Studies in the Behavioral Sciences. While teaching at Northwestern, he has also served as Fulbright lecturer in American History at Moscow University and as a Mellon visiting professor at Rice University.

R. Hal Williams

R. Hal Williams has been Dean of Dedman College at Southern Methodist University since 1980. He received his A.B. degree from Princeton University (1963) and his Ph.D. degree from Yale University (1968). His books include *The Democratic Party and California Politics, 1880–1896* (1973) and *Years of Decision: American Politics in the 1890s* (1978). He taught at Yale University from 1968 to 1975 and came to SMU in 1975 as Chair of the Department of History. He has received outstanding teaching awards at both Yale and SMU. Williams has received grants from the American Philosophical Society and the National Endowment for the Humanities, and he serves on the Texas Committee for the Humanities.

Preface

America: Past and Present is a history of the United States that tells the unfolding story of national development from the days of the earliest inhabitants to the present. We emphasize *telling the story* because we strongly believe in the value of historical narrative to provide a vivid sense of the past. Weaving the various strands of the American experience, we have sought in each chapter to blend the excitement and drama of that experience with insights into the underlying social, economic, and cultural forces that brought about change.

In a clear chronological organization, we have used significant incidents and episodes to reflect the dilemmas, the choices, and the decisions made by the people as well as by their leaders. After the colonial period, most of the chapters deal in short time periods, usually about a decade, that permit us to view major political and public events as points of reference and orientation around which social themes are integrated. This approach gives unity and direction to the text.

As the title suggests, our book is a blend of the traditional and the new. The strong narrative emphasis and chronological organization are traditional; the incorporation of the many fresh insights that historians have gained from the social sciences in the past two decades is new. In recounting the story of the American past we see a nation in flux. The early Africans and Europeans developed complex agrarian folkways that departed greatly from their experiences in the Old World—an evolution that established new cultural identities and finally led the settlers to accept the idea of political independence. People who had been subjects of the British Crown created a system of government that challenged later Americans to work out the full implications of social and economic equality. As we move to the growing sectional rift between North and South, the focus shifts to divergent modes of labor utilization and disparate social values that culminated in civil war. The westward movement and the accompanying industrial revolution severely tested the values of an agrarian society, while leading to an incredibly productive economic system. In the early twentieth century, progressive reformers sought to infuse the industrial order with social justice, and the First World War demonstrated the extent of American power in the world. The resiliency of the maturing American nation was tested by the Great Depression and World War II but despite setbacks, the United States overcame these challenges. The Cold War ushered in an era of crises, foreign and domestic, that revealed both the strengths and weaknesses of modern America.

The impact of change on human lives adds a vital dimension to historical understanding. We need to comprehend how the Revolution affected the lives of ordinary citizens; what it was like for both blacks and whites to live in a plantation society; how men and women fared in the shift from an agrarian to an industrial economy; and what impact technology, in the form of the automobile and the computer, has had on patterns of life in the twentieth century.

Our primary goal has been to write a clear, relevant, and balanced history of the United States. Our commitment is not to any particular ideology or point of view; rather, we hope to challenge our readers to rediscover the fascination of the American past and reach their own conclusions. At the same time, we have not tried to avoid controversial issues and have sought to offer reasoned judgments on such morally charged subjects as the nature of slavery and the advent of nuclear weapons. We believe that what happened in the entire nation, not just New England and the Northeast, deserves retelling, and thus we have given special emphasis to developments in the South and West. (Kenneth

Bain helped prepare the picture essay on the Mexican-American Experience in the Southwest.)

The structure and features of the book are intended to stimulate student interest and reinforce learning. Chapters begin with a **vignette** or incident that relates to the chapter themes stated in the introductory section, which also serves as an overview of the topics covered. Each chapter has a **chronology, recommended readings, bibliography,** and a two-page **special feature** on a topic that combines high interest and instructional value. In addition, the very extensive full-color map program, the many charts and graphs, and the full-color illustrations throughout are directly related to the narrative. They serve to advance and expand the themes, provide elaboration and contrast, tell more of the story, and generally add another dimension of learning. The illustrations also serve as a mini-survey of American painting styles. Eight **picture essays** explore facets of American life, and a six-page **map series** at the front of the text highlights the sweep of American history. The **Appendix** contains the vital documents, a ten-column chart on choosing the president and other political information, the cabinet members in every administration, and the Supreme Court justices.

Although this book is a joint effort, each author took primary responsibility for writing one section. T. H. Breen contributed the first eight chapters from the Native American period to the second decade of the nineteenth century; George M. Fredrickson wrote chapters 9 through 16, carrying the narrative through the Reconstruction era. R. Hal Williams is responsible for chapters 17 through 24, focusing on the industrial transformation and urbanization, and the events culminating in World War I; and Robert A. Divine wrote chapters 25 through 32, bringing the story through the Depression, World War II, and the Cold War to the present. Each contributor reviewed and revised the work of his colleagues and helped shape the material into its final form.

THE AUTHORS

Acknowledgments

This book owes much to the conscientious historians who reviewed chapters and sections, and offered valuable suggestions that led to many important improvements in the text. We are grateful to the following:

Frank W. Abbott
University of Houston

Kenneth G. Alfers
Mountain View College
Dallas

Thomas Archdeacon
University of Wisconsin-Madison

Kenneth R. Bain
Pan American University
Edinburg, Texas

Lois W. Banner
Hamilton College
Clinton, New York

Thomas Camfield
Sam Houston State University
Huntsville, Texas

Clayborne Carson
Stanford University

Jerald Combs
San Francisco State University

John Cooper
University of Wisconsin-Madison

Nancy F. Cott
Yale University

Eric Foner
Columbia University

Stephen Foster
Northern Illinois University

Sondra Herman
DeAnza Community College
Cupertino, California

John R. Howe
University of Minnesota

Nathan I. Huggins
Harvard University

John Kelley
Shawnee State Community College
Portsmouth, Ohio

Richard S. Kirkendall
Iowa State University

Herbert F. Margulies
University of Hawaii

Myron Marty
National Endowment for the Humanities
Washington, D.C.

John M. Murrin
Princeton University

John K. Nelson
University of North Carolina at Chapel Hill

Nora Ramirez
San Antonio Community College

Ronald Walters
Johns Hopkins University

Frank Wetta
Galveston Community College

We are also indebted to many people at Scott, Foresman, our publisher. Bruce Borland was instrumental in initiating the project and taking it from a gleam in the eyes of the authors to a final manuscript. His successor as history editor, Christine Silvestri, carried it through to its full development as an American history text. Developmental editor Charlotte Iglarsh did a marvelous job of keeping the authors faithful to their commitment to clear writing and compelling prose, as well as to their deadlines. Betty Slack expertly copyedited the manuscript and deftly guided it into production. Other members of the Scott, Foresman staff who gave valuable assistance include the photo research department, especially Nina Page and Leslie Cohn; designer Barbara Schneider, who is responsible for the visual clarity and elegance of the book design; cartographer Paul Yatabe, who conceived many of the maps; Cathy Wacaser, who served as editorial liaison to production; and Victoria Moon, the production coordinator.

Finally, each author received aid and encouragement from many colleagues, friends, and family members over the four years of research, reflection, drafting, and revising that went into this book.

Robert A. Divine wishes to thank Lisa Divine for typing and retyping his chapters, Barbara Renick Divine for superb editorial advice, Ricardo Romo for several helpful suggestions, and Brian Duchin and Louis Gomolak for preparing many of the special features in the last eight chapters of the book.

T. H. Breen wishes to thank John Williams, Robyn Muncy Champagne, E. Faber, James Axtell, Susan C. Breen, George Breen, Sarah Breen, and Bant Breen. Special appreciation goes to Chester Pach, Professor of History at Texas Tech, for assistance at all stages of the project.

George M. Fredrickson wishes to thank Keith Schlesinger and Barbara McElroy for help with map research and special features, and Hélène Fredrickson and Joan Stahl for typing drafts of his chapters.

R. Hal Williams wishes to thank Lewis L. Gould, Kathleen Triplett, Edith Duncan, Alice McCaulley, Dorothy Friedlander, N. Coulter, Pat Hurst, Ann Nurre, Linda, Lise, and Scott Williams. Special thanks go to Jane Yoder and John Nicholson, who participated in every stage, and to Henry L. Gray and Michael R. Best, who lightened the administrative burden and allowed a Dean to research and write.

Contents

Maps

Charts and Graphs

Maps

Map 1 Major Indian Tribes and Culture Areas in North America, 1500

ARCTIC OCEAN

Eskimo
Koyukon
Eskimo
Ingalik
Kutchin
Tanaina
Tanana
Eskimo
Aleut
Hare
Eyak
Tuchone
ARCTIC
Tlingit
Kaska
Eskimo
Mackenzie R.
Tahltan
Slave
Eskimo
NORTHWEST
Sekani
Chipewyan
Hudson Bay
Tsimshian
Beaver
SUB-ARCTIC
Naskapi
Haida Bella
Coola
Montagnais
COAST
Athabasca R.
Cree
Bella Bella Carrier Sarsi
Beothuk
Kwakiutl
Shuswap
Cree
Micmac
Nootka
Chilcotin
Malecite
Makah
Columbia R.
Okanagan
Blackfoot
Chippewa
(Ojibwa)
Salish Kutenai
Abnaki
Quinault PLATEAU Colville Blackfoot
Assiniboin
Algonquin
Mahican
Chehalis Spokane Gros Ventre
Chippewa
Ottawa Huron
Pennacook
Tillamook Yakima
(Ojibwa)
Klikitat Flathead
Missouri R.
Iroquois Mohawk
Massachusetts
Rogue Umpqua Nez
River Cayuse Percé Crow Hidatsa
Menominee
Oneida
Onondaga Wampanoag
Yurok Klamath Mandan
Sauk
Potawatomi Cayuga Narragansett
Shasta Modoc Northern Bannock
Arikara Santee
Fox Seneca
Pomo Paiute
Sioux
Winnebago EASTERN
Maidu Shoshoni
Northern
Kickapoo
Erie Susquehanna Delaware
Goshute
Cheyenne
Miami
Miwok Ponca
WOODLAND
GREAT BASIN
Omaha
Powhatan
Costanoan Arapaho Pawnee
Illinois
Yokuts Ute GREAT PLAINS
Tutelo
CALIFORNIA Southern
Southern Kansa Missouri
Shawnee
Tuscarora
Paiute Cheyenne
Ohio R.
Chumash
Cherokee Catawba
Navajo Jicarilla
Serrano Mohave Hopi Pueblo Apache Kiowa Osage
Cahuilla Yavapi Zuñi
Quapaw SOUTHEAST
Digueño Yuma Pima SOUTHWEST Wichita Chickasaw
ATLANTIC OCEAN
Papago Maricopa Mescalero
Caddo Choctaw Creek Yamasee
Western Apache
Tonkawa Natchez Timucua
Apache Lipan Apalachee
Opata Apache Biloxi
Cochimi Seri
Atakapa
Canita Concho
Seminole
Yaqui NORTHERN Karankawa
Gulf of Mexico
Lucayo
MEXICO
Ciboney Carib
Waiguri Acaxee Coahuiltec
Subtaino
Pericu Tepehuan Tamaulipec
Taino
Guachichil
CARIBBEAN
Totonac Maya
Otomí MIDDLE AMERICA
Tarascan Toltec
Caribbean Sea
Aztec Olmec
Mixtec
Zapotec Maya

Mosquito
Lenca
Cuna
Guaymí

PACIFIC
OCEAN

Tropic of Cancer
Arctic Circle

0   300   600 Miles
0   300   600 Kilometers

Map 2 Thirteen Colonies: Distribution of Major Immigrant Groups and Extent of Settlement

NOVA SCOTIA

MAINE
(part of Mass.)

QUEBEC

Lake Huron

Lake Ontario

Lake Erie

Lake Champlain

St. Lawrence R.

Proclamation Line of 1763

Connecticut R.

NEW
HAMPSHIRE

Portsmouth

NEW
YORK

Boston   MASSACHUSETTS

ATLANTIC
OCEAN

Hudson R.

Hartford   Providence

CONNECTICUT

Newport

New Haven   RHODE ISLAND

Susquehanna R.

Delaware R.

PENNSYLVANIA

Perth Amboy   New York

Philadelphia   Burlington   NEW JERSEY

New Castle

MARYLAND

Annapolis   DELAWARE

Potomac R.

INDIAN   RESERVE

Ohio R.

VIRGINIA

James R.

Williamsburg

Proclamation Line of 1763

NORTH CAROLINA

New Bern

Pee Dee R.

SOUTH
CAROLINA

Savannah R.

GEORGIA   Charles Town

Savannah

0   100   200 Miles

0   100   200 Kilometers

Major Immigrant Groups

English   Scottish

African   Scotch-Irish

German   Dutch

NOVA
SCOTIA

MAINE
(part of Mass.)

QUEBEC

Lake Huron

Lake Ontario

Lake Erie

N.H.

N.Y.   MASS.

R.I.
CONN.

PA.

N.J.

MD.

DEL.

INDIAN RESERVE

VA.

ATLANTIC
OCEAN

N.C.

S.C.

GA.

EAST
FLORIDA

Extent of Settlement

circa 1650

circa 1700

circa 1775

0   200 Miles

0   200 Kilometers

Map 3 The Advancing Frontier: America at Mid-nineteenth Century

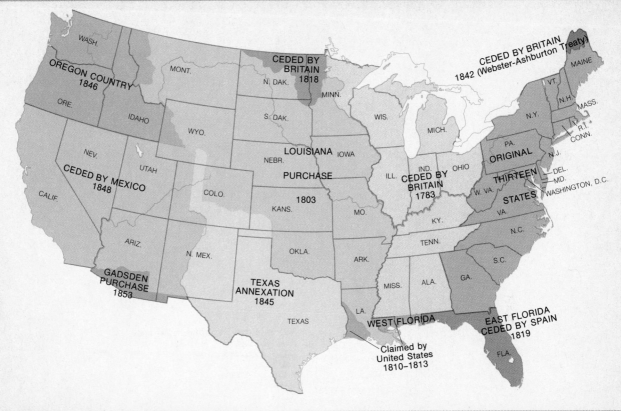

OREGON COUNTRY 1846

CEDED BY BRITAIN 1818

CEDED BY BRITAIN 1842 (Webster-Ashburton Treaty)

WASH.
MONT.
N. DAK.
MINN.
ORE.
IDAHO
WYO.
S. DAK.
WIS.
MICH.
MAINE
VT.
N.H.
MASS.
N.Y.
R.I.
CONN.
PA.
ORIGINAL

NEV.
UTAH
CEDED BY MEXICO 1848
COLO.
NEBR.
LOUISIANA IOWA
PURCHASE
1803
KANS.
ILL.
IND.
CEDED BY BRITAIN 1783
OHIO
THIRTEEN
W. VA.
N.J.
DEL.
MD.
WASHINGTON, D.C.

CALIF.
MO.
STATES
VA.
KY.
N.C.

ARIZ.
N. MEX.
OKLA.
ARK.
TENN.
S.C.
GA.

GADSDEN PURCHASE 1853
TEXAS ANNEXATION 1845
MISS.
ALA.

TEXAS
LA.
WEST FLORIDA
EAST FLORIDA CEDED BY SPAIN 1819
FLA.

Claimed by United States 1810–1813

Map 4 Secession: A Nation Divided

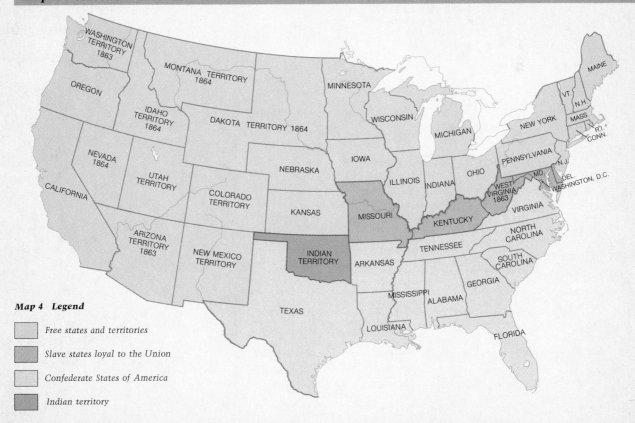

WASHINGTON TERRITORY 1863
MONTANA TERRITORY 1864
MINNESOTA
OREGON
IDAHO TERRITORY 1864
DAKOTA TERRITORY 1864
WISCONSIN
MICHIGAN
MAINE
VT.
N.H.
MASS.
R.I.
CONN.

NEVADA 1864
UTAH TERRITORY
NEBRASKA
IOWA
NEW YORK
PENNSYLVANIA
N.J.
DEL.
MD.
WASHINGTON, D.C.

CALIFORNIA
COLORADO TERRITORY
KANSAS
ILLINOIS
INDIANA
OHIO
WEST VIRGINIA 1863
VIRGINIA

MISSOURI
KENTUCKY

ARIZONA TERRITORY 1863
NEW MEXICO TERRITORY
INDIAN TERRITORY
ARKANSAS
TENNESSEE
NORTH CAROLINA
SOUTH CAROLINA
GEORGIA

TEXAS
MISSISSIPPI
ALABAMA

LOUISIANA
FLORIDA

Map 4   Legend

Free states and territories

Slave states loyal to the Union

Confederate States of America

Indian territory

NORTH AMERICA

Iceland 1941
Greenland 1941
U.S. troops land

UNITED STATES

Tunis
Algiers

MOROCCO
Wars Against
the Barbary States
1801–1805, 1815

Dominican Republic
1916–1924
U.S. occupation
1965
U.S. troops land

Vera Cruz 1914
Seized by U.S. Navy

Haiti
1915–1934
U.S. occupation

Grenada 1983
U.S. troops land

Nicaragua
1912–1925, 1927–1933
Marines enforce
U.S. position

ATLANTIC
OCEAN

Equator

SOUTH
AMERICA

PACIFIC
OCEAN

Map shows present-day boundaries

Murmansk 1919
U.S. troops intervene

Archangel 1918
U.S. troops intervene

EUROPE

ASIA

Vladivostok 1918
U.S. troops intervene

Greece 1947
U.S. military advisors arrive

Lebanon
1958
U.S. troops land
1982
Marines land as part of
multinational peacekeeping force

Tripoli

Peking 1900
U.S. helps to crush
Boxer Rebellion

Korean War 1950–1953
U.S. police action
in support of U.N.

AFRICA

Vietnam War
1965–1973

PACIFIC
OCEAN

Equator

INDIAN
OCEAN

AUSTRALIA

HARPER'S WEEKLY.
A JOURNAL OF CIVILIZATION.

Vol. XI.—No. 568.]   NEW YORK, SATURDAY, NOVEMBER 16, 1867.   [SINGLE COPIES TEN CENTS.
[$4.00 PER YEAR IN ADVANCE.

Entered according to Act of Congress, in the Year 1867, by Harper & Brothers, in the Clerk's Office of the District Court for the Southern District of New York.

chapter 16

THE
AGONY OF
RECONSTRUCTION

D. W. Griffith's *Birth of a Nation* (1915) was the most ambitious film yet made by the fledgling American film industry. An epic of the Civil War and Reconstruction produced a half-century after the events it portrays, the movie remains a technical masterpiece, combining impressive, realistic battle scenes with a heavy dose of political and racial propaganda. The villains are vindictive northern politicians, corrupt carpetbaggers, and ignorant ex-slaves lusting for power over their former masters. To make the message clear, words are flashed on the screen describing Reconstruction as a callous attempt to *"put the white South under the heel of the black South."* Later in the film leering blacks carry signs reading "Equality/Equal Rights/Equal Politics/Equal Marriage."

Lincoln is depicted as a wise statesman who would have spared the South the horrors of black rule, but his assassination gives power to a vengeful Republican congressman, meant to represent Thaddeus Stevens. Under the urging of his mulatto mistress, the congressman hatches a devilish plot to oppress and humiliate the white South. The fruits of this scheming are revealed in a scene portraying the South Carolina state legislature as a mob of grinning, barefooted blacks, carousing at the taxpayers' expense.

The melodramatic plot features two climactic episodes. In the first a southern maiden throws herself from a cliff to escape the embraces of a "renegade Negro," and in the second the Ku Klux Klan rescues the daughter of a northern Republican from a forced marriage with a mulatto politician. Even the father, a professed champion of black equality, rejoices in this triumph of racial purity. The message is unmistakable—the Klan saved the South and white civilization from a fate worse than death.

At a special White House screening, then President Woodrow Wilson, who was of southern birth and a professional historian as well as a politician, found the film impressive and rooted in fact. "It is like writing history with lightning," he announced. "And my only regret is that it is all so terribly true." The movie, undoubtedly helped by the presidential blurb, was a spectacular popular success. Black protests, organized by the recently founded National Association for the Advancement of Colored People (NAACP), forced censors in some northern cities to delete some of the more blatantly racist scenes, but millions of Americans saw and applauded the uncut version.

The picture of Reconstruction presented in *Birth of a Nation* developed from the image projected by the southern leaders who had overthrown Radical rule in the 1870s and then proceeded to put blacks "in their place" by stripping them of rights supposedly guaranteed by the Fourteenth and Fifteenth Amendments. Over the next forty years many Northerners became persuaded that their forebears made a terrible mistake in trying to enforce equal rights for blacks after the Civil War.

During the period between the 1890s and the 1940s, most professional historians agreed; they concluded that Reconstruction was one of the most disgraceful episodes in American history—a "tragic era" when misguided or opportunistic northern politicians had enfranchised a black population obviously unfit for citizenship, thereby condemning the long-suffering South to an orgy of misrule and corruption. Some black scholars of the 1920s and '30s disagreed vehemently with this view, notably W. E. B. Du Bois in his massive work *Black Reconstruction in America*, but not until the 1950s and '60s did a majority of Reconstruction historians reject the exaggerations, distortions, and racist assumptions of this image. Because they dissented vigorously from the old orthodoxy, these historians became known as "revisionists." Even today, however, some of the myths reflected in *Birth of a Nation* have a strong hold on the popular historical imagination.

Retelling the story of Reconstruction from a modern revisionist perspective does not require setting up a new myth of saintly Radical Republicans, model black officeholders, and totally vicious southern whites to replace the stereotypes in *Birth of a Nation*. Mixed motives, hypocrisy, blunders, and corruption were important aspects of the complex drama that unfolded between the end of the Civil War and the final collapse of Reconstruction in 1877. But there was another side, involving the heroic struggle of blacks and their white allies to achieve racial justice and equality against overwhelming odds. If Reconstruction was "tragic," it was not because what was attempted was wrong; it was rather because those who tried to form a more egalitarian society in the South lacked the sustained support and unfaltering will to achieve their aims.

The President Versus Congress

The problem of how to reconstruct the Union in the wake of the South's military defeat was one of the most difficult and perplexing challenges ever faced by American policymakers. The Constitution provided no firm guidelines, for the framers had not anticipated a division of the country into warring sections. Once emancipation became a northern war aim, the problem was compounded by a new issue: how far should the federal government go to secure freedom and civil rights for four million former slaves?

The debate that evolved led to a major political crisis. Advocates of a minimal Reconstruction policy favored quick restoration of the Union with no protection for the freed slaves beyond the prohibition of slavery. Proponents of a more radical policy wanted readmission of the southern states to be dependent on guarantees that "loyal" men would displace the Confederate elite and that blacks would acquire some of the basic rights of American citizenship. The White House favored the minimal approach, while Congress came to endorse the more radical and thoroughgoing form of Reconstruction. The resulting struggle between Congress and the chief executive was the most serious clash between two branches of government in the nation's history.

Wartime Reconstruction

Tension between the President and Congress over how to reconstruct the Union began during the war. Occupied mainly with achieving victory,

■ "The Union Christmas Dinner" appeared in Harper's Weekly in 1864. The cartoon illustrates the spirit of forgiveness and reconciliation that marked Lincoln's policy toward the South.

Lincoln never set forth a final and comprehensive plan for bringing the rebellious states back into the fold. But he did take some initiatives that indicated he favored a lenient and conciliatory policy toward Southerners who would give up the struggle and repudiate slavery. In December 1863 he issued a Proclamation of Amnesty and Reconstruction; it offered a full pardon to all Southerners (with the exception of certain classes of Confederate leaders) who would take an oath of allegiance to the Union and acknowledge the legality of emancipation. Once 10 percent or more of the voting population of any occupied state had taken the oath, they were authorized to set up a loyal government. Efforts to establish such regimes were quickly undertaken in states that were wholly or partially occupied by Union troops; by 1864 Louisiana and Arkansas had fully functioning Unionist governments.

Lincoln's policy was meant to shorten the war. The President hoped that granting pardon and political recognition to oath-taking minorities would weaken the southern cause by making it easy for disillusioned or lukewarm Confederates to switch sides. He also hoped to further his emancipation policy by insisting that the new governments abolish slavery, an action that might prove crucial if—as seemed possible before Lincoln's reelection in 1864 and Congress' subsequent passage of the Thirteenth Amendment—the courts or a future Democratic administration were to disallow or revoke the Emancipation Proclamation. When constitutional conventions operating under the 10 percent plan in Louisiana and Arkansas dutifully abolished slavery in 1864, emancipation came closer to being irreversible.

But Congress was unhappy with the President's reconstruction experiments and in 1864 refused to seat the Unionists elected to the House and Senate from Louisiana and Arkansas. A minority of congressional Republicans—the strongly anti-slavery Radicals—favored strong protection for black rights as a precondition for the readmission of southern states. These Republican militants were upset because Lincoln had not insisted that the constitution-makers provide for black suffrage. But a larger group in Congress was not yet prepared to implement civil and political equality for blacks. Most of these moderates also opposed Lincoln's plan, but they did so primarily because they did not trust the repentant Confederates who would play a major role in the new governments. No matter what their position on black rights, most congressional Republicans feared that hypocritical oath-taking would allow the old ruling class to return to power and cheat the North of the full fruits of its impending victory.

Also disturbing Congress was a sense that the President was exceeding his authority by using executive powers to restore the Union. Lincoln operated on the theory that secession, being illegal, did not place the Confederate states outside the Union in a constitutional sense. Since individuals and not states had defied federal authority, the President could use his pardoning power to certify a loyal electorate, which could then function as the legitimate state government.

The dominant view in Congress, on the other hand, was that the southern states had definitely withdrawn from the Union and that it was up to Congress to decide when and how they would be readmitted. The most popular justification for congressional responsibility was based on the clause of the Constitution providing that "the United States shall guarantee to every State in this Union a Republican Form of Government." By seceding, it was argued, the Confederate states had ceased to be republican, and it was now Congress' job to set the conditions to be met before they could be readmitted.

After refusing to recognize Lincoln's 10 percent governments, Congress passed a Reconstruction bill of its own in July 1864. Known as the Wade-Davis bill, this legislation required that 50 percent of the voters must take an oath of future loyalty before the restoration process could begin. Once this had occurred, those who could swear that they had never willingly supported the Confederacy could vote in an election for delegates to a constitutional convention. The bill in its final form did not require black suffrage, but it did give federal courts the power to enforce emancipation. Faced with this attempt to nullify his own program, Lincoln exercized a pocket veto by refusing to sign the bill before Congress adjourned. He justified his action by announcing that he did not wish to be committed to any single reconstruction plan. The sponsors of the bill responded with an angry manifesto, and Lincoln's relations with Congress reached their lowest ebb.

Congress and the President remained stalemated on the Reconstruction issue for the rest of the war. During his last months in office, however, Lincoln showed some willingness to compromise. He persisted in his efforts to obtain full recognition for the governments he had nurtured in Louisiana and Arkansas but seemed receptive to the setting of other conditions—perhaps including black suffrage—for readmission of those states where wartime conditions had prevented execution of his plan. However, he died without clarifying his intentions, leaving historians to speculate on whether his quarrel with Congress would have worsened or been resolved. Given Lincoln's past record of political flexibility, the best bet is that he would have come to terms with the majority of his party.

Andrew Johnson at the Helm

Andrew Johnson, the man suddenly made president by an assassin's bullet, attempted to put the Union back together on his own authority in 1865. But his policies eventually put him at odds with Congress and the Republican party and provoked the most serious internal crisis in the history of the federal government.

Johnson's approach to Reconstruction was shaped by his background. Born in dire poverty in North Carolina, he migrated as a young man to

The Agony of Reconstruction

■ *Nearly insurmountable problems with a Congress determined to enact its own Reconstruction policy plagued Andrew Johnson through his presidency. Impeached in 1868, he escaped conviction by a single vote.*

eastern Tennessee where he made his living as a tailor. Lacking formal schooling, he was barely able to read until adult life and subsequently entered politics as a Jacksonian Democrat. His effectiveness as a stump speaker railing against the planter aristocracy made him the spokesman for Tennessee's nonslaveholding whites and the most successful politician in the state. He advanced from state legislator to congressman to governor and in 1857 was elected to the United States Senate.

When Tennessee seceded in 1861, Johnson was the only senator from a Confederate state who remained loyal to the Union and continued to serve in Washington. But his Unionism and defense of the common people did not include antislavery sentiments. Nor was he friendly to blacks. While campaigning in Tennessee, he had objected only to the fact that slaveholding was

the privilege of a wealthy minority. He revealed his basic attitude when he expressed the extraordinary wish that "every head of family in the United States had one slave to take the drudgery and menial service off his family."

During the war, while acting as military governor of Tennessee, Johnson endorsed Lincoln's emancipation policy and carried it into effect. But he viewed it primarily as a means of destroying the power of the hated planter class rather than as a recognition of black humanity. He was chosen as Lincoln's running mate in 1864 because putting a proadministration Democrat, who was a southern Unionist in the bargain, on the ticket would broaden its appeal. No one expected Johnson to succeed to the presidency; it is one of the strange accidents of American history that a southern Democrat, a fervent white supremacist, came to preside over a Republican administration immediately after the Civil War.

What may seem even stranger is the fact that some Radical Republicans initially welcomed Johnson's ascent to the nation's highest office. But their hopes make sense in the light of Johnson's record of fierce loyalty to the Union and his apparent agreement with the Radicals that ex-Confederates should be severely treated. More than Lincoln, who had spoken of "malice toward none and charity for all," Johnson seemed likely to punish southern "traitors" and prevent them from regaining political influence. Only gradually did the deep disagreement between the President and the Republican majority in Congress become evident.

The Reconstruction policy that Johnson initiated on May 29, 1865, created some uneasiness among the Radicals, but most other Republicans, moderate and conservative, were willing to give it a chance. Johnson placed North Carolina and eventually other states under appointed provisional governors chosen from among prominent southern politicians who had opposed the secession movement and had rendered no conspicuous service to the Confederacy. The governors were responsible for calling constitutional conventions and ensuring that only "loyal" whites were permitted to vote for delegates. Participation required taking the oath of allegiance that Lincoln had prescribed earlier. Once again Confederate leaders and former officeholders who had participated in the rebellion were excluded. To regain their political and property rights, those in the exempted categories had to apply for individual presidential pardons. Johnson made one significant addition to the list of the excluded: all those possessing taxable property exceeding $20,000 in value. In this fashion, he sought to prevent his longtime adversaries—the planter class—from participating in the reconstruction of southern state governments.

Once the conventions met, Johnson urged them to do three things: declare the ordinances of secession illegal, repudiate the Confederate debt, and ratify the Thirteenth Amendment abolishing slavery. After governments had been reestablished under constitutions meeting these conditions, the President assumed that the process of Reconstuction would be complete and that the ex-Confederate states could regain their full rights under the Constitution.

The conventions, dominated by prewar Unionists and representatives of backcountry yeoman farmers, did their work in a way satisfactory to the President but troubling to many congressional Republicans. Rather than quickly accepting Johnson's recommendations, the delegates in several states approved them begrudgingly or with qualifications. Furthermore, all the resulting constitutions limited the suffrage to whites, disappointing the large number of Northerners who hoped, as Lincoln had, that at least some blacks—perhaps those who were educated or had served in the Union army—would be given the vote. Johnson on the whole seemed eager to give southern white majorities a free hand in determining the civil and political status of the freed slaves.

Republican uneasiness turned to disillusionment and anger when the state legislatures elected under the new constitutions proceeded to pass "Black Codes" subjecting the former slaves to a variety of special regulations and restrictions on their freedom. Especially troubling were vagrancy and apprenticeship laws that forced blacks to work and denied them a free choice of employers. Blacks in some states were also prevented from testifying in court against whites and were subject to a separate penal code. To Radicals, the Black Codes looked suspiciously like slavery under a new guise. More upsetting to northern public opinion in general was the fact that a number of prominent ex-Confederate leaders were elected to Congress in the fall of 1865.

Johnson himself was partly responsible for this turn of events. Despite his lifelong feud with the planter class, he was generous in granting pardons to members of the old elite who came to him, hat in hand, and asked for them. When former Confederate Vice-President Alexander Stephens and other proscribed ex-rebels were elected to Congress although they had not been pardoned, Johnson granted them special amnesty so that they could serve.

The growing rift between the President and Congress came into the open in December when the House and Senate refused to seat the recently elected southern delegation. Instead of endorsing Johnson's work and recognizing the state governments he had called into being, Congress established a joint committee, chaired by Senator William Pitt Fessenden of Maine, to review Reconstruction policy and set further conditions for readmission of the seceded states.

Congress Takes the Initiative

The struggle over how to reconstruct the Union ended with Congress doing the job all over again. The clash between Johnson and Congress was a matter of principle and could not be reconciled. Johnson's personality—his prickly pride, sharp tongue, intolerance of opposition, and stubborn refusal to give an inch—did not help his political cause. But the root of the problem was that he disagreed with the majority of Congress on what Reconstruction was supposed to accomplish. An heir of the Democratic states' rights tradition, he wanted to restore the prewar federal system as quickly as possible, with the single change that states would no longer have the right to legalize slavery.

Most Republicans, on the other hand, believed that the sectional conflict would not be resolved until there were firm guarantees that the old southern ruling class would not regain regional power and national influence by devising new ways to subjugate blacks. Since emancipation had nullified the three-fifths clause of the Constitution by which slaves had been counted as three fifths of a person, all blacks were now to be counted in determining representation. Consequently, unlike Johnson, the Republicans worried about increased southern strength in Congress

According to this cartoon, Congress' plan of Reconstruction was a bitter dose for the South, and the President, "Naughty Andy," urged Southerners not to accept the plan. Mrs. Columbia insisted, however, that Dr. Congress knew what was best.

and the electoral college. Congress favored a reconstruction policy that would give the federal government authority to limit the political role of ex-Confederates and provide some protection for black citizenship.

Republican leaders—with the exception of a few extreme Radicals like Charles Sumner—lacked any firm conviction that blacks were inherently equal to whites. They *did* believe, however, that a modern democratic state should provide the same basic rights and opportunities for all citizens, regardless of their natural abilities. Principle coincided easily with political expediency; southern blacks, whatever their alleged shortcomings, were likely to be loyal to the Republican party that had emancipated them. They could be used, if necessary, to counteract the influence of resurgent ex-Confederates, thus preventing the Democrats from returning to national dominance through control of the South.

The disagreement between the President and Congress became irreconcilable in early 1866 when Johnson vetoed two bills that had passed with overwhelming Republican support. The first extended the life of the Freedmen's Bureau—a temporary agency set up to aid the former slaves by providing relief, education, legal help, and assistance in obtaining land or employment. The second was a civil rights bill meant to nullify the black codes and guarantee to the freedmen "full and equal benefit of all laws and proceedings for the security of person and property as is enjoyed by white citizens."

The vetoes shocked moderate Republicans who had expected Johnson to accept these relatively modest measures as a way of heading off more radical proposals, such as black suffrage and a prolonged denial of political rights to ex-Confederates. Presidential opposition to policies that represented the bare minimum of Republican demands on the South alienated the moderates in the party and ensured a wide opposition to Johnson's plan of Reconstruction. Johnson succeeded in blocking the Freedmen's Bureau bill, although a modified version later passed. But the Civil Rights Act won the two-thirds majority necessary to override his veto, signifying that the President was now hopelessly at odds with most of the congressmen from what was supposed to be his own party.

Johnson soon revealed that he intended to abandon the Republicans and place himself at the head of a new conservative party uniting the small minority of Republicans who supported him with a reviving Democratic party that was rallying behind his Reconstruction policy. In preparation for the elections of 1866, Johnson helped found the National Union movement to promote his plan to readmit the southern states to the Union without further qualifications. A National Union convention meeting in Philadelphia in August 1866 called for the election to Congress of men who endorsed the presidential plan for Reconstruction.

Meanwhile, the Republican majority on Capitol Hill, fearing that Johnson would not enforce civil rights legislation or that the courts would declare such federal laws unconstitutional, passed the Fourteenth Amendment. This, the most important of all our constitutional amendments, gave the federal government responsibility for guaranteeing equal rights under the law to all Americans. The first section defined national citizenship for the first time as extending to "all persons born or naturalized in the United States."

The states were prohibited from abridging the rights of American citizens and could not "deprive any person of life, liberty, or property, without due process of law; nor deny to any person . . . equal protection of the laws."

The other sections of the amendment were important in the context of the time but had fewer long-term implications. Section two sought to encourage extension of voting rights to blacks by reducing the congressional representation of any state that formally deprived a portion of its male citizens of the right to vote. The third section denied federal office to those who had taken an oath of office to support the United States Constitution and then had supported the Confederacy, and the fourth repudiated the Confederate debt. The amendment was sent to the states with an implied understanding that Southerners would be readmitted to Congress only if their states ratified it.

The congressional elections of 1866 served as a referendum on the Fourteenth Amendment. Johnson opposed it on the grounds that it created a "centralized" government and denied the states the right to manage their own affairs; he also counselled southern state legislatures to reject it, and all except Tennessee followed his advice. The President's case for state autonomy was weakened by the publicity resulting from bloody race riots in New Orleans and Memphis. These and other reported atrocities against the former slaves made it clear that the existing southern state governments were failing abysmally to protect the "life, liberty, or property" of the ex-slaves.

Johnson further weakened his cause by taking the stump on behalf of candidates who supported his policies. In his notorious "swing around the circle," he toured the nation, slandering his opponents in crude language and engaging in undignified exchanges with hecklers. Enraged by southern inflexibility and the antics of a president who acted as if he were still campaigning in the backwoods of Tennessee, northern voters repudiated the administration. The Republican majority in Congress increased to a solid two thirds in both houses, and the radical wing of the party gained strength at the expense of moderates and conservatives.

Congressional Reconstruction Plan Enacted

Congress was now in a position to implement its own plan of Reconstruction. In 1867 it passed a series of acts that nullified the President's initiatives and reorganized the South on a new basis. Generally referred to as "Radical Reconstruc-

Reconstruction Amendments, 1865–1870

Amendment	Main Provisions	Congressional Passage (⅔ majority in each house required)	Ratification Process (¾ of all states including ex-Confederate states required)
13	Slavery prohibited in United States	January 1865	December 1865 (twenty-seven states, including eight southern states)
14	1. National citizenship 2. State representation in Congress reduced proportionally to number of voters disfranchised 3. Former Confederates denied right to hold office	June 1866	Rejected by twelve southern and border states, February 1867 Radicals make readmission of southern states hinge on ratification Ratified July 1868
15	Explicit prohibition of denial of franchise because of race, color, or past servitude	February 1869	Ratification required for readmission of Virginia, Texas, Mississippi, Georgia Ratified March 1870

With this cartoon, Petroleum V. Nasby satirized President Johnson's "swing around the circle" before the congressional elections of 1866. As a result of Johnson's unrestrained outbursts and crude behavior, support for the President nearly disappeared.

tion," these measures actually represented a compromise between genuine Radicals and the more moderate elements within the party.

Consistent Radicals like Senator Charles Sumner of Massachusetts and Congressmen Thaddeus Stevens of Pennsylvania and George Julian of Indiana wanted to shape southern society before readmitting ex-Confederates to the Union. Their program of "regeneration before reconstruction" required an extended period of military rule, confiscation and redistribution of large landholdings among the freedmen, and federal aid for schools that would educate blacks for citizenship. But the majority of Republican congressmen found such a program unacceptable because it broke with American traditions of federalism and regard for property rights.

The First Reconstruction Act, passed over Johnson's veto on March 2, 1867, did place the South under military rule—but only for a short period. The act opened the way for the readmission of any state that framed and ratified a new constitution providing for black suffrage. Ex-Confederates disqualified from holding federal office under the Fourteenth Amendment were prohibited from voting for delegates to the constitutional conventions or in the elections to ratify the conventions' work. Since blacks were allowed to participate in this process, Republicans thought they had found a way to ensure that

"loyal" men would dominate the new governments. Speed was essential because some Republican leaders anticipated that they would need votes from the reconstructed South in order to retain control of Congress and the White House in 1868.

"Radical Reconstruction" was based on the false assumption that once blacks had the vote, they would have the power to protect themselves against the efforts of white supremacists to deny them their rights. The Reconstruction Acts thus signaled a retreat from the true Radical position that a sustained use of federal authority was needed to complete the transition from slavery to freedom and prevent the resurgence of the South's old ruling class. The majority of Republicans were unwilling to embrace centralized government and an extended period of military rule over civilians. Such drastic steps went beyond the popular northern consensus on necessary and proper Reconstruction measures. Thus, despite strong reservations, Radicals like Thaddeus Stevens supported the plan of readmitting the southern states on the basis of black suffrage when they realized that this was as far as the party and the northern public were willing to go.

Even so, congressional Reconstruction did have a radical aspect. Although the program won Republican support partly because it promised practical political advantages, a genuine spirit of dem-

■ *Among the most influential of the Radicals was Congressman Thaddeus Stevens of Pennsylvania. He advocated seizing a portion of the property of southern whites and distributing it among the freed blacks.*

ocratic idealism gave legitimacy and fervor to the cause of black suffrage. The principle that even the poorest and most underprivileged should have access to the ballot box was a noble and enlightened one. The problem was how to enforce it under conditions then existing in the postwar South.

The Impeachment Crisis

The first obstacle to enforcement of congressional Reconstruction was resistance from the White House. Johnson thoroughly disapproved of the new policy and sought to thwart the will of Congress by administering the plan in his own obstructive fashion. He immediately began to dismiss officeholders who sympathized with Radical Reconstruction, and he countermanded the orders of generals in charge of southern military districts who were zealous in their enforcement of the new legislation. Some Radical generals were transferred and replaced by conservative Democrats. Congress responded by passing laws designed to limit presidential authority over Reconstruction matters. One of these measures was the Tenure of Office Act, requiring Senate approv-

al for the firing of cabinet officers and other officials whose appointment had needed the consent of the Senate. Another measure—a rider to an army appropriations bill—sought to limit Johnson's authority to issue orders to military commanders.

Johnson objected vigorously to these restrictions on the ground that they violated the constitutional doctrine of the separation of powers. When it became clear that the President was resolute in fighting for his powers and using them to resist the establishment of Radical regimes in the southern states, some congressmen began to call for his impeachment. A preliminary effort foundered in 1867, but when Johnson tried to discharge Secretary of War Edwin Stanton—the only Radical in the cabinet—and persisted in his efforts despite the disapproval of the Senate, the proimpeachment forces gained in strength.

In January 1868 Johnson ordered General Grant, who already commanded the army, to replace Stanton as head of the War Department. But Grant had his eye on the Republican presidential nomination and refused to defy Congress. Johnson subsequently appointed General Lorenzo Thomas, who agreed to serve. Faced with this apparent violation of the Tenure of Office Act, the House voted overwhelmingly to impeach the President on February 24, and he was placed on trial before the Senate.

Johnson narrowly avoided conviction and removal from office. Seven Republican senators broke with the party leadership and voted for acquittal. Thus, the impeachment effort fell one vote short of the necessary two thirds. This outcome resulted in part from a skillful defense. Attorneys for the President argued for a narrow interpretation of the constitutional provision that a president can be impeached only for a "high crime and misdemeanor," asserting that this referred only to an indictable crime. Responding to the charge that Johnson had deliberately violated the Tenure of Office Act, the defense contended that the law did not apply to the removal of Stanton because he had been appointed by Lincoln, not Johnson.

The prosecution countered with a different interpretation of the Tenure of Office Act, but the core of their case was that Johnson had abused the powers of his office in an effort to sabotage the congressional Reconstruction policy. Obstructing the will of the legislative branch, they claimed, was sufficient grounds for conviction even if no crime had been committed. The Republicans who broke ranks to vote for acquittal could not endorse such a broad view of the impeachment power. They feared that removal of a president for essentially political reasons would threaten the constitutional balance of powers and open the way to legislative supremacy over the executive.

Although Johnson's acquittal by the narrowest of margins protected the American presidency from congressional domination, the impeachment episode helped create an impression in the public mind that the Radicals were ready to turn the Constitution to their own use to gain their objectives. Conservatives were again alarmed when Congress took action in 1868 to deny the Supreme Court's appellate jurisdiction in cases involving the military arrest and imprisonment of anti-Reconstruction activists in the South. But the evidence of congressional ruthlessness and illegality is not as strong as most historians used to think. Modern legal scholars have found merit in the Radicals' claim that their actions did not violate the Constitution.

The failed impeachment effort was an embarrassment to congressional Republicans, but the episode did ensure that Reconstruction in the South would proceed as the majority in Congress intended. During the trial Johnson helped influence the verdict by pledging to enforce the Reconstruction Acts, and he held to this promise during his remaining months in office. Unable to depose the President, the Radicals had at least succeeded in neutralizing his opposition to their program.

Reconstruction in the South

The Civil War left the South devastated, demoralized, and destitute. Slavery was dead, but what this meant for future relationships between whites and blacks was still in doubt. The overwhelming majority of southern whites wanted to keep blacks adrift between slavery and freedom—without rights, in a status resembling that of the "free Negroes" of the Old South. Blacks sought to be independent of their former masters and viewed the acquisition of land, education, and the vote as the best means of achieving this goal. The

Political cartoonist Thomas Nast entitled this cartoon on Johnson's impeachment "The Political Death of the Bogus Caesar." Johnson was not convicted, but neither did his party nominate him for the presidency in 1868. It was not the end of his political career, however; he was elected to the Senate from Tennessee in 1874.

thousands of Northerners who went south after the war for economic or humanitarian reasons hoped to extend Yankee "civilization" to what they viewed as an unenlightened and barbarous region. For most of them this reformation required the aid of the freedmen; not enough southern whites were willing to accept the new order and embrace northern middle-class values.

The struggle of these groups to achieve their conflicting goals bred chaos, violence, and instability. Unsettled conditions meant that there were many opportunities for corruption, crime, and terrorism. This was scarcely an ideal setting for an experiment in interracial democracy, but one was attempted nonetheless. Its success depended on massive and sustained support from the federal government. To the extent that this was forthcoming, progressive reform could be achieved. When it faltered, the forces of reaction and white supremacy were unleashed.

Social and Economic Adjustments

The Civil War scarred the southern landscape and wrecked its economy. Central South Carolina looked to one 1865 observer "like a broad black streak of ruin and desolation"; the Tennessee Valley, according to another, "consists for the most part of plantations in a state of semi-ruin and plantations of which the ruin is for the present complete and total." Several major cities —including Atlanta, Columbia, and Richmond— were gutted by fire. Most factories were dismantled or destroyed, and long stretches of railroad were torn up.

Physical ruin would not have been so disastrous if investment capital had been available for rebuilding. But the substantial wealth represented by Confederate currency and bonds had melted away, and emancipation of the slaves had divested the propertied classes of their most valuable and productive assets. According to some estimates, the South's per capita wealth in 1865 was only about half what it had been in 1860.

Recovery could not even begin until a new labor system replaced slavery. It was widely assumed in both the North and the South that southern prosperity would continue to depend on cotton and that the plantation was the most efficient unit for producing the crop. But rebuilding the plantation economy was hindered by lack of capital to pay wages, the deep-rooted belief of southern whites that blacks would work only under compulsion, and the freedmen's resistance to labor conditions that recalled slavery.

Blacks strongly preferred to be small independent farmers rather than plantation laborers, and for a time they had reason to hope that the federal government would support their ambitions. General Sherman, hampered by the huge numbers of black fugitives that followed his army on its famous march, issued an order in January 1865 that set aside the islands and coastal areas of Georgia and South Carolina for exclusive black occupancy on forty-acre plots. Furthermore, the Freedmen's Bureau, as one of its many responsibilities, was given control of hundreds of thousands of acres of abandoned or confiscated land and authorized to make forty-acre grants to black settlers for three-year periods, after which they would have the option to buy at low prices. By June 1865, forty thousand black farmers were at work on three hundred thousand acres of what they thought would be their own land.

But the dream of "forty acres and a mule" was not to be realized. President Johnson pardoned the owners of most of the land consigned to the ex-slaves by Sherman and the Freedmen's Bureau, and proposals for an effective program of land confiscation and redistribution failed to get through Congress. Consequently, most blacks in physical possession of small farms failed to acquire title, and the mass of freedmen were left with little or no prospect of becoming landowners. Recalling the plight of southern blacks in 1865, an ex-slave later wrote that "they were set free without a dollar, without a foot of land, and without the wherewithal to get the next meal even."

For most ex-slaves no alternative remained except to return to the white-owned cotton fields. By mid to late 1865 the majority of freedmen had accepted this fate. The most common form of agricultural employment in 1865 and '66 was a contract labor system. Under this system workers committed themselves for a year in return for fixed wages, a substantial portion of which were withheld until after the harvest. Since many planters were inclined to drive hard bargains, abuse their workers, or cheat them at the end of the year, the Freedmen's Bureau assumed the role

For many former slaves, conditions were little changed after the Civil War. Lacking their own property, many blacks—like the cotton pickers above—were forced to work the lands of their former owners.

of reviewing the contracts and enforcing them. But bureau officials had differing notions of what it meant to protect blacks from exploitation. Some stood up strongly for the rights of the freedmen; others served as allies of the planters, rounding up available workers, coercing them to sign contracts for low wages, and then helping keep them in line.

After 1867, when the bureau's influence was waning (it was phased out completely by 1869), a new arrangement evolved out of direct negotiations between planters and freedmen. Unhappy with gang labor and constant white supervision, blacks demanded sharecropper status—in other words, the right to work a small piece of land independently in return for a fixed share of the crop produced on it, usually one half. Many landowners accepted this arrangement because it did not require much capital and forced the tenant to share the risks of crop failure or a fall in cotton prices. These considerations loomed larger after disastrous harvests in 1866 and '67.

Blacks initially viewed sharecropping as a step up from wage labor in the direction of landownership. But during the 1870s this form of tenancy evolved into a new kind of servitude. Croppers had to live on credit until their cotton was sold, and planters or merchants seized the chance to "provision" them at high prices and exorbitant rates of interest. Creditors were entitled to deduct what was owed to them out of the tenant's share of the crop and this left most sharecroppers with no net profit at the end of the year—more often than not with a debt that had to be worked off in subsequent years. Various methods, legal and extralegal, were eventually devised to bind indebted tenants to a single landlord for extended periods, and a system of virtual peonage resulted.

While landless blacks in the countryside were being reduced to economic dependence, those in towns and cities found themselves living in an increasingly segregated society. The Black Codes of 1865 attempted to require separation of the races in public places and facilities; when most of the codes were set aside by federal authorities as violations of the Civil Rights Act of 1866, the

Education was one route through which the former slaves believed they could escape the harsh economic and social conditions of the Reconstruction South. The earliest schools for the freedmen, like this primary school at Vicksburg, Mississippi, were usually staffed by white women from one of the northern abolitionist or missionary societies.

same end was often achieved through private initiative and community pressure. In some cities blacks successfully resisted being consigned to separate streetcars by appealing to the military during the brief period when it exercised authority or by organizing boycotts. But they found it almost impossible to gain admittance to most hotels, restaurants, and other privately owned establishments catering to whites. On railroads, separate black, or "Jim Crow," cars were not yet the rule, but Afro-Americans were normally denied first-class accommodations. When black-supported Republican governments came to power in 1868, some of them passed civil rights acts requiring equal access to public facilities, but little effort was made to enforce the legislation.

Some forms of racial separation were not openly discriminatory, and blacks accepted or even endorsed them. Freedmen who had belonged to white churches as slaves welcomed the chance to join all-black denominations like the African Methodist Episcopal Chuch, which provided freedom from white dominance and a more congenial style of worship. The first schools for ex-slaves were all-black institutions established by the Freedmen's Bureau and various northern missionary societies. Having been denied any education at all during the antebellum period, most blacks viewed separate schooling as an opportunity rather than as a form of discrimination. When the Radical governments set up public school systems, they condoned de facto educational segregation. Only in the city schools of New Orleans

and at the University of South Carolina were there serious attempts during Reconstruction to bring white and black students together in the same classrooms.

The upshot of all forms of racial separatism—whether produced by white prejudice or black accommodation—was to create a divided society, one in which blacks and whites lived much of the time in separate worlds. But there were two exceptions to this pattern: one was at work, where blacks necessarily dealt with white employers; the other was in the political sphere, where blacks sought to exercise their rights as citizens of a democracy.

Political Reconstruction in the South

The state governments that emerged in 1865 had little or no regard for the rights of the freed slaves. Some of their codes even made black unemployment a crime, which meant that blacks had to make long-term contracts with white employers or face judicial punishment. Others limited the rights of blacks to own property or engage in occupations other than those of servant or laborer. The codes were set aside by the actions of Congress, the military, and the Freedmen's Bureau, but private violence and discrimination against blacks continued on a massive scale unchecked by state authorities. Hundreds, perhaps thousands, of blacks were murdered by whites in

1865–1866, and few of the perpetrators were brought to justice.

The imposition of military rule in 1867 was designed in part to protect former slaves from violence and intimidation, but the task was beyond the capacity of the few thousand troops stationed in the South. When new constitutions were approved and states readmitted to the Union under the congressional plan in 1868, the problem became more severe. White opponents of Radical Reconstruction adopted systematic terrorism as a means of keeping blacks away from the polls. Yet the military presence was progressively reduced, leaving the new Republican regimes to fight a losing battle against armed white supremacists. In the words of historian William Gillette, "there was simply no federal force large enough to give heart to black Republicans or to bridle southern white violence."

Hastily organized in 1867, the southern Republican party dominated the constitution making of 1868 and the regimes that came out of it. The party was an attempted coalition of three social groups (which of course varied in their relative strength from state to state). One was the same class that was becoming the backbone of the Republican party in the North—businessmen with an interest in enlisting government on the side of private enterprise. Many Republicans of this stripe were recent arrivals from the North—so-called carpetbaggers—but some were former Whig planters or merchants who were born in the South or had immigrated to the region before the war and now saw a chance to realize their dreams for commercial and industrial development.

Poor white farmers, especially those from upland areas where Unionist sentiment had been strong during the Civil War, were a second element in the original coalition. These owners of small farms expected the party to favor their interests at the expense of the wealthy landowners and to come to their aid with special legislation when—as was often the case in this period of economic upheaval—they faced the loss of their homesteads to creditors. Newly enfranchised blacks were the third group to which the Republicans appealed. Blacks formed the vast majority of the Republican rank and file in most states and were concerned mainly with education, civil rights, and landownership.

Under the best of conditions, these coalitions

Race riots erupted in several southern cities as white Southerners turned to violence against the newly freed blacks. The scene above is from the Memphis riots of 1866.

would have been difficult to maintain. Each group had its own distinct goals and did not fully support the aims of the other segments. White yeomen, for example, had a bred-in-the-bone resistance to black equality. And for how long could one expect essentially conservative businessmen to support costly measures for the elevation or relief of the lower classes of either race? In some states, astute Democratic politicians exploited these divisions by appealing to disaffected white Republicans. As a result, Republican coalitions split, opening the way for the overthrow of Radical rule.

But during the relatively brief period when they were in power in the South—it varied from one to nine years depending on the state—the Republicans chalked up some notable achievements. They established (on paper at least) the South's first adequate systems of public education, democratized state and local government, and appropriated funds for an enormous expansion of public services and welfare responsibilities. They also sought to foster economic development by subsidizing the construction of railroads and other internal improvements.

These activities—particularly the grants to railroads—were often accompanied by inefficiency, waste, and corruption. Although the Radical regimes brought needed reforms to the South, it can scarcely be claimed that they were model governments. Embezzlement of public funds and bribery of state lawmakers or officials were common occurrences. State debts and tax burdens rose enormously, mainly because governments had undertaken heavy new responsibilities, but partly as a result of waste and graft. But the situation varied from state to state; ruling cliques in Louisiana and South Carolina were guilty of much wrongdoing, yet Mississippi had a relatively honest and frugal regime.

Furthermore, southern corruption was not exceptional, nor was it a special result of the extension of suffrage to uneducated blacks, as critics of Radical Reconstruction have claimed. It was part of a national pattern during an era when private interests considered buying government favors a part of the cost of doing business, and many politicians expected to profit by obliging them. The Louisiana governor who pocketed $100,000 in a single year on an $8000 salary was a small-time operator compared to Boss Tweed of New York City, whose notorious "Ring" probably stole more than was embezzled in all the southern states combined. If railroad magnate Jay Gould could bribe the majority of the New York state legislature to gain concessions for the Erie Railroad, it should come as no surprise that "Honest John" Patterson, representing the Blue Ridge Railroad, could do the same in South Carolina.

Blacks bore only a limited responsibility for the dishonesty of the Radical governments. Although sixteen blacks served in Congress—two in the Senate—between 1869 and 1880, only in South Carolina did blacks constitute a majority of even one house of the state legislature. Furthermore, no black governors were elected during Reconstruction (although P. B. S. Pinchback served for a time as acting governor of Louisiana). The biggest grafters were opportunistic whites—some of the most notorious were carpetbaggers but others were native Southerners. Businessmen offering bribes included members of the prewar gentry who were staunch opponents of Radical programs. Some black legislators went with the tide and accepted "loans" from those railroad lobbyists who would pay most for their votes, but the same men could usually be depended upon to vote the will of their constituents on civil rights or educational issues.

It was unfortunate, however, that blacks first entered American politics at a time when public ethics were at a low point. They served or supported corrupt and wasteful regimes because they had no alternative. Although the Democrats, or "Conservatives" as they called themselves in some states, made sporadic efforts to attract black voters, it was clear that if they won control, they would attempt to strip blacks of their civil and political rights. But opponents of Radical Reconstruction were able to capitalize on racial prejudice and persuade many Americans that "good government" was synonymous with white supremacy.

Contrary to myth, the small number of blacks elected to state or national office during Reconstruction demonstrated on the average more integrity and competence than their white counterparts. Most were fairly well educated, having been free Negroes or unusually privileged slaves before the war. Among the most capable were Senator Blanche K. Bruce of Mississippi—elected to the Senate in 1874 after rising to deserved prominence in the Republican party of his home state; Congressman Robert Brown Elliott of South Carolina—an adroit politician who was also a consistent champion of civil rights; and Congressman James T. Rapier of Alabama, who stirred Congress and the nation in 1873 with his eloquent appeals for federal aid to southern education and new laws to enforce equal rights for Afro-Americans.

The Age of Grant

Ulysses S. Grant was the only president between Jackson and Wilson to serve two full and consecutive terms. But unlike other chief executives so favored by fortune and the electorate, Grant is commonly regarded as a failure. Historians used to blame him mainly for the corruption that surfaced in his administration. More recently he has been condemned for the inconsistency and ultimate failure of his southern policy. The charges are valid, and no one is likely to make the case that he was a great statesman. Faced with the demands of the presidency, Grant found that he had no strong principles to guide him except

■ *In the Senate, Blanche K. Bruce (left) championed the causes of citizenship for the American Indians and improvement of the Mississippi River.* Electioneering in the South, *a sketch by W. L. Sheppard, depicts a black politician campaigning for votes among newly enfranchised freedmen.*

loyalty to old friends and to politicians who supported him. But the problems he faced were difficult, if not insoluble. A president with a clearer sense of duty and purpose might have done little better.

Rise of the Money Question

The impeachment crisis of 1868 represented the high point of popular interest in Reconstruction issues. Already competing for public attention was the question of how to manage the nation's currency, and more specifically, what to do about the greenbacks—paper money issued during the war. Hugh McCulloch, secretary of the Treasury under Johnson, favored a return to "sound" money and in 1866, he had initiated a policy of withdrawing greenbacks from circulation until they were on a par with gold, thus allowing a return to payments in silver or gold. Opposition to this hard-money policy and the resulting deflation came from a number of groups; it split both the major parties. In general, the "greenbackers"

were strongest in the credit-hungry West and among expansionist-minded manufacturers. Defenders of hard money were mostly the commercial and financial interests in the East; they received crucial support from intellectuals who regarded government-sponsored inflation as immoral or contrary to the natural laws of classical economics.

In 1868 the money question surged briefly to the forefront of national politics. Faced with a business recession blamed on McCulloch's policy of contracting the currency, Congress voted to stop the retirement of greenbacks. The Democratic party, responding to midwestern pressure, included in its platform a plan calling for the redemption of much of the Civil War debt in greenbacks rather than gold, despite the fact that bondholders had been assured of specie payment. But divisions within the parties prevented the money question from becoming a central issue in the presidential campaign. The Democrats nominated Governor Horatio Seymour of New York, a sound-money supporter, thus nullifying their progreenback platform. Republicans based their

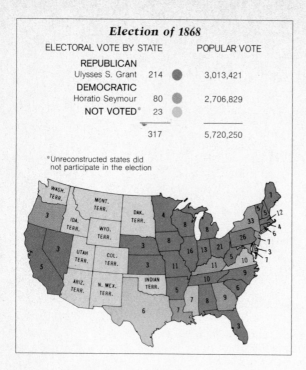

Election of 1868

ELECTORAL VOTE BY STATE   POPULAR VOTE

REPUBLICAN
Ulysses S. Grant   214   3,013,421

DEMOCRATIC
Horatio Seymour   80   2,706,829

NOT VOTED°   23

    317   5,720,250

°Unreconstructed states did
not participate in the election

campaign mainly on a defense of their reconstruction policy and a celebration of their popular candidate. With the help of votes from the Republican-dominated southern states, Grant won a decisive victory.

In 1869 and '70 a Republican-controlled Congress passed laws that assured payment in gold to most bondholders but eased the burden of the huge Civil War debt by refunding it, which meant that bonds soon coming due were exchanged for those that would not be payable for ten, fifteen, or thirty years. In this way the public credit was protected, but at the same time those who had purchased bonds during the war with depreciated paper currency were assured of great profits.

Still unresolved was the problem of what to do about the $356 million in greenbacks that remained in circulation. Hard-money proponents wanted to retire them quickly, while inflationists thought more should be issued to stimulate the economy. Both opinions were held by leading Republicans. The Grant administration followed the middle course of allowing the greenbacks to float until economic expansion would bring them to a par with gold, thus permitting a painless return to specie payments. But the panic of 1873, which brought much of the economy to its knees, led to a revival of agitation to inflate the curren-

cy. Debt-ridden farmers, who would be the backbone of the greenback movement for years to come, now joined the easy-money clamor for the first time.

Responding to the money and credit crunch, Congress moved in 1874 to authorize a modest issue of new greenbacks. But Grant, influenced by the opinions of hard-money financiers, vetoed the bill. In 1875, Congress, led by Senator John Sherman of Ohio, enacted the Specie Resumption Act which provided for a limited reduction of greenbacks leading to full resumption of specie payments by January 1, 1879. Although Congress softened the blow by permitting an expanded issue of national bank notes, its action was widely interpreted as deflation in the midst of depression. Farmers and workers, who were already suffering acutely from deflation, reacted with dismay and anger.

The Democratic party could not capitalize adequately on these sentiments because of the influence of its own hard-money faction, and in 1876 an independent Greenback party entered the national political arena. The party's nominee for president, Peter Cooper, received an insignificant number of votes, but in 1878 the Greenback Labor party polled more than a million votes and elected fourteen congressmen. Greenbackers kept the money issue alive through the next decade.

Retreat from Reconstruction

The Republican effort to make equal rights for blacks the law of the land culminated in the Fifteenth Amendment. Passed by Congress in 1869 and ratified by the states in 1870, the amendment prohibited any state from denying a citizen the right to vote because of race, color, or previous condition of servitude. A more radical version, requiring universal manhood suffrage, was rejected because it departed too sharply from traditional views of federal-state relations. States therefore could still limit the suffrage by imposing literacy tests, property qualifications, or poll taxes allegedly applying to all racial groups; such devices would eventually be used to strip southern blacks of the right to vote. But the makers of the amendment did not foresee this result. They believed that their action would prevent future Congresses or southern constitutional conven-

An engraving celebrating the passage of the Fifteenth Amendment, which provided for universal male suffrage. Passage of the amendment was troubling to many feminists since women were still denied the right to vote (see pp. 470–471).

THE RESULT OF THE FIFTEENTH AMENDMENT,
And the Rise and Progress of the African Race in America and its final Accomplishment, and Celebration on May 19? A.D. 1870.

tions from repealing or nullifying the provisions for black suffrage included in the Reconstruction Acts. A secondary aim was to enfranchise blacks in those northern states that still denied them the vote.

The Grant administration was charged with enforcing the amendment and protecting black voting rights in the reconstructed states. Since survival of the Republican regimes depended on black support, political partisanship dictated federal action, even though the North's emotional and ideological commitment to black citizenship was waning.

Between 1868 and 1872, the main threat to southern Republican regimes came from the Ku Klux Klan and other secret societies bent on restoring white supremacy by intimidating blacks who sought to exercise their political rights. First organized in Tennessee in 1866, the Klan spread rapidly to other states, adopting increasingly lawless and brutal tactics. A grassroots vigilance movement and not a centralized conspiracy, the Klan thrived on local initiative and gained support from whites of all social classes. Its secrecy, decentralization, popular support, and utter ruthlessness made it very difficult to suppress. As soon as blacks had been granted the right to vote, hooded night riders began to visit the cabins of those who were known to be active Republicans; some victims were only threatened, but others were whipped or even murdered. A typical incident was related by a black Georgian: "They broke my door open, took me out of bed, took me to the woods and whipped me three hours or more and left me for dead. They said to me, 'Do you think you will vote for another damned radical ticket?'"

These methods were first used effectively in the presidential election of 1868. Grant lost Louisiana and Georgia mainly because the Klan—or the Knights of the White Camelia as the Louisiana variant was called—launched a reign of terror to prevent prospective black voters from exercising their right. In Louisiana political violence claimed more than a thousand lives, and in Arkansas, which Grant managed to carry, more than two hundred Republicans, including a congressman, were assassinated.

Thereafter, Klan terrorism was directed mainly at Republican state governments. Virtual insurrections broke out in Arkansas, Tennessee, North Carolina, and parts of South Carolina. Republican governors called out the state militia to fight the Klan, but only the Arkansas militia succeeded in bringing it to heel. In Tennessee, North Carolina, and Georgia Klan activities helped undermine

■ Above, a member of the Ku Klux Klan, a secret white supremacist organization, in typical regalia. Before any election, hooded Klansmen terrorized blacks to discourage them from voting.

■ The White League was another organization formed to deny blacks their rights. Above, armed White Leaguers guard a ballot box to prevent black voters from depositing their ballots.

Republican control, thus allowing the Democrats to come to power in all of these states by 1870.

Faced with the violent overthrow of the southern Republican party, Congress and the Grant administration were forced to act. A series of laws passed in 1870–1871 sought to enforce the Fifteenth Amendment by providing federal protection for black suffrage and authorizing use of the army against the Klan. These "Ku Klux Klan" or "Force" Acts made interference with voting rights a federal crime and established provisions for government supervision of elections. In addition, the legislation empowered the president to call out troops and suspend the writ of habeas corpus to quell insurrection. In 1871–1872, thousands of suspected Klansmen were arrested by the military or U.S. marshals, and the writ was suspended in nine counties of South Carolina which had been virtually taken over by the secret order. Although most of the accused Klansmen either were never brought to trial, were acquitted, or received suspended sentences, the enforcement effort was vigorous enough to put a damper on hooded terrorism and ensure relatively fair and peaceful elections in 1872.

Radical Reconstruction in the South was obviously tottering by 1872, and further outbreaks of violence helped bring its total collapse. The surviving Republican governments were riddled by factionalism and tainted by charges of corruption, and the northern public became increasingly disenchanted with federal intervention on behalf of these regimes, even when their opponents were resorting to riot and murder.

Grant did intervene militarily in Louisiana in 1874 when an overt paramilitary organization known as the White League staged an armed insurrection against a Republican government accused of stealing an election. But when another unofficial militia—the White Line of Mississippi —instigated a series of bloody race riots prior to the state elections of 1875, Grant refused the governor's request for federal troops. As a result, black voters were successfully intimidated—one county registered only seven Republican votes where there had been a black majority of two thousand, and Mississippi fell to the Conservatives. According to one account, Grant decided to withhold troops because he had been warned that intervention might cost the Republicans the crucial state of Ohio in the same off-year elections.

By 1876 Republicans held on to only three southern states—South Carolina, Louisiana, and Florida. Partly because of Grant's hesitant and inconsistent use of presidential power but mainly because the northern electorate would no longer tolerate military action to sustain Republican governments and black voting rights, Radical Reconstruction was falling into total eclipse.

Spoilsmen Versus Reformers

One reason Grant found it increasingly difficult to take strong action to protect southern Republicans was the bad odor surrounding his stewardship of the federal government and the Republican party. Reformers charged that a corrupt national administration was propping up bad governments in the South for personal and partisan advantage. An apparent case in point was Grant's intervention in Louisiana in 1872 on behalf of an ill-reputed Republican faction headed by his wife's brother-in-law, who controlled federal patronage as collector of customs in New Orleans.

The Republican party in the Grant era was rapidly losing the idealism and high purpose associated with the crusade against slavery. By the beginning of the 1870s, the men who had been the conscience of the party—old-line radicals like Thaddeus Stevens, Charles Sumner, and Benjamin Wade—were either dead, out of politics, or at odds with the administration. New leaders of a different stamp, whom historians have dubbed "spoilsmen" or "politicos" were taking their place. When he made common cause with hard-boiled manipulators like Senators Roscoe Conkling of New York and James G. Blaine of Maine, Grant lost credibility with reform-minded Republicans.

During Grant's first administration, an aura of scandal surrounded the White House but did not directly implicate the President. In 1869 the financial buccaneer Jay Gould enlisted the aid of a brother-in-law of Grant to further his incredible scheme to corner the gold market. Gould failed in the attempt, but he did manage to save himself and come away with a huge profit.

Grant's first-term vice-president, Schuyler Colfax of Indiana, was directly involved in the notorious Crédit Mobilier scandal. Crédit Mobilier was a construction company that actually served as a fraudulent device for siphoning off profits that should have gone to the stockholders of the Union Pacific Railroad, which was the beneficiary of massive federal land grants. In order to forestall government inquiry into this arrangement, Crédit Mobilier stock was distributed to influential congressmen, including Colfax (who was Speaker of the House before he was elected vice-president). The whole business came to light just before the campaign of 1872.

Republicans who could not tolerate such corruption or had other grievances against the administration broke with Grant in 1872 and formed a third party committed to "honest government" and "reconciliation" between the North and the South. Led initially by high-minded reformers like Senator Carl Schurz of Missouri, the "Liberal Republicans" endorsed reform of the civil service to curb the corruption-breeding patronage system and advocated strict laissez-faire economic policies—which meant low tariffs, an end to government subsidies for railroads, and hard money. Despite their rhetoric of idealism and reform, the Liberal Republicans were extremely conservative in their notions of what government should do to assure justice for blacks and other underprivileged Americans.

The Liberal Republicans' national convention nominated Horace Greeley, editor of the respected *New York Tribune*. This was a curious and divisive choice since Greeley was at odds with the founders of the movement on the tariff question and indifferent to civil service reform. The Democrats also endorsed Greeley, mainly because he promised to end Radical Reconstruction by restoring "self-government" to the South.

But the journalist turned out to be a poor campaigner who failed to inspire enthusiasm from lifelong supporters of either party. Most

The Election of 1872

Candidate	Party	Popular Vote	Electoral Vote*
Grant	Republican	3,598,235	286
Greeley	Democrat and Liberal Republican	2,834,761	Greeley died before the electoral college voted.

Out of a total of 366 electoral votes. Greeley's votes were divided among the four minor candidates.

Woman's Rights and the Fifteenth Amendment

Extending citizenship and the right to vote to the newly freed slaves marked a milestone in their passage from slavery to freedom. The Fourteenth Amendment, adopted in 1868, defined citizenship and forbade the states from abridging the rights of citizens or denying them "equal protection of the laws." The amendment, in effect, extended to blacks the rights, privileges, and immunities of citizenship. The Fifteenth Amendment, proposed by Congress in 1869 and ratified by the states within a year, prohibited federal and state governments from denying the vote to anyone "on account of race, color, or previous condition of servitude." Of course, states could still restrict the right to vote, by property and literacy requirements, for example; hence the amendment prohibited one type of disfranchisement rather than requiring universal manhood suffrage.

Nonetheless, the amendment seemed to offer something to everyone with a stake in the Union's victory. For the abolitionists and other reformers, it meant the triumph of principles of human rights and the admission of blacks into political equality with whites. For Republican party leaders, it created a bloc of black voters in the South likely to be grateful to its northern liberators—and to demonstrate its gratitude at the polls. And to the slaves themselves, it gave some protection from their former masters, a chance to defend themselves against southern political action aimed at returning them to a form of slavery. But to the many women who had worked for emancipation, the amendment offered little. Congress had neglected their demands for woman suffrage while enfranchising the male members of a group that remained at the bottom of society in status and wealth.

Feminists and abolitionists had a long history of intermittent periods of cooperation and conflict. Women were active in the abolition movement from the first, forming female auxiliaries to the antislavery societies, collecting signatures on antislavery petitions, and raising money for the cause. As long as the women were willing to work behind the scenes, abolitionist leaders welcomed their support. But in the late 1830s, inspired by concern for the slaves and belief in their own abilities, women began to lecture against slavery in public, to take part in abolitionist debates, and to serve on abolitionist committees. Abolitionists then began to argue among themselves over the proper role of women in their organizations.

The women's issue divided abolitionists into

three main camps. William Lloyd Garrison and his radical followers saw abolitionism as part of a larger crusade for human rights and welcomed women's participation in the movement. They did not actively work for woman suffrage or make it a part of their program, but they insisted that anyone who wished might speak out on behalf of the slave. More conservative abolitionists like Lewis Tappan saw emancipation as removing the main blemish from a generally healthy society and feared the disruption of too much change. Both custom and divine law told them that women belonged at home in the family, under the protection of a husband or father. These conservatives believed that womankind neither needed nor deserved a public voice and thus had no place in official abolitionist activity. A third, smaller group of men, like Theodore Weld, endorsed feminism but urged caution and prudence on the radicals. The northern public, they reasoned, would not support emancipation if it were linked to other reforms. Women should keep silent until the slaves were freed, and then they could work for their own liberation.

The women who had started the controversy were drawn into a stronger commitment to their own rights. "What *then* can *woman* do for the slave," asked Angelina Grimké, "when she herself is under the feet of man and shamed into silence?" Continuing to work in the cause of the slave, these women developed a separate feminist movement as well, demanding—among other things—the vote.

These divisions reemerged in the late 1860s when Congress debated the future of the freedmen. Male antislavery advocates at last had a chance to influence national policy, and their doubts about how far reform should be carried took on a new importance. A few men supported the most radical position, that the demands of blacks and women were inseparable and must be met together. The more conservative abolitionists, who had never supported woman's rights, continued to work only for black men's suffrage. They found powerful allies among the many Republicans in Congress who saw no political advantage in giving the vote to women. But even former radicals now heeded the counsel of expediency, concluding that women must wait to act

until black freedom had been secured. It was "the Negro's hour," and the first priority of Reconstruction government must be to guarantee the black man's status as an American citizen. Blacks, as part of an enlarged and liberal voting public, would later aid the passage of woman suffrage.

Women were not so sure. Upset by language in the Fourteenth Amendment limiting its protections to "male citizens," they campaigned hard for a suffrage amendment that would include women as well as blacks. Their defeat caused a new division within their own ranks. Differences over the Fifteenth Amendment split feminists into two factions, each with its own organization. One, represented by Lucy Stone (p. 470 right), Julia Ward Howe, and the American Woman Suffrage Association, sided with the advocates of expediency and supported the Fifteenth Amendment. Though the amendment had been a disappointment, "I will be thankful in my soul if *any* body can get out of this terrible pit," proclaimed Lucy Stone. Susan B. Anthony (p. 470 left) disagreed, threatening to "cut off this right arm of mine before I will ever work for or demand the ballot for the Negro and not the woman." Anthony and Elizabeth Cady Stanton broke their ties with the abolitionists and Radical Republicans, who they felt had betrayed them. Speaking out vehemently against the amendment, they organized a movement led by women that concentrated on women's goals. In 1869 they formed the National Woman Suffrage Association, committed to passing a sixteenth amendment that would enfranchise women.

Leaders of both factions—Stanton and Anthony as well as Stone and Howe—had worked to bring about emancipation; Stanton and Anthony had even led a petition drive for the Thirteenth Amendment freeing the slaves. But their success as abolitionists convinced them of their abilities as women, and to see the black man given rights denied themselves seemed a brutal slap in the face. Women of education and status could not vote; freed*men* could. Feminists were faced with a painful choice between full loyalty to their own cause and full support for the rights of blacks. The decisions they made divided the women suffrage movement for a generation to come.

I BEG TO REPEAT THAT THESE FRAUDS ON THE GOVERNMENT SHALL BE PROBED TO THE VERY BOTTOM.

TAMMANY RING. CANAL RING. WHISKEY RING. INDIAN RING PRESS RING BELKNAP. FRAUD CLAIMS. STATE RING. COUNTY RING. TOWN RING. WARD RING. BACK PAY GRAB EMMA MINE WHISKEY FRAUDS BRIBERY

■ "In for It," a rare anti-Grant cartoon by Thomas Nast, shows the President falling headlong into the barrel of scandals that tainted his administration.

Republicans stuck with Grant, despite the corruption issue, because they still could not stomach the idea of ex-rebels returning to power in the South. Many Democrats, recalling Greeley's previous record as a staunch Republican, simply stayed away from the polls. The result was a decisive victory for Grant, whose 56 percent of the popular vote was the highest percentage won by any candidate between Andrew Jackson and Theodore Roosevelt.

Grant's second administration bore out the reformers' worst suspicions about corruption in high places. In 1875 the public learned that federal revenue officials had conspired with distillers to defraud the government of millions of dollars in liquor taxes. Grant's private secretary, Orville E. Babcock, was indicted as a member of the "Whiskey Ring" and was saved from conviction only by the President's personal intercession. The next year, Grant's Secretary of War William E.

Belknap was impeached by the House after an investigation revealed that he had taken bribes for the sale of Indian trading posts. He avoided conviction in the Senate only by resigning from office before his trial. Grant fought hard to protect Belknap, to the point of participating in what a later generation might call a "cover-up."

There is no evidence that Grant profited personally from any of the misdeeds of his subordinates. Yet he is not entirely without blame for the corruption in his administration. He failed to take action against the malefactors, and even after their guilt had been clearly established, he tried to shield them from justice.

Reunion and the New South

Congressional Reconstruction prolonged the sense of sectional division and conflict for a dozen years after the guns had fallen silent. Its final liquidation in 1877 opened the way to a reconciliation of North and South that some historians have celebrated as a culminating achievement of American nationalism. But the costs of reunion were high for less privileged groups in the South. The civil and political rights of blacks, left unprotected, were progressively and relentlessly stripped away by white supremacist regimes. Lower-class whites saw their interests sacrificed to those of capitalists and landlords. Despite the rhetoric hailing a prosperous "New South," the region remained poor and open to exploitation by northern business interests.

The Compromise of 1877

The election of 1876 pitted Rutherford B. Hayes of Ohio, a Republican governor untainted by the scandals of the Grant era, against Governor Samuel J. Tilden of New York, a Democratic reformer who had battled against Tammany Hall and the Tweed Ring. (For more on the Tweed Ring, see chapter 19.) Honest government was apparently the electorate's highest priority. When the returns came in, Tilden had clearly won the popular vote and seemed likely to win a narrow victory in the electoral college. But the result was placed in

Rutherford B. Hayes (above) was awarded the presidency in the disputed election of 1876 even though he won fewer popular votes than his opponent, Democrat Samuel Tilden.

be ratified by both houses of Congress. The Republican-dominated Senate readily approved it, but Democrats in the House planned a filibuster to delay the final counting of the electoral votes until after inauguration day. If the filibuster succeeded, neither candidate would have a majority and, as provided in the Constitution, the election would be decided by the House, where the Democrats controlled enough states to elect Tilden.

To ensure Hayes' election, Republican leaders negotiated secretly with conservative southern Democrats, some of whom seemed willing to abandon the filibuster if the last troops were withdrawn and "home rule" was restored to the South. Eventually an informal bargain was struck, which historians have dubbed "the Compromise of 1877." In a sense, Hayes did not really concede anything, because he had already decided to end federal support for the crumbling Radical regimes. But southern negotiators were heartened by firm assurances that this would indeed be the policy. Some were also influenced by vaguer promises involving federal support for southern railroads and internal improvements.

doubt when the returns from the three southern states still controlled by the Republicans—South Carolina, Florida, and Louisiana—were contested. If Hayes were to be awarded these three states, plus one contested electoral vote in Oregon, Republican strategists realized, he would triumph in the electoral college by a single vote.

The outcome of the election remained undecided for months, plunging the nation into a major political crisis. To resolve the impasse, Congress appointed a special electoral commission of fifteen members to determine who would receive the votes of the disputed states. Originally composed of seven Democrats, seven Republicans, and an independent, it fell under Republican control when the independent member resigned to run for the Senate, and a Republican was appointed to take his place. The commission split along party lines and voted 8 to 7 to award Hayes the disputed states. But this decision still had to

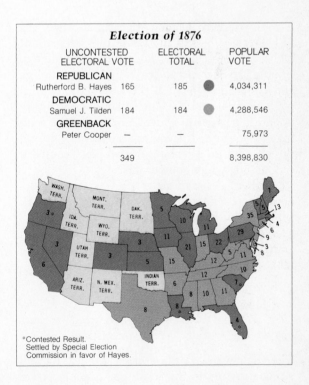

Election of 1876

	UNCONTESTED ELECTORAL VOTE	ELECTORAL TOTAL		POPULAR VOTE
REPUBLICAN				
Rutherford B. Hayes	165	185	●	4,034,311
DEMOCRATIC				
Samuel J. Tilden	184	184	●	4,288,546
GREENBACK				
Peter Cooper	—	—		75,973
		349		8,398,830

*Contested Result.
Settled by Special Election Commission in favor of Hayes.

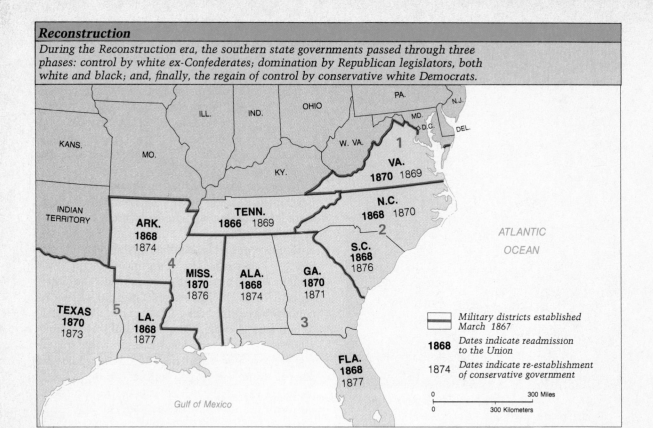

Reconstruction

During the Reconstruction era, the southern state governments passed through three phases: control by white ex-Confederates; domination by Republican legislators, both white and black; and, finally, the regain of control by conservative white Democrats.

PA.
N.J.
ILL. IND. OHIO
MD.
D.C.
DEL.
KANS.
W. VA. **1**
MO.
VA.
1870 1869
KY.
INDIAN TERRITORY
N.C.
1868 1870
ARK.
1868
1874
TENN.
1866 1869
2
ATLANTIC OCEAN
S.C.
1868
1876
4
MISS.
1870
1876
ALA.
1868
1874
GA.
1870
1871
TEXAS
1870
1873
5
LA.
1868
1877
3

Military districts established March 1867

1868 Dates indicate readmission to the Union

1874 Dates indicate re-establishment of conservative government

FLA.
1868
1877

0   300 Miles
0   300 Kilometers

Gulf of Mexico

With southern Democratic acquiescence, the filibuster was broken and Hayes took the oath of office. He immediately ordered the army not to resist a Democratic takeover in South Carolina and Louisiana. Thus fell the last of the Radical governments, and the entire South was firmly under the control of white Democrats. The trauma of the war and Reconstruction had destroyed the chances for a renewal of two-party competition among white Southerners.

Northern Republicans soon reverted to denouncing the South for its crimes against black suffrage. But this "waving of the bloody shirt" soon degenerated into an empty campaign ritual aimed at northern voters who could still be moved by sectional antagonism.

The New South

The men who led the crusade against Radical Reconstruction in the South and came to power after it fell in one state after another are usually referred to as the "Redeemers." They were predominantly upper class in origins and loyalties, but the elite that they represented was not identical to the ruling group of the Old South. Although planters who had been large slaveholders were conspicuous in their ranks, most Redeemers favored commercial and industrial interests over those that were strictly agrarian. Some were sharp-witted men who had seized the political and economic opportunities created by disordered conditions in the postwar South. Others were prewar aristocrats who had made the adjustment to a new age by adopting the values and practices of tough-minded businessmen.

The ideology of the Redeemers rested on two bases—white supremacy and industrial progress. The first was the principal rallying cry that brought them to power in the first place. Once the Redeemers were in office they found that they could stay there by charging that opponents of ruling Democratic cliques were trying to divide "the white man's party" and open the way to a

The first industries of the New South were usually processing plants for the agricultural products of the region. Above, blacks working on a sugar plantation in Louisiana are cutting sugar cane to be processed in the plantation's refinery.

return of "black domination." The gospel of industrial progress—the image of a "New South" where factories and railroads would bring prosperity to all—served to mask policies that favored employers over workers, landlords over tenants, and creditors over debtors. It also opened the doors to northern capital and encouraged absentee ownership of important segments of the southern economy.

The new governments were more economical than those of Reconstruction, mainly because they cut back drastically on appropriations for schools and other needed public services. But they were scarcely more honest—embezzlement of funds and bribery of officials continued to occur to an alarming extent. Louisiana, for example, suffered for decades from the flagrant corruption associated with a state-chartered lottery.

The Redeemer regimes of the late 1870s and '80s badly neglected the interests of small white farmers. Whites, as well as blacks, were suffering from the notorious "crop lien" system, which gave local merchants who advanced credit at high rates of interest during the growing season the right to take possession of the harvested crop on terms that buried farmers deeper and deeper in debt. As a result, increasing numbers of whites lost title to their homesteads and were reduced to tenancy. When a depression of world cotton prices added to the burden of a ruinous credit system, agrarian protesters began to challenge the ruling elite, first through the Southern Farmers' Alliance of the late 1880s and then by supporting its political descendant—the Populist party of the 1890s.

But the greatest hardships imposed by the new order were reserved for blacks. The Redeemers promised, as part of the understanding that led to the end of federal intervention in 1877, that they would respect the rights of blacks as set forth in the Fourteenth and Fifteenth amendments. Governor Wade Hampton of South Carolina was especially vocal in pledging that Afro-Americans would not be reduced to second-class citizenship by the new regimes. But when blacks tried to vote Republican in the "redeemed" states, they encountered renewed violence and intimidation. "Bulldozing" Afro-American voters remained common practice in state elections during the late 1870s and early '80s; those blacks who withstood the threat of losing their jobs or being evicted from tenant farms if they voted for the party of Lincoln were visited at night and literally whipped into line. The message was clear—vote Democratic or vote not at all.

Furthermore, white Democrats now controlled the electoral machinery and were able to manipulate the black vote by stuffing ballot boxes, discarding unwanted votes, or reporting fraudulent totals. Some states also imposed complicated new voting requirements to discourage black participation. Full-scale disfranchisement did not occur until literacy tests and other legalized obstacles to voting were imposed in the period from 1890 to 1910, but by that time less formal and comprehensive methods had already made a mockery of the Fifteenth Amendment.

Nevertheless, blacks continued to vote freely in some localities until the 1890s; a few districts even elected black Republicans to Congress during the immediate post-Reconstruction period.

The last of these, Representative George H. White of North Carolina, served until 1901. His farewell address eloquently conveyed the agony of southern blacks in the era of Jim Crow (strict segregation).

These parting words are in behalf of an outraged, heart-broken, bruised, and bleeding but God-fearing people, faithful, industrious, loyal people—rising people, full of potential force . . . The only apology that I have to make for the earnestness with which I have spoken is that I am pleading for the life, the liberty, the future happiness, and manhood suffrage of one-eighth of the entire population of the United States.

The dark night of racism that fell on the South after Reconstruction seemed to unleash all the baser impulses of human nature. Between 1889 and 1899 an average of 187 blacks were lynched every year for alleged offenses against white supremacy. Those convicted of petty crimes against property were often little better off; many were condemned to be leased out to private contractors

Lynching was responsible for more than three thousand deaths between 1889 and 1918. Nor were lynchings confined to the South. During that thirty-year-period, only seven states reported no lynchings.

Supreme Court Decisions Affecting Black Civil Rights, 1875–1900

Hall v. *DeCuir* (1878)	Struck down Louisiana law prohibiting racial discrimination by "common carriers" (railroads, steamboats, buses). Court declares the law a "burden" on interstate commerce, over which states had no authority.
United States v. *Harris* (1882)	Federal laws to punish crimes such as murder and assault declared unconstitutional. Such crimes declared to be the sole concern of local government. Court ignores the frequent racial motivation behind such crimes in the South.
Civil Rights Cases (1883)	Struck down Civil Rights Act of 1875. Congress may not legislate on civil rights unless a *state* passes a discriminatory law. Court declares the Fourteenth Amendment silent on racial discrimination by private citizens.
Plessy v. *Ferguson* (1896)	Louisiana statute requiring "separate but equal" accommodations on railroads upheld. Court declares that segregation is *not* necessarily discrimination.
Williams v. *Mississippi* (1898)	State law requiring a literacy test to qualify for voting upheld. Court refuses to find any implication of racial discrimination in the law. Using such laws, southern states rapidly disenfranchise blacks.

whose brutality rivaled that of the most sadistic slaveholders. (Annual death rates in the convict camps ranged as high as 25 percent.) Finally, the dignity of blacks was cruelly affronted by the wave of segregation laws passed in the 1890s, which served to remind them constantly that they were deemed unfit to associate with whites on any basis that implied equality.

The North and the federal government did little or nothing to stem the tide of racial oppression in the South. A series of Supreme Court decisions between 1875 and 1896 gutted the Reconstruction amendments and the legislation passed to enforce them, leaving blacks virtually defenseless against political and social discrimination.

At the same time, the wounds of the Civil War were healing, and white Americans were seized by the spirit of sectional reconciliation. By the late 1880s, Union and Confederate veterans were tenting together and celebrating their common Americanism. "Reunion" was becoming a cultural as well as political reality. But whites could come back together only because Northerners had tacitly agreed to give Southerners a free hand

in their efforts to reduce blacks to a new form of servitude. It was the "outraged, heart-broken, bruised, and bleeding" Afro-Americans of the South who paid the heaviest price for sectional reunion.

Recommended Reading

Two excellent short accounts of what happened during Reconstruction are Kenneth Stampp, *The Era of Reconstruction, 1865–1877* (1965), and John Hope Franklin, *Reconstruction: After the Civil War* (1961). Both incorporate modern "revisionist" interpretations. W. E. B. DuBois, *Black Reconstruction in America, 1860–1880* (1935) is not altogether reliable but remains brilliant and provocative. The section on Reconstruction in J. G. Randall and David Donald, *The Civil War and Reconstruction*, 2d ed. (1969) is valuable because it seeks a middle ground between traditional views of Reconstruction and revisionist interpretations. The latest reconsiderations of Reconstruction issues can be found in J. Morgan Kousser and James M. McPherson, eds. *Region, Race, and Reconstruction: Essays in Honor of C. Vann Woodward* (1982). Morton Keller, *Affairs of State: Public Life in Late Nineteenth Century America* (1977), provides a brilliant analysis of American government and politics during Reconstruction and afterward.

Chronology

1863 Lincoln sets forth 10 percent Reconstruction plan

1864 Wade-Davis Bill passes Congress, is pocket-vetoed by Lincoln

1865 Johnson moves to reconstruct the South on his own initiative
Congress refuses to seat representatives and senators elected from states reestablished under presidential plan (December)

1866 Johnson vetoes Freedmen's Bureau Bill (February)
Johnson vetoes Civil Rights Act; it passes over his veto (April)
Congress passes Fourteenth Amendment (June)
Republicans increase their congressional majority in the fall elections

1867 First Reconstruction Act is passed over Johnson's veto (March)

1868 Johnson is impeached; he avoids conviction by one vote (February-May)
Southern blacks vote and serve in constitutional conventions
Grant wins presidential election, defeating Horatio Seymour

1869 Congress passes Fifteenth Amendment, granting blacks the right to vote

1870–1871 Congress passes Ku Klux Klan Acts to protect black voting rights in the South

1872 Grant relected president, defeating Horace Greeley, candidate of Liberal Republicans and Democrats

1873 Financial panic plunges nation into depression

1875 Congress passes Specie Resumption Act
"Whiskey Ring" scandal exposed

1876–1877 Disputed presidential election resolved in favor of Republican Hayes over Democrat Tilden

1877 "Compromise of 1877" results in end to military intervention in the South and fall of the last Radical governments

Particular phases of Reconstruction are covered in Eric L. McKitrick, *Andrew Johnson and Reconstruction, 1865–1867* (1960); W. R. Brock, *An American Crisis: Congress and Reconstruction, 1865–1867* (1963); and William Gillette, *Retreat from Reconstruction, 1869–1879* (1979). Leon F. Litwack, *Been in the Storm So Long: The Aftermath of Slavery* (1979), provides a moving portrayal of the black experience of emancipation. The best introduction to the Grant era is William S. McFeeley, *Grant: A Biography* (1981). On the end of Reconstruction and the character of the post-Reconstruction South, see two classic works by C. Vann Woodward: *Reunion and Reaction*, rev. ed. (1956) and *Origins of the New South, 1877–1913* (1951).

Additional Bibliography

The Reconstruction era is surveyed in Rembert W. Patrick, *The Reconstruction of the Nation* (1967); Avery O. Craven, *Reconstruction: The Ending of the Civil War* (1969); and Harold M. Hyman, ed., *New Frontiers of the American Reconstruction* (1966).

The conflict between the President and Congress is examined in David Donald, *The Politics of Reconstruction, 1863–1867* (1965); Michael Les Benedict, *A Compromise of Principle: Congressional Republicans and Reconstruction* (1974) and *The Impeachment and Trial of Andrew Johnson* (1973); and Hans L. Trefousse, *Impeachment of a President* (1975). On constitutional issues, Stanley I. Kutler, *Judicial Power and Reconstruction Politics* (1968), and Harold M. Hyman, *A More Perfect Union: The Impact of the Civil War and Reconstruction on the Constitution* (1973), are useful.

Reconstruction in the South is surveyed in E. Merton Coulter, *The South During Reconstruction* (1947). Michael Perman, *Reunion Without Compromise: The South and Reconstruction, 1865–1868* (1973), deals effectively with southern politics in the immediate postwar years. On the Freedmen's Bureau, see George R. Bentley, *A History of the Freedmen's Bureau* (1965); William McFeeley, *Yankee Godfather: General O. O. Howard and the Freedmen* (1968); and Donald G. Nieman, *To Set the Law in Motion: The Freedmen's Bureau and Legal Rights for Blacks, 1865–1868* (1979).

Harold O. Rabinowitz, *Race Relations in the Urban South, 1865–1890* (1977); Roger A. Fischer, *The Segregation Struggle in Louisiana, 1862–1877* (1974); and C. Vann Woodward, *The Strange Career of Jim Crow*, 3d rev. ed. (1974) cover race relations in the postwar South. Economic adjustments are analyzed in Lawrence N. Powell, *New Masters: Northern Planters During the Civil War and Reconstruction* (1980); Roger L. Ransom and Richard Sutch, *One Kind of Freedom: The Economic Consequences of Emancipation* (1977); Stephen J. DeCanio, *Agriculture in the Postbellum South* (1974); and Daniel A. Novak, *The Wheel of Servitude: Black Forced Labor After Emancipation* (1978).

American labor during Reconstruction is the subject

of David Montgomery, *Beyond Equality: Labor and the Radical Republicans, 1861–1872* (1967). Liberal republicanism is examined in Ari A. Hoogenboom, *Outlawing the Spoils: A History of Civil Service Reform* (1961), and John G. Sproat, *"The Best Men": Liberal Reformers in the Gilded Age* (1968).

Keith I. Polakoff, *The Politics of Inertia* (1977), challenges C. Vann Woodward's interpretation of the Compromise of 1877. Woodward's conclusions on the Redeemer period have been confirmed or disputed in Paul M. Gaston, *The New South Creed* (1970); William Cooper, *The Conservative Regime: South Carolina, 1877–1890* (1968); Jonathan M. Weiner, *Social Origins of the New South: Alabama, 1860–1885* (1978); and J. Morgan Kousser, *The Shaping of Southern Politics: Suffrage Restriction and the Establishment of the One-Party South* (1974). Post-Reconstruction northern attitudes toward the South and blacks are treated in Vincent de Santis, *Republicans Face the Southern Question* (1959); Stanley P. Hirshson, *Farewell to the Bloody Shirt: Northern Republicans and the Southern Negro, 1877–1893* (1962); and Rayford W. Logan, *The Betrayal of the Negro: From Rutherford B. Hayes to Woodrow Wilson*, rev. ed. (1965).

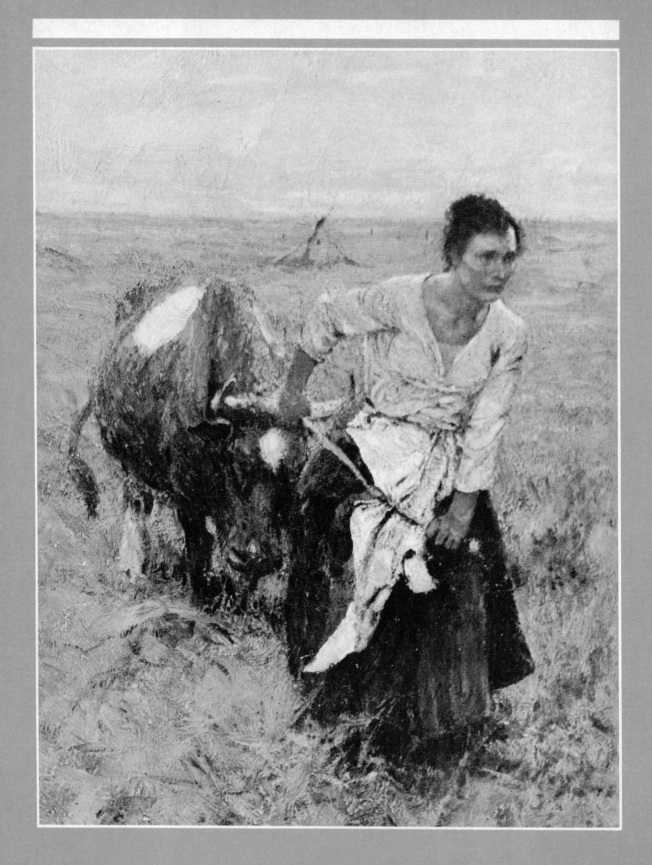

chapter 17
THE WEST: EXPLOITING AN EMPIRE

In the last three decades of the nineteenth century a flood of settlers ventured into America's newest and last West. James H. Kyner, a railroad contractor in Oregon, saw in the 1880s "an almost unbroken stream of emigrants from horizon to horizon. . . . Teams and covered wagons, horsemen, little bunches of cows, more wagons, some drawn by cows, men walking, women and children riding—an endless stream of hardy, optimistic folk, going west to seek their fortunes and to settle an empire."

Prospectors poured into unsettled areas in search of "paydirt," railroads crisscrossed the continent, eastern and foreign capitalists invested in cattle and land bonanzas, and farmers took up the promise of free western lands. In 1867 Horace Greeley, editor of the New York *Tribune*, told New York City's unemployed: "If you strike off into the broad, free West, and make yourself a farm from Uncle Sam's generous domain, you will crowd nobody, starve nobody, and neither you nor your children need evermore beg for something to do."

With the end of the Civil War, white Americans again claimed a special destiny to expand across the continent. In the process they crushed the culture of the American Indians and ignored the special contributions of those of other nationalities, such as the Chinese miners and laborers and the Mexican herdsmen. As millions moved west, the states of Colorado, Washington, Montana, the Dakotas, Idaho, Wyoming, and Utah were carved out of the vast lands across the Mississippi. At the turn of the century only Arizona, New Mexico, and Oklahoma remained as territories.

The West became a great colonial empire, harnessed to eastern capital and tied increasingly to national and international markets. Western economies depended to an unusual degree on the federal government, which subsidized their railroads, distributed their land, and spent millions of dollars for the upkeep of soldiers and Indians. Regional variations persisted; and Westerners remained proud of their hardy, individualistic traditions. Yet they imitated the East's social, cultural, and political patterns.

By the 1890s the West of the buffalo and Indian was gone, and instead there were cities and towns, health resorts, Paris fashions, and the latest magazines. As Francis Parkman, a New Englander who had made the dangerous crossing to Oregon in 1846, reflected sadly in 1892: "The Wild West is tamed, and its savage charms have withered."

Beyond the Frontier

The frontier line had reached the edge of the timber country of Missouri by 1840. Beyond lay an enormous land of rolling prairies, parched deserts, and rugged, majestic mountains. Emerging from the timber country, travelers first encountered the Great Plains—treeless, nearly flat, an endless "sea of grassy hillocks." The Prairie Plains, the eastern part of the region, enjoyed rich soil and good rainfall; it included parts of present-day Wisconsin, Minnesota, the Dakotas, Nebraska, Kansas, Oklahoma, and Texas. To the west— covering Montana, Wyoming, Colorado, New Mexico, and Arizona—were the High Plains, rough, semiarid, rising gently to the foothills of the Rocky Mountains.

Running from Alaska to central New Mexico, the Rockies presented a formidable barrier. There were valuable beaver in the streams and gold near Pike's Peak. But most travelers hurried through the northern passes, emerging in the desolate basin of present-day southern Idaho and Utah. Indians lived there—the Utes, Paiutes, Bannocks, and Shoshoni—scrabbling out a bare subsistence by digging for roots, seeds, and berries. Scornful whites called them "Digger Indians," a stern judgment on people trying their best to survive. On the west the lofty Coast ranges, the Cascades and Sierra Nevada, held back rainfall; beyond were the temperate lands of the Pacific Coast.

Early explorers like Zebulon Pike thought the country beyond the Mississippi was uninhabitable, fit only, Pike said, for "wandering and uncivilized aborigines." Mapmakers agreed; between 1825 and 1860 American maps showed this land as "The Great American Desert." Settlement paused on the edge of the Plains, and most settlers headed directly for California and Oregon.

The Plains daunted even those hurrying across them. "You look on, on, on, out into space, out almost beyond time itself," John Noble, a painter reared in Kansas, remarked.

You see nothing but the rise and swell of land and grass, and then more grass—the monotonous, endless prairie! A stranger traveling on the prairie would get his hopes up, expecting to see something different on making the next rise. To him the disappointment and monotony were terrible. "He's got loneliness," we would say of such a man.

Few rivers cut through the Plains; those that did raged in the winter and trickled in the summer. Rainfall usually did not reach fifteen inches a year, not enough to support extensive agriculture. There was little lumber for homes and fences, and the tools of eastern settlement—the cast-iron plow, the boat, and the ax—were virtually useless on the tough and treeless Plains soil. "East of the Mississippi," historian Walter Prescott Webb noted, "civilization stood on three legs—land, water, and timber; west of the Mississippi not one but two of these legs were withdrawn,—water and timber,—and civilization was left on one leg—land."

Hot winds seared the Plains in summer, and northers, blizzards, and hailstorms froze them in

Physiographic Map of the United States

In the Great Plains and Rocky Mountains, the topography, climate, altitudes, crops, and, especially, the drought led to changes in a mode of settlement that had been essentially uniform from the Atlantic Coast through Kentucky and Ohio and on to Missouri. The rectangular land surveys and the quarter-section lots that were traditional in woods and prairie could not accommodate Great Plains conditions.

winter. Wildlife roamed in profusion. Antelope shared the open prairies with wolves, coyote, and millions of jack rabbits and prairie dogs. The American bison, better known as the buffalo, grazed in enormous herds from Mexico to Canada. In 1865 perhaps fifteen million buffalo lived on the Plains, so many they seemed like "leaves in a forest" to an early observer. A single herd sighted in 1871 had four million head.

Crushing the Indians

When Greeley urged New Yorkers to move West and "crowd nobody," he—like almost all his white countrymen—ignored the fact that large numbers of people already lived there. At the close of the Civil War Indians inhabited nearly half the United States. By 1880 they had been driven onto smaller and smaller reservations and were no longer an independent people. A decade later even their culture had crumbled under the impact of white domination.

In 1865 nearly a quarter of a million Indians lived in the western half of the country. Tribes like the Winnebago, Menominee, Cherokee, and Chippewa were resettled there, forced out of their eastern lands by advancing white settlement. Other tribes were native to the region. In the Southwest there were the Pueblo groups, including the Hopi, Zuni, and Rio Grande Pueblos. Peaceful farmers and herders, they had built up complex traditions around a settled way of life.

The Pueblo groups were cultivators of corn. They lived on the subdesert plateau of present-day western New Mexico and eastern Arizona. Harassed by powerful neighboring tribes, they built communal houses of adobe brick on high mesas or in cracks in the cliffs. More nomadic were the Camp Dwellers, the Navajo and Jicarilla Apache who roamed eastern New Mexico and western Texas. Blending elements of the Plains and Plateau environments, they lived in teepees or mud huts, grew some crops to supplement their hunting, and moved readily from place to place. The Navajo herded sheep and produced beautiful ornamental silver, baskets, and blankets. Fierce fighters, Apache horsemen were feared by whites and fellow Indians across the southwestern Plains.

Farther west were the short, stout, dark-skinned natives of present-day California. Divided into many small bands, they eked out a difficult existence living on roots, grubs, berries, and small game. In the Pacific Northwest, where fish and forest animals made life easier, the Klamath, Chinook, Yurok, and Shasta tribes developed a rich civilization. They built plank houses and canoes, worked extensively in wood, and evolved a complex social and political organization. Settled and determined, they resisted the invasion of the whites.

By the 1870s most of these tribes had been destroyed or beaten into submission. The powerful Ute, crushed in 1855, ceded most of their Utah lands to the United States and settled on a small reservation near Great Salt Lake. The Navajo and Apache fought back desperately, but between 1865 and 1873 they too were confined to reservations. The California Indians succumbed to the contagious diseases carried by whites during the Gold Rush of 1849. Miners burned their villages and by 1880 there were less than twenty thousand Indians in California.

Life of the Plains Indians

Nearly two thirds of the Indians lived on the Great Plains. The Plains tribes included the Sioux of present-day Minnesota and the Dakotas, the Blackfoot of Idaho and Montana, the Cheyenne, Crow, and Arapaho of the central Plains, the Pawnee of western Nebraska, and the Kiowa, Apache, and Comanche of present-day Texas and New Mexico.

Nomadic and warlike, the Plains Indians depended on the buffalo and horse. The modern horse, first brought by Spanish explorers in the 1500s, spread north from Mexico onto the Plains, and by the 1700s had changed the Plains Indians' way of life. They gave up farming almost entirely to hunt the buffalo, ranging widely over the rolling plains. They also became superb warriors and horsemen, among the best light cavalry in the world.

Equipped with stout wood bows, three feet or less in length, Plains tribes made fierce warriors. Hiding their bodies behind their racing ponies, they drove deadly arrows clear through a buffalo. Against white troops or settlers, the skillful Co-

(Below) The Buffalo Hunt *by Charles M. Russell. At first the Plains Indians hunted the buffalo on foot; then, with the arrival of the horse, on horseback. After the buffalo was killed, women skinned the hide, cut up the meat, and then cured the hide as shown in the painting (right) by George Catlin. Women also decorated the teepees and preserved the meat by drying it on racks in the sun.*

manche rode three hundred yards and shot twenty arrows in the time it took a soldier to load his firearm once. The introduction of the new Colt six-shooters during the 1850s gave white troops a rapid-fire weapon but did not entirely offset the Indians' advantage.

Migratory in culture, the Plains Indians formed tribes of several thousand people but lived in smaller "bands" of three to five hundred. The Comanche, who numbered perhaps seven thousand, had thirteen bands with such names as Burnt Meat, Making Bags While Moving, and Those Who Move Often. Each band was governed by a chief and a council of elder men, and Indians of the same tribe transferred freely from band to band. Bands acted independently, making it difficult for the United States government to deal with the fragmented tribes.

The bands followed and lived off the buffalo. Buffalo provided food, clothing, and shelter; and the Indians, unlike later white hunters, used every part of the animal. The meat was dried or "jerked" in the hot Plains air. The skins made teepees, blankets, and robes. Buffalo bones became knives; tendons were made into bow strings; horns and hooves were boiled into glue. Buffalo "chips"—dried manure—were burned as fuel.

Warfare between tribes usually took the form of brief raids and skirmishes. Plains Indians fought few prolonged wars and rarely coveted territory. Most conflicts involved only a few warriors intent on stealing horses or "counting coups"—touching an enemy's body with the hand or a special stick. Tribes developed a fierce and trained warrior class, recognized for achievements in battle. Speaking different languages, Indians of various tribes were nevertheless able to communicate with one another through a highly developed sign language.

The Plains tribes divided labor tasks according to sex. Men hunted, traded, supervised ceremonial activities, and cleared ground for planting. Women were responsible for child-rearing and artistic activity. They also performed the camp work, grew vegetables, prepared buffalo meat and hides, and gathered berries and roots. Among tribes like the Sioux, there was little difference in status. Men were respected for hunting and war, women for their artistic skills with quill and paint.

Before the Civil War Americans used the land west of the Mississippi as "one big reservation." The government named the area "Indian Country," moved eastern tribes there with firm treaty guarantees, and in 1834 passed the Indian Intercourse Act which prohibited any white person from entering Indian country without a license.

The situation changed in the 1850s. Wagon trains wound their way to California and Oregon, miners pushed into western gold fields, and there was talk of a transcontinental railroad. To clear the way for settlement, the federal government in 1851 abandoned "One Big Reservation" in favor of a new policy of "concentration." For the first time it assigned definite boundaries to each tribe. The Sioux, for example, were given the Dakota country north of the Platte River, the Crows a large area near the Powder River, and the Cheyenne and Arapaho the Colorado foothills between the North Platte and Arkansas rivers for "as long as waters run and the grass shall grow."

The "concentration" policy lasted only a few years. Accustomed to hunt widely for buffalo, many Indians refused to stay within their assigned areas. White settlers poured into Indian lands, then called on the government to protect them. Indians were pushed out of Kansas and Nebraska in the 1850s, even as white reformers fought to hold those territories open for free blacks. In 1859 gold miners moved into the Pike's Peak country, touching off warfare with the Cheyenne and Arapaho.

In 1864, tired of the fighting, the two tribes asked for peace. Certain that the war was over, Chief Black Kettle led his seven hundred followers to camp on Sand Creek in southeastern Colorado. Early on the morning of November 29, 1864, a group of Colorado militia led by Colonel John M. Chivington attacked the sleeping Indians. "Kill and scalp all, big and little," Chivington told his men. "Nits make lice." Black Kettle tried to stop the ambush, raising first an American flag and then a white flag. Neither worked. Indian men, women, and children were clubbed, stabbed, and scalped.

The Chivington massacre set off angry protests in Colorado and the East. Congress appointed an investigating committee, and the government concluded a treaty with the Cheyenne and Arapaho condemning "the gross and wanton outrages." Still, the two tribes were forced to surrender their Sand Creek reservation in exchange for lands elsewhere. The Kiowa and Comanche were also ousted from areas they had been granted "forever" only a few years before. As the Sioux chief Spotted Tail said: "Why does not the Great Father put his red children on wheels so that he can move them as he will?"

Before long the powerful Sioux were on the warpath in the great Sioux War of 1865–1867. Once again an invasion of gold miners touched off the war, which flared even more intensely when the federal government announced plans to connect the various mining towns by building the Bozeman Trail through the heart of the Sioux hunting grounds in Montana. Red Cloud, the Sioux chief, determined to stop the trail. In December 1866, pursued by an army column under Captain William J. Fetterman, he lured the incautious Fetterman deep into the wilderness, ambushed him, and wiped out all eighty-two soldiers in his command.

The Fetterman massacre, coming so soon after the Chivington massacre, sparked a public debate over the nation's Indian policy. Like the policy itself, the debate reflected differing white views of the Indians. In the East some reform, humanitarian, and church groups wanted a humane peace policy, directed toward educating and "civilizing" the tribes. Many people, East and West, questioned this approach, convinced that Indians were savages unfit for civilization. Westerners in general favored firm control over the Indians, including swift punishment of any who rebelled.

In 1867 the peace advocates won the debate. Halting construction on the Bozeman Trail, Congress created a Peace Commission of four civilians and three generals to end the Sioux War and eliminate permanently the causes of Indian wars. Setting out for the West, the Peace Commissioners agreed that only one policy offered a permanent solution: a policy of "small reservations" to isolate the Indians on distant lands, teach them to farm, and gradually "civilize" them.

The commissioners chose two areas to hold all the Plains Indians. The fifty-four thousand Indi-

Indians in the West: Major Battles and Reservations

"They made us many promises, more than I remember, but they never kept but one; they promised to take our land, and they took it." So said Red Cloud of the Oglala Sioux, summarizing Indian-white relations in the 1870s.

ans on the northern Plains would be moved north of the Black Hills in Dakota Territory, far from prospective white settlement. On the southern Plains the eighty-six thousand Indians would be moved into present-day Oklahoma, a region also considered unattractive to whites. In both areas tribes would be assigned specific reservations where government agents could supervise them.

The Kiowa, Comanche, Cheyenne, and Arapaho agreed to the plan in 1867, the Sioux in 1868. Extending the policy beyond the Plains, the Ute, Shoshoni, Bannock, Navajo, and Apache also accepted small reservations. "We have now selected and provided reservations for all, off the great road," an army commander wrote. "All who cling to their old hunting-grounds are hostile and will remain so till killed off."

Final Battles on the Plains

Few Indians settled peacefully into life on the new reservations. Young warriors and minor chiefs denounced the treaties and drifted back to the open countryside. In late 1868 warfare broke out again, and it took over a decade of violence to beat the Indians into submission. The Kiowa and Comanche rampaged through the Texas Panhandle, looting and killing, until the army crushed them in the Red River War of 1874–1875 and ended warfare in the Southwest.

On the northern Plains fighting resulted from the Black Hills Gold Rush of 1875. As prospectors tramped across Indian hunting grounds, the Sioux gathered to stop them. They were led by Rain-in-the-Face, the great war chief Crazy Horse, and the famous medicine man Sitting Bull. The army sent several columns of troops after the Indians, but one, under flamboyant Lieutenant Colonel George A. Custer, pushed recklessly ahead, eager to claim the victory. On the morning of June 25, 1876, thinking he had a small band of Indians surrounded on the banks of the Little Bighorn River in Montana, Custer divided his column and took 265 men toward the Indian village. Instead of finding a small band, he discovered that he had stumbled on the main Sioux camp with 2500 warriors.

By mid-afternoon it was over; Custer and his men were dead. Custer was largely responsible for the loss, but "Custer's Last Stand," set in blazing

Sitting Bull (far left) led the Sioux against the U.S. cavalry at the Little Bighorn. The pictograph (below left), by Oglala Sioux Amos Bad Heart Bull, is an Indian version of that battle. Left, a photograph of Crow Indians taken prisoner after an unsuccessful uprising in Montana in 1877. Below is the mass grave of the two hundred Indian men, women, and children massacred at Wounded Knee. Twenty-nine soldiers also died in the battle. There was another victim at Wounded Knee. Black Elk, an Oglala Sioux, later recalled, "A people's dream died there."

headlines across the country, signaled a nation-wide demand for revenge. Within a few months the Sioux were surrounded and beaten, 3000 of them surrendering in October 1876. Sitting Bull and a few followers who had fled to Canada gave up in 1881.

The Sioux War ended the major Indian warfare in the West, but occasional outbreaks occurred for several years thereafter. In 1877 the Nez Percé tribe of Oregon, a people who had warmly welcomed Lewis and Clark in 1805, rebelled against government policy. Hoping to reach Canada, Chief Joseph led the tribe on a courageous flight covering 75 days and 1321 miles. They defeated the pursuing army at every turn but then ran out of food, horses, and ammunition. Surrendering, they were sent to barren lands in the Indian Country of Oklahoma, and there, most of them died from disease.

In 1890 the Teton Sioux of South Dakota, bitter and starving, became restless. Many of them turned to the "Ghost Dances," a set of dances and rites that grew from a vision of a Paiute messiah named Wovoka. Performance of the dances, Wovoka said, would bring back Indian lands and cause the whites to disappear. All Indians would reunite, the earth would be covered with dust, and a new earth would come upon the old. The vanished buffalo would return in great herds.

The army intervened to stop the dancing, touching off violence that killed Sitting Bull and a number of other warriors. Frightened Indians fled southwest to join other Ghost Dancers under the aging chief Big Foot. Moving quickly, troops of the Seventh Cavalry, Custer's old regiment, caught up with Big Foot's band who agreed to come to the army camp on Wounded Knee Creek in South Dakota. An Indian, it is thought, fired the first shot, returned by the army's new machine guns. Firing a shell a second, they shredded tepees and people. About two hundred men, women, and children were massacred in the snow.

The End of Tribal Life

The final step in Indian policy came in the 1870s and '80s. Some reformers had long argued against segregating the Indians on reservations, urging instead that the nation assimilate them individu-

Tom Torlino, a Navajo Indian photographed before and after his "assimilation." Torlino attended the Carlisle Indian School in Pennsylvania.

ally into white culture. These "assimilationists" wanted to use education, land policy, and federal law to eradicate tribal society.

Congress began to adopt the policy in 1871 when it ended the practice of treaty-making with Indian tribes. Since tribes were no longer separate nations, they lost many of their political and judicial functions, and the power of the chiefs was weakened. In 1882 Congress created a Court of Indian Offenses to try Indians who broke government rules, and soon thereafter it made Indians answerable in regular courts for certain crimes.

While Congress worked to break down the tribes, educators trained young Indians to adjust to white culture. In 1879 fifty Pawnee, Kiowa, and Cheyenne youths were brought east to the new Carlisle Indian School in Carlisle, Pennsylvania. Other Indian schools soon opened, including the Haskell Institute in Kansas and numerous day schools on the western reservations. The schools taught students to fix machines and farm; they forced them to trim their long hair, made them speak English, banned the wearing of tribal paint or clothes, and forbade tribal ceremonies and dances. "Kill the Indian and save the man," said Richard H. Pratt, the army officer who founded the Carlisle School.

Land ownership was the final and most important link in the new policy. Indians who owned land, it was thought, would become responsible, self-reliant citizens. Deciding to give each Indian a farm, Congress in 1887 passed the Dawes Severalty Act, the most important legal development in Indian-white relations in over three centuries.

Aiming to end tribal life, the Dawes Act divided tribal lands into small plots for distribution among members of the tribe. Each family head received 160 acres, single adults 80 acres, and children 40 acres. Once the land was distributed, any surplus was sold to white settlers, with the profits going to Indian schools. To keep the Indians' land from falling into the hands of speculators, the federal government held it in trust for twenty-five years. Finally, American citizenship was granted to Indians who accepted their land, lived apart from the tribe, and "adopted the habits of civilized life."

Through the Dawes Act, 47 million acres of land were distributed to Indians and their families. There were another 90 million acres in the reservations, and these lands, often the most fertile, were sold to white settlers. Speculators evaded the twenty-five-year rule, leasing rather than purchasing the land from the Indians. Many

Indians knew little about farming. Their tools were rudimentary, and in the culture of the Plains Indians, farming was women's work. In 1934 the government returned to the idea of tribal land ownership, but by then 138 million acres of Indian land had shrunk to 48 million acres, half of which was barren.

The final blow to tribal life came not in the Dawes Act but in the virtual extermination of the buffalo, the Plains Indians' chief resource and the basis for their unique way of life. The killing began in the 1860s as the transcontinental railroads pushed west, but in 1871 a Pennsylvania tannery discovered that buffalo hides made valuable leather. Professional hunters like William F. "Buffalo Bill" Cody swarmed across the Plains, killing millions of the helpless beasts.

Buffalo hunting became a favorite pastime. Churches and schools raised money by sponsoring hunts, such as the one, three hundred strong, that left Lawrence, Kansas, in October 1868. Chartering a train, the group took along the Lawrence Cornet Band for entertainment. For two days they saw no buffalo until suddenly the horizon filled with them. As the train chugged along, a hundred rifles fired and fired again; finally a buffalo fell. The train stopped, and the

A pile of forty thousand buffalo hides, Dodge City, Kansas, 1874. Before the arrival of white settlers, immense herds of millions of buffalo roamed the western Plains. By 1883 only a few thousand of the animals were left. When the buffalo disappeared, the way of life of the Plains Indians also came to an end.

Blacks in Blue:
The Buffalo Soldiers in the West

On Saturday afternoons youngsters used to sit in darkened movie theaters and cheer the victories of the United States cavalry over the Indians. Typically, the Indians were about to capture a wagon train, when army bugles suddenly sounded. Then the blue-coated cavalry charged over the hill. Few in the theaters cheered for the Indians; fewer still noticed the absence of black faces among the on-charging cavalry. But in fact, more than 2000 black cavalrymen served on the western frontier between 1867 and 1890. Known as the "buffalo soldiers," they made up a fifth of the U.S. cavalry.

Black troops were first used on a large scale during the Civil War (see chapter 15). Organized in segregated units, with white officers, they fought with distinction. Nearly 180,000 blacks served in the Union army; 34,000 of them died. When the war ended in 1865, Congress for the first time authorized black troops to serve in the regular peacetime army. In addition to infantry, it created two cavalry regiments—the Ninth and Tenth, which became known as the famous buffalo soldiers.

Like other black regiments, the Ninth and Tenth Cavalry had white officers who took special examinations before they could serve. The chaplains were assigned not only to preach but to teach reading, writing, and arithmetic. The food was poor; racism was widespread. The army stocked the first black units with worn-out horses, a serious matter to men whose lives depended on the speed and stamina of their mounts. "Since our first mount in 1867 this regiment has received nothing but broken down horses and repaired equipment," an officer said in 1870.

Many white officers refused to serve with black troops. George A. Custer, the handsome "boy general," turned down a position in the Ninth and joined the new Seventh Cavalry, headed for disaster at Little Bighorn. The *Army and Navy Journal* carried ads that told a similar story:

**A FIRST LIEUTENANT
OF INFANTRY**

(white)

stationed at a

very desirable post

in the Department of the South

desires a transfer with

an officer of the same grade

on equal terms

if in a white regiment

but if in a colored regiment

a reasonable bonus

would be expected.

There was no shortage of black troops for the officers to lead. Blacks enlisted because the army offered some advancement in a closed society. It also paid $13 a month, plus room and board.

In 1867 the Ninth and Tenth Cavalry were posted to the West, where they remained for two decades. Under Colonel Benjamin H. Grierson, a Civil War hero, the Tenth went to Fort Riley, Kansas; the regiment arrived in the midst of a great Indian war. Kiowas, Comanches, Cheyennes, Arapahoes, and Sioux were on the warpath. Troopers of the Tenth defended farms, stages, trains, and work crews building railroad tracks to the west. Cornered by a band of Cheyennes, they beat back the attack and won a new name. Earlier known as the "brunettes" or "Africans," the Cheyenne now called them the buffalo soldiers, a name that soon applied to all black soldiers in the West (some of the "buffalo soldiers" of the Tenth Cavalry are shown in the photo right).

From 1868 to 1874 the Tenth served on the Kansas frontier. The dull winter days were filled with drills and scouting parties outside the post. In spring and summer the good weather brought forth new forays. Indian bands raided farms and ranches and stampeded cattle herds on the way north from Texas. They struck and then melted back into the reservations.

The Ninth Cavalry also had a difficult job. Commanded by Colonel Edward Hatch, who had served with Grierson in the Civil War, it was stationed in West Texas and along the Rio Grande. The summers were so hot that men collapsed with sunstroke, the winters so cold that water froze in the canteens. Indians from outside the area frequently raided it. From the north Kiowa and Comanche warriors rode down the Great Comanche War Trail; Kickapoos crossed the Rio Grande from Mexico. Gangs of Mexican bandits and restless Civil War veterans roamed and plundered at will.

In 1874–1875 the Ninth fought in the great Red River War, in which the Kiowas and Comanches, fed up with conditions on the reservations, revolted against Grant's peace policy. Marching, fighting, then marching again, the soldiers harried and wore out the Indians, who finally surrendered in the spring of 1875. Herded into a new and desolate reservation, the Mescalero Apaches of New Mexico took to the warpath in 1877 and again in 1879. Each time it took a year of grueling warfare to effect their surrender. In 1886 black cavalrymen surrounded and captured the famous Apache chief Geronimo. In that and other campaigns, several buffalo soldiers won the Congressional Medal of Honor.

Black troops hunted Big Foot and his band before the slaughter at Wounded Knee in 1890 (see p. 490), and they served in many of the West's most famous Indian battles. While a third of all army recruits deserted between 1865 and 1890, the Ninth and Tenth Cavalry had few desertions. In 1880 the Tenth had the fewest desertions of any regiment in the country.

It was ironic that in the West black men fought red men to benefit white men. Once the Indian wars ended, the buffalo soldiers worked to keep illegal settlers out of Indian or government land; much of this land was later opened to settlement. Both regiments saw action in the Spanish-American War, the Ninth at San Juan Hill, the Tenth in the fighting around Santiago. The old buffalo soldiers were forgotten in retirement, although some of them had the satisfaction of settling on the western lands they had done so much to pacify.

Shrinkage of the Buffalo Herds

Fewer than two hundred buffalo roamed the West by 1883. By 1903 the number had dwindled to thirty-four.

Extent of buffalo range

- 1820's
- 1850's
- 1870's

unemployment were growing problems, and Indians, no longer able to live off the buffalo, became wards of the state. They lost their special distinctiveness as a culture. Once possessors of the entire continent, they had been crowded into smaller and smaller areas, overwhelmed by the demand to become settled, literate, and English-speaking. "Except for the internment of the West Coast Japanese during World War II," said historian Roger L. Nichols, "Indian removal is the only example of large-scale government-enforced migration in American history. For the Japanese, the move was temporary; for the Indians it was not."

Even as the Indians lost their identity, they entered the romantic folklore of the West. Dime novels, snapped up by readers young and old, told tales of Indian fighting on the Plains. Buffalo Bill Cody turned it all into a profitable business. Beginning in 1883, his Wild West Show ran for over three decades, playing to millions of viewers in the United States, Canada, and Europe. It featured Plains Indians chasing buffalo, performing a war dance, and attacking a settler's cabin. In 1885 Sitting Bull himself, victor over Custer at the battle of Little Bighorn, performed in the show.

Settlement of the West

Between 1870 and 1900 white—and some black—Americans settled the enormous total of 430 million acres west of the Mississippi; they occupied more land than in all the years before 1870.

People moved West for many reasons. Some sought adventure; others wanted to escape the drab routine of factory or city life. Many moved to California for their health. The Mormons settled Utah to escape religious persecution. Others followed the mining camps, the advancing railroads, and the farming and cattle frontier. "Most of the time we were solitary adventurers in a great land as fresh and new as a spring morning, and we were free and full of the zest of darers," said Charles Goodnight, a Texas cattleman and founder of the famous Goodnight Trail.

Whatever the specific reason, most people moved West to better their lot. On the whole, their timing was good, for as a nation's population grew, so did demand for the livestock and the agricultural, mineral, and lumber products of the

guests swarmed off. A hunter stood atop the kill. An observer described the scene: "Then came the ladies; a ring was formed; the cornet band gathered around, and, as if to tantalize the spirits of all departed buffalo, as well as Indians, played Yankee Doodle."

Between 1872 and 1874 professional hunters slaughtered three million buffalo a year. In a frontier form of a factory system, riflemen, skinners, and transport wagons pushed through the vast herds, which shrank steadily behind them. A good hunter killed a hundred buffalo a day; skinners took off the hides, removed the tongue, hump, and tallow, and left the rest. "I have seen their bodies so thick after being skinned," a hunter said, "that they would look like logs where a hurricane had passed through a forest."

By 1883 the buffalo were almost gone. When the government set out to produce the famous "buffalo nickel," the designer had to go to the Bronx Zoo in New York City to find a buffalo.

By 1900 there were only two hundred thousand Indians in the country, most of them on reservations. Many lived in poverty. Alcoholism and

494

expanding West. Contrary to older historical views, the West did not act as a major "safety valve," an outlet for social and economic tensions. The poor and unemployed did not have the means to move there and establish farms. "Moreover," as Douglass C. North, an economic historian, said, "most people moved West in good times . . . in periods of rising prices, of expanding demand, when the prospects for making money from this new land looked brightest; and this aspect characterized the whole pattern of settlement."

Men and Women on the Overland Trail

The first movement west aimed not for the nearby Plains but for California and Oregon on the continent's far shore. It started in the 1849 Gold Rush to California, and in the next three decades perhaps as many as half a million individuals made the long journey. Some walked; others rode horses alone or in small groups. About half joined great caravans, numbering 150 wagons or more, that inched across the 2000 miles between the Missouri River and the Pacific Coast.

More often than not, men made the decision to make the crossing. Wives either went with their husbands or faced being left behind. Four out of five men on the overland trail had picked up stakes and moved before, some of them several times. Most had little cash, but they needed only strong legs, a few staples, and a willingness to tighten the belt when game was scarce. The majority of people traveled in family groups, including in-laws, grandchildren, aunts, and uncles. As one historian said: "The quest for something new would take place in the context of the very familiar."

Individuals and wagon trains set out from various points along the Missouri River. Leaving in the spring and traveling through the summer, they hoped to reach their destination before the first snowfall. During April, travelers gradually assembled in spring camp just across the Missouri River, waiting for the new grass to ripen into forage. They packed and repacked the wagons and elected the train's leaders, who would set the line of march, look for water and campsites, and impose discipline. Some trains adopted detailed rules, fearing a lapse into savagery in the wild lands across the Missouri. "Every man to carry with him a Bible and other religious books, as we hope not to degenerate into a state of barbarism," one agreement said.

Setting out in early May, travelers divided the enormous route into manageable portions. The first leg of the journey followed the Platte River west to Fort Kearney in central Nebraska Territory, a distance of about three hundred miles. The land was even, with good supplies of wood, grass, and water. From a distance the white-topped wagons seemed driven by a common force, but in fact, internal discipline broke down almost immediately. Arguments erupted over the pace of the march, the choice of campsites, the number of guards to post, whether to rest or push on. Elected leaders quit; new ones were chosen. Every train was filled with individualists, and as the son of one train captain said, "if you think it's any snap to run a wagon train of 66 wagons with every man in the train having a different idea of what is the best thing to do, all I can say is that some day you ought to try it."

Men, women, and children had different tasks on the trail. Men concerned themselves almost entirely with hunting, guard duty, and transportation. They rose at four A.M. to hitch the wagons, and after breakfast began the day's march. At noon they stopped and set the teams to graze, while the women prepared the midday meal. The march continued until sunset. Then, while the men relaxed, the women fixed dinner and the next day's lunch, and the children kindled the fire, brought water to camp, and searched for wood or other fuel. Walking fifteen miles a day, in searing heat and mountain cold, travelers were exhausted by late afternoon. "We can all, as soon as we stop, lie down on the grass or anywhere and be asleep in less than no time almost," Rebecca Ketcham, an Oregon-bound emigrant, reported.

For women the trail was lonely, and they worked to exhaustion. Before long they adjusted their clothing to the harsh conditions, adopting the new bloomer pants, shortening their skirts, or wearing regular "wash dresses"—so called because they had shorter hemlines that did not drag on the wet ground on washday. Men hunted buffalo and antelope for fresh meat. Both men and women carried firearms in case of Indian attacks, but most emigrants saw few Indians en route.

Not every one was a crack shot. "The young men of our party . . . went out this morning for the purpose of hunting buffalo," Harriet Ward noted sardonically in her diary. "They soon discovered a herd of a hundred and fifty, rushed into their midst, fired their guns without effect and finally succeeded in capturing a cow."

The first stage of the journey was deceptively easy, and travelers usually reached Fort Kearney by late May. The second leg led another 300 miles up the Platte River to Fort Laramie on the eastern edge of Wyoming Territory. The heat of June had burned the grass, and there was no wood. Anxious to beat the early snowfalls, travelers rested a day or two at the fort, then hurried on to South Pass, 280 miles to the west, the best route through the forbidding Rockies. The land was barren. It was now mid-July, but the mountain nights were so cold that ice formed on top of the water buckets.

Beyond South Pass, some emigrants turned south to the Mormon settlements on Great Salt Lake, but most headed 340 miles north to Fort Hall on the Snake River in Idaho. It took another three months to cover the remaining 800 miles. California-bound travelers followed the Humboldt River through the summer heat of Nevada. Well into September they began the final arduous push: first, a 55-mile stretch of desert; then 70 difficult miles up the eastern slopes of the Sierra Nevada, hoisting wagons laboriously over massive outcrops of rock; and finally the last 100 miles down the western slopes to the welcome October greenness of the Sacramento Valley.

Under the best of conditions the trip took six months, sixteen hours a day, dawn to dusk, of hard, grueling labor. Walking halfway across the continent was no easy task, and it provided a never-to-be-forgotten experience for those who did it. The wagon trains, carrying the dreams of thousands of individuals, reproduced society in small focus: individualistic, hopeful, mobile, divided by age and sex roles, apprehensive, yet willing to strike out for the distant and new.

Land for the Taking

As railroads pushed west in the 1870s and '80s, locomotive trains replaced wagon trains, but the shift was gradual, and until the end of the century emigrants often combined both modes of travel. Into the 1890s travelers could be seen making their way across the West by any available means. Early railroad transportation was expensive, and the average farm family could not afford to buy tickets and ship supplies. Many Europeans traveled by rail to designated outfitting places, and then proceeded West with wagons and oxen. Traffic flowed in all directions. Eager settlers heading West passed defeated ones returning East.

Why did they come? "The motive that induced us to part with the pleasant associations and the dear friends of our childhood days," explained Phoebe Judson, an early emigrant, "was to obtain from the government of the United States a grant of land that 'Uncle Sam' had promised to give to the head of each family who settled in this new country." A popular camp song reflected the same motive:

Come along, come along—don't be alarmed,
Uncle Sam is rich enough to give us all a farm.

Uncle Sam owned about 1 billion acres of land in the 1860s, much of it mountain and desert land unsuited for agriculture. By 1900 the various land laws had distributed half of it. Between 1862 and 1890 the government gave away 48 million acres under the Homestead Act of 1862, sold about 100 million acres to private citizens and corporations, granted 128 million acres to railroad companies to tempt them to build across the unsettled West, and sold huge tracts to the states.

The Homestead Act of 1862, a law of great significance, gave 160 acres of land to anyone who would pay a $10 registration and pledge to live on it and cultivate it for five years. The offer set off a mass migration of land-hungry Europeans, dazzled by a country that gave its land away. Americans also seized on the act's provisions, and between 1862 and 1900 nearly 400,000 families claimed free homesteads under it.

Yet the Homestead Act did not work as Congress had hoped. Few farmers and laborers had the cash to move to the frontier, buy farm equipment, and wait out the year or two before the farm became self-supporting. Tailored to the timber and water conditions of the East, the act did not work as well in the semiarid West. In the fertile valleys of the Mississippi, 160 acres provided a generous farm. A farmer on the Great Plains needed either a larger farm for dry farming or a smaller one for irrigation.

The Timber Culture Act of 1873 attempted to adjust the Homestead Act to western conditions. It allowed homesteaders to claim an additional 160 acres if they planted trees on a quarter of it within four years. A successful act, it distributed 10 million acres of land, encouraged needed forestation, and enabled homesteaders to expand their farms to a workable size. Cattle ranchers lobbied for another law, the Desert Land Act of 1877, which allowed individuals to obtain 640 acres in the arid states for $1.25 an acre, provided they

irrigated part of it within three years. This act invited fraud. Irrigation sometimes meant a bucket of water dumped on the ground, and ranchers used their hired hands to claim large tracts. More than 2.6 million acres was distributed, much of it fraudulently.

The Timber and Stone Act of 1878 applied only to lands "unfit for cultivation" and valuable chiefly for timber or stone. It permitted anyone in California, Nevada, Oregon, and Washington to buy up to 160 acres of forestland for $2.50 an acre. Like ranchers, lumber companies used employees to file false claims. Company agents rounded up seamen on the waterfront, marched them to the land office to file their claims, took them to a notary public to sign over the claims to the company, and then marched them back to the waterfront for payment in beer or cash. By 1900, 3.6 million acres of rich forest land had been claimed under the measure.

Speculators made ingenious use of the land laws. Sending agents in advance of settlement, they moved along choice river bottoms or irrigable areas, accumulating large holdings to be held for high prices. In the arid West, where control of water meant control of the surrounding land, shrewd ranchers plotted their holdings accordingly. In Colorado one cattleman, John F. Iliff, owned only 105 small parcels of land, but by placing them around the few waterholes, he effectively dominated an empire stretching over 6000 square miles.

As beneficiaries of the government's policy of land grants for railway construction, the railroad companies were the West's largest landowners. Eager to have immigrants settle on the land they owned near the railroad right-of-way, and eager to boost their freight and passenger business, the companies sent agents to the East and Europe. Attractive brochures touted life in the West. The Union Pacific called the rocky Platte Valley in Nebraska "a flowery meadow of great fertility, clothed in nutritious grasses." The Burlington Railroad reminded women of the West's many unmarried men: "when a daughter of the East is once beyond the Missouri she rarely recrosses it except on a bridal tour."

Railroad lines set up Land Departments and Bureaus of Immigration. The Land Department priced the land, arranged credit terms, and even gave free farming courses to immigrants. The

Railroad companies distributed elaborately illustrated brochures and broadsides to lure people to the West, where they would settle on land owned by the railroad.

Bureau of Immigration employed agents in Europe, met immigrants at eastern seaports, and ran special cars for land-seekers heading West. In 1874 the Santa Fe Railroad convinced 1900 Russian Mennonites to bring $2 million in gold drafts and settle on the fertile plains of Kansas.

Half a billion acres of western land were given or sold to speculators and corporations. At the same time only 600,000 homestead patents were issued, covering 80 million acres. Thus, only one acre in every nine initially went to individual pioneers, the intended beneficiaries of the nation's largesse.

Territorial Government

As new areas of the West opened, they were organized as territories under the control of Congress and the president. The territorial system started with the famous Northwest Ordinance of 1787 (see chapter 6), which established the rules by which territories became states. Washington ran the territories like "a passive group of colonial mandates." The president appointed the governor and judges in each territory; Congress detailed their duties, set their budgets, and oversaw their activities. Territorial officials had almost absolute power over the territories.

Until statehood, then, the territories depended on the federal government for their existence. They became an important part of the patronage system, a place to give jobs to deserving politicians. Lew Wallace of Indiana, a Civil War hero, was named governor of New Mexico Territory in the 1870s. Unable to sleep in the stuffy governor's residence, Wallace wrote the bestselling novel *Ben Hur*.

The national political parties, especially the Republicans, funneled government funds into the territorial economies, and in areas like Wyoming and the Dakotas, where resources were scarce, economic growth depended on them. Many early settlers held patronage jobs or hoped for them, traded with government-supported Indians, sold supplies to army troops, and speculated in government lands.

As his advertisement suggested, E. P. Caldwell, a small-town attorney in Huron, Dakota Territory, made a living the way many Westerners did, by serving Washington and the East:

MONEY LOANED
for Eastern Capitalists
Taxes Paid for Nonresidents

**INVESTMENTS
CAREFULLY MADE**
for Eastern Capitalists

GENERAL LAW,
Land and Collection Business
Transacted

Buy and Sell Real Estate
U.S. Land Business
Promptly Attended to

In a large portion of the trans-Mississippi West, a generation grew up under territorial rule. Inevitably, they developed distinct ideas about politics, government, and the economy.

The Spanish-Speaking Southwest

In the nineteenth century almost all Spanish-speaking people in the United States lived in California, Arizona, New Mexico, Texas, and Colorado. Their numbers were small—California had only 8086 Mexican residents in 1900—but the influence of their culture and institutions was large. In some respects the Southwestern frontier was more Spanish-American than Anglo-American.

Pushing northward from Mexico, the Spanish brought to the Southwest irrigation, stock raising, weaving, and the rule of law. After winning independence in the 1820s, the Mexicans brought additional laws, ranching methods, chaps, and the burro. Both Spanish and Mexicans created the legal framework for distributing land and water, a precious resource in the Southwest. They gave large grants of land to communities for grazing, to individuals as rewards for service, and to the various Indian pueblos.

In Southern California the Californios, descendants of the original colonizers, began after the 1860s to lose their once vast landholdings to drought and mortgages. Some turned to crime and became feared bandidos; others, like José María Amador, lived in poverty and remembered better days:

When I was but a little boy I drained the chocolate pot,
But now I am a poor man and am condemned to slop.

In 1875 Romualdo Pacheco, an aristocratic native son, served as governor of California and then went on to Congress. But as the Californios died out, Mexican-Americans continued the Spanish-Mexican influence. In 1880 one quarter of the residents of Los Angeles County were Spanish speaking.

In New Mexico Spanish-speaking citizens remained the majority ethnic group until 1928, and the Spanish-Mexican culture dominated the territory. Contests over land grants became New Mexico's largest industry; lawyers who dealt in them amassed huge holdings. After 1888 *Las Gorras Blancas*, The White Caps, a secret organization of Spanish-Americans, attacked the movement of Anglo ranchers into the Las Vegas community land grant. Armed and hooded like a Ku Klux Klan, they rode at night—but to defend civil rights instead of stifle them.

Throughout the Southwest the Spanish-Mexican heritage gave a distinctive shape to society. It fostered a modified economic caste system, a strong Roman Catholic influence, and the primary use of the Spanish language. Spanish names and customs spread, even among Anglos. David Starr Jordan, arriving from Indiana to become the first president of Stanford University in California, bestowed Spanish names on streets, houses, and a Stanford dormitory. Spanish was the region's first or second language. Confronted by Sheriff Pat Garrett in a darkened room, New Mexico's famous outlaw, Billy the Kid, died saying *"Quien es? Quien es?"* ("Who is it? Who is it?")

The Bonanza West

Between 1850 and 1900 wave after wave of newcomers swept over the trans-Mississippi West. There were riches for the taking, hidden in gold-washed streams, spread lushly over grass-covered prairies, or available in the gullible minds of greedy newcomers. The nineteenth-century West took shape in the search for mining, cattle, and land bonanzas that drew eager settlers from the East and around the world.

As with all bonanzas, the consequences in the West were uneven growth, boom-and-bust economic cycles, and wasted resources. As a society it seemed constantly in the making. People moved here and there, following river bottoms, gold strikes, railroad tracks, and other opportunities. "Instant cities" arose. San Francisco, Salt Lake City, and Denver were the most spectacular examples, but every cow town and mining camp witnessed a similar phenomenon. San Francisco needed a little more than two decades to attract a third of a million people; Boston needed more than two centuries to do the same.

Most Westerners came to get rich quickly, and they adopted institutions that reflected that goal. As a contemporary poem said:

Love to see the stir an' bustle
In the busy town,
Everybody on the hustle

Before the California Gold Rush of 1849, San Francisco was a sleepy little Spanish-Mexican village called Yerba Buena. Gold-seekers turned it into a boom town with an international population. Here, Spanish-Mexican rancheros, white prospectors, Chinese laborers, and a top-hatted professional gambler mingle in a San Francisco saloon.

Saltin' profits down.
Everybody got a wad a'
Ready cash laid by;
Ain't no flies on Colorado—
Not a cussed fly.

In their lives the West was an idea as well as a region, and the idea molded them as much as they molded it.

The Mining Bonanza

Mining was the first important magnet to attract people to the West. Many came to "strike it rich" in gold and silver, but at least half the newcomers had no intention of working in the mines. Instead, they provided food, clothing, and services to the thousands of miners. Leland Stanford and Collis P. Huntington, who later built the Central Pacific Railroad, set up a general store in Sacramento where they sold shovels and supplies. Stephen J. Field, later a prominent justice of the United States Supreme Court, followed the Gold Rush to California to practice law.

The California Gold Rush of 1849 began the mining boom and set the pattern for subsequent experience. Individual prospectors made the first strikes, discovering pockets of gold along streams

flowing westward from the Sierra Nevada. To get the gold, they used a simple process called placer mining, which required little skill, technology, or capital. A placer miner needed only a shovel, washing pan, and a good claim. As the placers gave out, a great deal of gold remained, but it was locked in quartz or buried deep in the earth. Mining became an expensive business, far beyond the reach of the average miner.

Large corporations moved in to dig the deep shafts and finance costly equipment. Quartz mining required heavy rock crushers, mercury vats to dissolve the gold, and large retorts to recapture it. Eastern and European financiers assumed control, labor became unionized, and mining towns took on some of the characteristics of the industrial city. Individual prospectors meanwhile dashed on to the next find. Unlike other frontiers, the mining frontier moved from west to east, as the original California miners—the "yonder-siders," they were called—hurried eastward in search of the big strike.

In 1859 fresh strikes were made near Pike's Peak in Colorado and in the Carson River Valley of Nevada. News of both discoveries set off wild migrations—100,000 miners were in Pike's Peak country by June 1859. The gold there quickly played out, but the Nevada find uncovered a

With the "long tom," miners washed placer gold from pay dirt. These prospectors, photographed in 1852, are working at a stream bed near Auburn, California.

thick, bluish black ore that was almost pure silver and gold. A quick-witted drifter named Henry T. P. Comstock talked his way into partnership in the claim, and word of the Comstock Lode—with ore worth $3876 a ton—flashed over the mountains.

Thousands of miners climbed the Sierra Nevada that summer. On the rough slopes of Davidson Mountain they created Virginia City, the prototype of the tumultuous western mining town. Mark Twain was there and described the scene in *Roughing It* (1872): "The sidewalks swarmed with people. . . . Joy sat on every countenance, and there was a glad, almost fierce, intensity in every eye, that told of the money-getting schemes that were seething in every brain and the high hope that held sway in every heart."

The biggest strike was yet to come. In 1873 John W. Mackay and three partners formed a company to dig deep into the mountain, and at 1167 feet they hit the Big Bonanza, a seam of gold and silver more than 54 feet wide. It was the richest discovery in the history of mining. Between 1859 and 1879 the Comstock Lode produced gold and silver worth $306 million. Most of it went to financiers and corporations. Mackay himself became the richest person in the world, earning (according to a European newspaper) $25

a minute, $5 a minute more than Czar Alexander II of Russia.

In the 1860s and '70s important strikes were made in Washington, Idaho, Nevada, Colorado, Montana, Arizona, and Dakota. Extremely mobile, miners flocked from strike to strike, and new camps and mining towns sprang up overnight. "The miners of Idaho were like quicksilver," said Hubert Howe Bancroft, an early historian. "A mass of them dropped in any locality, broke up into individual globules, and ran off after any atom of gold in their vicinity. They stayed nowhere longer than the gold attracted them."

The final fling came in the Black Hills rush of 1874–1876. The army had tried to keep miners out of the area, the heart of the Sioux hunting grounds, and even sent a scientific party under Colonel George A. Custer to disprove the rumors of gold. Instead, Custer found gold all over the hills, and the rush was on. Miners, gamblers, desperadoes, and prostitutes flocked to Deadwood, the most lawless of all the mining camps. There, Martha Jane Canary—a crack shot who, as Calamity Jane, won fame as a scout and teamster —fell in love with Wild Bill Hickok; and Hickok himself—a western legend who had tamed Kansas cow towns, killed an unknown number of men, and toured in Buffalo Bill's Wild West Show

■ *Martha Jane Canary—Calamity Jane—in the uniform of a U.S. Army scout. She boasted of her marksmanship and her exploits as a pony express rider and a scout.*

—died, shot in the back of the head. Hickok was thirty-nine.

Towns such as Deadwood, in the Dakota Territory; Virginia City, Nevada; Leadville, Colorado; and Tombstone, Arizona, began a new process in the frontier experience. The farming frontier naturally took place in a rural setting. On the mining frontier, the camp—the germ of a city—appeared almost simultaneously with the first "strike." Periodicals, the latest fashions, theaters, schools, literary clubs, and lending libraries came quickly to the camps, providing civilized refinements not available on other frontiers. But urbanization also created the need for municipal government, sanitation, and law enforcement.

Mining camps were governed by a simple democracy. Soon after a strike, the miners in the area met to organize a mining "district" and adopted rules governing behavior in it. Rules regulated the size and boundaries of claims, established procedures for settling disputes, and set penalties for crimes. Petty criminals were banished from the district; serious offenders were hanged. In the case of a major dispute, the whole camp gathered, chose legal counsel for both sides, and heard the evidence. If all else failed, miners formed secret vigilance committees to hang a few offenders as a lesson to the rest. Early visitors to the mining country were struck by the way miners, solitary and competitive, joined together, founded a camp, and created a society.

The camps were mostly male, made up of "men who can rough it" and a few ladies of "spirit and energy." In 1870 men outnumbered women in the mining districts by more than two to one; there were few children. Prostitutes followed the camps around the West, and "respectable" women were an object of curiosity. Four arrived in Nevada City in 1853, and as one observed: "The men stand and gaze at us with mouth and eyes wide open, every time we go out." Some women worked claims, but more often they took jobs as cooks, housekeepers, and seamstresses—for wages considerably higher than in the East. There were advantages in scarcity. "I lead a life of great variety—full of agreeable, and stirring incidents," one woman said. "I think that I should find any other country very dull after this."

In most camps between one quarter and one half of the population was foreign-born. The lure of gold drew large numbers of Chinese, Chileans, Peruvians, Mexicans, French, Germans, and English. Experienced miners, the Latin Americans brought valuable mining techniques. At least six thousand Mexicans joined the California rush of 1849, and by 1852 there were twenty-five thousand Chinese in California. Painstaking, the Chinese profitably worked claims others had abandoned. In the 1860s almost one third of the miners in the West were Chinese.

Hostility often surfaced against foreign miners, particularly the French, Latin Americans, and Chinese. In 1850 California passed a Foreign Miners' Tax that charged foreign miners a $20 monthly licensing fee. As intended, it drove out Mexican and other miners. Riots against Chinese laborers occurred in the 1870s and '80s in Los Angeles, San Francisco, Seattle, Reno, and Denver. Responding to pressure, Congress passed the Chinese Exclusion Act of 1882, which suspended immigration of Chinese laborers for ten years. The number of Chinese in the United States fell drastically.

By the 1890s the early mining bonanza was over. All told, the western mines contributed billions of dollars to the economy. They helped finance the Civil War and provided needed capital for industrialization. The vast boost in silver production from the Comstock Lode changed the relative value of gold and silver, the base of American currency. Bitter disputes over the currency affected politics and led to the famous "battle of the standards," the presidential election of 1896 (see chapter 20).

The mining frontier populated portions of the West and sped its political organization. Nevada, Idaho, and Montana were granted early statehood because of mining. Merchants, editors, lawyers, and ministers accompanied the frontier and established permanent settlements. But the industry also left behind painful scars in the form of invaded Indian reservations, pitted hills, and lonely ghost towns.

Gold from the Roots Up

"There's gold from the grass roots down," said California Joe, a guide in the gold districts of Dakota in the 1870s, "but there's more gold from the grass roots up." Ranchers began to recognize the potential of the vast grasslands of the West. The Plains were covered with buffalo or grama grass, a wiry variety with short, hard stems. Cattle thrived on it.

For twenty years after 1865, cattle ranching dominated the "open range," a vast, fenceless

---

Mining Camps and Cattle Trails

Opportunistic, materialistic, and exploitative Westerners were always ready to seize the main chance. Lucky miners extracted gold from beneath the ground and cattle ranchers made fortunes from the grasslands above the ground.

The Bonanza West

Cowboys roping longhorns, a painting by James Walker. Roping was often the most difficult part of a cowboy's job. It required expert horsemanship, a good sense of timing, and great skill with the rope or lariat.

area extending from the Texas Panhandle north into Canada. The techniques of the business came from Mexico, where long before American cowboys moved herds north, their Mexican counterparts, the *vaqueros*, developed the essential techniques of branding, roundups, and roping. The cattle themselves, the famous Texas longhorns, also came from Mexico. Spreading over the grasslands of southern Texas, the longhorns multiplied rapidly. Although their meat was coarse and stringy, they fed a nation hungry for beef at the end of the Civil War.

The problem was to get the beef to eastern markets, and Joseph G. McCoy, a livestock shipper from Illinois, solved it. Looking for a way to market Texas beef, McCoy conceived the idea of taking the cattle to railheads in Kansas. He talked first with the president of the Missouri Pacific, who ordered him out of his office, and then with the head of the Kansas Pacific, who laughed at the idea. The persistent McCoy finally signed a contract in 1867 with the Hannibal and St. Joseph Railroad. Searching for an appropriate rail junction, he settled on the sleepy Kansas town of Abilene, "a very small, dead place," he remembered, with about a dozen log huts and one near-bankrupt saloon.

In September 1867, McCoy shipped the first train of twenty cars of longhorn cattle. By the end of the year a thousand carloads had followed, all headed for Chicago markets. In 1870 three hundred thousand head of Texas cattle reached Abilene, and the following year—the peak year—seven hundred thousand head. The Alamo Saloon, crowded with tired cowboys at the end of the drive, now employed seventy-five bartenders, working three eight-hour shifts.

The profits were enormous. Drivers bought cheap Texas steers for $7 a head and sold them for $60 or $70 a head at the northern railhead. The most famous trail was the Chisholm, running from southern Texas through Oklahoma Territory to Ellsworth and Abilene, Kansas, on the Kansas Pacific Railroad. Dodge City, Kansas, became the prime shipping center between 1875 and 1879.

Cowboys pushed steers northward in herds of two to three thousand. Novels and films have portrayed them as white, but at least a quarter were black and possibly another quarter were Mexicans. A typical crew on the trail north might have eight men, half of them black or Mexican. Most of the trail bosses were white; they earned about $125 a month. As James "Jim" Perry, a renowned black cowboy who worked for more than twenty years as a rider, roper, and cook for the XIT ranch, said: "If it weren't for my damned old black face, I'd have been a boss long ago."

Like miners, cattlemen lived beyond the formal reach of the law and so established their own. Before each drive Charles Goodnight drew up rules governing behavior on the trail. A cowboy who shot another was hanged on the spot. Ranchers adopted rules for cattle ownership, branding, roundups, and drives; and they formed associations to enforce them. The Wyoming Stock Growers' Association, the largest and most formidable, had four hundred members owning two million cattle; its reach extended well beyond Wyoming into Colorado, Nebraska, Montana, and the Dakotas. Throughout this vast territory the "laws" of the association were often the law of the land.

Hollywood to the contrary, there was little violence in the booming cow towns. The number

Nat Love, born a slave in Tennessee in 1854, claimed to be the original "Deadwood Dick," having won the title—he said—in a cowboy contest in Deadwood, South Dakota, in 1876.

of homicides in a year never topped five in any town, and in many years no one was killed. Doc Holliday and William B. (Bat) Masterson never killed anyone. John Wesley Hardin, a legendary teen-aged gunman, shot only one man, firing blindly through a hotel room wall to stop him from snoring. Famous western sheriffs had everyday duties. Wild Bill Hickok served as Abilene's street commissioner, and the Wichita city council made its lawmen, including Wyatt Earp, repair streets and sidewalks before each cattle season.

By 1880 more than six million cattle had been driven to northern markets. But the era of the great cattle drive was ending. Farmers were planting wheat on the old buffalo ranges; barbed wire, a recent invention, cut across the trails and divided up the big ranches. Mechanical improvements in slaughtering, refrigerated transportation, and cold storage modernized the industry. Ranchers bred the Texas longhorns with heavier Hereford and Angus bulls, and as the new breeds proved profitable, more and more ranches opened on the northern ranges.

By the mid-1880s some 4.5 million cattle grazed the High Plains, reminding people of the once great herds of buffalo. Stories of vast profits circulated, attracting outside capital. Large investments transformed ranching into big business, often controlled by absentee owners and subject to new problems.

By 1885 experienced cattlemen were growing alarmed. A presidential order that year forced stockmen out of the Indian Territory in Oklahoma, adding 200,000 cattle to the overcrowded northern ranges. The winter of 1885–1886 was cold, and the following summer was one of the hottest on record. Waterholes dried up; the grass turned brown. Beef prices fell. The *Rocky Mountain Husbandman* urged ranchers to sell: "Beef is low, very low, and prices are tending downward. . . . But for all that, it would be better to sell at a low figure, than to endanger the whole herd by having the range overstocked."

The winter of 1886–1887 was one of the worst in western history. Temperatures dropped to 45 degrees below zero, and cattle that once would have saved themselves by drifting ahead of the storms, came up against the new barbed wire fences. Herds jammed together, pawing the frozen ground or stripping bark from trees in search of food. Cattle died by the tens of thousands. In

■ *Cowboys' lives were brutal with long hours, dangerous conditions, and low pay. They earned between $25 and $40 a month and managed herds worth fortunes.*

the spring of 1887, when the snows thawed, ranchers found stacks of carcasses piled up against the fences.

The melting snows did produce a lush crop of grass for the survivors. The cattle business recovered, but it took different directions. Outside capital, so plentiful in the boom years, dried up. Ranchers began fencing their lands, reducing the size of their herds, and growing hay for winter food. To the dismay of cowboys, mowing machines and hay rakes became as important as chuck wagons and branding irons. "I tell you times have changed,"one cowboy said sadly.

The last roundup on the northern ranges took place in 1905. Ranches grew smaller, and some ranchers, mainly in the scrub country of the Southwest, switched to raising sheep. In Wyoming the number of cattle shrank from nine million in 1886 to three million in 1895, the same number as when the boom began. Homesteaders, armed with barbed wire and new strains of wheat, pushed onto the Plains, and the day of the open range was over.

Farming on the Frontier

Like miners and cattlemen, millions of farmers moved West in the decades after 1870 to seek crop bonanzas and new ways of life. Some realized their dreams; many fought just to survive.

Said a folk song from Greer County, Oklahoma:

Hurrah for Greer County! The land of the free,
The land of the bedbug, grasshopper, and flea;
I'll sing of its praises, I'll tell of its fame,
While starving to death on my government claim.

Between 1870 and 1900 farmers cultivated more land than ever before in American history. They peopled the Plains from Dakota to Texas, pushed the Indians out of their last sanctuary in Oklahoma, and poured into the basins and foothills of the Rockies. By 1900 the western half of the nation contained almost 30 percent of the population, compared to less than 1 percent just a half-century earlier.

Sodbusters on the Plains

Unlike mining, farm settlement often followed predictable patterns, taking population from states east of the frontier line and moving gradually westward. Crossing the Mississippi, farmers settled first in South Dakota, Minnesota, western Iowa, Nebraska, Kansas, and Texas. The movement slumped during the depression of the 1870s, but then a new wave of optimism carried thousands more west. Several years of above-average rainfall convinced farmers that the Dakotas, western Nebraska and Kansas, and eastern Colorado were the "rain belt of the Plains." Between 1870 and 1900 the population on the Plains tripled.

Farming there presented new problems. There was little surface water, and wells ranged between fifty and five hundred feet deep. Well drillers charged up to $2 a foot. Taking advantage of the steady Plains winds, windmills brought the water to the surface, but they too were expensive, and until 1900 many farmers could not afford them. Lumber for homes and fences was also scarce. Some settlers imported it from distant Wisconsin, but a single homestead of 160 acres cost $1000 to fence, an amount few could pay.

Unable to afford wood, farmers often started out in dreary sod houses. Cut into three-foot sections, the thick prairie sod was laid like brick, with space left for two windows and a door. Since glass was scarce, cloth hung over the windows; a blanket was hung from the ceiling to make two rooms. Sod houses were small, provided little light and air, and were impossible to keep clean. When it rained, water seeped through the roof. Yet a sod house cost only $2.78 to build.

Outside, the Plains environment sorely tested the men and women who moved there. Neighbors were distant; the land stretched on as far as the eye could see. Always the wind blew. "As long as I live I'll never see such a lonely country," a woman said of the Texas Plains; a Nebraska woman said: "These unbounded prairies have such an air of desolation—and the stillness is very oppressive."

In the winters savage storms swept the open grasslands. Ice caked on the cattle until their heads were too heavy to hold up. Summertime temperatures stayed near 110 degrees for weeks at a time. Fearsome rainstorms, building in the summer's heat, beat down the young corn and wheat. The summers also brought grasshoppers,

■ *A Nebraska farm couple plowing the corn in the dooryard of their sod house in 1888. Corn, which could fight its way through tough prairie grass, was often the prairie farmer's first crop.*

Farming on the Frontier

arriving without warning, flying in clouds so huge they shut out the sun. The grasshoppers ate everything in sight: crops, clothing, mosquito netting, tree bark, even plow handles. In the summer of 1874 they devastated the whole Plains from Texas to the Dakotas, eating everything "but the mortgage," as one farmer said.

New Farming Methods

Farmers adopted new techniques to meet these conditions. For one thing, they needed cheap and effective fencing material, and in 1874 Joseph F. Glidden, a farmer from De Kalb, Illinois, provided it with the invention of barbed wire. By 1883 his factory was turning out 600 miles of barbed wire every day, and farmers were buying it faster than it could be produced.

Dry farming, a new technique, helped compensate for the lack of rainfall. By plowing furrows twelve to fourteen inches deep, and creating a dust mulch to fill the furrow, farmers loosened the soil and slowed evaporation. Wheat farmers imported European varieties that could withstand the harsh Plains winters. Hard-kerneled varieties like "Turkey Red" wheat from Russia required new milling methods, developed during the 1870s. By 1881 Minneapolis, St. Louis, and Kansas City had become milling centers for the rich "New Process" flour.

Farm technology changed long before the Civil War, but later developments improved it. In 1877 James Oliver of Indiana patented a chilled-iron plow with a smooth-surface mold board that did not clog in the thick prairie soils. The spring-tooth harrow (1869) sped soil preparation; the grain drill (1874) opened furrows and scientifically fed seed into the ground. The lister (1880) dug a deep furrow, planted corn at the bottom, and covered the seed—all in one operation.

The first baling press was built in 1866, and the hay loader was patented in 1876. The first successful harvester, the cord binder (1878), cut and tied bundles of grain, enabling two men and a team of horses to harvest twenty acres of wheat a day. Invented earlier, threshers grew larger; employing as many as nine men and ten horses, they threshed three hundred bushels of grain a day.

In 1890 over 900 corporations manufactured farm machinery. Scientific agriculture flourished under new discoveries linking soil minerals and plant growth. Samuel Johnson of Yale University wrote books on *How Crops Grow* (1868) and *How Crops Feed* (1870), and one of his students pioneered work on nitrogen, the base of many modern fertilizers. The Hatch Act, passed in 1887, supported agricultural experiment stations that spread the discoveries among farmers. Four years later, these stations employed over 450 persons and distributed more than 300 published reports annually to some 350,000 readers.

In the late 1870s huge bonanza farms rose, run by the new machinery and financed with outside capital. Oliver Dalrymple, the most famous of the bonanza farmers, headed an experiment in North Dakota's Red River Valley in 1875, then moved on to manage the Grandin Bonanza of 61,000 acres, five times the size of Manhattan Island. Dalrymple hired armies of workers, bought machinery by the carload, and planted on a scale that dazzled the West. "You are in a sea of wheat," said one visitor to the Grandin Bonanza. "The railroad train rolls through an ocean of grain. . . . We encounter a squadron of war chariots . . . doing the work of human hands."

The bonanza farms—thanks to their size and machinery—captured the country's imagination. Using 200 pairs of harrows, 155 binders, and 16 threshers, Dalrymple produced 600,000 bushels of wheat in 1881. He and other bonanza managers profited from the economies of scale, buying materials at wholesale prices and receiving rebates from the railroads. Then a period of drought began. Rainfall dropped between 1885 and 1890, and the large-scale growers found it hard to compete with smaller farmers who diversified their crops and cultivated more intensively. Many of the large bonanzas slowly disintegrated, and Dalrymple himself went bankrupt in 1896.

Discontent on the Farm

Like the cattle boom, the farming boom ended sharply after 1887. A severe drought that year cut harvests, and other droughts followed in 1889 and 1894. Thousands of new farmers were wiped out on the western Plains. Between 1888 and 1892 more than half the population of western Kansas left. In the 1890s Nebraska lost fifteen thousand people and six thousand farms.

Thirty-two horses pull a harvester-thresher combine through a wheat field in Oregon. The huge machines combined the work of binding and threshing into one operation. Soon the animals were replaced by steam power.

Farmers grew angry and restless. They complained about declining crop prices, rising railroad rates, and heavy mortgages. In the wheat-growing Plains the economic problems were persistent. Returning home to Iowa in 1889, the author Hamlin Garland found his farming friends caught up "in a sullen rebellion against the government and against God."

Every house I visited had its individual message of sordid struggle and half-hidden despair. . . . All the gilding of farm life melted away. The hard and bitter realities came back upon me in a flood. Nature was as bountiful as ever . . . but no splendor of cloud, no grace of sunset, could conceal the poverty of these people.

Touring the South in the 1860s, Oliver H. Kelley, a clerk in the Department of Agriculture, was struck by the drabness of rural life. In 1867 he founded the National Grange of the Patrons of Husbandry, known simply as the Grange. The Grange provided social, cultural, and educational activities for its members. Its constitution banned involvement in politics, but Grangers often ignored it and supported railroad regulation and other measures.

The Grange grew rapidly during the depression of the 1870s, and by 1875 it had over 800,000 members in 20,000 local Granges. Most were in the Midwest and South. The Granges set up cooperative stores, grain elevators, warehouses, insurance companies, and farm machinery factories. Many failed, but in the meantime the organization made its mark. Farm-oriented groups like the Farmers' Alliance, with branches in both South and West, began to attract followers. Discontent grew, spilling over into the turbulent Populist movement of the 1890s. (See chapter 20 for a more detailed discussion.)

The peopling of the West transformed American agriculture. The states beyond the Mississippi became the garden land of the nation. California sent fruit, wine, and wheat to eastern markets. Under the Mormons, Utah flourished with irrigation. Texas beef stocked the country's tables, and vast wheat fields, stretching to the horizon, covered Minnesota, the Dakotas, Mon-

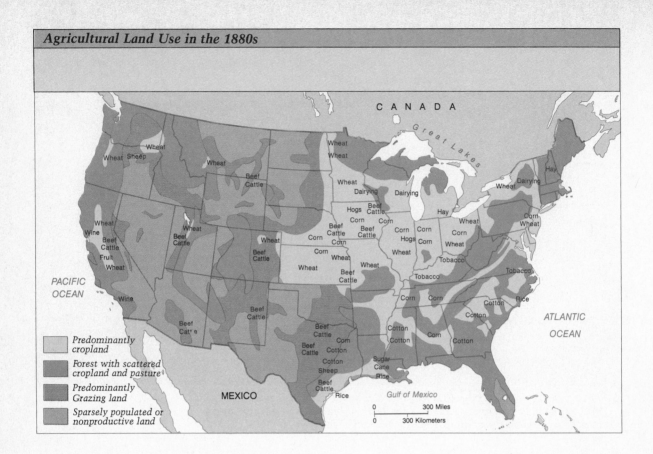

Predominantly cropland

Forest with scattered cropland and pasture

Predominantly Grazing land

Sparsely populated or nonproductive land

tana, and eastern Colorado. All produced more than Americans could consume. By 1890 American farmers were exporting large amounts of wheat and other crops.

Farmers became more commercial and scientific. They needed to know more and work harder. Mail-order houses and rural free delivery diminished their isolation and tied them ever closer to the national future. "This is a new age to the farmer," said a statistician in the Department of Agriculture in 1889. "He is now, more than ever before, a citizen of the world."

The Final Fling

As the West filled in with people, pressure mounted on the president and Congress to open the last Indian territory, Oklahoma, to settlers. In March 1889 Congress acted and forced the Creeks and Seminoles, two tribes who had been moved into Oklahoma in the 1820s, to surrender their rights. The arrangements complete, President Benjamin Harrison announced the opening of the Oklahoma District as of noon, April 22, 1889.

Preparations were feverish all along the frontier. "From all the West," historian Ray Allen Billington noted, "the homeless, the speculators, the adventurers, flocked to the still forbidden land." On the morning of April 22, nearly 100,000 people lined the Oklahoma borders; "for miles on end horsemen, wagons, hacks, carriages, bicycles, and a host of vehicles beggaring description stood wheel to wheel awaiting the signal." Fifteen Santa Fe trains were jammed with people from platform to roof.

At noon the starting flag dropped. Bugles and cannon signaled the opening of the "last" territory. Horsemen lunged forward, overloaded wagons collided and overturned. The trains steamed slowly forward, forced to keep a pace that would not give their passengers an undue advantage.

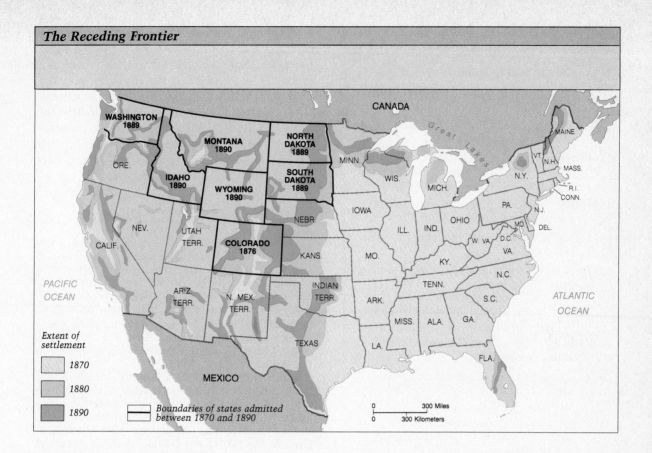

The Receding Frontier

WASHINGTON 1889 · ORE. · IDAHO 1890 · MONTANA 1890 · NORTH DAKOTA 1889 · WYOMING 1890 · SOUTH DAKOTA 1889 · COLORADO 1876 · NEV. · UTAH TERR. · CALIF. · NEBR. · IOWA · MINN. · WIS. · MICH. · CANADA · Great Lakes · MAINE · VT · N.H. · MASS. · N.Y. · R.I. · CONN. · PA. · N.J. · OHIO · MD · DEL. · W. VA · D.C. · VA. · ILL. · IND. · KY. · N.C. · ARIZ. TERR. · N. MEX. TERR. · KANS. · MO. · TENN. · S.C. · PACIFIC OCEAN · INDIAN TERR. · ARK. · MISS. · ALA. · GA. · ATLANTIC OCEAN · TEXAS · LA. · FLA. · MEXICO

Extent of settlement
1870
1880
1890
Boundaries of states admitted between 1870 and 1890

0 — 300 Miles
0 — 300 Kilometers

By sunset that day settlers claimed 12,000 homesteads, and the 1,920,000 acres of the Oklahoma District were officially settled. Homesteaders threw up shelters for the night. By evening, Oklahoma City, that morning merely a spot on the prairie with cottonwoods and grass, had 10,000 people; Guthrie to the north had 15,000. Speculators swiftly erected pay toilets, and drinking water cost as much as a beer.

The "Boomers" and "Sooners"—those who had jumped the gun—reflected the speed of western settlement. "Creation!" a character in Edna Ferber's novel *Cimarron* declared. "Hell! That took six days. This was done in one. It was History made in an hour—and I helped make it."

Between the Civil War and 1900 the West witnessed one of the greatest migrations in history. With the Indians driven into smaller and smaller areas, farms, ranches, mines, and cities took over the vast lands from the Mississippi to the Pacific. The 1890 census noted that for the first time in the country's history, "there can hardly be said to be a frontier line." Picking up the theme, Frederick Jackson Turner, a young history instructor at the University of Wisconsin, examined its importance in an influential 1893 paper, "The Significance of the Frontier in American History."

"The existence of an area of free land," Turner wrote, "its continuous recession, and the advance of American settlement westward, explain American development." It shaped customs and character; gave rise to independence, self-confidence, and individualism; and fostered invention and adaptation. Historians have substantially modified Turner's thesis by pointing to frontier conservatism and imitativeness, the influence of varying racial groups, and the persistence of European ideas and institutions. Yet there can be no doubt that the frontier and the West influenced American development.

Chronology

1849 Gold rush to California

1859 More gold discoveries, in Colorado and Nevada

1862 Congress passes Homestead Act, encouraging western settlement

1864 Nevada admitted to the Union
Colonel John Chivington leads massacre of Indians at Sand Creek, Colorado

1865–1867 Sioux fight against white miners and U.S. army in Great Sioux War

1866 "Long drive" of cattle touches off cattle bonanzas

1867 Horace Greeley urges Easterners to "Go West, young man"
National Grange of the Patrons of Husbandry (the Grange) founded to enrich farmers' lives

1867–1868 Policy of "small reservations" for Indians adopted

1873 Congress passes Timber Culture Act
Big Bonanza discovered on the Comstock Lode in Nevada

1874 Joseph F. Glidden invents barbed wire
Discovery of gold in Dakota Territory sets off Black Hills Gold Rush

1876 Colorado admitted to the Union
Custer and his men defeated and killed by the Sioux at battle of Little Bighorn (June)

1883 Museum expedition discovers fewer than 200 buffalo in the West
Buffalo Bill Cody organizes and begins touring with his Wild West Show

1886–1887 Severe drought and winter damage cattle and farming bonanzas

1887 Congress passes Dawes Severalty Act, making Indians individual landowners
Hatch Act provides funds for establishment of agricultural experiment stations

1889 Washington, Montana, and the Dakotas admitted to the Union
Oklahoma Territory opened to settlement

1890 Idaho and Wyoming admitted to Union
Teton Sioux massacred at battle of Wounded Knee, South Dakota (December)

1893 Young historian Frederick Jackson Turner analyzes closing of the frontier

Western lands attracted European, Latin American, and Asian immigrants, adding to the society's talent and diversity. The mines, forests, and farms of the West fueled the economy, sent raw materials to eastern factories, and fed the growing cities. Though defeated in warfare, Indian and Spanish influence persisted in art, architecture, law, and western folklore. The West was the first American empire, and it had a profound impact on the American mind and imagination.

Recommended Reading

The best general account of the movement West is Ray Allen Billington, *Westward Expansion* (1967), which also has a first-rate bibliography. See also Frederick Merk, *History of the Westward Movement* (1978). Frederick Jackson Turner's influential interpretation of frontier development, "The Significance of the Frontier in American History," is in his *Frontier in American History* (1920). Walter Prescott Webb, *The Great Plains* (1931), offers a fascinating analysis of development on the Plains.

Rodman W. Paul gives a thorough survey of the mining bonanza in *Mining Frontiers of the Far West* (1963), while Fred A. Shannon provides similar coverage for agriculture in *The Farmer's Last Frontier* (1945). Lewis Atherton, *The Cattle Kings* (1961), and E. S. Osgood, *The Day of the Cattleman* (1929), cover the cattle industry. Louis B. Wright, *Culture on the Moving Frontier* (1955), argues that settlers did not give up books and other cultural assets as they moved West; Henry Nash Smith, *Virgin Land: The American West as Symbol and Myth* (1950) is superb on the literary images of the West in the nineteenth century.

Recent authors have taken fresh and stimulating looks at older or ignored questions. Robert R. Dykstra, *The Cattle Towns* (1968), examines five Kansas cattle towns, with interesting results. Gunther Barth traces the rapid rise of San Francisco and Denver in *Instant Cities* (1975), and Earl Pomeroy, *The Pacific Slope* (1965), looks at urban and other developments in the Far West. Julie Roy Jeffrey, *Frontier Women: The Trans-Mississippi West* (1979), and Joanna L. Stratton, *Pioneer Women: Voices from the Kansas Frontier* (1981), are perceptive works on a neglected topic, and John Mack Faragher, *Women and Men on the Overland Trail* (1979), examines social and other relationships on the trails west.

Additional Bibliography

On the Indians, there are a number of valuable works, including William T. Hagan, *American Indians* (1961); Wilcomb E. Washburn, *The Indian in America* (1975); Robert M. Utley, *The Last Days of the Sioux Nation* (1963) and *Frontier Regulars: The United States Army* and the Indian (1973); and R. K. Andrist, *The Long Death: The Last Days of the Plains Indians* (1964). Helen Hunt Jackson, *A Century of Dishonor* (1881) is a stinging contemporary account.

Dwight W. Hoover, *The Red and the Black* (1976), and Leonard Dinnerstein, Roger L. Nichols, and David M. Reimers, *Natives and Strangers* (1979), contrast Indian policy with the treatment of other minorities. Leonard Pitt looks at *The Decline of the Californios: A Social History of the Spanish-Speaking Californians* (1966); Mario T. Garcia at the Mexican immigrants to El Paso in *Desert Immigrants* (1981); and Gunther Barth at the treatment of the Chinese in *Bitter Strength* (1964).

George R. Stewart, *The California Trail* (1962) and John D. Unruh, Jr., *The Plains Across: The Overland Emigrants and the Trans-Mississippi West, 1840–1860* (1979) are good, but read some of the extraordinary diaries, including David M. Potter, ed., *The Trail to California* (1962) and Dale Morgan, ed., *Overland in 1846* (1963). A. B. Guthrie, Jr., *The Way West* (1949) is an excellent fictional account based on considerable research.

Books on the mining bonanza include Rodman W. Paul, *California Gold* (1948); Charles H. Shinn, *Mining Camps* (1885); William T. Jackson, *Treasure Hill: Portrait of a Silver Mining Camp* (1963); Odie B. Faulk, *Tombstone: Myth and Reality* (1972); D. A. Smith, *Rocky Mountain Mining Camps: The Urban Frontier* (1967); Dan DeQuille, *History of the Big Bonanza* (1876); Eliot Lord, *Comstock Mining and Miners* (1883); and Mark Twain, *Roughing It* (1872).

The best works on the cowboy are E. E. Dale, *Cow Country* (1942); Andy Adams, *The Log of a Cowboy* (1902); and J. B. Franz and J. E. Choate, *The American Cowboy: The Myth and Reality* (1955). Ralph P. Bieber's edited version of Joseph G. McCoy, *Historic Sketches of the Cattle Trade of the West and Southwest* (1940) is indispensable on the man who claimed to start the great herds north. Gene M. Gressley, *Bankers and Cattlemen* (1966), details outside investment in cattle.

Federal land policy is surveyed in Roy M. Robbins, *Our Landed Heritage* (1942), and Paul Wallace Gates, *Fifty Million Acres* (1954). Valuable studies of farming include Gilbert C. Fite, *The Farmer's Frontier* (1966); Allan G. Bogue, *From Prairie to Corn Belt* (1963); Everett Dick, *The Sod-House Frontier* (1937); and H. M. Drache, *The Day of the Bonanza* (1964). Solon J. Buck, *The Granger Movement* (1913), studies early farm discontent and the Grange.

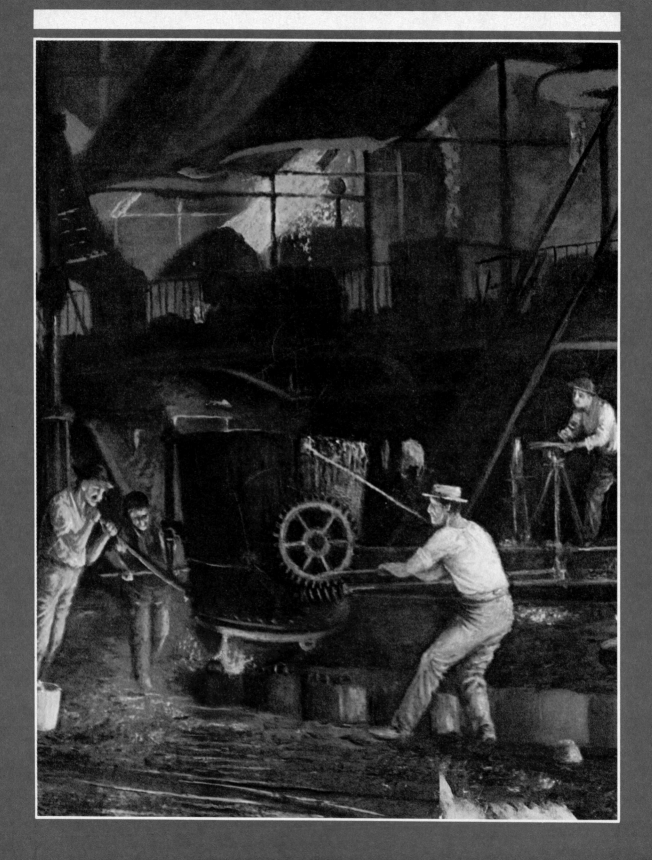

chapter 18
THE
INDUSTRIAL
SOCIETY

In 1876 Americans celebrated their first century of independence. Survivors of a recent civil war, they observed the centenary proudly and rather self-consciously, in song and speech, and above all in a grand Centennial Exposition held in Philadelphia, Pennsylvania.

Spread over thirteen acres of land, the exposition focused more on the present than the past. Fairgoers strolled through exhibits of life in colonial times, then hurried off to see the main attractions: machines, inventions, and new products. They saw linoleum, a new, easy-to-clean floor covering. For the first time they tasted root beer, supplied by a young druggist named Charles Hires, and the rare banana, wrapped in foil and selling for a dime. They saw their first bicycle, an awkward high-wheeled contraption with solid tires.

A Japanese Pavilion generated widespread interest in the culture of Japan. There was also a Women's Building, the first ever in a major exposition. Inside were displayed paintings and sculpture by women artists, along with rows of textile machinery staffed by female operators.

In the entire exposition, machinery was the focus and Machinery Hall the most popular building. Here were the products of an ever improving civilization. Long lines of the curious waited to see the telephone, Alexander Graham Bell's new device. ("My God, it talks!" the emperor of Brazil exclaimed.) Thomas A. Edison displayed several recent inventions, while nearby, whirring machines turned out bricks, chewing tobacco, and other products. Fairgoers saw the first public display of the typewriter, Elisha Otis' new elevator, and the Westinghouse railroad air brake.

But above all, they crowded around the mighty Corliss engine, the focal point of the exposition. A giant steam engine, it dwarfed everything in Machinery Hall, its twin vertical cylinders towering almost four stories in the air. Alone it supplied power for the eight thousand other machines, large and small, on the exposition grounds. Poorly designed, the Corliss was soon obsolete, but for the moment it captured the nation's imagination. It symbolized swift movement toward an industrial and urban society. John Greenleaf Whittier, the aging rural poet, likened it to the snake in the Garden of Eden and refused to see it.

As Whittier feared, the United States was fast becoming an industrial society. Developments earlier in the century laid the basis, but the most spectacular advances in industrialization came during the three decades after the Civil War. At the start of the war the country lagged well behind industrializing nations such as Great Britain, France, and Germany. By 1900 it had vaulted far into the lead, with a manufacturing output that exceeded the *combined* output of its three European rivals. Over the same years cities grew, technology advanced, and farm production rose. Developments in manufacturing, mining, agriculture, transportation, and communication changed society.

Many Americans eagerly sought the change. William Dean Howells, a leading novelist, visited

International Steel Production, 1880–1914

1880
1914

Millions of tons

Germany France Great Britain Russia United States

the Centennial Exposition and stood in awe before the Corliss. Comparing it to the paintings and sculpture on display, Howells preferred the machine: "It is in these things of iron and steel," he said, "that the national genius most freely speaks."

Industrial Development

American industry owed its remarkable growth to several considerations. It fed on an abundance of natural resources: coal, iron, timber, petroleum, waterpower. An iron manufacturer likened the nation to "a gigantic bowl filled with treasure." Labor was also abundant, drawn from American farm families and the hosts of European immigrants who flocked to American mines, cities, and factories. Nearly eight million immigrants arrived in the 1870s and 1880s; another fifteen million came between 1890 and 1914.

The burgeoning population led to expanded markets, which new devices like the telegraph and telephone helped to exploit. The swiftly growing urban populations devoured goods, and the railroads, spreading pell-mell across the land, linked the cities together and opened a national market. Within its boundaries the United States had the largest free-trade market in the world, while tariff barriers partially protected its producers from outside competition.

Expansive market and labor conditions buoyed the confidence of investors, European and American, who provided large amounts of capital. Technological progress, so remarkable in these years, doomed some older industries (tallow, for example) but increased productivity in others, such as the kerosene industry, and created entirely new industries as well. Through inventions like the harvester and the combine, it also helped foster a firm agricultural base, on which industrialization depends.

Eager to promote economic growth, government at all levels—federal, state, and local—gave manufacturers money, land, and other resources. Other benefits, too, flowed from the American system of government: stability, commitment to the concept of private property, and initially at least, a reluctance to regulate industrial activity. Unlike their European counterparts, American

manufacturers faced few legal or social barriers, and their main domestic rivals, the southern planters, had lost political power in the Civil War.

In this atmosphere entrepreneurs flourished. Taking steps crucial for industrialization, they organized, managed, and assumed the financial risks of the new enterprises. Admirers called them "captains of industry"; foes labeled them "robber barons." To some degree they were both —creative *and* acquisitive. If sometimes they seemed larger than life, they dealt in concepts, distances, and quantities often unknown to earlier generations.

Industrial growth, it must be remembered, was neither a simple nor steady nor inevitable process. It involved human decisions and brought with it large social benefits and costs. Growth varied from industry to industry and from year to year. It was concentrated in the North and East, from where in 1890 more than 85 percent of America's manufactured goods originated. The more sparsely settled West provided raw materi-

■ *A sectional view of the "beehive" headquarters of Montgomery Ward & Co., one of the emerging retail and mail-order giants of the '90s (see p. 530).*

als, while the South, although making major gains in iron, textiles, and tobacco, had to rebuild after wartime devastation. In 1890 the industrial production of the entire South amounted in value to about half that of the state of New York.

Still, industrial development proceeded at an extraordinary pace. Between 1865 and 1914 the real Gross National Product (GNP)—the total monetary value of all goods and services produced in a year, with prices held stable—grew at a rate of more than 4 percent a year, increasing about eightfold overall. As Robert Higgs, an economic historian, noted: "Never before had such rapid growth continued for so long."

An Empire on Rails

Genuine revolutions happen rarely, but a major one occurred in the nineteenth century: a revolution in transportation and communications. When the century began, people traveled and communicated much as they had for centuries; when it ended, the railroad, the telegraph, the telephone, and the ocean-going steamship had wrought enormous changes.

The steamship sliced in half the time of the Atlantic crossing and, not dependent on wind and tide, introduced new regularity in the movement of goods and passengers. The telegraph, flashing messages almost instantaneously along miles of wire (four hundred thousand miles of it in the early 1880s), transformed communications, as did the telephone a little later. But the railroad worked the largest changes of all. Along with Bessemer steel, it was the most significant technical innovation of the century.

"Emblem of Motion and Power"

More than most such innovations, the railroad dramatically affected economic and social life. Economic growth would have occurred without it, of course; canals, inland steamboats, and the country's superb system of interior waterways already provided the outlines of an effective transportation network. But the railroad added significantly to the network and contributed advantages all its own.

Those advantages included more direct routes, greater speed, greater safety and comfort than other modes of land travel, more dependable schedules, a larger volume of traffic, and year-round service. A day's land travel on stagecoach or horseback might cover fifty miles. The railroad covered fifty miles in about an hour, seven hundred miles in a day. It went where canals and rivers did not go—directly to the loading platforms of great factories or across the arid West. As construction crews pushed tracks onward, vast areas of the continent opened for settlement.

Railroad Construction, 1830–1920

Source: U.S. Bureau of the Census, Historical Statistics of the United States, Colonial Times to 1970, *Bicentennial Edition, Washington, D.C., 1975.*

Linking widely separated cities and villages, the railroad ended the relative isolation and self-sufficiency of the country's "island communities." It tied people together, brought in outside products, fostered greater interdependence, and encouraged economic specialization. Under its stimulus, Chicago supplied meat to the nation; Minneapolis, grain; and Saint Louis, beer. For these and other communities the railroad made possible a national market and in so doing pointed the way toward mass production and mass consumption, two of the hallmarks of twentieth-century society.

It also pointed the way toward later business development. The railroad, as Alfred D. Chandler, the historian of business, has written, was "the nation's first big business"; it worked out "the modern ways of finance, management, labor relations, competition, and government regulation."

A railroad corporation, far-flung and complex, was a new kind of business. It stretched over thousands of miles, employed thousands of people, dealt with countless customers, and required a scale of organization and decision making unknown in earlier business. Railroad managers never met most customers or even many employees; thus arose new problems in marketing and labor relations. Year by year railroad companies consumed large quantities of iron, steel, coal, lumber, and glass; purchases stimulated growth and employment in numerous industries.

No wonder, then, that the railroad captured so completely the country's imagination. Walt Whitman, the poet who celebrated American achievement, chanted the locomotive's praises:

Thy black cylindric body, golden brass and silvery steel . . .
Thy great protruding head-light fix'd in front,
Thy long, pale, floating vapor-pennants, tinged with delicate purple . . .
Thy knitted frame, thy springs and valves, the tremulous twinkle of thy wheels,
Thy train of cars behind, obedient, merrily following . . .
Type of the modern—emblem of motion and power—pulse of the continent . . .
Fierce-throated beauty!

For nearly a hundred years—the railroad era lasted through the 1940s—children gathered at depots, paused in the fields to wave as the fast express flashed by, listened at night to far-off whistles, and wondered what lay down the tracks. They lived in a world grown smaller.

Building the Empire

When Lee surrendered at Appomattox in 1865, the country already had 35,000 miles of track, and much of the railroad system east of the Mississippi River was in place (see chapter 13). Farther west, the rail network stood poised on the edge of settlement. Although southern railroads were in shambles from the war, the United States had nearly as much railroad track as the rest of the world.

After the Civil War, rail construction increased by leaps and bounds. From 35,000 miles in 1865, the network expanded to 93,000 miles in 1880; 166,000 in 1890; and 193,000 in 1900—more than in all Europe including Russia. Mileage peaked at 254,037 miles in 1916, just before the industry began its long decline into the mid-twentieth century.

To build such an empire took vast amounts of capital—over $4.5 billion by 1880, before even half of it was complete. American and European investors provided some of the money; government supplied the rest. In all, local governments gave railroad companies about $300 million, and

■ *The* Fast Mail, *with its hook out to seize the mail pouch, its brave engineer, its gleaming brass and belching smoke, fascinated Americans.*

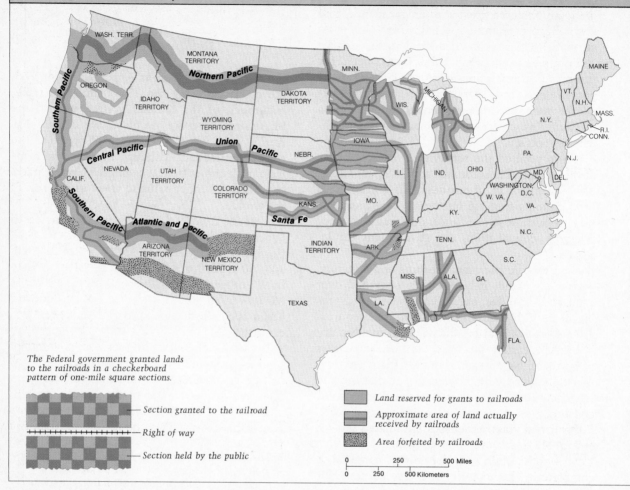

Federal Land Grants to Railroads as of 1871

Besides land, the government provided loans of $16,000 for each mile built on level land, $32,000 for each mile built on hilly terrain, and $48,000 for each mile in high mountain country.

The Federal government granted lands to the railroads in a checkerboard pattern of one-mile square sections.

— Section granted to the railroad

— Right of way

— Section held by the public

Land reserved for grants to railroads

Approximate area of land actually received by railroads

Area forfeited by railroads

state governments added $228 million more. The federal government loaned nearly $65 million to a half dozen western railroads and donated millions of acres of the public domain. Between 1850 and 1871, some eighty railroads received more than 170 million acres of land.

Almost 90 percent of the federal land grants lay in twenty states west of the Mississippi River. Federal land grants helped build 18,738 miles of track, less than 8 percent of the system. The land was frequently distant and difficult to market. Railroad companies sometimes sold it to raise cash but more often used it as security for bonds or loans.

Beyond doubt, the grants of cash and land

promoted waste and corruption. The companies built fast and wastefully, eager to collect the subsidies that went with each mile of track. Wanting quick profits, some owners formed separate construction companies to which they awarded lavish contracts. In this way the notorious Crédit Mobilier, a construction company controlled by an inner ring on the Union Pacific, enriched its owners in the 1860s, while the Contract and Finance Company did the same on the Central Pacific. The Crédit Mobilier bribed congressmen and state legislators in order to avoid congressional investigation of its activities (see chapter 16).

Yet, on balance, the grants probably worked

more benefits than evils. As Congress had hoped, the grants were the lure for railroad building across the rugged, unsettled West, where it would be years before revenues would repay construction. Farmers, ranchers, and merchants poured into the newly opened areas, settling the country and boosting the value of government and private land nearby. The grants seemed necessary in a nation which, unlike Europe, expected private enterprise to build the railroads. In return for aid, Congress required the railroads to carry government freight, troops, and mail at substantially reduced rates—resulting in savings to the government of almost $1 billion between 1850 and 1945. In no other cases of federal subsidies to carriers— canals, highways, and airlines—did Congress exact specific benefits in return.

Linking the Nation via Trunk Lines

The early railroads may seem to have linked different regions, but in fact they did not. Built with little regard for through traffic, they were designed more to protect local interests than to tap outside markets. Many extended fewer than fifty miles. To avoid cooperating with other lines, they adopted conflicting schedules, built separate depots, and above all, used different gauges. Gauges, the distance between the rails, ranged from 4 feet 8½ inches, which became the standard gauge, to 6 feet. Without special equipment, trains of one gauge could not run on tracks of another.

The Civil War showed the value of fast, long-distance transportation, and after 1865 railroad managers worked to provide it. In a burst of consolidation the large swallowed the small; integrated rail networks became a reality. Railroads also adopted standard schedules, signals, equipment, and finally in 1886, the standard gauge. In 1866, in a dramatic innovation to speed traffic, railroad companies introduced fast freight lines which pooled cars for service between cities.

In the Northeast four great trunk lines took shape, all intended to link eastern seaports with the rich traffic of the Great Lakes and western rivers. Like a massive river system, trunk lines drew traffic from dozens of tributaries (feeder lines) and carried it to major markets. The Baltimore and Ohio (B & O), which reached Chicago in 1874, was one; the Erie Railroad was another. Running from New York City to Chicago, the

This poster advertised the Erie Railroad as a great trunk line, renowned for its "double-tracked steel rails, scenic route, and well-appointed passenger cars, equipped with the celebrated Pullman hotel, drawing room and sleeping coaches."

Erie paralleled the route of Cornelius Vanderbilt —the "Commodore"—a crusty old multimillionaire from the shipping business who put together a third trunk line of his own.

Nearly seventy years old when he first entered railroading, Vanderbilt wasted no time. In 1867 he took over the New York Central Railroad and merged it with other lines to provide a track from New York City to Buffalo. When he died in 1877, his Central operated over forty-five hundred miles of track.

J. Edgar Thomson and Thomas A. Scott built the fourth trunk line, the Pennsylvania Railroad, which initially ran from Philadelphia to Pittsburgh. Restless and energetic, they dreamed of a rail empire stretching through the South and West. A brilliant business leader, Scott expanded the Pennsylvania system to Cincinnati, Indianapolis, Saint Louis, and Chicago in 1869, New York City in 1871, and Baltimore and Washington soon thereafter.

In the war-damaged South, consolidation took longer. As Reconstruction waned, northern and European capital rebuilt and integrated the southern lines, especially during the 1880s when rail construction in the South led the nation. By 1900 the South had five large systems: the Illinois Central, linking Chicago, New Orleans, and Savannah, Georgia; the Atlantic Coast Line and the Seaboard Air Line, both running from Virginia to Florida; the Louisville & Nashville, tapping the iron and coal regions of the middle South; and the Southern Railway, which ran from Washington, D.C., to New Orleans. Just four decades after the secession crisis, these systems tied the South into a national transportation network.

Over that rail system, passengers and freight moved in relative speed, comfort, and safety. Automatic couplers (1868), air brakes (1869), refrigerator cars (1867), dining cars, heated cars, electric switches, and stronger locomotives transformed railroad service. George Pullman's lavish sleeping cars became popular. Handsome depots, like New York's Grand Central and Washington's Union Station, were erected at major terminals. Passenger miles per year increased from five billion in 1870 to sixteen billion in 1900.

In November 1883, the railroads even changed time. Ending the crazy quilt jumble of local times that caused scheduling difficulties, the American Railway Association divided the country into four time zones and adopted the modern system of standard time. Congress took thirty-five years longer; it adopted standard time in 1918 in the midst of World War I.

Rails Across the Continent

The dream of a transcontinental railroad, linking the Atlantic and Pacific oceans, stretched back many years but had always succumbed to sectional quarrels over the route. In 1862 and 1864, with the South out of the picture, Congress passed legislation to build the first transcontinental. The act incorporated the Union Pacific Railroad Company to build westward from Nebraska to meet the Central Pacific Railroad Company, building eastward from the Pacific Coast. For each mile built, the two companies received from Congress twenty square miles of land in alternate sections along the track. For each mile they also received a thirty-year loan of $16,000, $32,000, or $48,000, depending on the difficulty of the terrain over which they built.

Construction began simultaneously at Omaha and Sacramento in 1863, lagged during the war, and moved vigorously ahead after 1865. It became a race, each company vying for land, loans, and potential markets. General Grenville M. Dodge, a tough Union army veteran, served as construction chief for the Union Pacific, while Charles Crocker, a former Sacramento dry-goods merchant, led the Central Pacific crews. Dodge organized an army of ten thousand workers, many of them ex-soldiers and Irish immigrants. Pushing rapidly westward, he encountered frequent Indian attacks but had the advantage of building over flat prairie.

Crocker faced more trying conditions in the high Sierra Nevada along California's eastern border. After several experiments he decided that Chinese laborers worked best, and he hired six thousand of them, most brought directly from China. "I built the Central Pacific," Crocker enjoyed boasting, but the Chinese crews did the awesome work. Under the most difficult conditions they dug, blasted, and pushed their way slowly east.

On May 10, 1869, the two lines met at Promontory Point, Utah, near the northern tip of the Great Salt Lake. Dodge's crews had built 1086

■ *After the last spike was hammered in at Promontory Point, the pilots of the two locomotives touched and exchanged champagne toasts. The chief engineers of the two lines are seen shaking hands.*

miles of track, Crocker's 689. The Union Pacific and Central Pacific presidents hammered in a golden spike (both missed it on the first try), and the dreamed-of connection was made. The telegraph flashed the news east and west, setting off wild celebrations.

The transcontinental railroad symbolized American unity and progress. Along with the Suez Canal, completed the same year, it helped knit the world together. Bret Harte, the exuberant poet of the West, wrote of Promontory Point:

What was it the Engines said,
Pilots touching,—head to head
Facing on the single track,
Half a world behind each back?

In the next twenty-five years four more railroads reached the coast: the Northern Pacific (completed in 1883), running from Minnesota to Oregon; the Atchison, Topeka and Santa Fe (1883), connecting Kansas City and Los Angeles; the powerful Southern Pacific (1883), running from San Francisco and Los Angeles to New

Orleans; and James J. Hill's superbly built Great Northern Railway (1893), running from Minneapolis-Saint Paul to Seattle, Washington.

By the 1890s business leaders talked comfortably of railroad systems stretching deep into South America and across the Bering Strait to Asia, Europe, and Africa. In an age of progress, anything seemed possible. "The American," said the Chicago *Tribune*, "intelligent and self-reliant, has banished forever the impossible from his philosophy."

Problems of Growth

Overbuilding during the 1870s and '80s caused serious problems for the railroads. Lines paralleled each other, and where they did not, speculators like Jay Gould often laid one down to force a rival line to buy it at inflated prices. While many managers worked to improve service, Gould and others bought and sold railroads like toys, watered their stock, and milked their assets. By

1885, almost one third of railroad stock represented "water," that is, stock distributed in excess of the real value of the assets.

Competition was severe, and managers fought desperately for traffic. They offered special rates and favors: free passes for large shippers; low rates on bulk freight, carload lots, and long hauls; and above all, rebates—secret, privately negotiated reductions below published rates. Fierce rate wars broke out frequently, convincing managers that ruthless competition helped no one. Rebates made more enemies than friends.

Managers like Albert Fink, the brilliant vice-president of the Louisville & Nashville, tried first to control competition by sharing traffic. Fink directed the Eastern Trunk Line Association (1877), which divided westbound traffic among the four trunk lines. Similar associations pooled traffic in the South and West, but none survived the intense pressures of competition. Customers grew adept at bargaining for rebates and other privileges, and railroads rarely felt able to refuse them. In the first six months of 1880 the New York Central alone granted six thousand special rates.

Failing to cooperate, railroad owners next tried to consolidate. Through purchase, lease, and merger, they gobbled up competitors and built "self-sustaining systems" that dominated entire regions. But many of these systems, expensive and unwieldy, collapsed in the panic of 1893. By mid-1894 a quarter of the railroads were bankrupt. The victims of the panic included such legendary names as the Erie, B & O, Santa Fe, Northern Pacific, and Union Pacific.

Needing money, railroads turned naturally to bankers, who finally imposed order on the industry. J. Pierpont Morgan, head of the New York investment house of J. P. Morgan and Company, took the lead. Massively built, with eyes so piercing they seemed like the headlights of an onrushing train, Morgan was the most powerful figure in American finance. He liked efficiency, combination, and order. He disliked "wasteful" competition. In 1885, during a bruising rate war between the New York Central and the Pennsylvania, Morgan invited the combatants to a conference aboard his palatial steam yacht, *Corsair*. Cruising on Long Island Sound, he arranged a traffic-sharing agreement and collected a million-dollar fee. Bringing peace to an industry could be profit-

■ *A 1903 photograph of J. P. Morgan by Edward Steichen. The photographer captured Morgan's awesome presence, the embodiment of power.*

able. It also satisfied Morgan's passion for stability.

After 1893 Morgan and a few other bankers refinanced ailing railroads, and in the process they took control of the industry. Their methods were direct: fixed costs and debt were ruthlessly cut; new stock was issued to provide capital; rates were stabilized; rebates and competition were eliminated; and control was vested in a "voting trust" of hand-picked trustees. Between 1894 and 1898 Morgan reorganized—critics said "Morganized"—the Southern Railway, the Erie, the Northern Pacific, and the B & O. In addition, he took over a half dozen other important railroads. By 1900 he dominated American railroading.

As the new century began, the railroads had pioneered the patterns followed by most other industries. Seven giant systems controlled nearly two thirds of the mileage, and they in turn answered to a few investment banking firms like the house of Morgan. For good and ill, a national transportation network, centralized and relatively efficient, was now in place.

An Industrial Empire

Along with railroads, the new industrial empire was based on steel. Harder and more durable than other kinds of iron, steel wrought changes in manufacturing, agriculture, transportation, and architecture. It permitted longer bridges, taller buildings, stronger railroad track, newer weapons, better plows, heavier machinery, and faster ships. Made in great furnaces by strong men, it symbolized the tough, often brutal nature of industrial society. From the 1870s onward, steel output became the worldwide accepted measure of industrial progress, and nations around the globe vied for leadership.

The Bessemer process, developed in the late 1850s by Henry Bessemer in England and independently by William Kelly in the United States, made it possible. Both Bessemer and Kelly discovered that a blast of air through molten iron burned off carbon and other impurities, resulting in steel of a more uniform and durable quality. The discovery transformed the industry. While earlier methods produced amounts a person could lift, a Bessemer converter dealt with five tons of molten metal at a time. The mass production of steel was now possible.

Carnegie and Steel

Bessemer plants demanded extensive capital investment, abundant raw materials, and sophisticated production techniques. Using chemical and other processes, they required research departments, which became critical components of later American industries. Costly to build, they limited entry into the industry to the handful who could afford them.

Great steel districts arose in Pennsylvania, Ohio, and Alabama—especially near Pittsburgh, which became the center of the industry. Output shot up. In 1874 the United States produced less than half the pig iron produced in Great Britain. By 1890 it took the lead, and in 1900 it produced four times as much as Britain.

Iron ore abounded in the fabulous deposits near Lake Superior, the greatest deposits in the world. In the mines of the Mesabi Range in Minnesota, giant steam shovels loaded ore on railroad cars for

■ *The Jones & Laughlin Steel Mills in Pittsburgh, around 1905. The haze of factory smoke darkens the sky and the horizon.*

transport to ships on the Great Lakes. Powered lifts, self-loading devices, and other innovations sped the process. "By the turn of the century," historian Peter Temin noted, "the transport of Lake ores had become an intricate ballet of large and complex machines."

Like the railroads, steel companies grew larger and larger. In 1880 only nine companies could produce more than 100,000 tons a year. By the early 1890s several companies exceeded 250,000 tons, and two—including the great Carnegie Steel Company—produced over a million tons a year. As operations expanded, managers needed greater skills. Product development, marketing, and consumer preferences became important. Competition was fierce, and steel companies, like the railroads, tried secret agreements, pools, and consolidation. During the 1880s and '90s they moved toward vertical integration, a type of organization in which a single company owns and controls the entire process from the unearthing of the raw materials to the manufacture and sale of the finished product. Such companies combined coal and iron mines, transportation companies, blast furnaces, and rolling mills into integrated networks.

■ *Of all the great industrial tycoons, Carnegie best combined intelligence, luck, and personal charm.*

Andrew Carnegie emerged as the undisputed master of the industry. Born in Scotland, he came to the United States in 1848 at the age of twelve. Settling near Pittsburgh, he went to work as a bobbin boy in a cotton mill, earning $1.20 a week. He soon took a job in a telegraph office, where in 1852 his hard work and skill caught the eye of Thomas A. Scott of the Pennsylvania Railroad. Starting as Scott's personal telegrapher, Carnegie spent a total of twelve years on the Pennsylvania, a training ground for company managers. By 1859 he had become a divisional superintendent. He was twenty-four.

Soon rich from shrewd investments, Carnegie plunged into the steel industry in 1872. On the Monongahela River south of Pittsburgh he built the giant J. Edgar Thomson Steel Works, named after the president of the Pennsylvania Railroad, his biggest customer. With his warmth and salesmanship, he attracted able subordinates such as Henry Clay Frick and Charles M. Schwab, whom he drove hard and paid well. Although he had written magazine articles defending the rights of workers, Carnegie kept the wages of the laborers in his mills low, disliked unions, and crushed a violent strike at his Homestead works in 1892 (see p. 539).

In 1878 he won the steel contract for the Brooklyn Bridge. During the next decade, as city building boomed, he converted the huge Homestead works near Pittsburgh to the manufacture of structural beams and angles, which went into the New York City elevated railway, the first skyscrapers, and the Washington Monument. Carnegie profits mounted: from $2 million in 1888 to $40 million in 1900. That year Carnegie Steel alone produced more steel than Great Britain. Employing twenty thousand people, it was the largest industrial company in the world.

In 1901 Carnegie sold it. Believing that wealth brought social obligations, he wanted to devote his full time to philanthropy. He found a buyer in J. Pierpont Morgan, who in the late 1890s had put together several steel companies, including Federal Steel, Carnegie's chief rival. Carnegie Steel had blocked Morgan's well-known desire for control, and in mid-1900, when a war loomed between the two interests, Morgan decided to buy Carnegie out. In early January 1901 Morgan told Charles M. Schwab: "Go and find his price." Schwab cornered Carnegie on the golf course, Carnegie listened, and the next day handed Schwab a note, scribbled in blunt pencil, asking almost a half billion dollars. Morgan glanced at it and said: "I accept this price."

Drawing other companies into the combination, Morgan on March 3, 1901, announced the creation of the United States Steel Corporation. The new firm was capitalized at $1.4 billion, the first billion-dollar company. It absorbed over 200 other companies, employed 168,000 people, and produced 9 million tons of iron and steel a year. It controlled three fifths of the country's steel business. Soon there were other giants, including Bethlehem Steel, Republic Steel, and National Steel. As the nineteenth century ended, steel products—rare just thirty years before—had altered the landscape. Huge firms, investment bankers, and professional managers dominated the industry.

Rockefeller and Oil

Petroleum worked comparable changes in the economic and social landscape, although mostly after 1900. Distilled into oil, it lubricated the machinery of the industrial age. There seemed

■ *This 1902 cartoon, hostile toward Morgan's control of railroads, steel, and shipping, labels him "Alexander the Great" looking for more worlds to conquer.*

refineries cost little, competition flourished. Output fluctuated dramatically; prices rose and fell with devastating effect. Refineries—usually a collection of wooden shacks and tanks—were centered in Cleveland and Pittsburgh, near the original oil-producing regions.

A young merchant from Cleveland named John D. Rockefeller imposed order on the industry. "I had an ambition to build," he later recalled, and beginning in 1863, at the age of twenty-four, he built the Standard Oil Company, soon to become one of the titans of corporate business. Like Morgan, Rockefeller considered competition wasteful, small-scale enterprise inefficient, and consolidation the path of the future. Consolidation "revolutionized the way of doing business all over the world," he said. "The time was ripe for it. It had to come, though all we saw at the moment was the need to save ourselves from wasteful conditions."

Methodically, Rockefeller absorbed or destroyed competitors in Cleveland and elsewhere. As ruthless in his methods as Carnegie, he lacked the steel master's spontaneous charm. He was distant and taciturn, a man of deep religious beliefs who taught Bible classes at Cleveland's Erie Street Baptist Church. Like Carnegie, he demanded efficiency, relentless cost-cutting, and the latest technology. He attracted exceptional lieutenants—although, as one said, he could see further ahead than any of them, "and then see around the corner."

"Nothing in haste, nothing ill-done," Rockefeller often said to himself. "Your future hangs on every day that passes." Paying careful attention to detail, he counted the stoppers in barrels, shortened barrel hoops to save metal, and in one famous incident, reduced the number of drops of solder on kerosene cans from forty to thirty-nine. In large-scale production, Rockefeller realized, even small reductions meant huge savings. Research uncovered other ways of lowering costs and improving products, and Herman Frasch, a brilliant Standard chemist, solved problem after problem in the refining of oil.

In the end, Rockefeller triumphed over his competitors by marketing products of high quality at the lowest unit cost. But he employed other, less savory methods as well. He threatened rivals and bribed politicians. He exploited railroad rebates, extorted other privileges, and employed

little use for gasoline (the internal combustion engine had only just been developed), but kerosene, another major distillate, brought inexpensive illumination into almost every home. Whale oil, cottonseed oil, and even tallow candles were expensive to burn; consequently, many people went to bed at nightfall. Kerosene lamps opened the evenings to activity, which altered the patterns of life.

Like other changes in these years, the oil boom happened with surprising speed. In the mid-1850s petroleum was a bothersome, smelly fluid that occasionally rose to the surface of springs and streams. Clever entrepreneurs bottled it in patent medicines; a few scooped up enough to burn. Other entrepreneurs soon found that drilling reached pockets of oil beneath the earth. In 1859 Edwin L. Drake drilled the first oil well near Titusville in northwest Pennsylvania, and the "black gold" fever struck. Chemists soon discovered ways to make lubricating oil, grease, paint, wax, varnish, naphtha, and paraffin. Within a few years there was a world market in oil.

At first, growth of the oil industry was chaotic. Early drillers and refiners produced for local markets, and since drilling wells and even erecting

An Industrial Empire

■ *John D. Rockefeller, satirized in a 1901* Punch *cartoon, is enthroned on oil, the base of his empire; his crown is girdled by other holdings.*

which dividends were paid. On January 2, 1882, the first of the modern trusts was born. As Dodd intended, it immediately centralized control of Standard's far-flung empire.

Competition almost disappeared; profits soared. A trust movement swept the country, as industries with similar problems—whiskey, lead, and sugar, among others—followed Standard's example. The word *trust* became synonymous with monopoly, amid vehement protests from the public. Antitrust became a watchword for a generation of reformers from the 1880s through the era of Woodrow Wilson. But Rockefeller's purpose had been *management* of a monopoly, not monopoly itself, which he had already achieved.

In 1897 Rockefeller retired with a fortune of nearly $900 million, but for Standard Oil and petroleum in general, the most expansive period was yet to come. The great oil pools of Texas and Oklahoma had not yet been discovered. Plastics and other oil-based synthetics were several decades in the future. There were only four usable automobiles in the country, and the day of the gasoline engine, automobile, and airplane lay just ahead.

The Business of Invention

"America has become known the world around as the home of invention," boasted the Commissioner of Patents in 1892. It had not always been so; until the last third of the nineteenth century, the country imported most of its technology. Then an extraordinary group of inventors and tinkerers—"specialists in invention," Thomas A. Edison called them—began to study the world around them. Some of their inventions gave rise to new industries; a few actually changed the quality of life.

The number of patents issued to inventors reflected the trend. During the 1850s fewer than 2000 patents were issued each year. By the 1880s and '90s, the figure reached more than 20,000 a year. Between 1790 and 1860 the Patent Office issued just 36,000 patents; in the decade of the 1890s alone, it issued more than 200,000.

Some of the inventions transformed communications. In 1866 Cyrus W. Field improved the transatlantic cable linking the telegraph net-

spies to harass the customers of competing refiners. By 1879 he controlled 90 percent of the country's oil-refining capacity.

Vertically integrated, Standard Oil owned wells, timberlands, barrel and chemical plants, refineries, warehouses, pipelines, and fleets of tankers and oil cars. Its marketing organization served as the model for the industry. Standard exported oil to Asia, Africa, and South America; and its five-gallon kerosene tin, like Coca-Cola during a later era, was a familiar sight in the most distant parts of the world.

To manage it all, the company developed a new plan of business organization, the trust, which had profound significance for American business. In 1881 Samuel T. C. Dodd, Standard's attorney, set up the Standard Oil Trust, with a board of nine trustees empowered "to hold, control, and manage" all Standard's properties. Stockholders exchanged their stock for trust certificates, on

Patents Issued, by Decade, 1850–1899 (in thousands)

1850–1859	1860–1869	1870–1879	1880–1889	1890–1899
19,591	64,302	124,672	195,104	221,277

Source: U.S. Bureau of the Census, Historical Statistics of the United States, Colonial Times to 1970, Bicentennial Edition, Washington, D.C. 1975.

works of Europe and the United States. By the early 1870s land and submarine cables ran to Brazil, Japan, and the China coast; in the next two decades they reached Africa and spread across South America. Diplomats and business leaders could now "talk" to their counterparts in Johannesburg or Saigon. Even before the telephone, the cables quickened the pace of foreign affairs, revolutionized journalism, and allowed businesses to expand and centralize.

The typewriter (1867), stock ticker (1867), cash register (1879), calculating machine (1887), and adding machine (1888) helped business transactions. High-speed spindles, automatic looms, and electric sewing machines transformed the clothing industry, which for the first time in history turned out ready-made clothes for the masses. In 1890 the Census Bureau first used machines to sort and tabulate data on punched cards, a portent of a new era of information storage and treatment.

In 1879 George Eastman patented a process for coating gelatine on photographic dry plates, which led to celluloid film and the motion pictures. By 1888 he was marketing the Kodak, which weighed 35 ounces, took 100 exposures, and cost only $25. Even though early Kodaks had to be returned to the factory, camera and all, for film developing, they revolutionized photogra-

phy. Now almost anyone could snap a picture. In the mid-1890s Eastman Kodak was an $8 million company which had changed the leisure habits of millions of Americans.

Other innovations improved the diet. There were new processes for flour, canned meat, vegetables, condensed milk, and even beer—an offshoot of Louis Pasteur's discoveries about bacteria. Packaged cereals appeared on breakfast tables. Refrigerated railroad cars, ice-cooled, brought fresh fruit from Florida and California to all parts of the country. In the 1870s Gustavus F. Swift, a Chicago meatpacker, hit on the idea of using the cars to distribute meat nationwide. Setting up "dissembly" factories to butcher meat (Henry Ford later copied them for his famous "assembly" lines), he started an "era of cheap beef," as a newspaper said.

No innovation, however, rivaled in importance the telephone and the use of electricity for light and power. The telephone was the work of Alexander Graham Bell, a shrewd and genial Scotsman who settled in Boston in 1871. Interested in the problems of the deaf, Bell experimented with ways to transmit speech electrically, and after several years developed electrified metal disks that, much like the human ear, converted sound waves to electrical impulses and back again. On March 10, 1876, he transmitted the first sentence over a telephone: "Mr. Watson, come here; I want you." Later that year he exhibited the new device to excited crowds at the Centennial Exposition in Philadelphia.

In 1878—the year a telephone was installed in the White House—the first telephone exchange opened in New Haven, Connecticut. Fighting off competitors who challenged the patent, the young Bell Telephone Company dominated the growing industry. By 1895 there were about 310,000 phones; a decade later, there were 10 million—one for almost every ten people. In 1915 Bell himself opened the first transcontinental telephone line from New York to San Francisco. By then American Telephone and Telegraph Company, formed by the Bell interests in 1885, had become a vast holding company, consolidating over a hundred local systems.

If the telephone dissolved communications barriers as old as the human race, Thomas Alva Edison, the "Wizard of Menlo Park," invented processes and products of comparable significance. Born in 1847, Edison had little formal education, although he was an avid reader. Like Carnegie, he went into the new field of telegraphy. Tinkering in his spare time, he made several important improvements, including a telegraph capable of sending four messages over a single wire. Gathering teams of specialists to work on specific problems, Edison built at Menlo Park, New Jersey, the first modern research laboratory. It may have been his most important invention.

The laboratory, Edison promised, would turn out "a minor invention every ten days and a big thing every six months or so." In 1877 it turned out a big thing. Worried about a telephone's high cost, Edison set out to invent a "telephone repeater," which became the phonograph. Those unable to afford a phone, he thought, could record their voices for replay from a central telephone station. Using tin foil wrapped around a grooved, rotating cylinder, he shouted the verses of "Mary had a little lamb" and then listened in awe as the machine played them back. "I was never so taken aback in all my life," he later said. "Everybody was astonished. I was always afraid of things that worked the first time."

In 1896 records made of hard rubber and shellac appeared on the market; the following year a phonograph sold for $20. In 1904 someone had the idea of recording on both sides of the record,

■ *Alexander Graham Bell (top) is seen making the first telephone call between New York City and Chicago in 1892. Thomas A. Edison (bottom) with his incandescent lamps. His discovery of the "Edison effect" revealed the basic principle on which modern electronics rests.*

and the phonograph record in its modern form was born. For the first time in history, people could listen again and again to a favorite symphony or piano solo. The phonograph made human experience repeatable in a way never before possible.

In 1879 came an even larger triumph, the incandescent lamp. Sir Joseph William Swan, an English inventor, had already experimented with the carbon filament, but Edison's task involved more than finding a durable filament. He set out to do nothing less than change light. A trial-and-error inventor, Edison tested sixteen hundred materials before producing, late in 1879, the carbon filament he wanted. Then he had to devise a complex system of conductors, meters, and generators, by which electricity could be divided and distributed to homes and businesses.

With the financial backing of J. Pierpont Morgan, he organized the Edison Illuminating Company and built the Pearl Street power station in New York City, the testing ground of the new apparatus. On September 4, 1882, as Morgan and others watched, Edison threw a switch and lit the house of Morgan, the stock exchange, the *New York Times*, and a number of other buildings. Power stations soon opened in Boston, Philadelphia, and Chicago. By 1900 there were 2774 stations, lighting some 2 million electric lights around the country. In a nation alive with light, the habits of centuries changed. A flick of the switch lit homes and factories at any hour of the day or night.

In a rare blunder, Edison based his system on low-voltage direct current, which could be transmitted only about two miles. George Westinghouse, the inventor of the railroad air brake, demonstrated the advantages of high-voltage alternating current, transmitted over great distances. In 1886 he formed the Westinghouse Electric Company and with the inventor Nikola Tesla, a Hungarian immigrant, developed an alternating-current motor that could convert electricity into mechanical power. Electricity could light a lamp or illuminate a skyscraper; pull a streetcar or drive an entire railroad; run a sewing machine or power a mammoth assembly line. Transmitted easily over long distances, it freed factories and cities from location near water or coal. Electricity, in short, brought a revolution.

Taking advantage of the new devices, Frank J. Sprague, a young engineer, electrified the Richmond, Virginia, streetcar system in 1887. Other cities quickly followed. Electric-powered subway systems opened in Boston in 1897 and New York City in 1904. Overhead wires and third-rails made urban transportation quieter, faster, and cleaner. Buried under pavement or strung from pole to pole, wires of every description—trolley, telephone, and power—marked the birth of the modern city.

The Sellers

The increased output of the industrial age was one thing, but the products still had to be sold, and that gave rise to a new "science" of marketing. Some business leaders—like Swift in meatpacking, James B. Duke in tobacco, and Rockefeller in oil—built extensive marketing organizations of their own. Others relied on retailers, merchandising techniques, and advertising, developing a host of methods to convince consumers to buy.

In 1867 businesses spent about $50 million on advertising; in 1900 they spent over $500 million, and the figure was increasing rapidly. The first advertising agency, N. W. Ayer and Son, of Philadelphia, began to service businesses in the mid-1870s, and it was followed by numerous imitators. The rotary press (1875) churned out newspapers and introduced a new era in newspaper advertising. Woodcuts, halftones, and photoengraving added illustrations to catch the consumer's eye. Brand names became popular, and already Kellogg was promising cornflake eaters "Genuine Joy, Genuine Appetite, Genuine Health and therefore Genuine Complexion."

Bringing producer and consumer together, nationwide advertising was the final link in the national market. Humorist Finley Peter Dunne's Irish characters poked fun at the ads for breakfast cereals:

Guff . . . ye've seen th' advertisement: "Out iv th' house wint Lucky Joe; Guff was th' stuff that made him go." Mother prefers Almost-food, a scientific preparation iv burlap. I used to take Sawd Ust . . . later I had a peeryod iv Hungareen, a chimically pure diet, made iv th' exterryor iv bath towels. We all have our little

*tastes an' enthusyasms in th' matter iv break-
fast foods, dependin' on what pa-a-pers we
read an' what billboords we've seen iv late.*

R. H. Macy in New York, John Wanamaker in
Philadelphia, and Marshall Field in Chicago
turned the department store into a national institution. There people could browse (a relatively
new concept) and buy. Innovations in pricing,
display, and advertising helped customers develop wants they did not know they had. In 1870
Wanamaker took out the first full-page newspaper
ad, and Macy, an aggressive advertiser, touted
"goods suitable for the millionaire at prices in
reach of the millions."

The "chain store"—an American term—spread
across the country. The A & P grocery stores,
begun in 1859, numbered sixty-seven by 1876, all
marked by the familiar red-and-gold facade. By
1915 there were a thousand of them. In 1880 F. W.
Woolworth, bored with the family farm, opened
the first "Five and Ten Cent Store" in Utica, New
York. He had fifty-nine stores in 1900, the year he
adopted the bright red storefront and heaping
counters to lure customers in and persuade them
to buy.

In similar fashion, Sears, Roebuck and Montgomery Ward sold to rural customers through
mail-order catalogs—a means of selling that depended on effective transportation and a high
level of customer literacy. As a traveler for a
dry-goods firm, Aaron Montgomery Ward had
seen an unfulfilled need of people in the rural
West. He started the mail-order trend in 1872,
with a one-sheet price list offered from a Chicago
loft. By 1884 he offered almost 10,000 items in a
catalog of 240 pages.

Richard W. Sears also saw the possibilities in
the mail-order business. Starting with watches
and jewelry, he gradually expanded his list. In the
early 1880s he moved to Chicago, and with Alvah
C. Roebuck, founded Sears, Roebuck and Company. Sears sold anything and everything, prospering in a business that relied on mutual faith
between unseen customers and distant distribu-
tors. Sears catalogs, soon over 500 pages long,
exploited four-color illustrations and other new
techniques. By the early 1900s, Sears distributed
6 million catalogs annually.

Advertising, brand names, chain stores, and
mail-order houses brought Americans of all varieties into a national market. Even as the country
grew, a certain homogeneity of goods bound it
together, touching cities and farms, East and
West, rich and poor. There was a common language of consumption. The market, some con-

*An early store of the Great
Atlantic & Pacific Tea
Company chain, 1898.
Displayed on the counters
and shelves are lamps and
fans to be given to customers
as premiums. Note the
sandwichboard man—a
walking advertisement.*

temporaries thought, also bridged ethnic and other differences. Alfred Marshall, a prominent English economist, wrote in 1919: "Widely as the Scandinavians are separated from the Italians, and the native Americans from the Poles, in sentiment, in modes of living, and even in occupations, they are yet purchasers of nearly the same goods. . . . [T]hey buy similar clothes, furniture, and implements."

The theory had limits, as Marshall himself knew; ethnic and racial differences remained deep in the society. But Americans *had* become a community of consumers, surrounded by goods unavailable just a few decades before, and able to purchase them. They had learned to make, want, and buy. "Because you see the main thing today is—shopping," Arthur Miller, a twentieth-century playwright, said in *The Price.*

Years ago a person, he was unhappy, didn't know what to do with himself—he'd go to church, start a revolution—something. Today you're unhappy? Can't figure it out? What is the salvation? Go shopping.

The Wage Earner

While entrepreneurs were important, it was the labor of millions of men and women that built the new industrial society. In their individual stories, nearly all unrecorded, lay much of the achievement, drama, and pain of these years.

In a number of respects, their lot improved during the last quarter of the nineteenth century. Real wages rose, working conditions got better, and the workers' influence in national affairs increased. Between 1880 and 1914, wages of the average worker rose about $7 a year, measured in constant dollars. Like others, workers also benefited from expanding health and educational services.

But life was not easy. Before 1900 most wage earners worked ten hours a day, six days a week. If skilled, they earned about 20¢ an hour; if unskilled, just half that. On average they earned between $400 and $500 a year. It took about $600 to live decently. Construction workers, machinists, government employees, printers, clerical workers, and western miners made more than the average. Eastern coal miners, agricultural work-

Average Annual Earnings, 1865–1900
(Non-farm employees)

Source: U.S. Bureau of the Census, Historical Statistics of the United States, Colonial Times to 1970, *Bicentennial Edition, Washington, D.C., 1975.*

ers, garment workers, and unskilled factory hands made considerably less.

There were few holidays or vacations and little respite from the grueling routine. Skilled workers could turn the system to their own ends—New York City cigarmakers, for example, paid someone to read to them while they worked—but the unskilled seldom had such luxury. They were too easily replaced. "A bit of advice to you," said a guidebook for immigrant Jews in the 1890s: "do not take a moment's rest. Run, do, work, and keep your own good in mind."

Work was not only grueling; it was highly dangerous. Safety standards were low, and accidents were common. On the railroads, 1 in every 26 workers was injured, 1 in every 399 killed per year. Thousands suffered from chronic illness, unknowing victims of dust, chemicals, and other pollutants. In the early 1900s Dr. Alice Hamilton established a link between jobs and disease, but meanwhile, illness weakened or struck down many a breadwinner.

The breadwinner might be a woman or child; both worked in increasing numbers. In 1870 about 15 percent of women over the age of sixteen were employed for wages; in 1900 20 percent (5.3 million women) were. Of 303 occupations listed in the 1900 census, women were represented in 296. Between 1870 and 1900 the number of working children rose nearly 130 percent to 1.8 mil-

In the early 1900s, photographer Lewis Hine documented many poignant scenes of child labor. These mill boys (left) had to climb up the machine frames to reach their work. A business office in 1907 (below). The female stenographer earned about $6 a week.

lion. In Paterson, New Jersey, an important industrial city, about half of all boys and girls aged eleven to fourteen had jobs.

Most working women were young and single. Many began work at sixteen or seventeen, worked a half-dozen years or so, married, and quit. In 1900 only 5 percent of all married women were employed outside the home, although black women were an important exception. Among them, 25 percent of married women worked in 1900, usually on southern farms or as low-paid laundresses and domestic servants. As clerical work expanded, women learned new skills like typing and stenography. Moving into formerly male occupations, they became secretaries, bookkeepers, typists, telephone operators, and clerks in the new department stores.

A few women—very few—became ministers, lawyers, and doctors. Arabella Mansfield, admitted to the Iowa bar in 1869, was the first woman lawyer in the country. But change was slow, and in the 1880s some law schools were still refusing to admit women because they "had not the mentality to study law." Among women entering the professions, the overwhelming majority became nurses, schoolteachers, and librarians. In such professions a process of *feminization* occurred, in which women became a majority of the workers, a small number of men took the management roles, and most men left for other jobs, lowering the profession's status.

In most jobs, status and pay were divided unequally between men and women. Many of both sexes thought a woman's place was in the home, "queen of a little house—no matter how humble —where there are children rolling on the floor." When employed in factories, women tended to occupy jobs that were viewed as natural extensions of household activity. They made clothes and textiles, processed food, and made cigars, tobacco, and shoes. In the ladies' garment industry, which employed large numbers of women, they were the sewers and finishers, jobs that paid less; men were the higher-paid cutters and pressers.

In *The Long Day: The Story of a New York Working Girl as Told by Herself* (1906), the girl, a young schoolteacher, earned $2.50 a week, paid $1.00 for her room, and had $1.50 for food, clothes, carfare, and any social life. For breakfast she had bread, butter, and coffee; for lunch bread and butter; for dinner potato soup, bread, and butter. In Pittsburgh a worker in a pickle factory said of her day: "I have stood ten hours; I have fitted 1,300 corks; I have hauled and loaded 4,000 jars of pickles. My pay is seventy cents." Exhausted, such workers fell into bed at night and crawled out again at dawn to begin another "long day."

In general, adults earned more than children, the skilled more than the unskilled, native-born more than foreign-born, Protestants more than Catholics or Jews, and whites more than blacks and Asians. On average, women made a little more than half as much as men, according to contemporary estimates. In some cases, employers defended the differences—the foreign-born, for example, might not speak English—but most simply reflected bias against race, creed, or sex. In the industrial society white, native-born Protestants—the bulk of the population—reaped the greatest rewards.

Blacks labored on the fringes, usually in menial occupations. The last hired and first fired, they earned less than other workers at almost every level of skill. On the Pacific Coast, the Chinese— and later the Japanese—lived in enclaves and

■ *This anti-Chinese cartoon in a weekly newspaper in San Francisco in 1877 shows the depth of workingmen's prejudice against Asians.*

suffered periodic attacks of discrimination. In 1879 the Workingmen's party of California got a provision in the state constitution forbidding corporations to employ Chinese, and in 1882 Congress prohibited the immigration of Chinese workers for ten years.

Culture of Work

Among almost all groups, industrialization shattered age-old patterns, including work habits and the culture of work, as Herbert G. Gutman, a social historian, has noted. It made people adapt "older work routines to new necessities and strained those wedded to premodern patterns of labor." Adaptation was difficult and often demeaning. Virtually everyone went through it, and newcomers repeated the experiences of those who came before.

Men and women fresh from farms were not accustomed to the factory's disciplines. Now they worked indoors rather than out, paced themselves to the clock rather than the movements of the sun, and followed the needs of the market rather than the natural rhythms of the seasons. They had foremen and hierarchies and strict rules. Piece work determined wages, and always—as Morris Rosenfeld, a clothing presser, wrote—there was the relentless clock:

> The Clock in the workshop,—it rests not a moment;
> It points on, and ticks on: eternity-time;
> Once someone told me the clock had a meaning,—
> In pointing and ticking had reason and rhyme. . . .
> At times, when I listen, I hear the clock plainly;—
> The reason of old—the old meaning—is gone!
> The maddening pendulum urges me forward
> To labor and still labor on.
> The tick of the clock is the boss in his anger.
> The face of the clock has the eyes of the foe.
> The clock—I shudder—Dost hear how it draws me?
> It calls me "Machine" and it cries [to] me "Sew"!

As industries grew larger, work became more impersonal. Machines displaced skilled artisans, and the unskilled tended them for employers they never saw. Workers picked up and left their jobs with startling frequency, and factories drew on a churning, highly mobile labor supply. Historian Stephan Thernstrom, who has carefully studied the census records, found that only about half the people recorded in any census still lived in the same community ten years later. "The country had an enormous reservoir of restless and foot-loose men, who could be lured to new destinations when opportunity beckoned."

Thernstrom and others have also found substantial economic and social mobility. The Horatio Alger stories, of course, had always said so, and careers like Andrew Carnegie's—the impoverished immigrant boy who made good—seemed to confirm it. The actual record was considerably more limited. Most business leaders in the period came from well-to-do or middle-class families of old American stock. Of 360 iron and steel barons in Pittsburgh, Carnegie's own city, only 5 fit the Carnegie characteristics, and one of those was Carnegie himself. Still, if few workers became steel magnates, many workers made major progress during their lifetimes. In Thernstrom's study, he discovered that a quarter of the manual laborers rose to middle-class posi-

tions, and working-class children were even more likely to move up the ladder. In Boston about half the Jewish immigrants rose from manual to middle-class jobs, and English, Irish, and Italian immigrants were not far behind.

The chance for advancement played a vital role in American industrial development. It gave workers hope, wedded them to the system, and tempered their response to the appeal of labor unions and working-class agitation. Very few workers rose from rags to riches, but a great many rose to better jobs and higher status.

Labor Unions

Weak throughout the nineteenth century, labor unions never included more than 2 percent of the total labor force nor more than 10 percent of industrial workers. To many workers, unions seemed "foreign," radical, and out of step with the American tradition of individual advancement. Craft, ethnic, and other differences fragmented the labor force, and its extraordinary mobility made organization difficult. Employers opposed unions. "I have always had one rule," said an executive of U.S. Steel. "If a worker sticks up his head, hit it."

As the national economy emerged, however, national labor unions gradually took shape. The early unions often represented skilled workers in local areas, but in 1866 William H. Sylvis, a Pennsylvania iron-molder, united several unions into a single national organization, the National Labor Union. Like many of the era's labor leaders, Sylvis sought long-range humanitarian reforms, such as the establishment of workers' cooperatives, rather than specific, bread-and-butter goals. A talented propagandist, he attracted many members—some 640,000 by 1868—but he died in 1869, and the organization did not long survive him.

The year Sylvis died, Uriah S. Stephens and a group of Philadelphia garment workers founded a far more successful organization, the Noble and Holy Order of the Knights of Labor. A secret fraternal order, it grew slowly through the 1870s, until Terence V. Powderly, the new Grand Master Workman elected in 1879, ended the secrecy and embarked on an aggressive program. Wanting to unite all labor, the Knights welcomed everyone who "toiled," regardless of skill, creed, sex, or color. Unlike most unions they organized female workers, and at their peak they had 60,000 black members.

Harking back to the Jacksonians, the Knights set the "producers" against monopoly and special privilege. As members they excluded only "nonproducers"—bankers, lawyers, liquor dealers, and gamblers. Since employers were "producers," they could join; and since workers and employers had common interests, workers should not strike. The order's platform included the eight-hour day and the abolition of child and prisoner labor, but more often it focused on uplifting, utopian reform. Powderly, the eloquent and idealistic leader, spun dreams of a new era of harmony and cooperation. He wanted to sweep away trusts and end drunkenness. Workers should pool their resources, establish worker-run factories, railroads, and mines, and escape from the wage system. "The aim of the Knights of Labor—properly understood—is to make each man his own employer," Powderly said.

Membership grew steadily—from 42,000 in 1882 to 110,000 in 1885. In March 1885, ignoring Powderly's dislike of strikes, local Knights in Saint Louis, Kansas City, and other cities won a victory against Jay Gould's Missouri Pacific Railroad, and membership soared. It soon reached almost 730,000 but neither Powderly nor the union's loose structure could handle the growth. In 1886 the wily Gould struck back, crushing the

■ Women delegates at a national meeting of the Knights of Labor in 1886. Women belonged to separate associations affiliated with local all-male unions.

Knights on the Texas and Pacific Railroad, and the boom was over. By 1890 the order had shrunk to 100,000 members, and a few years later it was virtually defunct.

Even as the Knights waxed and waned, another organization emerged that was to endure. Founded in 1881, the American Federation of Labor (AFL) was a loose alliance of national craft unions. Unlike the Knights, the AFL rejected industrial unionism. It organized only skilled workers along craft lines, avoided politics, and worked for specific practical objectives. "I have my own philosophy and my own dreams," Samuel Gompers, the founder and longtime president, said, "but first and foremost I want to increase the workingman's welfare year by year."

Born in a London tenement in 1850, Gompers was a child of the union movement. Settling in New York, he worked as a cigarmaker, took an active hand in union activities, and flirted for a time with socialism and working-class politics. As leader of the AFL, he adopted a pragmatic approach to labor's needs. Gompers accepted capitalism and did not argue for fundamental chang-

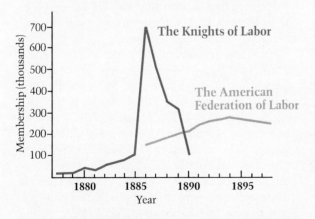

Rise and Decline of the Knights of Labor

The Knights of Labor

The American Federation of Labor

Membership (thousands): 100, 200, 300, 400, 500, 600, 700

Year: 1880, 1885, 1890, 1895

Source: From Leo Wolman, The Growth of American Trade Unions, 1924.

es in it. For labor he wanted simply a recognized place within the system and a greater share of the rewards.

Unlike Powderly, Gompers and the AFL assumed that most workers would remain workers throughout their lives. The task, then, lay in improving lives in "practical" ways: higher wages, shorter hours, and better working conditions. They offered some attractive assurances to employers. As trade unionists, they would use the strike and boycott, but only to achieve limited gains, and if treated fairly, they would provide a stable labor force. They would not oppose monopolies and trusts, as Gompers said, "so long as we obtain fair wages."

By the 1890s the AFL was the most important labor group in the country, and Gompers, the guiding spirit, stayed its president, except for one year, until his death in 1924. Membership expanded from 140,000 in 1886, past 250,000 in 1892, to over a million by 1901. The AFL then included almost a third of the country's skilled workers. By 1914 it had over 2 million members. The great majority of workers—skilled and unskilled—remained unorganized, but Gompers and the AFL had become a significant force in national life.

Few unions allowed women to join. The Knights of Labor had a Department of Woman's Work headed by Leonora M. Barry, a shrewd, enthusiastic organizer who established a dozen women's locals and investigated the condition of women's labor. The AFL either ignored or opposed women workers. Only two of its national affiliates—the Cigar Makers' Union and the Typographical Union—accepted women as members; others prohibited them outright, and Gompers himself often complained that women workers undercut the pay scales for men. Conditions improved after 1900, but even then unions were largely a man's world. The AFL did not expressly forbid black workers from joining, but member unions used high initiation fees, technical examinations, and other means to discourage black membership.

Labor Unrest

Workers used various means to adjust to the factory age. To the dismay of managers and "effi-ciency" experts, they often dictated the pace and quality of their work, and they set the tone of the workplace. Newly arrived immigrants got jobs for friends and relatives, taught them how to deal with factory conditions, and humanized the workplace.

Many employers believed in an "iron law of wages" in which supply and demand, not the welfare of their workers, dictated wages. "If I wanted boiler iron," a steelmaker said, "I would go out on the market and buy where I could get it the cheapest, and if I wanted to employ men I would do the same thing." Wanting a docile labor force, employers fired workers who joined unions, hired scabs to replace strikers, and used a powerful new weapon, the court injunction, to quell strikes. The injunction, which forbade workers to interfere with their employers' business, was used to break the great Pullman strike of 1894 (see chapter 20) and the Supreme Court upheld use of the injunction in *In re Debs* (1895). Court decisions also affected the legal protection offered to workers. In *Holden* v. *Hardy* (1896), the Court upheld a law limiting working hours for miners, but in *Lochner* v. *New York* (1905) it struck down a law limiting bakery workers to a sixty-hour week and ten-hour day.

As employers' attitudes hardened, strikes and violence broke out. Between 1880 and 1900 there were more than 23,000 strikes involving 6.6 million workers. The railroad strike of 1877 (see the special feature in this chapter) paralyzed railroads from West Virginia to California, resulted in the deaths of over 100 workers, and required federal troops to suppress it. Another outburst of labor unrest occurred during the mid-1880s; in 1886, the peak year, 610,000 workers were off the job because of strikes and lockouts.

The worst incident took place at Haymarket Square in Chicago. In early May 1886 police, intervening in a strike at the McCormick Harvester works, shot and killed two workers. The next evening, May 4, labor leaders called a protest meeting at Haymarket Square near downtown Chicago. The meeting was peaceful, even a bit dull; about three thousand people were there. Police ordered them to disperse; someone threw a dynamite bomb which instantly killed one policeman and fatally wounded six others. Police fired into the crowd and killed four people.

No one ever discovered who threw the bomb,

Steel Workers, an AFL affiliate, struck, and Frick responded by locking the workers out of the plant. The workers surrounded it, and Frick, furious, hired a small private army of Pinkerton detectives to drive them off. But alert workers spotted the approaching detectives, pinned them down with gunfire, and forced them to surrender. Three detectives and ten workers died in the battle.

A few days later the Pennsylvania governor ordered the state militia to impose peace at Homestead. On July 23 an anarchist named Alexander Berkman, who was not one of the strikers, walked into Frick's office and shot him. He fired twice, then stabbed him several times. Incredibly, Frick survived, watched the police take Berkman away, called in a doctor to bandage his wounds, and stayed in the office until closing time. "I do not think I shall die," he told reporters. "But if I

■ *Anarchists called for a protest meeting and distributed these bilingual handbills on the day of the Haymarket Square bombing in 1886.*

but many Americans—not just business leaders—demanded action against labor "radicalism." Cities strengthened their police forces and armories. In Chicago donors helped to establish nearby Fort Sheridan and the Great Lakes Naval Training Station to curb social turmoil. Uncertain who threw the bomb, Chicago police rounded up eight anarchists who were found guilty of murder. Four were hanged, one committed suicide, and three remained in jail until pardoned by the governor in 1893. Linking labor and anarchism in the public mind, the Haymarket Riot weakened the national labor movement.

Violence again broke out in the unsettled conditions of the 1890s. In 1892 federal troops crushed a strike of silver miners in the Coeur d'Alene district of Idaho. That same year Carnegie and Henry Clay Frick, his partner and manager, lowered wages nearly 20 percent at the Homestead steel plant. The Amalgamated Iron and

■ *This engraving in* Harper's Weekly, *July 16, 1892, depicts the surrender of Pinkerton detectives after a bloody battle with Homestead strikers. Thirteen men lay dead; ten strikers and three detectives. The strikers' victory was only temporary.*

The Great Railroad Strike of 1877

On May 24, 1877, in the midst of a nationwide depression, the Pennsylvania Railroad announced a 10 percent cut in pay. At the time engineers made about $3.25 a day for a twelve-hour day, conductors $2.75, firemen $1.90, and brakemen $1.75. Other railroads also cut pay; the Baltimore & Ohio announced cuts totaling 20 percent. For firemen and brakemen on the B & O, that meant a wage of $.90 a day.

Those wages hurt. As a worker on the B & O said: "We eat our hard bread and tainted meat two days on the sooty cars up the road, and when we come home, find our children gnawing bones and our wives complaining that they cannot even buy hominy and molasses for food."

When pay cuts on the B & O took effect on July 16, anger erupted. In Martinsburg, West Virginia, after one train crew walked off the job leaving their cattle train standing on the tracks, the stoppage spread to other crews. Trains backed up for two miles east and west of town, and at the request of B & O officials, the governor of West Virginia called out the state militia.

The next day, the militia stood guard as another crew took over the cattle train. Strikers boarded the train, and one of them fired a pistol. His fire was returned, and he fell, mortally wounded. The militiamen, many of them sympathetic to the strike, turned and left the yards. Alarmed,

West Virginia's governor called for federal troops to protect railroad property. President Rutherford B. Hayes hesitated, but on July 18 he issued the orders. For the first time since the 1830s the army was ordered out in peacetime to quell a strike.

As the strike spread along the B & O, jeering crowds threw stones at passing freights. At Cumberland, Maryland, west of Martinsburg, only one freight in sixteen got through. On July 20 the governor of Maryland, too, ordered out the state militia. As one regiment emerged from the Garden Street Armory in Baltimore, the city's factories let out for the day. Homeward-bound workers pelted the bewildered soldiers with stones. Blocks away, several thousand people penned up another regiment. Shooting started, and when it ended, eleven civilians were dead and forty were wounded. At the request of Maryland's governor, President Hayes that night sent army units to Baltimore. Portions of two states were now under federal protection.

The strike spread westward through New York, Pennsylvania, and Ohio. In each one of those states the militia was called out. Workers on the giant Pennsylvania system stayed on the job until Robert Pitcairn, the aggressive superintendent of the Pittsburgh division, ordered double-headers—trains with two locomotives—on all eastbound freights. Double-headers pulled more freight and required fewer crewmen, but they were difficult to handle.

The morning the order took effect, Augustus Harris, a veteran flagman, refused to take out the 8:40 double-header. Workers and sympathizers blocked the 9:40 trains; incoming crews joined the shutdown. At noon men from the steel mills mingled in the crowd.

During the night Pennsylvania state officials ordered in two trainloads of militia from Philadelphia to clear the key Twenty-eighth Street railroad crossing. Several thousand people massed at the crossing and on the hillsides above. There were revolver shots, and the militia opened fire. Within minutes, twenty people lay dead, including a woman and three small children. Fifteen soldiers were hurt.

The strike spread. On Monday, July 23, the New York Central, a vital link between New York City and Chicago, shut down. Cleveland, Buffalo, and other cities were cut off from fuel and supplies. The next day, a general strike paralyzed Saint Louis, and strikes hit major railroads to the West. That night, all freight traffic in and out of Chicago, a vital railroad hub, came to a halt.

Chicago factories closed; angry crowds paraded through the streets. Bankers and lawyers armed themselves with Springfield rifles from nearby government arsenals. On Wednesday evening, July 25, violence broke out when excited policemen fired into a crowd. Citizens' militias and working people battled across the city. Shooting continued through the next day; eighteen people died.

Determined to stop the violence, President Hayes sent six companies of soldiers to Chicago and ordered the army to open the Pennsylvania line between Philadelphia and Pittsburgh. On Saturday, July 28, the break came. Nine days after the original order, the first double-header left Pittsburgh with thirty-four cars of cattle and two cars of troops.

Within a matter of days the anger was spent and the Great Strike was over. It lasted about two weeks, touched eleven states, and affected two thirds of the country's railroad track. According to one estimate, it involved over 80,000 railroad workers and 500,000 workers in other occupations. More than a hundred people died.

Some employers responded to the strike by tightening hiring procedures, cracking down on labor unions, and stengthening police forces. Others, eager to avert another conflict, took measures to alleviate grievances. By 1880 most of the railroads had raised pay scales to earlier levels.

Many people here and abroad studied the significance of the strike. Did it mean, as some suggested, that war between capital and labor had begun? Did industrialization inevitably involve class dislocation, class tensions, and violence? Were federal troops required to maintain peace in the new industrial society?

Railroad strike violence: (above) devastation in Pittsburgh's railroad yards after a night of bloodshed; (opposite) Cincinnati's Union Station on fire.

Answers differed. One response was heightened demands for government intervention to regulate railroads and thereby lessen the hardships brought on by rapid industrial growth.

But like most events, the strike had the greatest impact on ordinary individuals whose opinions went unrecorded. In moments of individual decision, they stranded trains in Martinsburg, closed factories in Chicago, and shut down entire railroad networks.

Chronology

1859	First oil well drilled near Titusville, Pennsylvania
1866	William Sylvis establishes National Labor Union
1869	Transcontinental railroad completed at Promontory Point, Utah Knights of Labor organize
1876	Alexander Graham Bell invents the telephone Centennial Exposition held in Philadelphia
1877	Railroads cut workers' wages, leading to bloody and violent strike
1879	Thomas A. Edison invents the incandescent lamp
1881	Samuel Gompers founds American Federation of Labor (AFL)
1882	Rockefeller's Standard Oil Company becomes nation's first trust Edison opens first electric generating station in New York
1883	Railroads introduce standard time zones
1886	Labor protest erupts in violence in Haymarket Riot in Chicago Railroads adopt standard gauge
1892	Workers strike at Homestead steel plant in Pennsylvania
1901	J. P. Morgan announces formation of U.S. Steel Corporation, nation's first billion-dollar company

the American promise of abundance. National wealth grew from $16 billion in 1860 to $88 billion in 1900; wealth per capita more than doubled. For the bulk of the population, the standard of living—a particularly American concept—rose.

But industrialization also meant rapid change, social instability, exploitation of labor, and growing disparity in income between rich and poor. Industry flourished, but control rested in fewer and fewer hands. Maturing quickly, the young system became a new corporate capitalism: giant businesses, interlocking in ownership, managed by a new professional class, and selling an expanding variety of goods in an increasingly controlled market. As goods spread through the society, so did a sharpened, aggressive materialism. Workers felt the strains of the shift to a new social order. Now, in the last three decades of the century, Americans had to learn how to adjust to life in the industrial society.

Recommended Reading

Samuel P. Hays, *The Response to Industrialism: 1885–1914* (1957) is an influential interpretation of the period. A detailed survey is Edward C. Kirkland, *Industry Comes of Age: Business, Labor, and Public Policy, 1860–1897* (1967). Douglass C. North, *Growth and Welfare in the American Past: A New Economic History* (1966) is stimulating. Other valuable overviews include Stuart Bruchey's brief *Growth of the Modern Economy* (1975), W. Elliot Brownlee's more detailed *Dynamics of Ascent: A History of the American Economy* (1974), and Robert Higgs, *The Transformation of the American Economy, 1865–1914* (1971).

For stimulating interpretations of the period, see Robert H. Wiebe, *The Search for Order, 1877–1920* (1968) and John A. Garraty, *The New Commonwealth, 1877–1890* (1968). Thomas C. Cochran and William Miller, *The Age of Enterprise* (1942) and Alfred D. Chandler, *The Visible Hand: The Managerial Revolution in American Business* (1978) are perceptive. The railroad empire is treated in G. R. Taylor and I. D. Neu, *The American Railroad Network, 1861–1890* (1956) and John F. Stover, *American Railroads* (1961). On the steel industry, see Peter Temin, *Iron and Steel in Nineteenth-Century America* (1964) and Joseph F. Wall, *Andrew Carnegie* (1970).

For the techniques of selling, see Daniel J. Boorstin, *The Americans: The Democratic Experience* (1973). Two superb books by Sam B. Warner, Jr., *Streetcar Suburbs: The Process of Growth in Boston, 1870–1900* (1962) and *The Urban Wilderness: A History of the American City* (1973), examine technology and city

do or not, the company will pursue the same policy and it will win." In late July the Homestead works reopened under military guard, and in November the strikers gave up.

Events like those at Homestead troubled many Americans who wondered whether industrialization, for all its benefits, might carry a heavy price in social upheaval, class tensions, and even outright warfare. Most workers did not share in the immense profits of the industrial age, and as the nineteenth century came to a close, there were some who rebelled against the inequity.

In the half-century after the Civil War, the United States became an industrial nation—the leading one, in fact, in the world. On one hand, industrialization meant "progress," growth, world power, and in some sense, fulfillment of development. The wage earner is examined in Herbert G. Gutman, *Work, Culture, and Society in Industrializing America* (1976) and in two books by Stephan Thernstrom: *Poverty and Progress: Social Mobility in the Nineteenth-Century City* (1964) and *The Other Bostonians: Poverty and Progress in the American Metropolis, 1880–1970* (1973). Philip S. Foner, *Women and the American Labor Movement*, 2 vols. (1979); Lois W. Banner, *Women in Modern America: A Brief History* (1974); and Milton Cantor and Bruce Laurie, eds., *Class, Sex, and the Woman Worker* (1977) are excellent.

Additional Bibliography

Alfred D. Chandler, *The Railroads: The Nation's First Big Business* (1965), stresses the railroads' importance; Robert Fogel, *Railroads in American Economic Growth* (1964), questions it. Julius Grodinsky, *Jay Gould* (1957) and Albro Martin, *James J. Hill and the Opening of the Northwest* (1976) are superb.

For steel, see Carnegie's *Autobiography of Andrew Carnegie* (1920); Harold C. Livesay, *Andrew Carnegie and the Rise of Big Business* (1975); and John Ingham, *The Iron Barons: A Social Analysis of an American Urban Elite, 1874–1965* (1978). For the oil industry, see Carl Solberg, *Oil Power* (1976); H. F. Williamson and A. R. Daum, *The American Petroleum Industry: Age of Illumination* (1959); and Allan Nevins, *Study in Power: John D. Rockefeller*, 2 vols. (1953). For Morgan, see Lewis Corey, *The House of Morgan* (1930) and Frederick Lewis Allen, *The Great Pierpont Morgan* (1949).

On technological developments, Lewis Mumford, *Technics and Civilization* (1934); Charles Singer et al., eds., *History of Technology*, vol. 5, *The Late Nineteenth Century, c. 1850 to c. 1900* (1958); and W. P. Strassmann, *Risk and Technological Innovation: American Manufacturing Methods During the Nineteenth Century* (1959) are the places to begin. Useful studies include Matthew Josephson, *Edison* (1959); H. G. Prout, *A Life of George Westinghouse* (1921); John Brooks, *Telephone: The First Hundred Years* (1976); and Robert V. Bruce, *Alexander Graham Bell and the Conquest of Solitude* (1973).

Frank Presbrey, *The History and Development of Advertising* (1929) is the best general account; others include J. P. Wood, *The Story of Advertising* (1958); Ralph M. Hower, *History of Macy's of New York, 1858–1919* (1943); John K. Winkler, *Five and Ten: The Fabulous Life of F. W. Woolworth* (1940); and Boris Emmet and John E. Jeuck, *Catalogues and Counters: A History of Sears, Roebuck and Company* (1950). Also, David M. Potter, *People of Plenty: Economic Abundance and the American Character* (1954).

On labor, see David Brody, *Steelworkers in America: The Nonunion Era* (1960); Gerald N. Grob, *Workers and Utopia: A Study of Ideological Conflict in the American Labor Movement, 1865–1900* (1961); N. J. Ware, *The Labor Movement in the United States, 1860–1893* (1929); and S. B. Kaufman, *Samuel Gompers and the Origins of the American Federation of Labor* (1973). John Laslett, *Labor and the Left: A Study of Socialist and Radical Influences in the American Labor Movement, 1881–1924* (1970) is illuminating. Terence V. Powderly, *Thirty Years of Labor* (1889) and Samuel Gompers, *Seventy Years of Life and Labor*, 2 vols. (1925), give the flavor of their thought.

chapter 19

TOWARD AN URBAN SOCIETY: 1877–1890

Life in the United States, said the perceptive English statesman and historian James Bryce in the 1880s, "is in most ways pleasanter, easier, simpler than in Europe; it floats in a sense of happiness like that of a radiant summer morning."

Between 1877 and 1890 factories poured out consumer goods, and the newly invented cash registers rang up sale after sale. Electric lights and telephones enhanced social life. People eager for amusement discovered baseball, bicycling, and the great traveling circus. Public and private educational systems burgeoned; illiteracy declined. Life expectancy increased. "The old nations of the earth creep on at a snail's pace," wrote Andrew Carnegie in *Triumphant Democracy* (1886), "the Republic thunders past with the rush of an express."

Other voices raised somber warnings. "The time was," said Congressman John Reagan of Texas in 1877, "when none were poor and none rich. . . . Then the few became fabulously rich, the many wretchedly poor . . . and the poorer we are the poorer they would make us." In the 1870s and '80s social critics and reformers like Henry George, Edward Bellamy, Jacob Riis, and others poked among the dark corners of American life and questioned what they saw.

Opportunity was not open to all; wealth was an elusive goal. Corruption strained the political system, hard-pressed to respond to the extraordinary pace of change. Crime and violence were everywhere on the rise—among urban street gangs, Western bandits and vigilantes, and Southern night riders. Cities virtually exploded in population, and immigrants crowded by the millions into slums. Men, women, and children worked in factories from dawn to dusk; work-related accidents took an appalling toll of lives and limbs.

"Amid the greatest accumulations of wealth," wrote Henry George in *Progress and Poverty* (1879), one of the era's most influential books, "men die of starvation, and puny infants suckle dry breasts. . . . The promised land flies before us like a mirage." George described America as "the House of Have and the House of Want," almost in paraphrase of Lincoln's earlier metaphor of the "house divided." Could this house, unlike that one, stand?

Life in America, 1877

From 1877 to the 1890s the nation underwent sweeping changes that affected economic, political, and social life. Technology changed mores; bright lights and new careers drew young men and women to the cities; family ties loosened. Cities, suburbs, and factories took new forms. While many people worked harder and harder, others had increased leisure time. The roles of women and children changed in a number of ways, and immigrants molded the society and in turn were molded by it.

"We are in a period," President Rutherford B. Hayes said in 1878, "when old questions are settled, and the new ones are not yet brought forward." Old questions—questions of racial, social and economic justice, and of federal-state relations—were not settled, but people wanted new directions. Political issues lost the sharp focus of the Civil War and Reconstruction. For men and women of middle age in 1877, the issues of the Union and slavery had been the overriding public concerns throughout their adult lives. Now, with the end of Reconstruction, it seemed time for new concerns.

Change and movement were everywhere, in cities and factories, on farms that sprinkled the Western prairies, and along railroad tracks pushing into unsettled domain. Thanks to advancing technology, news flashed quickly across the oceans, and for the first time in history people shook open their evening newspapers to read of that day's events in distant lands.

In 1877 the country had 47 million people. A little more than a decade later there were nearly 63 million. Nine tenths of the population was white; just under one tenth was black. There were 66,000 Indians, 108,000 Chinese, and 148 Japanese. The bulk of the white population, most of whom were Protestant, came from the so-called Anglo-Saxon countries of northern Europe. WASPs—White Anglo-Saxon Protestants—dominated American society.

Most people still lived on farms or in small towns. Their lives revolved around the farm, the church, and the general store. In 1880 nearly 75 percent of the population lived in communities of fewer than twenty-five hundred people. In 1900, in the midst of city growth, 60 percent still did. The average family in 1880 had three children, and life expectancy was about forty-three years. By 1900 it had risen to forty-seven years, the result of improved health care. For blacks and other minorities, often living in unsanitary rural areas, life expectancy was substantially lower: thirty-three years in 1900.

Houses were usually made of wooden shingles or clapboard, set back from unpaved streets, whose dusty surfaces muffled the sounds of passing horses. Life was quiet. Many homes had a front porch for summertime sitting. In the backyard there were numerous outbuildings, including one—at the end of a well-worn path—with a

■ *State Street, Jacksonville, 1889. The quiet, tree-lined street reflects the unhurried pace of life in small-town America in the late nineteenth century.*

distinctive half-moon carved in the door. There was a vegetable garden and often a chicken coop or cowshed; families—even in the cities—needed backyard produce to supplement their diet. Inside the house, life centered in the kitchen with its enormous wood or coal stove.

Meals tended to be heavy and so did people. Even breakfast had several courses and could include steak, eggs, fish, potatoes, toast, and coffee. Food prices were low. Families ate fresh homegrown produce in the summer, and "put up" fruits and vegetables for the long winters. Toward the end of the century eating habits changed. New packaged breakfast cereals became popular; fresh fruit and vegetables came in on fast trains from Florida and California, and commercially canned food processing became safer and cheaper. The newfangled icebox, cooled by blocks of ice, kept food fresher and added new treats like ice cream.

Medical science was in the midst of a major revolution. Louis Pasteur's recent discovery that germs cause infection and disease created the new science of microbiology and led the way to the development of vaccines and other preventive measures. But tuberculosis, typhoid, diphtheria, and pneumonia—all are now curable—were still the leading causes of death. Many families knew the wrenching pain of a child's death. Infant mortality declined between 1877 and 1900, but the decline was gradual; the great drop did not come until after 1920.

1890 Retail Prices: Food		
BACON	1 lb.	**15.5¢**
BUTTER	1 lb.	**25.5¢**
EGGS	1 dozen	**20.8¢**
FLOUR	5 lbs.	**14.5¢**
MILK	½ gal. delivered	**13.6¢**
PORK CHOPS	1 lb.	**10.7¢**
POTATOES	10 lbs.	**16¢**
ROUND STEAK	1 lb.	**12.3¢**
SUGAR	5 lbs.	**34.5¢**

Source: U.S. Bureau of the Census, Historical Statistics of the United States, Colonial Times to 1970, Bicentennial Edition, Washington, D.C., 1975.

There were few hospitals and no hospital insurance. Most patients stayed at home, although medical practice, especially surgery, expanded rapidly. Once brutal and dangerous, surgery in these years became relatively safe and painless. Anesthetics—ether and chloroform—eliminated pain, and antiseptic practices helped prevent postoperative infections. Antiseptic practices at childbirth also cut down on puerperal fever, an infection that for centuries had killed many women and newborn infants. An earlier discovery—nitrous oxide, called laughing gas—eased the discomfort of dentistry. The new science of psychology began to explore the mind, hitherto uncharted (see the special feature on pp. 564–65). William James, a leading American psychologist and philosopher, laid the foundations of modern behaviorist psychology, which stressed the importance of the environment on human development.

Manners and Mores

The code of Victorian morality, its name derived from the British queen who reigned throughout the period, set the tone for the era. The code prescribed stern standards of dress, manners, and sexual behavior. It was both obeyed and disobeyed, and it reflected the tensions of a generation that was undergoing a change in moral standards.

In 1877 children were to be seen and not heard. They spoke when spoken to, listened rather than chattered—or at least that was the rule. Older boys and girls were often chaperoned, although they could always find moments alone. They played post office and spin the bottle; they puffed cigarettes behind the barn. William Allen White, later a famous journalist, recalled the high jinks of his boyhood. He and his friends smeared their naked bodies with mud and leaped out in full view of passengers on passing trains. Counterbalancing such youthful exuberance was strong pride in virtue and self-control. "Thank heaven I am absolutely pure," Theodore Roosevelt, the future president, wrote in 1880 after proposing to Alice Lee. "I can tell Alice everything I have ever done."

Gentlemen of the middle class dressed in heavy black suits, derby hats, and white shirts with

■ The slightest exertion on the part of women who wore the fashionable, tightly laced, steel-and-whalebone corset was likely to bring on a fainting spell.

paper collars. Women wore tight corsets, long, dark dresses, and black shoes reaching well above the ankles. As with so many things, styles changed dramatically toward the end of the century, spurred in part by new sporting fads such as golf, tennis, and bicycling, which required looser clothing. By the 1890s a middle-class woman wore a tailored suit or a dark skirt and a blouse, called a "shirtwaist," modeled after men's shirts. Her skirts still draped about the ankles, but more and more she removed or loosened the corset, the dread device that squeezed skin and internal organs into fashionable eighteen-inch waistlines.

Religious and patriotic values were strong. One of the centers of community life, the church often set the tenor for family and social relationships. On Sundays the family dressed in Sunday-best and attended a long morning service, followed by Sunday dinner, naps, reading, and another church service in the evening. In the 1880s eight out of ten church members were Protestants; most of the rest were Roman Catholics. Evangelists like Dwight L. Moody, a former Chicago shoe salesman, and Ira B. Sankey, an organist and singer, conducted mass revival meetings across the country. Enormously successful, Moody preached to millions and sparked a spiritual awakening on American college campuses.

With slavery abolished, reformers turned their attention to new moral and political issues. One group, known as the Mugwumps, worked to end corruption in politics. Drawn mostly from the educated and upper class, they included individuals like Thomas Nast, the famous political cartoonist, George William Curtis, editor of *Harper's Weekly*, and E. L. Godkin, editor of the influential *Nation*. Other zealous reformers campaigned for prohibition of the sale of intoxicating liquors, hoping to end the social evils that stemmed from drunkenness. In 1874, women who advocated total abstinence from alcoholic beverages formed the Women's Christian Temperance Union. Their leader, Frances E. Willard, served as president of the group from 1879 until her death in 1898. By then the WCTU had 10,000 branches and 500,000 members.

In New York City, Anthony Comstock formed the Society for the Suppression of Vice, which supervised public morality. At his request Congress passed the Comstock Law (1873) prohibiting the mailing or transporting of "obscene, lewd or lascivious" articles. The law was not successful; within a few years Comstock reported finding 64,094 "articles for immoral use," 700 pounds of "lead moulds for making obscene matter," 202,679 obscene photographs, and 26 "obscene pictures, framed on walls of saloons."

Leisure and Entertainment

In the 1870s people tended to rise early. On getting up, they washed from the pitcher and bowl in the bedroom, first breaking the layer of ice if it was winter. In winter, they often left their clothes in the kitchen near the warmth of the stove. After dressing and eating, they went off to work and school; without large refrigerators, housewives marketed almost daily. In the evenings, families gathered in the "second parlor" or living room, where the children did their lessons, played games, sang around the piano, and listened to that day's verse from the Bible.

Popular games included cards, dominoes, backgammon, chess, and checkers. Many homes had a packet of "author cards" that required knowledge of books, authors, and noted quotations. The latest fad was the stereopticon or "magic lantern," which brought three-dimensional life to art, history, and nature. Like "author cards" and other games, it was instructional as well as entertaining.

The newest outdoor game was croquet, so popular that candles were mounted on the wickets to allow play at night. Croquet was the first outdoor game designed for play by both sexes, and it frequently served as a setting for courtship. Early manuals advised girls how to assume attractive poses while hitting the ball. A popular song of the period told of a pair seated side by side as the

mallets and balls unheeded lay . . .
and I thought to myself, is that Croquet?

American taste in the theater ran to intrigue, swordplay, melodrama, and grandiloquent language. New York's Broadway—known as the Great White Way because of the sparkling new gaslights—had seventeen theaters in the early 1870s. Road shows took popular plays to many cities and towns; in 1887 Edwin Booth, the period's most acclaimed actor (and the brother of Lincoln's assassin), played to packed houses all across the Midwest. Most plays were imported from Europe; the United States had few serious playwrights.

Sentimental ballads such as "Silver Threads Among the Gold" (1873) remained the most popular musical form, but the insistent syncopated rhythms of ragtime were being heard. By the time the strains of Scott Joplin's "Maple Leaf Rag" (1899) popularized ragtime, critics complained that "a wave of vulgar, filthy and suggestive music has inundated the land." Classical music flourished. The New England Conservatory (1867), the Cincinnati College of Music (1878), and the Metropolitan Opera (1883) were new sources of civic pride; New York, Boston, and Chicago launched first-rate symphony orchestras between 1878 and 1891.

In the hamlets and small towns of America traveling circuses were enormously popular. Hamlin Garland, an author who grew up in small Iowa villages, recalled how the circus came "trailing clouds of glorified dust and filling our minds with the color of romance. . . . It brought to our ears the latest band pieces and taught us the

■ *Below, the third baseman makes a bare-handed catch as the runner slides safely into base. Right, the high-wheeled bicycles the men are riding were called "ordinaries."*

popular songs. It furnished us with jokes. It relieved our dullness. It gave us something to talk about." Larger circuses, run by entrepreneurs like P. T. Barnum and James A. Bailey, played the cities, but every town attracted its own smaller version. When the circus was not in town, Buffalo Bill's Wild West Show was, reenacting Indian battles and displaying frontier marksmanship.

Fairs, horse races, balloon ascensions, bicycle tournaments, and football and baseball contests attracted avid fans. The years between 1870 and 1900 saw the rise of organized spectator sports, a trend reflecting the new uses of leisure. Baseball's first professional team, the Cincinnati Red Stockings, appeared in 1869, and baseball soon became the preeminent national sport. Fans sang songs about it ("Take Me Out to the Ballgame"), wrote poems about it ("Casey at the Bat"), and made up riddles about it ("What has eighteen feet and catches flies?"). Modern rules were adopted. Umpires were designated to call balls and strikes; catchers wore masks and chest protectors and moved closer to the plate instead of staying back to catch the ball on the bounce. Fielders had to catch the ball on the fly rather than on one

bounce in their caps. By 1890 professional baseball teams were drawing crowds of sixty thousand daily.

In 1869 Princeton and Rutgers played the first intercollegiate football game. Soon other schools picked up the sport, and by the early 1890s crowds of fifty thousand or more attended the most popular contests. Basketball, invented in 1891, gained a large following. Boxing, a popular topic of conversation in saloons and schoolyards, was outlawed in most states. For a time championship prizefights were held in secret, with news of the result spread rapidly by word-of-mouth. Matches were long and bloody, fought with bare knuckles until the invention in the 1880s of the five-ounce boxing glove. John L. Sullivan, the Boston Strong Boy and the era's most popular champion, won the heavyweight title in 1882 in a brutal seventy-five-round victory over the stubborn Jake Kilrain.

As gas and electric lights brightened the night, and streetcars crisscrossed city streets, leisure habits changed. Delighted with the new technology, people took advantage of an increasing variety of things to do. They stayed home less often.

Steam, steel, and electricity transformed cities. In this W. Louis Sonntag, Jr., watercolor of New York City's Bowery in 1895, electric streetcars travel up and down the street while the elevated railroad rumbles overhead. Bright incandescent lamps light up the night.

New York City's first electric sign—"Manhattan Beach Swept by Ocean Breezes"—appeared in 1881, and people filled the streets on their way to the theater, vaudeville shows, dance halls, or just out for an evening stroll.

Family Life

In 1873 a writer said: "Whatever tends to deteriorate the marriage relation and consequently the home, tends to deteriorate the whole machinery of life, whether social or political." Nonetheless, under the impact of industrialization and urbanization, family relationships were changing. On the farm parents and children worked more or less together, and the family was a producing unit. In factories, family members rarely worked together. In working-class families, mothers, fathers, and children separated at dawn and returned, ready for sleep, at dark. Morris Rosenfeld, a clothing presser, lamented in "My Boy":

I have a little boy at home,
A pretty little son;

I think sometimes the world is mine
In him, my only one. . . .

'Ere dawn my labor drives me forth;
Tis night when I am free;
A stranger am I to my child;
And stranger my child to me.

Middle-class fathers began to move their families out of the city to the suburbs, while they commuted to work on the new streetcars, leaving wives and children at home and school.

As the middle-class family's economic function declined, it took on increased emotional significance. "In the old days," said a woman in 1907, "a married woman was supposed to be a frump and a bore and a physical wreck. Now you are supposed to keep up intellectually, to look young and well and be fresh and bright and entertaining." Magazines like the *Ladies' Home Journal*, which started in 1889, glorified motherhood and the home, but its articles and ads featured women as homebound, child-oriented consumers. While society's leaders spoke fondly of the value of homemaking, the status of housewives declined under the factory system, which emphasized money rewards and devalued household labor.

In and out of the family, there was growing recognition of the self-sufficient working woman, employed in factory, telephone exchange, and business office, who was entering the work force in increasing numbers. In 1880 there were 2.6 million women gainfully employed; in 1890, 4 million. In 1882 the Census Bureau took the first census of working women; most were single and worked out of necessity rather than choice.

This "New Woman" was seen by many as a corruption of the ideal vision of the American woman, in which man worshipped "a diviner self than his own," innocent, helpless, and good. Women were to be better than the world around them. They were brought up, said Ida Tarbell, a leading political reformer who went through it herself, "as if wrongdoing were impossible to them."

■ *Women operators, called "Hello Girls," were hired to work telephone switchboards after it was discovered that male operators tended to argue too much with the subscribers.*

Views changed, albeit slowly. One important change occurred in the legal codes pertaining to women, particularly in the common law doctrine of *femme couverte*. Under that doctrine, wives were chattel of their husbands; they could not legally control their own earnings, property, or children unless they had drawn up a specific contract before marriage. By 1890 many states had substantially revised the doctrine to allow wives control of their earnings and inherited property. In cases of divorce, the new laws also recognized women's rights to custody or joint custody of their children. Although divorce was still far from being socially acceptable, divorce rates more than doubled during the last third of the century. By 1905 one in twelve marriages was ending in divorce.

In the 1870s and '80s a growing number of women were asserting their own humanness. They fought for the vote, lobbied for equal pay, and sought self-fulfillment. The new interest in psychology and medicine strengthened their cause. Charlotte Perkins Gilman, author of *Women and Economics* (1898), joined other women in questioning the ideal of womanly "innocence," which, she argued, actually meant ignorance. In medical and popular literature, menstruation, sexual intercourse, and childbirth were becoming viewed as natural functions instead of taboo topics.

Edward Bliss Foote's *Plain Home Talk of Love, Marriage, and Parentage,* a best-seller that went through many editions between the 1880s and 1900s, challenged Victorian notions that sexual intercourse was unhealthy and intended solely to produce children. In *Plain Facts for Old and Young* (1881), Dr. John H. Kellogg urged parents to recognize the early awakening of sexual feelings in their children. Still, such matters were avoided in many American homes. Rheta Childe Dorr, a journalist, remembered that when a girl reached the age of fourteen, new rules were introduced, "and when you asked for an explanation you met only embarrassed silence."

Women espoused causes with new fervor. Susan B. Anthony, a veteran of many reform campaigns, tried to vote in the 1872 presidential election and was fined $100, which she refused to pay. In 1890 she helped form the National American Woman Suffrage Association to work for the enfranchisement of women (see chapter 22). On

New York's Lower East Side, the Ladies Anti-Beef Trust Association, formed to protest increases in the price of meat, established a boycott of butcher shops. When their demands were ignored, the women invaded the shops, poured kerosene on the meat, and set fire to it. "We don't riot," Rebecca Ablowitz told the judge. "But if all we did was to weep at home, nobody would notice it; so we have to do something to help ourselves."

Educating the Masses

Continuing a trend that stretched back a hundred years, childhood was becoming a distinct time of life. There was still only a vague concept of adolescence—the special nature of the teen-age years—but the role of children was changing. Less and less were children perceived as "little adults," valued for the additional financial gain they might bring into the family. Now children were to grow and learn and be nurtured rather than rushed into adulthood.

As a result, schooling became more important and American educators came closer than ever before to universal education. By 1900, thirty-one states and territories (out of fifty-one) had enacted laws making school attendance compulsory. In 1870 there were only 160 public high schools; in 1900 there were 6000. In the same years, public school budgets rose from $63 million to $253 million; illiteracy declined from 20 percent to just over 10 percent of the population. Still, even as late as 1900, the average adult had only five years of schooling.

Most schools stressed a highly structured curriculum, focused on discipline and routine. In 1892 Joseph Rice, a pediatrician, toured twelve hundred classrooms in thirty-six cities. In a typical classroom, he reported, the atmosphere was "damp and chilly," the teacher strict. "The unkindly spirit of the teacher is strikingly apparent; the pupils being completely subjugated to her will, are silent and motionless." One teacher asked her pupils, "How can you learn anything with your knees and toes out of order?"

School began early; boys attended all day, but girls often stayed home after lunch, since it was thought they needed less in the way of learning. On the teacher's command, students stood and recited from *Webster's Spellers* and *McGuffey's*

■ *Although education was growing in importance, in most schools the emphasis continued to be on conformity and deportment with the teacher acting as drillmaster and disciplinarian.*

Readers, the period's most popular textbooks. The work of William Holmes McGuffey, a professor of languages at Miami University in Ohio, *McGuffey's Readers* had been in use since 1836 (see chapter 11); 100 million copies were sold in the last half of the nineteenth century. Nearly every child read them; they taught not only reading but also ethics, values, and religion. In the *Readers* boys grew up to be heroes, girls to be mothers, and hard work always meant success:

Shall birds, and bees, and ants, be wise,
*   While I my moments waste?*
O let me with the morning rise,
*   And to my duty haste.*

The South lagged far behind in education. Family size was about twice as large as in the North, and a greater proportion of the population lived in isolated rural areas. State and local authorities mandated fewer weeks in the average school year, and many southern states refused to adopt compulsory education laws. Most important, Southerners insisted on maintaining separate school systems to segregate the races. Supported by the

United States Supreme Court decision in *Plessy v. Ferguson* (1896), segregated schooling added a devastating financial burden to education in the South.

North Carolina and Alabama mandated segregated schools in 1876, South Carolina and Louisiana in 1877, Mississippi in 1878, and Virginia in 1882. The laws often implied that the schools would be "separate but equal," but they rarely were. Black schools were usually dilapidated, the teachers in them paid considerably less than white teachers. In 1890 only 35 percent of black children attended school in the South; 55 percent of white children did. That year nearly two thirds of the country's black population was illiterate.

Educational techniques changed after the 1870s. Educators paid more attention to early elementary education, a trend that placed young children in school and helped the growing number of mothers who worked outside the home. The kindergarten movement, started in Saint Louis in 1873, spread across the country. In kindergartens, four- to six-year olds learned by playing, not by keeping their knees and toes in order. For older children, Jane Addams and other reformers advocated "practical" courses in manual training and homemaking. "We are impatient with the schools which lay all stress on reading and writing," Addams said, for "they fail to give the child any clew to the life about him."

For the first time education became a field of university study. European theorists like Johann Friedrich Herbart, a German educator, argued that learning occurred best in an atmosphere of freedom and confidence between teachers and pupils. Teacher training became increasingly professional. Only 10 normal schools, or teacher-training institutions, existed in the United States before the Civil War. By 1900 there were 345, and one in every five elementary teachers had graduated from a professional school.

Higher Education

Nearly 150 new colleges and universities opened in the twenty years between 1880 and 1900. The Morrill Land Grant Act of 1862 gave large grants of land to the states for the establishment of colleges to teach "agriculture and the mechanic arts." The act fostered 69 "land-grant" institutions, including the great state universities of Wisconsin, California, Minnesota, and Illinois.

Private philanthropy, born of the large fortunes of the industrial age, also spurred growth in higher education. Leland Stanford gave $24 million to endow Stanford University on his California ranch, and John D. Rockefeller, founder of the Standard Oil Company, gave $34 million to found the University of Chicago. Other industrialists established Cornell (1865), Vanderbilt (1873), and Tulane (1884).

As colleges expanded, their function changed, and their curriculum broadened. No longer did they exist primarily to train young men for the ministry. They moved away from the classical curriculum of rhetoric, mathematics, Latin, and Greek toward "reality and practicality," as President David Starr Jordan of Stanford University said. The Massachusetts Institute of Technology (M.I.T.), founded in 1861, focused on science and engineering.

Influenced by the new German universities, which emphasized specialized research, Johns Hopkins University in Baltimore opened the nation's first separate graduate school in 1876. Under President Daniel Coit Gilman, Johns Hopkins stressed the seminar and laboratory as teaching tools, bringing together student and teacher in close association. By 1900 more than nine thousand Americans had studied in Germany, and some of them returned home to become presidents of institutions such as Harvard, Yale, Columbia, the University of Chicago, and Johns Hopkins.

One of them, Charles W. Eliot, who became president of Harvard in 1869 at the age of thirty-five, moved to end, as an admirer said, the "old fogyism" that marked the institution. Revising the curriculum, Eliot set up the elective system in which students chose their own courses rather than following a rigidly prescribed curriculum. Lectures and discussions replaced rote recitation, and courses in the natural and social sciences, fine arts, and modern languages multiplied. In the 1890s Eliot's Harvard moved to the forefront of educational innovation.

Before the Civil War, only three private colleges admitted women to study with men. After the war educational opportunities increased for women. A number of women's colleges opened, including Vassar (1865), Wellesley (1875), Smith

■ *Unlike these Smith College chemistry students, most women who attended college in the 1870s and '80s were urged to take home economics rather than science courses.*

■ *W. E. B. Du Bois (top) argued against the accommodationist approach of Booker T. Washington and the emphasis on vocational training at Washington's Tuskegee Institute. Students in the wheelwright shop at Tuskegee are shown in the photo at bottom.*

(1875), Bryn Mawr (1885), Barnard (1889), and Radcliffe (1893). The land-grant colleges of the Midwest, open to women from the outset, spurred a nationwide trend toward coeducation, although some physicians, like Harvard Medical School's Dr. Edward H. Clarke in his popular *Sex in Education* (1873), continued to argue that the strain of learning made women sterile. By 1900 women made up about 40 percent of college students, and four out of five colleges admitted them.

Fewer opportunities existed for blacks and other minorities. Mrs. Jane Stanford encouraged the Chinese who had worked on her husband's Central Pacific Railroad to apply to Stanford University, but her policy was unusual. Most colleges did not accept minorities, and few applied. W. E. B. Du Bois, the brilliant black sociologist and civil rights leader, attended Harvard in the late 1880s but found the society of Harvard Yard closed against him. Disdained and disdainful, he "asked no fellowship of my fellow students." Chosen as one of the commencement speakers, Du Bois picked as his topic, "Jefferson Davis," treating it, said an onlooker, with "an almost contemptuous fairness."

Black students turned to black colleges such as the Hampton Normal and Industrial Institute in Virginia and the Tuskegee Institute in Alabama. Booker T. Washington, an ex-slave, put into practice his educational ideas at Tuskegee, which opened in 1881. Washington began Tuskegee with limited funds, four run-down buildings, and only thirty students; by 1900 it was a model industrial and agricultural school. Spread over forty-six buildings, it offered instruction in thirty trades to fourteen hundred students.

Washington stressed patience, manual training, and hard work. "No race," he said in 1895, "can prosper till it learns that there is as much dignity in tilling a field as in writing a poem. It is at the bottom of life we must begin, and not at the top." Rather than fighting for equal rights, blacks should acquire property, improve themselves through self-help, and show they were worthy of their rights. Many whites and blacks welcomed this philosophy; Du Bois, on the other hand, charged that Washington would simply create a black working class to till the farms and tend the machines of white society. But Washington did believe in black equality, and he bespoke a racial pride that contributed to the rise of black nationalism in the twentieth century.

Throughout higher education there was increased emphasis on professional training, particularly in medicine, dentistry, and law. Enrollments swelled, even as standards of admission tightened. The number of medical schools in the country rose from 75 in 1870 to 160 in 1900, and the number of medical students—including more and more women—almost tripled. Schools of nursing grew from only 15 in 1880 to 432 in 1900. Doctors, lawyers, and others became part of a growing middle class that shaped the concerns of the Progressive era (see chapter 22).

Although fewer than 5 percent of the college-age population attended college during the 1877–1890 period, the new trends had great impact. A generation of men and women encountered new ideas that changed their views of themselves and society. Courses never before offered, like Philosophy II at Harvard, "The Ethics of Social Reform," which students called "drainage, drunkenness, and divorce," heightened interest in social problems and the need for reform. Some graduating students burned with a desire to cure society's ills. "My life began . . . at Johns Hopkins University," Frederic C. Howe, an influential reformer, recalled. "I came alive, I felt a sense of responsibility to the world, I wanted to change things."

The Lure of the City

William Allen White left the small Kansas town of his boyhood in 1891 to go to the "gilded metropolis" of Kansas City. White was twenty-three years old, and the experience affected him for the rest of his life. He rode the cable cars and used the newfangled telephone—"always with the consciousness that I was tampering with a miracle," he said of the phone. He purchased a second-hand dress suit, listened to the music of a sixty-piece orchestra, attended plays, and heard James Whitcomb Riley recite poetry. "Life was certainly one round of joy in Kansas City," White said.

Between 1870 and 1900 the city—like the factory—became a symbol of a new America. Drawn from farms, small towns and foreign lands, newcomers swelled the population of older cities and created new ones almost overnight. At the beginning of the Civil War only one sixth of the American people lived in cities of 8,000 people or more. By 1900, one third did; by 1910, one half. "We live in the age of great cities," wrote the Reverend Samuel Lane Loomis in 1887. "Each successive year finds a stronger and more irresistible current sweeping in towards the centers of life."

The current brought growth of an explosive sort. Thousands of years of history had produced only a handful of cities with more than a half-million in population. In 1900 the United States

Urban and Rural Population, 1870–1900 (in millions)

Source: U.S. Bureau of the Census, Historical Statistics of the United States, Colonial Times to 1970, *Bicentennial Edition, Washington, D.C., 1975.*

had six such cities, including three—New York, Chicago, and Philadelphia—with a population over a million.

Strangers in a New Land

While some of the new city dwellers came from farms and small towns, many of them came from abroad. Most came from Europe, where unemployment, food shortages, and increasing threats of war sent millions fleeing across the Atlantic to make a fresh start in the United States. Italians first came in large numbers to escape an 1887 cholera epidemic in southern Italy; tens of thousands of Jews sought refuge from the anti-Semitic pogroms that swept Russia and Poland after 1880.

All told, the immigration figures were staggering. Between 1877 and 1890 more than 6.3 million people entered the United States. In one year alone, 1882, almost 789,000 people came. By 1890 about 15 percent of the population, 9 million people, were foreign-born.

Most newcomers were job seekers. Nearly two thirds were males, and the majority were between the ages of fifteen and forty. Most were unskilled laborers. Most settled on the eastern seaboard. In 1901 the Industrial Relocation Office was established to relieve overcrowding in the eastern cities; opening Galveston, Texas as a port of entry, it attracted many Russian Jews to Texas and the Southwest. But most immigrants preferred the shorter, more familiar journey to New York, and they tended to crowd into northern and eastern cities, settling in areas where others of their nationality or religion had settled.

They were often dazzled by what they saw. They stared at electric lights, indoor plumbing, soda fountains, streetcars, plush train seats for all classes, ice cream, lemons, and bananas. Relatives whisked them off to buy new "American" clothes and showed them the teeming markets, department stores, and Woolworth's new five and dime stores. "It seemed quite advanced compared with our home in Khelm," said a young Polish girl. "There was a sense of safety and hope that we had never felt in Poland."

Cities had increasingly large foreign-born populations. In 1900 three fourths of Chicago's population was foreign-born or of foreign-born parentage, two thirds of Boston's, and one half of Philadelphia's. New York City, where most immigrants arrived and many stayed, had more Italians than lived in Naples, more Germans than

Immigration to the United States, 1870–1900 (by area of origin)

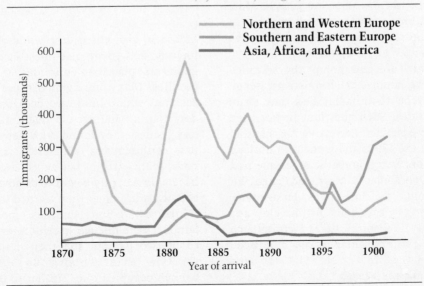

Source: U.S. Bureau of the Census, Historical Statistics of the United States, Colonial Times to 1970, Bicentennial Edition, Washington, D.C., 1975.

In a Puck cartoon entitled "Looking Backward," the shadows of their immigrant origins loom over the rich and powerful who wanted to deny the "new" immigrants from central and southern Europe admission to America. The caption on the cartoon reads, "They would close to the newcomer the bridge that carried them and their fathers over."

lived in Hamburg, and twice as many Irish as lived in Dublin. Four out of five New York City residents in 1890 were of foreign birth or foreign parentage.

Beginning in the 1880s, the sources of immigration shifted dramatically away from northern and western Europe, the chief source of immigration for over two centuries. More and more immigrants came from southern and eastern Europe: Italy, Greece, Austro-Hungary, Poland, and Russia. Between 1880 and 1910 approximately 8.4 million people came from these lands. The "new" immigrants tended to be Catholics or Jews rather than Protestants, unskilled rather than skilled, and they often spoke "strange" languages. Most were poor and uneducated; sticking together in closeknit communities, they clung to their native customs, languages, and religions.

More than any previous group, the so-called new immigrants troubled the mainstream society. Could they be assimilated? Did they share "American" values? Such questions preoccupied groups like the American Protective Association, which arose in the 1890s and worked to limit or end immigration. Sneering epithets became part of the national vocabulary: "wop" and "dago" for Italians, "bohunk" for Bohemians, Hungarians, and other Slavs, "grease-ball" for Greeks, and "kike" for Jews. "You don't call . . . an Italian a white man?" a congressman asked a railroad construction boss in 1890. "No, Sir," the boss replied. "An Italian is a Dago."

Anti-Catholicism and anti-Semitism flared up again, as they had in the 1850s (recall chapter 14).

Edward A. Ross, a prominent sociologist, publicly decried "the lower class of Jews of Eastern Europe [who] reach here [as] moral cripples, their souls warped and dwarfed." In 1889 the head of the Fresh Air Fund, a program that sent New York City children on vacations to the suburbs, noted that "no one asked for Italian children." The Immigration Restriction League, founded in 1894, demanded a literacy test for immigrants from southern and eastern Europe. Congress passed such a law in 1896, but President Cleveland vetoed it.

Immigrants and the City

Industrial capitalism—the world of factories and foremen and grimy machines—tested the immigrants and placed an enormous strain upon their families. Many immigrants came from peasant societies where life proceeded according to outdoor routine and age-old tradition. In their new city homes, they found both new freedoms and new confinements, a different language, and a novel set of customs and expectations. Historians have only recently begun to discover the remarkable ways in which they learned to adjust.

Like native-born families, most immigrant families were nuclear in structure—they consisted of two parents and their children. Though variations occurred from group to group, men and women occupied roles similar to those in native families; men were wage earners, women housekeepers and mothers. Margaret Boyington, who studied steelworkers' homes in Homestead in the early 1900s, learned that the father played relatively little role in child-rearing or managing the family's finances. "His part of the problem is to earn and hers to spend." In Chicago Jane Addams discovered that immigrant women made it "a standard of domestic virtue that a man must not touch his pay envelope, but bring it home unopened to his wife."

Although patterns varied between ethnic groups, and between economic classes within ethnic groups, immigrants tended to marry within the group more than did the native-born. In one New York community, only 2 percent of French Canadian and 7 percent of Irish working men married outside their ethnic group in 1880, compared to almost 40 percent of native-born working men. Immigrants also tended to marry at a later age than natives, and they tended to have more children, a fact that worried nativists opposed to immigration.

Immigrants shaped the city as much as it shaped them. Most of them tried to retain their traditional culture for themselves and their children while at the same time adapting to life in their new country. To do this, they spoke their native language, practiced their religious faith, read their own newspapers, and established special parochial or other schools. They observed traditional holidays and formed a myriad of social organizations to maintain ties between members of the group.

Immigrant associations—there were many of them in every city—offered fellowship in a strange land. They helped newcomers find jobs and homes; they provided important services such as unemployment and health insurance. In a Massachusetts textile town, the Irish Benevolent Society said: "We visit our sick, and bury our dead." Some groups were no larger than a neighborhood; others spread nationwide. In 1914 the Deutsch-Amerikanischer Nationalbund, the largest of them, had more than two million members in dozens of cities and towns. Many women belonged to and participated in the work of the immigrant associations; in addition, there were groups exclusively for women such as the Polish Women's Alliance, the Jednota Ceskyck Dam (Society of Czech Women), and the National Council of Jewish Women.

The Polish National Alliance (PNA), a typical

Ethnic Neighborhoods in Chicago, 1870

Immigrants coming to a big city settled in neighborhoods where people were familiar with the customs and traditions of their native land.

immigrant association, was founded in 1880. Like other organizations, it helped new immigrants on their arrival, offered insurance plans, established libraries and museums, sponsored youth programs, fielded baseball teams, and organized trips back to Poland. Each year the PNA published a sought-after calendar filled with Polish holidays, information, and proverbs. Extolling Poles' contributions to their new country, it erected monuments to distinguished Americans of Polish descent.

Every major city had dozens of foreign-language newspapers, with circulations large and small. The first newspaper published in the Lithuanian language appeared in the United States, not in Lithuania. Eagerly read, the papers carried news of events in the homeland, but they also reported on local ethnic leaders, told readers how to vote and become citizens, and gave practical tips on adjusting to life in the United States. In similar fashion, the Swedes, Poles, Czechs, and Germans established ethnic theaters that performed national plays and music. The Yiddish

(Jewish) Theater, the most famous, started in the 1880s in New York City and lasted for over fifty years.

The church and the school were the most important institutions in every immigrant community. East European Jews established synagogues and religious schools wherever they settled; they taught the Hebrew language and raised their children in a heritage they did not want to leave behind. Among groups like the Irish and the Poles, the Roman Catholic Church provided spiritual and educational guidance. In the parish schools, Polish priests and nuns taught Polish-American children about Polish as well as American culture in the Polish language.

Church, school, and fraternal societies shaped the way in which immigrants adjusted to life in America. By preserving language, religion, and heritage, they also shaped the country itself.

■ *The ten-story Home Insurance Building, designed by William LeBaron Jenney, showed that with elevators and a steel frame buildings could soar to almost any height.*

Skyscrapers and Suburbs

Beginning in the 1880s a revolution in technology transformed American cities. The age of steel and glass produced the skyscraper; the streetcar produced the suburbs and new residential patterns.

On the eve of the change, American cities were a crowded jumble of small buildings. Church steeples stood out on the skyline, clearly visible above the roofs of factories and office buildings. Buildings were usually made of masonry, and since the massive walls had to support their own weight, they could be no taller than a dozen or so stories. Steel frames and girders ended that limitation and allowed buildings to soar higher and higher. "Curtain walls," which concealed the steel framework, were no longer load-bearing; they were pierced by many windows that let in fresh air and light. Completed in 1885, the Home Insurance Building in Chicago was the country's first metal-frame structure.

To a group of talented Chicago architects the new trends served as a springboard for innovative forms. The leader of the movement was Louis H. Sullivan, who had studied at M.I.T. and in Paris before settling in Chicago, attracted by the chance to rebuild the city after the great fire of 1871. In 1886, at the age of thirty, he began work on the Chicago Auditorium, one of the last great masonry buildings. "Then came the flash of imagination which saw the single thing," he later said. "The trick was turned; and there swiftly came into being something new under the sun." Sullivan's skyscrapers, the "flash of imagination," changed the urban skyline.

In the Wainwright Building in Saint Louis (1890), the Schiller Building (1892) and the Carson, Pirie, and Scott department store (1899) in Chicago, and the Prudential Building in Buffalo (1895), Sullivan developed the new forms. Architects must discard "books, rules, precedents," he announced; responding to the new, they should design for a building's function. "Form follows function," Sullivan believed, and he passed the idea on to a talented disciple, Frank Lloyd Wright. The modern city should stretch to the sky. A skyscraper "must be every inch a proud and soaring thing, rising in sheer exaltation . . . from bottom to top . . . a unit without a single dissenting line."

Electric elevators carried passengers upward in the new skyscrapers. During the same years streetcars carried them outward to expanded boundaries that transformed urban life.

Cities were no longer largely "walking cities," confined to a radius of two or three miles, the distance an individual might walk. Streetcar systems extended the radius and changed the urban map. Cable lines, electric surface lines, and elevated rapid transit brought shoppers and workers into central business districts and sped them home again. Offering the cheap five-cent fare with a free transfer, these mass transit systems fostered commuting; widely separated business and residential districts sprang up. The middle class moved farther and farther out to the leafy greenness of the suburbs.

As the middle class moved out of the cities, the immigrants and working class poured in. They took over the older brownstones, row houses, and workers' cottages, turning them under the sheer weight of numbers into the slums of the central city. In the cities of the past classes and occupations had been thrown together; without streetcars and subways there was no other choice. The streetcar city, sprawling and specialized, became a more fragmented and stratified society with middle-class residential rings surrounding a business and working-class core.

Tenements and Privies

In the shadow of the skyscrapers grimy rows of tenements filled the central city. Exploring them in words and photographs, Jacob Riis described them in *How the Other Half Lives* (1890).

Be a little careful, please! The hall is dark and you might stumble. . . . Here where the hall turns and dives into utter darkness is . . . a flight of stairs. You can feel your way, if you cannot see it. Close? Yes! What would you have? All the fresh air that enters these stairs comes from the hall-door that is forever slamming. . . . Here is a door. Listen! That short, hacking cough, that tiny, helpless wail — what do they mean? . . . The child is dying of measles. With half a chance it might have lived; but it had none. That dark bedroom killed it.

Tenement houses on small city lots crowded people into cramped apartments. In the late 1870s architect James E. Ware won a competition for tenement design with the "dumbbell tenement." Rising seven or eight stories in height, the dumb-

bell tenement packed about thirty four-room apartments on a lot only 25 by 100 feet. Between four and sixteen families lived on a floor; two toilets in the hall of each floor served their needs. Narrowed at the middle, the tenement resembled a giant dumbbell in shape. The indented middle created an air shaft between adjoining buildings that provided a little light and ventilation. It also carried flames from one story to the next, making these buildings notorious firetraps. In 1890 nearly half the dwellings in New York City were tenements.

That year more than 1.4 million people lived on Manhattan Island, one of whose wards had a population density of 334,000 people per square mile. Many people lived in alleys and basements so dark they could not be photographed until flashlight photography was invented in 1887. Exploring the city, William Dean Howells, the prominent author, inhaled "the stenches of the neglected street . . . [and] the yet fouler and dreadfuller poverty smell which breathes from the open doorways."

Howells smelled more than poverty. In the 1870s and '80s cities stank. One problem was horse manure, hundreds of tons of it a day in every city. Another was the privy, "a single one of which," said a leading authority on public health, "may render life in a whole neighborhood almost unendurable in the summer."

Baltimore smelled "like a billion polecats," recalled H. L. Mencken, who grew up there. Said one New York City resident: "The stench is something terrible." Another wrote that "the stink is enough to knock you down." In 1880 the Chicago *Times* said that a "solid stink" pervaded the city. "No other word expresses it so well as stink. A stench means something finite. Stink reaches the infinite and becomes sublime in the magnitude of odiousness." In 1892 one neighborhood of Chicago, covering a third of a square mile, had only three bathtubs.

Cities dumped their wastes into the nearest body of water, then drew drinking water from the same site. Many built modern, purified waterworks but could not keep pace with spiraling growth. In 1900 fewer than one in ten city dwellers drank filtered water. Factories, the pride of the era, polluted the urban air. At night Pittsburgh looked and sounded like "Hell with the lid off," according to contemporary observers. Smoke

A WARNING TO LANDLORDS.

■ Impoverished immigrant families, like the one in the Jacob Riis photograph (top right), often lived in tiny, windowless rooms in crowded tenement districts like New York City's lower East Side (above). Disease, as indicated in the Harper's Weekly cartoon (right), was a frequent visitor to the tenements.

poured from seventy-three glass factories, forty-one iron and steel mills, and twenty-nine oil refineries. The choking air helped prevent lung diseases and malaria—or so the city's advertising claimed.

Crime was another growing problem. The nation's homicide rate nearly tripled in the 1880s, much of the increase coming in the cities. Slum youths formed street gangs with names like the Hayes Valley gang in San Francisco or the Baxter Street Dudes, the Daybreak Boys, and the Alley Gang in New York. The Daybreak Boys, all under

twelve years of age, rose up early to rob ships in the harbor. In San Francisco the gangs gave rise to the new word "hoodlums," described by a disgusted English traveler as "young embryo criminals" who robbed and murdered at night.

After remaining constant for many decades, the suicide rate rose steadily between 1870 and 1900, according to a recent study of Philadelphia. Alcoholism also rose, especially among men. A 1905 survey of Chicago counted as many saloons as grocery stores, meat markets, and dry goods stores combined.

Closely connected with explosive urban growth was the emergence of the powerful city political machine. As cities grew, lines of responsibility in city governments became hopelessly confused, increasing the opportunity for corruption and greed. Burgeoning populations required streets, buildings, and public services; immigrants needed even more services. In this situation party machines played an important role.

The machines traded services for votes. Loosely knit, they were headed by a strong, influential leader—the "boss"—who tied together a network of ward and precinct captains, each of whom looked after his local constituents. In New York "Honest" John Kelley, Richard Croker, and Charles F. Murphy led Tammany Hall, the famous Democratic party organization that dominated city politics from the 1850s to the 1930s. Other bosses included "Hinky Dink" Kenna and "Bathhouse John" Coughlin in Chicago, James McManes in Philadelphia, and Christopher A. Buckley—the notorious "Blind Boss," who used an exceptional memory for voices to make up for failing eyesight—in San Francisco.

William M. Tweed, head of the famed Tweed Ring in New York, provided the model for them all. Nearly six feet tall, weighing almost three hundred pounds, Tweed rose through the ranks of Tammany Hall. He served in turn as city alderman, member of Congress, and New York State assemblyman. A man of culture and warmth, he moved easily between the rough back alleys of New York and the parlors and clubs of the city's elite. Behind the scenes he headed a ring that plundered New York for tens of millions of dollars.

The New York County Courthouse—"The House that Tweed Built"—was his masterpiece. Nestled in City Hall Park in downtown Manhattan, the three-story structure was designed to cost $250,000, but the bills ran a bit higher. Furniture, carpets, and window shades alone came to more than $5.5 million. Three tables and forty chairs cost the city $180,000. Tweed's own quarry supplied the marble; the plumber got almost $1.5 million for fixtures. Andrew Garvey, the "Prince of Plasterers," charged $500,000 for plaster work, and then $1 million to repair the

same work. His total bill came to $2,870,464.06. (The *New York Times* suggested that the six cents be donated to charity.) In the end the building cost over $13 million—and in 1872, when Tweed fell, it was still not finished.

Some bosses were plainly corrupt; others believed in "honest graft," a term Tammany's George Washington Plunkitt coined to describe "legitimate" profits made from advance knowledge of city projects. Why did voters keep them in power? The answers are complex, involving skillful political organization and the type of constituency. Most immigrants had little experience with democratic government and proved easy prey for well-oiled machines. For the most part, however, the bosses stayed in power because they paid attention to the needs of the least privileged city voters. They offered valued services in an era when neither government nor business lent a hand.

If an immigrant, tired and bewildered after the long crossing, came looking for a job, bosses like Tweed, Plunkitt, or Buckley found him one in city offices or local businesses. If a family's breadwinner died or was injured, the bosses donated food and clothing and saw to it that the family made it through the crisis. If the winter was particularly cold, they provided free coal to heat tenement apartments. They ran picnics for slum children on hot summer days and contributed to hospitals, orphanages, and dozens of worthy neighborhood causes.

Most bosses became wealthy; they were not Robin Hoods who took from the rich to give to the poor. They took for themselves as well. Reformers occasionally ousted them. Tweed fell from power in 1872, "Blind Boss" Buckley in 1891, Croker in 1894. But reformers rarely stayed in power long. Drawn mainly from the middle and upper classes, they had little understanding of the needs of the poor. Before long they returned to private concerns, and the bosses, who had known it would happen all along, cheerily took power again.

"What tells in holdin' your grip on your district," the engaging Plunkitt once said, "is to go right down among the poor families and help them in the different ways they need help. . . . It's philanthropy, but it's politics, too—mighty good politics. . . . The poor are the most grateful people in the world."

Charles J. Guiteau and the Controversial Insanity Defense

Charles J. Guiteau was thirty-nine years old in 1881. Short and slightly built, he sported a mustache and a trim, dark beard. He did not smoke or drink, and he took particular pride in his neat appearance. In 1879 he had published a religious volume bearing the modest title, *The Truth, A Companion to the Bible.* "I had ideas but no reputation," he later said. A desire for political recognition and a hope of lasting fame were among his ideas. Although without political influence of any kind, he supported James A. Garfield in the presidential election of 1880, then persuaded himself that he deserved a handsome reward. He wrote Garfield to say that he would be happy to accept an ambassadorship in Europe.

Soon after taking office, Garfield became entangled in a fight with Senator Roscoe Conkling of New York and the Conkling wing of the Republican party (see chapter 20). The intraparty struggle disturbed Guiteau. "Like a flash" the idea came to him (he testified at his trial) that all would be well if only Garfield were "removed." On June 6, Guiteau purchased for $10 a British Bull Dog revolver and a box of cartridges. He chose a bone-handled revolver, thinking it would look nice in the museum case it was destined to occupy.

For three weeks in June, Guiteau stalked Garfield through the streets of Washington. Finally, on July 2, Guiteau could wait no longer. Garfield was scheduled to leave that day for Williams College, his alma mater, to deliver a commencement address. With his revolver in his pocket, Guiteau set out for the Baltimore and Potomac Railroad depot. As Garfield walked toward the train, Guiteau ran up behind him and fired two shots, hitting the President in the arm and lower back. "My God! What is that?" cried Garfield as he fell, partly conscious, to the depot floor.

An alert policeman arrested Guiteau immediately. In his pocket was the gun, and in the railway station, where he had left them for later discovery, were a copy of his book, *The Truth,* a biographical sketch for the convenience of the newspapers, and a letter addressed "To the White House," dated July 2. "The President's death," the letter stated, "was a sad necessity, but it will unite the Republican party and save the Republic. Life is a fleeting dream, and it matters little when one goes. A human life is of small value."

Taken to the White House, Garfield lay gravely ill throughout the summer as doctors probed unsuccessfully to find the bullet that had entered his back. Day by day this once powerful man wasted away, ravaged by internal infection. On September 19, 1881, eighty days after the shooting, he died.

Americans were horrified by the assassination. Many people assumed it was the work of a madman. Garfield himself thought Guiteau must be crazy. There was no other explanation.

Madman. Crazy. These were deceptively simple words in the 1880s when little was known about the mind and mental illness. In the weeks following the shooting, professionals in the developing field of psychology took a deep interest in Guiteau and his impending trial. Guiteau was likely, it seemed, to plead not guilty by reason of insanity. But much of the public viewed such a plea as the "insanity dodge," and American psychiatry itself was sharply divided over the proper definition of insanity and criminal responsibility.

In 1881 most psychologists agreed that mental illness was a physical disease, but one that could be caused by emotional pressures. They differed, however, over the interpretation of the *symptoms* of mental illness. So-called conservative psychologists like John P. Gray, the influential editor of the *American Journal of Insanity*, played down the emotional and behaviorial symptoms. Liberal psychologists, like Edward C. Spitzka, trained in Germany, stressed their importance.

The insanity defense often hinged on a defendant's previous record. If the record showed criminal activity, then it was believed that the crime at issue in the trial resulted most likely from evil impulses, not mental illness. If it showed, however, a blameless life (Guiteau, for example, boasted that he neither smoked nor drank), then the crime was thought to result from a disease that led to mental illness. Trials involving an insanity defense often became lengthy sessions in "competitive biography," as opposing psychiatrists recited the telling factors in the defendant's life and family background.

Guiteau's trial (the sketch opposite shows the defendant entertaining the jury with a comic story) became a test of the era's conflicting theories of mental illness. From the outset, government attorneys stressed the M'Naghten Rule, a legal rule that held a defendant responsible if he understood the nature of his act and knew it to be against the law. The prosecutors claimed that Guiteau's self-seeking motives and methodical planning could not be the products of a fevered, disordered mind.

The defense called eight psychiatrists, Spitzka among them, to the stand. Seven had little effect on the jury, but Spitzka was different. After examining Guiteau, he concluded that the defendant was, beyond all doubt, insane. "I concluded that I had an insane man to deal with on sight, before I asked him any questions. He has got the insane manner as well marked as I have ever seen it in an asylum." Guiteau's illness was hereditary, Spitzka testified, and very likely his brain from birth had unequal sides.

Taken aback by Spitzka's testimony, the prosecution called a flood of rebuttal witnesses to attest to Guiteau's sanity. Gray himself took the stand in the trial's final days and reported on a two-day interview with Guiteau from which he determined that Guiteau was obviously sane. Insanity was not hereditary. It was a physical disease whose symptoms reflected the disease itself, and in Guiteau there was no evidence of brain disease or anything except a sinful, dissolute life.

On January 5, 1882, the trial ended. The jury retired at 4:35 P.M., and at 5:40 it returned with a verdict of guilty. After the legal appeals were exhausted, Guiteau was hanged on June 30, 1882.

Guiteau's death allowed a closer look at the controversy. In apparent verification of Spitzka's theory, the autopsy showed that the left hemisphere of Guiteau's brain was larger than the right. Twentieth-century psychiatrists who have studied the case tend to agree that Guiteau was mentally ill, but by then insanity had become a common legal defense. "There is no such thing as a science of insanity, any more than a science of health," *The Nation*, an influential journal, reported in 1882.

As the years passed, heredity and emotional symptoms became more important in the diagnosis of mental illness. In 1981—one hundred years after Garfield and Guiteau—at the trial of John Hinckley, who shot and wounded President Ronald Reagan, Hinckley was found not guilty by reason of insanity.

When Henry George asked a friend what could be done about the problem of political corruption in American cities, his friend replied: "Nothing! You and I can do nothing at all. . . . We can only wait for evolution. Perhaps in four or five thousand years evolution may have carried men beyond this state of things."

This stress on the slow pace of change reflected the doctrine of Social Darwinism, based on the evolutionary theories of Charles Darwin and the writings of English social philosopher Herbert Spencer. In several influential books Spencer applied Darwinian principles of natural selection to society, combining biology and sociology in a theory of "social selection" that explained human progress. Like animals, society evolved, slowly, by adapting to the environment. The "survival of the fittest"—a term Spencer, not Darwin, invented—preserved the strong and weeded out the weak. "If they are sufficiently complete to live, they *do* live, and it is well they should live. If they are not sufficiently complete to live, they die, and it is best they should die."

Social Darwinism had a number of influential followers in the United States, including William Graham Sumner, a professor of political and social science at Yale University. One of the country's best-known academic figures, Sumner was forceful and eloquent. In writings such as *What Social Classes Owe to Each Other* (1883) and "The Absurd Effort to Make the World Over" (1894), he argued that government action on behalf of the poor or weak interfered in evolution and sapped the species. Reform tampered with the laws of nature. "It is the greatest folly of which a man can be capable to sit down with a slate and pencil to plan out a new social world," Sumner said.

The influence of Social Darwinism on American thinking has been exaggerated, but in the powerful hands of Sumner and others it did influence some journalists, ministers, and policymakers. Between 1877 and the 1890s, however, it came under increasing attack. In fields like religion, economics, politics, literature, and law, thoughtful people raised questions about established conditions and suggested the need for reform.

Read and reread, passed from hand to hand, Henry George's nationwide best-seller, *Progress and Poverty* (1879), led the way to a more critical appraisal of American society in the 1880s and beyond. The book jolted traditional thought. "It was responsible," one historian has said, "for starting along new lines of thinking an amazing number of the men and women" who became leaders of reform.

Born in 1839, the child of a poor Philadelphia family, George had little formal schooling. As a boy he went to sea, then worked as a prospector, printer, and journalist. Self-educated as an economist, he moved to San Francisco in the late 1850s and began to study "the fierce struggle of our civilized life." Disturbed by the depression of the 1870s and labor upheavals like the great railroad strikes of 1877, George saw modern society—rich, complex, with material goods hitherto unknown—as sadly flawed.

"The present century," he wrote "has been marked by a prodigious increase in wealth-producing power. . . . It was natural to expect, and it was expected, that . . . real poverty [would become] a thing of the past." Instead, he argued

it becomes no easier for the masses of our people to make a living. On the contrary, it is becoming harder. The wealthy class is becoming more wealthy; but the poorer class is becoming more dependent. The gulf between the employed and the employer is growing wider; social contrasts are becoming sharper; as liveried carriages appear, so do barefooted children.

George proposed a simple solution. Land formed the basis of wealth; a "single tax" on it, replacing all other taxes, would equalize wealth and raise revenue to help the poor. "Single-tax" clubs sprang up around the country, but George's solution, simplistic and unappealing, had much less impact than his analysis of the problem itself. He raised questions a generation of readers set out to answer.

New Currents in Social Thought

George's emphasis on deprivation in the environment excited a young country lawyer in Ashtabu-

■ *The rich and poor of Victorian America: Mrs. Cornelia Ward Hall and her children (above) and a tenement mother and her children trying to eke out a living by making paper roses (right).*

la, Ohio, Clarence Darrow. Unlike the Social Darwinists, Darrow was sure that criminals were made and not born. They grew out of "the unjust condition of human life." In the mid-1880s he left for Chicago and a forty-year career working to convince people that poverty lay at the root of crime. "There is no such thing as crime as the word is generally understood . . . ," he told a group of startled prisoners in the Cook County jail. "If every man, woman and child in the world had a chance to make a decent, fair, honest living there would be no jails and no lawyers and no courts."

As Darrow rejected the implications of Social Darwinism, in similar fashion did Richard T. Ely and a group of young economists poke holes in traditional economic thought. Fresh from graduate study in Germany, Ely in 1884 attacked classical economics for its dogmatism, simple faith in laissez-faire, and reliance on self-interest as a guide for human conduct. The "younger" economics, he said, must no longer be "a tool in the hands of the greedy and the avaricious for keeping down and oppressing the laboring classes. It does not acknowledge laissez-faire as an excuse for doing nothing while people starve."

Accepting a post at Johns Hopkins University, Ely assigned graduate students to study labor conditions in Baltimore and other cities; one of them, John R. Commons, went on to publish a massive four-volume study, *History of Labour in the United States*. In 1885 Ely led a small band of rebels in founding the American Economic Association, which linked economics to social problems and urged government intervention in economic affairs. Social critic Thorstein Veblen saw economic laws as a mask for human greed. In *The Theory of the Leisure Class* (1899), Veblen analyzed the "predatory wealth" and "conspicuous consumption" of the business class.

Edward Bellamy dreamed of a cooperative society where poverty, greed, and crime no longer existed. A lawyer from western Massachusetts, Bellamy published *Looking Backward, 2000–1887*, in 1887 and became a national reform figure virtually overnight. The novel's protagonist, Julian West, falls asleep in 1887 and awakes in the year 2000. Wide-eyed, he finds himself in a socialist utopia; the government owns the means of production, and citizens share the material rewards. Cooperation, rather than competition, is the watchword.

The world of *Looking Backward* had limits; it was regimented, paternalistic, and filled with the gadgets and material concerns of Bellamy's own day. But it had a dramatic effect on many readers. The book sold at the rate of ten thousand copies a week, and its followers formed Nationalist Clubs to work for its objectives. By 1890 there were such clubs in twenty-seven states, all calling for the nationalization of public utilities and a wider distribution of wealth.

Walter Rauschenbusch, a young Baptist minister, read widely from the writings of Bellamy and George, along with the works of other social reformers. When he took his first church post in Hell's Kitchen, a blighted area of New York City, he soon discovered the weight of the slum environment. "One could hear," he said, "human virtue cracking and crushing all around." In the 1890s Rauschenbusch became a professor at the Rochester Theological Seminary, and he began to expound on the responsibility of organized religion to advance social justice.

Traditional doctrines of Protestantism stressed individual salvation and a better life in the next world, not in this one. Poverty was evidence of sinfulness; the poor had only themselves to blame. "God has intended the great to be great and the little to be little," said Henry Ward Beecher, the country's best-known pastor. Wealth and destitution, suburbs and slums — all formed part of God's plan.

Challenging those traditional doctrines, a number of churches in the 1880s began establishing missions in the city slums. William Dwight Porter Bliss, an Episcopal clergyman, founded the Church of the Carpenter in a working-class district of Boston. Lewis M. Pease worked in the grim Five Points area of New York; Alexander Irvine, a Jewish missionary, lived in a flophouse in the Bowery. Irvine walked his skid row neighborhood every afternoon to lend a hand to those in need. Living among the poor and homeless, the urban missionaries grew impatient with religious doctrines that endorsed the status quo.

Many of the new trends were reflected in an emerging religious philosophy known as the "Social Gospel." As the name suggests, the Social Gospel focused on society as well as individuals, on improving living conditions as well as saving souls. Sermons in Social Gospel churches called upon church members to fulfill their social obligations, and adults met before and after the regular service to discuss social and economic problems. Children were excused from sermons, organized into age groups, and encouraged to make the church a center for social as well as religious activity. Soon, churches included dining halls, gymnasiums, and even theaters.

The most active Social Gospel leader was Washington Gladden, a Congregational minister and prolific writer. Linking Christianity to the social and economic environment, Gladden spent a lifetime working for "social salvation." He saw Christianity as a fellowship of love and the church as a social agency. In *Applied Christianity* (1886) and other writings, he denounced competition, urged an "industrial partnership" between employers and employees, and called for efforts to help the poor.

The Settlement Houses

A growing number of social workers, living in the urban slums, shared Gladden's concern. Like Tweed and Plunkitt, they appreciated the dependency of the poor; unlike them, they wanted to eradicate the conditions that underlay it.

Youthful, idealistic, and mostly middle-class, these social workers took as their model Toynbee Hall, founded in 1884 in the slums of East London. Stanton Coit, a moody and poetic graduate of Amherst College, was the first American to borrow the settlement-house idea; in 1886 he opened the Neighborhood Guild on the Lower East Side of New York. The idea spread swiftly. By 1900 there were over a hundred settlements in the country; five years later there were over two hundred, and by 1910 more than four hundred.

The settlements included Jane Addams' famous Hull House in Chicago (1889); Robert A. Woods' South End House in Boston (1892); and Lillian Wald's Henry Street Settlement in New York (1893). These reformers wanted to bridge the socioeconomic gap between rich and poor and to bring education, culture, and hope to the slums. They sought to create in the heart of the city the values and sense of community of small-town America. Of settlement workers, Wald said in *The House on Henry Street* (1915): "We were to live in a neighborhood . . . identify ourselves with it socially, and, in brief, contribute to it our citizenship."

Many of the settlement workers were women, some of them college graduates who found that society had little use for their talents and energy. Jane Addams, a graduate of Rockford College in Illinois, opened Hull House on South Halsted Street in the heart of the Chicago slums. Twenty-nine years old, endowed with a forceful and winning personality, she intended "to share the lives of the poor" and humanize the industrial city. "American ideals," she said, "crumbled under the overpowering poverty of the overcrowded city."

Occupying an old rundown mansion, Hull House had a "plainness that just escaped barrenness and just touched the artistic." Its staff stressed education, offering classes in elementary English and Shakespeare, lectures on ethics and the history of art, and courses in cooking, sewing, and manual skills. Hull House had university extension classes for college credit; John Dewey and Frank Lloyd Wright lectured there. Gradually it expanded to occupy a dozen buildings sprawling over more than a city block.

Like settlement workers in other cities, Addams and her colleagues studied the immigrants in nearby tenements. Laboriously they identified the background of every family in a one-third square mile area around Hull House. Finding people of eighteen different nationalities, they taught them American history and the English language, yet also encouraged them—through folk festivals and art—to preserve their heritage.

In Boston, Robert Woods of South End House focused on the problem of school dropouts. He offered manual training, formed clubs to get young people off the streets, and established a cheap restaurant where the hungry could eat. Lillian Wald, the daughter of a wealthy family and herself a graduate nurse, concentrated on providing health care for the poor. In 1898 the first Catholic-run settlement house opened in New York, and in 1900 Bronson House opened in Los Angeles to work in the Mexican-American community.

Florence Kelley, a spirited young graduate of Cornell, taught night school one winter in Chicago. Watching children break under the burden of poverty, she devoted her life to the problem of child labor. Convinced of the need for political activism, she worked with Addams and others to push through the Illinois Factory Act of 1893, which prohibited the employment of children under the age of fourteen for longer than eight hours a day.

A Crisis in Social Welfare

When the depression of 1893 struck (see chapter 20), it jarred the young settlement workers, many

■ *The first public playground in Chicago was started by Hull House in 1893. Medical care and day care nurseries were among the services offered at Hull House.*

of whom had just begun their work. Addams and the Hull House workers helped form the Chicago Bureau of Charities to coordinate emergency relief. Kelley, recently appointed the chief factory inspector of Illinois, worked even harder to end child labor, and in 1899 she moved to New York City to head the National Consumers League, which marshaled the buying power of women to encourage employers to provide better working conditions.

In cities and towns across the country traditional methods of helping the needy foundered in the crisis. Churches, Charity Organization Societies, and Community Chests did what they could, but their resources were limited, and they functioned on traditional lines. Many of them still tried to reform rather than aid individual families, and people were often reluctant to call on them for help.

Gradually, a new class of professional social workers arose to fill the need. Unlike the church and charity volunteers, these social workers wanted not only to feed the poor but to study their condition and alleviate it. Revealingly they called themselves "case workers" and daily collected data on the income, housing, jobs, health, and habits of the poor. Prowling tenement districts, they gathered information about the number of rooms, number of occupants, ventilation, and sanitation, putting together a fund of useful data.

Chronology

1862 Morrill Land Grant gives land to states for establishment of colleges

1869 Rutgers and Princeton play in nation's first intercollegiate football game
Cincinnati Red Stockings, baseball's first professional team, organized

1873 Comstock Law bans obscene articles from U.S. mail
Nation's first kindergarten opens in Saint Louis, Missouri

1874 Women's Christian Temperance Union formed to crusade against evils of liquor

1876 Johns Hopkins University opens first separate graduate school

1879 Henry George analyzes problems of urbanizing America in *Progress and Poverty*
Salvation Army arrives in United States

1880 Polish National Alliance formed to help Polish immigrants adjust to life in America

1881 Booker T. Washington opens Tuskegee Institute in Alabama
Dr. John H. Kellogg advises parents to teach their children about sex in *Plain Facts for Old and Young*

1883 Metropolitan Opera opens in New York

1885 Home Insurance Building, country's first metal-frame structure, erected in Chicago
American Economic Association formed to advocate government intervention in economic affairs

1887 Edward Bellamy promotes idea of socialist utopia in *Looking Backward, 2000–1887*

1889 Jane Addams opens Hull House in Chicago

1890 National American Woman Suffrage Association formed to work for women's right to vote

1894 Immigration Restriction League formed to limit immigration from southern and eastern Europe

1896 Supreme Court decision in *Plessy* v. *Ferguson* establishes constitutionality of "separate but equal" facilities
John Dewey's Laboratory School for testing and practice of new educational theory opens at University of Chicago

---

Studies of the poor popped up everywhere. Walter Wyckoff, a graduate of Princeton University, embarked in 1891 on what he called "an experiment in reality." For eighteen months he worked as an unskilled laborer in jobs from Connecticut to California. "I am vastly ignorant of the labor problems and am trying to learn by experience," he said as he set out. After working as a ditch digger, farmhand, and logger, Wyckoff summarized his findings in *The Workers* (1897), a book immediately hailed as a major contribution to sociology.

To investigate living issues, Wyckoff felt, one must investigate life, and so many others followed his example that sometimes it seemed the observers outnumbered those being observed. Lillian Pettengill took a job as a domestic servant to see "the ups and downs of this particular dog-life from the dog's end of the chain." Others became street beggars, miners, lumberjacks, and factory laborers. Bessie and Marie Van Vorst's *The Woman Who Toils: Being the Experiences of Two Gentlewomen as Factory Girls* (1903) studied female workers, as did Helen Campbell's *Women Wage-Earners: Their Past, Their Present and Their Future* (1893), which suggested that the conditions of factory employment prepared women mainly "for the hospital, the workhouse, and the prison."

William T. Stead, a prominent British editor, visited the Chicago World's Fair in 1893 and stayed to examine the city. He roamed the flophouses and tenements and dropped in at Hull House to drink hot chocolate and talk over conditions with Jane Addams. Later he wrote an influential book *If Christ Came to Chicago* (1894), and in a series of mass meetings during 1893, he called for a civic revival. In response, Chicagoans formed the Civic Federation, a group of forty leaders who aimed to make Chicago "the best governed, the healthiest city in this country." Setting up task forces for philanthropy, moral improvement, and legislation, the new group helped spawn the National Civic Federation (1900), a nationwide organization devoted to reform of urban life.

"The United States was born in the country and moved to the city," historian Richard Hofstadter said. Much of that movement occurred during the nineteenth century when the United

States was the most rapidly urbanizing nation in the western world. American cities bustled with energy; they absorbed millions of migrants from Europe and other parts of the world. That migration, and the urban growth that accompanied it, reshaped American politics and culture.

By 1920 the census showed that, for the first time, most Americans lived in cities. By then, too, almost half the population was descended from people who arrived after the American Revolution. As European, African, and Asian cultures met in the American city, a culturally pluralistic society emerged. Dozens of nationalities produced a hyphenated culture whose members considered themselves Polish-Americans, Afro-Americans, and Irish-Americans. The melting pot sometimes melted, but it only partially blended.

"Ah, Vera," said a character in Israel Zangwill's popular play, *The Melting Pot* (1908), "what is the glory of Rome and Jerusalem where all nations and races come to worship and look back, compared with the glory of America, where all races and nations come to labour and look forward!" Critics scorned the play as "romantic claptrap," and indeed it was. But the metaphor of the melting pot clearly depicted a new national image. In the decades after the 1870s a jumble of ethnic and racial groups responded to the challenges of industrialization and urbanization.

Recommended Reading

On urban America, see Sam Bass Warner, Jr.: *Streetcar Suburbs* (1962) and *The Urban Wilderness* (1972). Arthur M. Schlesinger, *The Rise of the City, 1878–1898* (1933) is a pioneering study; Blake McKelvey, *The Urbanization of America, 1860–1915* (1963); Constance M. Green, *The Rise of Urban America* (1965); and Howard P. Chudacoff, *The Evolution of American Urban Society*, rev. ed. (1981) are also valuable.

Russel B. Nye, *The Unembarrassed Muse: The Popular Arts in America* (1970), covers popular culture; Neil Harris, *Humbug: The Art of P. T. Barnum* (1973), is superb on both Barnum and the era. For family life, see Carl N. Degler, *At Odds: Women and the Family in America from the Revolution to the Present* (1980); Joseph Kett, *Rites of Passage: Adolescence in America* (1977); and Tamara K. Hareven and Maris Vinovskis, eds., *Family and Population in Nineteenth Century America* (1978). For education, see L. A. Cremin, *The Transformation of the School: Progressivism in American Education, 1876–1956* (1961); Lawrence Veysey, *The Emergence of the American University* (1965); and

David B. Tyack, *The One Best System: A History of American Urban Education* (1974).

Oscar Handlin, *The Uprooted*, 2d ed. (1973) and John Higham, *Strangers in the Land: Patterns of American Nativism* (1955) are classic studies. Robert H. Bremner, *From the Depths: The Discovery of Poverty in the United States* (1956); Allen F. Davis, *Spearheads for Reform: The Social Settlements and the Progressive Movement, 1890–1914* (1967); and *American Heroine: The Life and Legend of Jane Addams* (1973), also by Allen F. Davis, examine urban reform.

Treatments of intellectual currents include Richard Hofstadter, *Social Darwinism in American Thought*, rev. ed. (1955); Sidney Fine, *Laissez Faire and the General Welfare State* (1956); and Eric F. Goldman, *Rendezvous with Destiny* (1952).

Additional Bibliography

Robert H. Walker, *Life in the Age of Enterprise, 1865–1900* (1967), examines everyday life. On leisure and entertainment, see Gunther Barth, *City People* (1980); Harold Seymour, *Baseball*, 2 vols. (1960–1971); Foster R. Dulles, *America Learns to Play* (1966); and Ronald L. Davis, *A History of Music in American Life*, vol. 2: *The Gilded Years, 1865–1920* (1980). David J. Pivar, *Purity Crusade: Sexual Morality and Social Control, 1868–1900* (1973); Susan Estabrook Kennedy, *If All We Did Was To Weep At Home: A History of White Working Class Women in America* (1979); Barbara Mayer Wertheimer, *We Were There: The Story of Working Women in America* (1977); and Lois W. Banner, *Women in Modern America: A Brief History* (1974), are helpful.

On education, see Sidney Hook, *John Dewey* (1939); Frederick Rudolph, *The American College and University* (1962); C. W. Dabney, *Universal Education in the South* (1936); Donald Spivey, *Schooling for the New Slavery: Black Industrial Education, 1868–1915* (1978); and Louis R. Harlan, *Booker T. Washington: The Making of a Black Leader, 1865–1901* (1972).

For immigration and urban growth, consult Barbara Solomon, *Ancestors and Immigrants* (1956); Josef J. Barton, *Peasants and Strangers: Italians, Rumanians, and Slovaks in an American City* (1975); Leonard Dinnerstein, Roger L. Nichols, and David M. Reimers, *Natives and Strangers* (1979); Moses Rischin, *The Promised City: New York's Jews* (1962); David Ward, *Cities and Immigrants* (1971); Thomas L. Philpott, *The Slum and the Ghetto* (1978); William A. Bullough, *The Blind Boss and His City* (1979); and Leo Hershkowitz, *Tweed's New York: Another Look* (1977).

See also Dorothy Rose Blumberg, *Florence Kelley: The Making of a Social Pioneer* (1971); Roy M. Lubove, *The Progressives and the Slums: Tenement House Reform in New York City* (1962); Martin J. Schiesl, *The Politics of Efficiency: Municipal Administration and Reform in America* (1977); Henry F. May, *Protestant Churches and Industrial America* (1949); and R. C. White, Jr., and C. H. Hopkins, *The Social Gospel: Religion and Reform in Changing America* (1976).

chapter 20

POLITICAL REALIGNMENTS AND THE DECADE OF DECISION: THE 1890s

In mid-February 1893, panic suddenly hit the New York stock market. In one day investors dumped a million shares of a leading company, the Philadelphia and Reading Railroad, and it went bankrupt. Business investment dropped sharply in the railroad and construction industries, touching off the worst economic downturn to that point in the country's history.

Frightened, people hurriedly sold stocks and other assets to buy gold. The overwhelming demand depleted the gold reserve of the United States Treasury. Eroding almost daily in March 1893, the Treasury's reserve slumped toward the $100 million mark, an amount that stood for the government's commitment to maintain the gold standard. On April 22, for the first time since the 1870s, it fell below $100 million.

The news shattered business confidence—the stock market broke. On Wednesday, May 3, railroad and industrial stocks plummeted, and the next day several major firms went bankrupt.

When the market opened on Friday, crowds filled the galleries, anticipating a panic. Within minutes, leading stocks plunged to record lows, and there was pandemonium on the floor and in the streets outside. May 5, 1893, Wall Street's worst day until the Great Crash of 1929, became "Industrial Black Friday," "a day of terrible strain long remembered on the market."

Afterward, banks cut back on loans. Unable to get capital, businesses failed at an average rate of two dozen a day during the month of May. "The papers are full of failures—banks are breaking all over the country, and there is a tremendous contraction of credits and hoarding of money going on everywhere," an observer noted. On July 26 the Erie Railroad, one of the leading names in railroading history, failed.

August 1893 was the worst month. Across the country factories and mines shut down. In Orange, New Jersey, Thomas A. Edison, the symbol of the country's ingenuity, laid off 240 employees

■ *A run on a New York City bank during the Panic of 1893 (left). In Chicago the economic downturn and the Pullman strike forced many of the poor to live in hastily thrown-together shantytowns (right).*

at the Edison Phonograph Works. On August 15 the Northern Pacific Railroad went bankrupt; the Union Pacific and the Santa Fe soon followed. Some economists estimated unemployment at 2 million people or nearly 15 percent of the labor force.

"There are thousands of homeless and starving men in the streets," reported a young journalist in Chicago. "I have seen more misery in this last week than I ever saw in my life before." Charity societies and churches tried to help, but they could not handle the huge numbers of needy in the cities, and they did not even reach the farms. Susan Orcutt, a farm woman from Kansas, wrote in June 1894: "I take my pen in hand to let you know we are starving. . . . My husband went away to find work and came home last night and told me that he would have to starve. He has been in 10 counties and did not get no work. . . . I haven't had nothing to eat today and it is 3 o'clock."

Continuing through 1897, the depression was the decisive event of the decade. At its height, three million people were unemployed. The human costs were enormous, even among the well-to-do. "They were for me years of simple Hell," shattering "my whole scheme of life," said Charles Francis Adams, the descendant of two American presidents. "I was sixty-three years old and a tired man when at last the effects of the 1893 convulsion wore themselves out."

Thanks to city lights and new entertainment, the decade became known as the Gay Nineties, but it was hardly that. When it was over, prosperity had returned, and the United States had crushed Spain in a brief and popular war (see chapter 21). Yet the depression had profound and lasting effects. Attitudes changed and ideas were reshaped in many fields, above all in politics. A realignment of the American political system, which had been developing since the end of Reconstruction, finally reached its fruition in the 1890s, establishing new patterns that lasted well into the twentieth century.

Politics of Stalemate

Electoral politics was a major fascination of the Gilded Age, its mass entertainment and favorite sport. There were few other distractions, and politics was the arena for action and reform. Millions of Americans read party newspapers, listened to three-hour speeches by party leaders, and in elections turned out in enormous numbers to vote. In the six presidential elections from 1876 to 1896, an average of almost 79 percent of the electorate voted, a higher percentage than voted before or after.

White males made up the bulk of the electorate; until after the turn of the century women could vote in national elections only in Wyoming, Utah, Idaho, and Colorado. The National Woman Suffrage Association early sued for the vote, but in 1875 the Supreme Court (*Minor* v. *Happersett*) upheld the power of the states to deny this right to women. On several occasions Congress refused to pass a constitutional amendment for woman's suffrage, and between 1870 and 1910 nearly a dozen states defeated referenda to grant women the vote.

Black men were increasingly kept from the polls. In 1877 Georgia adopted the poll tax to make voters pay an annual tax for the right to vote. The technique, aimed at impoverished blacks, was quickly copied across the South. In 1882 South Carolina adopted the "eight box" law, also copied elsewhere, that required ballots for separate offices to be placed in separate boxes, a difficult task for illiterate voters.

In 1890 Mississippi required voters to be able to read and interpret the federal Constitution to the satisfaction of registration officials, all of them white. Eight years later Louisiana adopted the famous "grandfather clause," demanding a literacy test for all voters except the sons and grandsons of those who had voted in the state before 1867—a time, of course, when no blacks could vote. The number of black voters decreased dramatically. In 1896 there were 130,334 registered black voters in Louisiana; in 1904 there were 1342.

The Party Deadlock

The 1870s and '80s were still dominated by the Civil War generation, the unusual group of people who rose to power in the turbulent 1850s. In both the North and South they had ruled longer than most generations, with a consciousness that the war experience had set them apart. Five of the six presidents elected between 1865 and 1900 had served in the war, as had many civic, business, and religious leaders. In 1890 there were well over a million veterans of the Union army still alive, and Confederate veterans numbered in the hundreds of thousands.

Party loyalties—rooted in Civil War traditions, ethnic and religious differences, and perhaps class distinctions—were remarkably strong. Voters clung to their old parties, shifts were infrequent, and there were relatively few "independent" voters. Although linked to the defeated Confederacy, the Democrats revived quickly after the war. In 1874 they gained control of the House of Representatives, which they maintained for all but four of the succeeding twenty years. The Democrats rested on a less sectional base than did the Republicans. While identification with civil rights and military rule cut Republican strength in the South, the Democratic party's principles of states' rights, decentralization, and limited government won supporters everywhere.

If Democrats offered "the master-wisdom of governing little," the Republicans pursued policies in which local interests merged into nationwide patterns, and government became an instrument to promote moral and material wealth. The Republicans passed the Homestead Act (1862), granted subsidies to the transcontinental railroads, and pushed other measures to encourage economic growth. They enacted legislation and constitutional amendments to protect civil rights. They advocated a high protective tariff as a tool of economic policy, to keep out foreign products while "infant industries" grew.

In national elections, sixteen states, mostly in New England and the North, consistently voted Republican; fourteen states, mostly in the South, consistently voted Democratic. Elections, therefore, depended on a handful of "doubtful" states, which could swing elections either way. These states—New York, New Jersey, Connecticut, Ohio, Indiana, and Illinois—received special attention at election time. Politicians lavished money and time on them; presidential candidates usually came from them. From 1868 to 1912 eight of the nine Republican presidential candidates and six of the seven Democratic candidates came from the "doubtful" states, especially New York and Ohio.

The two parties were evenly matched, and elections were closely fought. In three of the five presidential elections from 1876 to 1892, the victor won by less than 1 percent of the vote; in 1876 and 1888 the losing candidates actually had more popular votes than the winners but lost in the electoral college. Knowing that small mistakes could lose elections, politicians became extremely cautious; it was difficult to govern. Only twice during these years did one party control both the presidency and the two houses of Congress—the Republicans in 1888 and the Democrats in 1892.

Historians once believed that politicians accomplished little between 1877 and 1900, but they were looking in the wrong location. With the impeachment of Andrew Johnson, the authority of the presidency dwindled in relation to congressional strength. For the first time in many years attention shifted away from Washington itself. North and South, people who were weary of the centralization brought on by war and Reconstruction looked first to state and local governments to deal with issues.

Experiments in the States

Across the country, state bureaus and commissions were established to regulate the new industrial society. Commodities shippers, especially farmers and merchants, in protest against the railroads' policies of rate discrimination and other corrupt practices—bribes and free passes given to public officials in exchange for favors—turned to the states for government action. In 1869 Massachusetts established the first commission to oversee the railroads; by 1900 twenty-eight states had taken such action. Most of the early commissions were advisory in nature; they collected statistics and published reports on rates and practices—serving, one commissioner said, "as a sort of lens" to focus public attention. Impatient with the results, legislatures in the Midwest and on the Pacific Coast established commissions with greater powers to fix rates, outlaw rebates, and investigate rate discrimination. These commissions, experimental in nature, served as models for later policy at the federal level.

Illinois had one of the most thoroughgoing provisions. Responding to local merchants who

"WHITE CITY" THE COLUMBIAN EXPOSITION OF 1893

On May 1, 1893, the World's Columbian Exposition opened in Chicago. A focal event of the decade, the Exposition commemorated the four-hundredth anniversary of Columbus' voyage to the New World. It also celebrated modern industrial progress and featured the latest mechanical inventions in acres of white plaster buildings modeled on Greek and Roman patterns. Called the White City, the Exposition cost $31 million and attracted twenty-seven million visitors.

Artists, architects, and engineers flocked to Chicago to participate in its creation. In contrast to the normal jumble of urban growth, the Exposition offered one of the first examples of a planned city. Ten leading architects set out to design it. Frederic Law Olmstead, the designer of New York's famed Central Park, produced his last major public landscape for it, a large lagoon and park along Lake Michigan. It touched off city-planning and "city-beautiful" movements that affected cities as far apart as Washington, Manila, and San Francisco. Chicago transformed itself under the farsighted Chicago Plan (1907–1909) of Daniel H. Burnham, one of the Exposition's chief architects. "City-beautiful" designers integrated transportation, sanitation, and urban architecture in a more "human" city; parks, playgrounds, and tree-lined boulevards proliferated.

The Grand Court at Night. *The Administration Building looms above the gondolas and illuminated fountains that shimmer in the lagoon at the main entrance to the Fair.*

Visitors stroll amid parkways, islands, commemorative columns, and shining white palaces mirrored in wide lagoons.

Louis Sullivan's Transportation Building. *Unique in its deviation from the Fair's classic style of porticoes and pillars.*

The Palace of Electricity. *Many fairgoers saw their first electric lamp here—a great pillar of light studded with colored globes that flashed kaleidoscopic patterns.*

Machinery Hall. *Bethlehem Iron Works' full-sized model of a 125-ton steam hammer, the largest in the world.*

Opening day attracted a crowd of two hundred thousand strong, eager to see the marvels. Jane Addams' purse was snatched; the crowd on the Midway saw the first Ferris wheel, commissioned as a feat of American engineering to rival the recently erected Eiffel Tower in Paris; visitors tasted the first grapefruit brought in on refrigerated railroad cars from Florida and California; American Bell Telephone, a fast-growing young company, offered the first long-distance calls to New York and Boston; Edison showed his latest phonographs and, more fascinating, his new Kinetoscope, a peep-show device that ran short motion pictures on the just-invented celluloid film. (The first Kinetoscope parlor opened the next month on Broadway in New York.)

Machinery at the Exposition went far beyond the famous Corliss steam engine that had impressed the world at the Philadelphia Exposition only seventeen years earlier. A much more "up-to-date" wonder—the new magic of electricity—generated the power for the marvels of machinery exhibited in Chicago. For the first time, visitors saw the electric dynamo and George Westinghouse's alternating-current generator. The Westinghouse Company tucked Edison's incandescent light bulbs in every nook and cranny. Opening the Exposition, President Grover Cleveland touched an ivory telegraph key and the electric current unfurled flags, lit ten thousand electric lights, and started engines throughout the grounds of the fair. In Machinery Hall, the thirty-seven steam engines started at once, producing, in a reporter's words, "a sound that will thrill every observer."

The Exposition represented "the transformation of power into beauty," one onlooker said. Elaborate in its symbolism, the White City celebrated social harmony, the union of architects, engineers, inventors, businessmen, and laborers to create the industrial society. It fused timeless classical forms with the turbulent progress of the new civilization.

For a dazzling moment in Chicago an era paid homage to its accomplishments. A moment was all it had. Three days after the opening ceremonies, the stock market broke, rallied, then broke again. The American economy, so lovingly celebrated by the White City in Chicago, was about to collapse into the worst depression in the history of the nation.

Midway Plaisance. *A favorite with visitors, the entertainment area of the Fair featured foreign villages where a babel of tongues could be heard. When feet gave out, wheeled chairs and "pushers" were available to drive people around.*

Ferris Wheel. *A 264-foot high wheel. Each glass car held sixty passengers. Several couples tried unsuccessfully to get married on the top car!*

Little Egypt. *She scored a triumph on the Midway despite debate about "whether the customs of Cairo would undermine the morals of the public."*

Phoenix House. *This exquisite small Japanese structure, erected by workmen sent by the emperor of Japan, influenced young American architects, notably Frank Lloyd Wright, whose "prairie style" incorporated features of Japanese architecture.*

This cartoon, entitled "The Scourge of the West" (1885) satirizes railroad monopolists. The robber baron astride his iron horse brandishes his weapons—land grants and federal funds—and shoots down workers and farmers.

were upset with existing railroad rate policies, the Illinois state constitution of 1870 declared railroads to be public highways and authorized the legislature to pass laws establishing maximum rates and preventing rate discrimination. In the important case of *Munn* v. *Illinois* (1877), the Supreme Court upheld the Illinois legislation, declaring that private property "affected with the public interest . . . must submit to being controlled by the public for the common good."

But the Court soon weakened that judgment. In the *Wabash* case of 1886 (*Wabash, St. Louis, & Pacific Railway Co.* v. *Illinois*), it narrowed the *Munn* rule and held that states could not regulate commerce extending beyond their borders. Only Congress could. The *Wabash* decision spurred Congress to pass the Interstate Commerce Act (1887), which created the Interstate Commerce Commission to investigate and oversee railroad activities. The act outlawed rebates and pooling agreements, and the ICC became the prototype of the federal commissions that today regulate many parts of the economy.

Reestablishing Presidential Power

Johnson's impeachment, the scandals of the Grant administrations, and the controversy surrounding the 1876 election (see chapter 16) weakened the presidency. During the last two decades of the nineteenth century presidents fought to reassert their authority, and by 1900, under William McKinley, they had succeeded to a remarkable degree. The late 1890s, in fact, marked the birth of the modern powerful presidency.

Rutherford B. Hayes entered the White House with his title clouded by the disputed election of 1876 (see chapter 16). Opponents called him "His Fraudulency" and "Rutherfraud B. Hayes," but soon he began to reassert the authority of the presidency. Hayes worked for reform in the civil service, placed well-known reformers in high offices, and ordering the last troops out of South Carolina and Louisiana, ended military Reconstruction. He hoped to revive the Republican party in the South by persuading business-oriented ex-Whigs to join a national party that would support their economic interests more effectively than the Democrats did. In this attempt, however, he failed. Committed to the gold standard—the only basis, Hayes thought, of a sound currency—in 1878 he vetoed the Bland–Allison Silver Purchase bill, which called for the partial coinage of silver, but Congress passed it over his veto.

James A. Garfield, a Union army hero and long-time member of Congress, succeeded Hayes. Winning by a handful of votes in 1880, he took office energetically, determined to unite the Republican party (which had been split by personality differences and disagreement over policy to-

The Election of 1880			
Candidate	Party	Popular Vote	Electoral Vote
Garfield	Republican	4,446,158	214
Hancock	Democrat	4,444,260	155
Weaver	Greenback	305,997	0

ward the tariff and the South) lower the tariff to reduce surplus revenues, and assert American economic and strategic interests in Latin America. Ambitious and eloquent, Garfield had looked forward to the presidency, yet within a few weeks he said to friends: "My God! What is there in this place that a man should ever want to get into it?"

Office seekers, hordes of them, evoked Garfield's anguish. Each one wanted a government job, and each one thought nothing of cornering the President on every occasion. The problem of government jobs also provoked a bitter fight with the powerful senator from New York, Roscoe Conkling, who resented some of Garfield's choices. On the verge of victory over Conkling, Garfield planned to leave Washington on July 2, 1881, for a vacation in New England. Walking toward his train, he was shot in the back by Charles J. Guiteau, a deranged lawyer and disappointed office seeker (see the special feature in chapter 19). Suffering through the summer, Garfield succumbed on September 19, 1881, and Vice-President Chester A. Arthur—an ally of Senator Conkling—became president.

Arthur was a better president than many had expected. Deftly he established his independence of Conkling. Conservative in outlook, he reversed Garfield's foreign policy initiatives in Latin America, but he approved the construction of the modern American navy. Arthur worked to lower the tariff, and in 1883, with his backing, Congress passed the Pendleton Act to reform the civil service. In part a reaction against Garfield's assassination, the act created a bipartisan Civil Service Commission to administer competitive examinations and appoint officeholders on the basis of merit.

In the election of 1884 Grover Cleveland, the Democratic governor of New York, narrowly defeated Republican nominee James G. Blaine, largely because of the continuing divisions in the Republican party. The first Democratic president

since 1861, Cleveland was slow and ponderous, known for his honesty, stubbornness, and hard work. His term in the White House from 1885 to 1889 reflected the Democratic party's desire to curtail federal activities. Cleveland vetoed over two thirds of the bills presented to him, more than all his predecessors combined.

The Election of 1884			
Candidate	Party	Popular Vote	Electoral Vote
Cleveland	Democrat	4,874,621	219
Blaine	Republican	4,848,936	182
Butler	Greenback	175,096	0
St. John	Prohibition	147,482	0

Forthright and sincere, he brought a new respectability to a Democratic party still tainted by its link with secession. Working long into the night, he reviewed veterans' pensions and civil service appointments. He continued Arthur's naval construction program and forced railroad, lumber, and cattle companies to surrender millions of acres of fraudulently occupied public domain. Late in 1887 he devoted his annual message to an attack on the tariff, "the vicious, inequitable, and illogical source of unnecessary taxation," and committed himself and the Democratic party to lower the tariff.

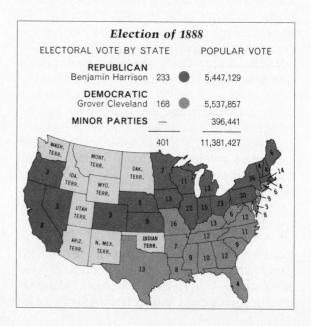

Election of 1888

	ELECTORAL VOTE BY STATE		POPULAR VOTE
REPUBLICAN Benjamin Harrison	233		5,447,129
DEMOCRATIC Grover Cleveland	168		5,537,857
MINOR PARTIES	—		396,441
	401		11,381,427

The Republicans accused him of undermining American industries, and in 1888 they nominated for the presidency Benjamin Harrison, a defender of the tariff. Cleveland garnered 90,000 more popular votes than Harrison but won the electoral votes of only two northern states and the South. Harrison won the rest of the North, most of the "doubtful" states, and the election.

Republicans in Power: The Billion-Dollar Congress

Despite Harrison's narrow margin, the election of 1888 was the most sweeping victory for either party in almost twenty years; it gave the Republicans the presidency and both houses of Congress. Eager to block Republican-sponsored laws, the Democrats in Congress used minority tactics, especially the "disappearing quorum" rule, which let members of the House of Representatives join in debate but then refuse to answer the roll call to determine if a quorum was present.

For two months the Democrats used the rule to bring Congress to a halt. The Republicans grew angry and impatient. On January 29, 1890, they fell two votes short of a quorum, and Speaker of the House Thomas B. Reed, a crusty veteran of Maine politics, made congressional history. "The Chair," he said, "directs the Clerk to record the following names of members present and refusing to vote." Democrats shouted "Czar! Czar!" a title that stuck to Reed for the rest of his life. Tumult continued for days, but in mid-February 1890 the Republicans adopted the Reed rules and proceeded to enact the party's program.

Tariffs, Trusts, and Silver

As if a dam had burst, law after law poured out of the Republican Congress during 1890. The Republicans passed the McKinley Tariff Act, which raised tariff duties about 4 percent, higher than ever before; it also included a novel reciprocity provision that allowed the president to lower duties if other countries did the same. In addition, the act used duties to promote new industries, like tinplate for packaging the new "canned" foods appearing on grocery-store shelves. A De-pendent Pensions Act granted pensions to Civil War veterans, their widows, and children. The pensions were modest—$6 to $12 a month—but the number of pensioners doubled by 1893, when nearly one million individuals received about $160 million in pensions.

The Republicans also passed the Sherman Antitrust Act, the first federal attempt to regulate big business. As the initial attempt to deal with the problem of trusts and industrial growth, the act shaped all later antitrust policy. It declared illegal "every contract, combination in the form of trust or otherwise, or conspiracy, in restraint of trade or commerce." Penalties for violation were stiff, including fines and imprisonment and the dissolution of guilty trusts. Experimental in nature, the act's terms were often vague and left precise interpretation to later experience and the courts.

One of the most important laws Congress has passed, the Sherman Antitrust Act made the United States virtually the only industrial nation to regulate business combinations. It tried to harness big business without harming it. The Supreme Court crippled the act in *U.S.* v. *E. C. Knight Co.* (1895), ruling that it applied only to commerce and not to manufacturing. But after the turn of the century it gained fresh power.

Another measure, the Sherman Silver Purchase Act, tried to end the troublesome problem of silver. As one of the two precious metals, silver had once played a large role in currencies around the world, but by the mid-1800s, it had slipped into disuse. With the discovery of the great bonanza mines in Nevada (see chapter 17), American silver production quadrupled between 1870 and 1890, glutting the world market and persuading many European nations to demonetize silver in favor of the scarcer metal, gold. The United States kept a limited form of silver coinage with congressional passage of the Bland-Allison Act in 1878.

Support for silver coinage was especially strong in the South and West, where people thought it might inflate the currency, raise wages and crop prices, and challenge the hated power of the gold-oriented Northeast. Eager to avert the free coinage of silver, which would require the coinage of all silver presented at the United States mints, President Harrison and other Republican leaders pressed for a compromise that took shape in the Sherman Silver Purchase Act of 1890.

The act directed the Treasury to purchase 4.5 million ounces of silver a month and to issue legal tender in the form of Treasury notes in payment for it. The act was a compromise; it satisfied both sides. Opponents of silver were pleased that it did not include free coinage. Silverites, on the other hand, were delighted that the monthly purchases would buy up most of the country's silver production. The Treasury notes, moreover, could be cashed for either gold or silver at the bank, a gesture toward a true bimetallic system based on silver and gold.

As a final measure, Republicans in the House passed a federal elections bill to protect the voting rights of blacks in the South. Although restrained in language and intent, it set off a storm of denunciation among the Democrats, who called it a "force bill" that would station army troops in the South. Because of the outcry, the bill failed in the Senate; it was the last major effort until the 1950s to enforce the Fifteenth Amendment to the Constitution.

The 1890 Elections

The Republican Congress of 1890 was one of the most important Congresses in American history, both because of the number of laws it passed and because many of the laws were so influential in shaping later policy. This Congress also asserted federal authority to a degree the country would not then accept. It passed a record number of significant laws, but the Democrats labeled it the "Billion-Dollar Congress" for spending that much in appropriations and grants.

"This is a billion-dollar country," Speaker Reed replied, but the voters disagreed. The 1890 elections crushed the Republicans, who lost seventy-eight seats in the House, an extraordinary loss. The elections also crushed Republicans in the Midwest where, again enlarging government authority, they had passed state laws prohibiting the sale of alcoholic beverages, requiring the closing of businesses on Sunday, and mandating the use of English in the public schools. Roman Catholics, German Lutherans, and other groups resented such laws, and they angrily deserted the Republicans.

Political veterans went down to defeat, and new leaders vaulted into sudden prominence.

Nebraska elected a Democratic governor for the first time in its history. The state of Iowa, once so staunchly Republican that a local leader had predicted that "Iowa will go Democratic when Hell goes Methodist," went Democratic in 1890.

The Rise of the Populist Movement

The elections of 1890 drew attention to a fast-growing movement among farmers that soon came to be known far and wide as Populism. The movement had begun rather quietly, in places distant from normal centers of attention, and for a time it went almost unnoticed in the press. But during the summer of 1890 wagonloads of farm families in the South and West converged on campgrounds and picnic areas to socialize and discuss common problems. They came by the thousands, weary of drought, mortgages, and low crop prices. At the campgrounds they picnicked, talked, and listened to recruiters from an organization called the National Farmers' Alliance and Industrial Union, which promised unified action to solve agricultural problems.

Farmers were joining the Alliance at the rate of a thousand a week; the Kansas Alliance alone claimed 130,000 members in 1890. The summer of 1890 became "that wonderful picnicking, speech-making Alliance summer," a time of fellowship and spirit long remembered by farmers.

The Farm Problem

Farm discontent was a worldwide phenomenon between 1870 and 1900. With the new means of transportation and communication, farmers everywhere were caught up in a complex international market they neither controlled nor entirely understood.

American farmers complained bitterly about declining prices for their products, rising railroad rates for shipping them, and burdensome mortgages. Some of the grievances were valid. Farm profits were certainly low; agriculture in general tends to produce low profits because of the ease of entry into the industry. The prices of farm commodities fell between 1865 and 1890—corn sold

Source: U.S. Bureau of the Census, Historical Statistics of the United States, Colonial Times to 1970, Bicentennial Edition, Washington, D.C., 1975.

at sixty-three cents a bushel in 1881 and twenty-eight cents in 1890—but they did not fall as low as did other commodity prices. Farmers received less for their crops, yet their purchasing power increased.

Neither was the farmers' second grievance—rising railroad rates—entirely justified. Railroad rates actually fell during these years, benefiting shippers of all products. Farm mortgages, while certainly burdensome, were common since many farmers mortgaged their property to expand their holdings or buy new farm machinery. Most mortgages were short, with a term of four years or less, after which farmers could renegotiate at new rates, and the new machinery enabled farmers to triple their output and increase their income.

The actual situation varied from area to area and year to year. New England farmers suffered from overworked land; many southern farmers were trapped in the lien system that kept them always in debt. A study of farms in the Midwest between 1860 and 1900 suggests that farm income rose substantially in the 1860s, fell during the devastating depression of the '70s, rose in the '80s, and remained roughly constant in the '90s. There were also large variations in farm profits from county to county, again indicating the absence of clear nationwide patterns. Farmers who had good land close to railroad transportation did well; others did not.

Still, many farmers were sure their condition had declined, and this perception sparked a growing anger. Everyone in the 1870s and '80s seemed excited about factories, not farms. Farmers were now "hayseeds," a word that first appeared in 1889, and they watched their offspring leave for city lights and new careers. Books like *The Spider and the Fly: or, Tricks, Traps, and Pitfalls of City Life by One Who Knows* (1873) warned against such a move, but still the children went. A literature of disillusionment emerged, most notably Hamlin Garland's *Son of the Middle Border* (1890) and *Main-Travelled Roads* (1891) which described the ugliness of farm life.

The Fast-Growing Farmers' Alliance

Originally a social organization for farmers, the Grange lost many of its members as it turned more and more toward politics in the late 1870s. In its place, a multitude of farm societies sprang into existence. By the end of the 1880s they had formed into two major organizations: the National Farmers' Alliance, located on the Plains west of the Mississippi and known as the Northwestern Alliance; and the Farmers' Alliance and Industrial Union, based in the South and known as the Southern Alliance.

■ *The Grange, personified as a farmer, rouses the sleeping citizenry to the dangers of the trusts in this 1880 engraving.*

The Southern Alliance began in Texas in 1875 but did not assume major proportions until Dr. Charles W. Macune, an energetic and farsighted leader, took over the leadership in 1886. Rapidly expanding, the Alliance absorbed other agricultural societies. Its agents spread across the South where farmers were fed up with crop liens, depleted lands, and sharecropping. They "seem like unto ripe fruit," an Alliance organizer said, "you can garner them by a gentle shake of the bush." In 1890 the Southern Alliance claimed more than a million members.

An effective organization, it published a newspaper, distributed Alliance material to hundreds of local newspapers, and in five years sent lecturers to forty-three states and territories where they spoke to two million farm families. It was "the most massive organizing drive by any citizen institution of nineteenth-century America." Like the Grange, the Alliance also established cooperative grain elevators, marketing associations, and retail stores—all designed to bring farmers to-

gether to make greater profits. Most of the projects were short-lived, but for a time between 1886 and 1892 cooperative enterprises blossomed in the South.

Loosely affiliated with the Southern Alliance, a separate Colored Farmers' National Alliance and Cooperative Union enlisted black farmers in the South. Claiming over a million members, it probably had closer to 250,000, but even that figure was sizable in an era when "uppity" blacks faced not merely defeat, but death. In 1891 black cotton pickers struck for higher wages near Memphis, Tennessee. Led by Ben Patterson, a thirty-year-old picker, they walked off several plantations, but a posse hunted them down and, following violence on both sides, lynched fifteen strikers, including Patterson. The abortive strike ended the Colored Farmers' Alliance.

On the Plains, the Northwestern Alliance, a smaller organization, was formed in 1880 by Milton George of Chicago. Its objectives were similar to those of the Southern Alliance, but it disagreed with the Southerners' emphasis on secrecy, centralized control, and separate organizations for blacks. In 1889 the Southern Alliance changed its name to the National Farmers' Alliance and Industrial Union and persuaded the three strongest state alliances on the plains— those in North Dakota, South Dakota, and Kansas —to join. Thereafter, the new organization dominated the Alliance movement.

The Alliance mainly sponsored social and economic programs, but it turned early to politics. In the West its leaders rejected both the Republicans and Democrats and organized their own party. In June 1890, Kansas organizers formed the first major People's party. The Southern Alliance resisted the idea of a new party for fear it might divide the white vote, thus undercutting white supremacy. The Southerners instead followed leaders such as Benjamin F. Tillman of South Carolina who wanted to capture control of the dominant Democratic party.

Thomas E. Watson and Leonidas L. Polk, two politically minded Southerners, reflected the high quality of Alliance leadership. Georgia-born, Watson was a talented orator and organizer; he urged Georgia farmers, black and white, to unite against their oppressors. The president of the National Farmers' Alliance, Polk believed in scientific farming and cooperative action. Jeremiah Simpson of Kansas, probably the most able of the western leaders, was reflective and well-read. A follower of reformer Henry George, he pushed for major social and economic change. Mary E. Lease—Mary Ellen to her friends, "Mary Yellin'" to her opponents—helped head a movement remarkably open to female leadership. A captivating speaker, she made 160 speeches during the summer of 1890, calling on farmers to rise against Wall Street and the industrial East.

Populist Mary E. Lease advised farmers to "raise less corn and more hell." She also said "... if one man has not enough to eat three times a day and another man has $25 million, that last man has something that belongs to the first."

Meeting in Ocala, Florida, in 1890, the Alliance adopted the Ocala Demands, the platform it pushed for as long as it existed. First and foremost, the demands called for the creation of a "sub-treasury system," which would allow farmers to store their crops in government warehouses. In return, they could claim Treasury notes for up to 80 percent of the local market value of the crop, a loan to be repaid when the crops were sold. Farmers could thus hold their crops for the best price. The Ocala Demands also urged the free coinage of silver, an end to protective tariffs and national banks, a federal income tax, the direct election of senators, and tighter regulation of railroad companies.

The Alliance strategy worked well in the elections of 1890. In Kansas the Alliance-related People's party, organized just a few months before, elected four congressmen and a United States senator. Across the South the Alliance won victories based on "the Alliance Yardstick," a demand that Democratic party candidates pledge support for Alliance measures. Alliance leaders claimed thirty-eight Alliance supporters elected to Congress, with at least a dozen more pledged to Alliance principles.

The People's Party

After the 1890 elections, Northern Alliance leaders urged the formation of a national third party to promote reform, although the Southerners remained reluctant, still hopeful of capturing control of the Democratic party. Plans for a new party were discussed at Alliance conventions in 1891 and the following year. In July 1892, a convention in Omaha, Nebraska, formed the new People's party. Southern Alliance leaders joined in, convinced now that there was no reason to cooperate with the Democrats who exploited Alliance popularity but failed to adopt its reforms.

In the South the Populists had worked to unite black and white farmers. "They are in the ditch just like we are," a white Texas Populist said. Blacks and whites served on Populist election committees; they spoke from the same platforms, and they ran on the same tickets. Populist sheriffs called blacks for jury duty, an unheard-of practice in the close-of-the-century South. In 1892 a black Populist was threatened with lynching; he took refuge with Tom Watson, and two thousand white farmers, some of whom rode all night to get there, guarded Watson's house until the threat passed.

Many of the delegates at the Omaha convention had planned to nominate Leonidas L. Polk for president, but he died suddenly in June, and the convention turned instead to James B. Weaver of Iowa, a former congressman, Union army general, and third-party candidate for president in 1880 (on the Greenback-Labor party ticket). As its platform, the People's party adopted many of the Ocala Demands.

Weaver waged an active campaign but with mixed results. He won 1,039,000 votes, the first third-party presidential candidate ever to attract more than a million votes. He carried Kansas, Idaho, Nevada, and Colorado, along with portions of North Dakota and Oregon, for a total of twenty-two electoral votes. The Populists elected

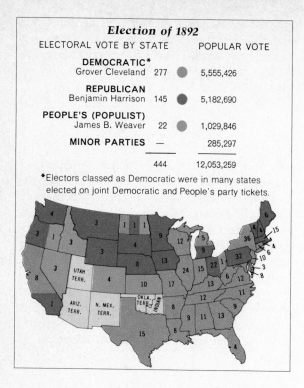

Election of 1892

ELECTORAL VOTE BY STATE		POPULAR VOTE
DEMOCRATIC* Grover Cleveland	277	5,555,426
REPUBLICAN Benjamin Harrison	145	5,182,690
PEOPLE'S (POPULIST) James B. Weaver	22	1,029,846
MINOR PARTIES	—	285,297
	444	12,053,259

*Electors classed as Democratic were in many states elected on joint Democratic and People's party tickets.

governors in Kansas and North Dakota, ten congressmen, five senators, and about fifteen hundred members of state legislatures.

Despite the Populists' victories, the election brought disappointment. Using fraud and manipulation, Southern Democrats deflected the Populists' efforts and simply wrote them off. Weaver was held to less than a quarter of the vote in every southern state except Alabama. In most of the country he lost heavily in urban areas with the exception of some mining towns in the Far West. He also failed to win over farmers in the settled Midwest. In no midwestern state did he win as much as 5 percent of the vote.

In the election of 1892 many voters switched parties, but they tended to switch to the Democrats rather than the Populists, whose platform on silver and other issues had no appeal among city dwellers or factory workers. Although the Populists did run candidates in the next three presidential elections, their heyday was over. In 1892 Farmers' Alliance membership dropped for the second year in a row, and the organization, once the breeding ground of the People's party, was broken.

The Crisis of the Depression

Building on the Democratic party's sweeping triumph in the midterm elections of 1890, Grover Cleveland decisively defeated incumbent President Benjamin Harrison in 1892. He won by nearly 400,000 votes, a large margin by the standards of the era, and the Democrats increased their strength in the cities and among working-class voters. For the first time since the 1850s, they controlled the White House and both branches of Congress.

Unfortunately for Cleveland, the panic of 1893 struck almost as he took office. The economy had expanded too rapidly in the 1870s and '80s. Railroads had overbuilt, gambling on future growth. Companies had grown beyond their markets; farms and businesses had borrowed heavily for expansion. The mood changed early in 1893. Business confidence sagged, and investors became timid and uneasy. Panic hit the stock market. During 1893 fifteen thousand business firms and more than six hundred banks closed.

The year 1894 was even worse. The gross national product dropped again, and by mid-year the number of unemployed stood at three million. One out of every five workers was unemployed. Unprecedented numbers of needy people taxed the ability of churches and charities to help. "Famine is in our midst," said the head of one city's relief committee. In the summer a heat wave and drought struck the farm belt west of the Mississippi River, creating conditions unmatched until the devastating Dust Bowl of the 1930s. Corn withered in the fields. In the South the price of cotton fell below five cents a pound, far under the break-even point.

People became restless and angry. As one newspaper said in 1896: "On every corner stands a man whose fortune in these dull times has made him an ugly critic of everything and everybody." There was even talk of revolution and bloodshed. "Everyone scolds," Henry Adams, the historian, wrote a British friend. "Everyone also knows what ought to be done. Everyone reviles everyone who does not agree with him, and everyone differs, or agrees only in contempt for everyone else. As far as I can see, everyone is right."

Coxey's Army and the Pullman Strike

Some of the unemployed wandered across the country—singly, in small groups, and in small armies. In February 1894, police ejected six hundred unemployed men who stormed the State House in Boston demanding relief. During 1894 there were some fourteen hundred strikes involving more than a half million workers.

On Easter Sunday, 1894, an unusual "army" of perhaps three hundred people left Massillon, Ohio. At its head rode "General" Jacob S. Coxey, a mild-looking, middle-aged businessman who wanted to put the nation's jobless to work building roads. Coxey wanted Congress to pass the Coxey Good Roads bill, which would authorize the printing of $500 million in paper money to finance road construction. His march to Washington—"a petition in boots," he called it—drew nationwide attention. Forty-three newspaper correspondents accompanied him, reporting every detail of the march.

Other armies sprang up around the country, and all headed for Washington to persuade the government to provide jobs on irrigation, road construction, or other projects. In the West they commandeered freight trains and headed east. Coxey himself reached Washington on May 1, 1894, after a difficult, tiring march. Police were everywhere, lining the streets and blocking the approaches to the Capitol. Coxey made it to the foot of the Capitol steps, but before he could do anything, the police were on him. He and a companion were clubbed, then arrested for trespassing. A week later Coxey was sentenced to twenty days in jail.

The armies melted away, but discontent did not. The great Pullman strike—one of the largest strikes in the country's history—began just a few days after Coxey's arrest when the employees of the Pullman Palace Car Company, living in a company town (a town in which everything was owned and everything was provided by the company) struck to protest wage cuts, continuing high rents, and layoffs. On June 26, 1894, the American Railway Union (ARU) under Eugene V. Debs joined the strike by refusing to handle trains that carried Pullman sleeping cars.

Within hours the strike paralyzed the western

■ The march on Washington by Coxey's "army" of unemployed men was an indication of the strength of Populist sentiment and the widespread unrest of the decade.

half of the nation. Grain and livestock could not reach markets. Factories shut down for lack of coal. The strike extended into twenty-seven states and territories, tying up the economy and renewing talk of class warfare. In Washington, President Cleveland decided to break it because it obstructed delivery of the mail.

On July 2 he secured a court injunction against the ARU, and he ordered troops to Chicago. When they arrived on the morning of Independence Day, the city was peaceful. Before long, however, violence broke out, and mobs composed mostly of nonstrikers overturned freight cars, looted, and burned. Restoring order, the army occupied railroad yards in Illinois, California, and other points. By late July the strike was over; Debs was jailed for violating the injunction. Many people applauded Cleveland's action, "nominally for the expedition of the mails," a newspaper said, but "really for the preservation of society."

The Pullman strike had far-reaching consequences for the development of the labor move-

Above, army cavalry troopers clear the way for a train to pass through the strikers' lines during the 1894 Pullman strike in Chicago. Eugene V. Debs (left), leader of the American Railway Union. When troops were ordered to Chicago, Debs' hopes for a nonviolent strike were dashed.

ment. Upholding Debs' sentence in *In re Debs* (1895), the Supreme Court endorsed the use of the injunction in labor disputes, thus giving business and government an effective antilabor weapon that hindered union growth in the 1890s. The strike's failure catapulted Debs into prominence. Working people resented Cleveland's actions in the strike, particularly as it became apparent that he sided with the railroads.

The Miners of the Midwest

The plight of coal miners in the Midwest illustrated the personal and social impact of the depression. Even in the best of times, mining was a dirty and dangerous business. One miner in twelve died underground; one in three suffered injury. Mines routinely closed for as long as six months a year, and wages fell with the depression. An Illinois miner earned $.97 per ton in 1889 and only $.80 in 1896. A bituminous coal miner made $282 a year.

Midwestern mining was often a family occupation, passed down from father to son. It demanded delicate judgments about when to blast, where to follow a seam, and how to avoid rockfalls. Until 1890 English and Irish immigrants dominated the business. They migrated from mine to mine, but nearly always lived in flimsy shacks owned by the company. Time and again the miners struck for higher wages—between 1887 and 1894 there were 116 major coal strikes in Illinois, 111 in Ohio.

After 1890 immigration from southern and eastern Europe, hitherto a trickle, became a flood. Italians, Lithuanians, Poles, Slovaks, Magyars, Russians, Bohemians, and Croatians came to the mines to find work. In three years nearly a thousand Italians settled in Coal City, Illinois; they comprised more than a third of the population. In other mining towns, Italian and Polish miners soon comprised almost half the population.

As the depression deepened, tensions grew between miners and their employers and between "old" miners and the "new." Many "new" miners spoke no English, and often they were "birds of passage," transients who had come to the United States to make money to take back home. Lacking the skills handed down by the "old" miners, they were often blamed for accidents, and they worked longer hours for less pay. At many a tavern after work, "old" miners grumbled about the different-looking newcomers and considered ways to get rid of them.

In April 1894 a wave of wage reductions sparked an explosion of labor unrest in the mines. The United Mine Workers, a struggling union formed just four years earlier, called for a strike of bituminous coal miners, and on April 21 virtually all Midwestern and Pennsylvania miners—some 170,000 in all—quit working. The flow of crucial coal slackened; cities faced blackouts; factories closed.

The violence that soon broke out followed a significant pattern. Over the years the English and Irish miners had built up a set of unspoken understandings with their employers. The "new" miners had not, and they were more prone to violent action to win a strike. The depression hit them especially hard, frustrating their plans to earn money and return home. In many areas, anger and frustration turned the 1894 strikes into outright war.

For nearly two weeks in June 1894 fighting rocked the Illinois, Ohio, and Indiana coalfields. Mobs ignited mine shafts, dynamited coal trains, and defied the state militias. While miners of all backgrounds participated in the violence, it often divided "old" miners and "new." In Spring Valley, Illinois, exiled Italian anarchists took over the strike leadership and incited rioting despite the opposition of the "old" miners. Elsewhere, a mine fired by arsonists burned because the "new" miners prevented the "old" ones from extinguishing the blaze.

Shocked by the violence, public opinion shifted against the strikers. The strike ended in a matter of weeks, but its effects lingered. English and Irish miners moved out into other jobs or up into supervisory positions. Jokes and songs poked cruel fun at the "new" immigrants, and the Pennsylvania and Illinois legislatures adopted laws to keep them out of the mines. Thousands of "old" miners voted Populist in 1894—the Populist platform called for restrictions on immigration—in one of the Populists' few successes that year. The United Mine Workers, dominated by the older miners, began in 1896 to urge Congress to stop the "demoralizing effects" of immigration.

Occurring at the same time, the Pullman strike pulled attention away from the crisis in the coalfields, yet the miners' strike involved three times as many workers and provided a revealing glimpse of the tensions within American society. The miners of the Midwest were the first large group of skilled workers seriously affected by the flood of immigrants from southern and eastern Europe. Buffeted by depression, they reflected the social and economic discord that permeated every industry.

A Beleaguered President

President Cleveland was sure that he knew the cause of the depression. The Sherman Silver Purchase Act of 1890, he believed, had damaged business confidence, drained the Treasury's gold reserve, and caused the panic. The solution to the depression was equally simple: repeal the act.

In June 1893, Cleveland summoned Congress into special session. India had just closed its mints to silver, and Mexico was now the only country in the world with free silver coinage. The silverites were on the defensive, although they pleaded for a compromise. Rejecting the pleas, Cleveland pushed the repeal bill through Congress, and on November 1, 1893, he signed it into law. Always sure of himself, he had staked everything on a single measure—a winning strategy if he succeeded, a devastating one if he did not.

Repeal of the Sherman Silver Purchase Act was probably a necessary action. It responded to the realities of international finance, reduced the flight of gold out of the country, and over the long run boosted business confidence. Unfortunately, it contracted the currency at a time when inflation might have helped. It also did not bring economic revival. The stock market remained listless, businesses continued to close, unemployment spread, and farm prices dropped. "We are hourly expecting the arrival of the benevolent man who is to pay ten cents a pound for cotton," a Virginia newspaper said.

The repeal battle of 1893, discrediting the conservative Cleveland Democrats who had dominated the party since the 1860s, reshaped the politics of the country. It confined the Democratic party largely to the South, helped the Republicans become the majority party in 1894, and strengthened the position of the silver Democrats in their bid for the presidency in 1896. It also focused national attention on the silver issue and thus intensified the silver sentiment Cleveland intended to dampen. In the end, repeal did not even solve the Treasury's gold problem. By January 1894, the reserve had fallen to $65 million. A year later it fell to $44.5 million.

In January 1894 Cleveland desperately resorted to a sale of $50 million in gold bonds to replenish the gold reserve; the following November he again sold bonds; and in February 1895, arousing outrage among many, he agreed to a third bond sale that allowed financier J. Pierpont Morgan and other bankers to reap large profits. A fourth bond sale in January 1896 also failed to stop the drain on the reserve, although it further sharpened the silverites' hatred of President Cleveland.

Depression Politics

In 1894 Cleveland and the Democrats tried to fulfill their long-standing promise to reduce the tariff. The Wilson-Gorman Tariff Act, passed by Congress in August 1894, contained only modest reductions in duties. It reduced the tariff on coal, iron ore, wool, and sugar, ended the McKinley Tariff Act's popular reciprocity agreements with other countries, and moved some duties higher than before. It also imposed a small income tax, a provision the Supreme Court overturned in 1895. Discouraged, Cleveland let the bill become law without his signature.

The Democrats were buried in the elections of 1894. Suffering the greatest defeat in congressional history, they lost 113 House seats, while the Republicans gained 117. In twenty-four states not a single Democrat was elected to Congress. Only one Democrat (Boston's John F. Fitzgerald, the grandfather of President John F. Kennedy) came from all of New England. The Democrats even lost some of the "Solid South," and in the Midwest, a crucial battleground of the 1890s, the party was virtually destroyed.

Wooing labor and the unemployed, the Populists made striking inroads in parts of the South and West, yet it was far from enough. In a year in which thousands of voters switched parties, the People's party elected only four senators or congressmen. Southern Democrats again used fraud and violence to keep the Populists' totals down. In the Midwest the Populists won double the number of votes they had received in 1894, yet still attracted less than 7 percent of the vote. Across the country the discontented tended to vote for the Republicans, not the Populists, a discouraging sign for the Populist party.

For millions of people, Grover Cleveland became a scapegoat for the country's economic ills. Fearing attack, he placed new police barracks on the White House grounds. The Democratic party split, and southern and western Democrats deserted him in droves. At Democratic conventions Cleveland's name evoked jeers. "He is an old bag of beef," Democratic Congressman "Pitchfork" Ben Tillman told a South Carolina audience, "and I am going to go to Washington with a pitchfork and prod him in his old fat ribs."

The elections of 1894 marked the end of the party deadlock that had existed since the 1870s. The Democrats lost, the Populists gained somewhat, and the Republicans became the majority party in the country. The Republican doctrines of activism and national authority, repudiated in the elections of 1890, became more attractive in the midst of depression.

Changing Attitudes

Across the country people were rethinking older ideas about government, the economy, and society. The depression, brutal and far-reaching, undermined traditional views. As men and women concluded that established ideas had failed to deal with the depression, they looked for new ones. There was, the president of the University of Wisconsin said, "a general, all-pervasive, restless discontent with the results of current political and economic thought."

In prosperous times Americans had thought of unemployment as the result of personal failure, affecting primarily the lazy and immoral. Now, in the midst of depression, everyone knew people who were both worthy *and* unemployed. Next door a respected neighbor might be laid off, down the block an entire factory shut down. People debated issues they had long taken for granted. New and reinvigorated local institutions—discussion clubs, women's clubs, reform societies, university extension centers, church groups, farmer's societies—gave people a place to discuss alternatives to the existing order. Pressures for reform increased, and demand grew for government intervention to help the poor and unemployed.

Everybody Works but Father

As husbands and fathers lost their jobs, more and more women and children went to work. Even as late as 1901, well after the depression had ended, a study of working-class families showed that more than half the principal breadwinners were out of work. So many women and children worked that in 1905 there was a popular song, "Everybody Works but Father."

During the 1890s the number of working women rose from 4 million to 5.3 million. Trying to make ends meet, they took in boarders and found jobs as laundresses, cleaners, or domestics. Where possible they worked in offices and factories. Far more black urban women than white worked to supplement their husbands' meager earnings. In New York City in 1900, nearly 60 percent of black women worked compared to 27 percent of the foreign-born and 24 percent of native-born white women. Men still dominated business offices, but during the 1890s more and more employers noted the relative cheapness of female labor. Women telegraph and telephone operators nearly tripled in number during the decade. Women worked as clerks in the new five-and-tens and department stores and as nurses; in 1900 half a million were teachers. They increasingly entered office work as stenographers and typists, occupations in which they earned between $6.00 and $15.00 a week, compared to factory wages of $1.50 to $8.00 a week.

The depression also caused an increasing number of children to work. During the 1890s the number of children employed in southern textile mills jumped more than 160 percent, and boys and girls under sixteen years of age made up nearly a third of the labor force of the mills. Youngsters of eight and nine years worked twelve hours a day for pitiful wages. In most cases children worked not in factories but in farming and city street trades like peddling and shoeshining. In 1900 the South had more than half the child laborers in the nation.

■ *Tiny barefoot children peddling newspapers and female domestics serving the rich—their meager earnings were desperately needed.*

Concerned about child labor, middle-class women in 1896 formed the League for the Protection of the Family, which called for compulsory education to get children out of factories and into classrooms. The Mothers Congress of 1896 gave rise to the National Congress of Parents and Teachers, the spawning-ground of thousands of local PTAs. The National Council of Women and the General Federation of Women's Clubs took up similar issues. By the end of the 1890s the Federation had 150,000 members who worked for various civic reforms in the fields of child welfare, education, and sanitation.

Changing Themes in Literature

The depression also gave point to a growing movement in literature toward realism and naturalism. In the years after the Civil War, literature often reflected the mood of romanticism—sentimental and unrealistic. Walt Whitman called it "ornamental confectionary" and "copious dribble," but it remained popular through the end of the century.

After the 1870s a number of talented authors rejected romanticism and turned instead to realism. Determined to portray life as it was, they studied local dialects, wrote regional stories, and emphasized the "true" relationships between people. In doing so, they reflected broader trends in the society, such as industrialism, evolutionary theory which emphasized the effect of the environment on humans, and the new philosophy of pragmatism which stressed the relativity of values. (See chapter 22 for a more detailed discussion of pragmatism.)

Regionalist authors like Joel Chandler Harris and George Washington Cable depicted life in the South; Hamlin Garland described the grimness of life on the Great Plains; and Sarah Orne Jewett wrote about everyday life in rural New England. Another regionalist, Bret Harte, achieved fame with stories that portrayed the local color of the California mining camps, particularly in his popular tale, "The Outcasts of Poker Flat."

Harte was joined by a more talented writer, Mark Twain, who became the country's most outstanding realist author. Growing up along the Mississippi River in Hannibal County, Missouri, the young Samuel Langhorne Clemens observed life around him with a humorous and skeptical eye. Adopting a pen name from the river term "mark twain" (two fathoms), he wrote a number of important works that drew on his own experiences. *Life on the Mississippi* (1883) described his career as a steamboat pilot. *The Adventures of Tom Sawyer* (1876) and *The Adventures of Huckleberry Finn* (1884) gained international prominence. In these books, Twain used dialect and common speech instead of literary language, touching off a major change in American prose style.

Illustrations from popular literary works of the time: Mark Twain (top left) created an idyllic setting for the adventures of the irrepressible Tom Sawyer, shown here convincing a gullible friend of the joys of whitewashing a fence (bottom left). A powerful drawing entitled "From the Depths" (above) illustrated J. Ames Mitchell's The Silent War (1906), which dealt with the class struggle. The tenement house alley gang (below) illustrated Stephen Crane's Maggie.

William Dean Howells—after Twain, the country's most famous author—came more slowly to the realist approach. At first he wrote about the happier sides of life, but he grew worried about the impact of industrialization. *A Traveler from Altruria* (1894), a utopian novel, described an industrial society that consumed lives. The poem, "Society" (1895), written in the midst of the depression, compared society to a splendid ball in which men and women danced on flowers covering the bodies of the poor:

And now and then from out the dreadful floor
An arm or brow was lifted from the rest,
As if to strike in madness, or implore
For mercy; and anon some suffering breast
Heaved from the mass and sank; and as before
The revellers above them thronged and prest.

Other writers became impatient even with realism. Pushing Darwinian theory to its limits, they wrote of a world in which a cruel and merciless environment determined human fate. Often focusing on economic hardship, naturalist writers studied the poor, the lower classes, and the criminal mind; they brought to their writing the social workers' passion for direct and honest experience.

Stephen Crane spent a night in a seven-cent lodging house on the Bowery and in "An Experiment in Misery" captured the smells and sounds of the poor. Crane depicted the carnage of war in *The Red Badge of Courage* (1895) and the impact of poverty in *Maggie: A Girl of the Streets* (1893). His poetry suggested the unimportance of the individual in an uncaring world:

A man said to the universe
"Sir, I exist!"
"However," replied the universe,
"The fact has not created in me
A sense of obligation."

Frank Norris assailed the power of big business in two dramatic novels, *The Octopus* (1901) and *The Pit* (1903), both the story of individual futility in the face of the heartless corporations. Norris' *McTeague* (1899) studied the disintegration of character under economic pressure. Jack London, another naturalist author, traced the power of nature over civilized society in novels like *The*

Sea Wolf (1904) and *The Call of the Wild* (1903), his classic tale of a sled dog that preferred the difficult life of the wilderness to the world of human beings.

Theodore Dreiser, the foremost naturalist writer, grimly portrayed a dark world in which human beings were tossed about by forces beyond their understanding or control. "My own ambition," Dreiser said, "is to represent my world, to conform to the large, truthful lines of life." In his great novel, *Sister Carrie* (1901), he followed a young farm girl who took a job in a Chicago shoe factory. He described the exhausting nature of factory work: "Her hands began to ache at the wrists and then in the fingers, and towards the last she seemed one mass of dull, complaining muscle, fixed in an eternal position, and performing a single mechanical movement."

Like other naturalists, Dreiser focused on environment and character. He thought writers should tell the truth about human affairs, not fabricate romance, and *Sister Carrie*, he said, was "not intended as a piece of literary craftsmanship, but was a picture of conditions."

The Presidential Election of 1896

The election of 1896 was known as "the battle of the standards" because it involved the gold and silver standards of value in the monetary system of the nation. New voting patterns replaced the old, a new majority party confirmed its control of the country, and national policy shifted to suit the new realities.

The Mystique of Silver

Sentiment for free silver coinage grew swiftly after 1894, dominating the South and West, appearing even in the farming regions of New York and New England. Prosilver literature flooded the country (see the special feature in this chapter on pp. 594–95). Pamphlets issued by the millions argued silver's virtues.

People wanted quick solutions to the economic crisis. During 1896 unemployment shot up; farm income and prices fell to the lowest point in the decade. "I can remember back as far as 1858," an Iowa hardware dealer said in February 1896, "and I have never seen such hard times as these are." The silverites offered a solution, simple but compelling: the free and independent coinage of silver at the ratio of sixteen to one. Free coinage meant that the United States mints would coin all the silver offered to them. Independent coinage meant that the country would coin silver regardless of the policies of other nations, nearly all of which were on the gold standard.

Above all, the silverites believed in a quantity theory of money: the amount of money in circulation determined the level of activity in the economy. A shortage of money meant declining activity and depression. Silver meant more money and thus prosperity. Added to the currency, it would increase the money supply and stir new economic activity. Farm prices would rise. "It means the reopening of closed factories, the relighting of fires in darkened furnaces; it means hope instead of despair; comfort in place of suffering; life instead of death."

By 1896 silver was a symbol. It had moral and patriotic dimensions and stood for a wide range of popular grievances. For many, it reflected rural values rather than urban ones, suggested a shift of power away from the Northeast, and spoke for the downtrodden instead of the well–to–do. Silver represented the common people, as the vast literature of the movement showed.

William H. Harvey's *Coin's Financial School* (1894), the most popular of all silver pamphlets, had the eloquent Coin, a wise but unknown youth, tutoring famous people on the currency. Bankers, lawyers, and scholars came to argue for gold, but left shaken, leaning toward silver. *Coin's Financial School* sold five thousand copies a day at its peak in 1895, with tens of thousands of copies distributed free by silver organizations. It "is being sold on every railroad train by the newsboys and at every cigar store . . . ," a Mississippi congressman said. "It is being read by almost everybody."

Silver was a social movement, one of the largest in American history, but its life span turned out to be brief. As a mass phenomenon, it flourished between 1894 and 1896, then succumbed to electoral defeat, the return of prosperity, and the onset of fresh concerns. But in its time it bespoke a national mood and won millions of followers.

The Republicans and Gold

Scenting victory over the discredited Democrats, numerous Republicans fought for the party's presidential nomination, including "Czar" Thomas B. Reed of the Billion-Dollar Congress. Reed picked up early support but suffered from his reputation for biting wit. William McKinley of Ohio, his chief rival, soon passed him in the race for the nomination.

Able, calm, and affable, McKinley had served in the Union army during the Civil War. In 1876 he won a seat in Congress where he became the chief sponsor of the tariff act named for him. In the months before the 1896 national convention, Marcus A. Hanna, his campaign manager and trusted friend, built a powerful national organization that featured McKinley as "the Advance Agent of Prosperity." When the convention met in June, McKinley had the nomination in hand, and he backed a platform that favored the gold standard against the free coinage of silver.

Republicans favoring silver proposed a prosilver platform, but the convention overwhelmingly defeated it. Twenty-three silverite Republicans, far fewer than prosilver forces had hoped, marched out of the convention hall. The remaining delegates waved handkerchiefs and flags and shouted "Good-bye" and "Put them out." Hanna stood on a chair screaming "Go! Go! Go!" William Jennings Bryan, who was there as a special correspondent for a Nebraska newspaper climbed on a desk to get a better view.

■ Supporters of William McKinley's gold-standard platform in 1896 sported handsome goldbug pins like the one shown here.

The Democrats and Silver

Despite President Cleveland's opposition, more than twenty Democratic state platforms came out for free silver in 1894. Power in the party shifted to the South, where it remained for decades. The party's base narrowed; its outlook increasingly reflected southern views on silver, race, and other issues. In effect, the Democrats became a sectional—no longer a national—party.

The anti-Cleveland Democrats had their issue, but they lacked a leader. Out in Nebraska, Bryan saw the opportunity. He was barely thirty-six years old and had relatively little political experience. But he had spent months wooing support, and he was a captivating public speaker—tall, slender, and handsome, with a resounding voice that in an era without microphones projected easily into every corner of an auditorium. Practicing at home before a mirror, he rehearsed his speeches again and again, as his wife, Mary, a bright, sharp, and politically astute woman, listened for errors.

From the outset of the 1896 Democratic convention, the silver Democrats were in charge, and they put together a platform that stunned the Cleveland wing of the party. It demanded the free coinage of silver, attacked Cleveland's actions in the Pullman strike, and censured his gold bond sales. On July 9, as delegates debated the platform, Bryan's moment came. Striding to the stage, he stood for an instant, a hand raised for silence, waiting for the applause to die down. He would not contend with the previous speakers, he began, for "this is not a contest between persons. The humblest citizen in all the land, when clad in the armor of a righteous cause, is stronger than all the hosts of error. I come to speak to you in defense of a cause as holy as the cause of liberty—the cause of humanity."

The delegates were captivated. Like a trained choir, they rose, cheered each point, and sat back to listen for more. They were there, Bryan said, "to enter up the judgment already rendered by the plain people of this country." The country praised businessmen but forgot that laborers, miners, and farmers were businessmen, too. Shouts rang through the hall and delegates pounded on chairs. Savoring each cheer, Bryan defended silver. Then came the famous closing: "Having behind us the producing masses of this

The Wonderful Wizard of Oz

A restless dreamer, Frank Baum tried his hand at several careers before he gained fame and fortune as a writer of children's literature. From 1888 to 1891 he ran a store and newspaper in South Dakota, where he experienced the desolation and grayness that accompanied agrarian discontent. An avid supporter of William Jennings Bryan in the "battle of the standards," Baum wrote an enduring allegory of the silver movement, *The Wonderful Wizard of Oz*. Published in April 1900, it was an immediate success.

The book opens with a grim description of Kansas:

When Dorothy stood in the doorway and looked around, she could see nothing but the great gray prairie on every side. Not a tree nor a house broke the broad sweep of flat country that reached the edge of the sky in all directions. The sun had baked the plowed land into a gray mass, with little cracks running through it. Even the grass was not green, for the sun had burned the tops of the long blades until they were the same gray color to be seen everywhere. Once the house had been painted,
but the sun blistered the paint and the rains washed it away, and now the house was as dull and gray as everything else.

Kansas had not always seemed that way. After 1854, when the Kansas-Nebraska Act opened to settlement its fifty million acres of rich grassland, people poured into the state to stake their claims. Many came from the hilly, timbered country to the east, and breaking onto the prairie, they saw "a new world, reaching to the far horizon without break of trees or chimney stack; just sky and grass and grass and sky . . . . The hush was so loud . . . . The heavens seemed nearer than ever before and awe and beauty and majesty over all."

In later years railroads crisscrossed the state, and advertisements touted the fertile soil. Land was plentiful, rainfall somehow seemed to increase each year, crop prices held at levels high enough to pay, new farming implements yielded larger crops, and property values increased.

Yet life on the prairie was never an easy matter. Flat, lonely, and windswept, the land affected people in ways that were hard to describe to the folks back East. When Aunt Em, Dorothy's aunt, came to Kansas to live, she was young and pretty, but the sun and wind soon changed her. "They had taken the sparkle from her eyes and left them a sober gray; they had taken the red from her cheeks and lips, and they were gray also." Like Aunt Em, Uncle Henry never laughed. "He worked hard from morning till night and did not know what joy was."

After 1887 a series of droughts struck Kansas, and as many as three out of four farms were mortgaged in some Kansas counties. Thousands of settlers like Aunt Em and Uncle Henry gave up and retraced their steps East; others trusted in the Farmers' Alliance and pinned their hopes on the free coinage of silver. While gold as a standard of currency symbolized the idle rich of the industrial Northeast, silver stood for the common folk. Added to the currency in the form of silver dollars, it meant more money, higher crop prices, and a return of prosperity.

Or so the supporters of silver coinage believed. In *The Wonderful Wizard of Oz*, Dorothy (every person) is carried by a cyclone (a victory of the silver forces at the polls) from drought-stricken Kansas to a marvelous land of riches and witches. Unlike dry, gray Kansas, Oz is beautiful, with rippling brooks, stately trees, colorful flowers, and bright-feathered birds. On arrival, Dorothy disposes of one witch, the Wicked Witch of the East (the Eastern money power and those favoring gold), and frees the Munchkins (the common people) from servitude. To return to Kansas, she must first go to the Emerald City (the national capital, greenback-colored).

Dorothy wears magical silver slippers and follows the yellow brick road, thus achieving a proper relationship between the precious metals, silver and gold. Like many of her countrymen, she does not at first recognize the power of the silver slippers, but a kiss from the Good Witch of the North (Northern voters) protects her on the road. Dorothy meets the Scarecrow (the farmer) who has been told he has no brain but actually possesses great common sense (no "hick" or "hayseed," he); the Tin Woodman (the industrial worker) who fears he has become heartless but discovers the spirit of love and cooperation; and the Cowardly Lion (reformers, particularly Wil-

liam Jennings Bryan) who turns out not to be very cowardly at all.

When the four companions reach the Emerald City, they meet the "Great and Terrible" Wizard who tells them that, to gain his help, they must destroy the Wicked Witch of the West (mortgage companies, heartless nature, and other things opposing progress there). Courageously, they set forth. Dorothy dissolves the witch with a bucket of water (what else for drought-ridden farmers?), but when they return to the Emerald City, they find that the Wizard (the money power) is only a charlatan, a manipulator, whose power rests on myth and illusion. "I thought Oz was a great Head," said Dorothy . . . "And I thought Oz was a terrible Beast," said the Tin Woodman. "And I thought Oz was a Ball of Fire," exclaimed the Lion. "No; you are all wrong," said the little man meekly. "I have been making believe."

Dorothy unmasks the wizard, and with the help of Glinda, the Good Witch of the South (support for silver was strong in the South), uses the silver slippers to return home to Kansas. Sadly, the shoes are lost in flight. Back in Oz, the Scarecrow rules the Emerald City (the triumph of the farmers), and the Tin Woodman reigns in the West (industrialism moves West). "Oz" was a familiar abbreviation to those involved in the 16 (ounces) to 1 fight over the ratio of silver to gold.

Baum wanted to write American fairy tales to "bear the stamp of our times and depict the progressive fairies of today." The land of Oz reflected his belief in the American values of freedom and independence, love of family, self-reliance, individualism, and sympathy for the underdog. *Oz*, he said in the original introduction, "aspires to being a modernized fairy tale, in which the wonderment and joy are retained and the heartaches and nightmares are left out."

The *Oz* stories have remained popular, and they still rest on many children's bookshelves. A 1939 film starring Judy Garland as Dorothy, with Ray Bolger as the Scarecrow, Jack Haley as the Tin Woodman, Bert Lahr as the Cowardly Lion, and Frank Morgan as the Wizard was spectacularly successful. Released in the midst of another depression, the film included songs designed, as Dorothy once had, to escape hardship "Somewhere Over the Rainbow."

nation and the world . . . we will answer their demand for a gold standard by saying to them: 'You shall not press down upon the brow of labor this crown of thorns, you shall not crucify mankind upon a cross of gold.'"

Bryan moved his fingers down his temples, suggesting blood trickling from his wounds. He ended with his arms outstretched as on a cross. Letting the silence hang, he dropped his arms, stepped back, then started to his seat. Suddenly, there was pandemonium. Delegates shouted and cheered. When the tumult subsided, they adopted the anti-Cleveland platform, and the next day, Bryan won the presidential nomination.

Campaign and Election

The Democratic convention presented the Populists with a dilemma. The People's party had staked everything on the assumption that neither major party would endorse silver. Now it faced a painful choice: nominate an independent ticket and risk splitting the silverite forces or nominate Bryan and give up its separate identity as a party.

The choice was unpleasant, and it shattered the People's party. Meeting late in July, the party's national convention nominated Bryan, but rather

■ *Although William Jennings Bryan was acclaimed enthusiastically as he campaigned throughout the nation, he failed to win the election.*

than accept the Democratic candidate for vice-president, it named Tom Watson instead. The Populists' endorsement probably hurt Bryan as much as it helped. It won him relatively few votes, since many Populists would have voted for him anyway. It identified him as a Populist, which he was not, and allowed the Republicans to accuse him of heading a ragtag army of malcontents. The squabble over Watson seemed to prove that the Democratic-Populist alliance could never stay together long enough to govern.

In August 1896, Bryan set off on a campaign that became an American legend. Much of the conservative eastern press had deserted him, and he took his campaign directly to the voters, the first presidential candidate in history to do so in a systematic way. By his own count, Bryan traveled 18,009 miles, visited 27 states, and spoke 600 times to a total of some 3 million people. He built skillfully on a new "merchandising" style of campaign in which he worked to educate and persuade voters.

Bryan summoned voters to an older America: a land where farms were as important as factories, where the virtues of rural and religious life outweighed the doubtful lure of the city, where common people still ruled, and opportunity existed for all. He drew on the Jeffersonian tradition of rural virtue, distrust of central authority, and abiding faith in the powers of human reason.

Urged to take the stump against Bryan, McKinley replied: "I might just as well put up a trapeze on my front lawn and compete with some professional athlete as go out speaking against Bryan." The Republican candidate let voters come to him. Railroads brought them by the thousands into McKinley's hometown of Canton, Ohio, and he spoke to them from his front porch. Through use of the press, he reached fully as many people as Bryan's more strenuous effort. Appealing to labor, immigrants, wealthy farmers, businessmen, and the middle class, McKinley defended economic nationalism and the advancing urban-industrial society.

On election day, voter turnout was extraordinarily high, a measure of the intense interest. By nightfall the outcome was clear: McKinley won 50 percent of the vote to Bryan's 46 percent. He won the Northeast and Midwest and carried four border states. In the cities McKinley crushed Bryan.

The election struck down the Populists, whose

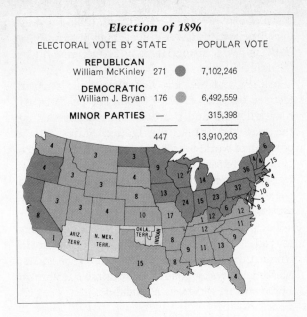

Election of 1896

ELECTORAL VOTE BY STATE		POPULAR VOTE
REPUBLICAN William McKinley	271	7,102,246
DEMOCRATIC William J. Bryan	176	6,492,559
MINOR PARTIES	—	315,398
	447	13,910,203

totals sagged nearly everywhere. Many Populist proposals were later adopted under different leadership. The graduated income tax, crop loans to farmers, the secret ballot, and direct election of United States senators all were early Populist ideas. But the People's party never could win over a majority of the voters, and failing that, it vanished after 1896.

The McKinley Administration

The election of 1896 cemented the voter realignment of 1894 and initiated a generation of Republican rule. For more than three decades after 1896, with only a brief Democratic resurgence under Woodrow Wilson, the Republicans remained the country's majority party.

McKinley took office in 1897 under favorable circumstances. To everyone's relief, the economy had begun to revive. The stock market rose, factories once again churned out goods, and farmers prospered. Farm prices climbed sharply during 1897 on bumper crops of wheat, cotton, and corn. Discoveries of gold in Australia and Alaska—together with the development of a new cyanide process for extracting gold from ore—enlarged the world's gold supply, decreased its price, and inflated the currency as the silverites had hoped.

For the first time since 1890, the 1897 Treasury statements showed a comfortable gold reserve.

McKinley and the Republicans basked in the glow. They became the party of progress and prosperity, an image that helped them win victories until another depression hit in the 1930s. McKinley's popularity soared. Open and accessible in contrast to Cleveland's isolation, he rode the Washington streetcars, walked the streets, and enjoyed looking in department store windows. Cleveland's special police barracks vanished from the White House lawn. McKinley became the first president to ride in an automobile, reaching the speed of eighteen miles an hour.

An activist president, he set the policies of the administration. Conscious of the limits of power, he maintained close ties with Congress and worked hard to educate the public on national choices and priorities. McKinley struck new relations with the press and traveled far more than previous presidents. In some ways he began the modern presidency.

Shortly after taking office, he summoned Congress into special session to revise the tariff. In July 1897 the Dingley Tariff passed the House and Senate. It raised average tariff duties to a record level, and as the final burst of nineteenth-century protectionism, it caused trouble for the Republican party. By the end of the 1890s consumers, critics, and the Republicans themselves were wondering if the tariff had outlived its usefulness in the maturing American economy.

From the 1860s to the '90s the Republicans had built their party on a pledge to *promote* economic growth through the use of state and national power. By 1900, with the industrial system firmly in place, the focus had shifted. The need to *regulate*, to control the effects of industrialism, became a central public concern of the new century. McKinley prodded the Republicans to meet that shift, but he died before his plans matured.

McKinley toyed with the idea of lowering the tariff, but one obstacle always stood in the way: the government needed revenue, and tariff duties were one of the few taxes the public would support. The Spanish-American War of 1898 (see chapter 21) persuaded people to accept greater federal power and, with it, new forms of taxation. In 1899 McKinley spoke of lowering tariff barriers in a world that technology had made smaller.

Chronology

1876 Mark Twain publishes *The Adventures of Tom Sawyer*; sets off major change in American literary style

1877 Disputed election of 1876 results in awarding of presidency to Republican Rutherford B. Hayes

1880 Republican James A. Garfield elected president

1881 Garfield assassinated; Vice-President Chester A. Arthur becomes president

1884 Democrat Grover Cleveland elected president, defeating Republican James G. Blaine

1887 Cleveland calls for lowering of tariff duties

1888 Republican Benjamin Harrison wins presidential election

1889 National Farmers' Alliance and Industrial Union formed to address problems of farmers

1890 Republican-dominated "Billion-Dollar" Congress enacts McKinley Tariff Act, Sherman Antitrust Act, and Sherman Silver Purchase Act
Farmers' Alliance adopts the Ocala Demands

1892 Democrat Cleveland defeats Republican Harrison for presidency
People's Party formed

1893 Financial panic touches off depression lasting until 1897
Sherman Silver Purchase Act repealed
World Columbian Exposition opens in Chicago

1894 Coxey's army marches on Washington
Employees of Pullman Palace Car Company strike

1896 Republican McKinley defeats William Jennings Bryan, Democratic and Populist candidate, in "Battle of the Standards"

1897 Gold discovered in Alaska
Dingley Tariff Act raises tariff duties

1900 McKinley reelected, again defeating Bryan
Gold Standard Act establishes gold as standard of currency

1901 McKinley assassinated; Vice-President Theodore Roosevelt assumes presidency
Naturalist writer Theodore Dreiser publishes *Sister Carrie*

"God and man have linked the nations together . . . ," he said in his last speech at Buffalo, New York, in 1901. "Isolation is no longer possible or desirable."

In 1898 and '99, the McKinley administration focused on the war with Spain, the peace treaty that followed, and the dawning realization that the war had thrust the United States into a position of world power (see chapter 21). In March 1900, Congress passed the Gold Standard Act, which declared gold the standard of currency and ended the silver controversy that had dominated the 1890s.

The presidential campaign of 1900 was a replay of the McKinley-Bryan fight of 1896. Bryan stressed the issues of imperialism and the trusts; McKinley stressed his record at home and abroad. The result in 1900 was a landslide.

The Election of 1900

Candidate	Party	Popular Vote	Electoral Vote
McKinley	Republican	7,218,039	292
Bryan	Democrat	6,358,345	155
Woolley	Prohibition	209,004	0
Debs	Socialist	86,935	0

On September 6, 1901, a few months after his second inauguration, McKinley stood in a receiving line at the Pan-American Exposition in Buffalo. Leon Czolgosz, a twenty-eight-year-old unemployed laborer and anarchist, moved through the line and, reaching the President, shot him. Surgeons probed the wound but could find nothing. A recent discovery called the X-ray was on display at the exposition, but it was not used. On September 14, McKinley died, and Vice-President Theodore Roosevelt became president. A new century had begun.

Reform movements begun in the 1890s flowered in the Progressive period after 1900. Political patterns shifted, the presidency acquired fresh power, and massive unrest prompted social change. The war with Spain brought worldwide responsibilities.

Technology continued to alter the way Americans lived. In 1896 Henry Ford produced a two-cylinder, four-horsepower car, the first of the

■ *Gold triumphs over silver in this* Puck *cartoon referring to the Gold Standard Act of 1900.*

famous line that bore his name. In 1899 the first automobile salesroom opened in New York, and some innovative thinkers were already imagining a network of service stations to keep the new cars running. At Kitty Hawk, North Carolina, Wilbur and Orville Wright, two bicycle manufacturers, neared the birth of powered flight.

The realignments that reached their peak in the 1890s seem distant, yet they are not. Important decisions in those years shaped nearly everything that came after them. In character and influence, the 1890s are as much a part of the twentieth century as of the nineteenth.

Recommended Reading

The most thorough account of the 1890s is in Harold U. Faulkner, *Politics, Reform and Expansion, 1890–1900* (1959), but see also Robert H. Wiebe, *The Search for Order, 1877–1920* (1967) and Samuel P. Hays, *The Response to Industrialism 1855–1914* (1957). David P. Thelen, *The New Citizenship: Origins of Progressivism in Wisconsin, 1885–1900* (1972), stresses the impact of the depression on ideas and attitudes.

The best study of the 1890s depression is Charles Hoffman, *The Depression of the Nineties: An Economic History* (1970). On politics, see H. Wayne Morgan, *From Hayes to McKinley: National Party Politics, 1877-1896* (1969), and Richard J. Jensen, *The Winning of the Midwest: Social and Political Conflict, 1888-1896* (1971). C. Vann Woodward examines the South in *Origins of the New South, 1887–1913* (1951).

Larzer Ziff, *The American 1890s: Life and Times of a Lost Generation* (1966); Henry Steele Commager, *The American Mind* (1950); and Justin Kaplan, *Mr. Clemens and Mark Twain: A Biography* (1966), examine literary currents. On Populism, see John D. Hicks, *The Populist Revolt: A History of the Farmers' Alliance and the People's Party* (1931) and Lawrence Goodwyn, *Democratic Promise: The Populist Moment in America* (1976). C. Vann Woodward, *Tom Watson: Agrarian Rebel* (1938), is a superb biography.

Additional Bibliography

On politics, see Morton Keller, *Affairs of State: Public Life in Late Nineteenth Century America* (1977); Paul John Kleppner, *The Cross of Culture: A Social Analysis of Midwestern Politics, 1850–1900* (1970); Robert D. Marcus, *Grand Old Party: Political Structure in the Gilded Age, 1880–1896* (1971); and R. Hal Williams, *Years of Decision: American Politics in the 1890s* (1978).

Biographies of the era's personalities include Allan Nevins, *Grover Cleveland: A Study in Courage* (1932); Paola E. Coletta, *William Jennings Bryan*, 3 vols. (1964–1969); Lewis L. Gould, *The Presidency of William McKinley* (1981); Stuart Noblin, *Leonidas Lafayette Polk* (1949); Peter H. Argersinger, *Populism and Politics: William Alfred Peffer and the People's Party* (1974); and Martin Ridge, *Ignatius Donnelly: The Portrait of a Politician* (1962).

On Populism, see Robert C. McMath, Jr., *Populist Vanguard: A History of the Southern Farmers' Alliance* (1975); James E. Wright, *The Politics of Populism: Dissent in Colorado* (1974); O. Gene Clanton, *Kansas Populism: Ideas and Men* (1969); Robert W. Larson, *New Mexico Populism* (1974); and Stanley B. Parsons, *The Populist Context: Rural Versus Urban Power on a Great Plains Frontier* (1973).

Social and labor unrest is covered in Almont Lindsey, *The Pullman Strike: The Story of a Unique Experiment and of a Great Labor Upheaval* (1942); Stanley Buder, *Pullman: An Experiment in Industrial Order and Community Planning, 1880–1930* (1967); Ray Ginger, *The Bending Cross: A Biography of Eugene Victor Debs* (1969); and Donald L. McMurry, *Coxey's Army: A Study of the Industrial Army Movement of 1894* (1929). Walter T. K. Nugent, *Money and American Society* (1968) and Allen Weinstein, *Prelude to Populism: Origins of the Silver Issue, 1867–1878* (1970), explain the silver-gold controversy.

Stanley L. Jones, *The Presidential Election of 1896* (1964); Paul W. Glad, *McKinley, Bryan, and the People* (1964); and Robert F. Durden, *The Climax of Populism: The Election of 1896* (1965) examine that election.

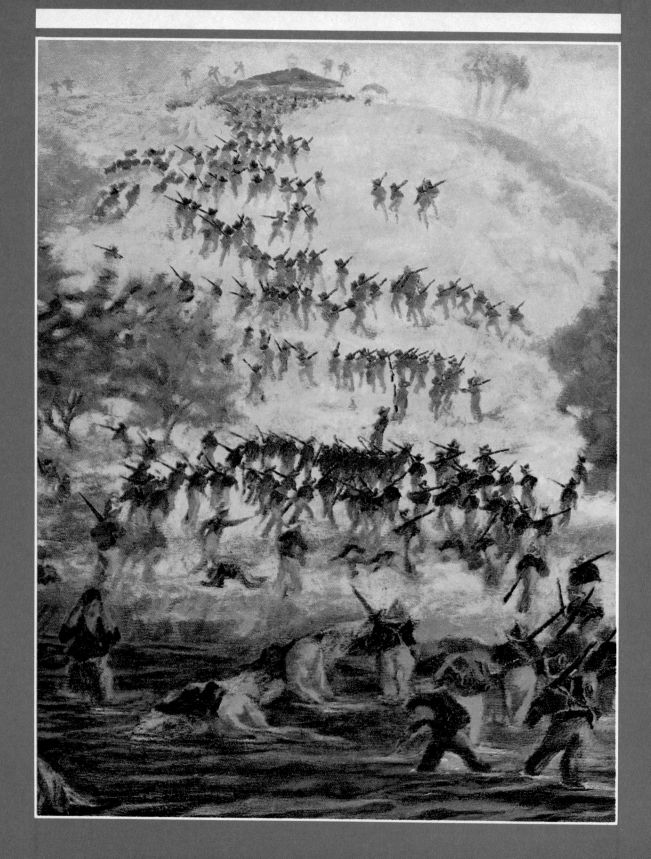

chapter 21

TOWARD EMPIRE

When war with Spain began in April 1898, many Americans regretted it, but many others welcomed it. War was different then, shorter and more personal than the all-encompassing, lengthy, and mechanistic wars of the twentieth century. There were many people—highly respected people—who thought that nations must fight every now and then to prove their power and test the national spirit.

Theodore Roosevelt, thirty-nine years old in 1898, was one of them. Nations needed to fight in order to survive, he thought. For months Roosevelt argued strenuously for war with Spain, first on grounds of freeing Cuba and expelling Spain from the hemisphere; second, because of "the benefit done to our people by giving them something to think of which isn't material gain"; and third, because the army and navy needed the practice.

In April 1898 Roosevelt was serving in the important post of assistant secretary of the navy. When war broke out he quickly resigned to join the army, rejecting the advice of the secretary of the navy who warned he would only "ride a horse and brush mosquitoes from his neck in the Florida sands." The secretary was wrong—dead wrong—and later had the grace to admit it. "Roosevelt was right," he said. "His going into the Army led straight to the Presidency."

In 1898 officers supplied their own uniforms, and Roosevelt, the son of well-to-do parents, wanted his to be stylish. He wired Brooks Brothers, the expensive New York clothier, for a "regular Lieutenant-Colonel's uniform without yellow on the collar and with leggings," to be ready in a week. Joining a friend, he chose to enlist his own regiment, and after a few telephone calls to friends and telegrams to the governors of Arizona, New Mexico, and Oklahoma asking for "good shots and good riders," he had more than enough men. The First United States Volunteer Cavalry, an intriguing mixture of Ivy League athletes and western frontiersmen, was born.

Known as the Rough Riders, it included men from the Harvard, Yale, and Princeton clubs of New York City, the Somerset Club of Boston, and New York's exclusive Knickerbocker Club. Former college athletes—football players, tennis players, and track stars—enlisted. Woodbury Kane, a wealthy yachtsman, signed up and promptly volunteered for kitchen duty.

Other volunteers came from the West—natural soldiers, Roosevelt called them, "tall and sinewy, with resolute, weather-beaten faces, and eyes that looked a man straight in the face without flinching." Among the cowboys, hunters, and prospectors, there was Bucky O'Neill, a legendary Arizona sheriff and Indian fighter, a half-dozen other sheriffs and Texas Rangers, a large number of Indians, a famous broncobuster, and an ex-marshal of Dodge City, Kansas.

Eager for war, the men trained hard, played harder, and rarely passed up a chance for an intellectual discussion—if Roosevelt's memoir of the war is to be believed. Once, he overheard Bucky O'Neill and a Princeton graduate "discussing Aryan word-roots together, and then sliding off into a review of the novels of Balzac, and a discussion as to how far Balzac could be said to be the founder of the modern realistic school of fiction." Roosevelt himself spent his spare time reading *Superiorité des Anglo-Saxons*, a French work that strove to prove the superiority of English-speaking peoples. In such a camp discipline was lax, and enlisted men got on easily with the officers.

The troops howled with joy when orders came to join the invasion army for Cuba. They won their first victories in Florida, fighting off other regiments to capture a train to take them to the wharf and then seizing the only available troopship to Cuba. The Rough Riders set sail on June 14, 1898, and Lieutenant Colonel Roosevelt, who had performed a war dance for the troops the night before, caught their mood: "We knew not whither we were bound, nor what we were to do; but we believed that the nearing future held for us many chances of death and hardship, of honor and renown. If we failed, we would share the fate of all who fail; but we were sure that we would win, that we should score the first great triumph in a mighty world-movement."

America Looks Outward

The overseas expansion of the 1890s differed in several important respects from earlier expansionist moves of the United States. The American Republic had expanded from its beginnings. After the first landings in Jamestown and Plymouth, settlers pushed westward: into the trans-Appalachian region, the Louisiana Territory, Florida, Texas, California, Arizona, and New Mexico. Most of these lands were contiguous with existing territories of the United States, and most were intended for settlement, usually agricultural.

The expansion of the 1890s moved into island possessions, the bulk of them already thickly populated. The new territories were held less for settlement than as naval bases, trading outposts, or commercial centers on major trade routes. More often than not, they were viewed as colonies, not as states-in-the-making.

Historian Samuel F. Bemis described the overseas expansion of the 1890s as "the great aberration," a time when the country adopted expansionist policies that did not fit with prior experience. Other historians, pointing to expansionist tendencies in thought and foreign policy that surfaced during the last half of the nineteenth century, have found a developing pattern that led naturally to the overseas adventures of the 1890s. In this view, "the United States did not set out on an expansionist path in the late 1890's in a sudden, spur-of-the-moment fashion. The overseas empire that Americans controlled in 1900 was not a break in their history, but a natural culmination."

Catching the Spirit of Empire

Most people in most times in history tend to look inward, and Americans in these years following the Civil War were no exception. Among other things, they focused on Reconstruction, the movement westward, and the growing industrial system. They took seriously the well-remembered advice of George Washington's Farewell Address to "steer clear" of foreign entanglements. Throughout the nineteenth century Americans enjoyed "free security" without fully appreciating it. Sheltered by two oceans and the British navy, they could enunciate bold policies like the Monroe Doctrine while remaining virtually impregnable to foreign attack.

Some people urged abolition of the foreign service, considering it an unnecessary expenditure, a dangerous profession that might lead to entanglement in the struggles of the world's great powers. A New York newspaper called it a "relic of medieval, monarchical trumpery," and if not that, it certainly became at times a dumping ground of the spoils system. Presidents named ambassadors from lists of politicians, journalists, and business leaders who, though successful in their own fields, had no training in languages or diplomatic relations.

In the 1870s and after, several developments combined to shift attention outward across the seas. The end of the frontier, announced officially in the census report of 1890, sparked fears about diminishing opportunities at home. Further growth, it seemed, must take place abroad, as John A. Kasson, an able and experienced diplomat, said in the *North American Review*: "We are rapidly utilizing the whole of our continental territory. We must turn our eyes abroad, or they will soon look inward upon discontent."

Factories and farms multiplied, producing more goods than the domestic market could consume. Both farmers and industrialists looked for new overseas markets, and the growing volume of exports—including more and more manufactured goods—changed the nature of American trade relations. American exports of merchandise amounted to $393 million in 1870, $858 million in 1890, and $1.4 billion in 1900. In 1898 the United States exported more than it imported, beginning a trend that lasted through the 1960s.

Political leaders—James G. Blaine was one—began to argue for the vital importance of foreign markets to continued economic growth. Blaine, secretary of state under Garfield and again under Harrison, aggressively sought a new empire of markets in Latin America and Asia. To some extent, he and others were also caught up in a worldwide scramble for empire. In the last third of the century Great Britain, France, and Germany divided up Africa and looked covetously at Asia. The idea of imperialistic expansion was in the air, and the great powers measured their greatness by the colonies they acquired. Inevitably, some Americans—certain business interests

■ *Entitled "The World Is My Market, My Customers Are All Mankind," this cartoon of the 1870s reflects America's growing interest in foreign markets.*

and foreign-policy strategists, for example—caught the spirit and wanted to enter the international hunt for territory (see p. 610).

Intellectual currents that supported expansion drew on Charles Darwin's theories of evolution. Adherents pointed, for example, to *The Origin of Species*, which mentioned in its subtitle *The Preservation of Favored Races in the Struggle for Life*. Applied to human and social development, biological concepts seemed to call for the triumph of the fit and the elimination of the unfit. "In this world," said Theodore Roosevelt, who thought of himself as one of the fit, "the nation that has trained itself to a career of unwarlike and isolated ease is bound, in the end, to go down before other nations which have not lost the manly and adventurous qualities."

Haeckel's Biogenetic Law, then a popular theory, suggested that the development of the individual repeated the development of the race. Primitive peoples thus were in the arrested stages of childhood or adolescence; they needed supervision and protective treatment. In a similar vein,

John Fiske, a popular writer and lecturer, argued for Anglo-Saxon racial superiority, a result of the process of natural selection. The English and Americans, Fiske said, would occupy every land on the globe that was not already "civilized," bringing the advances of commerce and democratic institutions.

Such views were widespread among the lettered and unlettered alike. In Cuba, one of the Rough Riders ushered a visiting Russian prince around the trenches, informing him with ill-considered enthusiasm: "You see, Prince, the great result of this war is that it has united the two branches of Anglo-Saxon people; and now that they are together they can whip the world, Prince! they can whip the world!" Eminent scholars like John W. Burgess, a professor of political science at Columbia University, argued in similar though more dignified fashion that people of English origin were destined to impose their political institutions on the world.

The career of Josiah Strong, a Congregational minister and fervent expansionist, suggested the strength of the developing ideas. A champion of overseas missionary work, Strong traveled extensively through the West for the Home Missionary Society, and in 1885, drawing on his experiences, he published a book entitled *Our Country: Its Possible Future and Its Present Crisis*. An immediate best-seller, the book called upon foreign missions to civilize the world under the Anglo-Saxon races. Strong became a national celebrity.

Our Country argued for expanding American trade and dominion. "The world is to be Christianized and civilized. And what is the process of civilizing but the creating of more and higher wants. Commerce follows the missionary." A special people, the bearers of civil liberty and Christianity, Americans were members of a God-favored race destined to lead the world. Anglo-Saxons already owned one third of the earth, Strong said, and in a famous passage he concluded that they must take more.

Then will the world enter upon a new stage of its history—the final competition of races for which the Anglo-Saxon is being schooled. If I do not read amiss, this powerful race will move down upon Mexico, down upon Central and South America, out upon the islands of the sea, over upon Africa and beyond. And can anyone doubt that the result of this competition of races will be the "survival of the fittest"?

Taken together, these developments in social, political, and economic thought prepared Americans for a larger role in the world. The change was gradual, and there was never a day when people awoke with a sudden realization of their interests overseas. But change there was, and by the 1890s Americans were ready to reach out into the world in a more determined and deliberate fashion than ever before. For almost the first time, they felt the need for a foreign "policy."

Foreign Policy Approaches: 1867–1900

Rarely consistent, American foreign policy in the last half of the nineteenth century took different approaches to different areas of the world. In relation to Europe, where the dominant world powers were, policymakers promoted trade and tried to avoid diplomatic entanglements. In North and South America, they based policy on the Monroe Doctrine, a recurrent dream of annexing Canada or Mexico, a hope for extensive trade, and Pan-American unity against the nations of the Old World. In Asia, they coveted Hawaii and other outposts on the sea lanes to China.

Secretary of State William Henry Seward, who served from 1861 to 1869, aggressively pushed an expansive foreign policy. "Give me . . . fifty, forty, thirty more years of life," he told a Boston audience in 1867, "and I will give you possession of the American continent and control of the world." Seward, it turned out, had only five more years of life, but he developed a vision of an American empire stretching south in Latin America and west to the shores of Asia. He wanted Canada and Mexico, islands in the Caribbean as strategic bases to protect a canal across the isthmus, and Hawaii and other islands as stepping-stones to Asia.

Seward tried unsuccessfully to negotiate a commercial treaty with Hawaii in 1867, and the same year he annexed the Midway Islands, a small atoll group twelve hundred miles west of Hawaii. In 1867 he concluded a treaty with Russia for the purchase of Alaska (which was promptly labeled "Seward's Folly") partly to sandwich western Canada between American territory and lead to its annexation. In all this, Seward's target remained the Asian market, which he and many others considered a virtually bottomless outlet for farm and manufactured goods. As the American empire spread, he thought, Mexico City would become its capital.

Mexico itself presented a difficult problem, for the French had taken advantage of the Civil War to create there a puppet state under Archduke Maximilian, the younger brother of Austria's Hapsburg emperor. Popular sentiment in the United States opposed the French adventure, and once the Civil War ended Seward's tone became firmer. By 1867 Napoleon III of France tired of the expense, and he withdrew his troops. Refusing to leave, Maximilian was captured and executed by the Mexicans. For the American public, the affair symbolized a victory for the Monroe Doctrine and growing American power in the hemisphere.

Secretary of State Hamilton Fish, an urbane New Yorker, followed Seward in 1869, serving under President Ulysses S. Grant. An avid expan-

■ *Cartoonists had a field day when Seward purchased Alaska. Here, he invites the Alaskan representative to "bring Mr. McSeal along with you to Washington."*

sionist, Grant wanted to extend American influence in the Caribbean and Pacific, though Fish, more conservative, often restrained him. They moved first to repair relations with Great Britain. The first business was settlement of the *Alabama* claims—demands that Britain pay the United States for damages caused by Confederate vessels which, like the *Alabama*, had been built and outfitted in British shipyards (see chapter 15). Negotiating patiently, Fish signed the Treaty of Washington in 1871, providing for arbitration of the *Alabama* issue and other nettlesome controversies. The treaty, one of the landmarks in the peaceful settlement of international disputes, marked a significant step in cementing Anglo-American relations.

Grant and Fish looked most eagerly to Latin America. In 1870 Grant became the first president to proclaim the nontransfer principle—"hereafter no territory on this continent shall be regarded as subject to transfer to a European power." Fish also promoted the independence of Cuba, restive under Spanish rule, while holding off the annexation desired by the more eager Grant. Influenced by speculators, Grant tried to annex Santo Domingo in 1869 but was thwarted by powerful Republicans in the Senate who disliked foreign involvement and feared a subsequent attempt to annex Haiti.

James G. Blaine served as secretary of state only six months, until Garfield's assassination, but laid extensive plans to establish closer commercial relations with Latin America. His successor, Frederick T. Frelinghuysen, changed Blaine's approach but not his strategy. Like Blaine, Frelinghuysen wanted to find Caribbean markets for American goods; he negotiated separate reciprocity treaties with Mexico, Cuba and Puerto Rico, the British West Indies, Santo Domingo, and Colombia. Using these treaties, Frelinghuysen hoped not only to obtain markets for American goods but to bind these countries to American interests.

When Blaine returned to the State Department in 1889 under President Benjamin Harrison, he moved again to expand markets in Latin America. Drawing on earlier ideas, he envisaged a hemispheric system of peaceful intercourse, arbitration of disputes, and expanded trade. He also wanted to annex Hawaii. "I think there are only three places that are of value and not already taken, that are not continental," he wrote Harrison in 1891. "One is Hawaii and the others are Cuba and Puerto Rico." The last two might take a generation to acquire, but "Hawaii may come up for decision at any unexpected hour and I hope we shall be prepared to decide it in the affirmative."

Harrison and Blaine toyed with naval acquisitions in the Danish West Indies, Santo Domingo, Haiti, and Peru, but in general they focused on Pan-Americanism and tariff reciprocity. Blaine presided over the first Inter-American Conference in Washington on October 2, 1889. Delegates from nineteen American nations were present, and Blaine urged them to unite Latin America and the United States in a customs union and create a way to settle conflicts. The delegates rejected both proposals but did create the International Bureau of the American Republics, later renamed the Pan-American Union, for the exchange of general information including political, scientific, and cultural knowledge. The conference, a major step in hemispheric relations, led to later meetings promoting trade and other agreements.

Reciprocity, Harrison and Blaine hoped, would divert Latin American trade from Europe to the United States. Working hard to sell the idea in Congress, Blaine lobbied for a reciprocity provision in the McKinley Tariff Act of 1890 (see chapter 20), and once that was enacted he negotiated important reciprocity treaties with most Latin American nations. The treaties suffered from the depression of the 1890s; nevertheless, they resulted in greater American exports of flour, grain, meat, iron, and machinery. Exports to Cuba jumped by a third between 1891 and 1893, then dropped precipitously when the 1894 Wilson-Gorman Tariff Act ended reciprocity.

Grover Cleveland, Harrison's successor, also pursued an aggressive policy toward Latin America. In 1895 he brought the United States precariously close to war with Great Britain over a boundary dispute between Venezuela and British Guiana. Cleveland sympathized with Venezuela, and he and Secretary of State Richard Olney urged Britain to arbitrate the dispute. When Britain failed to act, Olney drafted a stiff diplomatic note affirming the Monroe Doctrine and denying European nations the right to meddle in Western Hemisphere affairs.

Four months passed before Lord Salisbury,

A SIMPLE DEFINITION.

Master Johnny Bull. "MONROE DOCTRINE! WHAT *IS* THE 'MONROE DOCTRINE'?"
Master Jonathan. "WA-AL—GUESS IT'S THAT EVERYTHING EVERYWHERE BE-LONGS TO *US!*"

■ *John Tenniel's scathing definition of the Monroe Doctrine in this cartoon from* Punch *reflects the British view that the U.S. reserved exclusive rights to act like a colonial power in the Western Hemisphere.*

the British foreign secretary, replied. Rejecting Olney's arguments, he sent two letters, the first bluntly repudiating the Monroe Doctrine as international law. The second letter, carefully reasoned and sometimes sarcastic, rejected Olney's arguments for the Venezuelan boundary. Enraged, Cleveland defended the Monroe Doctrine, and he asked Congress for authority to appoint a commission to decide the boundary and enforce its decision. "I am fully alive to the responsibility incurred and keenly realize all the consequences that may follow," he told Congress, plainly implying war.

Preoccupied with larger diplomatic problems in Africa and Europe, Britain changed its position. In November 1896 the two countries signed a treaty of arbitration, under which Great Britain received much of the disputed territory and Venezuela retained control of the vital Orinoco River. Though the Cleveland-Olney approach was clumsy, the Venezuelan incident demonstrated growing American power of persuasion in the Western

Hemisphere. Cleveland and Olney persuaded Great Britain to recognize United States dominance, and they sharpened American influence in Latin America. The Monroe Doctrine assumed new importance. In averting war, an era of Anglo-American friendship was begun.

The Lure of Hawaii and Samoa

The islands of Hawaii offered a tempting way station to Asian markets. In the early 1800s they were already called the "Crossroads of the Pacific," and trading ships of many nations stopped there. In 1820 the first American missionaries arrived to convert the islanders to Christianity. Like missionaries elsewhere, they advertised Hawaii's economic and other benefits and attracted new settlers. Their children later came to dominate Hawaiian political life and played an important role in annexation.

After the Civil War the United States tightened its connections with the islands. The reciprocity treaty of 1875 allowed Hawaiian sugar to enter the United States free of duty and bound the Hawaiian monarchy to make no territorial or economic concessions to other powers. The treaty increased Hawaiian economic dependence on the United States; its political clauses effectively made Hawaii an American protectorate. In 1887 a new treaty reaffirmed these arrangements and granted the United States exclusive use of Pearl Harbor, a magnificent harbor that had early caught the eye of naval strategists.

Following the 1875 treaty, white Hawaiians became more and more influential in the islands' political life. The McKinley Tariff Act of 1890 ended the special status given Hawaiian sugar and in addition awarded American producers a bounty of two cents a pound. Hawaiian sugar production dropped dramatically, unemployment rose, and property values fell. The following year the weak King Kalakaua died, bringing to power a strong-willed nationalist, Queen Liliuokalani. Resentful of white minority rule, she decreed a new constitution that gave greater power to native Hawaiians.

Unhappy, the American residents revolted in early 1893 and called on the United States for help. John L. Stevens, the American minister in Honolulu, sent 150 marines ashore from the

Windjammers, loaded with a sugar cargo, shown in Honolulu Harbor in 1882.

Queen Liliuokalani, a fierce nationalist, composed the lovely Hawaiian song "Aloha Oe." Her stubborn resistance to annexation could only postpone, not prevent, it.

cruiser *Boston*, and within three days the bloodless revolution was over. Queen Liliuokalani surrendered "to the superior force of the United States," and the victorious rebels set up a provisional government. On February 14, 1893, Harrison's Secretary of State John W. Foster and delegates of the new government signed a treaty annexing Hawaii to the United States.

But only two weeks remained in Harrison's term, and the Senate refused to ratify the agreement. Five days after taking office, Cleveland withdrew the treaty; he then sent a representative to investigate the cause of the rebellion. The investigation revealed the American role in it, and Cleveland decided to restore the queen to her throne. He made that demand, but the provisional government in Hawaii politely refused and instead established the Republic of Hawaii, which the embarrassed Cleveland, unable to do otherwise, recognized.

The debate over Hawaiian annexation, continuing through the 1890s, foreshadowed the later debate over the treaty to end the Spanish-American War. People in favor of annexation pointed to Hawaii's strategic location, argued that Japan or other powers might seize the islands if the United States did not, and suggested that Americans had a responsibility to civilize and Christianize the native Hawaiians. Opponents warned that annexation might lead to a colonial army and colonial problems, the inclusion of a "mongrel" population in the United States, and rule over an area not destined for statehood.

Annexation came swiftly in July 1898 in the midst of excitement over victories in the Spanish-American War. The year before, President William McKinley had sent a treaty of annexation to the Senate. "We need Hawaii just as much and a good deal more than we did California," he said privately. "It is Manifest Destiny." But opposition quickly arose, and the treaty stalled. Japan protested against it, pointing out that Japanese made up a quarter of the Hawaiian population. Japan dispatched a cruiser to Honolulu; the Navy Department sent the battleship *Oregon* and ordered naval forces to take Hawaii if the Japanese made threatening moves.

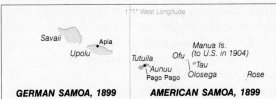

Hawaii and Samoa

The location of the Hawaiian Islands and Samoa in the Pacific Ocean is shown in the small-scale map at the top.

GERMAN SAMOA, 1899   AMERICAN SAMOA, 1899

the Samoan Islands, three thousand miles to the south, sat astride the sea lanes of the South Pacific. Americans showed early interest in Samoa, and in 1872 a naval officer negotiated a treaty granting the United States the use of Pago Pago, a harbor on the island of Tuitula. The Senate rejected it but six years later approved a similar agreement providing for a naval station there. The agreement bound the United States to use its good offices to adjust any disputes between the Samoan chiefs and foreign governments. Great Britain and Germany also secured treaty rights in Samoa, and thereafter the three nations jockeyed for position.

The situation grew tense in 1889 when warships from all three countries gathered in a Samoan harbor. But a sudden hurricane destroyed the fleets, and tensions eased. A month later delegates from Britain, Germany, and the United States met in Berlin to negotiate the problem. Britain and Germany wanted to divide up the islands; Secretary of State Blaine held out for some degree of authority by the indigenous population, with American control over Pago Pago.

The agreement, an uneasy one, ended in 1899 when the United States and Germany divided Samoa and compensated Britain with lands elsewhere in the Pacific. Germany claimed the two larger islands in the chain; the United States kept Tutuila and the harbor at Pago Pago.

The New Navy

Large navies were vital in the scramble for colonies, and in the 1870s the United States had almost no navy. One of the most powerful fleets in the world during the Civil War, the American navy had fallen into rapid decline. By 1880 there were fewer than two thousand vessels, only forty-eight of which could fire a gun. Ships rotted, and many officers left the service. "It was easy then," said George Dewey, later a hero of the war with Spain, "for an officer to drift along in his grade, losing interest and remaining in the navy only because he was too old to change his occupation."

Conditions changed during the 1880s. A group of rising young officers, steeped in a new naval philosophy, argued for an expanded navy equipped with fast, aggressive fleets capable of fighting battles across the seas. This group had its

In 1898 annexationists redoubled arguments about Hawaii's commercial and military importance. McKinley and congressional leaders switched strategies to seek a joint resolution, rather than a treaty, for annexation. A joint resolution required only a majority of both houses, while a treaty needed a two-thirds vote in the Senate. Bolstered by the new strategy, the annexation measure moved quickly through Congress, and McKinley signed it on July 7, 1898. His signature, giving the United States a naval and commercial base in the mid-Pacific, realized a goal of policymakers since the 1860s.

While Hawaii represented a step toward China,

An 1881 cartoon (left) depicts "our top-heavy navy," a decrepit vessel sinking with idle officers. Below, the ten thousand-ton battleship Oregon, one of the first steel ships constructed for the new navy.

greatest influence in a special Naval Advisory Board, formed by the secretary of the navy in 1881. Big-navy proponents pointed to the growing fleets of Great Britain, France, and Germany, arguing that the United States needed greater fleet strength to protect its interests in the Caribbean and Pacific.

In 1883 Congress authorized construction of four steel ships, marking the beginning of the new navy. Experts also worked to improve naval management and the quality of fleet personnel, and between 1885 and 1889 Congress budgeted funds for thirty additional ships. The initial building program focused on lightly armored, fast cruisers for raiding enemy merchant ships and protecting American shores, but after 1890 the program shifted to the construction of a seagoing, offensive battleship navy capable of challenging the strongest fleets of Europe.

Alfred Thayer Mahan and Benjamin F. Tracy were two of the main forces behind the new navy. Austere and scholarly, Mahan was the era's most influential naval strategist. After graduating from the Naval Academy in 1859, he devoted a lifetime to studying the influence of sea power in history;

for over two decades he headed the Newport Naval War College, where officers imbibed the latest in strategic thinking. A clear, logical writer, Mahan summarized his beliefs in three major books: *The Influence of Sea Power Upon History, 1660–1783* (1890), *The Influence of Sea Power Upon the French Revolution and Empire, 1793–1812* (1892), and *The Interest of America in Sea Power* (1897).

Mahan's reasoning was simple and persuasive. Industrialism, he argued, produced vast surpluses of agricultural and manufactured goods, for which markets must be found. Markets involved distant ports; reaching them required a large merchant marine and a powerful navy to protect it. Navies, in turn, needed coaling stations and repair yards. Coaling stations meant colonies, and colonies became strategic bases, the foundation of a nation's wealth and power. The bases might serve as markets themselves, but they were more important as stepping-stones to other objectives, the markets of Latin America and Asia.

Mahan called attention to the worldwide race for power, a race, he warned, the United States could not afford to lose. "All around us now is strife; 'the struggle of life,' 'the race of life' are phrases so familiar that we do not feel their significance till we stop to think about them. Everywhere nation is arrayed against nation; our own no less than others." To compete in the struggle the United States must expand. It needed strategic bases, a powerful, oceangoing navy, a canal across the isthmus to link the East coast with the Pacific, and Hawaii as a way station on the route to Asia.

Mahan influenced a generation of policymakers in the United States and Europe; one of them, Benjamin F. Tracy, became Harrison's secretary of the navy in 1889. Between then and 1893 Tracy organized the Bureau of Construction and Repair to design and build new ships, established the Naval Reserve in 1891, saved from a budget cut the Naval War College where Mahan lectured, and ordered construction of the first American submarine in 1893. He also started the first heavy rapid-fire guns, smokeless powder, torpedoes, and heavy armor. Above all, Tracy joined with big-navy advocates in Congress to push for a far-ranging battleship fleet capable of attacking distant enemies. He wanted two fleets of battleships, eight in the Pacific and twelve in the Atlantic. He got four first-class battleships.

In 1889, when Tracy entered office, the United States ranked twelfth among world navies; in 1893, when he left, it ranked seventh and was climbing rapidly. "The sea," he predicted in 1891, "will be the future seat of empires. And we shall rule it as certainly as the sun doth rise." By the end of the decade the navy had seventeen steel battleships, six armored cruisers, and many smaller craft. It ranked third in the world.

War with Spain

The war with Spain in 1898 built a mood of national confidence, altered older, more insular patterns of thought, and reshaped the way Americans saw themselves and the world. When the war ended, American possessions stretched into the Caribbean and deep into the Pacific. American influence went further still, and the United States was recognized as a "world power."

The Spanish-American War established the United States as a dominant force for the twenti-

■ Mr. Dooley, the irreverent Irish-American saloon keeper created by Finley Peter Dunne, often aimed his sardonic humor at the "Establishment."

eth century. It brought colonies and millions of colonial subjects; it brought imperial dreams and responsibilities. The war strengthened the office of the presidency, swept the nation together in a tide of emotion, and confirmed the long-standing belief in the superiority of the New World over the Old. Afterward, Americans looked outward as never before, touched, they were sure, with a special destiny.

They seemed a chosen people, as Mr. Dooley pointed out to his friend Hennessy over the Archey Road bar. "We're a gr-reat people" said Hennessy, in his rolling Irish brogue. "We ar-re that," replied Mr. Dooley. "We ar-re that. An th' best iv it is we know we ar-re."

A War for Principle

By the 1890s Cuba and the nearby island of Puerto Rico comprised nearly all that remained of Spain's once vast empire in the New World. Several times Cuban insurgents had rebelled against Spanish rule, including a decade-long rebellion from 1868 to 1878 (the Ten Years' War) that failed to settle the conflict. The depression of 1893 damaged the Cuban economy, and the Wilson-Gorman Tariff of 1894 prostrated it. Duties on sugar, Cuba's lifeblood, were raised 40 percent. With the island's sugar market in ruins, discontent with Spanish rule heightened, and in late February 1895 revolt again broke out.

Recognizing the importance of the nearby United States, Cuban insurgents established a junta in New York City to raise money, purchase weapons, and wage a propaganda war to sway American public opinion. Conditions in Cuba were grim. The insurgents pursued a hit-and-run, scorched-earth policy to force the Spanish to leave. Spain committed more than two hundred thousand soldiers; the Spanish commander, who had won with similar tactics in 1878, tried to pin the insurgents in the eastern part of the island where they could be cornered and destroyed.

When this strategy failed, Spain in January 1896 sent a new commander, General Valeriano Weyler y Nicolau. Relentless and brutal, Weyler gave the rebels ten days to lay down their arms. He then put into effect a "reconcentration" policy designed to move the native population into camps and destroy the rebellion's popular base. Herded into fortified areas, Cubans died by the thousands, victims of unsanitary conditions, overcrowding, and disease.

There was a wave of sympathy for the insurgents stimulated by the newspapers (see the special feature on pp. 614–15). But "yellow" journalism did not cause the war. It stemmed from larger conflicts in policies and perceptions between Spain and the United States. Grover Cleveland, under whose administration the rebellion began, preferred Spanish rule to the kind of turmoil that might invite foreign intervention. Opposed to the annexation of Cuba, he issued a proclamation of neutrality and tried to restrain public opinion. In 1896 Congress passed a resolution favoring recognition of Cuban belligerency, but Cleveland ignored it. Instead, he offered to mediate the struggle, an offer Spain declined.

Taking office in March 1897, President McKinley also urged neutrality but tilted more toward the insurgents. He immediately sent a trusted aide on a fact-finding mission to Cuba; the aide reported in mid-1897 that Weyler's policy had wrapped Cuba "in the stillness of death and the silence of desolation." The report in hand, McKinley offered to mediate the struggle, but concerned over the suffering, he protested against

■ *The illustration below appeared in* Harper's Weekly. *Entitled "Starvation by Proclamation," it shows Cubans being marched into one of General Weyler's "reconcentration" camps. Frederic Remington's article (right) in the* New York Journal *describes the cruel manner in which the "guerillas"—irregular troops employed by the Spanish—treated the Cubans ("Pacificos").*

SPANISH GUERILLAS BRINGING "PACIFICOS" INTO CAMP

GUINES, CUBA, *January 15, 1897.* The acts of the terrible savages, or irregular troops called "guerillas," employed by the Spaniards, pass all understanding by civilized man. The American Indian was never guilty of the monstrous crimes that they commit.

Their treatment of women is unspeakable, and as for the men captured by them alive, the blood curdles in my veins as I think of the atrocity, of the cruelty, practiced on these helpless victims.

My picture illustrates one case where the guerillas saw fit to bring their captives into the lines, trussed up at the elbows, after their fashion. *The New York* Journal, *January 24, 1897.*

Spain's "uncivilized and inhuman" conduct. The United States, he made clear, did not contest Spain's right to fight the rebellion but insisted it be done within humane limits.

Late in 1897 a change in government in Madrid brought a temporary lull in the crisis. The new government recalled Weyler and agreed to offer the Cubans some form of autonomy. It also declared an amnesty for political prisoners and released Americans in Cuban jails. The new initiatives pleased McKinley, though he again warned Spain that it must find a humane end to the rebellion. Then, in January 1898 Spanish army officers led riots in Havana against the new autonomy policy and shook his confidence in Madrid's control over conditions in Cuba.

McKinley ordered the battleship *Maine* to Havana as a gesture of strength and goodwill. On February 9, 1898, the *New York Journal*, a leader of the "yellow press," published a letter stolen from Enrique Dupuy de Lôme, the Spanish ambassador in Washington. The letter was a private letter to a friend, and in it de Lôme called McKinley "weak," "a would-be politician," and "a bidder for the admiration of the crowd." Many Americans were angered by the insult; McKinley himself was more worried about other sections of the letter which revealed Spanish insincerity in the negotiations. De Lôme immediately resigned and went home, but the damage was done.

A few days later, at 9:40 in the evening of February 15, an explosion tore through the hull of the *Maine*, riding at anchor in Havana harbor. The ship, a trim symbol of the new steel navy, sank quickly; 266 lives were lost. McKinley cautioned patience and promised an immediate investigation. Crowds gathered quietly on Capitol Hill and outside the White House, mourning the lost men. Soon there was a new slogan, "Remember the *Maine* and to Hell with Spain!"

The most recent study of the *Maine* incident blames the sinking on an accidental internal explosion, caused perhaps by spontaneous combustion in poorly ventilated coal bunkers. In 1898 Americans blamed it on Spain. Spaniards were hanged in effigy in many communities. Roosevelt, William Jennings Bryan, and others urged war, but McKinley delayed, hopeful that Spain might yet agree to an armistice and perhaps Cuban independence. "I have been through one war; I have seen the dead piled up; and I do not want to see another," he told a White House visitor.

In early March 1898, wanting to be ready for war if it came, McKinley asked Congress for $50 million in emergency defense appropriations, a request Congress promptly approved. The vote stunned Spain: it was unanimous, and allowing the President unusual latitude, it appropriated the money "for the National defense and for each and every purpose connected therewith to be expended at the discretion of the President." In late March the report of the investigating board blamed the sinking of the *Maine* on an external (and thus presumably Spanish) explosion. Pressures for war increased.

On March 27 McKinley cabled Spain his final terms. He asked Spain to declare an armistice, end the reconcentration policy, and—implicitly—move toward Cuban independence. When the Spanish answer came, it conceded some things, but not, in McKinley's judgment, the important ones. Spain offered a suspension of hostilities, not an armistice, and it left it to the Spanish commander in Cuba to set the length and terms of the

Headlines like these in William Randolph Hearst's New York Journal *left little doubt among his readers that Spain had sunk the* Maine.

Reporting the Spanish–American War

The force of the newspaper is the greatest force in civilization.

Under republican government, newspapers form and express public opinion.

They suggest and control legislation.

They declare wars.

They punish criminals, especially the powerful.

They reward with approving publicity the good deeds of citizens everywhere.

The newspapers control the nation because THEY REPRESENT THE PEOPLE.

So proclaimed William Randolph Hearst, owner of the *New York Journal* in the paper's September 25, 1898, issue. Proud of the power of the press, Hearst and a handful of other publishers built newspaper empires that not only reported events but also influenced their outcome.

Several of these empires took shape during the 1890s. The American population was growing rapidly, and so there were more people to read newspapers. In addition, more and more Americans were literate. Publishers did not hesitate to take advantage of the growing urban market. Technological improvements helped the spread of information: new machines made newspapers faster to print; larger type, a new half-tone engraving process for clearer pictures, and color cartoon supplements made them more appealing.

In 1865 there were about five hundred daily newspapers in the country with a total circulation of about two million. By 1900 there were over two thousand dailies with a circulation of over fifteen million. Papers sold for only one or two cents a copy. At that price publishers could not make money on the paper itself, so they recouped their losses on advertising. Advertisers wanted readers, and to attract more and more of them, publishers used new methods. They lured buyers with banner headlines and front-page photographs. Stories stressed sex and scandals, and more cartoons and comic strips appeared.

One of the first publishing magnates, Joseph Pulitzer bought the *New York World* in 1883 and within a year increased its sales from fifteen thousand a day to one hundred thousand. Pulitzer had little competition until 1895 when William Randolph Hearst, an aggressive publisher from San Francisco, bought the *New York Journal*. Hearst was thirty-two. The son of a multimillionaire, he had been expelled from Harvard, had traveled widely, and discovered a love for power and attention. Although he was shy and relatively inexperienced, money from his father and a desire to enter the world of newspaper publishing helped launch his career.

Fiercely competitive for "scoops" and circulation, Hearst and Pulitzer experimented with several new features: headlines that ran across the front page, profuse illustrations, a large Sunday paper with a comic section printed in color, and special sports' and women's sections. A cartoon character, "The Yellow Kid," appeared daily in both the *Journal* and the *World*, and they became known as "yellow journals." Stressing the sensational, "yellow journals" aimed to make news as well as report it. Hearst told his reporters: "Don't wait for things to turn up. Turn them up!"

The new journalism reached a peak in the crisis in Cuba between 1895 and 1898. When the short-lived rebellion of 1895 broke out, correspondents flocked to Cuba to cover it. Pulitzer sent the novelist Stephen Crane and printed reports from a young Englishman named Winston Churchill. Hearst sent the star *Journal* reporter Richard Harding Davis and the famous Western artist Frederic Remington to sketch scenes of Spanish cruelty. Both Hearst and Pulitzer sided with the rebels. Denouncing Spanish policy, they attacked General Valeriano Weyler—"Butcher," the *Journal* nicknamed him—and other Spanish generals.

SPANIARDS SEARCH WOMEN ON AMERICAN STEAMERS

Hearst was particularly proud of the story of Evangelina Cisneros, the seventeen-year-old niece of the rebellion's president. In August 1897, Evangelina was sentenced to twenty years in prison for aiding the rebels. Sensing the story's potential, Hearst started a letter-writing campaign to the queen of Spain to win her release. Soon he decided on a more direct method. He sent reporter Karl Decker to Havana to rescue Evangelina. Renting the house next door to the prison, Decker broke into the prison, freed Evangelina, and, disguising her as a boy, smuggled her out of Havana. On October 10, 1897, the *Journal* broke the news with the headline: "An American Newspaper Accomplishes at a Single Stroke What the Best Efforts of Diplomacy Failed Utterly to Bring About in Many Months."

Once war erupted between the United States and Spain, Hearst and his rivals stepped up their efforts. They employed hundreds of correspondents and hired a fleet of swift boats to carry stories to Florida for transmission back to New York. The correspondents both reported and fought in the war. At one point, Hearst considered sinking a ship in the Suez Canal to keep the Spanish fleet from reaching the Philippines, and from aboard a chartered steamer, he personally watched the destruction of Cervera's fleet off Santiago. Waving a revolver, he waded ashore to capture a handful of Spanish sailors who survived the battle. The efforts paid off in newspaper sales. When Hearst bought the *Journal*, it was selling 77,000 copies a day. At the war's height, its sales had increased to over 1.5 million daily.

After the war, Hearst cartoonists like Homer Davenport turned their skillful attention to the trusts and other issues. Showing the lack of restraint that characterized "yellow journalism," the *Journal*, a Democratic newspaper, again and again criticized President McKinley, even suggesting that assassination might be in order. In September 1901, McKinley was shot, and when reports circulated that the assassin had a copy of the *Journal* in his pocket, the public turned on Hearst. The *Journal*'s circulation dropped sharply. The new journalism continued into the twentieth century—Hearst himself went on to establish a famous publishing empire—but "yellow journalism" itself was never the same again.

suspension. It also revoked the reconcentration policy. But the Spanish response made no mention of a true armistice, McKinley's offer to mediate, or Cuba's independence.

Reluctantly McKinley prepared his war message. It was long and temperate—at seven thousand words even deliberately boring; it suggested the possibility of further negotiations. Congress heard it on April 11, 1898. On April 19 Congress passed a joint resolution declaring Cuba independent and authorizing the President to use the army and navy to expel the Spanish from Cuba. An amendment by Colorado Senator Henry M. Teller pledged that the United States had no intention of annexing the island.

On April 21, Spain severed diplomatic relations. The following day McKinley proclaimed a blockade of Cuba and called for 125,000 volunteers. On Monday, April 25, Congress passed a declaration of war. Late that afternoon McKinley signed it.

Some historians have suggested that in leading the country toward war McKinley was weak and indecisive, a victim of war hysteria in the Congress and country; others have called him a wily manipulator for war and imperial gains. In truth he was neither. Throughout the Spanish crisis McKinley pursued a moderate middle course that sought to protect American interests, promote Cuba's independence, and allow Spain time to adjust to the loss of the remnant of empire. He also wanted peace, but in the end the conflicting national interests of the two countries brought them to war.

"A Splendid Little War"

Ten weeks after the declaration of war the fighting was over. For Americans they were ten glorious, dizzying weeks, with victories to fill every headline and slogans to suit every taste. No war can be a happy occasion for those who fight it, but the Spanish-American War came closer than most. Declared in April, it ended in August. Relatively few Americans died, and the quick victory seemed to verify burgeoning American power. John Hay, soon to be McKinley's secretary of state, called it "a splendid little war."

At the outset the United States was militarily unprepared. Like the navy, the army had shrunk

drastically since the day twenty-three years before when Grant's great Civil War army marched sixty abreast, 200,000-strong, down Washington's Pennsylvania Avenue. In 1898 the regular army consisted of only 28,000 officers and men, most of them more experienced in quelling Indian uprisings than fighting large-scale battles. The Indian wars did produce effective, small-scale forces, well-trained and tightly disciplined, but the army was unquestionably too small for war against Spain.

When McKinley called for 125,000 volunteers, as many as 1 million young Americans responded. Ohio alone had 100,000 volunteers. Keeping the regular army units intact, War Department officials enlisted the volunteers in National Guard units that were then integrated into the national army. Men clamored to join. William Jennings Bryan, a pacifist by temperament, took command of a regiment of Nebraska volunteers; Roosevelt chafed to get to the front; and young Cordell Hull, who became secretary of state in the 1930s, was "wildly eager to leave at once." The secretary of war feared "there is going to be more trouble to satisfy those who are not going than to find those who are willing to go."

In an army inundated with men, problems of equipment and supply quickly appeared. The regulars had the new .30 caliber Krag-Jorgensen rifles, but National Guard units carried Civil War Springfield rifles that used old, black powder cartridges. The cartridges gave off a puff of smoke when fired, neatly marking the troops' position. Spanish troops were better equipped; they had modern Mausers with smokeless powder, which they used to devastating effect. Food was also a problem, as was sickness. The War Department fell behind in supplies and received many complaints about the canned beef it offered the men. Tropical disease felled many soldiers. Scores took ill after landing in Cuba and the Philippines, and it was not uncommon for half a regiment to be unable to answer the bugle call.

Americans then believed that "a foreign war should be fought by the hometown military unit acting as an extension of their community." Soldiers identified with their hometowns, dressed in the local fashion, and thought of themselves as members of a town unit in a national army. The poet Carl Sandburg, twenty years old in 1898, rushed to join the army and called his unit a "living part" of his hometown of Galesburg, Illinois. And the citizens of Galesburg, for their part, took a special interest in Sandburg's unit, in a fashion repeated in countless towns across the country.

Not surprisingly, then, National Guard units mirrored the social patterns of their communities. Since everyone knew each other, there was an easygoing familiarity, tempered by the deference that went with hometown wealth, occupation, education, and length of residence. Enlisted men resented officers who grabbed too much authority, and they expected officers and men to call each other by their first names. Sandburg knew most of the privates in his unit, had worked for his corporal, and had gone to school with the first lieutenant. "Officers and men of the Guard mingle on a plane of beautiful equality," said a visitor to one volunteer camp. "Privates invade the tents of their officers at will, and yell at them half the length of the street."

Each community thought of the hometown unit as *its* unit, an extension of itself. In later wars the government censored news and dominated press relations; there was little censorship in the war with Spain, and the freshest news arrived in the latest letter home. Small-town newspapers printed news of the men; townswomen knit special red or white bellybands of stitched flannel, thought to ward off tropical fevers; towns sent food, clothing, and occasionally even local doctors to the front. At the close of the war the Clyde (Ohio) Ladies Society collected funds to provide each member of the town's company a medal struck on behalf of the town.

"Smoked Yankees"

When the invasion force sailed for Cuba, nearly one fourth of it was black. In 1898 the regular army included four regiments of black soldiers, the Twenty-fourth and Twenty-fifth Infantry and the Ninth and Tenth Cavalry. Black regiments had served with distinction in campaigns against the Indians in the West. Most black troops in fact were posted in the West; no eastern community would accept them. A troop of the Ninth Cavalry was stationed in Virginia in 1891, but whites protested and the troop was ordered back to the West.

When the war broke out, the War Department called for five black volunteer regiments. The army needed men, and military authorities were sure that black men had a natural immunity to the climate and diseases of the tropics. But most state governors refused to accept black volunteers. Only Alabama, Ohio, and Massachusetts mustered in black units in response to McKinley's first call for volunteers. Company L of the Sixth Massachusetts Regiment took part in the invasion of Puerto Rico in July 1898, the only one of the black volunteer units to see action in the Caribbean. Black leaders, among them P. B. S. Pinchback, former acting governor of Louisiana, and George White of North Carolina, the lone black member of Congress, protested the discrimination. The McKinley administration intervened, and in the end the volunteer army included over ten thousand black troops.

Orders quickly went out to the four black regular-army regiments in the West to move to camps in the South to prepare for the invasion of Cuba. Crowds and cheers followed the troop trains across the Plains, but as they crossed into Kentucky and Tennessee, the cheering stopped. Welcoming crowds were kept away from the trains, and the troops were hustled onward. Station restaurants refused to serve them; all waiting rooms were segregated. "It mattered not if we were soldiers of the United States, and going to fight for the honor of our country," Sergeant Frank W. Pullen of the Twenty-fourth Infantry wrote; "we were 'niggers' as they called us and treated us with contempt."

Many soldiers were not prepared to put up with the treatment. Those stationed near Chickamauga Park, Tennessee, shot "at some whites who insulted them" and desegregated the railroad cars on the line into Chattanooga. Troops training near Macon, Georgia, refused to ride in the segregated "trailers" attached to the trolleys, and fights broke out. Discovering a Macon park with a sign saying "Dogs and niggers not allowed," they invaded it and removed the sign.

More than four thousand black troops trained near Tampa and Lakeland, Florida, where they found segregated saloons, cafes, and drugstores. "Here the Negro is not allowed to purchase over the same counter in some stores as the white man purchases over . . . ," George W. Prioleau, a chaplain, charged. "Why sir, the Negro of this country

The 24th and 25th Negro Infantry Divisions served with exceptional gallantry on San Juan Hill (left). Charles Young (below), an 1889 graduate of West Point, was the only black officer in the army, except for a few chaplains.

is a freeman and yet a slave. Talk about fighting and freeing poor Cuba and of Spain's brutality; of Cuba's murdered thousands, and starving recon-centradoes. Is America any better than Spain?"

Near Lakeland, units of the Tenth Cavalry pistol-whipped a drugstore owner who refused to serve a black soldier at the soda fountain. Just before the army's departure for Cuba, the tensions in Tampa erupted in a night of rioting. Drunken white soldiers from an Ohio regiment shot at a black child, black soldiers retaliated, and when the night ended, three white and twenty-seven black soldiers were wounded.

When the invasion force sailed a few days later, segregation continued on some of the troop ships. Blacks were assigned to the lowest decks, or whites and blacks were placed on different sides of the ship. But the confusion of war often ended the problem, if only temporarily. Blacks took command as white officers died, and Spanish troops soon came to fear the "smoked Yankees," as they called them. Black soldiers played a major role in the Cuban campaign and probably staved off defeat for the Rough Riders at San Juan Hill. In Cuba they won twenty-six Certificates of Merit and five Congressional Medals of Honor.

The Course of the War

Mahan's Naval War College had begun studying strategy for a war with Spain in 1895. By 1898 it had a detailed plan for operations in the Caribbean and Pacific. Naval strategy was simple: destroy the Spanish fleet, damage Spain's merchant marine, and harry the colonies or the coast of Spain. Planners were excited; two steam-powered armored fleets had yet to meet in battle anywhere in the world. The army's task was more difficult. It must defend the United States, invade Cuba and probably Puerto Rico, and undertake possible action in far-flung places like the Philippines or Spain.

Even before war was declared, the secretary of war arranged joint planning between the army and navy. Military intelligence was plentiful, and planners knew the numbers and location of the Spanish troops. Earlier they had rejected a proposal to send an officer in disguise to map Cuban harbors; such things, they said, were simply not done in peacetime. Still, the War Department's new Military Information Division, a sign of the increasing professionalization of the army, had detailed diagrams of Spanish fortifications in Havana and other points. On the afternoon of April 20, 1898, McKinley summoned the strategists to the White House, and to the dismay of those who wanted a more aggressive policy, they decided on the limited strategy of blockading Cuba, sending arms to the insurgents, and annoying the Spanish with small thrusts by the army.

Victories soon changed the strategy. In the case of war, long-standing naval plans had called for a holding action against the Spanish base in the Philippines. On May 1, 1898, with the war barely a week old, Commodore George Dewey, commander of the Asiatic Squadron located at Hong Kong, crushed the Spanish fleet in Manila Bay. Suddenly, Manila and the Philippines lay within American grasp. At home, Dewey portraits, songs, and poems blossomed everywhere, and his calm order to the flagship's captain—"You may fire when ready, Gridley"—hung on every tongue. Dewey had two modern cruisers, a gunboat, and a Civil War paddle steamer. He sank eight Spanish warships; one American sailor died —of heat stroke. Dewey had no troops to attack the Spanish army in Manila, but the War Department, stunned by the speed and size of the victory, quickly raised an expeditionary force. On August 13, 1898, the troops accepted the surrender of Manila, and with it, the Philippines.

McKinley and his aides were worried about Admiral Pascual Cervera's main Spanish fleet, thought to be headed across the Atlantic for an attack on Florida. On May 13 the navy found Cervera's ships near Martinique in the Caribbean but then lost them again. A few days later Cervera slipped secretly into the harbor of Santiago de Cuba, a city on the island's southern coast. But a spy in the Havana telegraph office alerted the Americans, and on May 28, a superior American force under Admiral William T. Sampson bottled Cervera up.

On June 14 an invasion force of about seventeen thousand men set sail from Tampa. Seven days later they landed at Daiquiri on Cuba's southeastern coast. All was confusion, but the Spanish offered no resistance. Immediately the Americans pushed west toward Santiago, which they hoped to surround and capture. At first the advance was peaceful, through the lush tropical countryside.

The first battle broke out at Las Guasimas, a

Spanish-American War: Pacific Theater

Commodore Dewey, promoted to admiral immediately after the naval victory at Manila Bay, was the first hero of the war.

crossroads on the Santiago road. After a sharp fight, the Spanish fell back. On July 1 the Rough Riders, troops from the four black regiments, and the other regulars reached the strong fortifications at El Caney and San Juan Hill. Black soldiers of the Twenty-fifth Infantry charged the El Caney blockhouses, surprising the Spanish defenders with Comanche yells. For the better part of a day the defenders fought stubbornly and held back the army's elite corps. In the confusion of battle, Roosevelt rallied an assortment of infantry and cavalry to take Kettle Hill, adjacent to San Juan Hill.

They charged directly into the Spanish guns, Roosevelt at their head, mounted on a horse, a blue polka-dot handkerchief floating from the brim of his sombrero. "I waved my hat and we went up the hill with a rush," he recalled in his autobiography. It was not quite so easy. Losses were heavy; eighty-nine Rough Riders were killed or wounded in the attack. Dense foliage concealed the enemy; smokeless powder gave no clue to their position. At nightfall the surviving Spanish defenders withdrew, and the Americans

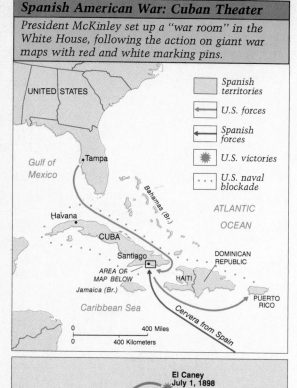

Spanish American War: Cuban Theater

President McKinley set up a "war room" in the White House, following the action on giant war maps with red and white marking pins.

UNITED STATES

Gulf of Mexico

Tampa

Havana

CUBA

Santiago

AREA OF MAP BELOW

Jamaica (Br.)

Caribbean Sea

Bahamas (Br.)

ATLANTIC OCEAN

DOMINICAN REPUBLIC

HAITI

PUERTO RICO

Cervera from Spain

Spanish territories

U.S. forces

Spanish forces

U.S. victories

U.S. naval blockade

0   400 Miles
0   400 Kilometers

El Caney
July 1, 1898

Santiago

Santiago Bay

San Juan Hill
July 1, 1898

Kettle Hill
July 1, 1898

Las Guasimas
June 24, 1898

Spanish fleet destroyed
July 3, 1898

Daiquiri

0   4 Miles
0   4 Kilometers

prepared for the counterattack. "We have won so far at a heavy cost," Roosevelt wrote home, "but the Spaniards fight very hard and charging these entrenchments against modern rifles is terrible. We are within measurable distance of a terrible military disaster."

American troops now occupied the ridges overlooking Santiago. They were weakened by sickness, but the Spanish, not knowing that, decided the city was lost. The Spanish command in Havana ordered Cervera to run for the open sea, although he knew the attempt was hopeless. On the morning of July 3 his squadron steamed down the bay and out through the harbor's narrow channel, but the waiting American fleet closed

in, and in a few hours every Spanish vessel was destroyed. Two weeks later Santiago surrendered.

Soon thereafter army troops, meeting little resistance, occupied Puerto Rico. Cervera had commanded Spain's only battle fleet, and when it sank, Spain was helpless against attacks on the colonies or even its own shores. The war was over. Lasting 113 days, it took relatively few lives, most of them the result of accident, yellow fever, malaria, and typhoid in Cuba. Of the 5500 Americans who died in the war, only 379 were killed in battle. The navy lost one man in the battle at Santiago Bay, and none at all in the stunning victory in Manila Bay.

Debate over Empire

Late in the afternoon of August 12, 1898, representatives of Spain and the United States met in McKinley's White House office to sign the preliminary instrument of peace. Secretary of State William R. Day beckoned a presidential aide over to a large globe, remarking: "Let's see what we get by this."

What the United States got was an expansion of its territory and an even larger expansion of its responsibilities. According to the preliminary agreement, Spain granted independence to Cuba, ceded Puerto Rico and the Pacific island of Guam to the United States, and allowed Americans to occupy Manila until the two countries reached final agreement on the Philippines. To McKinley, the Philippines were the problem. Puerto Rico was close to the mainland, and it appealed even to many of the opponents of expansion. Guam was small and unknown; it escaped attention. The Philippines, on the other hand, were huge, sprawling, and thousands of miles from America.

McKinley weighed a number of alternatives for the Philippines, but he liked none of them. He felt he could not give the islands back to Spain; public opinion would not allow it. He might turn them over to another nation, but then they would fall, as he later said, "a golden apple of discord, among the rival powers." Germany, Japan, Great Britain, and Russia had all expressed interest in acquiring them. Germany even sent a large fleet to Manila and laid plans to take the Philippines if the United States let them go.

Rejecting those alternatives, McKinley considered independence for the islands but was soon talked out of it. Nearly everyone who had been there believed the people were not ready for independence. He thought of establishing an American protectorate but discarded the idea, convinced it would bring American responsibilities without full American control. Sifting the alternatives, McKinley decided there was only one practical policy: annex the Philippines, with an eye to future independence after a period of tutelage.

At first hesitant, American opinion was swinging to the same conclusion. Religious and missionary organizations appealed to McKinley to hold on to the Philippines in order to Christianize them. Some merchants and industrialists saw them as the key to the China market and the wealth of Asia. Many Americans simply regarded them as the legitimate fruits of war. In October 1898, representatives of the United States and Spain met in Paris to discuss a peace treaty. Spain agreed to recognize Cuba's independence, assume the Cuban debt, and cede Puerto Rico and Guam to the United States.

Acting on instructions from McKinley, the American representatives demanded the cession of the Philippines. "Grave as are the responsibilities and unforeseen as are the difficulties which are before us, the President can see but one plain path of duty—the acceptance of the archipelago," the instructions said. In return, the United States offered a payment of $20 million. Spain resisted but had little choice, and on December 10, 1898, the American and Spanish representatives signed the Treaty of Paris.

Submitted to the Senate for ratification, the treaty set off a storm of debate throughout the country. Industrialist Andrew Carnegie, reformer Jane Addams, labor leader Samuel Gompers, prominent Republicans like Thomas B. Reed and John Sherman, Mark Twain, William Dean Howells, and a host of others argued forcefully against annexing the Phillipines. Carnegie felt so strongly he offered to buy Filipino independence with a personal check for $20 million. Annexation of the Philippines, the anti-imperialists protested over and over again, violated the very principles of independence and self-determination on which the country was founded.

Some labor leaders feared the importation of cheap labor from new Pacific colonies. Other anti-imperialists argued against assimilation of different races, "Spanish-Americans," as one said, 'with all the mixture of Indian and negro blood, and Malays and other unspeakable Asiatics, by the tens of millions!" Such racial views were at least as common among those favoring expansion, and in any event the anti-imperialists usually focused on different arguments. The exercise of tyranny abroad, they were sure, would result in tyranny at home. "This nation," declared William Jennings Bryan, "cannot endure half republic and half colony—half free and half vassal."

In November 1898, opponents of expansion formed the Anti-Imperialist League to fight against the peace treaty. Local leagues sprang up in Boston, New York, Philadelphia, and many other cities; the parent league claimed thirty thousand members and over half a million "contributors." Membership centered in New England; the cause was less popular in the West and South. It enlisted more Democrats than Republicans, though never a majority of either. The anti-imperialists lacked a coherent program. Some favored keeping naval bases in the conquered areas. Some wanted Hawaii and Puerto Rico but not the Philippines. Others wanted nothing to do with any colonies. Most simply

■ *A* Puck *cartoon entitled "School Begins" satirizes Uncle Sam's course in civilization, in which he assures his new class they will soon be glad they learned it.*

■ Aguinaldo's guerrilla fighters at an outpost (above). The Filipinos battled for three years before surrendering.

■ During the bitterly fought Philippine war, Americans shelled and then burned Manila (below).

wished that Dewey had sailed away after beating the Spanish at Manila Bay.

The debate in the Senate lasted a month. Pressing hard for ratification, McKinley earlier toured the South to rally support and consulted closely with senators. Though opposed to taking the Philippines, Bryan supported ratification in order to end the war; his support influenced some Democratic votes. Still, on the final weekend before the vote, the treaty was two votes short. That Saturday night, news reached Washington that fighting had broken out between American troops and Filipino insurgents who demanded immediate independence. The news increased pressure to ratify the treaty, which the Senate did on February 6, 1899, with two votes to spare. The United States had a colonial empire.

Guerrilla Warfare in the Philippines

Historians rarely write of the Philippine-American War, but it was an important event in American history. The war with Spain was over in a few months; war with the Filipinos lasted more than three years. Four times as many American soldiers fought in the Philippines as in Cuba. For the first time Americans fought men of a different color in an Asian guerrilla war. The Philippine-American War of 1898–1902 took a heavy toll: 4300 American lives and perhaps as many as 57,000 Filipino lives.

Emilio Aguinaldo, the Filipino leader, was twenty-nine years old in 1898. An early organizer of the anti-Spanish resistance, he had gone into exile in Hong Kong, from where he welcomed the outbreak of the Spanish-American War. Certain the United States would grant independence, he worked for an American victory. Filipino insurgents helped guide Dewey into Manila Bay, and Dewey himself sent a ship to Hong Kong to bring back Aguinaldo to lead a native uprising against the Spanish. On June 12, 1898, the insurgents proclaimed their independence.

Cooperating with the Americans, they drove the Spanish out of many areas of the islands. In the liberated regions Aguinaldo established local governments with appointed provincial governors. He waited impatiently for American recognition, but McKinley and others doubted the Filipinos were ready. Shortly thereafter fighting broke out between the Filipinos and Americans.

By late 1899 the American army had defeated and dispersed the organized Filipino army, but claims of victory proved premature. Aguinaldo and his advisers shifted to guerrilla tactics, striking suddenly and then melting into the jungle or friendly native villages. In many areas the Americans ruled the day, the guerrillas the night. The Americans found themselves using Weyler-like tactics. After any attack on an American patrol, they burned all the houses in the nearest district. They established protected "zones" and herded Filipinos into them. Seizing or destroying all food outside the zones, they starved many guerrillas into submission.

In 1900 McKinley sent a special Philippine Commission under William Howard Taft, a prominent Ohio judge. Directed to establish a civil government, the commission organized municipal administrations and in stages created a government for the Philippines. In March 1901 five American soldiers tricked their way into Aguinaldo's camp deep in the mountains and took him prisoner. Back in Manila, he signed a proclamation urging his people to end the fighting. Some guerrillas held out for another year but to no avail. On July 4, 1901, authority was transferred from the army to Taft, who was named civilian governor of the islands, and his civilian commission. McKinley reaffirmed his purpose to grant the Filipinos self-government as soon as they were ready for it.

Given broad powers, the Taft Commission introduced many changes. New schools provided education and vocational training for Filipinos of all social classes. The Americans built roads and bridges, reformed the judiciary, restructured the tax system, and introduced sanitation and vaccination programs. They established local governments built on Filipino traditions and hierarchies. Taft encouraged Filipino participation in government. During the following decades other measures broadened Filipino rights; independence came on July 4, 1946, nearly fifty years after Aguinaldo proclaimed it.

Governing the Empire

Ruling the colonies raised new and perplexing questions. How could—and how should—the distant dependencies be governed? Did their inhabitants have the rights of American citizens? Some people contended that acquisition did not automatically incorporate the new possessions into the United States and endow them with constitutional privileges. Others argued that "the Consti-

Chronology	
1867	United States purchases Alaska from Russia Midway Islands are annexed
1871	Treaty of Washington between United States and Great Britain sets precedent for peaceful settlement of international disputes
1875	Reciprocity treaty with Hawaii binds Hawaii economically and politically to United States
1878	United States acquires naval base in Samoa
1883	Congress approves funds for construction of first modern steel ships; beginning of modern navy
1887	New treaty with Hawaii gives United States exclusive use of Pearl Harbor
1889	First Inter-American Conference meets in Washington, D.C.
1893	American settlers in Hawaii overthrow Queen Liliuokalani; provisional government established
1895	Cuban insurgents rebel against Spanish rule
1898	Battleship *Maine* explodes in Havana harbor (February) Congress declares war against Spain (April) Commodore Dewey defeats Spanish fleet at Manila Bay (May) United States annexes Hawaii (July) Americans defeat Spanish at El Caney, San Juan Hill (actually Kettle Hill), and Santiago (July) Spain sues for peace (August) Treaty of Paris ends Spanish-American War (December)
1899	Congress ratifies Treaty of Paris United States sends "open-door" notes to Britain, Germany, France, Russia, Japan, and Italy Philippine-American War erupts
1900	Foraker Act establishes civil government in Puerto Rico
1901	Platt Amendment authorizes American intervention in Cuba
1902	Philippine-American War ends with American victory

American Empire, 1900

With the Treaty of Paris, the United States gained an expanded colonial empire stretching from the Caribbean to the far Pacific. It embraced Puerto Rico, Alaska, Hawaii, part of Samoa, Guam, the Philippines, and a chain of Pacific islands.

tution followed the flag," meaning that acquisition made the possessions part of the nation and thus entitled to all constitutional guarantees. A third group suggested that only "fundamental" constitutional guarantees—citizenship, the right to vote, and the right to trial by jury—not "formal" privileges—the right to use American currency, the right to be taxed, and the right to run for the presidency—were applicable to the new empire.

In a series of cases between 1901 and 1904 (*De Lima* v. *Bidwell, Dooley* v. *U.S.,* and *Downes* v. *Bidwell*), the Supreme Court asserted the principle that the Constitution did not automatically and immediately apply to the people of an annexed territory and did not confer upon them all

the privileges of United States citizenship. Instead, Congress could specifically extend such constitutional provisions as it saw fit.

Four dependencies—Hawaii, Alaska, Guam, and Puerto Rico—were organized quickly. In 1900 Congress granted territorial status to Hawaii, gave American citizenship to all citizens of the Hawaiian republic, authorized an elective legislature, and provided for a governor appointed from Washington. A similar measure made Alaska a territory in 1912. Guam and the island of Tutuila were simply placed under the control of naval officers.

Unlike the Filipinos, Puerto Ricans readily accepted the war's outcome, and McKinley early withdrew troops from the island. The Foraker Act of 1900 established civil government in Puerto Rico. It organized the island as a territory, made its residents citizens of Puerto Rico (United States citizenship was extended to them in 1917), and empowered the president to appoint a governor general and a council to serve as the upper house of the legislature. A lower house of delegates was to be elected.

Cuba proved a trickier matter. McKinley asserted the authority of the United States over conquered territory and promised to govern the island until the Cubans had established a firm and stable government of their own. "I want you to go down there to get the people ready for a republican form of government," he instructed General Leonard Wood, commander of the army in Cuba until 1902. "I leave the details of procedure to you. Give them a good school system, try to straighten out their ports, and put them on their feet as best you can. We want to do all we can for them and to get out of the island as soon as we safely can."

Wood moved quickly to implement the instructions. Early in 1900 he completed a census of the Cuban population, conducted municipal elections, and arranged the election of delegates to a constitutional convention. The convention adopted a constitution modeled on the U.S. Constitution and, at Wood's prodding, included provisions for future relations with the United States. Known as the Platt Amendment, the provisions stipulated that Cuba should make no treaties with other powers that might impair its independence, acquire no debts it could not pay, and lease naval bases to the United States. Most important, the amendment empowered the United States to intervene in Cuba to maintain orderly government.

Between 1898 and 1902 the American military government worked hard for the economic and political revival of the island. It repaired the damage of the civil war, built roads and schools, and established order in rural areas. A public health campaign headed by Dr. Walter Reed, an army surgeon, wiped out yellow fever. Most troops withdrew at the end of 1899, but a small American occupation force remained until May 1902. When it sailed for home, the Cubans at last had their independence, although they were under the clear domination of their neighbor to the north.

The Open Door

Poised in the Philippines, the United States had become an Asian power on the doorsteps of China. Weakened by years of warfare, China in 1898 and 1899 was unable to resist foreign influence. Japan, England, France, Germany, and Russia eyed it covetously, dividing the country into "spheres of influence." They forced China to grant "concessions" that allowed them exclusive rights to develop particular areas and threatened American hopes for extensive trade with the country.

McKinley first outlined a new China policy in September 1898 when he said that Americans sought more trade, "but we seek no advantages in the Orient which are not common to all. Asking only the open door for ourselves, we are ready to accord the open door to·others." In September 1899 Secretary of State John Hay addressed identical diplomatic notes to England, Germany, and Russia, and later to France, Japan, and Italy, asking them to join the United States in establishing the "Open Door." The policy urged three

European Spheres of Influence in China

The international grab for economic and territorial control of China led in 1900 to the Boxer Rebellion, a violent antiforeign movement.

RUSSIA

Mongolia   Manchuria

Singkiang

Port Arthur (Russ.)   KOREA
Peking   Dairen (Russ.)
                          Wei-hai-wei
                          (Br.)
CHINA   Tsingtao
             (Ger.)   JAPAN

Tibet   East
         China
NEPAL   Sea

BHUTAN   FORMOSA
                    (Japanese)
BRITISH INDIA   Macao
                 (Port.)   Hong Kong (Br.)

0   500 Miles   PHILIPPINE IS.
                              (U.S.)
0   500 Kilometers   FRENCH
              SIAM   INDOCHINA   Kuang-chou-wan
                                   (Fr.)

British sphere of influence   Japanese sphere of influence

French sphere of influence   Russian sphere of influence

German sphere of influence   ■ Major treaty ports

The United States broadened its Open Door policy in 1900 with a second round of notes that included all China, not just the areas under European spheres of influence.

agreements: nations possessing a sphere of influence would respect the rights and privileges of other nations in that sphere; the Chinese government would continue to collect tariff duties in all spheres; and nations would not discriminate against other nations in levying port dues and railroad rates within their respective spheres of influence.

Under the Open Door policy, the United States would retain many commercial advantages that were endangered by the partition of China into spheres of influence. McKinley and Hay also attempted to preserve for the Chinese some semblance of national authority. Great Britain most nearly accepted the principle of the Open Door. Russia declined to approve it, and the other powers, sending evasive replies, stated they would only agree if all the other nations did. Hay turned the situation to American advantage by boldly announcing in March 1900 that all the powers had accepted the Open Door policy.

The war over, Roosevelt and the Rough Riders sailed for home in mid-August 1898. They sauntered through the streets of New York, the heroes of the city. A few weeks later Roosevelt bade them farewell. They presented him with a reproduction of Frederick Remington's famed bronze, *The Bronco-Buster*, and close to tears, he told them: "I am proud of this regiment beyond measure." Roosevelt later wrote an account of the war in which he played so central a role that Mr. Dooley suggested "If I was him, I'd call th' book 'Alone in Cubia.'" By then Roosevelt was already

governor of New York and on his way to the White House.

Other soldiers were also glad to be home, although sometimes resentful of the reception they found. "The war is over now," said Winslow Hobson, a black trooper from the Ninth Ohio, "and Roosevelt . . . and others (white of course) have all there is to be gotten out of it." Bravery in Cuba and the Philippines won some recognition for black soldiers, but the war itself set back the cause of civil rights. It spurred talk about "inferior" races, at home and abroad, and united whites in the North and South. "The Negro might as well know it now as later," a black editor said, "the closer the North and South get together by this war, the harder he will have to fight to maintain a footing." A fresh outburst of segregation and lynching occurred during the decade after the war.

McKinley and the Republican party soared to new heights of popularity. Firmly established, the Republican majority dominated politics until the 1930s. Scandals arose about the canned beef and the conduct of the War Department, but there was none of the sharp sense of deception and betrayal that was to mark the years after World War I. In a little more than a century the United States had grown from thirteen states stretched along a thin Atlantic coastline into a world power that reached from the Caribbean to the Pacific. As Seward and others had hoped, the nation now dominated its own hemisphere, dealt with European powers on more equal terms, and was a major power in Asia.

Recommended Reading

The best general account of the development of American foreign policy during the last part of the nineteenth century is Walter LaFeber, *The New Empire: An Interpretation of American Expansion, 1860–1898* (1963). Robert L. Beisner, *From the Old Diplomacy to the New, 1865–1900* (1975), and Charles S. Campbell, Jr., *Transformation of American Foreign Relations, 1865–1900* (1976), give useful overviews that suggest important changes that took place in the 1890s. J. A. S. Grenville and George Berkeley Young present a series of significant essays in *Politics, Strategy and American Diplomacy: Studies in Foreign Policy, 1873–1917* (1966).

Ernest R. May analyzes the causes of the Spanish-American War in *Imperial Democracy: The Emergence of America as a Great Power* (1961); for a briefer treatment, see H. Wayne Morgan, *America's Road to Empire: The War with Spain and Overseas Expansion* (1965). Lewis L. Gould persuasively reassesses McKinley's diplomacy and wartime leadership in *The Presidency of William McKinley* (1980).

Graham A. Cosmas presents a detailed account of military organization and strategy in *An Army for Empire: The United States Army in the Spanish-American War* (1971), while Willard B. Gatewood, Jr., *"Smoked Yankees" and the Struggle for Empire: Letters from Negro Soldiers, 1898–1902* (1971), offers a fascinating glimpse of the thoughts of some black soldiers in the war. Gerald F. Linderman relates the war to the home front in *The Mirror of War: American Society and the Spanish-American War* (1974).

Additional Bibliography

On American foreign policy during this period, see David M. Pletcher, *The Awkward Years: American Foreign Relations under Garfield and Arthur* (1962); David F. Healy, *U.S. Expansionism: The Imperialist Urge in the 1890's* (1970); Milton Plesur, *America's Outward Thrust: Approaches to Foreign Affairs, 1865–1890* (1971); Richard W. Leopold, *The Growth of American Foreign Policy* (1962); and Tom E. Terrill, *The Tariff, Politics, and American Foreign Policy, 1874–1901* (1973).

For policies toward specific areas, see R. P. Gilson, *Samoa 1830 to 1900: The Politics of a Multi-Cultural Community* (1970); Charles S. Campbell, Jr., *Anglo-American Understanding, 1898–1903* (1957); Thomas J. McCormick, *China Market: America's Quest for Informal Empire, 1893–1901* (1967); Marilyn B. Young, *Rhetoric of Empire: American China Policy, 1895–1901* (1968); Merze Tate, *The United States and the Hawaiian Kingdom: A Political History* (1965); and William A. Russ, Jr., *The Hawaiian Republic, 1894–98 and Its Struggle to Win Annexation* (1961).

Books on naval and military developments during these years include J. D. Hittle, *The Military Staff* (1949); Walter R. Herrick, *The American Naval Revolu-*tion (1966); William R. Braisted, *The United States Navy in the Pacific, 1897–1909* (1958); Peter Karsten, *The Naval Aristocracy* (1972); Benjamin J. Cooling, *Gray Steel and Blue Water Navy* (1979); and Kenneth J. Hagan, *American Gunboat Diplomacy and the Old Navy, 1877–1889* (1973).

For the background of the war with Spain, see Julius W. Pratt, *Expansionists of 1898: The Acquisition of Hawaii and the Spanish Islands* (1936); Walter Millis, *The Martial Spirit: A Study of Our War with Spain* (1931); Philip S. Foner, *The Spanish-Cuban-American War and the Birth of American Imperialism, 1895–1902*, 2 vols. (1972); J. E. Wisan, *The Cuban Crisis as Reflected in the New York Press, 1895–1898* (1934); and Hyman G. Rickover, *How the Battleship Maine Was Destroyed* (1976).

Biographies of the period's leading personalities include H. Wayne Morgan, *William McKinley and His America* (1963); Margaret Leech, *In the Days of McKinley* (1959); Robert Seager, II, *Alfred Thayer Mahan* (1977); and Ronald Spector, *Admiral of the New Empire: The Life and Career of George Dewey* (1974). See also Theodore Roosevelt, *The Rough Riders* (1899); Russell A. Alger, *The Spanish-American War* (1901); John D. Long, *The New American Navy*, 2 vols. (1903); and H. Wayne Morgan, ed., *Making Peace with Spain: The Diary of Whitelaw Reid, September-December 1898* (1965).

The course of the war itself can be followed in Frank Freidel, *The Splendid Little War* (1958); Orestes Femara, *The Last Spanish War* (1937); Frederick Funston, *Memories of Two Wars: Cuba and Philippine Experiences* (1914); Charles H. Brown, *The Correspondents' War: Journalists in the Spanish-American War* (1967); David A. Gerber, *Black Ohio and the Color Line, 1860–1915* (1976); and Herschel V. Cashin et al., *Under Fire with the Tenth U.S. Cavalry* (1899).

For the debate over expansion and the treaty with Spain, consult Richard E. Welch, Jr., *George Frisbie Hoar and the Half-Breed Republicans* (1971); E. Berkeley Tompkins, *Anti-Imperialism in the United States: The Great Debate, 1890–1920* (1970); Daniel B. Schirmer, *Republic or Empire: American Resistance to the Philippine War* (1972); Thomas J. Osborne, *"Empire Can Wait": American Opposition to Hawaiian Annexation, 1893–1898* (1981); and Göran Rystad, *Ambiguous Imperialism: American Foreign Policy and Domestic Politics at the Turn of the Century* (1975).

Policy toward Cuba and the Philippines is covered in Richard E. Welch, Jr., *Response to Imperialism: The United States and the Philippine-American War, 1899–1902* (1979); David F. Healy, *The United States in Cuba, 1898–1902* (1963); James H. Hitchman, *Leonard Wood and Cuban Independence, 1898–1902* (1971); John Morgan Gates, *Schoolbooks and Krags: The United States Army in the Philippines, 1898–1902* (1973); Glenn A. May, *Social Engineering in the Philippines* (1980); and Peter W. Stanley, *A Nation in the Making: The Philippines and the United States, 1899–1921* (1974). Willard B. Gatewood, Jr., *Black Americans and the White Man's Burden, 1898–1903* (1975) is a thorough and thought-provoking study.

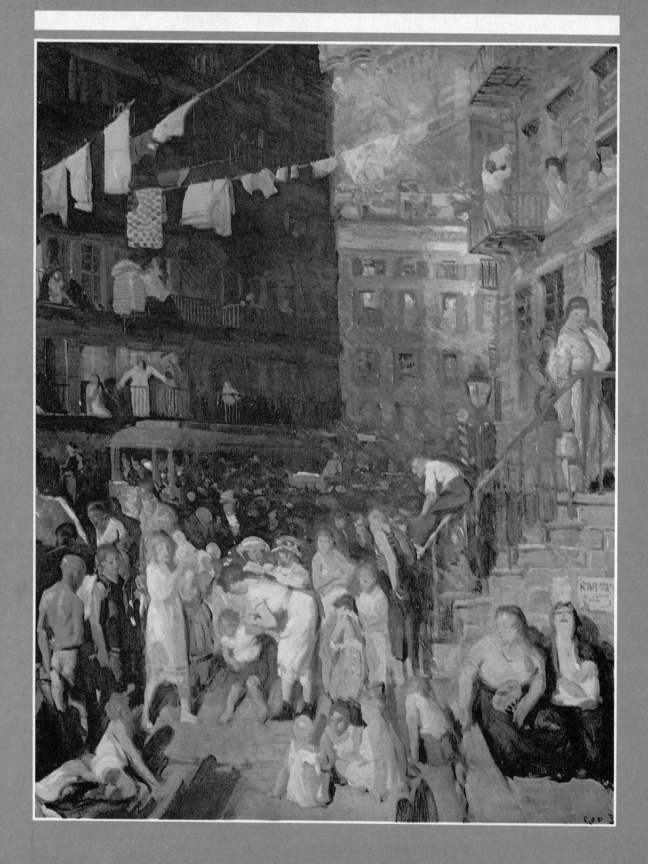

chapter 22

THE
PROGRESSIVE
ERA

In 1902 Samuel S. McClure, the shrewd owner of *McClure's Magazine*, sensed something astir in the country that his reporters were not covering. Like *Life, Munsey's*, the *Ladies' Home Journal*, and *Cosmopolitan, McClure's* was reaching more and more people—more than a quarter of a million readers a month. Americans were snapping up the new popular magazines filled with eye-catching illustrations and up-to-date fiction. Advances in photoengraving during the 1890s dramatically reduced the cost of illustrations; at the same time income from advertisements rose sharply. By the turn of the century some magazines earned as much as $60,000 an issue from advertising alone, and publishers could price them as low as $.10 a copy.

McClure was always chasing new ideas and readers, and in 1902, certain that something was happening in the public mood, he told one of his editors, thirty-six-year-old Lincoln Steffens, a former Wall Street reporter, to find out what it was. "Get out of here, travel, go—somewhere . . . ," he said to Steffens. "Buy a railroad ticket, get on a train, and there, where it lands you, there you will learn to edit a magazine."

McClure's, it turned out, had an unpaid bill from the Lackawanna Railroad, and Steffens traveled west. In Saint Louis he came across a young district attorney named Joseph W. Folk who had found a trail of corruption linking politics and some of the city's respected business leaders. Eager for help, Folk did not mind naming names to the visiting editor from New York. "It is good business men that are corrupting our bad politicians . . . ," he stressed again and again. "It is the leading citizens that are battening on our city." Steffens' story, "Tweed Days in St. Louis," appeared in the October 1902 issue of *McClure's*.

The November *McClure's* carried the first installment of Ida Tarbell's scathing "History of the Standard Oil Company," and in January 1903 Steffens was back with "The Shame of Minneapolis," another tale of corrupt partnership between business and politics. McClure had what he' wanted, and in the January issue he printed an editorial, "Concerning Three Articles in this

Number of *McClure's*, and a Coincidence that May Set Us Thinking." Steffens on Minneapolis, Tarbell on Standard Oil, and an article on abuses in labor unions—all, McClure said, on different topics but actually on the same theme: corruption in American life. "Capitalists, workingmen, politicians, citizens—all breaking the law, or letting it be broken."

Readers were enthralled, and articles and books by other muckrakers—Theodore Roosevelt coined the unflattering term in 1906 to describe the practice of exposing the corruption of public and prominent figures—spread swiftly. *Collier's* had articles on questionable stock-market practices, patent medicines, and the beef trust. Novelist Upton Sinclair tackled the meat packers in *The Jungle* (1906). In 1904 Steffens collected his *McClure's* articles in *The Shame of the Cities*, with an introduction expressing confidence that reform was possible, "that our shamelessness is superficial, that beneath it lies a pride which, being real, may save us yet."

Muckraking flourished from 1903 to 1909, and while it did, good writers and bad investigated almost every corner of American life: government, labor unions, big business, Wall Street, health care, the food industry, child labor, women's rights, prostitution, ghetto living, and life insurance. "Time was," Mr. Dooley, the fictional character of humorist Finley Peter Dunne, said to Mr. Hennessy, when magazines

was very ca'ming to the mind. Angabel an' Alfonso dashin' f'r a marriage license. Prom'nent lady authoresses makin' pomes at the moon. . . . Th' idee ye got fr'm these here publications was that life was wan glad sweet song. . . .

But now whin I pick me fav-rite magazine off th' flure, what do I find? Ivrything has gone wrong. . . . All th' pomes by th' lady authoresses that used to begin: "Oh, moon, how fair!" now begin: "Oh, Ogden Armour, how awful!" . . . Graft ivrywhere. "Graft in th' Insurance Companies," "Graft in Congress," "Graft be an Old Grafter," "Graft in Its Relations to th' Higher Life". . . .

During the progressive era, McClure's Magazine was at the front of the journalistic crusade for reform, which took the form of muckraking articles by such writers as Ida Tarbell (right). Her exposé of the Standard Oil Company ran side by side with Lincoln Steffens' article on the alliances between business and corrupt political machines in several cities.

An' so it goes, Hinnissy . . . till I don't thrust anny man anny more. . . . I used to be nervous about burglars, but now I'm afraid iv a night call fr'm th' prisidint iv th' First National Bank.

The muckrakers were a journalistic voice of a larger movement in American society. Called *progressivism*, it lasted from the mid-1890s through World War I. Like muckraking itself, it reflected concern with the state of society and a conviction that human compassion and scientific investigation could bring problems to light and solve them. Progressivism took on the character of Theodore Roosevelt and Woodrow Wilson, two important national spokesmen, but it affected large numbers of people and expressed at many levels the excitement of progress and change.

The Spirit of Progressivism

In one way or another, progressivism touched all aspects of society. Politically, it fostered a reform movement that sought cures for the problems of city, state, and nation. Intellectually, it drew on the expertise of the new social sciences and reflected a shift from older absolutes of class and religion to newer schools of thought that emphasized physiological explanations for behavior, the role of the environment in human development, and the relative nature of truth. Culturally, it inspired fresh modes of expression in dance, film, painting, literature, and architecture. Touching individuals in different ways, progressivism became a set of attitudes as well as a definable movement.

Unlike Populism, which grew mostly in the rural South and West, progressivism drew support across society. "The thing that constantly amazed me," said William Allen White, a leading progressive journalist, "was how many people were with us." Progressivism appealed to the expanding middle class, prosperous farmers, and skilled laborers; it also attracted significant support in the business community.

Leadership came mainly from young, educated men and women. Many of them belonged to the professions—law, medicine, religion, business, teaching, and social work—and they thought they could use their expertise to improve society. They believed in progress and disliked waste. No single issue or concern united them all. Some progressives wanted to clean up city governments, others to clean up city streets. Some wanted to purify politics or control corporate abuses, others to eradicate poverty or prostitution. Some demanded social justice in the form of woman's rights, child labor laws, temperance, and factory safety. They were Democrats, Republicans, Socialists, and independents.

Progressives believed in a better world and in the ability of people to achieve it. They paid to people, as a friend said of social reformer Florence Kelley, "the high compliment of believing that, once they knew the truth, they would act upon it." Progress depended on knowledge. The progressives stressed individual morality and collective action, the scientific method, and the value of expert opinon. Like contemporary business leaders, they valued system, planning, management, and predictability. They wanted not only reform but efficiency. In the introduction to *The Shame of the Cities*, Steffens said the cure for American ills lay in "good conduct in the individual, simple honesty, courage, and efficiency."

Progressivism also fed on an organizational impulse that encouraged people to join forces, share information, and solve problems. Between 1890 and 1920, a host of national societies and associations took shape—nearly four hundred of them in just three decades. Many new associations such as the American Medical Association (reorganized in 1901) and the U.S. Chamber of Commerce (1912) reflected the increasingly authoritative voice of the professions. Other groups such as the National Child Labor Committee, which lobbied for legislation to regulate the employment and working conditions of children, were formed to attack specific issues.

Believing in government as an agent of change, the progressives wanted to curb the influence of "special interests" and make government follow the public will. Once it did, they welcomed government action at whatever level was appropriate. The use of federal power increased, along with the power and prestige of the presidency. Most important, the progressives believed in the ability of experts to solve problems. At every level—local, state, and federal—thousands of commissions and agencies took form. Staffed by trained experts, they oversaw a multitude of matters ranging from railroad rates to public health.

Historians once viewed progressivism as the triumph of one group in society over another. In this view, farmers took on the hated and powerful railroads; upstart reformers challenged the city bosses; business interests fought for favorable legislation; youthful professionals carved out their place in society. Now historians stress the way progressivism brought people together rather than driving them apart. Disparate groups united in an effort to improve the well-being of many groups in society.

Reform in the Cities and States

Progressivism began in the cities during the 1890s. It first took form around settlement workers and others interested in freeing individuals from the crushing impact of cities and factories. Ministers, intellectuals, social workers, and lawyers joined in a social-justice movement that focused national attention on the need for tenement house laws, more stringent child labor legislation, and better working conditions for women. They brought pressure on municipal agencies for more and better parks, playgrounds, day nurseries, schools, and community services. Blending private and public action, settlement leaders turned increasingly to government aid. "Private beneficence," Jane Addams said, "is totally inadequate to deal with the vast numbers of the city's disinherited."

The Social-Justice Movement

Social-justice reformers were more interested in social cures than individual charity. They saw problems as endless and interrelated; individuals became part of a city's larger patterns. With that insight, social-service casework shifted from a focus on an individual's well-being to a scientific analysis of neighborhoods, occupations, and classes.

In the spring of 1900 the Charity Organization Society of New York held a tenement-house exhibition that graphically presented the new kind of sociological data. Put together by Lawrence Veiller, a young social worker, the exhibition included over a thousand photographs, detailed maps of slum districts, statistical tables and charts, and graphic cardboard depictions of tenement blocks. Never before had so much information been pulled together in one place. Veiller correlated data on poverty and disease with housing conditions, and he pointed out that new slums were springing up in more areas of the city.

An Infant Welfare Society nurse treats the baby of an immigrant family in Chicago. A host of medical discoveries and the growth of the quality medical education fostered an interest in public health work among the social-justice reformers.

Stirred by the public outcry, Governor Theodore Roosevelt appointed the New York State Tenement House Commission to do something about the problem.

With Veiller's success as a model, study after study analyzed the condition of the poor. Books and pamphlets like *The Standard of Living Among Working Men's Families in New York City* (1909) contained pages of data on family budgets, women's wages and working conditions, child labor, and other matters. Between 1910 and 1913 the U.S. Commissioner of Labor issued a massive nineteen-volume report on *Conditions of Women and Children Wage-Earners in the United States.*

Banding together to work for change, social-justice reformers formed the National Conference of Charities and Corrections, which in 1915 became the National Conference of Social Work. Controlled by social workers, the conference reflected the growing professionalization of reform. Through it, social workers discovered each other's efforts, shared methodology, and tried to establish themselves as a separate field within the social sciences. Once content with informal training sessions in a settlement-house living room, they now formed complete professional schools at Chicago, Harvard, and other universities. After 1909 they had their own professional magazine, the *Survey,* and instead of piecemeal reforms they aimed at a comprehensive program

of minimum wages, maximum hours, workers' compensation, and widows' pensions.

Women played a very large role in the social-justice movement. Feminists were particularly active, especially in the political sphere, between 1890 and 1914—feminists were more active then, in fact, than at any time until the 1960s. Some working-class women pushed for higher wages and better working conditions. College-educated women—five thousand a year graduated after 1900—took up careers in the professions, from which some of them supported reform. From 1890 to 1910 the work of a number of national women's organizations, including the National Council of Jewish Women, National Congress of Mothers, and the Women's Trade Union League, furthered the aims of the progressive movement.

The National Association of Colored Women was founded in 1895, fifteen years before the better known, male-oriented National Association for the Advancement of Colored People (NAACP). Aimed at social welfare, the women's organization was the first black social-service agency in the country. At the local level, black women's clubs established kindergartens, day nurseries, playgrounds, and retirement homes.

From two hundred thousand members in 1900, the General Federation of Women's Clubs grew to over one million by 1912. The clubs met, as they had before, for coffee and literary conversation, but they also began to look closely at conditions around them. In 1904 Mrs. Sarah P. Decker, the federation's new president, told the national convention: "Ladies, you have chosen me your leader. Well, I have an important piece of news to give you. Dante is dead. He has been dead for several centuries, and I think it is time that we dropped the study of his *Inferno* and turned our attention to our own."

Forming an Industrial Section and a Committee on Legislation for Women and Children, the federation supported reforms to safeguard child and women workers, improve schools, ensure pure food, and beautify the community. Reluctant at first, it finally lent support in 1914 to woman suffrage, a cause that dated back to the first woman's rights convention in Seneca Falls, New York, in 1848. Divided over tactics, the suffrage movement suffered from disunity, male opposition, indecision over whether to seek action at the state or at the national level, resistance from the Catholic Church, and opposition from liquor interests, who linked the cause to prohibition.

In 1900 Carrie Chapman Catt, a superb organizer, became president of the National American Woman Suffrage Association, which by 1920 had nearly two million members. Catt and Anna Howard Shaw, who became the association's head in 1904, believed in organization and peaceful lobbying to win the vote. Alice Paul and Lucy Burns, founders of the Congressional Union, were more militant; they interrupted public meetings, focused on Congress rather than the states, and in 1917 picketed the White House. The issue attracted many progressives who believed woman's suffrage would purify politics. In 1918 the House passed a constitutional amendment stating simply that the right to vote shall not be denied "on account of sex." The Senate and enough states followed, and the Nineteenth Amendment took effect in 1920.

The social-justice movement had most success in passing state laws limiting the working hours of women. By 1913 thirty-nine states set maximum working hours for women or banned the employment of women at night. Illinois had a ten-hour law; California and Washington, eight-hours. Wisconsin, Oregon, and Kansas allowed expert commissions to set different hours depending on the degree of strain in various occupations. As early as 1900, thanks to groups such as the National Child Labor Committee, twenty-eight

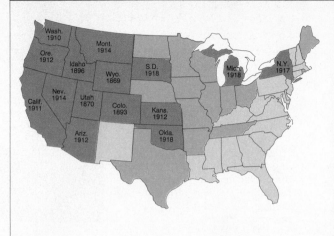

Woman Suffrage Before 1920

State by state gains in woman suffrage were limited to the Far West and were agonizingly slow in the early years of the twentieth century.

Equal suffrage with effective date

Partial woman suffrage

No woman suffrage

■ *A woman suffrage parade, New York, October 23, 1915. Women finally won the right to vote in 1920, seventy-two years after the idea was proposed at Seneca Falls.*

states had laws regulating child labor. But the courts often ruled against such laws, and families —needing extra income—sometimes ignored them. Parents sent children off to jobs with orders to lie about their age.

In 1916 President Woodrow Wilson backed a law to limit child labor, the Keating-Owen Act, but in *Hammer* v. *Dagenhart* (1918) the Supreme Court overturned it as an improper regulation of local labor conditions. In 1919 Congress tried again in the Second Child Labor Act, also struck down by the Court in *Bailey* v. *Drexel Furniture Company* (1922). Not until the 1930s did Congress succeed in passing a Court-supported national child labor law.

A Ferment of Ideas

A dramatic shift in ideas became one of the most important forces behind progressive reform. Building on the developments of the 1890s (see chapter 19), writers in law, economics, history, sociology, psychology, and a host of other fields advanced ideas that together challenged the status quo and called for change.

A new doctrine, called pragmatism, emerged in this ferment of ideas. A famous Harvard psychologist, William James, popularized the pragmatic approach to knowledge. Pragmatists posited that the human mind is not a fixed structure but is constantly changing. Moreover, its thoughts have meaning only in relation to their consequences— the actions they inspire. James' question was "what is the 'cash value' of a thought, idea or belief?" Does it work? Does it make a difference to the individual who experiences it? "The ultimate test for us of what a truth means," said James, "is the conduct it dictates."

The most influential educator of the Progressive era, John Dewey, applied pragmatism to educational reform. He argued that thought evolves in relation to the environment and that education is directly related to experience. In 1896 he and his wife founded a separate School of Pedagogy at the University of Chicago, with a laboratory where educational theory based on the newer philosophical and psychological studies could be tested and practiced.

Dewey introduced an educational revolution that stressed children's needs and capabilities. He described his beliefs and methods in a number of books, notably *School and Society* (1899) and *Democracy and Education* (1916). New ideas in education, he said, are "as much a product of the changed social situation, and as much an effort to meet the needs of the society that is forming, as are changes in modes of industry and commerce." He opposed memorization and dogmatic, authoritarian teaching methods; he emphasized personal growth, free inquiry, and creativity.

Providing an overarching framework within which others could fit, William James and Dewey had a great effect on other thinkers. Edward A. Ross, a reform sociologist, called in *Sin and Society* (1907) for "pure environmentalism" and a new standard of morality. Economist Richard T. Ely (see chapter 19) rejected the conservative "laws" of classical economics and developed theories that placed economics in a changing environment. In *The Theory of the Leisure Class* (1899) and *The Instinct of Workmanship* (1914) Thorstein Veblen argued that everything was flux, the only law was the lack of laws, and modern business was an anarchic struggle for profit. Reform was not only permissible; it could provide order and efficiency in an industrial and entrepreneurial system characterized by disorder.

Rejecting the older view of the law as universal and unchanging, lawyers and legal theorists instead viewed it as a reflection of the environment —an instrument for social change. Law reflected the environment that shaped it. A movement grew among judges for "sociological jurisprudence" that related the law to social reform.

In Denver, Colorado, after Judge Ben Lindsey sentenced a boy to reform school for stealing coal, the boy's mother rushed forward and, in grief, beat her head against the wall. Lindsey investigated the case; he found that the father was a smelting worker dying of lead poisoning; the family needed coal for heat. Children, he concluded, were not born with a genetic tendency to crime; they were made good or bad by the environment in which they grew. Lindsey "sentenced" youthful offenders to education and good care. He worked for playgrounds, slum clearance, public baths, and technical schools. Known as the "Kids' Judge," he attracted visitors from as far away as Japan.

Louis D. Brandeis graduated from Harvard Law School in 1878 and became a corporation lawyer

■ *Laundry owner Curt Muller (above, arms folded) challenged an Oregon law limiting the length of the working day for women to ten hours. Lawyer Louis D. Brandeis (right, top), using a mass of statistics, sociological data, and expert testimony compiled with the help of Lillian Wald (right, bottom), defended the law before the Supreme Court.*

and near-millionaire. But like many others, he changed his mind about social issues during the depression of the 1890s, and as the "People's Attorney," he fought corporate abuses and political corruption. In 1908 he accepted an invitation from the National Consumers' League to defend an Oregon law limiting working hours for women to ten hours a day.

Brandeis decided on a new kind of argument. With the help of Lillian Wald, he compiled masses of medical and sociological data, and when he submitted to the Court a 104-page brief, only 2 pages examined traditional legal precedents. The rest included reports from factory inspectors, health and hygiene commissioners, and expert commissions—all showing that the ten-hour law was necessary to protect the health, safety, and morals of women in Oregon.

Agreeing, the Supreme Court in *Muller* v. *Oregon* (1908) upheld the Oregon statute, and the famous "Brandeis Brief," based on environmental data rather than legal precedent, influenced law-yers and courts across the country. Like so many other reform efforts during these years, it focused on the effects of the environment, suggesting that changes in the way in which people lived and worked—through social and political reforms—could improve their condition.

Socialism, a reformist political philosophy, grew dramatically before the First World War. Organized in 1901, the Socialist party of America doubled in membership between 1904 and 1908, then tripled in the four years after that. Torn by factions, it enlisted some intellectuals, factory workers, disillusioned Populists, miners, and lumberjacks. By 1911 there were socialist mayors in thirty-two cities, including Berkeley, California; Butte, Montana; and Flint, Michigan. Although its doctrines were aimed at an urban proletariat, the Socialisty party drew support in rural Texas, Missouri, Arkansas, Idaho, and Washington. In Oklahoma it attracted as much as a third of the vote.

Eugene V. Debs, five times the party's presidential candidate, offset the popular image of the wild-eyed radical. Gentle and reflective, he was thrust into prominence by the Pullman strike (see chapter 20). Like the party he led, Debs never developed a cohesive platform, nor was he an effective organizer. But he was eloquent, passionate, and visionary. An excellent speaker, he captivated audiences, attacking the injustices of capitalism and urging a workers' republic. Running for president, he gained 100,000 votes in 1900; 400,000 in 1904; and 900,000 in 1912, the party's peak year.

Reform in the Cities

In the early years of the twentieth century, urban reform movements, many of them born in the 1890s, spread across the nation. In 1894 the National Municipal League was organized, and it became the forum for debate over civic reform, changes in the tax laws, and municipal ownership of public utilities. Within a few years nearly every city had a variety of clubs and organizations directed at improving the quality of city life.

"For two generations," Frederic C. Howe said in 1905, "we have wrought out the most admirable laws and then left the government to run itself. This has been our greatest fault." In the 1880s reformers like Howe would call an evening conference, pass resolutions, and then go home; after 1900 they formed associations, adopted long-range policies, and hired employees to achieve them. In the mid-1890s only Chicago had an urban reform league with a full-time paid executive; within a decade there were such leagues in every major city.

In city after city reformers reordered municipal government. Tightening controls on corporate activities, they broadened the scope of utility regulation and restricted city franchises. They updated tax assessments, often skewed in favor of corporations, and tried to clean up the electoral machinery. Devoted to efficiency, they developed a trained civil service to oversee planning and operations. The generation of the 1880s also believed in civil service, but the goal then was mostly negative: to get spoilsmen out and "good" people in. Now the goal was efficiency and above all, results.

In constructing their model governments,

urban reformers often turned to recent advances in business management and organization. They stressed continuity and expertise, a system in which professional experts staffed a government overseen by elective officials. At the top the elected leader surveyed the breadth of city, state, or national affairs and defined directions. Below, a corps of experts—trained in the various disciplines of the new society—funneled the definition into specific, scientifically based policies.

Reformers thus created a growing number of regulatory commissions and municipal departments. They hired engineers to oversee utility and water systems, physicians and nurses to improve municipal health, and city planners to oversee park and highway development. They created specialized "academies" to train police and firefighters. Imitated by the state and federal governments, the proliferation of experts and commissions widened the gap between voters and decision makers but dramatically improved the efficiency of government.

As cities exploded in size, they freed themselves from the tight controls of state legislatures and began to experiment with their governments. Struggling to recover from a devastating hurricane in 1900, Galveston, Texas, pioneered the commission form of government: a form of municipal government in which commissions of appointed experts, rather than elected officials, ran the city. Wanting nonpartisan expertise, Staunton, Virginia, was the first city to hire a city manager. Other cities followed, and by 1910 over a hundred cities were using either the commission or manager type of government.

In the race for reform, a number of city mayors won national reputations—among them Seth Low in New York City and Hazen S. Pingree in Detroit—working to modernize taxes, clean up politics, lower utility rates, and control the awarding of valuable city franchises. In Toledo, Ohio, Mayor Samuel M. ("Golden Rule") Jones, a wealthy manufacturer, took billy clubs away from the police, established free kindergartens, playgrounds, and night schools, and improved wages for city workers.

In Cleveland, Ohio, Tom L. Johnson showed an innovative approach to city government. A millionaire who had made his fortune manipulating city franchises, Johnson one day read Henry George's *Progress and Poverty* (see chapter 19) and turned to reform. Elected mayor of Cleveland, he served from 1901 to 1909 and collected a group of aggressive and talented young advisers. Frederic C. Howe, Newton D. Baker, and Edward Bemis—all of whom later won national reputations—shaped Johnson's ideas on taxes, prison reform, utility regulation, and other issues facing the city.

Johnson combined shrewdness and showmanship. Believing in an informed citizenry, he held outdoor meetings in huge tents. He used colorful charts to give Cleveland residents a course in utilities and taxation. He cut down on corruption, cut off special privilege, updated taxes, and gave Cleveland a reputation as the country's best-governed city.

Finding it difficult to regulate powerful city utilities and keep their costs down, Johnson and mayors in other cities turned more and more to public ownership of gas, electricity, water, and transportation. Called "gas and water socialism," the idea spread swiftly. In 1896 fewer than half of American cities owned their own waterworks; by 1915 almost two thirds did.

Action in the States

Reformers soon discovered, however, that many problems lay beyond a city's boundaries, and they turned for action to the state and federal governments. From the 1890s to 1920 they worked to stiffen state laws regulating the labor of women and children, create and strengthen commissions to regulate railroads and utilities, impose corporate and inheritance taxes, improve mental and penal institutions, and allocate more funds for state universities, the training ground for the experts and educated citizenry needed for the new society.

Maryland passed the first workers' compensation law in 1902; soon most industrial states had such legislation. After 1900 many states adopted factory inspection laws, and by 1916 almost two thirds of the states mandated insurance for the victims of factory accidents. By 1914, twenty-five states had enacted employers' liability laws.

To regulate business, virtually every state created regulatory commissions, empowered to examine corporate books and hold public hearings. Building on earlier experience, after 1900 they

were given new power to initiate actions, rather than await complaints, and in some cases to set maximum prices and rates. Dictating company practices, they pioneered regulatory methods later adopted in federal legislation of 1906 and 1910. Some business leaders supported the federal laws in order to get rid of "the intolerable supervision" of dozens of separate state commissions.

Historians have long praised the regulation movement, but the commissions did not always act wisely or even in the public interest. Elective commissions often produced commissioners who had little knowledge of corporate affairs. To win election, some promised specific rates or reforms, a violation of the commission's investigative functions. Appointive commissions sometimes fared better, but they too had to oversee extraordinarily complex businesses like the railroads. Shaping everything from wages to train schedules, the commissions affected railroad profits and growth. In the end, the regulatory commissions damaged the railroad industry.

Emphasizing people's involvement in politics, progressives backed three measures to make officeholders responsive to popular will: the initiative, which allowed voters to propose new laws; the referendum, which allowed them to accept or reject a law at the ballot box; and the recall, which gave them a way to remove an elected official from office. Oregon adopted the initiative and referendum in 1902; by 1912 twelve states had them. That year Congress added the Seventeenth Amendment to the Constitution to provide for the direct election of U.S. senators. By 1916 all but three states had direct primaries, which allowed the people, rather than nominating conventions, to choose candidates for office.

As attention shifted from the cities to the states, reform governors throughout the country won growing reputations. Joseph Folk, Steffens' hero in Saint Louis, became the governor of Missouri in 1904. Hiram Johnson won fame in California for his shrewd and forceful campaign against the Southern Pacific Railroad. In the East were Charles Evans Hughes in New York and Woodrow Wilson, the former president of Princeton University, in New Jersey.

Robert M. La Follette became the most famous reform governor. A graduate of the University of Wisconsin, La Follette served three terms in Congress during the late 1880s. A staunch Republican, he supported the tariff and other Republican doctrines but the Democratic landslide of 1890 turned him out of office. Moving to state politics, he became interested in reform, and in 1901 he became governor of Wisconsin. Then forty-five years old, La Follette was talented, aggressive, and a superb stump speaker.

In the following six years, he put together the "Wisconsin Idea," one of the most important reform programs in the history of state government. He established an industrial commission, the first in the country, to regulate factory safety and sanitation. He improved education, workers' compensation, public utility controls, and resource conservation. He lowered railroad rates and raised railroad taxes. Under La Follette's prodding, Wisconsin became the first state to adopt a direct primary for all political nominations. It also became the first to adopt a state income tax.

Like other progressives, La Follette drew on expert advice and relied on academic figures like Richard Ely and Edward Ross at the University of Wisconsin. La Follette supporters established the first Legislative Reference Bureau in the university's library; the bureau stocked the governor and his allies with facts and figures to support the measures they wanted. Theodore Roosevelt called La Follette's Wisconsin "the laboratory of democracy," and the "Wisconsin Idea" soon spread to many other states, including New York, California, Michigan, Iowa, and Texas.

■ *The most famous of the reform leaders in the states was Wisconsin's Robert M. "Fighting Bob" La Follette.*

The Mass Society

"Life in the States," an English visitor said in 1900, "is one perpetual whirl of telephones, telegrams, phonographs, electric bells, motors, lifts, and automatic instruments." If not quite that, conditions were better than just a few years before. Farms and factories were once again prosperous; in 1901, for the first time in years, the economy reached full capacity. Farm prices rose almost 50 percent between 1900 and 1910. Unemployment dropped. "In the United States of today," a Boston newspaper said in 1904, "everyone is middle class. The resort to force, the wild talk of the nineties are over. Everyone is busily, happily getting ahead."

The start of a new century influenced people's outlook. Excited about beginning the twentieth century, people believed that technology and enterprise would shape a better life. Savoring the word "new," they talked of the new poetry, new cinema, new history, new democracy, new woman, new art, new immigration, new morality, and new city. Magazines picked up the word; there were the *New Republic* and the *New Statesman*. Presidents Roosevelt and Wilson called their political programs the New Nationalism and the New Freedom.

The word "mass" also cropped up frequently. Victors in the recent war with Spain, Americans took pride in teeming cities, burgeoning corporations, and other marks of the mass society. They flocked more and more to mass entertainment, enjoyed the fruits of mass production, read mass-circulation newspapers and magazines, and took mass transit from the growing spiral of suburbs into the central cities.

An Urban Nation

In 1920 the median age of the population was only twenty-five. (It is now thirty.) Immigration accounted for part of the youthfulness, since most immigrants were young, and so did death rates. Thanks to medical advances and better living conditions, death rates dropped in the early years of the century; the average life span in-

Life Expectancy, 1900–1920

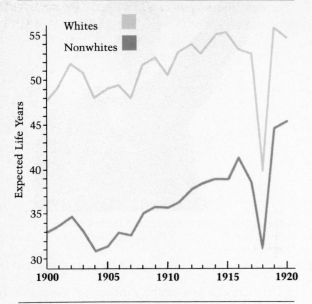

creased. Between 1900 and 1920, life expectancy rose from forty-nine to fifty-six years for white women and from forty-seven to fifty-four years for white men. It rose from thirty-three to forty-five years for blacks and other racial minorities.

Infant mortality remained high; nearly 10 percent of white babies and 20 percent of minority babies died in their first year of life. In comparison to today, fewer babies on average survived to adolescence, and fewer people survived beyond middle age. In 1900 the death rate among people between forty-five and sixty-five was more than twice the modern rate. As a result, there were relatively fewer older people—in 1900 only 4 percent of the population was older than sixty-five compared to nearly 12 percent today. Fewer children than today knew their grandparents. Still, improvements in health care helped people live longer, and as a result, the incidence of cancer and heart disease increased.

In 1900 six of every ten Americans lived on farms or in towns of fewer than twenty-five hundred people. But the flight from the farms continued, and a decade later only five in ten still lived there. By 1920 fewer than a third of all Americans lived on farms; fewer than half lived in rural areas.

Cities grew, and by any earlier standards, they grew on a colossal scale. Downtowns became a central hive of skyscrapers, department stores, warehouses, and hotels. Strips of factories radiated from the center. As street railways spread, cities took on a systematic pattern of socioeconomic segregation, usually in rings. The innermost ring filled with immigrants, circled by a belt of working-class housing. The remaining rings marked areas of rising affluence outward toward wealthy suburbs, which themselves formed around shopping strips and grid patterns of streets that restricted social interaction.

The giants were New York, Chicago, and Philadelphia, industrial cities that turned out every kind of product from textiles to structural steel. Smaller cities like Rochester, New York, or Cleveland, Ohio, specialized in manufacturing a specific line of goods or processing regional products for the national market. Railroads instead of highways tied things together; in 1916 the rail network, the leading one in the world, reached its peak—254,000 miles of track that carried over three fourths of intercity freight tonnage.

Step by step cities adopted their twentieth-century forms. Between 1909 and 1915 Los Ange-

Urban and Rural Population, 1900–1920 (in millions)

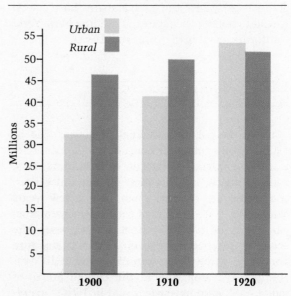

Source: U.S. Bureau of the Census, Historical Statistics of the United States, Colonial Times to 1970, Bicentennial Edition, Washington, D.C., 1975.

Annexation: Patterns of City Expansion

After 1900, dwellers in the suburban commuter belt around Chicago created by improved transit systems began to resist annexation by the city.

Old shoreline
Present-day shoreline
Lake Michigan
North Av.

City of Chicago, 1837
Annexations:
By 1860
By 1880
By 1900
By 1920
Present-day boundary

Western Av.
State St.
63rd St.

0   5 Miles
0   5 Kilometers

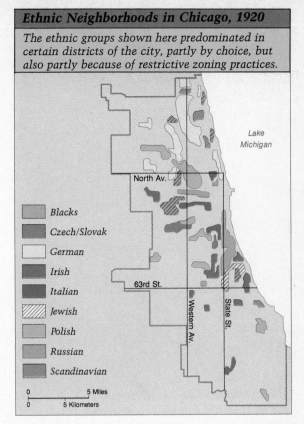

Ethnic Neighborhoods in Chicago, 1920

The ethnic groups shown here predominated in certain districts of the city, partly by choice, but also partly because of restrictive zoning practices.

Lake Michigan
North Av.

Blacks
Czech/Slovak
German
Irish
Italian
Jewish
Polish
Russian
Scandinavian

Western Av.
State St.
63rd St.

0   5 Miles
0   5 Kilometers

les, a city of three hundred thousand people, passed a series of ordinances that gave rise to modern urban zoning. For the first time the ordinances divided a city into three districts of specified use: a residential area, an industrial area, and an area open to residence and a limited list of industries. Other cities followed. Combining several features, the New York Zoning Law of 1916 became the model for the nation; within a decade 591 cities copied it.

Zoning ordered city development, keeping skyscrapers out of factory districts, factories out of the suburbs. It also had powerful social repercussions. In the South zoning became a tool to extend racial segregation; in northern cities it acted against ethnic minorities. Jews in New York, Italians in Boston, Poles in Detroit, blacks in Chicago—zoning laws held them all at arm's length. Like other migrants, blacks often preferred to settle together, but zoning also helped put them there. By 1920 ten districts in Chicago were more than three-quarters black. In Los An-

geles, Cleveland, Detroit, and Washington, D.C., most blacks lived in only two or three wards.

While many people fled the farm, farmers themselves prospered, the beneficiaries of greater production and expanding urban markets. Rural Free Delivery, begun in 1893, helped diminish the farmers' sense of isolation. In ways since forgotten, it changed farm life. The delivery of mail to the farm door opened that door to a wider world; it exposed farmers to urban thinking, national advertising, and political events. In 1911 over a billion newspapers and magazines were delivered over RFD routes.

Parcel post (1913) permitted the sending of packages through the U.S. mail. Mail-order houses flourished; rural merchants suffered. Packages went both ways—President Woodrow Wilson's first parcel-post delivery had eight pounds of New Jersey apples—and within a year 300 million packages were being mailed annually. While telephones and electricity did not reach most rural areas for decades, better roads, mail-order cata-

■ *With rural free delivery people in even the most remote areas had access to the world of goods described in the catalogues of the large mail-order houses.*

logs, and other innovations knit farmers into the larger society. Early in the new century Mary E. Lease—who in her Populist days had urged Kansas farmers to raise less corn and more Hell—moved to Brooklyn.

Life on the farm was tiring and often difficult. Land prices rose with crop prices, and farm tenancy increased, especially in the South. Tenancy grew from one quarter of all farms in 1880 to more than one third in 1910. In South Carolina, Georgia, Alabama, and Mississippi, it amounted to nearly two thirds. Many southern tenant farmers were black, and they suffered from farm-bred diseases. In 1909 the Rockefeller Sanitary Commission, acting on recent scientific discoveries, began a sanitation campaign that eventually wiped out the hookworm disease, and in 1912 the U.S. Public Health Service began work on rural malaria.

Improvements in telescopes and microscopes allowed scientists to look farther out and closer up than ever before. Using the new 100-inch telescope on Mount Wilson in California, Edwin P. Hubble showed that galaxies existed beyond the Milky Way. Other astronomers proved empirically what Copernicus had claimed centuries before: the earth revolves around the sun. Biologists concentrated upon the cell; they studied the protoplasm that formed the basis of life, and terms like chromosome, gene, and hormone became household words. "A few years ago the possibility of investigating by direct experiment the internal structure of atoms, or the topographical grouping of heredity units in the germ cells would have seemed a wild dream," Edmund B. Wilson, a Columbia University scientist, said in 1915. "Today these questions stand among the substantial realities of scientific inquiry."

Toward a Consumer Society

As factories produced more, people bought more. In 1900 business firms spent about $95 million on advertising; twenty years later they spent over $500 million. Ads and billboards touted cigarettes, cars, perfumes, and cosmetics. Advertising agencies boomed, and using new sampling techniques, they developed modern concepts of market testing and research. In an important side effect, sampling customer preferences also made business more responsive to public opinion on social and political issues.

Mass production swept the clothing industry and dressed more Americans better than any people ever before. Using lessons learned in making uniforms during the Civil War, manufacturers for the first time developed standard clothing and shoe sizes that fit most bodies. Clothing prices dropped; the availability of inexpensive, "off-the-rack" clothes lessened distinctions between rich and poor. By 1900 nine of every ten men and boys wore the new "ready-to-wear" clothes.

In 1900 people employed in manufacturing earned on average $418 a year. Two decades later they earned $1342 a year, though inflation took much of the increase. While the middle class expanded, the rich also grew richer. In 1920 the new income tax showed the first accurate tabulation of income, and it confirmed what many had suspected all along. Five percent of the population received almost one fourth of all income.

Kuppenheimer Clothes

SOLD BY

■ *A 1910 advertisement for men's ready-to-wear clothing features two collegians sporting the latest styles.*

Society's Masses

National networks of products and consumers helped fuel the mass society. But it also depended on an enormous increase in the labor force to work in the factories, mines, and forests. Women and blacks played larger roles. Immigration soared. Between 1901 and 1910 nearly 8.8 million immigrants entered the United States; between 1911 and 1920 another 5.7 million came.

Women worked in larger and larger numbers. In 1900 more than 5 million worked—one fifth of all adult women—and among those aged fourteen to twenty-four, the work rate was almost one third. Of those employed, single women outnumbered married women by seven to one; yet more than a third of married women worked. Most women held service jobs. Only a small number held higher paying jobs as professionals or managers.

In the 1890s women made up over a quarter of medical school graduates. Adopting rigid standards, men gradually squeezed them out, and by the 1920s only about 5 percent of the graduates were women. Few women taught in colleges and universities, and those that did were expected to resign if they married. In 1906 Harriet Brooks, a promising physicist at Barnard College in New York, became engaged and refused to resign; the dean told her icily that Barnard expected a married woman to "dignify her home-making into a profession, and not assume that she can carry on two full professions at a time."

More women than men graduated from high school, and with professions like medicine and science largely closed to them, they often turned to the new "business schools" that offered training in stenography, typing, and bookkeeping. In 1920 over a quarter of all employed women held clerical jobs. Many others taught school.

In 1907 and 1908 investigators studied 22,000 women workers in Pittsburgh; 60 percent of them earned less than $7 a week, a minimum for "decent living." Fewer than 1 percent held skilled jobs; most tended machines, wrapped and labeled, or did handwork that required no particular skill. In New York, many women toiled as garment workers from eight in the morning to six in the evening, with an hour off on Saturdays. They earned $7 to $12 a week, nothing at all during slack season. They had to buy their own needles and thread and pay for electricity and chairs to sit on.

Critics charged that women's employment endangered the home, threatened their reproductive functions, and even, as one man said, stripped them of "that modest demeanor that lends a charm to their kind." Adding to the fears, the birth rate continued to drop between 1900 and 1920, and the divorce rate soared, in part because working-class men took advantage of the newer moral freedom and deserted their families in growing numbers. By 1916 there was one divorce for every nine marriages as compared to one for twenty-one in 1880.

David Graham Phillips, a novelist troubled by the woman's problem, depicted a husband's oppression of his wife in *The Hungry Heart*, published in 1909. "He kissed her, patted her cheek, went back to his work." When the wife grew restless, the husband knew why: "A few more years'll wash away the smatter she got at college, and this restlessness of hers will yield to nature, and she'll be content and happy in her womanhood. . . . As grandfather often said, it's a dreadful mistake, educating women beyond their sphere." Such views, mild as they were, got Phillips assassinated by a lunatic who claimed the novelist was "trying to destroy the whole ideal of womanhood."

Many children worked. In 1900 about three million children—nearly 20 percent of those between the ages of five and fifteen—held full- or almost full-time jobs. Twenty-five thousand boys under sixteen worked in mining; twenty thousand children under twelve, mainly girls, worked in southern cotton mills. Gradually the use of child labor shrank, reflecting in part the growing recognition of the importance of childhood. Families focused greater and greater attention on the children, and child-rearing became a central— perhaps *the* central—concern of family life.

As the middle-class family changed from an economic to an emotional unit, middle-class women claimed increasing pride in homemaking and motherhood. Mother's Day, the national holiday, was formally established in 1913. With families preferring smaller numbers of children, birth control became a more acceptable practice. Margaret Sanger, a nurse and social reformer, led a campaign to give physicians broad discretion in prescribing contraceptives. When Sanger became involved in the birth-control movement, the federal Comstock Law banned the interstate transport of contraceptive devices and information (see the special feature on pp. 646–47).

Blacks and Mexican-Americans

At the turn of the century eight of every ten blacks lived in rural areas, mainly in the South. Most were poor sharecroppers. "Jim Crow" laws segregated many schools, railroad cars, hotels, and hospitals. Poll taxes and other devices disfranchised blacks and many poor whites. Violence was common; between 1900 and 1914, white mobs murdered over a thousand black people.

Two murders occurred near Vicksburg, Mississippi, in 1904. Looking for the killer of a white planter, a mob captured a black man and woman, their guilt or innocence unknown. They were tied to trees, and their fingers and ears were cut off as souvenirs. "The most excruciating form of punishment consisted in the use of a large corkscrew in the hands of some of the mob. This instrument was bored into the flesh of the man and the woman, in the arms, legs and body, and then pulled out, the spirals tearing out big pieces of raw, quivering flesh every time it was withdrawn." Finally, both people were thrown on a fire and burned to death, "a relief," a witness said, "to the maimed and suffering victims."

Many blacks labored in the cotton farms, railroad camps, sawmills, and mines of the South

LAD FELL TO DEATH IN BIG COAL CHUTE

Dennis McKee Dead and Arthur Allbecker Had Leg Burned In the Lee Mines.

Falling into a chute at the Chauncey colliery of the George S. Lee Coal Company at Avondale, this afternoon, Dennis McKee, aged 11 of West Nanticoke, was smothered to death and

He was removed to his home at Avondale.

Both boys were employed as breaker boys, and going too close to the chutes fell in. Fellow workmen rushed to their assistance and soon

Breaker boys, who picked out pieces of slate from the coal as it rushed past, often became bent-backed after years of working fourteen hours a day in the coal mines. Accidents—and death—were common.

PICKING SLATE

under conditions of peonage. Peons traded their lives and labor for food and shelter. Often illiterate, they were forced to sign contracts allowing planters "to use such force as he or his agents may deem necessary to require me to remain on his farm and perform good and satisfactory services." Armed guards patrolled the camps and whipped those trying to escape. "In the woods," a peon said, "they can do anything they please, and no one can see them but God."

Few blacks belonged to labor unions, and almost always blacks earned less than whites in the same job. In Atlanta white electricians earned $5.00 a day, blacks $3.50. Black songs like "I've Got a White Man Workin' for Me" (1901) voiced more hope than reality. The illiteracy rate among blacks dropped from 45 percent in 1900 to 30 percent in 1910, but nowhere were they given equal school facilities, teachers' salaries, or educational materials. In 1910 scarcely eight thousand black youths were attending high schools in all the states of the Southeast. South Carolina spent $13.98 annually for the education of each white child, $1.13 for each black child.

In 1905 a group of black leaders met near Niagara Falls, New York, and pledged action on behalf of voting, equal access to economic opportunity, integration, and equality before the law. At their head was sociologist W. E. B. Du Bois, now a professor of history and economics at Atlanta University. The Niagara movement rejected Booker T. Washington's gradualist approach, which, Du Bois said, would produce "a voteless herd to run the machines and wash the dishes for the new aristocracy. Negroes would be educated enough to be useful but not enough, or not in the right way, to be able to assert self-respect." In *The Souls of Black Folk* (1903) and other works, Du Bois eloquently called for justice and equality. "By every civilized and peaceful method," he said, "we must strive for the right which the world accords to man."

Race riots broke out in Atlanta, Georgia, in 1906 and Springfield, Illinois, in 1908, the latter the home of Abraham Lincoln. Unlike the riots of the 1960s, white mobs invaded black neighborhoods, burning, looting, and killing. They lynched two blacks—one eighty-four years old—in Springfield. Mary Ovington, a white anthropology student, was outraged, and along with other reformers, white and black, issued a call for

■ *The wish to have "our children . . . enjoy fairer conditions than have fallen to our lot" was the impetus behind both the Niagara movement (top) and the NAACP, which sponsored the 1917 parade in New York City, pictured at bottom.*

Margaret Sanger and the Birth Control Movement

At the start of the twentieth century, birth control was an issue fraught with social and religious controversy. Devout Christians—Protestants and Catholics—opposed it as a violation of God's law; the overseers of society's moral behavior feared it might foster, if not promiscuity, an overindulgence in sexual activity. Theodore Roosevelt said it meant "race death: a sin for which there is no atonement." The Comstock Act of 1873 banned from the U.S. mails all information on contraceptives and birth control, and by 1914 twenty-two states had enacted laws that prohibited outright or greatly inhibited the dissemination of such information. That year Margaret Sanger formally launched her campaign for birth control.

Born in 1883, Sanger grew up in Corning, New York, an upstate factory town. Her father, an Irish-born stonecutter, encouraged his children to think for themselves. "Leave the world better because you, my child, have dwelt in it," he told Margaret. One of eleven children, Margaret from an early age linked poverty to large families. "Our childhood," she said, "was one of longing for things that were always denied."

Sanger became a nurse; eager for excitement and romance, she settled in New York City, married, and had three children. Restless, and finding her marriage confining, she discovered Greenwich Village, a favorite haunt of the period's intense young radicals. On McDougal Street in the Village, Sanger met Socialist leader Eugene V. Debs; young reporter and revolutionary, John Reed, later to be honored by the Bolsheviks and buried in the Kremlin; William D. "Big Bill" Haywood of the radical Industrial Workers of the World (IWW); and feminist and socialist agitator, Emma Goldman.

The Village was filled with vibrant people determined to improve the world. Stimulated by the exciting talk, Sanger joined the Socialist party and worked to organize women for socialism in New York City. In 1912 she marched in the IWW picket lines in the great strike at the textile mills in Paterson, New Jersey. Pursuing her nursing career, Sanger worked on the lower East Side of New York where thousands upon thousands of people were crowded into tenement houses. Struck by the ignorance of tenement women about their own bodies, she wrote in 1912 a series of newspaper articles about venereal disease and personal hygiene, entitled "What Every Girl Should Know"; the Post Office Department banned it from the mails.

That same year Sanger watched at the bedside of Sadie Sachs, a poor working woman dying from a self-induced abortion. Warned that she might not survive another pregnancy, Sachs had asked for contraceptive advice, but the doctor had suggested only that she make her husband sleep on the roof. After Sachs died, Sanger spent hours walking the streets and thinking about birth and children and poverty. She resolved that night, she later said, "to seek out the root of the evil, to do something to change the destiny of mothers whose miseries were as vast as the sky."

The answer was birth control—a term she and several friends coined in 1914. Sanger spent a year absorbing medical opinion and learning about contraceptives, and then began publishing the journal *Woman Rebel*. Aimed at the working class, the journal touched on birth control, but its chief focus was on social revolution, particularly on raising the social consciousness of working women, encouraging them "to think for themselves" and "to have an ideal." It ran for only seven issues before it was banned by the post office. Sanger, indicted under the Comstock Act, fled to Europe.

There, after considerable reflection, she decided that birth control was a medical matter, not a social or revolutionary one. It belonged in the hands of physicians and their patients, with physicians free to prescribe contraception and other measures when appropriate. Women should "decide for themselves whether they shall become mothers, under what conditions, and when." Working through the National Birth Control League and other groups, Sanger broadened the movement's base beyond the socialists and feminists who had originally backed it. Settlement-house workers had been cool to birth control at first, but soon they too lent support.

Sanger returned to the United States, and the government, preoccupied with other issues, dropped the indictment against her. In October 1916, again defying the law, she opened the nation's first birth-control clinic in the teeming Brownsville section of Brooklyn, New York. Police soon raided the clinic, and Sanger was sentenced to thirty days in jail. On appeal, the New York State Court of Appeals upheld the sentence, but in an important victory for Sanger, it ruled that physicians should have greater discretion in prescribing birth control.

Late in 1916 Sanger formed the New York Birth Control League to push for legislation to give physicians even broader discretion. The league's argument that birth control would be an effective means of promoting the social welfare was a persuasive idea that convinced a wide variety of groups. Some reformers thought that smaller families would raise the standard of living of the poor. Other people thought birth control might limit the number of "undesirables" in the population. Eugenicists who wanted to improve the human species through genetic control saw it as a way to reduce the proportion of the unwanted and unfit in the society. Gradually Sanger herself reflected such arguments. "More children from the fit, less from the unfit—that is the chief issue," she said in 1919.

In 1921 Sanger organized a nationwide movement through the American Birth Control League; it held clinics and conferences to educate the public. In the photo above, volunteers are selling the "Birth Control Review." Although the Catholic Church remained opposed, the movement spread among Protestants, Jews, and those who did not attend church. In 1940 Eleanor Roosevelt, the popular First Lady, came out in support of family planning, and by the 1940s every state except Massachusetts and Connecticut had legalized the distribution of birth-control information.

When Margaret Sanger died in 1966, the birth-control pill had the approval of the Federal Drug Administration, and its use was widespread. The cause she had championed—once so shocking and radical—was won in American society.

the conference that organized the National Association for the Advancement of Colored People. Created in 1910, within four years the NAACP grew to fifty branches and over six thousand members. The eight top officers included one black—Director of Publicity and Research W. E. B. Du Bois.

At the beginning of the twentieth century, Mexicans for the first time immigrated in large numbers, especially after a revolution in 1909 forced many to flee across the northern border into Texas, New Mexico, Arizona, and California. Their exact numbers were unknown. American officials did not count border crossings until 1907, and even then, many migrants avoided the official immigration stations. Almost all came from the Mexican lower class, eager to escape peonage and violence in their native land. Labor agents—called *coyotes*—usually in the employ of large corporations or working for ranchers, recruited Mexican workers. After the turn of the century, almost 10 percent of the total population of Mexico moved to the American Southwest.

Mexican Immigration to the United States, 1900–1920

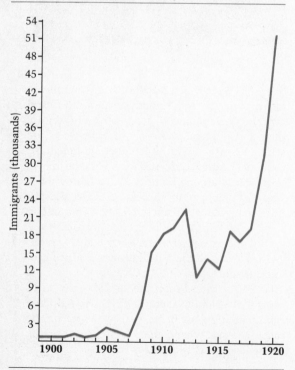

The "New" Immigration

Between 1901 and 1920 the extraordinarily high total of 14.5 million immigrants entered the country, more than in any previous twenty-year period. Continuing the recent trend (see chapter 19), many came from southern and eastern Europe. Still called the "new" immigrants, they met hostility from "older" immigrants of northern European stock who questioned their values and appearance.

From 1901 to 1914, some 3 million Italians and 1.5 million Jews and 4 million Slavs from central and eastern Europe entered the country. In 1907, the year of greatest influx, 1.3 million immigrants entered; about half of them came from Italy, Austria-Hungary, Poland, and Russia. Most were Catholic or Jewish in religion. More than a third were illiterate, and most, coming from peasant backgrounds, were unskilled. Over two thirds were males.

Labor agents—called *padroni* among the Italians, Greeks, and Syrians—recruited immigrant workers, found them jobs, and deducted a fee from their wages. Headquartered in Salt Lake City, Leonidas G. Skliris, the "Czar of the Greeks," provided workers for the Utah Copper Company and the Western Pacific Railroad. In Chicago at the turn of the century *padroni* employed more than one fifth of all Italians; in New York City they controlled two thirds of the entire labor force.

Immigrant patterns often departed from traditional stereotypes. Immigrants, for example, moved both ways. Fifty percent or more of some groups returned home, although the numbers varied among groups. Jews and Czechs often brought their families to resettle in America; Serbs and Poles tended to come singly, intent on earning enough money to make a fresh start at home. Many Italian men virtually commuted, "birds of passage" who returned home every slack season. However, the outbreak of World War I interrupted the practice and trapped hundreds of thousands of Italians and others who had planned to return to Europe.

Older residents lumped the newcomers together, ignoring geographic, religious, and other differences. Preserving important regional distinctions, Italians tended to settle as Calabreses, Venetians, Abruzzis, and Sicilians. Native Americans viewed them all simply as Italians. Henry Ford and other employers tried to erase the differences through English classes and deliberate "Americanization" programs. The Ford Motor Company ran a school where immigrant employees were first taught to say: "I am a good American." At the graduation ceremony, the pupils acted out a gigantic pantomime in which, clad in their old-country dress, they filed into a

■ *The Pledge of Allegiance, adopted in 1882, was part of the Americanization process for millions of immigrant children.*

Immigration to the United States, 1900–1920 (by area of origin)

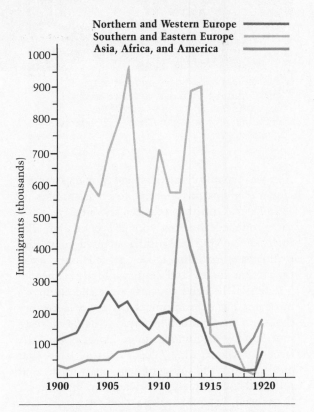

Northern and Western Europe
Southern and Eastern Europe
Asia, Africa, and America

Note: For purposes of classification, Northern and Western Europe includes Great Britain, Ireland, Scandinavia, the Netherlands, Belgium, Luxembourg, Switzerland, France and Germany. Southern and Eastern Europe includes Poland, Austria-Hungary, Russia and the Baltic States, Rumania, Bulgaria, European Turkey, Italy, Spain, Portugal, and Greece. Asia, Africa, and America includes Asian Turkey, China, Japan, India, Canada, the Caribbean, Latin America, and all of Africa.

Source: U.S. Bureau of the Census, Historical Statistics of the United States, Colonial Times to 1970, Bicentennial Edition, Washington, D.C., 1975.

large "melting pot." When they emerged, they were wearing identical American-made clothes, and each was waving a little American flag.

In similar fashion, the International Harvester Corporation taught Polish laborers to speak English, but it had other lessons in view as well. According to "Lesson One," drilled into the Polish "pupils":

I hear the whistle. I must hurry.
I hear the five minute whistle.
It is time to go into the shop.
I take my check from the gate board and hang it on the department board.
I change my clothes and get ready to work.
The starting whistle blows.
I eat my lunch.
It is forbidden to eat until then.
The whistle blows at five minutes of starting time.
I get ready to go to work.
I work until the whistle blows to quit.
I leave my place nice and clean.
I put all my clothes in the locker.
I must go home.

Nativist sentiment, which had accompanied earlier waves of immigrants, intensified. Old-stock Americans sneered at the newcomers' dress and language. Racial theories emphasized the superiority of northern Europeans (see chapter 21) and the new "science" of eugenics suggested controls over the population growth of "inferior" peoples. Hostility against Catholics and Jews was common but touched other groups as well.

Congress passed statutes requiring literacy tests designed to curtail immigration from southern and eastern Europe, but they were vetoed by William Howard Taft in 1913, and Woodrow Wilson in 1915 and 1917. In 1917 Congress passed such a measure over Wilson's veto. Other measures tried to limit immigration from Mexico and Japan, and in 1902 a law passed that prohibited immigration from China.

■ *The movies became the nation's mass entertainment. Here, an audience enjoys a Keystone Comedy while a piano player accompanies the silent action with appropriate sound effects.*

Entertainment for the Masses

Thanks to changing work rules and mechanization, many Americans benefited from more leisure time. The average work week for manufacturing laborers fell from sixty hours in 1890 to fifty-one in 1920. By the early 1900s white-collar workers might spend only eight to ten hours a day at work and a half-day on weekends. The new leisure time gave more people more opportunity to play.

Baseball entrenched itself as the national pastime. Automobiles and streetcars carried growing numbers of fans to ballparks; attendance at major-league games doubled between 1903 and 1920. Football also drew fans, although critics attacked the sport's violence and the use of "tramp athletes," nonstudents whom colleges paid to play. In 1905, the worst year, 18 players were killed and 150 seriously injured.

Alarmed, President Theodore Roosevelt—who had once said, "I am the father of three boys [and] if I thought any one of them would weigh a possible broken bone against the glory of being chosen to play on Harvard's football team I would disinherit him"—called a White House conference to clean up college sports. The conference founded the Intercollegiate Athletic Association, which in 1910 became the National Collegiate Athletic Association.

Movie theaters opened everywhere. By 1910 there were ten thousand of them, drawing a weekly audience of ten million people. Admission was usually five cents, and movies stressing laughter and pathos appealed to a mass market. In 1915 D. W. Griffith, a talented and creative director, produced the first movie spectacular, *The Birth of a Nation.* Griffith adopted new film techniques, including close-ups, fade-outs, artistic camera angles, and dramatic battle scenes.

Before 1910 band concerts were the country's most popular entertainment. As many as twenty thousand amateur bands played in parks on summer Sunday afternoons. John Philip Sousa, the famous "March King," led a touring band that profited from the self-confident nationalism that followed the Spanish-American War. "A march," Sousa said, "should make a man with a wooden leg step out," and robust, patriotic marches like "The Stars and Stripes Forever" (1896) earned him wealth and popularity.

Soon, automobiles, phonographs, and radios began to lure audiences away from the concerts. By 1901 phonograph and record companies included the Victor Talking Machine Company, the Edison Speaking Machine Company, and Columbia Records. Ornate mahogany Victrolas became standard fixtures in middle-class parlors. Early records were usually of vaudeville skits; orchestral recordings began in 1906. In 1919 2.25 million phonographs were produced; two years later more than 100 million records were sold.

As record sales grew, families sang less and listened more. Music became a business. In 1909 Congress enacted a copyright law that provided a two-cent royalty on each piece of music on phonograph records or piano rolls. The royalty, small as it was, offered welcome income to composers and publishers, and in 1914 composer Victor Herbert and others formed the American Society of Composers, Authors and Publishers (ASCAP) to protect musical rights and royalties.

The faster rhythms of syncopated ragtime became the rage, especially after 1911 when Irving Berlin, a Russian immigrant, wrote "Alexander's Ragtime Band." Ragtime set off a nationwide dance craze. Secretaries danced on their lunch hour, the first night clubs opened, and restaurants and hotels introduced dance floors. Waltzes and polkas gave way to a host of new dances, many with animal names: the Fox Trot, Bunny Hop, Turkey Trot, Snake, and Kangaroo Dip. Partners were not permitted to dance too close; bouncers tapped them on the shoulder if they got closer than nine inches. The aging John D. Rockefeller hired a private instructor to teach him the tango,

■ *Although they were denounced as indecent and disgusting, the turkey trot and other "animal" dances were extremely popular. A young woman in New Jersey was jailed for fifty days for doing the turkey trot.*

although Yale University banned that dance at its 1914 Junior Prom.

Vaudeville, increasingly popular after 1900, reached maturity around 1915. Drawing on the immigrant experience, it voiced the variety of city life and included skits, songs, comics, acrobats, and magicians. Dances and jokes showed an earthiness new to mass audiences. By 1914 stage runways extended into the crowd; performers had bared their legs and were beginning to show signs of the midriff. Fanny Brice, Ann Pennington, the "shimmy" queen, and Eva Tanguay—who sang "It's All Been Done Before but Not the Way I Do It"—starred in Florenz Ziegfeld's *Follies*, the peak of vaudeville.

In songs like "St. Louis Blues" (1914), W. C. Handy took the black southern folk music of the blues to northern cities. Gertrude "Ma" Rainey, the daughter of minstrels, sang in black vaudeville for nearly thirty-five years. Performing in Chattanooga, Tennessee, about 1910, she came across a twelve-year-old orphan, Bessie Smith, who became the "Empress of the Blues." Smith's voice was huge and sweeping. Recording for the "Race" division of Columbia Records, she made over eighty records that together sold nearly ten million copies.

Another musical innovation came north from New Orleans. Charles (Buddy) Bolden, a cornetist, Ferdinand "Jelly Roll" Morton, a pianist, and a youngster named Louis Armstrong played an improvisational music that had no formal name. Reaching Chicago, it became "jas," then "jass," and finally, "jazz." Jazz jumped, and jazz musicians relied on feeling and mood. A restaurant owner once asked "Jelly Roll" Morton to play a waltz. "*Waltz?*" Morton exclaimed. "Man, these people want to *dance*! And you talking about waltz. This is the *Roll* you're talking to."

Popular fiction reflected changing interests. Kate Douglas Wiggins' *Rebecca of Sunnybrook Farm* (1903) and Lucy M. Montgomery's *Anne of Green Gables* (1908) showed the continuing popularity of rural themes. Westerns also sold well, but readers turned more and more to detective thrillers with hard-bitten city detectives and science fiction tales featuring the latest dream in technology. The Tom Swift series, begun in 1910, looked ahead to spaceships, ray guns, and gravity nullifiers.

Edward L. Stratemeyer, the mind behind Tom

Swift, brought the techniques of mass production to book writing. In 1906 he formed the Stratemeyer Literary Syndicate that employed a stable of writers to turn out hundreds of Tom Swift, Rover Boys, and Bobbsey Twins stories for young readers. Burt Standish, another prolific author, took the pen name of Gilbert Patten and created the character of Frank Merriwell, wholesome college athlete. As Patten said: "I took the three qualities I most wanted him to represent—frank and merry in nature, well in body and mind—and made the name Frank Merriwell." The Merriwell books sold twenty-five million copies.

The Fine Arts

"There is a state of unrest all over the world in art as in all other things," the director of New York's Metropolitan Museum said in 1908. "It is the same in literature, as in music, in painting, and in sculpture."

Isadora Duncan and Ruth St. Denis transformed the dance. Departing from traditional ballet steps, both women stressed improvisation, emotion, and the human form. "Listen to the music with your soul . . .," Duncan told her students. "Unless your dancing springs from an inner emotion and expresses an idea, it will be meaningless." Draped in flowing robes, she revealed more of her legs than some thought tasteful, while she proclaimed the "noblest art is the nude." After a triumphant performance with the New York Symphony in 1908, her ideas and techniques swept the country. Duncan died tragically in 1927; her neck broken when her long red scarf caught in the wheel of a racing car.

The lofts and apartments of New York's Greenwich Village attracted artists, writers, and poets interested in experimentation and change. To these artists, the city was the focus of national life and the sign of a new culture. Robert Henri and the realist painters—known to their critics as the Ashcan School—relished the city's excitement. They wanted, a friend said, "to paint truth and to paint it with strength and fearlessness and individuality."

To the realists, a painting carried into the future the look of life as it happened. With the same feel for the environment that Brandeis and other reformers had shown, their paintings de-

■ Hairdresser's Window by John Sloan. One of the Ashcan realists, Sloan found his subject matter in the tenements, cafes, and barrooms of the modern city.

picted street scenes, colorful crowds, and slum children swimming in the river. In paintings like the "Cliff Dwellers," George W. Bellows captured the color and excitment of the tenements; John Sloan, one of Henri's most talented students, painted the vitality of ordinary people and familiar scenes.

In 1913 a show at the New York Armory presented sixteen hundred modernist paintings, prints, and sculptures. The work of Picasso, Cézanne, Matisse, Brancusi, Van Gogh, and Gauguin dazed and dazzled American observers. Critics attacked the show as worthless and depraved; a Chicago official wanted it banned from the city because the "idea that people can gaze at this sort of thing without [it] hurting them is all bosh."

The Post-Impressionists changed the direction of twentieth-century art and influenced adventuresome American painters. John Marin, Max Weber, Georgia O'Keeffe, Arthur Dove, and other modernists experimented in ways foreign to Henri's realists. Defiantly avant garde, they shook off convention and experimented with new forms. Using bold colors and abstract patterns, they worked to capture the energy of urban life. "I see great forces at work, great movements," Marin said, "the large buildings and the small buildings, the warring of the great and the small. . . . I can hear the sound of their strife, and there is a great music being played."

There was an extraordinary outburst of poetry. In 1912 Harriet Monroe started the magazine *Poetry* in Chicago, the hotbed of the new poetry; Ezra Pound and Vachel Lindsay, both daring experimenters with ideas and verse, published in the first issue. T. S. Eliot published the classic "Love Song of J. Alfred Prufrock" in *Poetry* in 1915. Attacked bitterly by conservative critics, the poem established Eliot's leadership among a group of poets, many of them living and writing in London, who rejected traditional meter and rhyme as artificial constraints. Eliot, Pound, and Amy Lowell, among others, believed that the poet's task was to capture fleeting images in verse.

Others experimenting with new techniques in poetry included Robert Frost (*North of Boston*, 1915), Edgar Lee Masters (*Spoon River Anthology*, 1915), and Carl Sandburg (*Chicago Poems*, 1916). Sandburg's poem "Chicago" celebrated the vitality of the city:

Come and show me another city with lifted head singing so proud to be alive and coarse and strong and cunning.
Fierce as a dog with tongue lapping for action, cunning as a savage pitted against the wilderness,

. . . .

Bareheaded,
Shoveling,
Wrecking,
Planning,
Building, breaking, rebuilding,

. . . .

Bragging and laughing that under his wrist is the pulse, and under his ribs the heart of the people,

■ Brooklyn Bridge *by Joseph Stella. Stella used fragments of color and dynamic patterns to capture the movement and intensity of a big city.*

Laughing!
Laughing the stormy, husky, brawling laughter of Youth, half-naked, sweating, proud to be Hog Butcher, Tool Maker, Stacker of Wheat, Player with Railroads and Freight Handler to the Nation.

Manners and morals change slowly, and many Americans overlooked the importance of the first two decades of this century. Yet sweeping change was underway; anyone who doubted it could visit a gallery, see a film, listen to music, or read one of the new literary magazines. Garrets and galleries were filled with a breathtaking sense of change. "There was life in all these new things," Marsden Hartley, a modernist painter, recalled. "There was excitement, there was healthy revolt, investigation, discovery, and an utterly new world out of it all."

The ferment of progressivism in city, state, and nation reshaped the country. In a burst of reform, people built playgrounds, restructured taxes, regulated business, won the vote for women, short-

Chronology

1894 National Municipal League formed to work for reform in cities

1900 Galveston, Texas, is first city to try commission form of government

1901 Tom L. Johnson elected reform mayor of Cleveland
Robert M. La Follette elected reform governor of Wisconsin

1902 Socialist party of America organized
Maryland is first state to pass workers' compensation law
Oregon adopts the initiative and referendum

1903 W. E. B. Du Bois calls for justice and equality for blacks in *The Souls of Black Folk*

1905 Black leaders inaugurate Niagara movement, advocating integration and equal opportunity for blacks

1906 Upton Sinclair attacks meat-packing industry in *The Jungle*

1908 Supreme Court upholds Oregon law limiting working hours for women in *Muller v. Oregon*

1909 Sanitation campaign by Rockefeller Sanitary Commission wipes out hookworm disease

1910 NAACP founded
National Collegiate Athletic Association formed

1911 Irving Berlin popularizes rhythm of ragtime with "Alexander's Ragtime Band"

1912 Harriet Monroe begins publishing magazine *Poetry*
Congress passes Seventeenth Amendment allowing direct election of U.S. senators

1913 Parcel post service begins
Mother's Day becomes a national holiday

1915 D. W. Griffith produces the first movie spectacular, *The Birth of a Nation*
T. S. Eliot publishes "The Love Song of J. Alfred Prufrock"

1916 Margaret Sanger forms New York Birth Control League

1917 Congress passes law requiring literacy test for all immigrants

1920 Nineteenth Amendment granting women the right to vote adopted

ened working hours, altered political systems, opened kindergartens, and improved factory safety. They tried to fulfill the national promise of dignity and liberty.

At most, the years of progressive reform lasted from the 1890s to 1921, and in large measure they were compressed into a single decade between 1906 and American entry into World War I. Many problems the progressives addressed, they did not solve; and some important ones, like race, they did not even tackle. Yet their regulatory commissions, direct primaries, city improvements, and child-labor laws marked an era of important, gradual, and measured reform.

After 1905 the progressives looked more and more to Washington. For one thing, Teddy Roosevelt was there, with his zest for publicity and alluring grin. But progressives also had a growing sense that many concerns—corporations and conservation, factory safety and child labor—crossed state lines. Federal action seemed desirable; specific reforms fit into a larger plan perhaps best seen from the nation's center. Within a few years La Follette and Hiram Johnson became senators, and while reform went on back home, the focus of progressivism shifted to Washington.

Recommended Reading

There are several important analyses of the progressive era, including Robert H. Wiebe, *The Search for Order, 1877–1920* (1967); Richard Hofstadter, *The Age of Reform* (1955); Samuel P. Hays, *The Response to Industrialism* (1957); and Gabriel Kolko, *The Triumph of Conservatism* (1963). C. Vann Woodward, *Origins of the New South, 1877–1913* (1951) is a superb account of developments in the South. Lewis L. Gould, ed., *The Progressive Era* (1974), covers the period from varying perspectives; William L. O'Neill, *The Progressive Years* (1975) is a useful overview. C. Vann Woodward, *The Strange Career of Jim Crow* (1955), traces the civil-rights setbacks of the Progressive years.

Samuel P. Hays offers an influential interpretation of progressivism in *Conservation and the Gospel of Efficiency* (1959). Albro Martin, *Enterprise Denied: Origins of the Decline of American Railroads, 1897–1917* (1971), argues persuasively that reformers damaged as well as regulated. Intellectual currents are traced in Charles Forcey, *The Crossroads of Liberalism* (1961); social justice reforms in Harold U. Faulkner, *The Quest for Social Justice, 1898–1914* (1931); and the important tax issue in Clifton K. Yearley, *The Money Machines: The Breakdown and Reform of Governmental and Party Finance in the North, 1860–1920* (1970).

Additional Bibliography

Studies of the muckrakers include David M. Chalmers, *The Social and Political Ideas of the Muckrackers* (1964) and Harold S. Wilson, *McClure's Magazine and the Muckrakers* (1970). Lincoln Steffens, *The Shame of the Cities* (1904) and *Autobiography of Lincoln Steffens* (1931) and Upton Sinclair, *The Jungle* (1906), give contemporary flavor.

Sam Bass Warner, Jr., *Streetcar Suburbs* (1962) and *The Urban Wilderness* (1972) are excellent on urban developments, including zoning and industrial growth. On urban reform, see John D. Buenker, *Urban Liberalism and Progressive Reform* (1973); Roy M. Lubove, *The Progressive and the Slums* (1962); and Martin J. Schiesl, *The Politics of Efficiency: Municipal Administration and Reform in America, 1880–1920* (1977). Bradley R. Rice, *Progressive Cities: The Commission Government Movement in America, 1901–1920* (1977) is recent and helpful.

Books on specific cities include Melvin Holli, *Reform in Detroit: Hazen S. Pingree and Urban Politics* (1969); James B. Crooks, *Politics and Progress: The Rise of Urban Progressivism in Baltimore, 1895 to 1911* (1968); Zane L. Miller, *Boss Cox's Cincinnati* (1968); and Jack Tager, *The Intellectual as Urban Reformer: Brand Whitlock and the Progressive Movement* (1968).

Statewide movements are covered in George E. Mowry's influental study, *The California Progressives* (1951); Spencer C. Olin, Jr., *California's Prodigal Sons: Hiram Johnson and the Progressives, 1911–1917* (1968); David P. Thelen, *The New Citizenship: Origins of Progressivism in Wisconsin, 1885–1900* (1972); Herbert Margulies, *The Decline of the Progressive Movement in Wisconsin, 1890–1920* (1968); Ransom E. Noble, Jr., *New Jersey Progressivism Before Wilson* (1946); Sheldon Hackney, *Populism to Progressivism in Alabama* (1969); Richard M. Abrams, *Conservatism in a Progressive Era: Massachusetts Politics, 1900–1912* (1964); and H. L. Warner, *Progressivism in Ohio, 1897–1917* (1964).

Studies of youth, age, and family life include Joseph Kett, *Rites of Passage: Adolescence in America* (1977); W. Andrew Achenbaum, *Old Age in the New Land* (1978); William L. O'Neill, *Divorce in the Progressive Era* (1967); Carl N. Degler, *At Odds: Women and the Family in America* (1980); Michael Gordon, ed., *The American Family in Social-Historical Perspective* (1973); Tamara K. Hareven, ed., *Anonymous Americans* (1971) and *Transitions: The Family and Life Course in Historical Perspective* (1978). For birth control, see Linda Gordon, *Woman's Body, Woman's Right: A Social History of Birth Control in America* (1976) and David M. Kennedy, *Birth Control in America: The Career of Margaret Sanger* (1970).

See also Eleanor Flexner, *Century of Struggle: The Women's Rights Movement in the United States* (1959); William L. O'Neill, *Everyone Was Brave: The Rise and Fall of Feminism in America* (1969); Leslie Woodcock Tentler, *Wage-Earning Women: Industrial Work and Family Life in the United States, 1900–1930* (1979); Sheila M. Rothman, *Woman's Proper Place* (1978); and Ellen Condliffe Lagemann, *A Generation of Women: Education in the Lives of the Progressive Reformers* (1979).

On Du Bois, see Elliot M. Rudwick, *W. E. B. Du Bois* (1968). Other useful books include George M. Frederickson, *The Black Image in the White Mind* (1971); Charles F. Kellogg, *NAACP: A History of the National Association for the Advancement of Colored People, 1909–1920* (1967); Louis R. Harlan, *Separate and Unequal: Public School Campaigns and Racism in the Southern Seaboard States, 1900–1915* (1968); Allen H. Spear, *Black Chicago* (1967); and Idus A. Newby, *Jim Crow's Defense: Anti-Negro Thought in America, 1900–1930* (1965).

Leonard Dinnerstein, Roger L. Nichols, and David M. Reimers, *Natives and Strangers: Ethnic Groups and the Building of America* (1979), offer a useful overview of Mexican-Americans and the "new" immigrants. See also Oscar Handlin, *The Uprooted* (1951); John Higham, *Strangers in the Land: Patterns of American Nativism* (1955); Josef J. Barton, *Peasants and Strangers* (1975); Donald B. Cole, *Immigrant City: Lawrence, Massachusetts, 1845–1921* (1963); and John E. Bodnar, *Immigration and Industrialization* (1977). Thomas Kessner, *The Golden Door, Italian and Jewish Immigrant Mobility in New York City, 1880–1915* (1977), is excellent.

For the ways in which Americans entertained themselves, see Gunther Barth, *City People* (1980); Allison Danzig, *History of American Football* (1956); Russel B. Nye, *The Unembarrassed Muse: The Popular Arts in America* (1970); John E. DiMeglio, *Vaudeville U.S.A.* (1973); Ronald L. Davis, *A History of Music in American Life, Volume II: The Gilded Years, 1865–1920* (1980); and Robert Sklar, *Movie-Made America: A Social History of the American Movies* (1975).

chapter 23

FROM ROOSEVELT TO WILSON: NATIONAL POLITICS IN THE AGE OF PROGRESSIVISM

On a sunny spring morning in 1909 Theodore Roosevelt, wearing the greatcoat of a colonel of the Rough Riders, left New York for a safari in Africa. An ex-president at the age of fifty, he had turned over the White House to his chosen successor, William Howard Taft (see page 656), and was now off for "the joy of wandering through lonely lands, the joy of hunting the mighty and terrible lords" of Africa, "where death broods in the dark and silent depths."

Some hoped he would not return. "I trust some lion will do its duty," Wall Street magnate J. P. Morgan said. Always prepared, Roosevelt took nine extra pairs of eyeglasses, and just in case, several expert hunters accompanied him. When the nearsighted Roosevelt took aim, three others aimed at the same moment. "Mr. Roosevelt had a fairly good idea of the general direction," the safari leader said, "but we couldn't take chances with the life of a former president." Though he had built a reputation as an ardent conservationist, Roosevelt shot nine lions, five elephants, thirteen rhinoceroses, seven hippopotamuses, and assorted other game—acquiring nearly three hundred trophies in all.

It was good fun, and afterward Roosevelt set off on a tour of Europe. He argued with the pope, dined with the king and queen of Italy—an experience he likened to "a Jewish wedding on the East Side of New York"—and happily spent five hours reviewing troops of the German empire. Less happily, he followed events back home where, in the judgment of many friends, Taft was not working out as president. Gifford Pinchot, Roosevelt's close companion in the conservation movement, came to Italy to complain personally about Taft, and at almost every stop there were letters from other disappointed Republicans.

Taft was puzzled by it all. Honest and warm-hearted, he had intended to continue Roosevelt's policies, even writing Roosevelt that he would "see to it that your judgment in selecting me as your successor and bringing about that succession shall be vindicated . . ." But events turned out differently. The conservative and progressive wings of the Republican party split, and Taft often sided with the conservatives. Among progressive Republicans, Taft's troubles stirred talk of a Roosevelt "Back from Elba" movement, akin to Napoleon's return from exile.

Thousands gathered to greet Roosevelt on his return from Europe. He sailed into New York harbor on June 18, 1910, to the sound of naval guns and loud cheers. In characteristic fashion, he had helped make the arrangements: "If there is to be a great crowd, do arrange it so that the whole crowd has a chance to see me and that there is as little disappointment as possible." Greeting Pinchot, one of Taft's leading opponents, with a hearty "Hello, Gifford," Roosevelt slipped away

Former President Theodore Roosevelt (center) was welcomed as a conquering hero and hailed as "the world's first citizen" on his return from his tour abroad. Young Franklin and Eleanor Roosevelt are at far right.

to his home in Oyster Bay, New York, where other friends awaited him.

He carried with him a touching letter from Taft, received just before he left Europe. "I have had a hard time—I do not know that I have had harder luck than other Presidents, but I do know that thus far I have succeeded far less than have others. I have been conscientiously trying to carry out your policies but my method of doing so has not worked smoothly." Taft invited Teddy to spend a night or two at the White House, but Roosevelt declined—saying that ex-presidents should not visit Washington. Relations between the two friends cooled. "It is hard, very hard," Taft said in 1911, "to see a devoted friendship going to pieces like a rope of sand."

A year later there was no longer thought of friendship, only a desperate fight between Taft and Roosevelt for the Republican presidential nomination. Taft chided Roosevelt for saying in his speeches nothing but "I, I, I" and called him a demagogue. Roosevelt in turn labeled Taft a puzzlewit and fathead. The name-calling was "pleasant and homelike," Mr. Dooley said. "Ivrybody callin' each other liars and crooks not like pollyytical inimies, d'ye mind, but like old frinds that has been up late dhrinkin' together."

The Changing Face of Industrialism

Businesses were large in the three decades after the Civil War, but in the years between 1895 and 1915 they became mammoth, employing thousands of workers and equipped with assembly lines to turn out huge numbers of the company's product. Inevitably, management attitudes changed, as did business organization and worker roles.

The Innovative Model T

Mass production of automobiles began in the first years of the century. Using an assembly-line system that foreshadowed later techniques, Ransom E. Olds turned out five thousand Olds runabouts in 1904. But Olds' days of leadership were numbered. In 1903 Henry Ford and a small group

of associates formed the Ford Motor Company, the firm that transformed the business.

Ford was forty years old. He had tried farming and hated it; during the 1890s he worked as an engineer for Detroit's Edison Company but spent his spare time designing internal combustion engines and automobiles. At first, like many others in the industry, he concentrated on luxury and racing cars. Racing his own cars, Ford became the "speed demon" of Detroit; in 1904 he set the world's land speed record—over ninety miles per hour—in the 999, a large red racer that shot flames from the motor.

In 1903 Ford sold the first Ford car. The price was high, and in 1905 Ford raised prices still higher. Sales plummeted. In 1907 he lowered the price; sales and revenues rose. Ford learned an important lesson of the modern economy: a smaller unit profit on a large number of sales meant enormous revenues. Early in 1908 he introduced the Model T, a four-cylinder, twenty-horsepower "Tin Lizzie," costing $850, and available only in black. Eleven thousand were sold the first year.

"I am going to democratize the automobile," Ford proclaimed. "When I'm through everybody will be able to afford one, and about everyone will have one." The key was mass production, and after many experiments, Ford copied the techniques of meat packers who moved animal carcasses along overhead trolleys from station to station. Adapting the process to automobile assembly, Ford in 1913 set up moving assembly lines in his plant in Highland Park, Michigan, that dramatically reduced the time and cost of producing cars. Emphasizing continuous movement, he strove for a nonstop flow from raw material to finished product. In 1914 he sold 248,000 Model T's.

That year Ford workers assembled a car in ninety-three minutes, one tenth the time it had taken just eight months before. By 1925 the Ford plant turned out 9109 Model T's, a new car for every ten seconds of the working day.

While Ford was putting more and more cars on the road, the 1916 Federal Aid Roads Act, a little-noticed measure, set the framework for road building in the twentieth century. Removing control from county governments, it required every state desiring federal funds to establish a highway department to plan routes, oversee construction, and maintain roads. In states that had such departments, the federal government paid half the cost of building the roads. Providing for a planned highway system, the act produced a national network of two-lane, all-weather intercity roads.

The Burgeoning Trusts

As businesses like Ford's grew, capital and organization became increasingly important, and the result was the formation of a growing number of trusts. Standard Oil started the trend in 1882 (see chapter 18), but the greatest momentum came two decades later. Between 1898 and 1903 a series of mergers and consolidations swept the economy. Many smaller firms disappeared, swallowed up in giant corporations. By 1904 large-scale combinations of one form or another controlled nearly two fifths of the capital in manufacturing in the country.

The result was not monopoly, but oligopoly—control of a commodity or service by a small

■ (Top) Assembling magnetos on the Ford line. One worker could do it in twenty minutes; twenty-nine workers, properly arranged, could do it in five minutes. (Bottom) One day's output of car chassis at the Ford Highland Park plant in 1913.

■ (Right) As early as 1886 cartoonist Thomas Nast attacked trusts. Here the people's welfare is sinking as the Statue of Liberty is defaced.

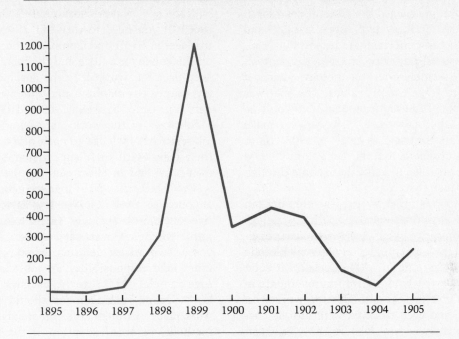

number of large, powerful companies. Six great financial groups dominated the railroad industry; a handful of holding companies controlled utilities and steel. Rockefeller's Standard Oil owned about 85 percent of the oil business. Large companies like Standard Oil and American Tobacco weathered the depression of the 1890s, and after 1898, financiers and industrialists followed their example and formed the Amalgamated Copper Company, Consolidated Tobacco, U.S. Rubber, and a host of others.

By 1909 just 1 percent of the industrial firms were producing nearly half the manufactured goods. Giant businesses reached abroad for raw materials and new markets. United Fruit, an empire of plantations and steamships in the Caribbean, exploited opportunities created by victory in the war with Spain. U.S. Steel worked with overseas companies to fix the price of steel rails, an unattainable dream just a few years before. For decades competition had sent rail prices up and down; now they stayed at $28 a ton, and through the famous "Gary dinners" in which Elbert H. Gary of U.S. Steel brought steel executives together, market conditions were fixed over wide areas of the industry.

Though the trend has been overstated, finance capitalists like J. P. Morgan tended to replace the industrial capitalists of an earlier era. Able to finance the mergers and reorganizations, investment bankers played a greater and greater role in the economy. A multibillion-dollar financial house, J. P. Morgan and Company operated a network of control that ran from New York to every industrial and financial center in the nation. Like other investment firms, it held directorships in many corporations, creating "interlocking directorates" that allowed it to control many businesses. In 1913 two banking groups—Morgan's and Rockefeller's—held 341 directorships in 112 corporations with an aggregate capital of more than $22 billion.

Massive business growth set off a decade-long debate over what government should do about the trusts. Some critics who believed that the giant companies were responsible for stifling individual opportunity and raising prices wanted to break them up into small competitive units. Others argued that large-scale business was a mark of the times; it produced more goods and better lives. The debate over the trusts influenced politics throughout the Progressive era.

Managing the Machines

Mass production changed the direction of American industry. Size, system, organization, and marketing became increasingly important. Management focused on speed and product, not on workers. Assembly-line technology changed tasks and, to some extent, values. The goal was no longer to make a unique product that would be better than the one before. "The way to make automobiles," Ford said as early as 1903, "is to make one automobile like another automobile, to make them all alike, to make them come through the factory just alike."

In a development that rivaled assembly lines in importance, businesses established industrial research laboratories where scientists and engineers developed new products. General Electric founded the first one in 1900 in a barn. It soon attracted experts who designed improvements in light bulbs, invented the cathode tube, worked on early radio, and even tinkered with atomic theory. Du Pont opened its labs in 1911, Eastman Kodak in 1912, and Standard Oil in 1919. As the source of new ideas and technology, the labs altered life in the twentieth century.

Through all this, business became large-scale, mechanized, and managed. While many shops still employed fewer than a dozen workers, the proportion of such shops shrank. By 1920 close to one half of all industrial workers worked in factories employing more than 250 people. More than a third worked in factories that were part of multiplant companies.

Industries that processed materials—iron and steel, paper, cement, and chemicals—were increasingly continuous and automatic. In the glass industry, machines ended the domination of highly skilled and well-paid craft workers. In 1908 Irving W. Colburn invented a machine to manufacture plate glass; the Libbey-Owens-Ford Company bought the patent; and Ford soon had a glassmaking machine from which emerged every day for two years a 3½-mile ribbon of automobile window glass, eventually reaching a length of almost 2000 miles.

Workers tending such ribbons could not fall behind. Foremen still managed the laborers on the factory floor, but more and more the rules came down from a central office where trained, professional managers supervised production flow. Systematic record keeping, cost accounting, and inventory and production controls became widespread. Workers lost control of the work pace. "If you need to turn out a little more," a manager at Swift and Company said, "you speed up the conveyor a little and the men speed up to keep pace." It worked. In the automobile industry, output per manhour multiplied an extraordinary four times between 1909 and 1919.

Folkways of the work place—workers passing job-related knowledge to each other, performing their tasks with little supervision, setting their own pace, and in effect running the shop—gave way to "scientific" labor management. More than anyone else, Frederick Winslow Taylor, an inventive mechanical engineer, strove to extract maximum efficiency from each worker. Taylor proposed two major reforms. First, management must take responsibility for job-related knowledge and classify it into "rules, laws, and formulae." Second, management should control the work place "through *enforced* standardization of methods, *enforced* adoption of the best implements and working conditions, and *enforced* cooperation."

Taylor's methods included time-and-motion studies, training workers for particular tasks, and differential pay rates that rewarded those who worked fastest. "In the past," he stated in *The Principles of Scientific Management* (1911), "the man has been first; in the future the system must be first." Armed with stopwatches, his disciples reduced a factory's operations to the simplest tasks, then devised the most efficient way to perform them. Although few factories wholly adopted Taylor's principles, he had great influence, and the doctrines of scientific management spread through American industry.

Workers caught up in the changing industrial system experienced the benefits of efficiency and productivity; in some industries they earned more. But they suffered important losses as well. Performing repetitive tasks, they seemed part of the machinery, to whose pace and needs they moved. Bored, they might easily lose pride of workmanship, though many workers, it is clear, did not. Efficiency engineers experimented with tools and methods, a process many workers found unsettling. Yet the goal was to establish routine—to work out, as someone said of a garment worker, "one single precise motion each second, 3600 in one hour, and all exactly the same." Praising that worker, the manager said: "She is a sure machine."

Jobs became not only monotonous but dangerous. Under the pressure of speed, boredom or miscalculation could bring disaster. Meat cutters sliced fingers and hands. Illinois steel mills, a magazine said, were "Making Steel and Killing Men"; one mill had forty-six deaths in 1906 alone. Injuries were part of many jobs. "The machines go like mad all day," a garment worker said, "because the faster you work the more money you get. Sometimes in my haste I get my finger caught and the needle goes right through it . . . I bind the finger up with a piece of cotton and go on working."

In March 1911 a fire at the Triangle Shirtwaist Company in New York focused attention on unsafe working conditions. When the fire started, five hundred men and women—mostly Italians, and Jews from eastern Europe—were just finishing their workday. Firefighters arrived within minutes, but they were already too late. Terrified seamstresses raced to the exits to try to escape the flames; most exit doors were closed, locked by the company to prevent theft and shut out union organizers. Many died in the stampede down the narrow stairways or the single fire escape. Still others, trapped on the building's top stories far above the reach of the fire department's ladders, jumped to their death on the street below. One hundred forty-six people died.

A few days later eighty thousand people marched silently in the rain in a funeral procession up Fifth Avenue. A quarter million people watched. New York's governor appointed a State Factory Investigating Commission that recommended laws to shorten the workweek and improve safety conditions in factories and stores.

■ *Fire nets were of no avail to the Triangle garment workers who jumped from the upper stories to escape the flames.*

Conflict and Conciliation

Strikes and absenteeism increased after 1910; labor productivity dropped 10 percent between 1915 and 1918, the first such decline in memory. In many industries labor turnover became a serious problem; workers changed jobs in droves. Union membership grew. In 1900 only about 1 million workers belonged to unions—less than 4 percent of the work force. By 1920 5 million belonged, about 13 percent of the work force. There were 8 million female workers in 1910, but only 125,000 belonged to unions. Most unions did not want them, and through outright prohibition or other techniques, they discouraged female applicants.

Samuel Gompers' American Federation of Labor increased from 250,000 members in 1897 to 1.7 million in 1904. By far the largest union organization, it remained devoted to the interests of skilled craftsmen. While it aimed partly at better wages and working conditions, it also sought to limit entry into the craft and protect worker prerogatives. Within limits, the AFL found acceptance among giant business corporations eager for conservative policies and labor stability.

Unlike the AFL, the Industrial Workers of the World (IWW) tried to organize the unskilled and foreign-born laborers working in the mass-production industries. Founded in Chicago in 1905, it aimed to unite the American working class into a mammoth union to promote labor's interests. Its motto—"an injury to one is an injury to all"—stressed labor solidarity as had the earlier Knights of Labor. But unlike the Knights, the IWW, or Wobblies as they were often known, urged social revolution.

Labor Union Membership, 1897–1920

for a massive labor pageant. IWW leaders welcomed the revolutionary tumult sweeping Russia and other countries. In the United States, they thought, a series of local strikes would bring about capitalist repression, then a general strike, and eventually a workers' commonwealth.

The IWW fell short of these objectives, but during its lifetime—from 1905 to the mid-1920s—it made major gains among immigrant workers in the Northeast, migrant farm labor on the Plains, and loggers and miners in the South and Far West. In factories like Ford's, it recruited workers resentful of the speed-ups on the assembly lines. Although IWW membership probably amounted to no more than one hundred thousand at any one time, workers came and left so often that its total membership may have reached as high as one million.

Concerned about labor unrest, business leaders turned to the new fields of applied psychology and personnel management. A school of industrial psychology emerged. As Taylor had, industrial psychologists studied workers' routines, but they showed that output was also affected by job satisfaction. While most businesses pushed ahead

As Joe Hill, the IWW's legendary folk poet, wrote:

> If the workers took a notion
>   They could stop all speeding trains;
> Every ship upon the ocean
>   They can tie with mighty chains.
>
> Every wheel in the creation
>   Every mine and every mill;
> Fleets and armies of the nation,
>   Will at their command stand still.

IWW leaders included "Mother" Jones, a famous veteran of battles in the Illinois coalfields; Elizabeth Gurley Flynn, a fiery young radical who joined as a teen-ager; and William D. (Big Bill) Haywood, the strapping, one-eyed founder of the Western Federation of Miners.

The IWW led a number of major strikes. The Lawrence, Massachusetts (1912), and Paterson, New Jersey (1912), strikes attracted national attention: Lawrence when the strikers sent their children, ill-clad and hungry, out of the city to stay with sympathetic families; Paterson when they rented New York's Madison Square Garden

■ *Elizabeth Gurley Flynn, labor's "Joan of Arc," addresses textile workers on strike at Paterson, New Jersey.*

with efficiency campaigns, a few established industrial-relations departments, hired public relations firms to improve their corporate image, and linked productivity to job safety and happiness.

Ivy L. Lee, a pioneer in the field of corporate public relations, advised clients like the Pennsylvania Railroad and Standard Oil on how to improve relations with labor and the public. Calling himself, a "physician to corporate bodies," Lee urged complete openness on the company's part. To please employees, companies printed newsletters and organized softball teams; they awarded prizes and celebrated retirements. Ford created a "Sociology Department" staffed by 150 experts who showed workers how to budget their incomes and care for their health. They even taught them how to shop for meat.

On January 5, 1914, Ford took another significant step. He announced the Five-Dollar Day, "the greatest revolution," he said, "in the matter of rewards for workers ever known to the industrial world." With a stroke, he doubled the wage rate for common labor, reduced the working day from nine hours to eight, and established a personnel department to place workers in appropriate jobs. The next day, ten thousand applicants stood outside the gates.

As a result, Ford had the pick of the labor force. Turnover declined; absenteeism, previously as much as a tenth of all Ford workers every day, fell to .3 percent. Output increased; the IWW at Ford collapsed. At first scornful of the "utopian" plan, business leaders across the country soon copied it, and on January 2, 1919, Ford announced the Six-Dollar Day.

■ *State troopers confront millhands on strike at Lawrence, Massachusetts, in 1912. The IWW reached its peak membership of 250,000 during the Lawrence strike.*

Amoskeag

In size, system, and worker relations, the record of the Amoskeag Company textile mills was revealing. Located beside the Merrimack River in Manchester, New Hampshire, the mills—an enormous complex of factories, warehouses, canals, and machinery—had been built in the 1830s. By the turn of the century they were producing nearly fifty miles of cloth an hour, more cloth each day than any other mills in the world. Amoskeag Manufacturing Company was the area's largest employer.

The face of the mills, an almost solid wall of red brick, stretched nearly a mile in length. Archways and bridges pierced the façade. Amoskeag resembled a walled, medieval city within which workers found "a total institution, a closed and almost self-contained world." At first the mills employed young women, but by 1900 more and more immigrant males staffed the machines. French Canadians, Irish, Poles, and Greeks—seventeen thousand in all—worked there, and their experiences revealed a great deal about factory work and life at the turn of the century.

The company hired and fired at will, and it demanded relentless output from the spindles and spinning frames. Yet it also viewed employees as its "children" and looked for total loyalty in return, an expectation often realized. Workers identified with Amoskeag and, decades later, still called themselves Amoskeag men and women. "We were all like a family," one said.

Most Amoskeag workers preferred the industrial world of the mills to the farms they had left behind. They did not feel displaced; they knew the pains of industrial life; and they adapted in ways that fit their own needs and traditions. Families played a large role. They neither disintegrated nor lost their relationships. French Canadians and others often came in family units. One or two family members left the farm for the mills, maintained close ties with those back home, and then sent for others in a form of "chain migration."

Once in Manchester, families often worked in the same workrooms. Looking after each other, they asked foremen for transfers and promotions for relatives; they taught their children technical skills and how to get along with bosses and fellow workers. Although low-paid, Amoskeag employees took pride in their work, and for many of them, a well-turned out product provided dignity and self-esteem.

The company long showed a paternal interest in employee welfare, and in 1910 it inaugurated a deliberate welfare and efficiency program. The program aimed to increase productivity, accustom immigrants to industrial work, instill company loyalty, and curb labor unrest. Playgrounds and visiting nurses, home-buying plans, a cooking school, and dental service were part of the plan.

Amoskeag workers' fair. Employees exhibited craft items and baked goods at an annual company event. Many firms between 1910 and 1917 adopted employee programs similar to those introduced at Amoskeag.

The Amoskeag Textile Club held employee dinners and picnics, organized shooting clubs and a baseball team, sponsored Christmas parties for the children, and put out the *Amoskeag Bulletin*, a monthly magazine of employee news and achievements.

From 1885 to 1919 no strike touched the mills. Therafter, however, labor unrest increased. Overproduction and foreign competition took their toll, and Amoskeag closed in 1935.

The Republican Roosevelt

In September 1901 President William McKinley died of gunshot wounds (see chapter 20); Vice-President Theodore Roosevelt succeeded him in the White House. McKinley and Roosevelt had moved in similar directions, and the new President initially vowed to carry on McKinley's policies. He continued some, developed others of his own, and in the end brought to them all the particular exuberance of his own personality.

At age forty-three, Roosevelt was then the youngest president in American history. In contrast to the dignified McKinley, he was open, aggressive, and high-spirited. At his desk by 8:30 every morning, he worked through the day, and there were usually visitors for breakfast, lunch, and dinner. Politicians, labor leaders, industrial-ists, poets, artists, and writers paraded through the White House.

In personal conversation Roosevelt was persuasive and charming. He read widely and he held opinions on every issue—literature, art, marriage, divorce, conservation, business, football, and even spelling. An advocate of simplified spelling, he once instructed government printers to use "thru" for "through" and "dropt" for "dropped." Public opposition forced him to withdraw the order, and shortly afterward, as he was watching a naval review in Long Island Sound, a launch marked "Pres Bot" steamed by. Roosevelt laughed with delight.

If McKinley cut down on presidential isolation, Roosevelt virtually ended it. The presidency, he thought, was "the bully pulpit," a forum of ideas and leadership for the nation. The president was "a steward of the people bound actively and affirmatively to do all he could for the people." Self-confident, Roosevelt enlisted talented associates, including Elihu Root, secretary of war and later secretary of state; William Howard Taft, secretary of war; Gifford Pinchot, the nation's chief forester and leading conservationist; and Oliver Wendell Holmes, Jr., whom he named to the Supreme Court.

In 1901 Roosevelt invited Booker T. Washington, the prominent black educator, to lunch at the White House. Many Southerners protested— "a crime equal to treason," a newspaper said—

Theodore Roosevelt is shown here addressing a group of black businessmen in 1910. Booker T. Washington is seated next to Roosevelt.

and they protested again when Roosevelt appointed several blacks to important federal offices in South Carolina and Mississippi. At first Roosevelt tried to build a biracial, "black-and-tan" southern Republican party, hoping it would foster racial progress and his own renomination in 1904. He also denounced lynching and ordered the Justice Department to act against peonage.

But Roosevelt soon retreated. In some areas of the South he supported "lily-white" Republican organizations, and his policies often reflected his own belief in black inferiority. He said nothing when a race riot broke out in Atlanta in 1906, although twelve persons died. He joined others in blaming black soldiers stationed near Brownsville, Texas, after a night of violence there in August 1906. Acting quickly and on little evidence, he discharged "without honor" three companies of black troops. Six of the soldiers who were discharged held the Congressional Medal of Honor.

Busting the Trusts

"There is a widespread conviction in the minds of the American people that the great corporations known as trusts are in certain of their features and tendencies hurtful to the general welfare," Roosevelt reported to Congress in 1901. Like most people, however, the President wavered on the trusts. Large-scale production and industrial growth, he believed, were natural and beneficial; they needed only to be controlled. Still he distrusted the trusts' impact on local enterprise and individual opportunity. Distinguishing between "good" and "bad" trusts, he pledged to protect the former while controlling the latter.

At first Roosevelt hoped the glare of publicity would be enough to uncover and correct business evils, and in public he both praised and attacked the trusts. Mr. Dooley poked fun at his wavering: "'Th' trusts,' says he, 'are heejous monsthers built up be th' enlightened intherprise iv th' men that have done so much to advance progress in our beloved country,' he says. 'On wan hand I wud stamp thim undher fut; on th' other hand not so fast.'"

In 1903 Roosevelt asked Congress to create a Department of Commerce and Labor, with a Bureau of Corporations empowered to investigate corporations engaged in interstate commerce. Congress balked; Roosevelt called in reporters, and in an off-the-record interview, charged that John D. Rockefeller had organized the opposition to the measure. After that accusation, editorials and many public figures clamored for action, and the proposal passed easily in a matter of weeks.

Roosevelt also undertook more direct legal action. On February 14, 1902, he instructed the Justice Department to bring suit against the Northern Securities Company for violation of the Sherman Antitrust Act. It was a shrewd move. A mammoth holding company, Northern Securities controlled the massive rail networks of the Northern Pacific, Great Northern, and Chicago, Burlington & Quincy railroads. Some of the most prominent names in business were behind the giant company—J. P. Morgan and Company, the Rockefeller interests, Kuhn, Loeb and Company, and railroad operators James J. Hill and Edward H. Harriman.

Shocked by Roosevelt's action, Morgan charged that the President had not acted like a "gentleman," and Hill talked glumly of having "to fight for our lives against the political adventurers who have never done anything but pose and draw a salary." Morgan rushed to Washington to complain and to ask whether there were plans to "attack my other interests," notably U.S. Steel. "No," Roosevelt replied, "unless we find out they have done something that we regard as wrong."

In 1904 the Supreme Court, in a five to four decision, upheld the suit against Northern Securities and ordered the company dissolved. Roosevelt was jubilant, and he followed up the victory with several other antitrust suits. In 1902 he had moved against the beef trust, an action applauded by western farmers and urban consumers alike. After a lull, he initiated suits in 1906 and 1907 against the American Tobacco Company, the Du Pont Corporation, the New Haven Railroad, and Standard Oil.

But Roosevelt's policies were not always clear, nor his actions always consistent. He invited Morgan to the White House to confer with him and allowed the president of National City Bank to preview a draft of his third annual message to Congress. Roosevelt also asked for (and received) business support in his bid for reelection in 1904. Large donations came in from industrial leaders, and Morgan himself later testifed that he gave

A 1904 cartoon depicts TR as "Jack the Giant-Killer" battling the Wall Street titans. Actually Roosevelt dissolved relatively few trusts.

$150,000 to Roosevelt's campaign. In 1907 the President permitted Morgan's U.S. Steel to absorb the Tennessee Coal and Iron Company, an important competitor.

Roosevelt, in truth, was not a "trust-buster," although he was frequently called that. William Howard Taft, his successor in the White House, initiated forty-three antitrust indictments in four years—nearly twice as many as the twenty-five Roosevelt initiated in the seven years of his presidency.

"Square Deal" in the Coalfields

A few months after announcing the Northern Securities suit, Roosevelt intervened in a major labor dispute involving the anthracite coal miners of northeastern Pennsylvania. Led by John Mitchell, a moderate labor leader, the United Mine Workers demanded wage increases, an eight-hour workday, and company recognition of the union. The coal companies refused, and in May 1902, 140,000 miners walked off the job. The mines closed.

As the months passed and the strike continued, coal prices rose. With winter coming on, schools, hospitals, and factories ran short of coal. Public opinion turned against the companies. Morgan and other industrial leaders privately urged them to settle, but George F. Baer, head of one of the largest companies, refused: "The rights and interests of the laboring man," Baer said, "will be protected and cared for—not by the labor agitators, but by the Christian men to whom God in his infinite wisdom has given the control of the property interests of this country."

Roosevelt was furious. Complaining of the companies' arrogance, he invited both sides in the dispute to an October 1902 conference at the White House. There, Mitchell took a moderate tone and offered to submit the issues to arbitration, but the companies again refused to budge. Roosevelt ordered the army to prepare to seize the mines and then leaked word of his intent to Wall Street leaders.

Alarmed, Morgan and others again urged settlement of the dispute, and at last the companies retreated. They agreed to accept the recommendations of an independent commission the President would appoint. In late October the strikers returned to work, and in March 1903 the commission awarded them a 10-percent wage increase and a cut in working hours. It recommended, however, against union recognition. The coal companies, in turn, were encouraged to raise prices to offset the wage increase.

More and more Roosevelt saw the federal government as an honest and impartial "broker" between powerful elements in society. Rather than leaning toward labor, he pursued a middle way to curb corporate or labor abuses, abolish privilege, and enlarge individual opportunity. Often he backed reforms in part to head off more radical measures.

During the 1904 campaign Roosevelt called his actions in the coal miners' strike a "square deal" for both labor and capital, a term that stuck to his administration. His actions stood in powerful contrast to Grover Cleveland's in the 1894 Pullman strike (see chapter 20). Roosevelt was not the first president to take a stand for labor, but he was

■ *President Roosevelt with mine workers after the settlement of the 1902 strike in the coalfields. His conciliatory position improved his standing with the working classes.*

the first to bring opposing sides in a labor dispute to the White House to settle it. He was the first to threaten to seize a major industry, and he was the first to appoint a commission whose decision both sides agreed to accept.

Another Term

In the election of 1904, the popular Roosevelt soundly drubbed his Democratic opponent, Alton B. Parker of New York, and the Socialist party candidate, Eugene V. Debs of Indiana. Roosevelt attracted a large campaign chest, campaigned strenuously, and won votes everywhere. In a landslide victory he received 57 percent of the vote to Parker's 38 percent, and on election night

The Election of 1904

Candidate	Party	Popular Vote	Electoral Vote
T. Roosevelt	Republican	7,626,593	336
Parker	Democrat	5,082,898	140
Debs	Socialist	402,489	0
Swallow	Prohibition	258,596	0

he savored the public's confidence. Overjoyed, he pledged that "under no circumstances will I be a candidate for or accept another nomination," a statement he later regretted.

Following his election, Roosevelt in late 1904 laid out a reform program that included railroad regulation, employers' liability for federal employees, greater federal control over corporations, and laws regulating child labor, factory inspection, and slum clearance in the District of Columbia. He turned first to railroad regulation. In 1903 he had worked with Congress to pass the Elkins Act to prohibit railroad rebates and increase the powers of the Interstate Commerce Commission (ICC). The Elkins Act, a moderate law, was framed with the consent of railroad leaders. In 1904 and 1905 the President wanted much more, and he urged Congress to empower the ICC to set reasonable and nondiscriminatory rates and prevent inequitable practices.

Widespread demand for railroad regulation strengthened Roosevelt's hand. In the Midwest and Far West the issue was a popular one, and reform Governors La Follette in Wisconsin, Albert C. Cummins in Iowa, and Hiram Johnson in California (see chapter 22) urged federal action. Roosevelt maneuvered cannily. As the legislative battle opened, he released figures showing that Standard Oil had reaped $750,000 a year from rebates. He also skillfully traded congressional support for a strong railroad measure in return for his promise to postpone a reduction of the tariff, a stratagem that came back to plague President Taft.

Triumph came with passage of the Hepburn Act of 1906. A significant achievement, the act strengthened the rate-making power of the Interstate Commerce Commission. It increased membership on the ICC from five to seven, empowered it to fix reasonable maximum railroad rates, and broadened its jurisdiction to include oil-pipeline, express, and sleeping-car companies. ICC orders were binding, pending any court appeals, thus placing the burden of proof upon the companies. Delighted, Roosevelt viewed the Hepburn Act as a major step in his plan for continuous, expert federal control over industry.

President Roosevelt signed two important laws to regulate the food and drug industries. Both laws reflected public outcry over adulterated and poisonous food and drugs. Muckraking articles

670

had touched frequently on filthy conditions in meat-packing houses, and Upton Sinclair's *The Jungle* (1906) described them in terms graphic enough to send people reeling from the dinner table:

> There would be meat stored in great piles in rooms; and the water from leaky roofs would drip over it, and thousands of rats would race about on it. It was too dark in these storage places to see well, but a man could run his hand over these piles of meat and sweep off handfuls of the dried dung of rats. These rats were nuisances, and the packers would put poisoned bread out for them; they would die, and then rats, bread, and meat would go into the hoppers together.

After reading *The Jungle*, Roosevelt ordered an investigation. The result, he said, was "hideous," and he threatened to publish the entire "sickening report" if Congress did not act. Meat sales plummeted in the United States and Europe. Demand for reform grew. Alarmed, the meat packers themselves supported a reform law, which they hoped would be just strong enough to still the clamor. The Meat Inspection Act of 1906, stronger than the packers wanted, set rules for sanitary meat packing and government inspection of meat products.

A second measure, the Pure Food and Drug Act, passed more easily on June 30, 1906 (see the special feature in this chapter).

An expert on birds, Roosevelt loved nature and the wilderness, and some of his most enduring accomplishments came in the field of conservation. Working closely with Pinchot, Chief of the Forest Service, he established the first comprehensive national conservation policy. He undertook a major reclamation program, created the federal Reclamation Service, and strengthened the forest preserve program in the Department of Agriculture. Broadening the concept of conservation, he placed power sites, coal lands, and oil reserves as well as national forests in the public domain.

When Roosevelt took office in 1901 there were 45 million acres in government preserves. In 1908 there were almost 195 million. That year he called a National Conservation Congress attended by forty-four governors and hundreds of experts. Roosevelt formed the National Commis-

Early twentieth-century meat-processing scenes like this are idyllic compared to those described in Upton Sinclair's The Jungle, *which became the most successful of the muckraking books.*

sion on the Conservation of Natural Resources to look after waters, forests, lands, and minerals. With Pinchot as head, it drew up an inventory of the nation's natural resources.

As 1908 approached, Roosevelt became increasingly strident in his demand for sweeping reforms. He attacked "malefactors of great wealth," urged greater federal regulatory powers, criticized the conservatism of the federal courts, and called for laws protecting factory workers. Many business leaders blamed him for a severe financial panic in the autumn of 1907, and conservatives in Congress stiffened their opposition. Divisions between Republican conservatives and progressives grew.

The Election of 1908			
Candidate	Party	Popular Vote	Electoral Vote
Taft	Republican	7,676,258	321
Bryan	Democrat	6,406,801	162
Debs	Socialist	420,380	0
Chafin	Prohibition	252,821	0

Immensely popular, Roosevelt prepared in 1908 to turn over the White House to William Howard Taft, his close friend and colleague. "The Roosevelt policies will not go out with the Roosevelt administration," a party leader said. "If Taft weakens, he will annihilate himself." As expected, Taft soundly defeated the Democratic standard-bearer William Jennings Bryan, who was making his third try for the presidency. The Republicans retained control of Congress. Taft prepared to move into the White House, ready and willing to carry on the Roosevelt legacy.

The Ordeal of William Howard Taft

The Republican national convention that nominated Taft had not satisfied either Roosevelt or Taft. True, Taft won the presidential nomination as planned, but conservative Republicans beat back the attempts of progressive Republicans to influence the convention. They named a conservative for vice-president, and the platform reflected conservative views on labor, the courts, and other issues. Taft wanted a pledge to lower the tariff but got only a promise of revision, which might lower—or raise—it. La Follette, Cummins, and other progressive Republicans were openly disappointed.

Taking office in 1909, Taft felt "just a bit like a fish out of water." The son of a distinguished Ohio family, and a graduate of Yale Law School, he became an Ohio judge, solicitor general of the United States, and a judge of the federal circuit court. In 1900 McKinley asked him to head the Philippine Commission, charged with the difficult and challenging task of forming a civil government in the Philippines. Later Taft was named the first governor general of the Philippines. In 1904 Roosevelt appointed him secretary of war.

In all these positions Taft made his mark as a skillful administrator. He worked quietly behind the scenes, avoided controversy, and shared none of Roosevelt's zest for politics. A good-natured man, Taft had personal charm and infectious humor. He fled from fights rather than seeking them out and disliked political maneuvering, preferring instead quiet solitude. "I don't like politics," he said. "I don't like the limelight."

■ *Taft played golf with gusto, despite his inability to place the ball on a tee and his habit of losing all the balls before the end of the match.*

Weighing close to three hundred pounds, Taft enjoyed conversation, golf and bridge, good food, and plenty of rest. Compared to Roosevelt and Wilson, he was lazy. He was also honest, kindly, and amiable, and in his own way he knew how to get things done. Reflective, he preferred the life of a judge, but his wife, Helen H. Taft, who enjoyed politics, prodded him toward the White House. When a Supreme Court appointment opened in 1906, Taft reluctantly turned it down. "Ma wants him to wait and be president," his youngest son said.

Taft's years as president were not happy. Mrs. Taft's health soon collapsed, and as it turned out, Taft presided over a Republican party torn with tensions that Roosevelt had either brushed aside or concealed. The tariff, business regulation, and other issues split conservatives and progressives and Taft often wavered or sided with the conservatives. Taft revered the past and distrusted change . Although an ardent supporter of Roosevelt, he never had Roosevelt's faith in the ability of government to impose reform and alter individual behavior. He named five corporation attorneys to his cabinet, leaned more to business than to labor, and spoke of a desire to "clean out the unions."

At the time and later, Taft's reputation suffered in contrast to the flair of Roosevelt and the moral majesty of Woodrow Wilson. He deserved better. Taft was an honest and sincere president, who— sometimes firm, sometimes befuddled—faced a series of important and troublesome problems during his term of office.

Party Insurgency

Taft started his term with an attempt to curb the powerful Republican Speaker of the House, Joseph "Uncle Joe" Cannon of Illinois. Using the powers of his position, Cannon set House procedures, appointed committees, and virtually dictated legislation. Straightforward and crusty, he often opposed reform. In March 1909 thirty Republican congressmen joined Taft's effort to curb Cannon's power, and the President sensed success. But Cannon retaliated and, threatening to block all tariff bills, forced a compromise. Taft stopped the anti-Cannon campaign in return for Cannon's pledge to help with tariff cuts.

Republicans were divided over the tariff, and there was a growing party insurgency against high rates. The House quickly passed a bill providing for lower rates, but in the Senate, protectionists raised them. Senate leader Nelson A. Aldrich of Rhode Island introduced a revised bill that added over eight hundred amendments to the House rates. It placed no duties on curling stones, false teeth, canary-bird seed, and hog bristles, which brought a chuckle from Mr. Dooley. "Th' new Tariff Bill," he said, "put these familyar commodyties within th' reach iv all."

Angry, La Follette and other Republicans attacked the bill as the child of special interests. In speeches on the Senate floor they called themselves "progressives," invoked Roosevelt's name,

and urged Taft to defeat the high-tariff proposal. Caught between protectionists and progressives, Taft wavered, then tried to compromise. In the end he backed Aldrich. The Payne-Aldrich Act, passed in November 1909, called for higher rates than the original House bill, though it lowered them from the Dingley Tariff of 1897 (see chapter 20). An unpopular law, it helped discredit Taft and revealed the tensions in the Republican party.

Republican progressives and conservatives drifted apart. Taft tried to find middle ground but leaned more and more toward the conservatives. During a nationwide speaking tour in the autumn of 1909 he praised Aldrich, scolded the low-tariff insurgents, and called the Payne-Aldrich Act "the best bill that the Republican party ever passed." Traveling through the Midwest, he pointedly ignored La Follette, Cummins, and other progressive Republicans.

When Congress met in 1910, progressive Republicans no longer looked to Taft for leadership. As before, they challenged Cannon's power, and again Taft wavered. In an outcome embarrassing to the President, the progressives won, managing to curtail Cannon's authority to dictate committee assignments and schedule debate. In progressive circles there was growing talk of a Roosevelt return to the White House.

■ *A 1910 cartoon shows Taft snarled in the intricacies of office as his disapproving mentor looks on.*

The Ordeal of William Howard Taft

Patent Medicines and the Pure Food and Drug Act

Around 1900, at the same time the science of medicine was making enormous strides, patent medicines were selling in record volume. Everybody was curing everything with Mrs. Winslow's Soothing Syrup, Perkins' Infallible Aromatic and Disinfectory Pastile, and of course Lydia E. Pinkham's famous Vegetable Compound for women. Often suspicious of doctors, and eager for quick, inexpensive cures, Americans in 1904 spent almost $100 million on patent medicines. About 50,000 such medicines were sold in the United States.

By the beginning of the twentieth century, the germ theory of disease was several decades old, and it was known that different germs cause different diseases. But no one seemed surprised that each patent medicine—according to the ads, at least—could cure almost everything. Ads for Helmbold's Buchu, one of the period's popular remedies, claimed it cured "General Debility, Mental and Physical Depression, Imbecility, Determination of Blood to the Head, Confused Ideas, Hysteria, General Irritability, . . . Dyspepsia, Emaciation, Low Spirits, Disorganization or Paralysis of the Organs of Generation," and several other ills.

Some patent medicine makers quickly recognized the marketing potential of the germ theory. Germ-killing medicines, including William Radam's hot-selling Microbe Killer, soon appeared. A gardener in Austin, Texas, Radam decided that all diseases had a single, germ-related cause—and thus a single cure. He mixed water with hydrochloric and sulphuric acid taken from his gardening shed, added a dash of red wine, and produced the Microbe Killer. Patented as a gardening aid, Radam sold the concoction as a medicine. By the early 1890s seventeen factories were producing gallon jugs of the mixture. Radam left Austin for a mansion on Fifth Avenue in New York City.

Other patent medicines contained cocoa, axle grease, beet sugar, glue, or castor oil. Some contained cocaine or morphine; many had large amounts of alcohol. Hostetter's Bitters was a popular medicine, and no wonder: nearly a third of each dose was alcohol. "You could get drunk on one bottle," the poet Carl Sandburg said. Hostetter's sold nearly a million bottles a year. In some towns, saloons served it at the bar.

Before long people began questioning the effectiveness of such medicines. Temperance groups were among the first to raise questions, sure that the medicines were little more than hard liquor in disguise. (Indeed, patent medicine sales had a way of booming wherever prohibition was adopted.) In 1905 the American Medical Association (AMA), a group that reflected the growing professionalization of medicine, created a special council of chemists and pharmacists to analyze patent medicine ingredients. The American Pharmaceutical Association also urged a listing of ingredients on the label of each bottle.

Involving greedy entrepreneurs who fed on the fears of gullible consumers, the patent medicines were a target tailor-made for the muckrakers. Samuel Hopkins Adams, a reporter for *Collier's*, had once considered a career in medicine; he resented the way in which patent medicine makers misled people who needed proper medical treatment. Like other muckrakers, he combined a zeal for facts with a desire to improve the lot of mankind. During 1904 and 1905 he studied ads, interviewed manufacturers, and sent samples of medicines to scientists for analysis.

On October 7, 1905, Adams broke the story in *Collier's* under the title "The Great American Fraud." "Gullible America," he began, "will spend this year some seventy-five millions of dollars in the purchase of patent medicines. In consideration of this sum it will swallow huge quantities of alcohol, an appalling amount of opiates and narcotics . . . and, far in excess of all other ingredients, undiluted fraud." Running until February 1906, the story included ten articles, in which Adams named 264 medicines, doctors, and companies. Newspapers summarized the findings; editorials demanded action. The AMA printed Adams' articles in a booklet that sold half a million copies.

While researching the story, Adams had sent medicine samples to Dr. Harvey W. Wiley, the chief chemist of the Department of Agriculture. A physician as well as a chemist, Wiley was energetic and innovative, with a flair for the dramatic—he was the third person in Washington to drive a car and the first to have a collision. He and his twelve young assistants became known as the "Poison Squad" in 1902, when they tested various food preservatives, determined to put an end to adulterated foods.

Wiley and the Poison Squad then began testing patent medicines. Wiley published the results of those tests, lectured on the issue to women's clubs and other groups, and urged Congress and President Theodore Roosevelt to curb the industry. In his 1905 message to Congress—issued in the midst of Adams' stories in *Collier's*—Roosevelt recommended federal regulation of "misbranded and adulterated foods, drinks, and drugs."

In February 1906 the Senate quickly passed a pure food and drug bill, amid indications that opponents planned to kill it in the House. If that was their plan, Upton Sinclair's *The Jungle*, which appeared in late February, created a sensation that aroused the public. Far from killing the bill, the House strengthened it, and on June 30, 1906, Roosevelt signed the new law. It required manufacturers to list the amount of alcohol, cocaine, morphine, and certain other ingredients on the label.

The law did not ban patent medicines. Instead, it relied on an assumption underlying much of the legislation of the progressive era—once people knew the facts, they would safely choose the right course. The assumption was not always correct, and patent medicines continued to sell after 1906. Kickapoo Cough *Cure*—one of the first medicines seized under the new law—simply changed its name to Kickapoo Cough *Syrup* and went on selling. Even today Americans spend almost $1 billion a year on products similar to those Adams and Wiley questioned in 1906.

The Ballinger-Pinchot Affair

The conservation issue dealt another blow to relations between Roosevelt and President Taft. In 1909 Richard A. Ballinger, Taft's secretary of the interior, offered for sale a million acres of public land that Pinchot, who had stayed on as Taft's chief forester, had withdrawn from sale. Pinchot protested and, seizing on a report that Ballinger had helped sell valuable Alaskan coal lands to a syndicate that included J. P. Morgan, asked Taft to intervene. After investigating, Taft supported Ballinger on every count, although he asked Pinchot to remain in office.

Pinchot refused to drop the matter. Behind the scenes he provided material for two anti-Ballinger magazine articles, and he wrote a critical public letter that Senator Dolliver of Iowa read to the Senate. Taft had had enough. He fired the insubordinate Pinchot, an appropriate action, but again lost in the process. Although a conservationist himself, the President had fired one of the nation's leading conservationists. Newspapers followed the controversy for months, and muckrakers assailed the administration's "surrender" to Morgan and other "despoilers of the national heritage."

The Ballinger-Pinchot controversy obscured Taft's important contributions to conservation. He won from Congress the power to remove lands from sale, and he used it to conserve more land than Roosevelt did. Still, the controversy tarred Taft, and it upset his old friend Roosevelt. Pinchot hurried to Italy where Roosevelt was on tour; he talked again with Roosevelt within days of TR's arrival home in June 1910.

Taft's Final Years

Interested in railroad regulation, Taft backed a bill in 1910 to empower the ICC to fix maximum railroad rates. Progressive Republicans favored that plan but attacked Taft's suggestion of a special Commerce Court to hear appeals from ICC decisions because most judges were traditionally conservative in outlook and usually rejected attempts to regulate railroad rates. Democratic and Republican progressives tried to amend the bill to strengthen it; Taft made support of it a test of party loyalty.

The Mann-Elkins Act of 1910 gave something to everyone. It gave the ICC power to set rates, stiffened long- and short-haul regulations, and placed telephone and telegraph companies under ICC jurisdiction. These provisions delighted progressives. The act also created a Commerce Court, pleasing conservatives. In a trade-off, conservative Republican Senate leaders pledged their support for a statehood bill for Arizona and New Mexico, which were both predicted to be Democratic. In return, enough Democratic senators promised to vote for the Commerce Court provision to pass the bill. While pleased with the act, Taft and the Republican party lost further ground. In votes on its key provisions, Taft raised the issue of party regularity, and progressive Republicans defied him.

Withholding patronage, Taft attempted to defeat the progressive Republicans in the 1910 elections. He helped form antiprogressive organizations, and he campaigned against progressive Republican candidates for the Senate. In California he opposed Hiram Johnson, the progressive Republican champion; in Wisconsin, the home of La Follette, he sent Vice-President James S. Sherman to take control of the state convention. Progressive Republicans retaliated by organizing a nationwide network of anti-Taft Progressive Republican Clubs.

The 1910 election results were a major setback for Taft and the Republicans—both conservatives and progressives. In party primaries, progressive Republicans overwhelmed most Taft candidates, and in November, the Democrats beat virtually everyone. They swept the urban-industrial states from New York to Illinois. New York, New Jersey, Indiana, and even Taft's Ohio elected Democratic governors. For the first time since 1894, Republicans lost control of both the House and the Senate. In all, they lost fifty-eight seats in the House and ten in the Senate. Disappointed, Taft called it "not only a landslide, but a tidal wave and holocaust all rolled into one general cataclysm."

Despite the defeat, Taft pushed through several important measures before his term ended. With the help of the new Democratic House, he backed laws to regulate safety in mines and on railroads, create a Children's Bureau in the federal government, establish employers' liability for all work done on government contracts, and mandate an eight-hour workday for government workers. In 1909 Congress initiated a constitutional amendment authorizing an income tax, perhaps the most significant legislative measure of the twentieth century. The Sixteenth Amendment took effect early in 1913.

An ardent supporter of competition, Taft relentlessly pressed a campaign against trusts. The Sherman Antitrust Act, he said in 1911, "is a good law that ought to be enforced, and I propose to enforce it." That year the Supreme Court in cases against Standard Oil and American Tobacco established the "rule of reason," which allowed the Court to determine whether a business was a "reasonable" restraint on trade. Taft thought the decisions gave the Court too much discretion, and he pushed ahead with the antitrust effort.

In October 1911, he sued U.S. Steel for its acquisition of the Tennessee Coal and Iron Company in 1907. Roosevelt had approved the acquisition (see p. 669), and the suit seemed designed to impugn his action. Enraged, he attacked Taft, and Taft, for once, fought back. He accused Roosevelt of undermining the conservative tradition in the country and began working to undercut the influence of the progressive Republicans. Increasingly now, Roosevelt listened to anti-Taft Republicans who urged him to run for president in 1912. In the following months he sounded Republican sentiment for a presidential bid. In February 1912 he announced: "My hat is in the ring."

Differing Philosophies in the Election of 1912

Delighted Democrats looked on as Taft and Roosevelt fought for the Republican nomination. As the incumbent president, Taft controlled the party machinery, and when the Republican convention met in June 1912, he took the nomination. In early July the Democrats met in Baltimore and, confident of victory for the first time in two decades, struggled through forty-six ballots before finally nominating Woodrow Wilson, the reform-minded governor of New Jersey.

A month later the anti-Taft and progressive Republicans—now calling themselves the Progressive Party—whooped it up in Chicago. Roosevelt himself was there to give a stirring "Confession of Faith" and listen to the delegates sing:

Thou wilt not cower in the dust,
   Roosevelt, O Roosevelt!
Thy gleaming sword shall never rust,
   Roosevelt, O Roosevelt!

Naming Roosevelt for president, the Progressive —soon known as the "Bull Moose"—party convention set the stage for the first important three-cornered presidential contest since 1860.

Saddened, Taft was out of the running before the campaign even began. "I think I might as well give up so far as being a candidate is concerned," he said in July. "There are so many people in the country who don't like me." Taft stayed at home and made no speeches before the election. Roosevelt campaigned strenuously, even completing one speech after being shot in the chest. "I have a message to deliver," he said, "and will deliver it as long as there is life in my body."

Roosevelt's message involved a program he called the New Nationalism. An important phase in the shaping of twentieth-century American political thought, it demanded a national approach to the country's affairs and a strong president to deal with them. The New Nationalism called for efficiency in government and society. It exalted the executive and the expert, urged social-justice reforms to protect workers, women, and

■ *The Bull Moose party's highly recognizable candidate is characterized in this cartoon as "the latest arrival at the political zoo."*

■ *To overcome the impression of him as an austere scholar, Wilson campaigned vigorously in 1912, stumping the country from the rear of a train.*

election of 1912 offered competing philosophies of government. Both Roosevelt and Wilson saw the central problem of the American nation as economic growth and its effect on individuals and society. Both focused on the government's relation to business; both believed in bureaucratic reform; and both wanted to use government to protect the ordinary citizen. But Roosevelt welcomed federal power, national planning, and business growth; Wilson distrusted them all.

On election day Wilson won 6.3 million votes to 4.1 million for Roosevelt and 900,000 for Eugene V. Debs, the Socialist party candidate. Taft, the incumbent president, finished third with 3.5 million votes; he carried only Vermont and Utah for 8 electoral votes. The Democrats also won outright control of both houses.

Woodrow Wilson's New Freedom

children, and accepted "good" trusts. The New Nationalism encouraged large concentrations of labor and capital, serving the nation's interests under a forceful federal executive.

For the first time in the history of a major political party, the Progressive campaign enlisted women in its organization. Some labor leaders, who saw potential for union growth, and some business leaders, who saw relief from destructive competition and labor strife, supported the new party.

Wilson, in contrast, set forth a program called the New Freedom that emphasized business competition and small government. A states' rights Democrat, he wanted to rein in federal authority, using it only to sweep away special privilege, release individual energies, and restore competition. Drawing on the thinking of Louis D. Brandeis, the brilliant shaper of reform-minded law, he echoed the Progressive party's social-justice objectives, while continuing to attack Roosevelt's planned state. For Wilson the vital issue was not a planned economy but a free one. "The history of liberty is the history of the limitation of governmental power . . .," he said in October 1912. "If America is not to have free enterprise, then she can have freedom of no sort whatever."

In the New Nationalism and New Freedom, the

If under Roosevelt social reform took on the excitement of a circus, "under Wilson," one historian said, "it acquired the dedication of a sunrise service." Born in Virginia in 1856, Wilson was the son of a Presbyterian minister. As a young man he wanted a career in public service, and he trained himself carefully in history and oratory. At age sixteen he became fascinated with the English parliamentary system, a fascination that shaped his scholarly career and perhaps his diplomacy in the First World War (see chapter 24). A moralist, he reached judgments easily, and once reached, almost nothing shook them. Opponents called him stubborn and smug. "He gives me the creeps," a Maryland ward boss said. "The time I met him, he said something to me, and I didn't know whether God or him was talking."

After graduating from Princeton University and the University of Virginia Law School, Wilson found that practicing law bored him. Shifting to history, from 1890 to 1902 he served as professor of jurisprudence and political economy at Princeton. In 1902 he became president of the university. Eight years later he was governor of New Jersey, where he led a campaign to reform election procedures, abolish corrupt practices, and strengthen railroad regulation.

Wilson's rise was rapid, and he knew relatively

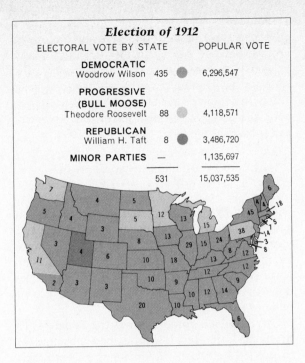

Election of 1912

	ELECTORAL VOTE BY STATE		POPULAR VOTE
DEMOCRATIC Woodrow Wilson	435		6,296,547
PROGRESSIVE (BULL MOOSE) Theodore Roosevelt	88		4,118,571
REPUBLICAN William H. Taft	8		3,486,720
MINOR PARTIES	—		1,135,697
	531		15,037,535

little about national issues and personalities. But he learned fast, and in some ways the lack of experience served him well. He had few political debts to repay, and he brought fresh perspectives to older issues. Ideas intrigued Wilson; details bored him. Although he was outgoing at times, he could also be cold and aloof, and aides soon learned that he preferred loyalty and flattery to candid criticism.

Prone to self-righteousness, Wilson often turned differences of opinion into bitter personal quarrels. Like Roosevelt, he believed in strong presidential leadership. A scholar of the party system, he cooperated closely with Democrats in Congress, and his legislative record placed him among the most effective presidents. Forbidding in individual conversation, Wilson could move crowds with graceful oratory. Unlike Taft, and even more than Roosevelt, he could inspire.

His inaugural address was eloquent. "The Nation," he said, "has been deeply stirred, stirred by a solemn passion, stirred by the knowledge of wrong, of ideals lost, of government too often debauched and made an instrument of evil. The feelings with which we face this new age of right and opportunity sweep across our heartstrings like some air out of God's own presence."

On the day of his inauguration, Wilson called Congress into special session to lower the tariff. When the session opened on April 8, 1913, Wilson himself was there, the first president since John Adams in 1801 to appear personally before Congress. In forceful language, he urged Congress to reduce tariff rates.

As the bill moved through Congress, Wilson showed exceptional skill. He worked closely with congressional leaders, and when lobbyists threatened the bill in the Senate, he appealed for popular support. The result was a triumph for Wilson and the Democratic party. The Underwood Tariff Act passed in 1913. The first tariff cut in nineteen years, it lowered rates about 15 percent and removed duties from sugar, wool, and several other consumer goods.

To make up for lost revenue, the act also levied a modest, graduated income tax, authorized under the just-ratified Sixteenth Amendment. Marking a significant shift in the American tax structure, it imposed a 1 percent tax on individuals and corporations earning more than $4000 annually and an additional 1 percent tax on incomes over $20,000. Above all, the act reflected a new unity within the Democratic party which, unlike its experience under Grover Cleveland, had worked together to pass a difficult tariff law.

Wilson himself emerged as an able leader. "At a single stage," a foreign editor said, "[he went] from the man of promise to the man of achievement." Encouraged by his success, Wilson decided to keep Congress in session through the hot Washington summer. Now he focused on banking reform, and the result in December 1913 was the Federal Reserve Act, the most important domestic law of his administration.

Meant to provide the United States with a sound yet flexible currency, the act established the country's first efficient banking system since Andrew Jackson killed the Second Bank of the United States in 1832 (see chapter 10). It created twelve regional banks, each to serve the banks of its district. The regional banks, in turn, answered to a Federal Reserve Board, appointed by the president, which governed the nationwide system.

A compromise law, the act blended public and private control of the banking system. Private bankers owned the federal reserve banks but answered to the presidentially appointed Federal Reserve Board. The reserve banks were authorized to issue currency and through the discount rate—the interest rate at which they loaned money to member banks—could raise or lower the amount of money in circulation. Monetary affairs no longer depended solely on the price of gold. Within a year nearly half the nation's banking resources were in the Federal Reserve System.

The Clayton Antitrust Act (1914) completed Wilson's initial legislative program. Like previous antitrust measures, it reflected confusion over how to discipline a growing economy without putting a brake on output. In part it was a response to the revelations of the Pujo Committee of the House, a congressional committee investigating Wall Street. Publicized by Brandeis in a disquieting series of articles, "Other People's Money," the committee discovered a pyramid of money and power capped by the Morgan-Rockefeller empire that, through "interlocking directorates," controlled companies worth $22 billion, over one tenth of the national wealth.

The Clayton Act outlawed such directorates and prohibited unfair trade practices. It forbade pricing policies that created monopoly, and it made corporate officers personally responsible for antitrust violations. Delighting Samuel Gompers and the labor movement, the act declared that unions were not conspiracies in restraint of trade, outlawed the use of injunctions in labor disputes unless necessary to protect property, and approved lawful strikes and picketing. To Gompers' dismay, the courts continued to rule against union activity.

A related law established a powerful Federal Trade Commission to oversee business methods. Composed of five members, the commission could demand special and annual reports, investigate complaints, and order corporate compliance, subject to court review. At first Wilson opposed the commission concept, which was an approach more suitable to Roosevelt's New Nationalism, but he changed his mind and, along with Brandeis, called it the cornerstone of his antitrust plan. To reassure business leaders, he appointed a number of conservatives to the new commission and to the Federal Reserve Board.

In November 1914 Wilson proudly announced the completion of his New Freedom program.

Tariff, banking, and antitrust laws promised a brighter future, he said, and it was now "a time of healing because a time of just dealing." Many Progressives were aghast. To think society's ills were so easily cured, the *New Republic* said, "casts suspicion either upon his own sincerity or upon his grasp of the realities of modern social and industrial life."

Retreat and Advance

Distracted by the start of war in Europe, Wilson gave less attention to domestic issues for over a year. When he returned to concern with reform, he adopted more and more of Roosevelt's New Nationalism and blended it with the New Freedom in ways that set it off from his earlier policies.

One of Wilson's problems was the Congress. To his dismay, the Republicans gained substantially in the 1914 elections. Reducing the Democratic majority in the House, they swept key industrial and farm states. At the same time a recession struck the economy, which had been hurt by the outbreak of the European war in August 1914. Some business leaders blamed the tariff and other New Freedom laws. On the defensive, Wilson soothed business sentiment and invited bankers and industrialists to the White House. He allowed companies fearful of antitrust actions to seek advice from the Justice Department.

Preoccupied with such problems, Wilson blocked significant action in Congress through most of 1915. He refused to support a bill providing minimum wages for women workers, sidetracked a child-labor bill on the ground that it was unconstitutional, and opposed a bill to establish long-term credits for farmers. He also refused to endorse woman suffrage, arguing that the right to vote was a state, not a federal matter.

Wilson's record on race disappointed blacks and many progressives. He had appealed to black voters during the 1912 election, and a number of black leaders campaigned for him. Soon after the inauguration, Oswald Garrison Villard, a leader of the NAACP, proposed a National Race Commission to study the problem of race relations. Initially sympathetic, Wilson rejected the idea because he feared he might lose southern Democratic votes in Congress. A Virginian himself, he appointed many Southerners to high office, and for the first time since the Civil War, southern views on race dominated the nation's capital.

At one of Wilson's first cabinet meetings the postmaster general proposed the segregation of all blacks in the federal service. No one dissented, including Wilson. Several government bureaus promptly began to segregate workers in offices, shops, restrooms, and restaurants. Employees who objected were fired. Black leaders protested, and they were joined by progressive leaders and clergymen. Surprised at the protest, Wilson backed quietly away from the policy, although he continued to insist that segregation benefited blacks.

As the year 1916 began, Wilson again pushed for reform, and the result—a virtual river of reform laws—began the second, national-minded phase of the New Freedom. In part Wilson was motivated by the approaching presidential election. A minority president, he owed his victory in 1912 to the split in the Republican party, now almost healed. Roosevelt was moving back into Republican ranks, and there were issues connected with the war in Europe that he might use against Wilson (see the next chapter). Moreover, many progressives were voicing disappointment with Wilson's limited reforms and his failure to support more advanced reform legislation such as farm credits, child labor, and women's suffrage.

Moving quickly to patch up the problem, Wilson named Brandeis to the Supreme Court in January 1916. Popular among progressives, Brandeis was also the first person of Jewish faith to serve on the Court. When conservatives in the Senate tried to defeat the nomination, Wilson stood firm and won, earning further praise from progressives, Jews, and others. In May he reversed his stand on farm loans and accepted a rural credits bill to establish farm-loan banks backed by federal funds. The Federal Farm Loan Act of 1916 created a Federal Farm Loan Board to give farmers credit similar to the Federal Reserve's benefits for trade and industry.

Wilson was already popular within the labor movement. Going beyond Roosevelt's policies, which had sought a balance between business and labor, he defended union recognition and collective bargaining. In 1913 he appointed William B. Wilson, a respected leader of the United Mine

Chronology

1900	General Electric founds the first industrial research laboratory
1901	Theodore Roosevelt becomes president
1902	Roosevelt sues the Northern Securities Company for violation of antitrust act Coal miners in northeastern Pennsylvania strike for wage increases, eight-hour day, and union recognition
1903	Department of Commerce and Labor created Ford Motor Company formed
1904	Roosevelt elected president
1905	Industrial Workers of the World (IWW) established
1906	Hepburn Act strengthens power and authority of ICC Congress passes Meat Inspection Act and Pure Food and Drug Act
1908	Taft elected president
1909	Payne-Aldrich Tariff Act divides Republican party
1910	Mann-Elkins Act passed to regulate railroads Taft fires Gifford Pinchot, head of U.S. Forest Service Democrats sweep midterm elections
1911	Frederick Winslow Taylor publishes *The Principles of Scientific Management* Fire at the Triangle Shirtwaist Company kills 146 people
1912	Progressive party formed; nominates Roosevelt for president Woodrow Wilson elected president IWW leads strikes in Massachusetts and New Jersey
1913	Underwood Tariff Act lowers rates Federal Reserve Act reforms U.S. banking system Ford introduces the moving assembly line in Highland Park plant Sixteenth Amendment authorizes Congress to collect taxes on incomes
1914	Clayton Act strengthens antitrust legislation Ford workers assemble an automobile in 93 minutes
1916	Wilson wins reelection Federal Aid Roads Act creates national road network

■ (Top) Strikers' tent colony at Ludlow before the militia and mine guards charged it on April 20, 1914. (Bottom) The ruins of Ludlow after the fourteen-hour attack that killed twenty-six people.

Workers, as the first head of the Labor Department, and he strengthened the department's Division of Conciliation. In 1914 in Ludlow, Colorado, state militia and mine guards fired machine guns into a tent colony of coal strikers, killing twenty-six men, women, and children. Outraged, Wilson stepped in and used federal troops to end the violence while negotiations to end the strike went on.

In August 1916 a threatened railroad strike again revealed Wilson's sympathies with labor. Like Roosevelt, he invited the two sides to the White House where he urged the railroad companies to grant an eight-hour day and labor leaders to abandon the demand for overtime pay. Labor leaders accepted the proposal; railroad leaders did not. "I pray God to forgive you, I never can," Wilson said as he left the room. Soon he signed the Adamson Act (1916) that imposed the eight-hour day on interstate railways and established a federal commission to study the railroad problem. Ending the threat of a strike, the act marked a milestone in the expansion of the federal government's authority to regulate industry.

With Wilson leading the way, the flow of reform legislation continued until the election. The Federal Workmen's Compensation Act established workers' compensation for government employees. The Keating-Owen Act, the first federal child-labor law, prohibited the shipment in interstate commerce of products manufactured by children under the age of fourteen. It too expanded the authority of the federal government. The Warehouse Act, similar to the subtreasury proposal the Populists urged in the 1890s (see chapter 20), authorized licensed warehouses to issue negotiable receipts for farm products deposited with them.

In September Wilson signed the Tariff Commission Act creating an expert commission to recommend tariff rates. The same month, the Revenue Act of 1916 boosted income taxes and furthered tax reform. Four thousand members of the National American Woman Suffrage Association cheered when Wilson finally came out in support of woman suffrage. "You touched our hearts and won our fealty," Carrie Chapman Catt, the association's president, told him. Two weeks later he endorsed the eight-hour day for all the nation's workers.

The 1916 presidential election was close, but Wilson won it on the issues of peace and progressivism (see chapter 24). By the end of 1916 he and the Democratic party had enacted most of the important parts of Roosevelt's Progressive party platform of 1912. To do it, Wilson abandoned portions of the New Freedom and accepted much of the New Nationalism, including greater federal power and commissions governing trade and tariffs. In mixing the two programs, he blended some of the competing doctrines of the progressive era, established the primacy of the federal government, and foreshadowed the pragmatic outlook of Franklin D. Roosevelt's New Deal.

In 1909 Taft rode to his inauguration in a horse and carriage; in 1913 Wilson rode in an automobile. In May 1918, the post office began airmail service between New York City and Washington, D.C. Change was evident throughout the country, as Americans and their institutions continued to adjust to a life of cities and suburbs, factories and mass production.

The institution of the presidency expanded. The president replaced Congress and the states as the center of national authority. From the White House radiated executive departments that guided a host of activities. Independent commissions, operating within flexible laws, supplemented executive authority.

Government at all levels accepted responsibility for the welfare of various elements in the social order. A reform-minded and bureaucratic society took shape, in which men and women, labor and capital, political parties and social classes competed for shares in the expansive framework of twentieth-century life.

After Napoleon's defeat in 1815, a century of peace began in western Europe, and as the decades passed, war seemed a dying institution. "It looks as though this were going to be the age of treaties rather than the age of wars," an American said in 1912, "the century of reason rather than the century of force." It was not to be. Two years later the most devastating of wars broke out in Europe, and in 1917 Americans were fighting on the battlefields of France.

Recommended Reading

George Mowry, *The Era of Theodore Roosevelt* (1958), and Arthur S. Link, *Woodrow Wilson and the Progressive Era* (1954), trace the social and economic conditions of the period. See also Henry F. Pringle's biography, *Theodore Roosevelt* (1931), John M. Blum's perceptive and brief *The Republican Roosevelt* (1954), and William H. Harbaugh's thoughtful *The Life and Times of Theodore Roosevelt*, rev. ed. (1975). Donald E. Anderson, *William Howard Taft* (1973), and Paolo E. Coletta, *The Presidency of William Howard Taft* (1973), study Taft. The definitive biography of Wilson is Arthur S. Link, *Wilson*, 5 vols. (1947–1965).

Work, workers, and the industrial society are perceptively treated in Herbert G. Gutman, *Work, Culture and Society in Industrializing America* (1977); David Montgomery, *Workers' Control in America: Studies in the History of Work, Technology, and Labor Struggles* (1979); and David Brody, *Workers in Industrial America: Essays on the Twentieth Century Struggle* (1980). Stephan Thernstrom, *The Other Bostonians* (1973), is the best study of social and economic mobility.

Additional Bibliography

Roger Burlingame, *Henry Ford* (1954) and Allan Nevins and Frank E. Hill, *Ford*, 3 vols. (1954–1963) cover Ford's career, while Alfred D. Chandler, *Strategy and Structure: Chapters in the History of American Industrial Enterprise* (1962); Samuel Haber, *Efficiency and Uplift: Scientific Management in the Progressive Era* (1964); and Frederick A. White, *American Industrial Research Laboratories* (1961), provide useful overviews. See also Tamara K. Hareven and Randolph Langenbach, *Amoskeag: Life and Work in an American Factory-City* (1978).

The labor movement is covered in Harold Livesay, *Samuel Gompers and Organized Labor in America* (1978); Melvyn Dubofsky, *We Shall Be All: A History of the Industrial Workers of the World* (1969); Susan Estabrook Kennedy, *If All We Did Was To Weep At Home: A History of White Working Class Women in America* (1979); and Barbara Mayer Wertheimer, *We Were There: The Story of Working Women in America* (1977).

On specific issues, see O. E. Anderson, *The Health of a Nation: Harvey W. Wiley and the Fight for Pure Food* (1958); Craig West, *Banking Reform and the Federal Reserve, 1863–1923* (1977); Aileen Kraditor, *The Ideas of the Woman Suffrage Movement, 1890–1920* (1981); David W. Southern, *The Malignant Heritage: Yankee Progressives and the Negro Question, 1901–1914* (1968); James H. Timberlake, *Prohibition and the Progressive Crusade* (1963); and Walter I. Trattner, *Crusade for the Children* (1970).

On politics, see George E. Mowry, *Theodore Roosevelt and the Progressive Movement* (1946); Kenneth W. Hechler, *Insurgency: Personalities and Politics of the Taft Era* (1940); Norman M. Wilensky, *Conservatives in the Progressive Era: The Taft Republicans of 1912* (1965); and L. J. Holt, *Congressional Insurgents and the Party System, 1909–1916* (1967).

Helpful biographies include David P. Thelen, *Robert M. La Follette and the Insurgent Spirit* (1976); R. S. Maxwell, *La Follette and the Rise of the Progressives in Wisconsin* (1956); G. Wallace Chessman, *Theodore Roosevelt and the Politics of Power* (1969); Edmund Wilson, *The Rise of Theodore Roosevelt* (1979); William Manners, *TR and Will* (1969); John M. Blum, *Woodrow Wilson and the Politics of Morality* (1962); John M. Mulder, *Woodrow Wilson: The Years of Preparation* (1978); and Henry F. Pringle, *Life and Times of William Howard Taft*, 2 vols. (1939).

Alpheus Thomas Mason, *Brandeis: A Free Man's Life* (1946); Harold W. Currie, *Eugene V. Debs* (1976); and Dewey W. Grantham, Jr., *Hoke Smith and the Politics of the New South* (1958) are valuable studies.

Contemporary accounts include Herbert Croly, *The Promise of American Life* (1909); Walter Lippmann, *Drift and Mastery* (1914); William Allen White, *The Old Order Changeth* (1910) and *The Autobiography of William Allen White* (1946); and Charles Seymour, ed., *The Intimate Papers of Colonel House*, 4 vols. (1926–1928).

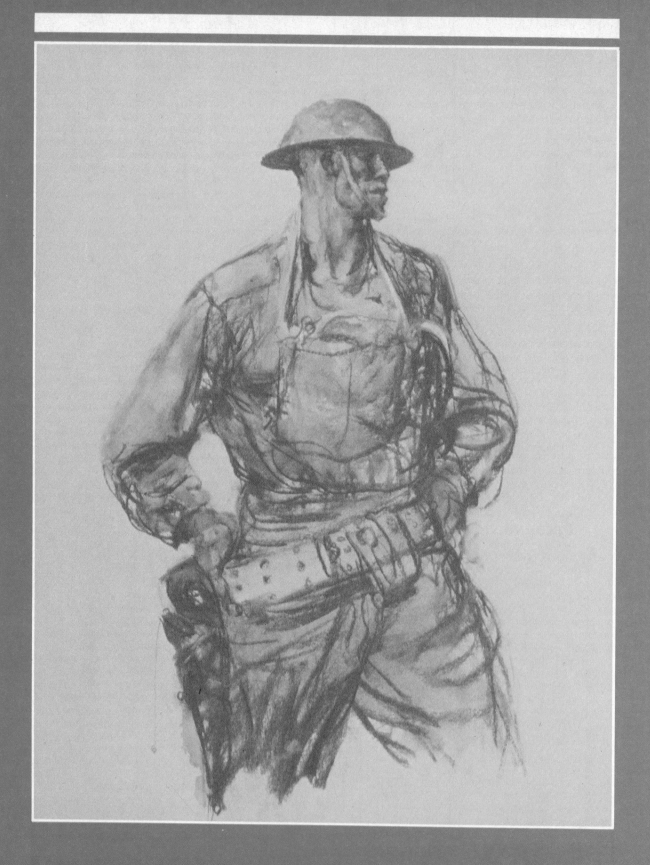

chapter 24
THE
NATION
AT WAR

On the morning of May 1, 1915, the German government printed an important advertisement in the *New York World*:

NOTICE—
Travellers intending to embark on the Atlantic voyage are reminded that a state of war exists between Germany and her allies and Great Britain and her allies; that the zone of war includes the waters adjacent to the British Isles; that, in accordance with formal notice given by the Imperial German Government, vessels flying the flag of Great Britain, or of any of her allies, are liable to destruction in those waters and that travellers sailing in the war zone on ships of Great Britain or her allies do so at their own risk.

At 12:30 that afternoon, the British steamship *Lusitania* set sail from New York to Liverpool.

The steamer was two hours late, but it held several speed records and could easily make up the time. The passenger list of 1257 was the largest since the outbreak of war in Europe. Alfred G. Vanderbilt, the millionaire sportsman, was aboard; so were Charles Frohman, a famous New York theatrical producer, and Elbert Hubbard, a popular writer who jested that a submarine attack might help sell his new book. While some passengers chose the *Lusitania* for speed, others liked the modern staterooms, more comfortable than the older ships of the competing American Line.

Six days later, the *Lusitania*, on schedule, reached the coast of Ireland. German U-boats patrolled these dangerous waters. When the war began in 1914, Great Britain imposed a naval blockade of Germany. In return, Germany in February 1915 declared the area around the British Isles a war zone; all enemy vessels, armed or unarmed, were at risk. Germany had only a handful of U-boats, but submarine warfare was new and frightening. On behalf of the United States President Woodrow Wilson protested the German action, and on February 10 he warned Germany of its "strict accountability" for any American losses resulting from U-boat attacks.

Off Ireland, the passengers lounged on the deck of the *Lusitania*. As in peacetime, the ship sailed straight ahead, with no zigzag maneuvers to throw off pursuit. But the submarine U-20 was there, and the commander, seeing a large ship, fired a single torpedo. Seconds after it hit, a boiler exploded and blew a hole in the *Lusitania's* side. The ship listed immediately, hindering the launching of lifeboats, and in eighteen minutes it sank. Nearly 1200 people died, including 128 Americans. As the ship's bow lifted and went under, the U-20 commander for the first time read the name: *Lusitania*.

The sinking, the worst since the *Titanic* went down with 1500 people in 1912, horrified Americans. Theodore Roosevelt called it "an act of piracy" and demanded war. On the French front the Germans had just introduced poison gas, another alarming new weapon, and there were reports of German atrocities in Belgium. Still, most Americans wanted to stay out of war; like Wilson, they hoped negotiations could solve the problem. "There is such a thing," Wilson said a few days after the sinking, "as a man being too proud to fight. There is such a thing as a nation being so right that it does not need to convince others by force."

In a series of diplomatic notes Wilson demanded a change in German policy. The first *Lusitania* note (May 13, 1915) called on Germany to abandon unrestricted submarine warfare, disavow the sinking, and compensate for lost American lives. Germany sent an evasive reply, and Wilson drafted a second *Lusitania* note (June 9) insisting on specific pledges. Fearful that the demand would lead to war, Secretary of State William Jennings Bryan resigned rather than sign the note. Wilson sent it anyway and followed with a third note (July 21)—almost an ultimatum—warning Germany that the United States would view similar sinkings as "deliberately unfriendly."

Unbeknown to Wilson, Germany had already ordered U-boat commanders not to sink passenger liners without warning. In August 1915 a U-boat mistakenly torpedoed the British liner *Arabic*, killing two Americans. Wilson protested,

With the sinking of the Lusitania, the American people learned first-hand of the horrors of total war. President Wilson's decision to protest the incident through diplomacy kept the United States out of the war—but only temporarily.

New York Tribune

First in Last—the Truth: News · Editorials · Advertisements

SATURDAY, MAY 8, 1915.   PRICE ONE CENT

900 Die as Lusitania Goes to Bottom; 400 Americans on Board Torpedoed Ship; Washington Stirred as When Maine Sank

CAPITAL AROUSED, SITUATION GRAVEST YET FACED IN WAR

Washington Determined That Germany Shall Not Be Allowed to Shirk Responsibility for Deaths.

GREATLY FEARS LOSS OF AMERICANS

President Shows Nervousness as Bulletins of Disaster Come In—Strongest Protest Yet Made Planned Even if No U.S. Citizens Were Lost

THE LUSITANIA, SUNK BY GERMAN TORPEDO, WITH HEAVY LOSS OF LIFE.

Dying and Injured Brought in with Other Survivors to Queenstown—Some Landed at Kinsale and Clonakilty.

TWO TORPEDOES FIRED, SAYS STEWARD

Attack Made About Eight Miles from Irish Coast in Broad Daylight and in Fine Weather—Survivor Tells of Bravery of Cunard Officers.

and Germany, eager to keep the United States out of the war, backed down. The *Arabic* pledge (September 1) promised to stop and warn liners, unless they tried to resist or escape. Germany also apologized for American deaths on the *Arabic*, and for the rest of 1915 U-boats hunted freighters, not passenger liners.

Although Wilson's diplomacy had achieved his immediate goal, the *Lusitania* and *Arabic* crises contained the elements that led to war. Trade and travel tied the world together, and Americans no longer hid behind safe ocean barriers. New weapons, such as the submarine, strained old rules of international law. But while Americans sifted the conflicting claims of Great Britain and Germany, they hoped for peace. A generation of progressives, inspired with confidence in human progress, did not easily accept war.

Wilson also hated war, but he found himself caught up in a worldwide crisis that demanded the best in American will and diplomacy. In the end diplomacy failed, and in April 1917 the United States entered a war that changed the nation's history.

East, and Latin America. It dominated the Caribbean.

In 1898 the United States left the peace table possessing the Philippines, Puerto Rico, and Guam. Holding distant possessions required a colonial policy; it also required a change in foreign policy, reflecting an outward approach. From the Caribbean to the Pacific, policymakers paid attention to issues and countries they had earlier ignored. Like other nations in these years, the United States built a large navy, protected its colonial empire, and became increasingly involved in international affairs.

The nation also became more and more involved in economic ventures abroad. Turning out goods from textiles to steel, mass-production industries sold products overseas, and financiers invested in Asia, Africa, Latin America, and Europe. During the years between the Spanish-American War and World War I, investments abroad rose from $445 million to $2.5 billion. While investments and trade never wholly dictated American foreign policy, they fostered greater involvement in foreign lands.

A New World Power

American foreign policy from 1901 to 1920 was aggressive and nationalistic. During these years the United States intervened in Europe, the Far

"I Took the Canal Zone"

Convinced the United States should take a more active international role, Theodore Roosevelt spent his presidency preparing the nation for

687

world power. Along with Secretary of War Elihu Root, he modernized the army, using lessons from the war with Spain. Roosevelt and Root established the Army War College, imposed stiff tests for the promotion of officers, and in 1903 created a general staff to oversee military planning and mobilization. Determined to end dependence on the British fleet, Roosevelt doubled the navy's strength during his term in office.

Stretching his authority to the limits, Roosevelt took steps to consolidate the country's new position in the Caribbean and Central America. European powers, which had long resisted American initiatives there, now accepted American supremacy. Preoccupied with problems in Europe and Africa, Great Britain agreed to United States plans for an isthmian canal in Central America and withdrew much of its military force from the area.

Roosevelt wanted a canal to link the Atlantic and Pacific oceans across the isthmus connecting North and South America. When the war with Spain started in 1898, it took the battleship *Oregon* seventy-one days to sail from San Francisco

around Cape Horn to its battle station in the Atlantic; years later naval experts still shuddered at the thought. Secretary of State John Hay negotiated with Britain the Hay-Pauncefote Treaty of 1901 that permitted the United States to construct and control an isthmian canal, providing it would be free and open to ships of all nations.

Delighted, Roosevelt began selecting the route. One route, fifty miles long, wandered through the rough, swampy terrain of the Panama region of Colombia. A French company had recently tried and failed to dig a canal there. Northwest of Panama, another route ran through mountainous Nicaragua. Although two hundred miles in length, it followed natural waterways, a factor that would make construction easier.

An Isthmian Canal Commission investigated both routes in 1899 and recommended the shorter route through Panama. Roosevelt backed the idea, and he authorized Hay to negotiate an agreement with the Colombian chargé d'affaires, Tomas Herrán. The Hay-Herrán Convention (1903) gave the United States a ninety-nine-year lease, with option for renewal, on a canal zone six miles in width. In exchange, the United States agreed to pay Colombia a one-time fee of $10 million and an annual rental of $250,000.

To Roosevelt's dismay, the Colombian Senate rejected the treaty, in part because it infringed upon Colombian sovereignty. The Colombians also wanted more money. Calling them "jack rabbits" and "contemptible little creatures," Roosevelt considered seizing Panama, then hinted he would welcome a Panamanian revolt from Colombia. In November 1903 the Panamanians took the hint, and Roosevelt moved quickly to support them. Sending the cruiser *Nashville* to prevent Colombian troops from putting down the revolt, he promptly recognized the new Republic of Panama.

Two weeks later the Hay–Bunau-Varilla Treaty with Panama granted the United States control of a canal zone ten miles wide across the Isthmus of Panama. In return, the United States guaranteed the independence of Panama and agreed to pay the same fees offered Colombia. Using giant steam shovels and thousands of black laborers from Jamaica, engineers cut their way across the isthmus. On August 15, 1914, the first ocean steamer sailed through the completed canal, which cost $275 million to build.

The Panama Canal Zone

Construction of the canal began in 1904, and despite landslides, steamy weather, and yellow fever, work was completed in 1914.

CARIBBEAN SEA

PANAMA

Colón
Cristobal

Gatun Locks

Gatun Lake

Chagres River

PANAMA CANAL ZONE

Pedro Miguel Locks

Miraflores Locks

Panamá
Balboa

PANAMA

0   10 Miles
0   10 Kilometers

PACIFIC OCEAN

Panama Canal

Locks

Railroad

NICARAGUA   CARIBBEAN SEA

Panama Canal   PANAMA CANAL ZONE

COSTA RICA

PANAMA

COLOMBIA

PACIFIC OCEAN

■ *The battleship* Ohio *sailing in the Panama Canal in 1915.*

Roosevelt's actions angered many Latin Americans. Trying to soothe feelings, Wilson agreed in 1914 to pay Colombia $25 million in cash, give it preferential treatment in using the canal, and express "sincere regret" over American actions. Roosevelt was furious, and his friends in the Senate blocked the agreement. Colombian-American relations remained strained until 1921, when the two countries signed a treaty that included Wilson's first two provisions but omitted the apology.

For his part, Roosevelt took great pride in the canal, calling it "by far the most important action in foreign affairs." Defending his methods, he said in 1911: "If I had followed traditional conservative methods, I would have submitted a dignified state paper of 200 pages to Congress and the debate on it would have been going on yet; but I took the Canal Zone and let Congress debate; and while the debate goes on the Canal does also."

The Roosevelt Corollary

With interests in Puerto Rico, Cuba, and the canal, the United States developed a Caribbean policy to ensure its dominance in the region. It established protectorates over some countries and subsidized others to keep them dependent. When necessary, it purchased islands to keep them out of the hands of other powers, as in the case of the Danish West Indies (now the Virgin Islands), bought in 1917 to prevent the Germans from acquiring them.

From 1903 to 1920 the United States intervened often in Latin America to protect the canal, promote regional stability, and exclude foreign influence. One problem worrying American policymakers was the scale of Latin American debts to European powers. Many countries in the Western Hemisphere owed money to European governments and banks, but often these nations were poor, prone to revolution, and unable to pay. The situation invited European intervention. In 1902 Venezuela defaulted on debts; England, Germany, and Italy sent Venezuela an ultimatum and blockaded its ports. American pressure forced a settlement of the issue, but the general problem remained.

Roosevelt was concerned about it, and in 1904, when the Dominican Republic defaulted on its debts, he was ready with a major announcement. Known as the Roosevelt Corollary of the Monroe Doctrine, the policy warned Latin American nations to keep their affairs in order or face American intervention.

Applying the new policy immediately, Roosevelt in 1905 took charge of the Dominican Republic's revenue system. American officials collected customs and saw to the payment of debt. Within two years Roosevelt also established protectorates in Cuba and Panama. In 1912 the United States Senate added the Lodge Corollary, which warned foreign corporations not to purchase harbors and other sites of military significance in Latin America. Continued by Taft, Wilson, and other presidents, the Roosevelt Corollary guided American policy in Latin America until the 1930s, when Franklin D. Roosevelt's Good Neighbor policy replaced it.

Ventures in the Far East

The Open Door policy toward China (see chapter 21) and possession of the Philippine Islands shaped American actions in the Far East. Congress refused to arm the Philippines, and the islands were vulnerable to the growing power of Japan. Roosevelt wanted to balance Russian and Japanese power, and he was not unhappy at first when war broke out between them in 1904. As

■ *A cartoon from* Judge *entitled "The World's Constable." The Roosevelt Corollary claimed the right of the U.S. to exercise "an international police power."*

Pacific, uphold the Open Door, and support Chinese independence.

In later years tensions grew in the Far East. The segregation of Japanese children in San Francisco schools in 1906 aroused Japan's resentment; anger mounted in 1913 when the California legislature prohibited Japanese residents from owning property in the state. At the start of the First World War, Japan seized some German colonies, and in 1915 it issued the Twenty-One Demands insisting on authority over China. Coveting an Asian empire, Japan eyed American possessions in the Pacific.

Taft and Dollar Diplomacy

In foreign as well as domestic affairs, President Taft tried to continue Roosevelt's policies. For secretary of state he chose Philander C. Knox, Roosevelt's attorney general, and together they pursued a policy of "dollar diplomacy" to promote American financial and business interests abroad. The policy had profit-seeking motives, but it also aimed to substitute economic ties for military alliances and bring lasting peace.

Intent, like Roosevelt, on supremacy in the Caribbean, Taft worked to replace European loans with American ones, thereby reducing the danger of outside meddling. In 1909 he asked American bankers to assume the Honduran debt in order to fend off English bondholders. A year later he persuaded them to take over the assets of the National Bank of Haiti, and in 1911 he helped Nicaragua secure a large loan in return for American control of Nicaragua's National Bank. When Nicaraguans revolted against the agreement, Taft sent marines to put them down. A marine detachment remained in the country intermittently until the 1930s.

In the Far East, Knox worked closely with Willard Straight, an agent of American bankers, who argued that dollar diplomacy was the financial arm of the Open Door. Straight had close ties to Edward H. Harriman, the railroad magnate, who wanted to build railroads in Manchuria. Roosevelt had tacitly promised Japan he would keep American investors out of the area, and Knox's plan reversed the policy. Trying to organize an international syndicate to loan China money to purchase the Manchurian railroads,

Japan won victory after victory, however, Roosevelt grew worried. He offered to mediate the conflict, and both Russia and Japan accepted: Russia because it was losing, and Japan because it was financially drained.

In August 1905 Roosevelt convened a peace conference at Portsmouth, New Hampshire. The conference ended the war, but Japan emerged as the dominant force in the Far East. Adjusting policy, Roosevelt sent Secretary of War Taft to Tokyo to negotiate the Taft-Katsura Agreement (1905), which recognized Japan's dominance over Korea in return for its promise not to invade the Philippines. Giving Japan a free hand in Korea violated the Open Door policy, but Roosevelt argued that he had little choice.

In a show of strength, he sent the American fleet around the world, including a stop in Tokyo in October 1908. Critics at home predicted dire consequences, and European naval experts felt certain Japan would attack the fleet. Instead, the Japanese welcomed it, even posting ads to sell the sailors Mitsukoshi washing powder to "rid yourselves of the seven blemishes on the way home." For the moment Japanese-American relations improved. In 1908 the two nations signed the comprehensive Root-Takahira Agreement in which they promised to maintain the status quo in the

Knox approached England, Japan, and Russia. In January 1910 all three turned him down.

The outcome was a blow to American policy and prestige in Asia. Russia and Japan found reasons to cooperate with each other, and they staked out spheres of influence in violation of the Open Door. Japan resented Taft's initiatives in Manchuria, and China's distrust of the United States deepened. Instead of cultivating friendship, as Roosevelt had envisioned, Taft started an intense rivalry with Japan for commercial advantage in China.

Foreign Policy Under Wilson

When he took office in 1913, Woodrow Wilson knew little about foreign policy. As a Princeton professor, he had studied Congress and the presidency, but his books made only passing reference to foreign issues, and during the 1912 campaign he mentioned foreign policy only when it affected domestic concerns. "It would be the irony of fate if my administration had to deal chiefly with foreign affairs," he said to a friend just before becoming president. And so it was. During his two terms Wilson faced crisis after crisis in foreign affairs, including the outbreak of World War I.

A supremely self-confident man, Wilson conducted his own diplomacy. He composed important diplomatic notes on his own typewriter, sent personal emissaries abroad, and carried on major negotiations without the knowledge of his secretaries of state. Failing to find the right persons for key diplomatic posts, he filled these positions with party regulars like James W. Gerard, his ambassador to Germany, for whom he had contempt. On Gerard's dispatches, Wilson penciled notes: "Ordinarily our Ambassador ought to be backed up as [a matter] of course, but—this ass? It is hard to take it seriously." Or, the next day: "Who can fathom this? I wish they would hand this idiot his passports!"

The idealistic Wilson believed in a principled, ethical world in which militarism, colonialism, and war were brought under control. He stressed moral purposes over material interests and said during one crisis: "The force of America is the force of moral principle." Rejecting the policy of dollar diplomacy, Wilson initially chose a course of moral diplomacy, designed to bring right to the world, preserve peace, and extend to other peoples the blessings of democracy.

Conducting Moral Diplomacy

William Jennings Bryan, whom Wilson appointed as secretary of state, was also an amateur in foreign relations. Trusting in the common people, he was skeptical of experts in the State Department. To key posts abroad he appointed "deserving Democrats," believing they could do the job as well as career diplomats. Bryan was a fervent pacifist, and like Wilson, he believed in the American duty to "help" less-favored nations.

In 1913 and 1914 he embarked on an idealistic campaign to negotiate treaties of arbitration throughout the world. Known as "cooling-off" treaties, they provided for submitting all international disputes to permanent commissions of investigation. Neither party could declare war or increase armaments until the investigation ended, usually within one year. The idea drew on the era's confidence in commissions and the sense that human reason, given time for emotions to fade, could settle problems without war. Bryan negotiated cooling-off treaties with thirty nations, including Great Britain, France, and Italy. Germany refused to sign one. Based on a generous idea, the treaties were naive, and they did not work.

Wilson and Bryan promised a dramatic new approach in Latin America, concerned not with the "pursuit of material interest" but with "human rights" and "national integrity." Signaling the change, in 1913 they negotiated the treaty with Colombia apologizing for Roosevelt's Panamanian policy. Yet in the end Wilson, distracted by other problems and impatient with the results of his idealistic approach, continued the Roosevelt-Taft policies. He defended the Monroe Doctrine, gave unspoken support to the Roosevelt Corollary, and intervened in Latin America more than had either Roosevelt or Taft.

In 1914 Wilson negotiated a treaty with Nicaragua to grant the United States exclusive rights to build a canal and lease sites for naval bases. This treaty made Nicaragua an American satellite. In 1915 he sent marines into Haiti to quell a revolution; they stayed until 1934. In 1916 he occupied

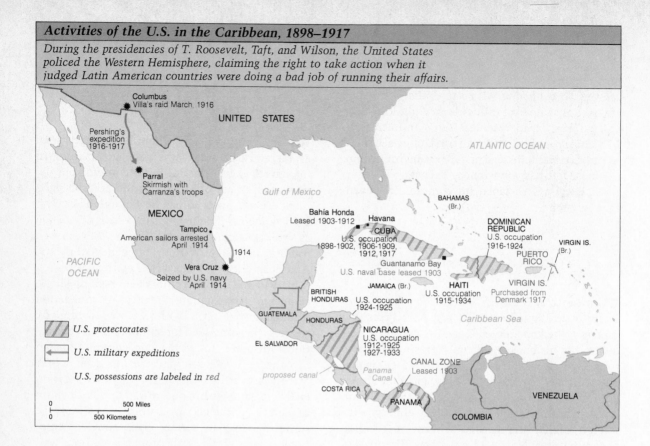

Activities of the U.S. in the Caribbean, 1898–1917

During the presidencies of T. Roosevelt, Taft, and Wilson, the United States policed the Western Hemisphere, claiming the right to take action when it judged Latin American countries were doing a bad job of running their affairs.

the Dominican Republic, establishing a protectorate that lasted until 1924. By 1917 American troops "protected" Nicaragua, Haiti, the Dominican Republic, and Cuba—four nations that were U.S. dependencies in all but name.

Troubles Across the Border

Porfirio Díaz, president of Mexico for thirty-seven years, was overthrown in 1911. Díaz had encouraged foreign investments in Mexican mines, railroads, oil, and land; by 1913 Americans had invested over $1 billion. Most Mexicans remained poor and uneducated, however; his overthrow led to a decade of violence that tested Wilson's policies and brought the United States close to war with Mexico.

A liberal reformer, Francisco I. Madero, followed Díaz as president in 1911. But Madero could not keep order in the troubled country, and opponents of his reforms undermined him. With support from wealthy landowners, the army, and

the Catholic Church, General Victoriano Huerta ousted Madero in 1913, threw him in jail, and murdered him. Most European nations immediately recognized Huerta, but Wilson, calling him a "butcher," refused to do so. Instead, he announced a new policy toward revolutionary regimes in Latin America. To win American recognition, they must not only exercise power but reflect "a just government based upon law, not upon arbitrary or irregular force."

On that basis Wilson withheld recognition from Huerta and maneuvered to oust him. Early in 1914 he stationed naval units off Mexico's ports to cut off arms shipments to the Huerta regime, but the action produced trouble. On April 9, 1914, several American sailors, ashore in Tampico to purchase supplies, were arrested. They were promptly released, but the American admiral demanded an apology and a twenty-one-gun salute to the American flag. Huerta agreed—if the Americans also saluted the Mexican flag.

Wilson asked Congress for authority to use military force if needed; then just as Congress

■ *The goal of his policy in Latin America, Wilson once said, was "to teach the South American republics to elect good men." In the cartoon, Wilson shakes his finger at Mexico in obvious disapproval of the Mexican Revolution and Huerta's government. The President fared little better with Carranza, Huerta's successor. The troops that Wilson ordered into Mexico to seize Pancho Villa clashed twice with Carranza's army.*

acted, he learned that a German ship was landing arms at Vera Cruz on Mexico's eastern coast. With Wilson's approval, American warships shelled the harbor, and marines went ashore. Against heavy resistance, they took the city. Outraged, Mexicans of all factions denounced the invasion, and for a time the two countries hovered on the edge of war.

Retreating hastily, Wilson explained that he desired only to help Mexico. Argentina, Brazil, and Chile came to his aid with an offer to mediate the dispute, and tensions eased. In July 1914, cut off from funds, Huerta resigned. Wilson recognized the new government, headed by Venustiano Carranza, an associate of Madero. Early in 1916, Francisco ("Pancho") Villa, one of Carranza's generals, revolted. Hoping to goad the United States into an action that would help him seize power, he raided border towns, injuring American civilians. In January, he removed seventeen Americans from a train in Mexico and murdered them. Two months later he invaded Columbus, New Mexico, killing sixteen Americans and burning

the town. (See the picture essay on the Mexican-American experience following p. 704.)

Stationing militia along the border, Wilson ordered General John J. Pershing on a punitive expedition to seize Villa in Mexico. Pershing led six thousand troops deep into Mexican territory. At first, Carranza agreed to the drive, but as the Americans pushed farther and farther into his country he changed his mind. As the wily Villa eluded Pershing, Carranza protested bitterly, and Wilson, worried about events in Europe, ordered Pershing home.

Wilson's policy had laudable goals; he wanted to help the Mexicans achieve political and agrarian reform, but his motives and methods were condescending. Wilson tried to impose gradual, progressive reform on a society sharply divided along class and other lines. With little forethought, he interfered in the affairs of another country, and in doing so he revealed the themes—moralism, combined with pragmatic self-interest and a desire for peace—that also shaped his policies in Europe.

Toward War

In May 1914, Colonel Edward M. House, Wilson's close friend and personal adviser, sailed to Europe on a fact-finding mission. Tensions there were rising. "The situation is extraordinary," he reported to Wilson. "It is jingoism [extreme nationalism] run stark mad. . . . There is too much hatred, too many jealousies."

Large armies dominated the European continent. A web of alliances entangled nations, maximizing the risk that a local conflict could produce a wider war. In Germany the ambitious Kaiser Wilhelm II coveted a world empire to match those of Britain and France. Germany had military treaties with Turkey and Austria-Hungary, a sprawling Central European country of many nationalities. Linked in another alliance, England, France, and Russia agreed to aid each other in case of attack.

On June 28, 1914, a Balkan assassin in the service of Serbia murdered Archduke Franz Ferdinand, heir to the Austro-Hungarian throne. With-

in weeks Germany, Turkey, and Austria-Hungary (the Central Powers) were at war with England, France, and Russia (the Allied Powers). Americans were shocked at the events. "I had a feeling that the end of things had come . . . ," one of Wilson's cabinet members said. "I stopped in my tracks, dazed and horror-stricken." Wilson immediately proclaimed neutrality and asked Americans to remain "impartial in thought as well as in action."

The war, he said, was one "with which we have nothing to do, whose causes cannot touch us." In private, Wilson was stunned. A man who loved peace, he had long admired the British parliamentary system, and he respected the leaders of the British Liberal party, who supported social programs akin to his own. "Everything I love most in the world," he said, "is at stake."

The Neutrality Policy

In general Americans accepted neutrality. They saw no need to enter the conflict, especially after

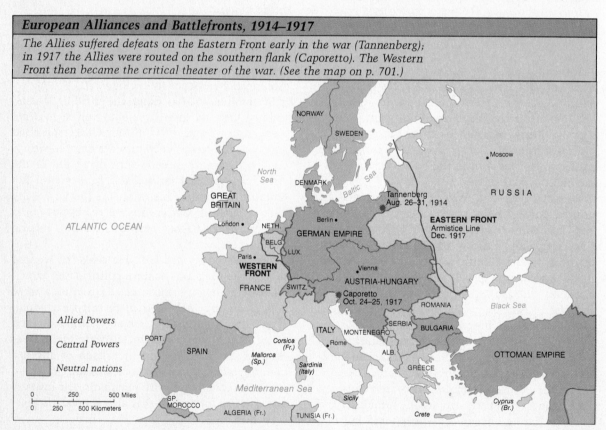

European Alliances and Battlefronts, 1914–1917

The Allies suffered defeats on the Eastern Front early in the war (Tannenberg); in 1917 the Allies were routed on the southern flank (Caporetto). The Western Front then became the critical theater of the war. (See the map on p. 701.)

the Allies in September 1914 halted the first German drive toward Paris. They resisted involvement in other countries' problems and had a tradition of freedom from foreign entanglements. Among progressives, there was added reason to resist. War violated the very spirit of progressive reform. Why demand safer factories and then kill men by the millions in war?

To many progressives, England represented international finance, an institution they detested. Germany, on the other hand, had pioneered some of their favorite social reforms. Furthermore, progressives and others tended to put the blame for war on the greed of "munition manufacturers, stockbrokers, and bond dealers" eager for wartime profits. "Do you want to know the cause of the war?" Henry Ford, who was no progressive, asked. "It is capitalism, greed, the dirty hunger for dollars." Above all, progressives were sure that war would end reform. It consumed money and attention; it inflamed emotions.

As a result, Jane Addams, Florence Kelley, Frederic C. Howe, Lillian Wald, and other progressives fought to keep the United States out of war. In late 1915 they formed the American Union Against Militarism, to throw, they said, "a monkey wrench into the machinery" of war. Throughout 1915 and 1916 *La Follette's Magazine*, the voice of the progressive leader, railed against the Morgans, Rockefellers, Du Ponts, and "the thirty-eight corporations most benefited by war orders." In 1915 Addams and Wald helped organize the League to Limit Armament, and shortly thereafter, Addams and Carrie Chapman Catt formed the Woman's Peace Party to organize women against the war.

The war's outbreak also tugged at the emotions of millions of immigrant Americans. Those who came from the British Isles tended to support the Allies; those from Ireland tended to support Germany, hoping that Britain's wartime troubles might free their homeland from British domination. The large population of German-Americans often sympathized with the Central Powers. But many people thought that, in a nation of immigrants, a policy of neutrality offered benefits from a domestic point of view as well as from the viewpoint of foreign policy.

At the deepest level, a majority in the country, bound by common language and institutions, sympathized with the Allies and blamed Germa-

Although Germany's invasion of Belgium and reports of German atrocities shocked Americans, most still adhered to the attitude expressed in the cartoon above: "Don't mix in a family quarrel."

ny for the war. Like Wilson, many Americans admired English literature, customs, and law; they remembered Lafayette and the times when France had helped the United States in its early years. Germany, on the other hand, seemed arrogant and militaristic. When the war began, it invaded Belgium to strike at France and violated a treaty which the German chancellor called "just a scrap of paper." Many Americans resented the violation, and they liked it even less when German troops executed Belgian civilians who resisted.

Both sides sought to sway American opinion, and fierce propaganda campaigns flourished. The German Literary Defense Committee distributed over a million pamphlets during the first year of the war. German propaganda tended to stress strength and will; Allied propaganda called on historical ties and took advantage of German atrocities, both real and alleged. In the end, the propaganda probably made little difference. Ties of heritage and the course of the war, not propaganda, decided the American position. At the outset, whichever side they cheered for, Americans of all persuasions preferred simply to remain at peace.

Freedom of the Seas

The demands of trade tested American neutrality and confronted Wilson with difficult choices. Under international law, neutral countries were permitted to trade in nonmilitary goods with all belligerent countries. But Great Britain controlled the seas, and it intended to cut off shipments of war materials to the Central Powers.

As soon as war broke out, Britain blockaded German ports and limited the goods Americans could sell to Germany. American ships had to carry cargoes to neutral ports from which, after examination, they could be carried to Germany. As time passed, Britain stepped up the economic sanctions by forbidding the shipment to Germany of all foodstuffs and most raw materials, seizing and censoring mail, and "blacklisting" American firms that dealt directly with the Central Powers. British ships often stopped American ships and confiscated cargoes.

Again and again Wilson protested against such infringements on neutral rights. Sometimes Britain complied, sometimes not, and Wilson often grew angry. But needing American support and supplies, Britain pursued a careful strategy to disrupt German-American trade without disrupting Anglo-American relations. After forbidding cotton shipments to Germany in 1915, it agreed to buy enough cotton to make up for the losses. When necessary it also promised to reimburse American businesses after war's end.

Other than the German U-boats, there were no constraints on trade with the Allies, and a flood of Allied war orders fueled the American economy. England and France bought huge amounts of arms, grain, cotton, and clothing. To finance the purchases, the Allies turned to American bankers for loans. By 1917 loans to Allied governments exceeded $2 billion, while loans to Germany came to only $27 million.

Loans and trade drew the United States ever closer to the Allied cause. And even though Wilson often protested English maritime policy, the protests involved American goods and money whereas Germany's submarine policy threatened American lives.

The U-Boat Threat

A relatively new weapon, the *Unterseeboot*, or submarine, strained the guidelines of international law. Traditional law required a submarine to surface, warn the target to stop, send a boarding party to check papers and cargo, then allow time for passengers and crew to board lifeboats before sinking the vessel. Flimsy and slow, submarines could ill-afford to surface while the prey radioed for help. If they did surface, they might be rammed or blown up by deck guns.

When Germany announced the submarine campaign in February 1915, Wilson protested sharply, calling the sinking of merchant ships without checking cargo "a wanton act." The Germans promised not to sink American ships—an agreement that lasted until 1917—and thereafter the issue became the right of Americans to sail on the ships of belligerent nations. In March an American citizen aboard the British liner *Falaba* perished when the ship was torpedoed off the Irish coast. Bryan urged Wilson to forbid Americans to travel in the war zones, but the President, determined to stand by the principles of international law, refused.

Wilson reacted more harshly in May and August of 1915 when U-boats sank the *Lusitania* and *Arabic*. He demanded that the Germans protect passenger vessels and pay for American losses. Fearing war, Bryan resigned as secretary of state and was replaced by Robert Lansing, a lawyer and counselor in the State Department. Lansing favored the Allies and believed that democracy was threatened in a world dominated by Germany. He urged strong stands against German violations of American neutrality.

In February 1916 Germany declared unrestricted submarine warfare against all *armed* ships. Lansing protested and told Germany it would be held strictly accountable for American losses. A month later, a U-boat torpedoed the unarmed French channel steamer, *Sussex*, without warning, injuring several Americans. Arguing that the sinking violated the *Arabic* pledge, Lansing urged Wilson to break relations with Germany. Wilson rejected the advice, but on April 18 sent an ultimatum to Germany that unless it immediately called off attacks on cargo and passenger ships, the United States would sever relations.

The kaiser, convinced he did not yet have enough submarines to risk war, yielded. In the *Sussex* pledge of May 4, 1916, he agreed to Wilson's demands and promised to shoot on sight only ships of the enemy's navy. But he attached the condition that the United States compel the Allies to end their blockade and comply with international law. Wilson accepted the pledge but turned down the condition.

The *Sussex* pledge marked the beginning of a short period of friendly relations between Germany and the United States. The agreement applied not only to passenger liners, but to *all* merchant ships, belligerent or not. There was one problem: Wilson had taken such a strong position that if Germany renewed submarine warfare on merchant shipping, war was likely. But most Americans viewed the agreement as a diplomatic stroke for peace by Wilson, and the issues of peace and preparedness dominated the presidential election of 1916.

"He Kept Us Out of War"

The "preparedness" issue pitted antiwar groups against those who wanted to prepare for war. The American Rights Committee, the National Security League, and other groups urged stepped-up military measures in case of war. In the summer of 1915 they persuaded the War Department to hold a training camp in Plattsburg, New York, in which regular army officers trained twelve hundred civilian volunteers in modern warfare. The following summer sixteen thousand volunteers participated in such training camps.

Bellicose as always, Teddy Roosevelt led the preparedness campaign. He called Wilson "yellow" for not pressing Germany harder and scoffed at the popular song "I Didn't Raise My Boy to Be a Soldier," which he compared to singing "I Didn't Raise My Girl to Be a Mother." Defending the

■ *Roosevelt's campaign for preparedness became a personal attack on Wilson, whom he called a "coward" and "weakling."*

military's state of readiness, Wilson refused to be stampeded just because "some amongst us are nervous and excited." In fact, when government revenue dropped in 1915, he cut military appropriations.

Wilson's position was attacked from both sides as preparedness advocates charged cowardice, while pacifists denounced any attempt at military readiness. The difficulty of his situation, plus the growing U-boat crisis, soon changed Wilson's mind. In mid-1915 he asked the War Department to increase military planning, and he quietly notified congressional leaders of a switch in policy. Later that year Wilson approved large increases in the army and navy, a move that upset many peace-minded progressives. In January 1916 he toured the country to promote preparedness, and in June, with an American flag draped over his shoulder, he marched in a giant preparedness parade in Washington.

For their standard-bearer in the presidential election of 1916, the Republicans nominated Charles Evans Hughes, a moderate justice of the Supreme Court. Hughes seemed to have all the qualifications for victory. A former reform governor of New York, he could lure back the Roosevelt Progressives, while at the same time appealing to the Republican conservatives. To woo the Roosevelt wing, Hughes called for a tougher line against Germany, thus allowing the Democrats to label him the "war" candidate. Even so, Roosevelt and others considered Hughes a "bearded iceberg," a dull campaigner who wavered on important issues.

The Democrats renominated Wilson in a convention marked by spontaneous demonstrations for peace. Determined to outdo Republican patriotism, Wilson himself had ordered the convention's theme to be "Americanism." The delegates were to sing "America" and "The Star-Spangled Banner," and to cheer any mention of America and the flag. They did it all dutifully but then broke into spontaneous applause at the mention of Wilson's careful diplomatic moves. As the keynote speaker reviewed them, the delegates shouted: "What did we do? What did we do?" The speaker shouted back: "We didn't go to war! We didn't go to war!"

Picking up the theme, perhaps with reservation, Wilson said in October: "I am not expecting this country to get into war." The campaign slogan, "He kept us out of war" was repeated again and again, and just before the election, the Democrats took full-page ads in leading newspapers:

You Are Working—Not Fighting!
Alive and Happy;—Not Cannon Fodder!
Wilson and Peace with Honor?
          or
Hughes with Roosevelt and War?

On election night, Hughes had swept most of the East, and Wilson retired at 10 P.M., thinking he had lost. During the night the results came in from California, New Mexico, and North Dakota; all supported Wilson—California by a mere 3773 votes. Wilson won with 9.1 million votes against 8.5 million for Hughes. Holding the Democratic South, he carried key states in the Midwest and West and took large portions of the labor and progressive vote. Women—who were then allowed to vote in presidential elections in twelve states—also voted heavily for Wilson.

The Final Months of Peace

Just before election day Great Britain further limited neutral trade, and there were reports from Germany of a renewal of unrestricted submarine

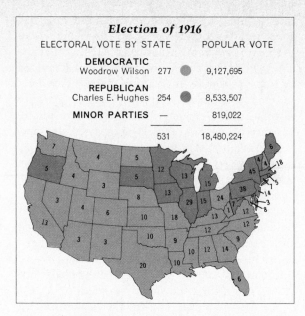

Election of 1916

ELECTORAL VOTE BY STATE		POPULAR VOTE
DEMOCRATIC Woodrow Wilson	277	9,127,695
REPUBLICAN Charles E. Hughes	254	8,533,507
MINOR PARTIES	—	819,022
	531	18,480,224

warfare. Fresh from his election victory, Wilson redoubled his efforts for peace. Aware that time was running out, he hoped to start negotiations to end the bloodshed and create a peaceful postwar world.

In December 1916, he sent messages to both sides asking them to state their war aims. Should they do so, he pledged the "whole force" of the United States to end the war. The Allies refused, although they promised privately to negotiate if the German terms were reasonable. The Germans replied evasively and in January 1917 revealed their real objectives. Close to forcing Russia out of the war, Germany sensed victory and wanted teritory in eastern Europe, Africa, Belgium, and France.

On January 22, in an eloquent speech before the Senate, Wilson called for a "peace without victory." Outlining his own aims, he urged respect for all nations, freedom of the seas, arms limitations, and a league of nations to keep the peace. "Only a peace between equals can last, only a peace the very principle of which is equality and a common participation in a common benefit." The speech made a great impression on many Europeans, but it was too late. The Germans had decided a few weeks before to unleash the submarines and gamble on a quick end to the war. Even as Wilson spoke, U-boats were in the Atlantic west of Ireland, preparing to attack.

On January 31, the German ambassador in Washington informed Lansing that beginning Feb-

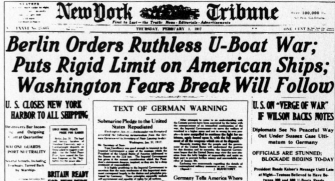

■ *A new and terrifying weapon of the war was the German U-boat, which attacked silently and without warning. Germany's decision to wage unrestricted submarine warfare provoked Wilson into asking for a declaration of war.*

ruary 1, U-boats would sink on sight all ships—passenger or merchant, neutral or belligerent, armed or unarmed—in the waters around England and France. Staking everything on a last effort, the Germans calculated that if they could sink six hundred thousand tons of shipping a month, they could defeat England in six months. As he had pledged in 1916, Wilson broke off relations with Germany, although he still hoped for peace.

On February 25 the British government privately gave Wilson a telegram intercepted from Arthur Zimmermann, the German foreign minister, to the German ambassador in Mexico. A day later, Wilson asked Congress for authority to arm merchant ships to deter U-boat attacks. When La Follette and a handful of others threatened to filibuster, Wilson divulged the contents of the Zimmermann telegram. It proposed an alliance with Mexico in case of war with the United States, offering financial support and recovery of Mexico's "lost territory" in New Mexico, Texas, and Arizona.

Spurred by a wave of public indignation, the House passed Wilson's measure, but La Follette and others still blocked action in the Senate. On March 9, 1917, Wilson ordered merchant ships armed on his own authority. Three days later he announced the arming, and on March 13 the navy instructed all vessels to fire on submarines. Between March 12 and March 21, U-boats sank five American ships, and Wilson decided to wait no longer.

He called Congress into special session and at 8:30 in the evening on April 2, 1917, asked for a declaration of war. "It is a fearful thing to lead this great peaceful people into war, into the most terrible and disastrous of all wars, civilization itself seeming to be in the balance. But the right is more precious than peace, and we shall fight for the things which we have always carried nearest our hearts,—for democracy, . . . for the rights and liberties of small nations, for a universal dominion of right by such a concert of free peoples as shall bring peace and safety to all nations and make the world itself at last free."

Congressmen broke into applause and crowded the aisles to congratulate Wilson. "My message today was a message of death for our young men," he said afterward. "How strange it seems to applaud that."

Over There

With a burst of patriotism, the United States entered a war its new allies were in danger of losing. That same month, the Germans sank 881,000 tons of Allied shipping, the highest amount of the war. There were mutinies in the French army; a costly British drive in Flanders stalled. In November the Bolsheviks seized power in Russia and soon signed a separate peace treaty with Germany (see the map on p. 694), freeing German troops to fight in

American Losses to the German Submarine Campaign, 1916–1918

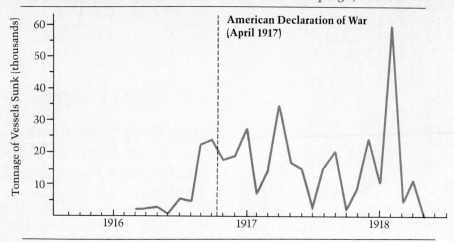

Source: U.S. Department of the Navy, American Ship Casualties of the World War *(1923).*

the West. German and Austrian forces routed the Italian army on the southern flank and the Allies braced for a spring 1918 offensive.

Mobilization

The United States was not prepared for war. Some Americans hoped the declaration of war itself might daunt the Germans; others hoped money and arms, not troops, would be sufficient to produce victory. "Good Lord!" one senator exclaimed just after war was declared. "You're not going to send soldiers over there, are you?"

Bypassing older generals, Wilson named "Black Jack" Pershing, leader of the Mexican campaign, to head the American Expeditionary Force (AEF). Pershing inherited an army unready for war. In April 1917 it had 200,000 officers and men, equipped with 300,000 old rifles, 1500 machine guns, 55 out-of-date airplanes, and 2 field radio sets. Its most recent battle experience had been chasing Pancho Villa around northern Mexico. It had not caught him.

The armed forces had two war plans: War Plan Orange that provided for a defensive war against Japan in the Pacific, and War Plan Black that countered a possible German attack in the Caribbean. Wilson had ordered military commanders not to plan because it violated neutrality. "When

the Acting Chief of Staff went to look at the secret files where the plans to meet the situation that confronted us should have been found," Pershing later said, "the pigeonhole was empty."

Although some in Congress preferred a voluntary army of the kind that had fought in the Spanish-American War, Wilson turned to conscription, which he felt was both efficient and democratic. In May 1917 Congress passed the Selective Service Act, providing for the registration of all men between the ages of twenty-one and thirty. Early in June 9.5 million men registered. The act ultimately registered 24.2 million men, about 2 million of whom were inducted into the army. Defending the draft, Wilson said it was not really a draft at all, but a "selection from a nation which has volunteered in mass."

War in the Trenches

World War I may have been the most terrible war of all time, more terrible even than the vast devastation of World War II. After the early offensives, the European armies dug themselves into trenches, in places only hundreds of yards apart. Artillery, poison gas, hand grenades, and a new weapon—rapid-fire machine guns—kept them pinned down.

Even in moments of respite, the mud, rats, cold, fear, and disease took a heavy toll. Deafening bombardments shook the earth, and there was a high incidence of shell shock. From time to time troops went "over the top" in an effort to break through, but the costs were enormous. The German offensive at Verdun in 1916 killed 600,000 men; the British lost 20,000 dead on the first day of an offensive on the Somme.

The first American soldiers reached France in June 1917. By March of the following year, 300,000 Americans were there, and by war's end, 2 million men had crossed the Atlantic. No troop ships were sunk, a credit to the British and American navies. In the summer of 1917 Admiral William S. Sims, a brilliant strategist, pushed through a convoy plan that used Allied destroyers to escort merchant vessels across the ocean. At first resisted by English captains who liked to sail alone, the plan soon cut shipping losses in half.

As expected, on March 21, 1918, the Germans launched a massive assault in western Europe. Troops from the Russian front added to the force, and by May they had driven Allied forces back to the Marne River, just fifty miles from Paris. More than 27,000 Americans, including four black regiments, saw their first action. They blocked the Germans at the town of Château-Thierry, and four weeks later forced them out of Belleau Wood, a crucial strongpoint. On July 15 the Germans threw everything into a last drive for Paris, but in three days they were finished. "On the 18th," the German chancellor said, "even the most optimistic among us knew that all was lost. The history of the world was played out in three days."

With the German drive stalled, the Allies counterattacked along the entire front. On September 12, 1918, half a million Americans and a smaller contingent of French drove the Germáns from the St. Mihiel salient, twelve miles south of Verdun. Two weeks later, 896,000 Americans attacked between the Meuse River and the Argonne Forest. Focusing on a main railroad supply line for the German army in the West, they broke through in early November, cut the line, and drove the Germans back along the whole front.

The Western Front: U.S. Participation, 1918

The turning point of the war came in July, when the German advance was halted at the Marne. The "Yanks," now a fighting force, were thrown into the breach. They played a dramatic role in stemming the tide and mounting the counteroffensives that ended the war.

Over There

■ *Soldiers in the front-line trenches at the Meuse, October 1918. A scant 1200 yards separated the Allied and the German lines.*

■ *German prisoners and American wounded returning from the front lines of the Meuse-Argonne. More Americans died in that campaign than in the rest of the war.*

The German high command knew that the war was lost. On October 6, 1918, Germany appealed to Wilson for an armistice, and by the end of the month, Turkey, Bulgaria, and Austria-Hungary were out of the war. At 4 A.M. on November 11, Germany signed the armistice. The AEF lost 48,909 dead and 230,000 wounded; losses to disease brought the total of dead to over 112,000.

The American contribution, although small in comparison to the enormous costs to European nations, was vital. Fresh, enthusiastic American troops raised Allied morale; they helped turn the tide at a crucial point in the war. American troops marched down the boulevards of Paris in the parade celebrating victory, but no black soldiers were allowed to march. They were also left out of a French mural depicting the different races in the war, even though black servicemen from the English and French colonies were represented.

Over Here

Victory at the front depended on economic and emotional mobilization at home. Consolidating federal authority, Wilson moved quickly in 1917 and 1918 to organize war production and distribution. An idealist who knew how to sway public opinion, he also recognized the need to enlist American emotions. To him, the war for people's minds, the "conquest of their convictions," was as vital as events on the battlefield.

The Conquest of Convictions

A week after war was declared, Wilson formed the Committee on Public Information (CPI) and asked George Creel, an outspoken progressive journalist, to head it. Creel hired other progressives like Ida Tarbell and Ray Stannard Baker and recruited thousands of people in the arts, advertising, and film industries to publicize the war. He worked out a system of voluntary censorship with the press, plastered walls with colorful posters, and issued more than 75 million pamphlets.

Creel also enlisted 75,000 "four-minute men" to give quick speeches at public gatherings and places of entertainment on "Why We Are Fighting" and "The Meaning of America." At first they were instructed to stress facts and stay away from hate, but by the beginning of 1918 the instructions shifted to portray the Germans as blood-

■ *Film actor Douglas Fairbanks calls for the purchase of war bonds at a rally on Wall Street.*

thirsty Huns bent on world conquest. Exploiting a new medium, the CPI promoted films like *The Prussian Cur* and *The Kaiser, the Beast of Berlin*. Creel secretly subsidized several prowar groups and formed the CPI's Division of Industrial Relations to rally labor to the war.

Helped along by the propaganda campaign, anti-German sentiment spread rapidly. Many schools stopped offering instruction in the German language, California's state education board calling it a language "of autocracy, brutality, and hatred." Sauerkraut became "liberty cabbage"; saloon-keepers removed pretzels from the bar. Orchestral works by Bach, Beethoven, and Brahms vanished from some symphonic programs, and the New York Philharmonic agreed not to perform the music of living German composers. Government agents harassed Karl Muck, the conductor of the Boston Symphony, imprisoned him for over a year, and then after the war ended, deported him. German-Americans and antiwar figures were badgered, beaten, and in some cases killed.

Vigilantism, sparked often by superpatriotism of a ruthless sort, flourished. Frequently it focused on radical antiwar figures like Frank Little, an IWW official in Butte, Montana, who was taken from his boardinghouse in August 1917, tied to the rear of an automobile, and dragged through the streets until his kneecaps were scraped off. Little was then hanged from a railroad trestle. In April 1918 a Missouri mob seized Robert Prager, a young man whose sole crime was being born in Germany. They bound him with an American flag, paraded him through town, and then lynched him. A jury acquitted the mob's members—who wore red, white, and blue ribbons to court—as one juror shouted: "Well, I guess nobody can say we aren't loyal now."

Rather than curbing the repression, Wilson encouraged it. "Woe be to the man or group of men that seeks to stand in our way," he told peace advocates soon after the war began. At his request, Congress passed the Espionage Act of 1917, which imposed sentences of up to twenty years in prison for persons found guilty of aiding the enemy, obstructing recruitment of soldiers, or encouraging disloyalty. It allowed the postmaster general to remove from the mails materials that incited treason or insurrection. The Trading-with-the-Enemy Act of 1917 authorized the government to censor the foreign-language press.

In 1918 Congress passed the Sedition Act, imposing harsh penalties on anyone using "disloyal,

■ *"The return of the Goth," an illustration by Boardman Robinson, expresses what many Americans really thought of Germany.*

profane, scurrilous, or abusive language" about the government, flag, or uniform. In all, over fifteen hundred persons were arrested under the new laws. People indicted or imprisoned included a Californian who laughed at rookies drilling at an army camp, a woman who greeted a Red Cross solicitor in a "hostile" way, and an editor who printed the sentence: "We must make the world safe for democracy even if we have to 'bean' the Goddess of Liberty to do it."

The sedition laws clearly went beyond any clear or present danger. There were, to be sure, German spies in the country, and the Germans wanted to encourage strikes in American arms factories. But the danger did not warrant a nationwide program of repression. Conservatives seized on the laws to stamp out socialists. Wilson's postmaster general banned from the mails more than a dozen socialist publications, including the *Appeal to Reason* which went to over half a million people weekly. In 1918 Eugene V. Debs, the Socialist party leader, delivered a speech denouncing capitalism and the war. He was convicted for violation of the Espionage Act and spent the war in a penitentiary in Atlanta. Nominated as the Socialist party candidate in the presidential election of 1920, Debs—prisoner 9653—won nearly a million votes, but the Socialist movement never fully recovered from the repression of the war.

A Bureaucratic War

Quick, effective action was needed to win the war, and to meet the need, Wilson and Congress set up an array of new federal agencies, nearly five thousand in all. Staffed largely by businessmen, the agencies drew on funds and powers of a hitherto unknown scope. At night the secretary of the treasury sat in bed, a yellow pad on his knees, adding up the money needed to finance the war. "The noughts attached to the many millions were so boisterous and prolific," he later said, "that, at times, they would run clear over the edge of the paper."

The War Industries Board, one of the most powerful of the agencies, oversaw the production of all American factories. Headed by millionaire Bernard M. Baruch, a Wall Street broker and speculator, it determined priorities, allocated raw materials, and fixed prices. It told manufacturers what they could and could not make. The WIB set the output of steel and regulated the number of stops on elevators. Working closely with business, Baruch for a time acted as the dictator of the American economy.

Herbert Hoover, the hero of a campaign to feed starving Belgians, headed a new Food Administration, and he set out with customary energy to supply food to the armies overseas. Appealing to the "spirit of self-sacrifice," Hoover convinced people to save food by observing "meatless" and "wheatless" days. He fixed prices to boost production, bought and distributed wheat, and encouraged people to plant "victory gardens" behind homes, churches, and schools. He sent half a million persons door-to-door to get housewives to sign cards pledging their cooperation. One householder—Wilson—set an example by grazing sheep on the White House lawn.

At another new agency, the Fuel Administration, Harry A. Garfield, the president of Williams College, introduced daylight saving time, rationed coal and oil, and imposed gasless days when motorists could not drive. To save coal, he shut down nonessential factories one day a week, and in January 1918, he closed all factories east of

MEXICAN-AMERICAN EXPERIENCE IN THE SOUTHWEST

From California to Texas in the early 1820s, one could enter the northern fringes of a rich civilization born out of three centuries of contacts between the Spanish and the Indians. Already a distinctly Mexican culture was emerging from the blend of European and native societies. Spaniards, with little concept of race, had mated and married Indian girls much more frequently than had Englishmen. They had fathered children (called Mestizos) who grew up knowing two worlds and who had developed a culture that reflected both. Missionaries had carried Spanish language, customs, manners, and morals to Apaches, Tilijaes, and other Indian tribes. Because the lower clergy had often championed the freedom of Indians from the tyranny of Spanish landlords, many natives had flocked to the church. Indians had blended Catholic beliefs with their own, while teaching Spaniards about both foods and farming methods.

By the early 1830s this borderlands Hispanic society flourished among thirty thousand people thinly spread from the Rio Grande Valley in Texas to northern California. Most of these people lived on *ranchos* (several hundred thousand others still lived as Indians) where cattle and horses produced colorful traditions. Here the American cowboy, or *vaquero* as the Mexicans called him, was born. His hat, his fine leather tooling of saddles, boots, and belts reflected the ornate artistry of Spanish culture. To fight boredom on these sprawling and lonely spreads, *vaqueros* made sport of roping and branding, the stuff of later rodeos. Both men and women became expert equestrians and, especially in California, took to the ancient Spanish sport of bull-baiting.

Americans who visited the West in the period often painted a romantic picture of a life both lavish and violent among colorful people. On wealthy *ranchos* it could be all that. On other

One of the last of the Spanish viceroys in Mexico, Don Jose de Iturrigara shown here with his family, about 1805.

Widespread and well-accepted, intermarriage between Spaniards and Indians in the early colonial period produced an interesting blend of racial types. Here an anonymous artist depicts a mestizo father, Spanish mother, and their child.

vast tracts of sun-baked land, especially in south Texas, *ranchero* families and the *vaqueros* lived among mesquites and cacti. Houses were made of mud bricks. Luxuries were few.

Life usually revolved around an extended family of several generations residing together. Children and young adults, even after marriage, accepted leadership and discipline from parents. They respected elders and valued family solidarity. Fathers headed these clans, but women enjoyed a status their English-American counterparts at the time never had. Wives held half-title to all property in a marriage (producing community property laws in many southwestern states). Women often ran business affairs on the *ranchos*.

When the United States conquered this civilization in the 1840s, there were immense differences between rich and poor. But soon wealthy landowners, middle-class farmers, and poverty-stricken peasants all shared the common fate of conquered people. Over the next half-century, Americans stripped the Mexicans of their land. They passed laws barring Chinese and Mexicans from working in the California mines. Squatters carved up ranches and then established English-speaking courts and boards to approve their thefts. Armed mobs sometimes lynched Mexican gold miners or burned crops and slaughtered cattle. In Texas, racist white settlers believed Mexicans were too inferior to deserve the land. So they taxed the *rancheros* out of business or used Texas Rangers to scare them away.

The mounted herdsmen (vaquero) tended the great cattle herds of the California (ranchero) landowners.

Early nineteenth-century drawing of a monk giving alms to an Indian child.

This intrepid Californio horsewoman is hoping to ground the bull by twisting his tail.

Such violence produced Mexican folk heroes who fought back. In California in the 1850s Joaquin Murieta killed Anglos suspected of mistreating Mexicans while Juan Cortina did the same in south Texas. To white authorities these men were bandits. To Mexican-Americans they were gallant heroes, defenders of home and hearth, inspirations for folk songs and legends.

Conquest disrupted families, drove most Mexican-Americans into poverty, and even undermined many extended families. Yet Mexican-Americans clung to their traditional culture: religious ceremonies for the living and the dead, unique foods and festivals, respect for tradition and authority, and a brightly hued palette of artistic expression.

At the turn of the century, fewer than three hundred thousand Mexican-Americans lived in the United States. In the next thirty years more than a million newcomers joined their ranks, fleeing the poverty of Mexico or the revolution that erupted there in 1910 and produced bloodshed for a decade. Between 1900 and 1910 the Mexican population of Texas and New Mexico nearly doubled; in Arizona it more than doubled; in California it quadrupled. In all four states it doubled again between 1910 and 1920. In time, this fresh class of Mexican-Americans and their children transformed the Southwest. They built most of the early highways in Texas, New Mexico, and Arizona; dug the irrigation ditches that produced an agricultural miracle in the Lower Rio

San Antonio was a Mexican city of lime-washed adobe houses in 1843 when Theodore Gentilz painted these scenes: a religious procession at the funeral of an infant; a busy market street and a festival featuring the rousing fandango dance.

Grande Valley of Texas; laid railroad track; and picked the cotton and vegetables that clothed and fed millions of other Americans. Many lived in shacks and shanties along the railroad tracks, isolated in a separate Spanish-speaking world.

Yet American society imposed harsh rules on these people. Segregation laws and practices often kept them out of hotels and other public accommodations. Schools either barred them or, ironically, tried to anglicize them in segregated facilities. Teachers changed Juan to Johnny, Araceli to Sally, and permitted no Spanish to be spoken on the playground. Yet again, Mexican-Americans clung to their culture. Their overcrowded *barrios* (neighborhoods) were both pockets of poverty and cultural islands of emotional comforts—family life, foods, and festivals remained familiar. During World War I many Mexican-Americans carried their culture into northern cities—Saint Louis, Chicago, Detroit, and Pittsburgh—as jobs opened there. Barrios developed in all these cities and elsewhere.

Joachin Murietta, seen here with reward poster, was killed in 1853.

New Mexico, 1897. No costly machinery, but goats, thresh the crop.

The Lugo family, Mexican-Americans of Southern California, 1888.

the Mississippi for four days to divert coal to munitions ships stranded in New York harbor. A fourth agency, the Railroad Administration, dictated rail traffic over nearly four hundred thousand miles of track—standardizing rates, limiting passenger travel, and speeding arms shipments. The War Shipping Board coordinated shipping, the Emergency Fleet Corporation supervised shipbuilding, and the War Trade Board oversaw foreign trade.

As never before, the government intervened in American life. When strikes threatened the telephone and telegraph companies, it simply seized and ran them. Businessmen, paid a nominal dollar a year, flocked to Washington to run the new agencies, and the partnership between government and business grew closer. As government expanded, business expanded as well, responding to wartime contracts. Industries like steel, aluminum, and cigarettes boomed in a war that displayed the triumph of large-scale industrial organization.

Labor in the War

The war also brought organized labor into the partnership with government, although the results were more limited than in the business-government alliance. Samuel Gompers, president of the AFL, served on Wilson's Council of National Defense, an advisory group formed to unify business, labor, and government. Gompers hoped to trade labor peace for labor advances, and he formed a War Committee on Labor to enlist workers' support for the war. With the blessing of the Wilson administration, membership in the AFL and other unions grew from about 2.7 million in 1916 to more than 4 million in 1919.

Hoping to encourage production and avoid strikes, Wilson adopted many of the objectives of the social-justice reformers. He supported an eight-hour day in war-related industries and improved wages and working conditions. In May 1918, he named Felix Frankfurter, a brilliant young law professor, to head a new War Labor Board. The agency standardized wages and hours, and at Wilson's direction, it protected the right of labor to organize and bargain collectively. Although it did not forbid strikes, it used various tactics to discourage them. It enforced decisions

■ War brought the mobilization of American railroads, farms, and factories. (Top) Brass shell casings fabricated at a plant in Toledo, Ohio, are readied for shipment to the Western Front. (Bottom) A woman worker in a defense plant welding with an acetylene torch.

Measuring the Mind

"Average"

"Inferior" "Superior"

IQ Score

From 1870 to 1920 scientists and physicians explored new ideas about the mind. In Europe the Viennese psychiatrist Sigmund Freud studied the unconscious, which, he thought, shaped human behavior. Russia's Ivan Pavlov tested the conditioned reflex in mental activity (Pavlov's dogs), and in the United States William James, the psychologist and philosopher, examined emotions and linked psychology to everyday problems.

As one way of understanding *the mind*, psychologists studied the mental processes of a great many minds, a task to which the relatively new science of statistics lent a hand. Testing large samples of subjects, they developed the concept of the "normal" and "average," helpful boundaries used to determine an individual's place in the population. In 1890 the psychologist James McKeen Cattell tested one hundred freshmen at the University of Pennsylvania for vision and hearing, sensitivity to pain, reaction time, and memory. He called these examinations by a new name—"mental tests"—and the idea spread. In 1895 the American Psychological Association (APA) set up a special committee to promote the nationwide collection of mental statistics.

Work was underway on both sides of the ocean,

and in 1905 Alfred Binet and Théodore Simon, two French psychologists, devised a metric intelligence scale. Seizing on the idea that until maturity, intelligence increases with age, they tested children of various ages to find an average level of performance for each age. Once they had determined the average, they could compare any child's test performance with it and thus distinguish between the child's "mental age" and chronological age. In 1912 William Stein, a German psychologist, introduced the "Intelligence Quotient," found by dividing a person's mental age by the chronological age. In 1916 Lewis M. Terman of Stanford University improved Binet's test, and the term *I.Q.* became part of the American vocabulary.

Employers and educators, however, remained skeptical of measuring intelligence. Thus, when the United States entered World War I, psychologists at once saw the opportunity to overcome the doubts and prove their theories. Huge numbers of men needed to be recruited, classified, and assigned to units quickly. Why not use the new mental tests? APA leaders formed twelve committees, including one on the Psychological Examination of Recruits, to explore the military uses of psychology.

Preferring to issue promotions on the basis of seniority, the army resisted the "mental meddlers," but the APA persuaded the War Department to make use of the tests. In early 1918 psychological examiners were posted at all training camps to administer the Alpha Test to literates and the Beta Test (with instructions given in pantomime) to illiterates and those who did not understand English. At the start of each Alpha Test, the examiners put the men at ease by explaining that the army was "not looking for crazy people. The aim is to help find out what we are best fitted to do." On the Beta Test, which was made up largely of pictures, the examiners were reminded that Beta men "sometimes sulk and refuse to work."

On the basis of the tests, the examiners classified recruits as "superior," "average," or "inferior." From the "superior" category, they selected men for officer training, a helpful winnowing process in an army that expanded quickly from 9000 officers to 200,000. That task done, they distributed the remaining "superior," "average," and "inferior" men among each military unit. In all, the examiners tested 1.7 million men—by far the largest testing program in human history to that time. To some degree the tests served their purpose, but they also seemed to raise questions about the education and mental ability of many American men.

For one thing, there was the extent of illiteracy —nearly a quarter of the draft-age men in 1918 could neither read nor write. (A third, incidentally, were physically unfit for service.) There was also the limited schooling of the recruits, most of whom had left school between the fifth and seventh grades. More alarming, according to the test results, 47 percent of the white draftees and 89 percent of the black draftees had a "mental age" of twelve years or under, which classified them as "feeble-minded." Did that mean half or more of the American population was feeble-minded?

The tests also turned up racial and national distinctions—or so some of the examiners concluded. Men of "native" backgrounds and "old" immigrant stock (from Northern Europe and the British Isles) tended to score well and fall in the "superior" category; "new" immigrants (from central and southern Europe) tended to score less well and rank as "inferior." Among Russian, Polish, and Italian draftees, more than half were classified as "inferior." Such results came as no surprise to those who had long doubted the intelligence of the "new" immigrants, nor did the fact that 80 percent of the blacks taking the Alpha Test scored in the inferior range.

Some observers, however, wondered what the tests really measured. The APA examiners claimed they measured "native intelligence," but questions about Edgar Allan Poe's poem "The Raven" or the paintings of Rosa Bonheur required answers that native intelligence alone could not supply. When blacks and whites scored comparably on the early Beta Test, the examiners decided that something must be wrong with the test, so they changed the questions until the scores showed the expected racial differences. Most of those taking the Beta Test had never taken a written test before; many had probably never held a pencil.

Still skeptical, the army discontinued the tests the moment the war ended, but what the army rejected, the nation adopted. Businesses, government, and above all, educational institutions found greater and greater uses for intelligence testing. In 1926 the College Entrance Examination Board (CEEB) administered the first Scholastic Aptitude Test (SAT), designed to test "intelligence" and predict performance in college. In 1935 it established scoring ranges from 200 to 800, with the average score set at 500. During World War II SAT tests were widely used. In 1947 the CEEB became part of a new Educational Testing Service that spurred an educational revolution by making intelligence instead of social or economic standing the main criterion of college admissions.

Before long, intelligence testing—the measuring of minds—touched every aspect of American life. Shaping lives and careers, it pushed some people forward and held others back, in the military, industry, the civil service, and higher education. "Intelligence tests . . . " an expert said in 1971, "have more and more become society's instrument for the selection of human resources."

in well-publicized cases; when the Smith and Wesson arms factory in Massachusetts and the Western Union telegraph company disobeyed the WLB's union rules, it took them over.

The WLB also ordered that women be paid equal wages for equal work in war industries. In 1914 the flow of European immigrants suddenly stopped because of the war, and in 1917 the draft began to take large numbers of American men. The result was a labor shortage, filled by women, blacks, and Mexican-Americans. A million women worked in war industries. Some of them took jobs previously held by men, but for the most part, they moved from one set of "women's jobs" into another. From the beginning of the war to the end, the number of women in the work force held steady at about eight million, and unlike the experience in World War II, large numbers of housewives did not leave the home for machine shops and arms plants.

Still, there were some new opportunities and in some cases higher pay. In food, airplane, and electrical plants, women made up a fifth or more of the work force. As their wages increased, they also increased their expectations; some became more militant, and there was growing conflict with male co-workers. To set standards for female employment, a Women's Bureau was established in the Department of Labor, but the government's influence varied. In the federally run railroad industry, women often made wages equal to those of men; in the federally run telephone industry, they did not.

Looking for more people to fill wartime jobs, corporations found another major source among southern blacks. Beginning in 1916, northern labor agents traveled across the South, promising jobs, high wages, and free transportation. Soon the word flashed from town to town, and the movement northward became a flood. Between 1916 and 1918 over 450,000 blacks left the Old South for the booming industrial cities of Saint Louis, Chicago, Detroit, and Cleveland. In the decade before 1920, Detroit's black population grew by over 600 percent, Cleveland's by over 300 percent, and Chicago's by 150 percent.

Most of the newcomers were young, unmarried, and skilled or semiskilled. The men found jobs in factories, railroad yards, steel mills, packing houses, and coal mines; black women worked in textile factories, department stores, and restaurants. In their new homes, blacks found greater racial freedom but also different living conditions. If the South was often hostile, the North could be impersonal and lonely. Accustomed to the pace of the farm—ruled by the seasons and the sun—those blacks who were able to enter the industrial sector now worked for hourly wages in mass-production industries, where time clocks and foremen dictated the daily routine.

Racial tensions increased, resulting in part from growing competition for housing and jobs. In mid-1917 a race war in East Saint Louis, Illinois, killed nine whites and about forty blacks. In July 1919, the month President Wilson returned from the peace conference in Paris, a race riot in Washington, D.C., killed six people. Riots in Chicago that month killed thirty-eight— fifteen whites and twenty-three blacks—and there were later outbreaks in New York City and Omaha. Lynch mobs killed forty-eight blacks in 1917, sixty-three in 1918, and seventy-eight in 1919. Ten of the victims in 1919 were war veterans, several still in uniform.

Blacks were more and more inclined to fight back. Two hundred thousand blacks served in France—42,000 as combat troops. Returning home, they expected better treatment. "I'm glad I went," a black veteran said. "I done my part and I'm going to fight right here till Uncle Sam does his." Roscoe Jameson, Claude McKay, and other black poets wrote biting poetry, some of it—like Fenton Johnson's "The New Day"—drawn from the war experience:

> For we have been with thee in No Man's Land,
> Through lake of fire and down to Hell itself;
> And now we ask of thee our liberty,
> Our freedom in the land of Stars and Stripes.

"Lift Ev'ry Voice and Sing," composed in 1900, became known as the "Negro National Anthem." Parents bought black dolls for their children, and W. E. B. Du Bois spoke of a "New Negro," proud and more militant: "We return. We return from fighting. We return fighting."

Eager for cheap labor, farmers and ranchers in the Southwest persuaded the federal government to relax immigration restrictions, and between 1917 and 1920 over 100,000 Mexicans migrated into Texas, Arizona, New Mexico, and California. The Mexican-American population grew from

■ *A wounded doughboy is welcomed home, New York City, March 1919. Most of the black combat troops in the war served with units assigned to the French command.*

385,000 in 1910 to 740,000 in 1920. Tens of thousands of Mexican-Americans moved to Chicago, Saint Louis, Omaha, and other northern cities to take wartime jobs. Often scorned and insecure, they created urban *barrios*, similar to the Chinatowns and Little Italys around them.

Like most wars, World War I affected patterns at home as much as abroad. Business profits grew, factories expanded, and industries turned out huge amounts of war goods. Government authority swelled, and people came to expect different things of their government. Labor made some gains, as did women and blacks. Society assimilated some of the shifts, but social and economic tensions grew, and when the war ended, they spilled over in the strikes and violence of the "Red Scare" of 1919 (see chapter 25).

The United States emerged from the war the strongest economic power in the world. In 1914 it was a debtor nation, and American citizens owed foreign investors about $3 billion. Five years later the United States had become a creditor nation. Foreign governments owed over $10 billion, and foreign citizens owed American investors nearly $3 billion. The war marked a shift in economic power rarely equaled in history.

The Treaty of Versailles

Long before the fighting ended, Wilson began to formulate plans for the peace. On January 8, 1918, appearing before Congress to rebut Bolshevik arguments that the war was merely a struggle among imperialists, the President outlined terms for a far-reaching, nonpunitive settlement. Wilson's Fourteen Points (see p. 710) were generous and farsighted, but they failed to satisfy wartime emotions.

England and France distrusted Wilsonian idealism as the basis for peace. They wanted Germany disarmed and crippled; they wanted its colonies; and they were skeptical of the principle of self-determination. As the end of the war neared, the Allies, who had made secret commitments with one another, balked at making the Fourteen Points the basis of peace. When Wilson threatened to negotiate a separate treaty with Germany, however, they accepted.

Wilson had won an important victory, but difficulties lay ahead. As Georges Clemenceau, the seventy-eight-year-old French premier, said: "God gave us the Ten Commandments, and we broke them. Wilson gives us the Fourteen Points. We shall see."

A Peace at Paris

Just before the peace conference began, Wilson appealed to voters to elect a Democratic Congress in the 1918 elections—"if you have approved of my leadership and wish me to continue to be your unembarrassed spokesman in affairs at home and abroad . . ." The Democrats lost both the House and Senate, enabling Wilson's opponents to announce that voters had rejected his policies. In fact, the Democratic losses stemmed largely from domestic problems, such as the price of wheat and cotton. But they hurt Wilson, who soon would be negotiating with European leaders buoyed by rousing victories at their own polls.

Two weeks after the elections, Wilson announced that he would attend the peace conference. This was a dramatic break from tradition, and his personal involvement drew attacks from Republicans. They renewed the criticism when he named the rest of the delegation: Secretary of State Lansing, Colonel House, General Tasker H.

Woodrow Wilson's Fourteen Points, 1918: Success and Failure in Implementation

1. Open covenants of peace openly arrived at	Not fulfilled
2. Absolute freedom of navigation upon the seas in peace and war	Not fulfilled
3. Removal of all economic barriers to the equality of trade among nations	Not fulfilled
4. Reduction of armaments to the level needed only for domestic safety	Not fulfilled
5. Impartial adjustment of colonial claims	Not fulfilled
6. Evacuation of all Russian territory; Russia to be welcomed into the society of free nations	Not fulfilled
7. Evacuation and restoration of Belgium	**Fulfilled**
8. Evacuation and restoration of all French lands; return of Alsace-Lorraine to France	**Fulfilled**
9. Readjustment of Italy's frontiers along lines of Italian nationality	Compromised
10. Self-determination for the former subjects of the Austro-Hungarian Empire	Compromised
11. Evacuation of Rumania, Serbia, and Montenegro; free access to the sea for Serbia	Compromised
12. Self-determination for the former subjects of the Ottoman Empire; secure sovereignty for Turkish portion	Compromised
13. Establishment of an independent Poland, with free and secure access to the sea	**Fulfilled**
14. Establishment of a League of Nations affording mutual guarantees of independence and territorial integrity	Not fulfilled

Source: Data from G. M. Gathorne-Hardy, The Fourteen Points and the Treaty of Versailles (Oxford Pamphlets on World Affairs, no. 6, 1939), pp. 8–34; Thomas G. Paterson et al., American Foreign Policy, A History Since 1900, 2d ed., Vol. 2, pp. 282–93.

Bliss, a military expert, and Henry White, a career diplomat. Wilson named no member of the Senate, and the only Republican in the group was White.

In selecting the delegation, Wilson passed over Henry Cabot Lodge, the powerful Republican senator from Massachusetts who opposed the Fourteen Points and would soon head the Senate Foreign Relations Committee. He also decided not to appoint Elihu Root or ex-President Taft, both of them enthusiastic internationalists. Never good at accepting criticism or delegating authority, Wilson wanted a delegation he could control—an advantage at the peace table but not in any battle over the treaty at home.

Upon his arrival in Europe, Wilson received a tumultuous welcome in England, France, and Italy. Never before had such crowds acclaimed a democratic political figure. In Paris two million people lined the Champs-Elysées, threw flowers at him, and shouted "Wilson le Juste [the just]" as his carriage drove by. Overwhelmed, Wilson was sure that people shared his goals, but he was wrong: like their leaders, they hated Germany and wanted victory unmistakably reflected in the peace.

Opening in January 1919, the Peace Conference at Paris continued until May. Although twenty-seven nations were represented, the "Big Four" dominated it: Wilson; Clemenceau of France, tired and stubborn, determined to end the German threat forever; David Lloyd George, the crafty British prime minister who had pledged to squeeze Germany "until the pips squeak"; and the Italian prime minister, Vittorio Orlando. A clever negotiator, Wilson traded various "small" concessions for his major goals—national self-determination, a reduction in tensions, and a League of Nations to enforce the peace.

Wilson had to surrender some important prin-

When Wilson arrived in Europe in December 1918, cheering crowds in England, France, and Italy hailed him as the "peacemaker from America." The painting (right) by Sir William Orpen recreates the signing of the treaty in the Hall of Mirrors at the palace of Versailles. The German delegates, Dr. Johannes Bell (seated, back to artist) and Herman Müller (next to Bell), sign under the watchful eyes of the Allied delegates. At the left are the five American delegates: General Tasker Bliss, Colonel House, Henry White, Secretary of State Lansing, and President Wilson.

Europe After the Treaty of Versailles, 1919

The treaty changed the map of Europe, creating a number of new and reconstituted nations. (Note boundary changes from prewar map on p. 694.)

ciples. Departing from the Fourteen Points, the treaty created two new independent nations—Poland and Czechoslovakia—with large German-speaking populations, a violation of self-determination. It divided up the German colonies in Asia and Africa. Instead of a peace without victory, it made Germany accept responsibility for the war and demanded enormous reparations —which eventually totaled $33 billion. It made no mention of disarmament, free trade, or freedom of the seas. Instead of an open covenant openly arrived at, the treaty was drafted behind closed doors.

But Wilson deflected some of the most extreme Allied demands, and he won his coveted Point 14, a League of Nations, designed, "to achieve international peace and security." The League included a general Assembly; a smaller Council composed of the United States, Great Britain, France, Italy, Japan, and four nations to be elected by the

711

The Treaty of Versailles

Assembly; and a court of international justice. League members pledged to submit to arbitration every dispute threatening peace and to enjoin military and economic sanctions against nations resorting to war. Article X, for Wilson the heart of the League, obligated members to protect each other's independence and territorial integrity.

The draft treaty in hand, Wilson returned home in February 1919 to discuss it with Congress and the people. Most Americans, the polls showed, favored the League; thirty-three governors endorsed it. But over dinner with the Senate and House Foreign Relations Committees, Wilson learned of the strength of congressional opposition to it. On March 5, Senator Lodge produced a "round robin" signed by thirty-seven senators declaring they would not vote for the treaty without amendment. Should those numbers hold up, Lodge had enough votes to defeat it.

Returning to Paris, Wilson attacked his critics, while privately he worked for changes to improve the chances of Senate approval. The Allies won major concessions in return, but they amended the League draft treaty, agreeing that domestic affairs remained outside League jurisdiction, exempting the Monroe Doctrine, and allowing nations to withdraw after two years' notice. On June 28, 1919, they signed the treaty in the Hall of Mirrors at Versailles, and Wilson started home for his most difficult fight.

Rejection in the Senate

There were ninety-six senators in 1919, forty-nine of them Republicans. Fourteen Republicans, led by William E. Borah of Idaho, were the "irreconcilables" who opposed the League on any grounds. "If the Savior of man," Borah said, "would revisit the earth and declare for a League of Nations, I would be opposed to it." Frank B. Kellogg of Minnesota led a group of twelve "mild reservationists" who accepted the treaty but wanted to insert several reservations that would not greatly weaken it. Finally, there were the Lodge-led "strong reservationists," twenty-three of them in all, who wanted major changes that the Allies would have to approve.

With only four Democratic senators opposed to the treaty, the Democrats and compromise-minded Republicans had enough votes to ratify it,

once a few reservations were inserted. Biding for time to allow public opposition to grow, Lodge scheduled lengthy hearings and spent two weeks reading the 268-page treaty aloud. Democratic leaders urged Wilson to appeal to the Republican "mild reservationists," but he angrily refused. "Anyone who opposes me in that I'll crush!"

Fed up with Lodge's tactics, Wilson set out in early September to take the case directly to the people. Crossing the Midwest, his speeches aroused little emotion, but on the Pacific Coast he won ovations, which heartened him. On his way back to Washington, he stopped in Pueblo, Colorado, where he delivered one of the most eloquent speeches of his career. People wept as he talked of Americans who died in battle and the hope that they would never fight again in foreign lands. That night Wilson felt ill. He returned to Washington, and on October 2, Mrs. Wilson found him lying unconscious on the floor of the White House, the victim of a stroke that paralyzed his left side.

After the stroke, Wilson could not work more than an hour or two at a time. No one was allowed to see him except family members, his secretary, and his physician. For over seven months he did not meet with the cabinet. Secretary of State Lansing convened cabinet meetings, but when Wilson learned of them, he ordered Lansing to stop and then cruelly forced him to resign. Focusing his remaining energy on the fight over the treaty, Wilson lost touch with other issues, and critics charged that his wife, Edith Bolling Wilson, ran the government.

On November 6, 1919, while Wilson convalesced, Lodge finally reported the treaty out of committee, along with "Fourteen Reservations," one for each of Wilson's points. The most important reservation stipulated that implementation of Article X, Wilson's key article, required the action of Congress in each case.

That day the President's floor leader in the Senate told him that the Democrats could not pass the treaty without reservations. "Is it possible?" Wilson asked sadly. "It might be wise to compromise," the senator said. "Let Lodge compromise!" Wilson replied. When Mrs. Wilson urged her husband to accept the Lodge reservations, he said: "Better a thousand times to go down fighting than to dip your colors to dishonorable compromise."

In this cartoon, Humanity points the finger of blame at the U.S. Senate, the ogre responsible for killing the peace treaty.

aside. The Democrats nominated Governor James M. Cox of Ohio, along with the young and popular Franklin D. Roosevelt, assistant secretary of the navy, for vice-president. Wilson called for "a great and solemn referendum" on the treaty. The Democratic platform endorsed the treaty but agreed to accept reservations to clarify the American role in the League.

On the Republican side, Senator Warren G. Harding of Ohio, who had nominated Taft in 1912, won the presidential nomination. Harding waffled on the treaty, but it made little difference. Voters wanted a change. Harding won in a landslide, taking 61 percent of the vote and beating Cox by 7 million votes. Without a peace treaty, the United States remained technically at war, and it was not until July 1921, almost three years after the last shot was fired, that Congress passed a joint resolution ending the war.

A hearty, down-to-earth handshaker, Warren G. Harding loved meeting and greeting people. An althorn player, the President poses here with a tuba.

On November 19, the treaty—with the Lodge reservations—failed, 39 to 55. Following Wilson's instructions, the Democrats voted against it. A motion to approve without the reservations lost 38 to 53, with only one Republican voting in favor. The defeat brought pleas for compromise, but neither Wilson nor Lodge would back down. When the treaty with reservations again came up for vote on March 19, 1920, Wilson ordered the Democrats to hold firm against it. Although twenty-one of them defied him, enough obeyed his orders to defeat it, 49 to 35, seven votes short of the necessary two-thirds majority.

To Wilson, walking now with the help of a cane, one chance remained: the presidential election of 1920. For a time he thought of running for a third term himself, but his party shunted him

The Election of 1920

Candidate	Party	Popular Vote	Electoral Vote
Harding	Republican	16,133,314	404
Cox	Democrat	9,140,884	127
Debs	Socialist	913,664	0

After 1919 there was disillusionment. World War I was feared before it started, popular while it lasted, and hated when it ended. To a whole generation that followed, it appeared futile, killing without cause, sacrifice without benefit. Books, plays, and movies—Hemingway's *A Farewell to Arms*, John Dos Passos' *Three Soldiers* (1921), Laurence Stallings and Maxwell Anderson's *What Price Glory?* (1924) among others—showed it as waste, horror, and death.

The war and its aftermath damaged the humanitarian, progressive spirit of the early years of the century. It killed "something precious and perhaps irretrievable in the hearts of thinking men and women." Progressivism survived well into the 1920s and the New Deal, but it no longer had the old conviction and broad popular support. Bruising fights over the war and the League drained people's energy and enthusiasm.

Confined to bed, Woodrow Wilson died in Washington in 1924, three years after Harding, the new president, promised "not heroics but healing; not nostrums but normalcy; not revolution but restoration." Nonetheless, the "war to end all wars," and the spirit of Woodrow Wilson left an indelible imprint on the country.

Recommended Reading

American foreign policy between 1901 and 1921 has been the subject of considerable study. Richard W. Leopold, *The Growth of American Foreign Policy* (1962) is balanced and informed. Howard K. Beale, *Theodore Roosevelt and the Rise of America to World Power* (1956), traces foreign policy during the early years; Robert E. Osgood, *Ideals and Self-Interest in America's Foreign Relations* (1953), and William Appleman Williams, *Roots of the Modern American Empire* (1969), explore the forces underlying American foreign policy.

David McCullough gives a lively account of the building of the Panama Canal in *The Path Between the Seas* (1977). For American policy toward Latin America, see Dana G. Munro's detailed account, *Intervention and Dollar Diplomacy in the Caribbean, 1900–1920* (1964). Arthur S. Link examines Wilson's foreign policy in his exceptional five-volume biography, *Wilson* (1947–1965) and in *Woodrow Wilson: Revolution, War, and Peace* (1979). N. Gordon Levin, Jr., *Woodrow Wilson and World Politics: America's Response to War and Revolution* (1968), places Wilson in the larger context of world events.

Ernest R. May studies American policy before the war in *The World War and American Isolation, 1914–*

1917 (1959). Bradford Perkins, *The Great Rapprochement: England and the United States, 1895–1914* (1968), examines the growing friendship between the two countries. Studies of events at home during the war include David M. Kennedy, *Over Here* (1980); Robert D. Cuff, *The War Industries Board* (1973); and Maurine W. Greenwald, *Women, War, and Work* (1980).

Woodrow Wilson and the Lost Peace (1944) and *Woodrow Wilson and the Great Betrayal* (1945) by Thomas A. Bailey are dated but thorough on Wilson's efforts at Versailles. Arthur Walworth, *America's Moment, 1918: American Diplomacy at the End of World War I* (1977), also examines Wilson's attempt to create a peaceful world order.

Additional Bibliography

For background to American policy in these years, see Richard D. Challener, *Admirals, Generals, and American Foreign Policy, 1898–1914* (1973) and Paul P. Abrahams, *The Foreign Expansion of American Finance and Its Relationship to the Foreign Economic Policies of the United States, 1907–1921* (1976). David H. Burton, *Theodore Roosevelt, Confident Imperialist* (1968); Frederick Marks III, *Velvet on Iron: The Diplomacy of Theodore Roosevelt* (1979); and C. E. Neu, *An Uncertain Friendship: Theodore Roosevelt and Japan, 1906–1909* (1967), trace Roosevelt's policies.

On Taft and Wilson, see Ralph E. Minger, *William Howard Taft and United States Foreign Policy* (1975); Walter V. Scholes and Marie V. Scholes, *The Foreign Policies of the Taft Administration* (1970); and John Morton Blum, *Woodrow Wilson and the Politics of Morality* (1956). For relations with Latin America, see Dexter R. Perkins, *The United States and the Caribbean*, rev. ed. (1966) and two books by Lester D. Langley: *Struggle for the American Mediterranean* (1975) and *The United States and the Caribbean, 1900–1970* (1980).

On Mexico, see Peter Calvert, *The Mexican Revolution, 1910–1914* (1968); Lloyd Gardner, *Wilson and Revolutions, 1913–1921* (1976); and Robert E. Quirk, *An Affair of Honor: Woodrow Wilson and the Occupation of Veracruz* (1962). Several books deal with policies in the Far East, including Charles Vevier, *United States and China, 1906–1913* (1955); Charles S. Campbell, *Special Business Interests and the Open Door Policy* (1951); Warren I. Cohen, *America's Response to China*, 2d ed. (1980); Raymond A. Esthus, *Theodore Roosevelt and Japan* (1966); and Jerry Israel, *Progressivism and the Open Door: America and China, 1905–1921* (1971).

Historians have long debated the reasons for America's entry into the war; see, for example, Charles Seymour, *American Diplomacy During the World War* (1934) and *American Neutrality, 1914–1917* (1935); Patrick Devlin, *Too Proud to Fight: Woodrow Wilson's Neutrality* (1974); David M. Smith, *Robert Lansing and American Neutrality* (1958); Ross Gregory, *The Origins of American Intervention in the First World War* (1971); and Jeffrey J. Safford, *Wilsonian Maritime Diplomacy* (1978).

The war at home is followed in John G. Clifford, *The Citizen Soldiers* (1972); William Preston, Jr., *Aliens and Dissenters: Federal Suppression of Radicals, 1903–1933* (1963); H. C. Peterson and Gilbert C. Fite, *Opponents of War, 1917–1918* (1957); Carol S. Gruber, *Mars and Minerva: World War I and the Uses of Higher Learning in America* (1975); and Stephen Vaughn, *Holding Fast the Inner Lines: Democracy, Nationalism, and the Committee on Public Information* (1980).

On military intervention, see Harvey DeWeerd, *President Wilson Fights His War* (1968); E. M. Coftman, *The War to End All Wars* (1968); Frank E. Vandiver, *Black Jack: The Life and Times of John J. Pershing*, 2 vols. (1977); Russell F. Weigley, *The American Way of War* (1973); Laurence Stallings, *The Doughboys* (1963); and Arthur E. Barbeau and Henri Florette, *The Unknown Soldiers: Black American Troops in World War I* (1974).

The Treaty of Versailles and the struggle for ratification are covered in Arno J. Mayer, *Politics and Diplomacy of Peacemaking* (1967); Charles L. Mee, Jr., *The End of Order, Versailles, 1919* (1980); Warren F. Kuehl, *Seeking World Order* (1969); L. W. Martin, *Peace Without Victory* (1958); and Ralph A. Stone, *The Irreconcilables* (1970).

Wesley M. Bagby, *The Road to Normalcy* (1962); Seward W. Livermore, *Politics Is Adjourned: Woodrow Wilson and the War Congress, 1916–1918* (1966); and David Burner, *The Politics of Provincialism: The Democratic Party in Transition, 1918–1932* (1967) are excellent studies of domestic politics of the era.

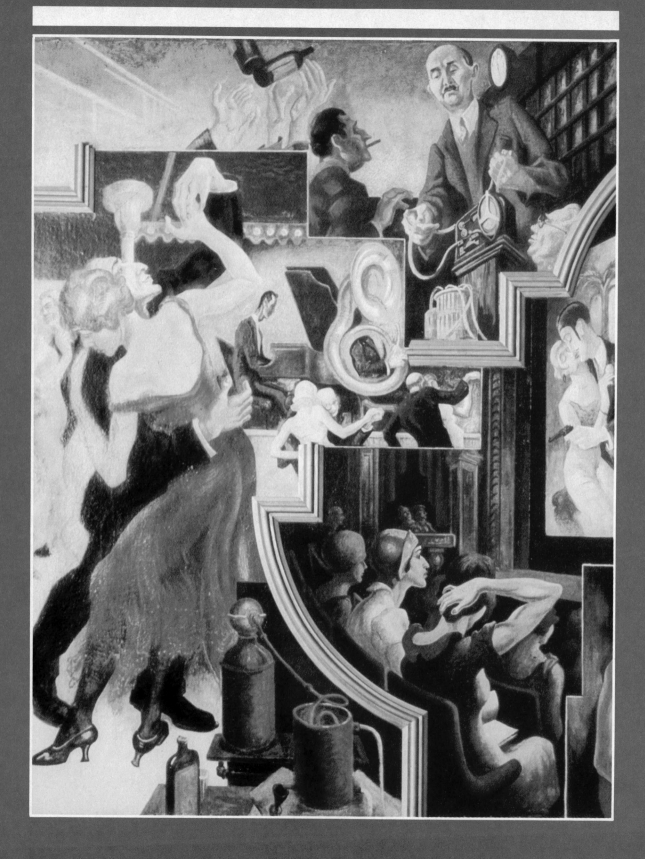

chapter 25
TRANSITION TO MODERN AMERICA

The moving assembly line that Henry Ford perfected in 1914 for manufacture of the Model T marked only the first step toward full mass production and the beginning of America's worldwide industrial supremacy. A year later, Ford began buying large plots of land along the Rouge River southeast of Detroit, Michigan. He already had a vision of a vast industrial tract where machines, moving through a sequence of carefully arranged manufacturing operations, would transform raw materials into finished cars, trucks, and tractors. The key would be control over the flow of goods at each step along the way, from lake steamers and railroad cars bringing in the coal and iron ore, to overhead conveyor belts and huge turning tables carrying the moving parts past the stationary workers on the assembly line. "Everything must move," Ford commanded, and by the mid-1920s at River Rouge, as the plant became known, it did.

Ford began fulfilling his industrial dream in 1919 when he built a blast furnace and foundry to make engine blocks for both the Model T and his tractors. By 1924, more than forty thousand workers were turning out nearly all the metal parts used in making Ford vehicles. A tractor factory was so efficient that it took just over twenty-eight hours to convert raw ore into a new farm implement.

Visitors from all over the world came to marvel at River Rouge. Some were disturbed by the jumble of machines (by 1926, there were forty-three thousand in operation) and the apparent congestion on the plant floor, but industrial experts recognized that the arrangement led to incredible productivity because "the work moves and the men stand still." A trained engineer summed it up best when he wrote that a visitor "sees each unit as a carefully designed gear which meshes with other gears and operates in synchronism with them, the whole forming one huge, perfectly-timed, smoothly-operating industrial machine of almost unbelieveable efficiency."

In May 1927, after producing over fifteen million Model Ts, Ford closed the assembly line at Highland Park. For the next six months, his engineers worked on designing a more compact and efficient assembly line at River Rouge for the Model A, which went into production in November. By then River Rouge had more than justified Ford's vision. "Ford had brought together everything at a single site and on a scale no one else

The tall smokestacks of the River Rouge plant rose more than three hundred feet into the sky, and the sprawling series of buildings eventually covered nearly two thousand acres of land. Every day ships, trains, and trucks brought to the plant a steady stream of raw materials for transformation into cars, trucks, and tractors going out to consumers all over the world.

had ever attempted," concluded historian Geoffrey Perrett. "The Rouge plant became to a generation of engineers far more than a factory. It was a monument."

Mass production, born in Highland Park in 1914 and perfected at River Rouge in the 1920s, became the hallmark of American industry. Other car makers copied Ford's methods and soon his emphasis on the flow of parts moving past stationary workers became the standard in nearly every American factory. The moving assembly line—with its emphasis on uniformity, speed, precision, and coordination—took away the last vestiges of craftsmanship and turned workers into near robots. It led to amazing efficiency that produced both high profits for manufacturers and low prices for buyers. By the mid-1920s, the cost of the Model T had dropped from $950 to only $290.

Most important, mass production led to a consumer-goods revolution. American factories turned out a flood of automobiles and electric appliances that made life easier and more pleasant for the vast majority of the American people. The result was the creation of a new America, one in which individualism was sacrificed to conformity as part of the price to be paid for a new era of abundance.

The twenties, often seen as a time of escape and frivolity before the onset of the Depression, actually marked a beginning, a time when the American people learned to adapt to life in the city, when they decided (wisely or not) to center their existence upon the automobile, and when they rejected their rural past while still longing for the old values it had created. It is in the 1920s that we can find the roots of modern America—the America we know today.

The Second Industrial Revolution

The first Industrial Revolution in the late nineteenth century had catapulted the United States into the forefront of the world's richest and most highly developed nations. With the advent of the new consumer-goods industries, the American people by the 1920s enjoyed the highest standard of living of any nation on earth. After a brief postwar depression, 1922 saw the beginning of a great boom that peaked in 1927 and lasted until 1929. In this brief period, American industrial output nearly doubled, and the gross national product rose by 40 percent. Most of this explosive growth took place in industries producing goods for consumers—automobiles, appliances, furniture, clothing. Equally important, the national per-capita income increased by 30 percent to $681 in 1929. American workers became the highest paid in history and thus were able to buy the

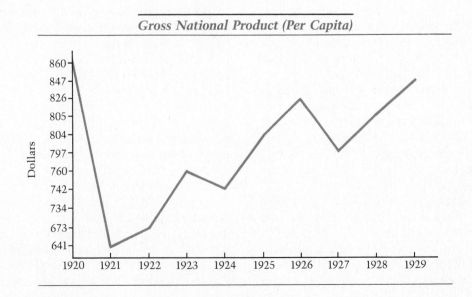

Gross National Product (Per Capita)

flood of new goods they were turning out on the assembly lines.

The key to the new affluence lay in technology. The moving assembly line pioneered by Ford became the standard feature in nearly all American plants. Electric motors replaced steam engines as the basic source of energy in factories; by 1929, 70 percent of all industrial power came from electricity. Efficiency experts broke down the industrial process into minute parts in time and motion studies and then showed managers and workers how to maximize the output of their labor. Production per man-hour increased an amazing 75 percent over the decade; in 1929, a work force no larger than that of 1919 was producing almost twice as many goods.

Patterns of Economic Growth

Automobiles were the most conspicuous of the consumer products that flourished in the 1920s but certainly not the only ones. The electrical industry grew nearly as quickly. Central power stations, where massive steam generators converted coal into electricity, brought current into the homes of city and town dwellers. Two thirds of all American families enjoyed electricity by the end of the decade, and they spent vast sums on washing machines, vacuum cleaners, refrigerators, and ranges. The new appliances eased the burdens of the housewife and ushered in an age of leisure.

Radio broadcasting and motion-picture production also boomed in the 1920s. The early success of KDKA in Pittsburgh stimulated the growth of more than eight hundred independent radio stations, and by 1929 NBC had formed the first successful radio network. Five nights a week "Amos 'n Andy," a comic serial featuring two "blackface" vaudevillians, held the attention of millions of Americans. The film industry thrived in Hollywood, reaching its maturity in the mid-1920s when in every large city there were huge theaters seating as many as four thousand people. With the advent of the "talkies" in 1929, average weekly movie attendance climbed to nearly one hundred million.

Other industries prospered as well. Production of light metals such as aluminum and magnesium grew into a major business. Chemicals came

■ For "a dollar down and a dollar a week" Americans of the 1920s could purchase the latest household electrical appliance—a washing machine, for example, or a fan or an iron or a refrigerator.

of age with the invention of synthetics, ranging from rayon for clothing to cellophane for packaging. Americans found a whole new spectrum of products to buy—cigarette lighters, wristwatches, heat-resistant glass cooking dishes, and rayon stockings to name just a few.

The corporation continued to be the dominant economic unit in the 1920s. Growing corporations now had hundreds of thousands of stockholders, and one individual or family rarely held more than 5 percent of the stock. The enormous profits generated by these corporations enabled their managers to finance growth and expansion internally, thus freeing companies from their earlier dependence on investment bankers like J. P. Morgan. Voicing a belief in social responsibility and enlightened capitalism, the new professional class operated independently of outside restraint. In the last analysis, the corporate managers were accountable only to other managers.

Another wave of mergers accompanied the

growth of corporations during the 1920s. From 1920 to 1928, some eight thousand mergers took place as more and more small firms proved unable to compete effectively with the new giants. By the end of the decade, the two hundred largest nonfinancial corporations owned almost half of the country's corporate wealth. The oligopoly in the automobile industry set the example for other areas. The greatest abuses took place in public utilities where promoters like Samuel Insull built vast paper empires by gaining control of operating power companies and then draining them of their assets.

The most distinctive feature of the new consumer-oriented economy was the stress on marketing. Advertising earnings rose from $1.3 billion in 1915 to $3.4 billion in 1926. Skillful practitioners like Edward Bernays and Bruce Barton sought to control public taste and consumer spending by identifying the good life with the possession of the latest product of American industry, whether a car, a refrigerator, or a cigarette. Chain stores advanced rapidly at the expense of small retail shops. A&P dominated the retail food industry, growing from 400 stores in 1912 to 15,500 by 1932. Woolworth's "five and tens" spread almost as rapidly, while such drugstore chains as Rexall and Liggetts—both owned by one huge holding company—opened outlets in nearly every town and city in the land.

Uniformity and standardization, the characteristics of mass production, now prevailed. The farmer in Kansas bought the same kind of car, the same groceries, and the same pills as the factory worker in Pennsylvania. Sectional differences in dress, food, and furniture began to disappear. Even the regional accents that distinguished Americans in different parts of the country were threatened with extinction by the advent of radio and films which promoted a standard national dialect devoid of any local flavor.

Economic Weaknesses

The New Era, as businessmen labeled the decade, was not as prosperous as it first appeared. The revolution in consumer goods disguised the decline of many traditional industries in the 1920s. Railroads, overcapitalized and poorly managed, suffered from internal woes and from the competition of the growing trucking industry. Coal was another troubled industry, with petroleum and natural gas beginning to replace it as a fuel. Cotton textiles declined with the development of rayon and other synthetic fibers. The New England mills moved south in search of cheap labor, leaving behind thousands of unemployed workers and virtual ghost towns in the nation's oldest industrial center.

Hardest hit of all was agriculture. American farmers had expanded production to meet the demands of World War I, when they fed a nation at war and most of Europe as well. A sharp cutback in exports in 1919 caused a rapid decline in prices. By 1921, farm exports had fallen by more than $2 billion. Throughout the 1920s, the farmers' share of the national income dropped until by 1929 the per-capita farm income was only $273, compared to the national average of $681.

Workers were better off in the 1920s, but they did not share fully in the decade's affluence. The industrial labor force remained remarkably steady for a period of economic growth; the technical innovations meant that the same number of workers could produce far more than before. Most of the new jobs came in the lower-paying service industry. During the decade, factory wage rates rose only a modest 11 percent; by 1929 nearly half of all American families had an income of less than $1500. At the same time, however, conditions of life improved. Prices remained stable, even dropping somewhat in the early twenties, so that workers enjoyed a gain in real wages.

Organized labor proved unable to advance the interests of workers in the 1920s. Conservative leadership in the AFL neglected the task of organizing the vast number of unskilled laborers in the mass-production industries. Aggressive management weakened the appeal of unions by portraying them as radical after a series of strikes in 1919. Many businessmen used the injunction and "yellow-dog" contracts, which forbade employees from joining unions, to establish open shops and deny workers the benefits of collective bargaining. Other employers wooed their workers away from unions using techniques of welfare capitalism, spending money to improve plant conditions and winning employee loyalty with pensions, paid vacations, and company cafeterias. The net result was a decline in union membership from a postwar high of five million to less than three million by 1929.

Black workers remained on the bottom, both economically and socially. Nearly half a million blacks had migrated northward from the rural South during World War I. Some found jobs in northern industries, but many more worked in menial service areas, collecting garbage, washing dishes, and sweeping floors. Yet even these jobs offered them a better life than they found on the depressed southern farms, where millions of blacks still lived in poverty, and so the migration continued. The black ghettos in northern cities grew rapidly in the 1920s; Chicago's black population doubled during the decade, while New York's rose from 152,467 to 327,706, with most blacks living in Harlem.

Middle- and upper-class Americans were the groups who thrived in the 1920s. The rewards of the second Industrial Revolution went to the managers—the engineers, bankers, and executives who directed the new industrial economy. Corporate profits nearly doubled in ten years, and income from dividends rose 65 percent, nearly six times the rate of workers' wages. Bank accounts, reflecting the accumulated savings of the upper-middle and wealthy classes, rose from $41.1 billion to $57.9 billion. These were the people who bought the fine new houses in the suburbs and who could afford more than one car. Their conspicuous consumption helped fuel the prosperity of the 1920s, but their disposable income eventually became greater than their material wants. The result was speculation, as those with idle money began to invest heavily in the stock market to reap gains from the industrial growth.

The economic trends of the decade had both positive and negative implications for the future. On the one hand, there was the solid growth of new consumer-based industries. Automobiles and appliances were not passing fancies; their production and use became a part of the modern American way of life, creating a high standard of living that evoked the envy of the rest of the world. The future pattern of American culture—cars and suburbs, shopping centers and skyscrapers—was determined by the end of the 1920s.

But at the same time there were ominous signs of danger. The unequal distribution of wealth, the saturation of the market for consumer goods, and the growing speculation all created economic instability. The boom of the twenties would end in a great crash; yet the achievements of the decade would survive even that dire experience to shape the future of American life.

The New Urban Culture

The city replaced the countryside as the focal point of American life in the 1920s. The 1920 census revealed that for the first time slightly more than half of the population lived in cities, defined broadly to include all places of more than 2500 people. During the decade, the metropolitan areas grew rapidly as both whites and blacks from rural areas came seeking jobs in the new consumer industries. Between 1920 and 1930 cities with populations of 250,000 or more had added some 8 million people to their ranks. New York alone grew by nearly 25 percent, while Detroit more than doubled its population during the decade.

The skyscraper soon became the most visible feature of the city. Faced with inflated land prices, builders turned upward—developing a distinctively American architectural style in the process. New York led the way with the ornate Woolworth Building in 1913. The sleek 102-story Empire State Building, completed in 1930, was for years the tallest building in the world. Other cities erected their own jagged skylines. By 1929, there were 377 buildings over 20 stories tall across the nation. Most significantly, the skyscraper came to symbolize the new mass culture. "The New York skyscrapers are the most striking manifestation of the triumph of numbers," wrote one French observer. "One cannot understand or like them without first having tasted and enjoyed the thrill of counting or adding up enormous totals and of living in a gigantic, compact and brilliant world."

In the metropolis, life was different. The old community ties of home, church, and school were loosening, but there were important gains—new ideas, new creativity, new perspectives. Some city dwellers became lost and lonely without the old institutions; others thrived in the urban environment.

■ *Its 102 stories rising 1250 feet into the sky (222 feet were added in 1950), the Empire State Building had space for 25,000 tenants.*

creased, and even though women earned nearly one third of all graduate degrees, only 4 percent of the full professors were female. For the most part, the professions were reserved for men, with women relegated to such stereotypical fields as teaching and nursing.

To be sure, women had won the right to vote in 1919, but the Nineteenth Amendment proved to have less impact than its proponents had hoped. Once achieved, it robbed women of a unifying cause, and the suffrage itself did little to change the prevailing sex roles in society. Men remained the principal breadwinners in the family; women cooked, cleaned, and reared the children. "The creation and fulfillment of a successful home," a *Ladies Home Journal* writer advised women, "is a bit of craftsmanship that compares favorably with building a beautiful cathedral."

■
One of the hard-won rights that women finally realized in 1920 was the right to vote, celebrated here in a cover from Leslie's Illustrated Weekly Newspaper.

Family Life in the 1920s

The urban culture of the 1920s witnessed important changes in the American family. This vital institution began to break down under the impact of economic and social change. A new freedom for women and children seemed to be emerging in its wake.

Women had already begun to leave the home in the early twentieth century as the second Industrial Revolution opened up new jobs for them. World War I speeded up the process, but in the 1920s there was no great permanent gain in the number of working women. Although two million more women were employed in 1930 than in 1920, this represented an increase of only 1 percent. Most women workers, moreover, had lower-paying jobs, ranging from stenographers to maids. The number of women doctors actually de-

The feminist movement, however, still showed signs of vitality in the 1920s. One group, led by Alice Paul's National Woman's Party (NWP), lobbied for full equality for women under the law. In 1923, the NWP succeeded in having an Equal Rights Amendment introduced in Congress. The amendment stated: "Men and women shall have equal rights throughout the United States and every place subject to its jurisdiction." Other women's organizations, notably the League of

Women Voters, opposed the amendment on the grounds that women needed legal protection, especially laws guaranteeing them at least a minimum wage and limiting the maximum length of the workday.

The drive for the ERA failed in the twenties, but social feminists were more successful in pushing for humanitarian reform, notably the Sheppard-Towner Act of 1921 which provided for federal aid to establish state programs for maternal and infant health care. Although the failure to enact the child-labor amendment in 1925 marked the beginning of a decline in humanitarian reform, for the rest of the decade women's groups continued to work for good-government measures, for the inclusion of women on juries, and for consumer legislation.

A generational change had a profound impact on feminism in the 1920s. Instead of crusading for social progress, young women concentrated on individual self-expression by rebelling against Victorian restraints. Some quickly adopted what critic H. L. Mencken called the flapper image, portrayed most strikingly by artist John Held, Jr. Cutting their hair short, raising their skirts above the knee, and binding their breasts, "flappers" set out to compete on equal terms with men on the golf course and in the speakeasy. Young women delighted in shocking their elders—they rouged their cheeks and danced the Charleston. For the first time, women smoked cigarettes and drank alcohol in public. The flappers assaulted the traditional double standard in sex, demanding that equality with men should include sexual fulfillment before and during marriage. The new permissiveness led to a sharp rise in the divorce rate; by 1928, there were 166 divorces for every 1000 marriages, compared to only 81 in 1900.

The sense of woman's emancipation was heightened by a drop in the birthrate and the abundance of consumer goods. With fewer children to care for and with washing machines and vacuum cleaners to ease their household labor, women of the 1920s seemed to have more leisure time. Yet appearances were deceptive. Advertisers eagerly sought out women as buyers of consumer products, but wives exercised purchasing power only as delegated by their husbands. Many women could not enjoy the new labor-saving devices—one fourth of the homes in Cleveland lacked running water in the twenties, and three

John Held, Jr.'s Sweet Girl Graduate combined the innocence of ruffled skirts with the sophistication of rouged cheeks, bobbed hair, and long cigarette.

quarters of the nation's families did not have washing machines. The typical childless woman spent between forty-three and fifty hours a week on household duties; for mothers, the average work week was fifty-six hours, far longer than that of their husbands. And despite the talk of the "new woman," the flappers fell victim to the sex-role conditioning of their parents. Boys continued to play with guns and grew up to head their families; girls played with dolls and looked forward to careers as wives and mothers. "In the 1920s, as in the 1790s," concluded historian June Sochen, "marriage was the only approved state for women."

The family, however, did change. It became smaller as new techniques of birth control enabled couples to limit their offspring. More and more married women took jobs outside the home, bringing in an income and gaining a measure of independence (although their rate of pay was always lower than that for men). Young people, who had once joined the labor force when they entered their teens, now discovered adolescence as a stage of life. A high-school education was no longer uncommon, and college attendance increased.

This prolonged adolescence led to new strains on the family in the form of youthful revolt. Freed of the traditional burden of earning a living at an early age, youth in the 1920s went on a great spree. Heavy drinking, casual sex encounters, and a constant search for excitement became the hallmarks of the upper-class youth immortalized by F. Scott Fitzgerald. "I have been kissed by dozens of men," one of his characters commented. "I suppose I'll kiss dozens more." The theme of rebellion against parental authority, which runs through all aspects of the 1920s, was at the heart of the youth movement.

■ "It's broccoli, dear." "I say it's spinach, and I say the hell with it." This New Yorker cartoon captures perfectly the spirit of the '20s.

■ In the George Bellows painting (right), Argentina's Luis Firpo knocks Jack Dempsey out of the ring. Dempsey came back to win the fight in the second round.

Frivolity and excitement ran high in the cities as crime waves and highly publicized sports events flourished. Prohibition ushered in such distinctive features of the decade as speakeasies, bootleggers, and bathtub gin. Crime rose sharply as middle- and upper-class Americans willingly broke the law to gain access to alcoholic beverages. City streets became the scene of violent shootouts between rival bootleggers; by 1929, Chicago had witnessed over five hundred gangland murders. Underworld czars like Al Capone controlled illicit empires; Capone's produced revenue of $60 million a year.

Sports became a national mania in the 1920s as people found more leisure time. Golf boomed, with some two million men and women playing on nearly five thousand courses across the country. Spectator sports attracted even more attention. Boxing drew huge crowds to see fighters like Jack Dempsey and Gene Tunney. Baseball attendance soared. More than twenty million fans attended games in 1927, the year Babe Ruth became a national idol by hitting sixty home runs. On college campuses, football became more popular than ever. Universities vied with each other in building massive stadiums, seating upward of seventy thousand people.

In what Frederick Lewis Allen called "the ballyhoo years," the popular yearning for excitement led people to seek vicarious thrills in all kinds of ways—applauding Charles Lindbergh's solo flight

Lindbergh Flies the Atlantic

At 7:52 A.M., Friday, May 20, 1927, Charles A. Lindbergh took off in the *Spirit of St. Louis*, a small single-engine airplane, from Roosevelt Field on Long Island. It was the first break in the weather after a long week of waiting in New York. Thirty-three hours and thirty minutes later, he landed at Le Bourget Aerodrome just outside Paris, completing the first solo Atlantic crossing in a heavier-than-air craft and winning the $25,000 Orteig Prize for the first nonstop flight between New York and Paris.

Lindbergh had been the dark horse in the transatlantic race. His career as a barnstormer, army air corps reserve officer, and air mail pilot could not compare to the reputations of the famous explorers and war aces planning to make the flight, and his late arrival among the ranks of the competitors relegated him to the back pages of newspapers. But a series of disasters befell the larger, more expensive multiengined aircraft flown by his better-known rivals, opening the way for this latecomer. Reporters, impressed by a pilot flying solo in a comparatively inexpensive single-engine plane, nicknamed Lindbergh "the Flyin' Fool."

More than a hundred thousand people awaited his landing at Le Bourget. Lindbergh was carried off on the shoulders of the crowd before his feet touched French soil. He was feted by the French people, decorated by their government and, when he flew on to Belgium and England, received similar laurels. Upon returning to the United States, Lindbergh led a parade through Washington, D. C.; at its end, he joined President and Mrs. Coolidge on a large reviewing stand at the base of the Washington Monument. Cheering crowds filled the Capitol Mall. In an uncharacteristically long and glowing speech, Coolidge described the young pilot's achievement as another chapter in "the same story of valor and victory by a son of the people that shines through every page of American history." At the conclusion of his address, Coolidge presented Lindbergh with the Distinguished Flying Cross, the first of such medals to be bestowed upon an American aviator. Two days later, in New York, there was another parade; police estimated the crowd to be in excess of 3 million, and Lindbergh received similar if somewhat smaller receptions throughout the country on his forty-eight-state tour. Lindbergh's flight had captured the imagination of the American people.

But the public fascination with Lindbergh and his flight represented more than the preoccupation with adventure and excitement so common in the 1920s. It was not just hero worship. To Europeans, Lindbergh was an unofficial goodwill ambassador whose bravery enhanced the American image in Europe. To his fellow citizens, he personified traditional American virtues in the modern industrial world.

Lindbergh's flight, as the President noted, *was* a shining example of the American tradition of individual initiative and self-reliance. The press reveled in Lindbergh's "conquest," describing him in terms reminiscent of those used in the winning of the West: as a "pioneer" of aviation opening a new "frontier." The theme was heroic individualism. Such references to America's hallowed past demonstrated a continuity between the values that had made America great and Lindbergh's successful Atlantic crossing. Industrialization and urbanization in the twentieth century had not sapped the American spirit, as many had feared. The nation could rejoice in the vitality of traditional American virtues.

But that was only half the story. While the pilot may have embodied what many Americans considered best in the past, his plane was a product of the technological and industrial progress that was their future. Lindbergh did not attribute his success merely to individual effort; the plane that carried him to France was, in his own words, "the culmination of twenty years of aeronautical research." Giving the *Spirit of St. Louis* its due, he entitled his autobiographical account *We*, referring to his plane and himself as partners in an epochal achievement. In his Washington address, Coolidge praised "American genius and industry" as the "silent partner" in Lindbergh's flight.

The significance of Charles Lindbergh's flight lay in harmonizing America's past with its future —the integration of a tradition of individual initiative with progress, technology, and industry. Lindbergh and the *Spirit of St. Louis* represented the best of both worlds. The days of the self-sufficient individual as an American norm may have ended, but modern America now at least had a symbolic manifestation that the cherished ideal still lived. Lindbergh's flight, moreover, provided an exciting look into the ever greater human command of the machine. (The picture below is of the enthusiastic reception Lindbergh received at Croydon, England.)

across the Atlantic, cheering Gertrude Ederle's swim across the English Channel, and flocking to such bizarre events as six-day bicycle races, dance marathons, and flagpole-sittings. It was a time of pure pleasure-seeking, when people sought to escape from the increasingly drab world of the assembly line by worshiping heroic individuals.

Sex became another focal point in the 1920s as Victorian standards began to crumble. Sophisticated city dwellers seemed to be intent on exploring a new freedom in sexual expression. Plays and novels focused on adultery, and the new urban tabloids—led by the *New York Daily News*—delighted in telling their readers about love nests and kept women. The popular songs of the decade, like "Hot Lips" and "Burning Kisses," were less romantic and more explicit. Hollywood exploited the obsession with sex by producing movies with such provocative titles as *Up in Mable's Room, A Shocking Night,* and *Women and Lovers.* Theda Bara and Clara Bow, the "vamp" and the "it" girl, set the model for feminine seductiveness while Rudolph Valentino became the heartthrob of millions of American women. Young people embraced the new permissiveness joyfully, with the automobile giving couples an easy way to escape parental supervision.

There is considerable debate, however, over the extent of the sexual revolution in the '20s. Later

■ *Clara Bow was selected by author Elinor Glyn as the girl with "It"—a quality defined as "that strange magnetism which attracts both sexes."*

studies by Dr. Alfred C. Kinsey (see the special feature in chapter 29) showed that premarital intercourse was twice as common among women born after 1900 than for those born before the turn of the century. But a contemporary survey of over two thousand middle-class women by Katherine B. Davis found that only 7 percent of those who were married had had sexual relations before marriage and that only 14 percent of the single women had engaged in intercourse. Actual changes in sexual behavior are beyond the historian's reach, hidden in the privacy of the bedroom, but the old Victorian prudery was a clear casualty of the 1920s. Sex was no longer a taboo subject; men and women now could and did discuss it openly.

The Literary Flowering

The greatest cultural advance of the 1920s was the outpouring of literature. The city gave rise to a new class of intellectuals—writers who commented on the new industrial society. Many had been uprooted by World War I. They were bewildered by the rapidly changing social patterns of the 1920s and appalled by the materialism of American culture. Some fled to Europe to live as expatriates, congregating in Paris cafes to bemoan the loss of American innocence and purity. Others stayed at home, observing and condemning the excesses of a business civilization. All shared a sense of disillusionment and wrote pessimistically of the flawed promise of American life. Yet, ironically, their body of writing revealed a profound creativity that suggested that America was coming of age intellectually.

The exiles included the poets Ezra Pound and T. S. Eliot and the novelist Ernest Hemingway. Pound discarded rhyme and meter in a search for clear, cold images that conveyed reality. Like many of the writers of the 1920s, he reacted against World War I, expressing a deep regret for the tragic waste of a whole generation in defense of a "botched civilization."

Eliot, who was born in Missouri but became a British citizen, displayed even more profound despair. In *The Waste Land,* which appeared in 1922, he evoked images of fragmentation and sterility that had a powerful impact on the other disillusioned writers of the decade. He reached the depths in *The Hollow Men* (1925), a biting description of the emptiness of modern man.

Ernest Hemingway sought redemption from the modern plight in the romantic individualism of his heroes. Preoccupied with violence, he wrote of men alienated from society who found a sense of identity in their own courage and quest for personal honor. His own experiences, ranging from driving an ambulance in the war to stalking lions in Africa, made him a legendary figure; his greatest impact on other writers, however, came from his sparse, direct, and clean prose style.

The writers who stayed home were equally disdainful of contemporary American life. F. Scott Fitzgerald chronicled American youth in *This Side of Paradise* (1920) and *The Great Gatsby* (1925), writing in bittersweet prose about "the beautiful and the damned." Amid the glitter of life among the wealthy on Long Island's North Shore came the haunting realization of emptiness and lack of human concern.

Sinclair Lewis became the most popular of the critical novelists. *Main Street*, published in 1920, satirized the values of small-town America as dull, complacent, and narrow-minded; *Babbitt*, which appeared two years later, poked fun at the commercialism of the 1920s, portraying George Babbitt as the stereotype of the energetic, go-getting businessman who hailed the decade as a New Era.

Most savage of all was H. L. Mencken, the Baltimore newspaperman and literary critic who founded the *American Mercury* in 1923. Declaring war on the "homo boobiens," Mencken mocked everything he found distasteful in America from the Rotary Club to the Ku Klux Klan. "From Boy Scouts, and from Home Cooking, from Odd Fellows' funerals, from Socialists, from Christians—Good Lord, deliver us," he pleaded. It was not difficult to discover what Mencken disliked; the hard part was finding out what he affirmed, other than wit and a clever turn of phrase. A born cynic, he served as a zealous guardian of public integrity in an era of excessive boosterism.

The cultural explosion of the 1920s was surprisingly broad. It included novelists like Sherwood Anderson and John Dos Passos—who described the way the new machine age undermined such traditional American values as craftsmanship and a sense of community—and

Chronicler of the Jazz Age, F. Scott Fitzgerald, shown here (above) with his wife Zelda and daughter Scottie, became a living symbol of the era.

The novels and short stories of Edith Wharton (right) are noted for their careful structure and penetrating social satire.

playwrights such as Eugene O'Neill, Maxwell Anderson, and Elmer Rice who added greatly to the stature of American theater. Women writers were particularly effective in dealing with regional themes. Edith Wharton continued to write penetratingly about eastern aristocrats in books like *The Age of Innocence* (1921), while Willa Cather and Ellen Glasgow focused on the plight of women in the Midwest and the South respectively in their short stories and novels. These writers portrayed their heroines in the traditional roles of wives and mothers, but playwright Zona Gale (who won the Pulitzer Prize for drama in 1920 for *Miss Lulu Bett*) used her title character to depict the dilemmas facing an unmarried woman in American society.

Art and music lagged behind literature but still made significant advances. Edward Hopper and Charles Burchfield captured the ugliness of city life and the loneliness of its inhabitants in their realistic paintings. Aaron Copland and George Gershwin added a new vitality to American music, but the greatest contribution came from the spread of jazz as blacks migrated northward—first to Saint Louis, Kansas City, and Chicago, and finally to New York. The form of jazz known as the blues, so expressive of the suffering of American blacks, became an authentic national folk music, and performers like Louis Armstrong enjoyed worldwide popularity.

The cultural growth of the 1920s was the work of blacks as well as whites. W. E. B. Du Bois, the editor of *Crisis*, became the intellectual voice of the black community developing in New York City's Harlem. In 1917, James Weldon Johnson, who had been a professor of literature at Fisk University, published *Fifty Years and Other Poems* in which the title poem commented on the half-century of suffering that had followed the Emancipation Proclamation. As other black writers gathered around them, Du Bois and Johnson became the leaders of the Harlem Renaissance. The NAACP moved its headquarters to Harlem, and in 1923 the Urban League began publishing *Opportunity*, a magazine devoted to scholarly studies of racial issues.

A black literary flowering quickly developed. In 1922, critics hailed the appearance of Claude McKay's book of verses, *White Shadows*. In stark images, McKay expressed both his resentment against racial injustice and his pride in blackness. Countee Cullen and Langston Hughes won critical acclaim for the beauty of their poems and the eloquence of their portrayal of the black tragedy.

Art and music also flourished during Harlem's golden age. Plays and concerts at the 135th Street YMCA; floor shows at Happy Rhone's nightclub (attended by many white celebrities); rent parties where jazz musicians played to raise money for writers, artists, and neighbors to help them pay their bills—all were part of the ferment that made Harlem "the Negro Capital of the World" in the 1920s. "Almost everything seemed possible above 125th Street in the early twenties for these Americans who were determined to thrive separately to better proclaim the ideals of integration," comments historian David Lewis. "You could be black and proud, politically assertive and economically independent, creative and disciplined—or so it seemed."

Although its most famous writers were identified with New York's Harlem, the new black cultural awareness spread to other cities in the form of poetry circles and theater groups. The number of black college graduates rose from 391 in 1920 to 1903 by 1929. Although blacks were still an oppressed minority in American life, a few were beginning in the 1920s to take the first steps toward achieving cultural and intellectual fulfillment.

In retrospect, there is a striking paradox about the literary flowering of the twenties. Nearly all the writers, black as well as white, cried out against the conformity and materialism of the contemporary scene. They were critical of mass production and reliance on the machine; they wrote wistfully of the disappearance of the artisan and of a more relaxed way of life. Few took any interest in politics or in social reform. They retreated instead into individualism, seeking an escape from the prevailing business civilization in their art. Whether they went abroad or stayed home, the writers of the '20s turned inward to avoid being swept up in the consumer-goods revolution. Yet despite their withdrawal, and indeed perhaps because of it, they produced an astonishingly rich and varied body of work. American writing had a greater intensity and depth than in the past; American writers, despite their alienation, had placed their country in the forefront of world literature.

The Rural Counterattack

Dominance by the urban centers led to a response that produced an ugly side of the twenties—a side where prejudice and bigotry, hate and intolerance flourished. For millions of Americans who lived in the countryside, either on farms or in small towns, the city came to represent all that was evil in contemporary life. Largely Anglo-Saxon and steeped in traditional Protestantism, these rural folk condemned the urban-centered crime, radicalism, and modernism which they felt were threatening their own way of life. Saloons, whorehouses, little Italys and little Polands, Communist cells, free love, and atheism—all were identified with the city. As the urban areas grew in population and influence, the countryside struck back in a deliberate if doomed attempt to restore a lost purity to American life.

Other factors contributed to the intensity of rural counterattack. The war had unleashed a nationalistic spirit that craved unity and conformity. In a nation where one third of the people were foreign-born, the attack on immigrants and the call for 100 percent Americanism took on a frightening zeal. When the war was over, groups like the American Legion tried to root out "un-American" behavior and insisted on cultural as well as political conformity. And the prewar progressive reform spirit added to the social tension. Stripped of much of its former idealism, progressivism focused on such social problems as drinking and illiteracy to justify repressive measures like Prohibition and immigration restriction. The result was tragic. Amid the emergence of a new urban culture, a wave of rural-inspired movements sought to preserve the values of an earlier America. They succeeded only in complicating life in an already difficult period of cultural transition.

The "Red Scare"

The first and most intense outbreak of national alarm came in 1919. The heightened nationalism of World War I, aimed at achieving unity at the expense of ethnic diversity, found a new target in bolshevism. The Russian Revolution and the triumph of Marxism frightened many Americans. A growing turn to communism among American radicals (especially the foreign-born) accelerated the fears, although the numbers involved were tiny—at most there were sixty thousand Communists in the United States in 1919. But they were located in the cities, and their influence appeared to be magnified with the outbreak of widespread labor unrest.

A general strike in Seattle, a police strike in Boston, and a violent strike in the iron and steel industry thoroughly alarmed the American people in the spring and summer of 1919. A series of bombings led to panic. First the mayor of strike-bound Seattle received a small brown package containing a homemade bomb; then an alert New York postal employee detected sixteen bombs addressed to a variety of famous citizens (includ-

"UNGRATEFUL SCUM!"

■ *With flagrant disregard for due process of law and basic civil liberties, Attorney General A. Mitchell Palmer ordered raids on "dangerous aliens" and "foreign subversives."*

ing John D. Rockefeller); and finally, on June 2, a bomb shattered the front of Attorney General A. Mitchell Palmer's home. Although the man who delivered it was blown to pieces, authorities quickly identified him as an Italian anarchist from Philadelphia.

In the ensuing public outcry, Attorney General Palmer led the attack on the alien threat. A Quaker and progressive, Palmer abandoned his earlier liberalism to launch a massive roundup of foreign-born radicals. In a series of raids that began on November 7, federal agents seized suspected anarchists and Communists and held them for deportation with no regard for due process of law. In December, 249 aliens—including such well-known radical leaders as Emma Goldman and Alexander Berkman—were sent to Russia aboard the *Buford*, dubbed the "Soviet Ark" by the press. Nearly all were innocent of the charges against them. A month later, Palmer rounded up nearly four thousand suspected Communists in a single evening. Federal

agents broke into homes, meeting halls, and union offices without search warrants. Many native-born Americans were caught in the dragnet and spent several days in jail before being released; aliens rounded up were deported without hearings or trials.

For a time, it seemed that this Red Scare reflected the prevailing views of the American people. Instead of condemning their government's action, citizens voiced their approval and even urged more drastic steps. One patriot said his solution to the alien problem was simple: "S.O.S.—ship or shoot." General Leonard Wood, the army chief of staff, favored placing Bolsheviks on "ships of stone with sails of lead," while evangelist Billy Sunday preferred to take "these ornery, wild-eyed Socialists" and "stand them up before a firing squad and save space on our ships." Inflamed by public statements like these, a group of legionnaires in Centralia, Washington, dragged a radical from the town jail, castrated him, and hanged him from a railway bridge. The coroner's report blandly stated that the victim "jumped off with a rope around his neck and then shot himself full of holes."

The very extremism of the Red Scare led to its rapid demise. Courageous government officials in the Department of Labor insisted on due process and full hearings before anyone else was deported. Prominent public leaders began to speak out against the acts of terror. Charles Evans Hughes, the defeated GOP candidate in 1916, offered to defend six Socialists expelled from the New York legislature; Ohio Senator Warren G. Harding, the embodiment of middle-class values, expressed his opinion that "too much has been said about bolshevism in America." Finally, Palmer himself, with evident presidential ambition, went too far. In April 1920, he warned of a vast revolution to occur on May 1; the entire New York City police force, some eleven thousand strong, was placed on duty. When no bombings or violence took place on May Day, the public began to react against Palmer's hysteria. Despite a violent explosion on Wall Street in September that killed thirty-three people, the Red Scare died out by the end of 1920. Palmer passed into obscurity, the tiny Communist party became torn with factionalism, and the American people tried hard to forget their momentary loss of balance.

Yet the Red Scare exerted a continuing influence on American society in the 1920s. The foreign-born lived in the uneasy realization that they were viewed with hostility and suspicion. Two Italian aliens in Massachusetts, Nicola Sacco and Bartolomeo Vanzetti, were arrested in May 1920 for a payroll robbery and murder. They faced a prosecutor and jury who condemned them more for their ideas than for any evidence of criminal conduct and a judge who referred to them as "those anarchist bastards." Despite a worldwide effort that became the chief liberal cause of the 1920s, the courts rejected all appeals. Sacco and Vanzetti, a shoemaker and a fish peddler, died in the electric chair on August 23, 1927. Their fate symbolized the bigotry and intolerance that lasted through the '20s and made this decade one of the least attractive in American history.

■ *Ben Shahn's* The Passion of Sacco and Vanzetti *(1931–1932) depicts the members of the committee who investigated the trial and confirmed its fairness.*

Prohibition

In December 1917, Congress adopted the Eighteenth Amendment, prohibiting the manufacture and sale of alcoholic beverages. A little over a year later, Nebraska became the necessary thirty-sixth state to ratify, and Prohibition became the law of the land.

As implemented under the Volstead Act, beginning January 16, 1920, it was illegal for anyone to make, sell, or transport any drink that contained more than half of 1 percent alcohol by volume. Prohibition was the result of both a rural effort of the Anti-Saloon League, backed by Methodist and Baptist clergymen, and the urban Progressive concern over the social disease of drunkenness, especially among industrial workers. The moral issue had already led to the enactment of Prohibition laws in twenty-six states by 1920; the real tragedy would occur in the effort to extend this "noble experiment" to the growing cities, where it was deeply resented by ethnic groups like the Germans and the Irish and nearly totally disregarded by the well-to-do and the sophisticated.

Prohibition did in fact lead to a decline in drinking. Americans consumed much less alcohol in the twenties than in the prewar years. Rural areas became totally dry, and in the cities the consumption of alcoholic beverages dropped sharply among the lower classes, who could not afford the high prices for bootleg liquor. Among the middle class and the wealthy, however, drinking became fashionable. Bootleggers supplied whiskey, which quickly replaced lighter spirits like wine and beer. The alcohol was either smuggled from abroad (a $40-million business by 1924) or illicitly manufactured in America. Such exotic products as Jackass Brandy, Soda Pop Moon, and Yack Yack Bourbon were common—and all could be fatal. Despite the risk of illness or death, Americans consumed some 150 million quarts of liquor a year in the twenties as bootleggers took in nearly $2 billion annually, about 2 percent of the gross national product.

Urban resistance to Prohibition finally led to its repeal in 1933. But in the intervening years, it damaged American society by breeding a profound disrespect for the law. The flamboyant excesses of bootleggers were only the more obvious evils spawned by Prohibition. In city after city, police openly tolerated the traffic in liquor, and judges and prosecutors agreed to let bootleggers pay merely token fines, creating almost a system of licenses. The countryside felt vindicated, yet rural and urban America alike suffered from this overzealous attempt to legislate morals.

The Ku Klux Klan

The most ominous expression of rural protest against the city was the rebirth of the Ku Klux Klan. On Thanksgiving night in 1915, on Stone Mountain in Georgia, Colonel William J. Simmons and thirty-four followers founded the modern Klan. Only "native born, white, gentile Americans" were permitted to join "the Invisible Empire, Knights of the Ku Klux Klan." Membership grew slowly during World War I, but after 1920, fueled by postwar fears and shrewd promotional techniques, the Klan mushroomed. In villages, towns, and small cities across the South and West, Anglo-Saxon Protestant men flocked into the newly formed chapters, seeking to relieve their anxiety over a changing society by embracing the weird rituals and by demonstrating their hatred against blacks, aliens, Jews, and Catholics.

The Klan of the 1920s, unlike the night riders of the post-Civil War era, was not just antiblack; the threat to American culture, as Klansmen perceived it, came from aliens—Italians and Russians, Jews and Catholics. They attributed much of the tension and conflict in society to the prewar flood of immigrants, foreigners who spoke different languages, worshiped in strange churches, and lived in distant, threatening cities. The Klansmen struck back by coming together and enforcing their own values. They punished blacks who did not know their place, women who practiced the new morality, and aliens who refused to conform. Beating, flogging, burning with acid—even murder—were condoned. But they also tried more peaceful methods of coercion, formulating codes of behavior and seeking communitywide support.

The Klan entered politics, at first hesitantly, then with growing confidence. The KKK gained control of the legislatures in Texas, Oklahoma, Oregon, and Indiana; in 1924, it blocked a resolution of censure at the Democratic National Convention. With nearly five million members by the mid-1920s, the Klan seemed to be fully established.

Its appeal lay in the sanctuary it offered to insecure and anxious people. Protestant to the core, the members found in the local Klavern a reassurance missing in their churches. The poor and ignorant became enchanted with the titles, ranging from Imperial Wizard to Grand Dragon, and gloried in the ritual that centered around the letter "K." Thus each Klan had its own Klalendar, held its weekly Klonklave in the local Klavern, and followed the rules set forth in the Kloran. Members found a sense of identity in the group activities, whether they were peaceful picnics, ominous parades in white robes, or fiery cross-burnings at night.

Although it was a male organization, the Klan did not neglect the family. There was a Women's Order, a Junior Order for boys, and a Tri-K Klub for girls. Members had to be born in America, but foreign-born Protestants were allowed to join a special Krusaders affiliate. Only blacks, Catholics, Jews, and prostitutes were beyond redemption to these lonely and anxious men who came together to chant:

> United we stick
> Divided we're stuck.
> The better we stick
> The better we Klux!

The Klan fell even more quickly than it rose. Its more violent activities—which included kidnap-

■ *A KKK initiation ceremony. Only native-born white Americans "who believe in the tenets of the Christian religion" were admitted into the Klan.*

ing, lynching, setting fire to synagogues and Catholic churches, and in one case, the murder of a priest—began to offend the nation's conscience. Misuse of funds and sexual scandals among Klan leaders, notably in Indiana, repelled many of the rank and file; effective counterattacks by traditional politicians ousted the KKK from control in Texas and Oklahoma. Membership declined sharply after 1925; by the end of the decade, the Klan had virtually disappeared. But its spirit lived on, testimony to the recurring demons of nativism and hatred that have surfaced periodically throughout the American experience.

Immigration Restriction

The nativism that permeated the Klan found its most successful outlet in the immigration legislation of the 1920s. The sharp increase in immigration in the late nineteenth century had led to a broad-based movement, spearheaded by organized labor and by New England aristocrats like Henry Cabot Lodge, to restrict the flow of people from Europe. In 1917, over Wilson's veto, Congress enacted a literacy test which reduced the number of immigrants. The war caused a much more drastic decline—from an average of 1 million a year between 1900 and 1914 to only 110,000 in 1918.

After the armistice, however, rumors began to spread of an impending flood of people seeking to escape war-ravaged Europe. Kenneth Roberts, a popular historical novelist, warned that all Europe was on the move, with only the limits of available steamship space likely to stem the flow. Worried congressmen spoke of a "barbarian horde" and a "foreign tide" that would inundate the United States with "dangerous and deadly enemies of the country." Even though the actual number of immigrants, 810,000 in 1920 (less than the prewar yearly average), did not match these projections, Congress responded in 1921 by passing an emergency immigration act. The new quota system restricted immigration from Europe to 3 percent of the number of nationals from each country living in the United States in 1910.

The 1921 act failed to satisfy the nativists. The quotas still permitted more than 500,000 Europeans to come to the United States in 1923, nearly half of them from southern and eastern Europe. The declining percentage of Nordic immigrants alarmed writers like Madison Grant, who warned the American people that the Anglo-Saxon stock that had founded the nation was about to be overwhelmed by lesser breeds with inferior genes. "These immigrants adopt the language of the native American, they wear his clothes and are beginning to take his women, but they seldom adopt his religion or understand his ideals," Grant wrote.

Psychologists, relying on primitive IQ tests used by the army in World War I, confirmed this judgment (see the special feature on "Measuring the Mind" in chapter 24). One senator claimed that all the nation's ills were due to an "intermingled and mongrelized people" as he demanded that racial purity replace the older reliance on the melting pot. In 1924, Congress adopted the National Origins Quota Act, which limited immigration from Europe to 150,000 a year; allocated most of the places to immigrants from Great Britain, Ireland, Germany, and Scandinavia; and banned all Oriental immigrants. The measure passed Congress with overwhelming rural support; not a single congressman south of the Mason-Dixon line or west of the Mississippi River voted against it.

The new restrictive legislation marked the most enduring achievement of the rural counterattack. Unlike the Red Scare, Prohibition, and the Klan, the quota system would survive until the 1960s, enforcing a racist bias that excluded Asians and limited the immigration of Italians, Greeks, and Poles to a few thousand a year while permitting a steady stream of Irish, English, and Scandinavian immigrants. The large corporations, no longer dependent on armies of unskilled immigrant workers, did not object to the 1924 law; the machine had replaced the immigrant on the assembly line. Yet even here the rural victory was not complete. A growing tide of Mexican laborers, exempt from the quota act, flowed northward across the Rio Grande to fill the continuing need for unskilled workers on the farms and in the service trades. The Mexican immigrants, as many as 100,000 a year, marked the strengthening of an element in our national ethnic mosaic that would grow in size and influence until it became a major force in modern American society.

The Fundamentalist Controversy

The most famous of all the rural attacks on the new urban culture was the Scopes trial held in Dayton, Tennessee. There in 1925, William Jennings Bryan, who had unsuccessfully run for president several times in previous decades, engaged in a crusade against the theory of evolution, appearing as a chief witness against John Scopes, a high-school biology teacher who had initiated the case by deliberately violating a new Tennessee law that forbade the teaching of Darwin's theory.

In the trial, Bryan testified under oath that he believed Jonah had been swallowed by a big fish and declared, "It is better to trust in the Rock of Ages than in the age of rocks." Chicago defense attorney Clarence Darrow succeeded in making Bryan look ridiculous. The court found Scopes guilty but let him off with a token fine; Bryan, exhausted by his efforts, died a few days later. H. L. Mencken, who covered the trail in person, rejoiced in the belief that fundamentalism was dead.

GATHERING DATA FOR THE TENNESSEE TRIAL

■ *Religious fundamentalism, which experienced a rebirth of popularity after World War I, clashed with current scientific theory in the Scopes trial.*

In reality, however, the traditional rural religious beliefs were stronger than ever. As middle- and upper-class Americans drifted into a genteel Christianity which stressed good works and respectability, the Baptist and Methodist churches continued to hold on to the old faith. In addition, aggressive fundamentalist sects such as the Churches of Christ, the Pentecostals, and Jehovah's Witnesses grew rapidly. The number of churches actually declined during the decade but church membership increased from 41.9 million in 1916 to 54.5 million in 1926. More and more rural dwellers drove their cars into town instead of going to the local crossroads chapel.

Many of those who came to the city in the twenties brought their religious beliefs with them and found new outlets for their traditional ideas. Thus evangelist Aimee Semple McPherson enjoyed amazing success in Los Angeles with her "Four-Square Gospel," building the Angelus Temple to seat over five thousand worshipers. And in Fort Worth, the Reverend J. Frank Norris erected a six-thousand-seat sanctuary for the First Baptist Church, bathing it in spotlights so that it could be seen for thirty miles across the north Texas prairie.

Far from dying out, as divinity professor Thomas G. Oden noted, biblical fundamentalism retained "remarkable grass-roots strength among the organization men and the industrialized mass society of the 20th century." The rural counterattack, while challenged by the city, did enable some older American values to survive in the midst of the new mass-production culture.

Politics of the Twenties

The tensions between the city and the countryside also shaped the course of politics in the 1920s. On the surface, it was a Republican decade. The GOP controlled the White House from 1921 to 1933 and had majorities in both houses of Congress from 1918 to 1930. The Republicans used their return to power after World War I to halt further reform legislation and to establish a friendly relationship betwen government and business. Important shifts were taking place, however, in the American electorate. The Democrats, although divided into competing urban and rural wings, were laying the groundwork for the future by winning over millions of new voters, especially among the ethnic groups in the cities. The rising tide of urban voters indicated a fundamental shift away from the Republicans toward a new Democratic majority.

Harding, Coolidge, and Hoover

The Republicans regained the White House in 1920 with the election of Warren G. Harding of Ohio. A dark-horse contender, Harding won the GOP nomination when the convention deadlocked and he became the compromise choice. Handsome and dignified, Harding reflected both the virtues and blemishes of small-town America. Originally a newspaper publisher in Marion, he had made many friends and few enemies throughout his career as a legislator, lieutenant governor, and finally, after 1914, a United States senator. Conventional in outlook, Harding was a genial man who lacked the capacity to govern and who delegated power broadly as president.

He made some good cabinet choices, notably Charles Evans Hughes as secretary of state and Herbert C. Hoover as secretary of commerce, but two corrupt offficials—Attorney General Harry Daugherty and Secretary of the Interior Albert Fall—sabotaged his administration. Daugherty became involved in a series of questionable deals that led ultimately to his forced resignation; Fall was the chief figure in the Teapot Dome scandal. Two oil promoters gave Fall nearly $400,000 in loans and bribes; in return, he helped them secure leases on naval oil reserves in Elk Hills, California, and Teapot Dome, Wyoming. The scandal came to light after Harding's death from a heart attack in 1923. Fall eventually served a year in jail, and the reputation of the Harding administration never recovered.

Vice-President Calvin Coolidge assumed the presidency upon Harding's death, and his honesty and integrity quickly reassured the nation. Coolidge, born in Vermont of old Yankee stock, had first gained national attention in 1919 as governor of Massachusetts when he had dealt firmly with a Boston police strike by declaring, "There is no right to strike against the public safety by anybody, anywhere, any time." A reserved, reticent man, Coolidge became famous for his epigrams,

■ *In this cartoon, Attorney General Daugherty struggles to keep the skeletons of corruption—the scandals of the Harding administration—hidden in the closet.*

which contemporaries mistook for wisdom. "The business of America is business," he proclaimed. "The man who builds a factory builds a temple; the man who works there worships there." Consistent with this philosophy, he believed his duty was simply to preside benignly, not govern the nation. Calvin Coolidge, one observer noted, "aspired to become the least President the country ever had; he attained his desire." Satisfied with the prosperity of the mid-twenties, the people responded favorably. Coolidge was elected to a full term by a wide margin in 1924.

When Coolidge announced in 1927 that he did not "choose to run," Herbert Hoover became the Republican choice to succeed him. By far the ablest GOP leader of the decade, Hoover epitomized the American myth of the self-made man. Orphaned as a boy, he had worked his way through Stanford University and had gained both wealth and fame as a mining engineer. During World War I, he had displayed admirable administrative skills in directing Wilson's food program at home and relief activities abroad. Sober, intelli-

gent, and immensely hard-working, Hoover embodied the nation's faith in individualism and free enterprise.

As secretary of commerce under Harding and Coolidge, he had sought cooperation between government and business. He used his office to assist American manufacturers and exporters in expanding their overseas trade, and he strongly supported a trade association movement to encourage cooperation rather than cutthroat competition among smaller American companies. He did not view business and government as antagonists. Instead, he saw them as partners, working together to achieve efficiency and affluence for all Americans. His optimistic view of the future led him to declare in his speech accepting the Republican presidential nomination in 1928 that "we in America today are nearer to the final triumph over poverty than ever before in the history of any land."

Republican Policies

During the 1920 campaign, Warren Harding urged a return to "not heroism, but healing, not nostrums, but normalcy." Misreading his speechwriter's "normality," he coined a new word that became the theme for the Republican administrations of the '20s. Aware that the public was tired of zealous reform-minded presidents like Teddy Roosevelt and Woodrow Wilson, Harding and his successors sought a return to traditional Republican policies. In some areas they were successful, but in others they were forced to adjust to the new realities of a mass-production society. The result was a mixture of traditional and innovative measures that was neither wholly reactionary nor entirely progressive.

The most obvious attempt to go back to the Republicanism of William McKinley came in tariff and tax policy. Fearful of a flood of postwar European imports, Congress passed an emergency tariff act in 1921 and followed it a year later with the protectionist Fordney-McCumber Tariff Act. The net effect was to raise the basic rates substantially over the moderate Underwood Tariff schedules of the Wilson period.

Secretary of the Treasury Andrew Mellon, a wealthy Pittsburgh banker and industrialist, worked hard to achieve a similar return to

Calvin Coolidge hosts an informal press conference on the porch of his Vermont home. Reserved and aloof—a complete contrast to the affable Harding—Coolidge believed in silence and inactivity. "Four fifths of all our troubles in this life would disappear," he said, "if we would just sit down and be still."

"normalcy" in taxation. Condemning the high wartime tax rates on businesses and wealthy individuals, Mellon pressed for repealing an excess-profits tax on corporations and slashing personal rates on the very rich. Using the new budget system adopted by Congress in 1921, he reduced government spending from its World War I peak of $18 billion to just over $3 billion by 1925, thereby creating a slight surplus. Congress responded in 1926 by cutting the highest income-tax bracket to a modest 20 percent.

The revenue acts of the 1920s greatly reduced the burden of taxation; by the end of the decade, the government was collecting a third less than it had in 1921, and the number of people paying income taxes dropped from over 6.5 million to 4 million. Yet the greatest relief went to the wealthy. The public was shocked to learn in the 1930s that J. P. Morgan and his nineteen partners had paid no income tax at all during the depths of the Depression.

The growing crisis in American farming during the decade forced the Republican administrations to seek new solutions. The end of the European war led to a sharp decline in farm prices and a return to the problem of overproduction. South-ern and western lawmakers formed a farm bloc in Congress to press for special legislation for American agriculture. The farm bloc supported the higher tariffs, which included protection for constituents' crops, and helped secure passage of legislation to create federal supervision over stockyards, packinghouses, and grain trading.

This special-interest legislation failed to get at the root of overproduction, however. Farmers then supported more controversial measures designed to raise domestic crop prices by having the government sell the surplus overseas at low world prices. Coolidge vetoed the legislation on grounds that it involved unwarranted government interference in the economy.

Yet the government's role in the economy increased rather than lessened in the 1920s. Republicans widened the scope of federal activity and nearly doubled the ranks of government employees. Herbert Hoover led the way in the Commerce Department, establishing new bureaus to help make American industry more efficient in housing, transportation, and mining. Under his leadership, the government encouraged corporations to develop welfare programs that undercut trade unions, and he tried to minimize labor disturbances by devising new federal machinery to mediate disputes. Instead of going back to the laissez-faire tradition of the nineteenth century, the Republican administrations of the twenties were pioneering a close relationship betwen government and private business.

The Divided Democrats

While the Republicans ruled in the 1920s, the Democrats seemed bent on self-destruction. The Wilson coalition fell apart in 1920 as pent-up dissatisfaction stemming from the war enabled Harding to win by a landslide. The pace of the second Industrial Revolution and the growing urbanization in the twenties split the party in two. One faction centered in the rural South and West. Traditional Democrats who had supported Wilson stood for Prohibition, fundamentalism, the Klan, and other facets of the rural counterattack against the city. In contrast, a new breed of Democrat was emerging in the metropolitan areas of the North and Midwest. Immigrants and their descendants began to become active in the Democratic party. Catholic or Jewish in religion and strongly opposed to Prohibition, they had little in common with their rural counterparts.

The split within the party surfaced dramatically at the national convention in New York in 1924. Held in Madison Square Garden, a hall built in the 1890s and too small and cramped for the more than one thousand delegates, the convention soon degenerated into what one observer described as a "snarling, cursing, tenuous, suicidal, homicidal roughhouse." City slickers mocked the "rubes and hicks" from the "sticks"; populist orators struck back by denouncing the city as "wanting in national ideals, devoid of conscience . . . rooted in corruption, directed by greed and dominated by selfishness." An urban resolution to condemn the Ku Klux Klan led to a spirited response from the rural faction and its defeat by a single vote. Then for nine days, in the midst of a stifling heat wave, the delegates divided between Alfred E. Smith, the governor of New York, and William G. McAdoo of California, Wilson's secretary of the treasury. When it became clear that neither the city nor the rural candidate could win a majority, both men withdrew; on the 103rd ballot, the weary Demo-crats finally chose John W. Davis, a former West Virginia congressman and New York corporation lawyer, as their compromise nominee.

In the ensuing election, the conservative Davis had difficulty in distinguishing his views from those of Republican President Calvin Coolidge. For the discontented, Senator Robert LaFollette offered an alternative by running on an independent Progressive party ticket. Coolidge won the election easily, receiving fifteen million votes to eight million for Davis and nearly five million for LaFollette. Davis had made the poorest showing of any Democratic candidate in the twentieth century.

The Election of 1924

Candidate	Party	Popular Vote	Electoral Vote
Coolidge	Republican	15,717,553	382
Davis	Democrat	8,386,169	136
LaFollette	Progressive	4,814,050	13

Yet the Democrats were in far better shape than this setback indicated. Beginning in 1922, the party had made heavy inroads into the GOP majority in Congress. The Democrats took seventy-eight seats away from Republicans in that election, many of them in the cities of the East and Midwest. In New York alone, they gained thirteen new congressmen, all but one in districts with heavy immigrant populations. Even in 1924, the Republican vote in the nation's largest cities declined as many urban voters chose LaFollette in the absence of an attractive Democratic candidate. By 1926, the Democrats were within one vote of controlling the Senate and had picked up nine more seats in the House in metropolitan areas. The large cities were swinging clearly into the Democratic column; all the party needed was a charismatic leader who could fuse the older rural elements with the new urban voters.

The Election of 1928

The selection of Al Smith as the Democratic candidate in 1928 indicated the growing power of the city. Born on the lower east side of Manhattan of mixed Irish-German ancestry, Smith was the prototype of the urban Democrat. He was Catholic; he was associated with a big-city machine; he was a wet who wanted to end Prohibition. Starting out in the Fulton Fish Market as a boy, he had joined Tammany Hall and gradually climbed the political ladder, rising from subpoena server to state legislator to governor, a post he held with distinction for nearly a decade. Rejected by rural Democrats in 1924, he still had to prove that he could unite the South and West behind his leadership. His lack of education, poor grammar, and distinctive New York accent all hurt him, as did his eastern provincialism. When reporters asked him about his appeal in the states west of the Mississippi, he replied, "What states *are* west of the Mississippi?"

The choice facing the American voter in 1928 seemed unusually clear-cut. Herbert Hoover was a Protestant, a dry, and an old-stock American who stood for efficiency and individualism; Smith was a Catholic, a wet, and a descendant of immigrants who was closely associated with big-city politics. Just as Smith appealed to new voters in the cities, so Hoover won the support of many old-line Democrats who feared the city, Tammany Hall, and the pope.

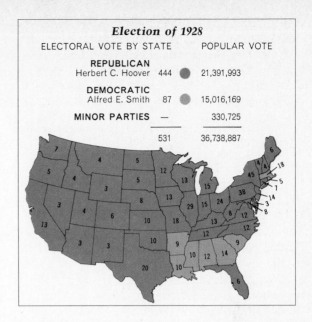

Election of 1928

ELECTORAL VOTE BY STATE		POPULAR VOTE
REPUBLICAN Herbert C. Hoover	444	21,391,993
DEMOCRATIC Alfred E. Smith	87	15,016,169
MINOR PARTIES	—	330,725
	531	36,738,887

■ *Republican candidate Herbert Hoover (below) campaigned on a platform that stressed continued economic prosperity.*

■ *The happy warrior, Al Smith, in his familiar brown derby, campaigning from a train platform in 1928.*

Chronology

1919 U.S. agents arrest 1700 in Red Scare raids
Congress passes Volstead Act over Wilson's veto (October)

1920 Budget Bureau set up to oversee federal spending
Nineteenth Amendment passed, granting women the right to vote
Transcontinental airmail service inaugurated (September)
WWJ-Detroit broadcasts first commercial radio program (November)

1921 Congress enacts quotas for European immigrants

1923 Newspapers expose KKK graft, torture, murder
Henry Luce begins publishing *Time* magazine (March)

1924 Senate probes Teapot Dome scandal
Veterans' World War I bonus bill passed

1925 John Scopes convicted of teaching theory of evolution in violation of Tennessee law (July)

1926 First Martha Graham modern dance recital (April)

1927 Charles Lindbergh completes first non-stop transatlantic flight from New York to Paris (May)
Coolidge vetoes farm price-control bill
Sacco and Vanzetti executed (August)
The movie *The Jazz Singer* features singing-talking soundtrack

Yet beneath the surface, as Allan J. Lichtman points out, there were "striking similarities between Smith and Hoover." Both were self-made men who embodied the American belief in freedom of opportunity and upward mobility. Neither advocated any significant degree of economic change nor any redistribution of national wealth or power. Though religion proved to be the most important issue in the minds of the voters, hurting Smith far more than Prohibition or his identification with the city, the Democratic candidate's failure to spotlight the growing cracks in prosperity and offer alternative economic policies ensured his defeat.

The 1928 election was a dubious victory for the Republicans. Hoover won easily, defeating Smith by more than six million votes and carrying such traditionally Democratic states as Oklahoma, Texas, and Florida. But Smith succeeded for the first time in winning a majority of votes for the Democrats in the nation's twelve largest cities. A new Democratic electorate was emerging, consisting of Catholics and Jews, Irish and Italians, Poles and Greeks. Now the task was to unite the traditional Democrats of the South and West with the urban voters of the Northeast and Midwest.

The 1920s marked a major transition in American politics as well as in social and economic development. The moving assembly line, the consumer-goods revolution, and the urban-centered culture all became permanent hallmarks of modern American life. Yet despite the very real economic progress achieved in the '20s, the decade ended in a grave depression that lasted all through the '30s. Only after World War II would the American people enjoy an abundance and prosperity rooted in the industrial transformation that began in the 1920s.

Recommended Reading

William Leuchtenburg provides the best overview of the 1920s in *The Perils of Prosperity, 1914–1932* (1958). He stresses the theme of rural-urban conflict and claims that the achievements of the decade were more significant than its failures. The essays in John Braeman, Robert H. Bremner, and David Brody, eds., *Change and Continuity in Twentieth Century America: The 1920s* (1968) illuminate important aspects of the period.

A fully detailed account of economic developments in the decade is George Soule, *Prosperity Decade* (1947). Two classic studies, Frederick Lewis Allen, *Only Yesterday* (1931) and Helen Lynd and Robert Lynd, *Middletown* (1929), offer valuable insights into social and cultural trends. The most recent overview of the decade is Geoffrey Perrett, *America in the Twenties* (1982).

The spirit of rural discontent with the new urban society is captured best in Lawrence Levine, *Defender of the Faith* (1965), an account of the last ten years of William Jennings Bryan's life. For changing political alignments of the 1920s, see David Burner, *The Politics of Provincialism* (1968).

Additional Bibliography

General surveys of the 1920s include Ellis W. Hawley, *The Great War and the Search for a Modern Order* (1979) and Donald McCoy, *Coming of Age* (1973). Books on economic themes are John B. Rae, *The American Automobile* (1965); James J. Flink, *The Car Culture* (1975); Allen Nevins and Frank E. Hill, *Ford: Expansion and Challenge, 1915–1933* (1957); James Prothro, *The Dollar Decade* (1954); Otis A. Pease, *The Responsibilities of American Advertising* (1959); and Alfred D. Chandler, Jr., *Strategy and Structure* (1962). The best books on labor are Irving Bernstein, *The Lean Years* (1960) and Robert H. Zieger, *Republicans and Labor, 1919–1929* (1969). James Shideler discusses the postwar agricultural depression in *Farm Crisis* (1957).

Social history is covered in Preston Slosson, *The Great Crusade and After* (1930); Paul Carter, *Another Part of the Twenties* (1976); and Elizabeth Stevenson, *Babbitts and Bohemians* (1967). For family life, see John Sirjamaki, *The American Family in the 20th Century* (1953) and Paula S. Fass, *The Damned and the Beautiful* (1977).

The role of women in the 1920s is examined in William Chafe, *The American Woman* (1972); J. Stanley Lemons, *The Woman Citizen* (1973); Susan D. Becker, *The Origins of the Equal Rights Amendment* (1981); and Winifred D. Wandersee, *Women's Work and Family Values, 1920–1940* (1981). For blacks in the 1920s, see Nathan Huggins, *Harlem Renaissance* (1971); Gilbert Osofsky, *Harlem* (1966); and David Levering Lewis, *When Harlem Was in Vogue* (1981), a lively account of black culture.

Frederick Hoffman, *The Twenties* (1955) and Alfred Kazin, *On Native Grounds* (1942) survey the literary trends during the decade. Other studies of this subject are Roderick Nash, *The Nervous Generation* (1969); Robert Crunden, *From Self to Society* (1972); Malcolm Cowley, *Exile's Return* (1934); and Edmund Wilson, *Shores of Light* (1952). Biographies of major literary figures of the period include William Manchester, *Disturber of the Peace* (1951) on H. L. Mencken; Arthur Mizener, *The Far Side of Paradise* (1951) on F. Scott Fitzgerald; Mark Shorer, *Sinclair Lewis* (1961); and Carlos Baker, *Hemingway* (1956).

Studies of political fundamentalism include Robert K. Murray, *Red Scare* (1955) and Stanley Coben, *A. Mitchell Palmer* (1963) on the postwar panic over radicalism; Andrew Sinclair, *Prohibition* (1962) and Herbert Asbury, *The Great Illusion* (1950) on the noble experiment; David Chalmers, *Hooded Americans* (1965), Arnold S. Rice, *The Ku Klux Klan in American Politics* (1962), and Kenneth T. Jackson, *The Ku Klux Klan in the City* (1967) on the KKK; Robert A. Divine, *American Immigration Policy* (1957) and John Higham, *Strangers in the Land* (1955) on nativism and immigration restriction; and Norman Furniss, *The Fundamentalist Controversy* (1954) and Ray Ginger, *Six Days or Forever?* (1956) on the attack on Darwinism and the Scopes trial.

For political developments during the 1920s, see Robert Murray, *The Harding Era* (1969) and *The Politics of Normalcy* (1973); Burl Noggle, *Teapot Dome* (1962); Francis Russell, *The Shadow of Blooming Grove: Warren G. Harding and His Times* (1968); Joan H. Wilson, *Herbert Hoover* (1975); and David Burner, *Herbert Hoover: A Public Life* (1979). Allan Lichtman, *Prejudice and the Old Politics* (1979) and Kristi Andersen, *The Creation of a Democratic Majority, 1928–1936* (1979) offer contrasting interpretations of the election of 1928.

chapter 26

FRANKLIN D. ROOSEVELT AND THE NEW DEAL

The prosperity of the twenties came to an abrupt halt in October 1929. The stock market, which had boomed during the decade, suddenly faltered. Investors who had borrowed heavily to take part in the speculative mania which swept Wall Street suddenly were forced to sell their securities to cover their loans. The wave of selling triggered an avalanche. On October 24, later known as Black Thursday, nearly thirteen million shares were traded as highfliers like RCA and Westinghouse lost nearly half their value. Bankers had only brief success in trying to stem the decline; panic overcame their feeble efforts on October 29, the worst day in stock-exchange history, when sellers dumped over sixteen million shares and the industrial average fell by forty-three points. The panic ended in November, with stocks at 1927 levels. For the next four years, there was a steady drift downward, until by 1932 prices were 80 percent below their 1929 highs.

The Great Depression which followed the crash of 1929 was the most devastating economic blow that the nation ever suffered. It lasted for ten years, dominating every aspect of American life during the thirties. Unemployment rose to twelve million by 1932, and though it dipped midway through the decade, it still stood at ten million by 1939. Children grew up thinking that economic deprivation was the norm rather than the exception in America. Year after year, people kept looking for a return to prosperity, but the outlook remained bleak and dismal. Intractable and all-encompassing, the Depression loosened its grip on the nation only after the outbreak of World War II. And even then, it left enduring psychological scars—never again would the Americans who lived though it be quite so optimistic about their economic future.

The Depression led to a profound shift in American political loyalties. The Republicans, dominant since the 1890s, gave way to a new Democratic majority. The millions of immigrants who had come to the United States before World War I became more active politically, as did their children when they reached voting age. The result was the election of Franklin D. Roosevelt to the presidency and the development of the New Deal, a broad program of relief, recovery, and reform that greatly increased the role of government in American life.

The Great Depression

The economic collapse altered American attitudes. In the twenties, optimism had prevailed as people looked forward to an ever increasing flow of consumer goods and a better way of life. But after 1929, bleak despair set in. Factories closed, machines fell silent, and millions upon millions of people walked the streets, looking for jobs that did not exist.

The Great Bull Market

The consumer-goods revolution contained the seeds of its own collapse. The steady expansion of the automobile and appliance industries led gradually to a saturation of the market. Each year after 1924, the rate of increase in the sale of cars and refrigerators and ranges slowed, a natural consequence of more and more people already owning these durable goods. Production began to falter, and in 1927, the nation underwent a mild recession. The sale of durable goods declined, and construction of houses and buildings fell slightly. If corporate leaders had heeded these warning signs, they might have responded by raising wages or lowering prices, both effective ways to stimulate purchasing power and sustain the consumer-goods revolution. Or if government officials had recognized the danger signals and forced a halt in installment-buying and slowed bank loans, the nation might have experienced a sharp but brief depression.

Neither government nor business leaders were so farsighted. The Federal Reserve Board lowered the discount rate, charging banks less for loans in an attempt to stimulate the economy. Much of this additional credit, however, went not into solid investment in factories and machinery but instead into the stock market, touching off a new wave of speculation that obscured the growing economic slowdown and ensured a far greater crash to come.

Individuals with excess cash began to invest heavily in the stock market, betting that the already impressive rise in security prices would bring them even greater windfall profits. The market had advanced in spurts during the decade; the value of all stocks listed on the New York Stock Exchange rose from $27 billion in 1925 to $67 billion in early 1929. The strongest surge began in the spring of 1928, when investors ignored the declining production figures in the belief that they could make a killing in the market. People took their savings and bet on speculative stocks. Corporations used their large cash reserves to supply money to brokers who in turn loaned it to investors on margin; in 1929, for example, the Standard Oil Company of New Jersey loaned out $69 million a day in this fashion.

Investors could now play the market on credit, buying stock listed at $100 a share with $10 down and $90 on margin, the broker's loan for the balance. If the stock advanced to $150, the investor could sell and reap a gain of 500 percent on the $10 investment. And in the bull-market climate of the twenties, everyone was sure that the market would go up.

By 1929, it seemed that the whole nation was engaged in speculation. In city after city, brokers opened branch offices, each complete with a stock ticker and a huge board covered with the latest Wall Street quotations. People crowded into the customers' rooms, filling the seats and greeting the latest advances of their favorite stocks with shouts of approval. So great was the public's interest in the stockmarket that newspapers carried the stock averages on their front pages.

In reality, though, more people were spectators than speculators; fewer than three million Americans owned stocks in 1919, and only about five hundred thousand were active buyers and sellers. But the bull market became a national obsession, assuring everyone that the economy was healthy and preventing any serious analysis of its underlying flaws. When the market soared to over $80 billion in total value by mid-summer, the *Wall Street Journal* discounted any possibility of a

■ *At their height, the 1920s were a zany, get-rich-quick era in which millions of Americans either played or watched the stock market.*

decline, proclaiming, "The outlook for the fall months seems brighter than at any time."

The great crash in October 1929 put a sudden and tragic end to the speculative mania. The false confidence that had kept the economy from collapsing in 1927 evaporated overnight. Suddenly, corporations and financial institutions were no longer willing to provide capital for stock-market purchases. More important, investors and bankers cut off consumer credit as well, drying up buying power and leading to a sharp decline in the sales of consumer goods. Factories began to cut back production, laying off some workers and reducing hours for others. The layoffs and cutbacks lowered purchasing power even further, so fewer people bought cars and appliances. More factory layoffs resulted, and some plants closed entirely, leading to even less money for the purchase of consumer goods.

This downward economic spiral continued for four years. By 1932, unemployment had swelled to 25 percent of the work force. Steel production was down to 12 percent of capacity, and the vast assembly lines in Detroit produced only a trickle of cars each day. The Gross National Product fell to 67 percent of the 1929 level. The bright promise of mass production had ended in a nightmare.

The basic explanation for the Great Depression lies in the fact that U.S. factories produced more goods than the American people could consume. There were other contributing causes—unstable economic conditions in Europe, the agricultural decline since 1919, corporate mismanagement, and excessive speculation—but at bottom people simply did not have enough money to buy the consumer products coming off the assembly lines. The market for such products was not fully saturated. In 1929, there were still millions of Americans who did not own a car or radio or a refrigerator. But they lacked the money to buy any of these creature comforts. Installment sales had helped bridge the gap, but by 1929 the burden of debt was just too great.

The failure of the new economic system to distribute wealth more broadly was the chief difficulty. Too much money had gone into profits, dividends, and industrial expansion, and not enough into the hands of the workers, who were also consumers. Factory productivity had increased 43 percent during the decade, but the wages of industrial workers had only gone up 11 percent (see chapter 25). If the billions that went into stock-market speculation had been used instead to increase wages—which would then have increased consumer purchasing power—production and consumption could have been brought into balance. Yet it is too much to expect that the prophets of the New Era could have foreseen this flaw and corrected it. They were pioneering a new industrial system, and only out of the bitter experience of the Depression would they discover the full dynamics of the consumer-goods economy.

Effect of the Depression

It is difficult to measure the human cost of the Great Depression. The material hardships were bad enough. Men and women lived in lean-tos made of scrap wood and metal, and families went without meat and fresh vegetables for months, existing on a diet of soup and beans. The psychological burden was even greater: Americans suffered through year after year of grinding poverty with no letup in sight. The unemployed stood in line for hours waiting for a relief check; veterans sold apples or pencils on street corners, their manhood—once prized so highly by the nation—now in question. People left the city for the countryside, but they found no salvation on the farm. Crops rotted in the fields because prices were too low to make harvesting worthwhile; sheriffs fended off angry crowds as banks foreclosed long-overdue mortgages on once-prosperous farms.

Few escaped the suffering. Blacks who had left the poverty of the rural South for factory jobs in the North were among the first to be laid off. Mexican-Americans, who had flowed in to replace European immigrants, met with competition from angry citizens, now willing to do stoop labor in the fields and work as track layers on the

Unemployment, 1929–1942

■ Unemployment devastated thousands, who turned to selling apples or advertising their labor. The suddenly homeless gathered in hobo camps, like the New York City "Hooverville" above, while others crowded together on The Park Bench, as shown in this detail of the painting by Reginald Marsh (left).

railroads. Immigration officials used technicalities to halt the flow across the Rio Grande and even to reverse it; nearly a half million Mexicans were deported in the 1930s, including families with children born in the United States.

The poor—black, brown, and white—survived because they knew better than most Americans how to exist in poverty. They stayed in bed in cold weather, both to keep warm and to avoid unnecessary burning up of calories; they patched their shoes with pieces of rubber from discarded tires, heated only the kitchens of their homes, and ate scraps of food that others would reject.

The middle class, which had always lived with high expectations, was hit hard. Professionals and white-collar workers refused to ask for charity even while their families went without food; one New York dentist and his wife turned on the gas and left a note saying, "We want to get out of the way before we are forced to accept relief money." People who fell behind in their mortgage payments lost their homes and then faced eviction when they could not pay the rent. Health care declined. Middle-class people stopped going to doctors and dentists regularly, unable to make the required cash payment in advance for services.

Even the well-to-do were affected, giving up many of their former luxuries and weighed down with guilt as they watched former friends and business associates join the ranks of the impoverished. "My father lost everything in the Depression" became an all-too-familiar refrain among young people who dropped out of college.

Many Americans sought escape in movement. Men and boys, and even women, rode the rails in search of jobs, hopping freights to move south in the winter or west in the summer. On the Missouri Pacific alone, the number of vagrants increased from just over thirteen thousand in 1929 to nearly two hundred thousand in 1931. One town in the Southwest hired special policemen to keep vagrants from leaving the boxcars. Those who became tramps had to keep on the move, but they did find a sense of community in the hobo jungles that sprang up along the major railroad routes. Here a man could find a place to eat and sleep and people with whom to share his misery. Louis Banks, a black veteran, told interviewer Studs Terkel what these informal camps were like:

Black and white, it didn't make any difference who you were, 'cause everybody was poor. All friendly, sleep in a jungle. We used to take a big pot and cook food, cabbage, meat and beans all together. We all set together, we made a tent. Twenty-five or thirty would be out on the side of the rail, white and colored. They didn't have no mothers or sisters, they didn't have no home, they were dirty, they had overalls on, they didn't have no food, they didn't have anything.

Fighting the Depression

The Great Depression presented an enormous challenge for American political leadership. The inability of the Republicans to overcome the economic catastrophe provided the Democrats with the chance to regain power. Although they failed to achieve full recovery before the outbreak of World War II, the Democrats did succeed in alleviating the suffering and establishing their political dominance.

Hoover and Voluntarism

Herbert Hoover was the Depression's most prominent victim. When the downturn began in late 1929, he tried to rally the nation with bold forecasts of better days ahead. His repeated assertion that prosperity was just around the corner bred cynicism and mistrust. Expressing complete faith in the American economic system, Hoover relied primarily on voluntary cooperation with business to halt the slide. He called the leaders of industry to the White House and secured their agreement to maintain prices and wages at high levels. Yet within a few months, employers were reducing wages and cutting prices in a desperate effort to survive.

Hoover also believed in voluntary efforts to relieve the human suffering brought about by the Depression. He called on private charities and local governments to help feed and clothe those in need. But when these sources were exhausted, he rejected all requests for direct federal relief, asserting that such handouts would undermine the character of proud American citizens.

As the Depression deepened, Hoover reluctantly began to move beyond voluntarism to undertake more sweeping governmental measures. A new Federal Farm Board loaned money to aid cooperatives and bought up surplus crops in the open market in a vain effort to raise farm prices. At Hoover's request, Congress cut taxes in an attempt to restore public confidence and adopted a few federal public-works projects, such as Boulder Dam, to provide jobs for idle men.

To help imperiled banks and insurance companies, Hoover proposed and Congress established the Reconstruction Finance Corporation established in early 1932. The RFC loaned government money to financial institutions to save them from bankruptcy. Hoover's critics, however, pointed out that while he favored aid to business, he still opposed measures such as direct relief and massive public works that would help the millions of unemployed.

By 1932, Hoover's efforts to overcome the Depression had clearly failed. The Democrats had gained control of the House of Representatives in the 1930 elections and were pressing the President to take bolder action, but Hoover stubbornly resisted. His public image suffered its sharpest blow in the summer of 1932 when he ordered General Douglas MacArthur to clear out a group of ragged World War I veterans who had marched on Washington in a vain effort to get a bonus bill passed in Congress. Mounted troops drove the bonus marchers out of their shanties in Anacostia Flats along the Potomac, blinding the veterans with tear gas and burning their shacks.

Meanwhile, the nation's banking structure approached collapse. Bank failures rose steadily in 1931 and 1932 as customers responded to rumors of bankruptcy by rushing in to withdraw their deposits, thereby causing a bank's failure. The banking crisis completed the nation's disenchantment with Hoover; the people were ready for a new leader in the White House.

The Emergence of Roosevelt

The man who stepped forward to meet this national need was Franklin D. Roosevelt. Born into the old Dutch colonial aristocracy of New York, FDR was a distant cousin of the Republican Teddy. He grew up with all the advantages of wealth—private tutors, his own sailboat and pony, frequent trips to Europe, and education at Groton and Harvard. His strong-willed mother smoothed all the obstacles in the path of her only child and gave him a priceless sense of inner security. After graduation from Harvard, he briefly attended law school but left to plunge into politics. He served in the New York legislature and then went to Washington as assistant secretary of the navy under Wilson, a post he filled

Bank Failures, 1929–1933

Year	Failures
1933	5190
1932	2294
1931	1456
1930	1352
1929	659

Source: Data compiled from C. D. Bremer, American Bank Failures *(New York: Columbia University Press, 1935), p. 42.*

capably during World War I. He met with defeat in 1920 as the Democratic vice-presidential candidate and had begun a banking career when an attack of polio crippled him in the summer of 1921. Refusing to give in, he fought back bravely, and though he never again walked unaided, he reentered politics in the mid-twenties and was elected governor of New York in 1928.

Roosevelt's dominant trait was his ability to persuade and convince other people. He possessed a marvelous voice, deep and rich, a winning smile, and a buoyant confidence that he could easily transmit to others. Some felt he was too vain and superficial as a young man, but his bout with polio gave him both an understanding of human suffering and a broad political appeal as a man who had faced heavy odds and overcome them. He understood the give-and-take of politics, knew how to use flattery to win over doubters, and was especially effective in exploiting the media, whether in bantering with newspaper reporters or reaching out to the American people on the radio. Although his mind was quick and agile, he had little patience with philosophical nuances; he dealt with the appearance of issues, not their deeper substance, and he displayed a flexibility toward political principles that often dismayed even his warmest admirers.

Roosevelt took advantage of the opportunity offered by the Depression. With the Republicans discredited, he cultivated the two wings of the divided Democrats, appealing to both the traditionalists from the South and West and the new urban elements in the North. After winning the party's nomination in 1932, he broke with tradition by flying to Chicago and accepting in person, telling the cheering delegates, "I pledge you—I pledge myself to a new deal for the American people."

In the fall, he defeated Herbert Hoover in a near landslide for the Democrats. Roosevelt tallied 472 electoral votes as he swept the South and West and carried nearly all the large industrial states as well. Farmers and workers, Protestants and Catholics, immigrants and native-born rallied behind the new leader who promised to restore prosperity. Roosevelt not only met the challenge of the Depression but also solidified the shift to the Democratic party and created an enduring coalition that would dominate American politics for a half-century.

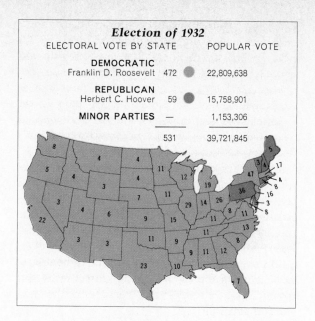

Election of 1932

ELECTORAL VOTE BY STATE		POPULAR VOTE
DEMOCRATIC Franklin D. Roosevelt	472	22,809,638
REPUBLICAN Herbert C. Hoover	59	15,758,901
MINOR PARTIES	—	1,153,306
	531	39,721,845

The Hundred Days

When Franklin Roosevelt took the oath of office on March 4, 1933, the nation's economy was on the brink of collapse. Unemployment stood at nearly thirteen million, one fourth of the labor force; banks were closed in thirty-eight states. On inauguration morning, the governors of New York and Illinois closed the banks in the nation's two largest cities, thus bringing the country's financial transactions to a halt. Speaking from the steps of the Capitol, FDR declared boldly, "First of all, let me assert my firm belief that the only thing we have to fear is fear itself—nameless, unreasoning, unjustified terror." Then he announced that he would call Congress into special session and request "broad executive power to wage a war against the emergency, as great as the power that would be given to me if we were in fact invaded by a foreign foe."

Within the next ten days, Roosevelt won his first great New Deal victory by saving the nation's banks. On March 5, he issued a decree closing the banks and called Congress back into session. His aides drafted new banking legislation and presented it to Congress on March 9; a few hours later, both houses passed it, and FDR signed the new legislation that evening. The measure provided for government supervision

Through his fireside chats, FDR became the first president to use the immediacy of the national media to reach and reassure the American public.

of nationalizing the banks, he had simply thrown the government's resources behind them and preserved private ownership. Though some other New Deal measures would be more radical, Roosevelt set the tone in the banking crisis. He was out to reform and restore the American economic system, not change it drastically.

For the next three months, until it adjourned in June, Congress responded to a series of presidential initiatives. During these "Hundred Days," Roosevelt sent fifteen major requests to Congress and received back fifteen pieces of legislation. A few created permanent agencies that have become a part of American life: the Federal Deposit Insurance Corporation (FDIC) to protect bank deposits and the Tennessee Valley Authority (TVA) to build dams that would both control floods and provide electricity to modernize a poverty-stricken area of the upper South. Other New Deal agencies were temporary in nature, designed to meet the specific economic problems of the Depression. None were completely successful; the Depression would continue for another six years, immune even to Roosevelt's magic. But psychologically the nation turned the corner in the spring of 1933. Under FDR, the government seemed to be responding to the economic crisis, enabling people for the first time since 1929 to look to the future with hope.

and aid to the banks. Strong ones would be reopened with federal support, weak ones closed, and those in difficulty bolstered by government loans.

On March 12, FDR addressed the nation by radio in the first of his fireside chats. In conversational tones, he told the public what he had done. Banks would begin to reopen the next day, with the government standing behind them. Other banks, once they became solvent, would open later, and the American people could safely put their money back into these institutions. The next day, March 13, the nation's largest and strongest banks opened their doors; at the end of the day, customers had deposited more cash than they withdrew. The crisis was over; gradually other banks opened, and the runs and failures ceased.

"Capitalism was saved in eight days," boasted one of Roosevelt's advisers. Most surprising was the conservative nature of FDR's action. Instead

Legislation Enacted During the Hundred Days (March 9–June 16, 1933)

Emergency Banking Relief Act	March 9
Beer-Wine Revenue Act	March 22
Unemployment Relief Act	March 31
Agricultural Adjustment Act	May 12
Federal Emergency Relief Act	May 12
Tennessee Valley Authority Act	May 18
Securities Act of 1933	May 27
Gold Repeal Joint Resolution	June 5
Home Owners' Refinancing Act	June 13
Farm Credit Act	June 16
Banking Act of 1933	June 16
Emergency Railroad Transportation Act	June 16
National Industrial Recovery Act	June 16

Two major New Deal programs launched during the Hundred Days were aimed at industrial and agricultural recovery. The first was the National Recovery Administration (NRA), FDR's attempt to achieve economic advance through planning and cooperation between government, business, and labor. In the midst of the Depression, businessmen were intent on stabilizing production and raising prices for their goods. Spokesmen for labor were equally determined to spread work through maximum hours and to put a floor under workers' income with minimum wages. The NRA hoped to achieve both goals by permitting companies in each major industry to cooperate in writing codes of fair competition which would set realistic limits on production, allocate percentages to individual producers, and set firm guidelines on prices. Section 7a of the enabling act mandated protection for labor in all the codes by establishing maximum hours, minimum wages, and the guarantee of collective bargaining by unions. No company could be compelled to join, but the New Deal sought complete participation by appealing to patriotism. Each firm that took part could display a blue eagle and stamp this symbol on its products. With energetic Hugh Johnson in charge, the NRA quickly enrolled the nation's leading companies and unions. By the summer of 1933, more than 500 industries had adopted codes that covered 2.5 million workers.

■ *Although the NRA quickly bogged down in a bureaucratic morass, the NRA blue eagle became a widely respected symbol of a business' patriotism.*

The NRA quickly bogged down in a huge bureaucratic morass. The codes proved to be too detailed to enforce easily. Written by the largest companies, these rules favored big business at the expense of smaller competitors. Labor quickly became disenchanted with Section 7a. The minimum wages were often near the starvation level, while business got around the requirement for collective bargaining by creating company unions that did not represent the real needs of workers. After a brief upsurge in the spring of 1933, industrial production began to sag as disillusionment with the NRA grew. By 1934, more and more businessmen were complaining about the new agency, calling it the "National Run Around." When the Supreme Court finally invalidated the NRA in 1935 on constitutional grounds, few mourned its demise. The idea of trying to overcome the Depression by relying on voluntary cooperation between competing businessmen and labor leaders had collapsed in the face of individual self-interest and greed.

The New Deal's attempt at farm recovery fared a little better. Henry A. Wallace, FDR's secretary of agriculture, came up with an answer to the farmers' old dilemma of overproduction. The government would act as a clearinghouse for producers of major crops, arranging for them to set production limits for wheat, cotton, corn, and other leading crops. Under the Agricultural Adjustment Act (AAA) passed by Congress in May 1933, the government would allocate acreage among individual farmers, encouraging them to take land out of production by paying them subsidies (raised by a tax on food processors). Unfortunately, Wallace preferred not to wait until the 1934 planting season to implement this program, and so farmers were paid in 1933 to plow under crops they had already planted and to kill livestock they were raising. Faced with the problem of hunger in the midst of plenty, the New Deal seemed to respond by destroying the plenty.

The AAA program worked better in 1934 and 1935 as land removed from production led to smaller harvests and rising farm prices. Farm income rose for the first time since World War I, increasing from $2 billion in 1933 to $5 billion by 1935. Severe weather, especially dust-bowl conditions in the Great Plains, contributed to the crop-limitation program, but most of the gain in farm income came from the subsidy payments themselves rather than from higher market prices.

On the whole, large farmers benefited most from the program. Possessing the capital to buy machinery and fertilizer, they were able to farm more efficiently than before on fewer acres of land. Small farmers, tenants, and sharecroppers did not fare as well, receiving very little of the government payments and often being driven off the land as owners took the acreage previously cultivated by tenants and sharecroppers out of production. Some three million people left the land in the thirties, crowding into the cities where they swelled the relief rolls. In the long run, the New Deal reforms improved the efficiency of American agriculture, but at a real human cost.

The Supreme Court eventually found the AAA unconstitutional in 1936, but Congress reenacted it in modified form that year and again in 1938. The system of allotments, now financed directly by the government, became a standard feature of the farm economy. Other New Deal efforts to assist the rural poor, notably the Farm Security Administration (FSA), sought to loan tenants and sharecroppers money to acquire land of their own, but the sums appropriated by Congress were too modest. The FSA was able to extend loans to fewer than 2 percent of the nation's tenant farmers. "Obviously," the FSA director informed Roosevelt, "this . . . program can be regarded as only an experimental approach to the farm tenancy problem." The result of the New Deal for American farming was to hasten its transformation into a business in which only the efficient and well-capitalized would thrive.

Roosevelt and Relief

The New Deal was far more successful in meeting the most immediate problem of the 1930s—relief for the millions of unemployed and destitute citizens. Roosevelt never shared Hoover's distaste for direct federal support; on May 12, 1933, in response to FDR's March request, Congress authorized the RFC to distribute $500 million to the states to help individuals and families in need.

Roosevelt brought in Harry Hopkins to direct the relief program. A former social worker who

"Hunger is not debatable," said Harry Hopkins, the brash but selfless New Dealer who distributed $5 million of relief in his first two hours in office.

seemed to live on black coffee and cigarettes, Hopkins set up a desk in the hallway of the RFC building and proceeded to spend over $5 million in less than two hours. By the end of 1933, Hopkins had cut through red tape to distribute money to nearly one sixth of the American people. The relief payments were modest in size, but they enabled millions to avoid starvation and stay out of humiliating breadlines.

Another, more imaginative early effort was the Civilian Conservation Corps (CCC), which was Roosevelt's own idea. The CCC enrolled youth from city families on relief and sent them to the nation's parks and recreational areas to build trails and improve public facilities. Ultimately, more than two million young men served in the CCC, contributing both to their families' incomes and to the nation's welfare.

Hopkins realized the need to do more than just keep people alive, and he soon became an advocate of work relief. Hopkins argued that the government should put the jobless to work, not just to encourage self-respect, but also to enable them to earn enough to purchase consumer goods and thus stimulate the entire economy. A Public Works Administration (PWA) headed by Secretary of the Interior Harold Ickes had been authorized

Federal work relief programs helped millions maintain their self-respect. Workers in the CCC (left) received $30 a month for planting trees and digging drainage ditches, while the WPA provided work for artists and writers.

in 1933, but Ickes, intent on the quality of the projects rather than human needs, failed to put many people to work. In the fall of 1933, Roosevelt created the Civil Works Administration (CWA) and charged Hopkins with getting people off the unemployment lines and relief rolls and back to work. Hopkins had over four million men and women at work by January 1934, building roads, schools, playgrounds, and athletic fields. Many of the workers were unskilled, and some of the projects were shoddy, but at least the CWA enabled people to work and earn enough money to survive the winter. Roosevelt, appalled at the huge expenditures involved, ended the CWA in 1934 and forced Hopkins to return to federal relief payments as the only source of aid to the jobless.

The final commitment to the idea of work relief came in 1935 when Roosevelt established the Works Progress Administration (WPA) to spend nearly $5 billion authorized by Congress for emergency relief. The WPA, under Hopkins, put the unemployed on the federal payroll so that they could earn enough to meet their basic needs and help stimulate the stagnant economy. Conservatives complained that the WPA amounted to nothing more than hiring the jobless to do make-work tasks with no real value. But Hopkins cared less about what was accomplished than about helping those who had been unemployed for years

to get off the dole and gain self-respect by working again.

In addition to the usual construction and conservation projects, the WPA tried to preserve the skills of American artists, actors, and writers. The Federal Theatre Project produced plays, circuses, and puppet shows that enabled entertainers to practice their crafts and to perform before people who often had never seen a professional production before. Similar projects for writers and artists led to a series of valuable state guidebooks and to murals that adorned public buildings across the land. A separate National Youth Administration (NYA) found part-time jobs for young people still in school and developed projects—ranging from automobile repairing in New York City to erecting tuberculosis isolation units in Arizona—for 2.5 million young adults.

The WPA helped ease the burden for the unemployed, but it failed to overcome the Depression. Rather than spending too much, as his critics charged, Roosevelt's greatest failure was not spending enough. The WPA never employed at any one time more than three million of the ten million jobless. The wages, although larger than relief payments, were still pitifully low, averaging only $52 a month. Thus the WPA failed to prime the American economy by increasing consumer purchasing power. Factories remained closed and machinery idle because the American people did not have the money, either from relief or the WPA, to buy cars, radios, appliances, and the other consumer goods that had been the basis for the prosperity of the 1920s. By responding to basic human needs, Roosevelt had made the Depression bearable. The New Deal's failure, however, to go beyond relief to achieve prosperity led to a growing frustration and the appearance of more radical alternatives that challenged the conservative nature of the New Deal and forced FDR to shift to the left.

■ *As the Depression continued, it became apparent that the stopgap measures of the New Deal would have to be replaced by more sweeping reforms.*

Democratic victory in the 1934 congressional elections, FDR responded by embracing a reform program that marked the climax of the New Deal.

Roosevelt and Reform

In 1935 the focus of the New Deal shifted from relief and recovery to reform. During his first two years in office, FDR had concentrated on fighting the Depression by shoring up the sagging American economy. Only a few new agencies, notably TVA, sought to make permanent changes in national life. Roosevelt was developing a "broker-state" concept of government, responding to pressures from organized elements such as corporations, labor unions, and farm groups while ignoring the needs and wants of the dispossessed who had no clear political voice. The early New Deal tried to assist bankers and industrialists, large farmers, and members of the labor unions, but it did little to help unskilled workers and sharecroppers.

The continuing depression and the high unemployment began to build pressures for more sweeping changes. Roosevelt faced the choice of either providing more radical programs, ones designed to end historical inequities in American life, or deferring to others who put forth solutions to the nation's ills. Bolstered by an impressive

Angry Voices

The signs of discontent were visible everywhere by 1935. In the upper Midwest, progressives and agrarian radicals, led by Minnesota Governor Floyd Olson, were calling for government action to raise farm and labor income. "I am a radical in the sense that I want a definite change in the system," Olson declared. "I am not satisfied with patching." Upton Sinclair, the muckraking novelist, nearly won the governorship of California in 1934 running on the slogan "End Poverty in California," while in the East a violent strike in the textile industry shut down plants in twenty states. The most serious challenge to Roosevelt's leadership, however, came from three demagogues who captured national attention in the mid-thirties.

The first was Father Charles Coughlin, a Roman Catholic priest from Detroit, who had originally supported FDR. Speaking to a rapt nationwide radio audience in his rich, melodious voice, Coughlin appealed to the discontented with a strange mixture of crank monetary schemes and anti-Semitism. He broke with the

New Deal in late 1934, denouncing it as the "Pagan Deal," and founded his own National Union for Social Justice. Increasingly vitriolic, he called for monetary inflation and the nationalization of the banking system in his weekly radio sermons to an audience of more than thirty million.

A more benign but equally threatening figure appeared in California. Dr. Francis Townsend, a sixty-seven-year-old physician, came forward in 1934 with a scheme to assist the elderly, who were suffering greatly during the Depression. The Townsend Plan proposed giving everyone over the age of sixty a monthly pension of $200 with the proviso that it must be spent within thirty days. Although designed less as an old-age pension plan than as a way to stimulate the economy, the proposal understandably had its greatest appeal among the elderly. They embraced it as a holy cause, joining Townsend Clubs across the country. Despite the criticism from economists that the plan would transfer over half the national income to less than 10 percent of the population, more than ten million people signed petitions endorsing the Townsend Plan, and few politicians dared oppose it.

The third new voice of protest was that of Huey Long, the flamboyant senator from Louisiana. Like Coughlin an original supporter of the New Deal, Long turned against FDR and by 1935 had become a major political threat to the President. A shrewd, ruthless, yet witty man, Long had a remarkable ability to mock those in power. The Kingfish (a nickname he borrowed from "Amos 'n Andy") announced a nationwide "Share the Wealth" movement in 1934. He spoke grandly of taking from the rich to make "Every Man a King," guaranteeing each American a home worth $5000 and an annual income of $2500. To finance the plan, Long advocated seizing all fortunes of more than $5 million and levying a tax of 100 percent on incomes over $1 million. By 1935, Long claimed to have founded twenty-seven thousand Share the Wealth Clubs and had a mailing list of over seven million people, including workers, farmers, college professors, and even bank presidents. Threatening to run as a third-party candidate in 1936, Long generated fear among Democratic leaders that he might attract three or four million votes, possibly enough to swing the election to the Republicans.

Social Security

When the new Congress met in January 1935, Roosevelt was ready to support a series of reform measures designed to take the edge off national dissent. The recent elections had increased Democratic congressional strength significantly, with the Republicans losing thirteen seats in the House and retaining less than one third of the Senate. Many of the Democrats were to the left of Roosevelt, favoring increased spending and more sweeping federal programs. "Boys—this is our hour," exulted Harry Hopkins. "We've got to get everything we want . . . now or never." Congress quickly appropriated $4.8 billion for the WPA and was prepared to enact virtually any proposal that Roosevelt offered.

The most significant reform enacted in 1935 was the Social Security Act. The Townsend movement had reminded Americans that the United States, alone among modern industrial nations, had never developed a welfare system to aid the aged, the disabled, and the unemployed. A cabinet committee began studying the problem in 1934, and President Roosevelt sent its recommendations to Congress the following January.

The proposed legislation had three major parts. First, it provided for old-age pensions financed equally by a tax on employers and workers, with no government contributions. Second, it set up a system of unemployment compensation on a federal-state basis, with employers paying a payroll tax and with each state setting the benefit levels and administering the program locally. Finally, it provided for direct federal grants to the states, on a matching basis, for welfare payments to the blind, handicapped, needy elderly, and dependent children.

Although there was criticism from conservatives who mourned the passing of traditional American reliance on self-help and individualism, the chief objections came from those who argued that the administration's measure did not go far enough. Democratic leaders, however, defeated efforts to incorporate Townsend's proposal for $200-a-month pensions and increases in unemployment benefits. Congress then passed the Social Security Act by overwhelming margins.

Ever since, critics have pointed out its shortcomings. The old-age pensions were paltry. Designed to begin in 1942, they ranged from $10 to

Join the march to OLD AGE SECURITY

Return YOUR APPLICATION FOR A SOCIAL SECURITY ACCOUNT NUMBER through the post office NOT LATER THAN DEC. 5 TH 1936

WHO IS ELIGIBLE EVERYBODY WORKING FOR SALARY OR WAGES (WITH ONLY A FEW EXCEPTIONS, SUCH AS AGRICULTURE, DOMESTIC SERVICE, AND GOVERNMENT WORK). APPLICATIONS FOR SOCIAL SECURITY ACCOUNTS ARE AVAILABLE THROUGH EMPLOYERS. IF YOU DO NOT GET ONE FROM YOUR EMPLOYER, ASK FOR ONE AT THE POST OFFICE.

HOW TO RETURN APPLICATION
1. HAND IT BACK TO YOUR EMPLOYER, or
2. HAND IT TO ANY LABOR ORGANIZATION OF WHICH YOU ARE A MEMBER, or
3. HAND IT TO YOUR LETTER CARRIER, or
4. DELIVER IT TO LOCAL POST OFFICE, or
5. MAIL IT IN A SEALED ENVELOPE ADDRESSED: POST MASTER, LOCAL DO IT NOW. NO POSTAGE NEEDED.

— Social Security Board

■ *Despite the administration's boosterism, many felt that Social Security could not fulfill its promises.*

$85 a month. Nor was everyone covered; those who most needed protection in their old age, such as farmers and domestic servants, were not included. The regressive feature of the act was even worse. All participants, regardless of income or economic status, paid in at the same rate, with no supplement from the general revenue. The trust fund also took out of circulation money that was desperately needed to stimulate the economy in the 1930s.

Other portions of the act were equally open to question. The cumbersome unemployment system offered no aid to those currently out of work, only to people who would lose their jobs in the future, and the benefits (depending on the state) ranged from barely adequate to substandard. The outright grants to the handicapped and dependent children were minute in terms of the need; in New York City, for example, a blind person received only $5 a week in 1937.

The conservative nature of the legislation reflected Roosevelt's own fiscal orthodoxy, but even more it was a product of his political realism. Despite the severity of the Depression, he realized that establishing a system of federal welfare went against deeply rooted American convictions. He insisted on a tax on participants to give those involved in the pension plan a vested interest in Social Security. He wanted them to feel that they had earned their pensions and that in the future no one would dare take them away. "With those taxes in there," he explained privately, "no damned politician can ever scrap my social security program." Above all, FDR had succeeded in establishing the principle of governmental responsibility for the aged, the handicapped, and the unemployed. Whatever the defects of the legislation, Social Security stood as a landmark of the New Deal, creating a system to provide for the welfare of individuals in a complex industrial society.

Labor Legislation

The other major reform achievement in 1935 was passage of the National Labor Relations Act. Senator Robert Wagner of New York introduced legislation in 1934 to outlaw company unions and other unfair labor practices in order to ensure collective bargaining for unions. FDR, who had little knowledge of labor-management relations and apparently little interest in them, opposed the bill. In 1935, however, Wagner began to gather broad support for his measure, which passed the Senate in May with only twelve opposing votes, and the President, seeing passage as likely, gave it his approval. The bill moved quickly through the House, and Roosevelt signed it into law in July.

The Wagner Act, as it became known, created a National Labor Relations Board to preside over labor-management relations and enable unions to engage in collective bargaining with federal support. The act outlawed a variety of union-busting tactics and in its key provision decreed that whenever the majority of a company's workers voted for a union to represent them, management would be compelled to negotiate with the union on all matters of wages, hours, and working conditions. With this unprecedented government sanction, labor unions could now proceed to recruit the large number of unorganized workers throughout the country. The Wagner Act, the most far-reaching of all New Deal measures, led to the revitalization of the American labor movement and a permanent change in labor-management relations.

Three years later, Congress passed a second law which had a lasting impact on American workers —the Fair Labor Standards Act. A long-sought goal of the New Deal, this measure aimed to establish both minimum wages and maximum hours of work per week. Since labor unions usually were able to negotiate adequate levels of pay and work for their members, the act was aimed at unorganized workers and met with only grudging support from unions. Southern conservatives opposed it strongly, both on ideological grounds (it meant still greater government involvement in private enterprise) and because it threatened the very low wages in the South which had attracted northern industry since Reconstruction.

Roosevelt finally succeeded in winning passage of the Fair Labor Standards Act in 1938, but only at the cost of exempting many key industries from its coverage. The act provided for a minimum wage of forty cents an hour by 1940 and a standard work week of forty hours, with time and a half for overtime. Despite its loopholes, the legislation did lead to pay raises for the twelve million workers earning less than forty cents an hour. More important, like Social Security it set up a system—however inadequate—which Congress could build upon in the future to reach more generous and humane levels.

Other New Deal reform measures met with a mixed reception in Congress. Proposals to break up the huge public-utility holding companies created by promoters in the 1920s and to levy a "soak-the-rich" tax on the wealthy stirred up bitter debate, and these bills were passed only in greatly weakened form. Roosevelt was more successful in passing a banking act that made important reforms in the Federal Reserve System. He also gained congressional approval of the Rural Electrification Administration (REA), which helped to bring electricity to the 90 percent of American farms without it in the 1930s.

All in all, Roosevelt's record in reform was similar to that in relief and recovery—modest success but no sweeping victory. A cautious and pragmatic leader, FDR moved far enough to the left to overcome the challenges of Coughlin, Townsend, and Long without venturing too far from the mainstream. His reforms improved the quality of life in America significantly, but he made no effort to correct all the nation's social and economic wrongs.

Impact of the New Deal

The New Deal had a broad influence on the quality of life in the United States in the 1930s. Government programs reached into areas hitherto untouched. Many of them brought about long overdue improvements, but others failed to make any significant dent in historic inequities. The most important advances came with the dramatic growth of labor unions; failure to help women and minorities was the most disappointing result.

Rise of Organized Labor

Trade unions were weak at the onset of the Depression, with a membership of fewer than three million workers. Most were in the American Federation of Labor (AFL), composed of craft unions which served the needs of skilled workers. The nation's basic industries like steel and automobiles were unorganized; the great mass of unskilled workers thus fared poorly in terms of

---

Later New Deal Legislation

1934 Farm Mortgage Refinancing Act
Gold Reserve Act
Civil-Works Emergency Relief Act
Home Owners' Loan Act
Farm Mortgage Foreclosure Act
Bank Deposit Insurance Act
Silver Purchase Act
Securities Exchange Act
Labor Dispute Joint Resolution
Railway Pension Act
Communication Act

1935 Emergency Relief Appropriation Act
Wagner-Connery Labor Relations Act
Social Security Act
Public Utility Holding Company Act
Work Relief Act

1937 National Housing Act
Bankhead-Jones Farm Tenancy Act

1938 Fair Labor Standards Act

wages and working conditions. Section 7a of the NRA had led to some growth in AFL ranks, but the Federation's conservative leaders, eager to cooperate with business, failed to take full advantage of the opportunity to organize the mass-production industries.

John L. Lewis, head of the United Mine Workers, took the lead in forming the Committee on Industrial Organization (CIO) in 1935. The son of a Welsh coal miner, Lewis was a dynamic and ruthless man. He had led the mine workers since 1919 and was determined to spread the benefits of unions throughout industry. Lewis first battled with the leadership of the AFL, and then—after being expelled—he renamed his group the Congress of Industrial Organizations and announced in 1936 that he would use the Wagner Act to extend collective bargaining to the nation's auto and steel industries.

Within five years, Lewis had scored a remarkable series of victories. Some came easily. The big steel companies, led by U.S. Steel, surrendered without a fight in 1937; management realized that with federal support the unions were in a strong position. There was greater resistance in the automobile industry. When General Motors, the first target, resisted, the newly created United Automobile Workers (UAW) developed an effective strike technique. In January 1937, GM workers in Flint, Michigan, simply sat down in the factory, refusing to leave until the company rec-

A dynamic and ruthless labor organizer, John L. Lewis (top) resolved to use the Wagner Act to unionize unskilled workers in the steel and auto industries. The first opponent, General Motors, succumbed peaceably to a sit-down strike, but other employers used police to forcibly remove unarmed pickets. Philip Evergood's 1937 painting, The American Tragedy *(left), depicts the violence of the Republic Steel strike.*

ognized their union and threatening to destroy the valuable tools and machines if they were removed forcibly. When the Michigan governor refused to call out the National Guard, General Motors conceded defeat in the sit-down strike and signed a contract with the UAW. Chrysler quickly followed suit, but Henry Ford refused to give in and fought the UAW, hiring strikebreakers and beating up organizers. In 1941, however, Ford finally recognized the UAW. Smaller steel companies, led by Republic Steel, engaged in even more violent resistance; in one incident in 1938 police shot ten strikers. The companies eventually reached a settlement with the steelworkers' union in 1941.

By the end of the 1930s, the CIO had some five million members, slightly more than the AFL. The successes were remarkable—in addition to the auto-making and steel, organizers for the CIO and the AFL had been successful in the textile, rubber, electrical, and metal industries. For the first time, unskilled as well as skilled were unionized. Women and blacks benefited from the creation of the CIO, not because the union followed enlightened policies, but simply because they made up a substantial proportion of the unskilled work force.

Yet despite these impressive gains, only 28 percent of all Americans (excluding farm workers) belonged to unions by 1940. Millions in the restaurant, retail, and service trades remained unorganized, working long hours for very low wages. Employer resistance and traditional hostility to unions blocked further progress, as did the aloof attitude of President Roosevelt, who commented, "A plague on both your houses" during the steel strike. The Wagner Act had helped open the way, but labor leaders like Lewis, Philip Murray of the Steel Workers Organizing Committee, and Walter Reuther of the United Automobile Workers deserved most of the credit for the gains that were achieved.

The New Deal and Minorities

The Roosevelt administration's attempts to aid the downtrodden were least effective with blacks and other racial minorities. The Depression had hit blacks with special force. Sharecroppers and tenant farmers had seen the price of cotton drop from eighteen to six cents a pound, far below the level to sustain a family on the land. In the cities, the saying "First Fired, Last Hired" proved all too true; by 1933, over 50 percent of urban blacks were unemployed. Hard times sharpened racial prejudice. "No Jobs for Niggers Until Every White Man Has a Job" became a rallying cry for whites in Atlanta.

The New Deal helped blacks survive the Depression, but it never tried to confront squarely the racial injustice built into the federal relief programs. Although the programs served blacks as well as whites, in the South the weekly payments blacks received were much smaller. In the early days, NRA codes permitted lower wage scales for blacks, while the AAA led to the eviction of thousands of Negro tenants and sharecroppers. Black leaders referred to the NRA as standing for "Negro Robbed Again" and dismissed the AAA as "a continuation of the same old raw deal." Nor did later reform measures help very much. Neither the minimum wage nor Social Security covered those working as farmers or domestic servants, categories that comprised 65 percent of all black workers. Thus an NAACP official commented that Social Security "looks like a sieve with the holes just large enough for the majority of Negroes to fall through."

Despite this bleak record, blacks rallied behind Roosevelt's leadership, abandoning their historic ties to the Republican party. In 1936, over 75 percent of those blacks who voted supported FDR. In part, this switch came in response to Roosevelt's appointment of a number of prominent blacks to high-ranking government positions, such as William H. Hastie in the Interior Department and Mary McLeod Bethune (founder and president of Bethune-Cookman College) in the National Youth Administration. Eleanor Roosevelt spoke out eloquently throughout the decade against racial discrimination, most notably in 1939 when the Daughters of the American Revolution refused to let black contralto Marian Anderson sing in Constitution Hall. The First Lady and Interior Secretary Harold Ickes arranged for the singer to perform at the Lincoln Memorial, where seventy-five thousand gathered to hear her on Easter Sunday.

Perhaps the most influential factor in the blacks' political switch was the color-blind policy of Harry Hopkins. He had over one million blacks

■ *With the statue of Abraham Lincoln as a backdrop, black contralto Marian Anderson sings on the steps of the Lincoln Memorial in a concert given April 9, 1939.*

working for the WPA by 1939, many of them in teaching and artistic positions as well as in construction jobs. Overall, the New Deal provided assistance to 40 percent of the nation's blacks during the Depression. Uneven as his record was, Roosevelt had still done more to aid this oppressed minority than any previous president since Lincoln. One black newspaper commented that while "relief and WPA are not ideal, they are better than the Hoover bread lines and they'll have to do until the real thing comes along."

The New Deal did far less for Mexican-Americans. Engaged primarily in agricultural labor, these people found their wages in California fields dropping from thirty-five to fourteen cents an hour by 1933. The pool of migrant labor expanded rapidly with dust-bowl conditions in the Great Plains and the subsequent flight of "Okies" and "Arkies" to the cotton fields of Arizona and the truck farms of California. The Roosevelt administration cut off any further influx from Mexico by barring entry of any immigrant "likely to become a public charge"; local authorities rounded up migrants and shipped them back to Mexico to relieve their welfare rolls.

The New Deal relief program, however, did aid many thousands of Mexican-Americans in the Southwest in the 1930s, although migrant workers had difficulty meeting state requirements. The WPA hired Mexican-Americans for a variety of construction and cultural programs, but after 1937 such employment was denied to aliens. Overall, the pattern was one of very great economic hardship and relatively little federal assistance for Mexican-Americans.

The American Indian, after decades of neglect, fared slightly better under the New Deal. Roosevelt appointed John Collier, a social worker who championed Indian rights, to serve as commissioner of Indian affairs. In 1934, Congress passed the Indian Reorganization Act, a reform measure designed to stress tribal unity and autonomy instead of attempting (as previous policy had done) to transform Indians into self-sufficient farmers by granting them small plots of land (see chapter 17). Collier employed more Native Americans in the Indian Bureau, supported educational programs on the reservations, and encouraged tribes to produce native handiwork such as blankets and jewelry. Modest gains occurred, but the one third of a million Indians remained the nation's most impoverished citizens.

Women in the Thirties

The decade witnessed a continued decline in the status of American women. In the midst of the Depression, there was little concern expressed for protecting or extending their rights. The popular idea that women worked for "pin money" while men were the breadwinners for their families led employers to discriminate in favor of men when cutting the work force. Working women "are holding jobs that rightfully belong to the God-intended providers of the household," declared a Chicago civic group. More than three fourths of the nation's school boards refused to hire wives, and more than half of them fired women teachers who married. Federal regulations prohibited more than one member of a family from working in the civil service, and almost always it was the wife who had to defer to her husband. A Gallup poll revealed that 82 percent of the people disapproved of working wives, with 75 percent of the women polled agreeing.

Many of the working women in the 1930s were either single or the sole support of an entire family. Yet their wages remained lower than those for men, and their unemployment rate ran higher than 20 percent throughout the decade. Women over thirty-five found it particularly hard to find or retain jobs during the Depression. The New Deal offered little encouragement. NRA codes sanctioned lower wages for women, permitting laundries, for example, to pay them as little as fourteen cents an hour. The minimum wage did help those women employed in industry, but too many worked as maids and waitresses, jobs not covered by the law. By 1940, the percentage of women in the work force was no higher than it had been in 1910, and the traditional sexual inequities in the marketplace were as great as ever.

The one area of advance in the 1930s came in government. Eleanor Roosevelt set an example which encouraged millions of American women. Instead of presiding sedately over the White House, she traveled continually around the country, always eager to uncover wrongs and bring them to the President's attention (see the special feature in this chapter). Frances Perkins, the secretary of labor, became the first woman cabinet member, and FDR appointed women as ambassadors and federal judges for the first time.

Women also were elected to office in larger numbers in the thirties. Hattie W. Carraway of Arkansas succeeded her husband in the Senate, winning a full term in 1934. That same year voters elected six women to the House of Representatives. Public service, however, was one of the few professions open to women. The nation's leading medical and law schools discouraged women from applying, and the percentage of female faculty members in colleges and universities continued to decline in the 1930s. In sum, the decade was a grim one for American women.

End of the New Deal

The New Deal reached its high point in 1936, when Roosevelt was overwhelmingly reelected and the Democratic party strengthened its hold on Congress. But this political triumph was deceptive. In the next two years, Roosevelt met with a series of defeats in Congress. Yet despite

■ *The few advances made by working women in the 1930s came in government, as personified by Secretary of Labor Frances Perkins, the first woman cabinet member, shown here greeting steelworkers in Pittsburgh.*

these setbacks, he remained a popular political leader who had restored American self-confidence as he attempted to meet the challenges of the Depression.

The Election of 1936

Franklin Roosevelt enjoyed his finest political hour in 1936. A man who loved the give-and-take of politics, FDR faced challenges from both the left and the right as he sought reelection. Father Coughlin and Gerald L. K. Smith, who inherited Huey Long's following after the senator's assassination in 1935, organized a Union party, with North Dakota Progressive Congressman William Lemke heading the ticket. At the other extreme, a group of wealthy industrialists formed the Liberty League to fight what they saw as the New Deal's assault on property rights. The Liberty League attracted prominent Democrats, including Al Smith, but in 1936 it endorsed the Republican presidential candidate, Governor Alfred M. Landon of Kansas. A moderate, colorless figure, Landon disappointed his backers by refusing to campaign for repeal of the popular New Deal reforms.

Roosevelt ignored Lemke and the Union party, focusing attention instead on the assault from the right. Democratic spokesmen condemned the Liberty League as a "millionaire's union" and reminded the American people of how much Roosevelt had done for them in fighting unemployment and providing relief. In his speeches, FDR condemned the "economic royalists" who were "unanimous in their hatred for me." "I welcome their hatred," he declared, and promised that in his second term these forces would meet "their master."

This frank appeal to class sympathies proved enormously successful. Roosevelt won easily, receiving five million more votes than he had gotten in 1932 and outscoring Landon in the electoral college by 523 to 8. The Democrats did almost as well in Congress, piling up margins of 331 to 89 in the House and 76 to 16 in the Senate (with 4 not aligned with either major party).

Equally important, the election marked the creation of a new political coalition that would dominate American politics for the next three decades. FDR, building on the inroads into the Republican majority that Al Smith had begun in 1928, carried urban areas by impressive margins, winning 3.6 million more votes than his opponents in the nation's twelve largest cities. He held on to the traditional Democratic votes in the

Presidential Voting in Chicago by Ethnic Groups, 1924–1932 (Percent Democratic)

	1924	1928	1932
Czechoslovakians	40	73	83
Poles	35	71	80
Lithuanians	48	77	84
Yugoslavs	20	54	67
Italians	31	63	64
Germans	14	58	69
Jews	19	60	77

Source: John M. Allswang, A House for All Peoples: Ethnic Politics in Chicago, 1890–1936 (Lexington: University Press of Kentucky, 1971).

South and West and added to them by appealing strongly to the diverse religious and ethnic groups in the northern cities—Catholics and Jews, Italians and Poles, Irish and Slavs. The strong support of labor, together with three quarters of the black vote, indicated that the nation's new alignment followed economic as well as cultural lines. The poor and the oppressed, who in the Depression years included many middle-class Americans, became attached to the Democratic party, leaving the GOP in a minority position, limited to the well-to-do and to rural and small-town Americans of native stock.

The Supreme Court Fight

FDR proved to be far more adept at winning electoral victories than in achieving his goals in Congress. In 1937, he attempted to use his recent success to overcome the one obstacle remaining in his path—the Supreme Court. During his first term, the Court had ruled several New Deal programs unconstitutional, most notably the NRA and the AAA. Only three of the nine justices were sympathetic to the need for emergency measures in the midst of the Depression. Two others were unpredictable, sometimes approving New Deal measures and sometimes opposing them. Four justices were bent on using the Constitution to block Roosevelt's proposals. All were elderly men, and one, Willis Van Devanter, had planned to retire in 1932 but remained on the Court because he believed Roosevelt to be "unfitted and unsafe for the Presidency."

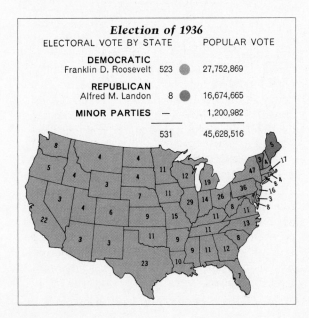

Election of 1936

ELECTORAL VOTE BY STATE — POPULAR VOTE

DEMOCRATIC
Franklin D. Roosevelt 523 — 27,752,869

REPUBLICAN
Alfred M. Landon 8 — 16,674,665

MINOR PARTIES — 1,200,982

531 — 45,628,516

Eleanor Roosevelt and the Quest for Social Justice

Eleanor Roosevelt entered public life as a reformer long before she became the First Lady. Although she loved and admired her uncle Theodore, her side of the Roosevelt family was more active in New York society than politics. In a family environment where the social graces were highly prized, Eleanor grew up shy and insecure. She turned to voluntary social work for fulfillment, where her relationships were based on common interests and ideals rather than social standing. Before her marriage to Franklin Roosevelt in 1905, she had been active in the New York settlement-house movement and the Consumers' League. Like many reformers of her day, she found her sense of social justice upset by the existence of poverty and inequality. Avoiding politics, which she then considered a "sinister affair," she limited her activities to nonpartisan reform and relief organizations.

After her marriage, she curtailed her social work, placing her responsibilities as a wife and mother first, as she believed a woman should. Though always a supportive partner, Mrs. Roosevelt did not develop a taste for politics despite her husband's tenure in the New York State Senate and later as assistant secretary of the navy during World War I. But when FDR was stricken with polio in 1921, she was determined that he return to political life as soon as possible; such a goal, she thought, was the best antidote to his pain and depression. While she worked tirelessly to speed his physical recovery, she also struck out on her own to keep the Roosevelt name alive in New York politics. In the newly formed League of Women Voters, the Women's City Club, the Non-Partisan Legislative Committee, and the New York State Democratic party, Eleanor Roosevelt brought her reformer's impulse to politics. In these organizations she formed the nucleus of an "old-girls' network" that she would employ entensively during the New Deal years. Her newly acquired political and organizational skills as well as her knowledge and speeches served her husband well in his gubernatorial and presidential campaigns.

In a speech delivered in 1928, Mrs. Roosevelt commented on the need to "bring government closer to the people" and to "develop the human side of government." Focusing on those whose needs were greatest, Eleanor Roosevelt was an advocate for the dispossessed. She advanced their interests within the administration, working hardest for women and blacks, whose voices were least often heard.

FDR appealed to the "forgotten man"; his wife concerned herself with the "forgotten woman." She worked with Harry Hopkins to achieve equity for women on relief and to create more jobs for women under the auspices of the CWA and the WPA. With Frances Perkins, she arranged to establish camps for unemployed girls patterned after the CCC while she continued to work with the Women's Trade Union League to guarantee women equal pay for equal work on federal projects. In her syndicated newspaper column "My Day," she often dealt with the problems faced by women during the Depression. She even held press conferences to which only women reporters were invited to ensure employment for at least a handful of female journalists.

The First Lady's office became, in effect, a clearing house for federally sponsored programs for women, and her endorsement often meant the difference between success or failure. She took advantage of her position to expedite the programs she thought most important. She saw to it that whenever possible women administrators were hired to supervise projects for women, but there were precious few programs for women to be administered. Although Mrs. Roosevelt was instrumental in the few gains made by women through the New Deal, her advocacy could not overcome the sexual stereotypes that continued to limit the role of women in the work force.

She worked equally hard for blacks, but with little more to show for her efforts. "We can have no group beaten down, underprivileged," said the First Lady in a radio address in 1934, "without reaction on the rest." In one sentence, she captured the essence of her appeal for justice and equality for blacks. Social justice was not merely desirable for blacks; it was necessary to ensure the vitality of American democracy. She spoke eloquently in favor of equal opportunity for blacks and sought their inclusion in New Deal programs. She worked with Hopkins to include more blacks in federal projects and lobbied within the administration for the appointment of black men and women to administer the programs designed specifically for them. Publicly, she endeavored to set an example for all Americans by addressing black audiences throughout the country, presiding over a more egalitarian

White House, and resigning her membership in the DAR over the Marian Anderson incident (see p. 762).

In her struggle against racial discrimination, Mrs. Roosevelt sometimes found her desires in conflict with her husband's attempts to keep the coalition of Democratic voters intact. His fear of alienating southern supporters caused him to temporize on the antilynching bill and abolition of the poll tax, both of which he considered desirable but not "must" legislation. Mrs. Roosevelt's support of these measures, however, put the Roosevelt name behind them. In her efforts to secure passage of the legislation, she arranged for meetings between FDR and Walter White of the NAACP. She briefed White to prepare him for FDR's objections in his conference with the President. When she asked FDR if he minded her public support of the antilynching bill, he replied, "Certainly not. . . . I can always say, 'Well, that is my wife; I can't do anything about her.'" Thus it appears that the President and Mrs. Roosevelt were of one mind, but she was able to support a cause that he felt it impolitic to advocate himself.

This distinction between the First Lady's activities as a representative of the Roosevelt administration and her actions as a private citizen was often a difficult one to establish. It is even harder to assess accurately her impact on the policies of the New Deal. Eleanor Roosevelt was revered by millions of Americans who saw in her the very essence of American ideals. Her support of women and blacks was instrumental in swaying their support to the Roosevelt coalition. Still, the telling fact remains that the plight of the two groups to which she devoted the lion's share of her attention during the Depression—women and blacks—was only slightly relieved. This is not to minimize her achievements. As the self-appointed conscience of the Roosevelt administration, she exposed the areas where the New Deal had not been realized. Her accessibility to the public and her willingness to serve its interests gave encouragement to those who had lost all hope. Her courage and vitality in the pursuit of human rights and equality made her the embodiment of reform and social justice in the New Deal.

FDR's battle with the Supreme Court provoked both sympathy and contempt among political cartoonists of the day. In the cartoon on the left, the NRA blue eagle lies dead, nailed to the wall by the Supreme Court. The cartoon on the right, entitled "That's the kind of sailor he is," satirizes FDR's Court-packing scheme.

When Congress convened in 1937, the President offered a startling proposal to overcome the Court's threat to the New Deal. Instead of seeking a constitutional amendment either to limit the Court's power or to clarify the constitutional issues, FDR chose an oblique attack. Declaring that the Court was falling behind schedule because of the age of its members, he asked Congress to appoint a new justice for each member of the Court over the age of seventy, up to a maximum of six.

Although this "Court-packing" scheme, as critics quickly dubbed it, was perfectly legal, it outraged not only conservatives but liberals as well, who realized it could set a dangerous precedent for the future. Republicans wisely kept silent, letting prominent Democrats such as Senator Burton Wheeler of Montana lead the fight against Roosevelt's plan. Despite all-out pressure from the White House, resistance in the Senate blocked early action on the proposal.

The Court defended itself well. Chief Justice Charles Evans Hughes testified tellingly to the Senate Judiciary Committee, pointing out that in fact the Court was up-to-date and not behind schedule as Roosevelt charged. The Court then surprised observers with a series of rulings approving such controversial New Deal measures as

the Wagner Act and Social Security. In the midst of the struggle, Justice Van Devanter resigned, enabling FDR to make his first appointment to the Court since taking office in 1933. Feeling that he had proved his point, the President allowed his Court-packing plan to die in the Senate.

During the next few years, four more vacancies occurred, and Roosevelt was able to appoint such distinguished jurists as Hugo Black, William O. Douglas, and Felix Frankfurter to the Supreme Court. Yet the price was high. The Court fight had badly weakened the President's relations with Congress, opening up deep rifts with members of his own party. Many senators and representatives who had voted reluctantly for Roosevelt's measures during the depths of the Depression new felt free to oppose any further New Deal reforms.

The New Deal in Decline

The legislative record during Roosevelt's second term was meager. Aside from the minimum wage and a maximum-hour law passed in 1938, Congress did not extend the New Deal into any new areas. Attempts to institute national health insurance met with stubborn resistance, as did

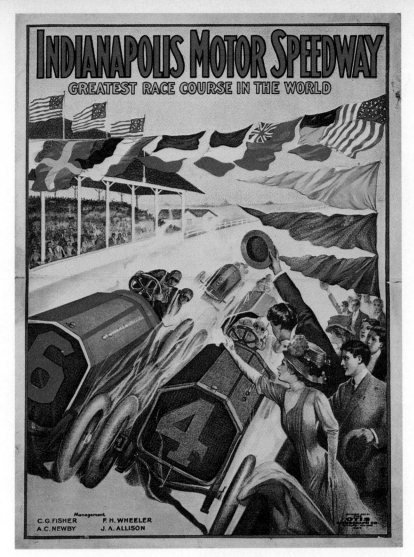

Culture of the Automobile

The nature of the consumer-goods revolution in the transition to modern America is epitomized in the "car culture." In 1920, there were ten million cars in the nation; by the end of the decade, twenty-six million autos were on the road. Production jumped from less than two million a year to over five million by 1929.

The automobile boom, at its peak from 1922 to 1927, depended on the apparently insatiable appetite of the American people for cars. But as the decade continued, the market became saturated as more and more of those who could afford the novel luxury had become car owners. Marketing became as crucial as production. Automobile makers began to rely heavily on advertising and annual model changes, seeking to make customers dissatisfied with their old vehicles and eager to order new ones. Installment buying helped prolong the boom. By 1925,

The first Indy 500-mile auto race at the speedway was held in 1911. Ray Harroun won, driving a Marmon Wasp that averaged 74.59 miles per hour.

LUXURY in a car is as much a matter of engine building as it is of upholstery. Luxury as expressed in a Pierce-Arrow means efficiency first, attractive design second, a perfectly appointed car, built around a thoroughly tried-out machine.

THE PIERCE-ARROW MOTOR CAR COMPANY, BUFFALO, N. Y.
Licensed under Selden Patent

Makers of the Pierce Arrow, the Duesenberg, and the Stutz Bearcat were squeezed out in the 1930s.

Traffic jam on a country lane, 1928. Despite vast road projects, highway construction lagged behind car sales.

An Oriental rug in the showroom of the prestigious Marmon auto emphasizes the car's elegance.

nearly 75 percent of all new cars were bought on credit as American consumers went into debt to satisfy their compulsion. An industry advertisement recognized the importance of this trend: "Take Off Your Hat to the Man Who Buys on Time."

Despite these efforts, the automobile industry revealed a basic weakness in the consumer-goods economy; once people bought an item with a long life, they were out of the market for a few years. Perishable and soft goods sold steadily year after year, but durables led to peaks and valleys in sales volume.

Few noticed the emerging economic instability until the 1930s. During the affluent 1920s, contemporary observers focused on the great stimulus the automobile had on the rest of the economy. Entire new rolling mills had to be built to supply sheet steel for car bodies. Rubber factories boomed with the demand for tires; paint and glass suppliers also benefited. The automobile helped create a boom in road construction. States began to levy new gasoline taxes to build the paved roads and highways needed for the cars. The auto changed the whole pattern of city life, leading to a suburban explosion as real-

Los Angeles area developers lay out Santa Monica Boulevard and Westwood Village in 1922.

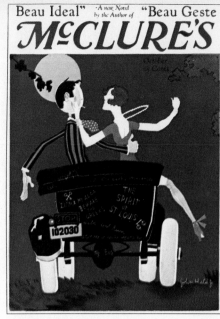

"Six-cylinder love" was a popular image of the 1920s.

A city-owned tourist park in Winona, Minnesota, 1929. Note the camper at left.

Roadside artistry in a 1930s second-hand tire display in San Marcos, Texas.

estate developers—no longer limited to areas served by streetcars and railway lines—could now build houses in ever wider concentric circles around the central cities. Americans were now bonded together by ribbons of concrete.

Filling stations appeared on the main streets, replacing the blacksmiths and the stables of the past. Tourist cabins, forerunners of the modern motel, appeared on the outskirts of cities; the drive-in restaurant soon became a familiar sight in nearly every American town. In Kansas City, Jess C. Nichols built the first shopping center, Country Club Plaza, and thus set an example quickly followed by other suburban developers.

In just a few short years, the automobile had become the very center of community life. Men drove cars to work, women did their shopping in them, and young people used them for their recreation. In Muncie, Indiana, site of a famous sociological survey in the 1920s, one elder replied when asked what was taking place, "I can tell you what's happening in just four letters:

A-U-T-O!"

The auto is an indispensable part of the public service message in this 1937 highway billboard.

During the Depression years most Americans could not heed the message of this poster; they had to hang on to their old cars.

Their vintage car piled high, migrant farm workers in California travel from one job to another.

The end of the road. Early auto graveyard on Lincoln Highway near Lancaster, Pennsylvania.

Not even the Great Depression could shake the grip of the car culture on American life, even though sales of new cars dropped by 75 percent between 1929 and 1932. Instead of buying new automobiles, owners nursed along their old ones so that by 1939 there were nearly thirty million vehicles on the road, three million more than in 1929. It is no accident that the word "jalopy" was coined in the 1930s to describe the decrepit Dodges and battered Model T Fords that still chugged down American streets and highways. Even the Okies went West on wheels, riding in old flivvers piled high with mattresses and household goods, children, and pets.

Despite economic near-paralysis, there were innovations. Manufacturers began to soften their boxlike designs with curved, "streamlined" styling. Each fall millions of Americans waited for next year's models to appear, eager to see what fresh wonders Detroit had created. A nation that had always revered symbols of movement, from the *Mayflower* to the covered wagon, now had a new icon to worship.

efforts by civil-rights advocates to pass antilynching legislation. Disturbed by this growing congressional resistance, Roosevelt set out in the spring of 1938 to defeat a number of conservative Democratic congressmen and senators. His targets gleefully charged the President with interference in local politics; only one of the men he sought to defeat lost in the primaries. The failure of this attempted purge further undermined Roosevelt's strained relations with Congress.

The worst blow came in the economic sector. The slow but steady improvement in the economy suddenly gave way to a sharp recession in the late summer of 1937. In the next ten months, industrial production fell by one third, and nearly four million workers lost their jobs. Critics of the New Deal quickly labeled the downturn "the Roosevelt recession," and businessmen claimed it reflected a lack of confidence in FDR's leadership.

Actually, Roosevelt was at fault. In an effort to reduce expanding budget deficits, he had cut back sharply on WPA and other government programs after the election. Federal contributions to consumer purchasing power fell from $4.1 billion in 1936 to less than $1 billion in 1937. For several months, Roosevelt refused to heed calls from economists to renew heavy government spending. Finally, in April 1938, Roosevelt asked Congress for a $3.75-billion relief appropriation, and the economy began to revive. But FDR's premature attempt to balance the budget had meant two more years of hard times and had marred his reputation as the energetic foe of the Depression.

The political result of the attempted purge and the recession was a strong Republican upsurge in 1938. The GOP won an impressive 81 seats in the House and 8 more in the Senate, as well as 13 governorships. The party many thought dead suddenly had new life. The Democrats still held a sizable majority in Congress, but their margin in the House was particularly deceptive. There were 262 Democratic representatives to 169 Republicans, but 93 southern Democrats held the balance of power. After 1938, more and more often anti-New Deal Southerners voted with Republican conservatives to block social and economic reform measures. Thus not only was the New Deal over by the end of 1938, but a new bipartisan conservative coalition that would prevail for a quarter century had formed in Congress.

Chronology

1932 Franklin D. Roosevelt elected president

1933 Emergency Banking Relief Act passed in one day (March)
Twenty-first Amendment repeals Prohibition (December)

1934 Securities and Exchange Commission authorized (June)

1935 Works Progress Administration (WPA) hires unemployed (April)
Wagner Act grants workers collective bargaining (July)
Congress passes Social Security Act (August)

1936 FDR wins second term as president

1937 Auto Workers' sit-down strike forces General Motors contract (February)
FDR loses Court-packing battle (July)
Roosevelt recession begins (August)

1938 Congress sets minimum wage at forty cents an hour (June)

Evaluation of the New Deal

The New Deal lasted a brief five years, and most of its measures came in two legislative bursts in the spring of 1933 and the summer of 1935. Yet its impact on American life was enduring. Nearly every aspect of economic, social, and political development in the decades that followed bore the imprint of Roosevelt's leadership.

The least impressive achievement of the New Deal came in the economic realm. Whatever credit Roosevelt is given for relieving human suffering in the depths of the Depression must be balanced against his failure to achieve recovery in the 1930s. The moderate nature of his programs, especially the unwieldy NRA, led to only slow and halting industrial recovery. Although much of the advance came as a result of government spending, FDR never embraced the concept of planned deficits, striving instead for a balanced budget. As a result, the nation had barely reached the 1929 level of production a decade later, and there were still nearly ten million men and women unemployed.

Equally important, Roosevelt refused to make any sweeping changes in the American economic system. Aside from the TVA, there were no broad experiments in nationalization and no attempt to alter free enterprise beyond imposing some limited forms of governmental regulation. The New Deal did nothing to alter the basic distribution of wealth and power in the nation. The outcome was the preservation of the traditional capitalist system with a thin overlay of federal control.

More significant change occurred in American society. With the adoption of Social Security, the government acknowledged for the first time its responsibility to provide for the welfare of those unable to care for themselves in an industrial society. The Wagner Act helped stimulate the growth of labor unions to balance corporate power, and the minimum-wage law provided a much-needed floor for many workers.

Yet the New Deal tended to help only the more vocal and organized groups, such as union members and commercial farmers. Those without effective voices or political clout—blacks and Mexican-Americans, women, sharecroppers, restaurant and laundry workers—received little help from the New Deal. For all the appealing rhetoric about the "forgotten man," Roosevelt did little more than Hoover in responding to the long-term needs of the dispossessed.

The most lasting impact of the Roosevelt leadership came in politics. Taking advantage of emerging ethnic voters and capitalizing on the frustration growing out of the Depression, FDR proved to be a genius at forging a new coalition. He overcame the friction between rural and urban Democrats that had prolonged Republican supremacy in the 1920s and attracted new groups to the Democratic party, principally blacks and organized labor. His political success led to a major realignment that lasted long after he left the scene.

His political achievement also reveals the true nature of Roosevelt's success. He was a brilliant politician who recognized the essence of leadership in a democracy—appealing directly to the people and infusing them with a sense of purpose. Thus despite his limitations as a reformer, Roosevelt proved to be the man the American people needed in the 1930s—the leader who helped them endure and survive the Great Depression.

Recommended Reading

The best overall account of political developments in the 1930s is William Leuchtenburg, *Franklin D. Roosevelt and the New Deal* (1963). Leuchtenburg offers a balanced treatment but concludes by defending Roosevelt's record. For a more critical view, see James MacGregor Burns, *Roosevelt: The Lion and the Fox* (1956), which portrays FDR as an overly cautious political leader. An exhaustive study of the New Deal through 1936 is Arthur M. Schlesinger, Jr., *The Age of Roosevelt*, 3 vols. (1957–1960), written from a sympathetic point of view. The best critique of Roosevelt's policies is the brief but perceptive book by Paul Conkin, *The New Deal* (1967).

Additional Bibliography

General accounts of the 1930s include Broadus Mitchell, *Depression Decade* (1947) on economic developments; Dixon Wecter, *The Age of the Great Depression* (1948) on social themes; John Braeman, Robert H. Bremner, and David Brody, eds., *The New Deal*, 2 vols. (1975), a collection of essays on both national and state trends; and John Allswang, *The New Deal and American Politics* (1978), a political survey.

Books on the Great Depression include John Kenneth Galbraith, *The Great Crash* (1955); Robert Sobel, *The Great Bull Market* (1968); Caroline Bird, *The Invisible Scar* (1963); and Studs Terkel, *Hard Times* (1970). Harris Warren, *Herbert Hoover and the Great Depression* (1959); Jordan Schwartz, *Interregnum of Despair* (1970); and Albert Romasco, *The Poverty of Abundance* (1965) all deal with Hoover's failure to stem the Depression.

Frank Freidel, *Franklin D. Roosevelt*, 4 vols. (1952–1976) is the most comprehensive biography of FDR, but the most recent volume only covers through mid-1933. Other biographical accounts of value are Rexford G. Tugwell, *The Democratic Roosevelt* (1957) and Alfred B. Rollins, *Roosevelt and Howe* (1962). The rich memoir literature for the New Deal includes Frances Perkins, *The Roosevelt I Knew* (1946); Raymond Moley, *The First New Deal* (1966); and Samuel I. Rosenman, *Working with Roosevelt* (1952). For biographies of Eleanor Roosevelt, see Joseph Lash, *Eleanor and Franklin* (1971) and Tamara K. Hareven, *Eleanor Roosevelt* (1968). Susan Ware traces the role of women in the New Deal in *Beyond Suffrage* (1981). J. Joseph Huthmacher has written a fine biography of a major New Deal figure, *Senator Robert Wagner and the Rise of Urban Liberalism* (1968).

The transition from Hoover and the beginning of the New Deal is traced in Elliot Rosen, *Hoover, Roosevelt and the Brains Trust* (1977). The best of many books dealing with farm problems in the 1930s are Richard Kirkendall, *Social Scientists and Farm Politics in the Age of Roosevelt* (1966); Paul Conkin, *Tomorrow a New*

World (1959); Van Perkins, *Crisis in Agriculture (1969);* Sidney Baldwin, *Poverty and Politics* (1968); and Donald Worster, *Dust Bowl* (1979). Searle F. Charles traces Harry Hopkins' role in the New Deal in *Minister of Relief* (1963), while William McDonald describes the WPA's cultural activities in detail in *Federal Relief Administration and the Arts* (1969). For labor developments, see Sidney Fine, *Sit Down: The General Motors Strike of 1936-37* (1969) and two books by Irving Bernstein: *The New Deal's Collective Bargaining Policy* (1950) and *The Turbulent Years* (1970).

Among the many books surveying the various New Deal programs, the most useful are John Salmond, *The Civilian Conservation Corps, 1933–1942* (1967); Thomas K. McCraw, *TVA and the Power Fight, 1933–1939* (1971); and Jane D. Mathews, *The Federal Theatre, 1935–1939* (1967). Two other important books on the New Deal are Otis L. Graham, Jr., *An Encore for Reform* (1967) and Ellis Hawley, *The New Deal and the Problem of Monopoly, 1933–1939* (1965).

Studies by critics of the New Deal include George Wolfskill, *Revolt of the Conservatives* (1962); T. Harry Williams, *Huey Long* (1969); Abraham Holtzman, *The Townsend Movement* (1963); Charles Tull, *Father Coughlin and the New Deal* (1965); Sheldon Marcus, *Father Coughlin* (1973); and Alan Brinkley, *Voices of Protest: Huey Long, Father Coughlin, and the Great Depression* (1982). For intellectual radicalism in the 1930s, see Daniel Aaron, *Writers on the Left* (1960) and Richard Pells, *Radical Visions and American Dreams* (1973).

Raymond Wolters offers a critical view of Roosevelt's policies toward blacks in *Negroes and the Great Depression* (1970); Harvard Sitkoff is more positive in *A New Deal for Blacks* (1978). Abraham Hoffman deals with the repatriation issue in *Unwanted Mexican-Americans in the Great Depression* (1974). For the impact of the Depression on women, see William H. Chafe, *The American Woman* (1972); Winifred Wandersee, *Women's Work and Family Values, 1920–1940* (1981); and Lois Sharf, *To Work and to Wed* (1980).

Leonard Baker describes Roosevelt's attempt to pack the Supreme Court in *Back to Back* (1967). The best account of the waning of the reform impulse in Congress is James T. Patterson, *Congressional Conservatism and the New Deal* (1967).

chapter 27

AMERICA AND THE WORLD, 1921–1945

On August 27, 1928, U.S. Secretary of State Frank B. Kellogg, French Foreign Minister Aristide Briand, and representatives of twelve other nations met in Paris to sign a treaty outlawing war. Several hundred spectators crowded into the ornate clock room of the Quai d'Orsay to watch the historic ceremony. Six huge kleig lights illuminated the scene so that photographers could record the moment for a world eager for peace. Briand opened the ceremony with a speech in which he declared, "Peace is proclaimed," and then Kellogg signed the document with a foot-long gold pen given to him by the citizens of Le Havre as a token of Franco-American friendship. In the United States, a senator called the Kellogg-Briand Treaty "the most telling action ever taken in human history to abolish war."

In reality, the Pact of Paris was the result of a determined American effort to avoid involvement in the European alliance system. In June 1927, Briand had sent a message to the American people inviting the United States to join with France in signing a treaty to outlaw war between the two nations. The invitation struck a sympathetic response, especially among pacifists who had advocated the outlawing of war throughout the 1920s, but the State Department feared correctly that Briand's true intention was to establish a close tie between France and the United States. The French had already created a network of alliances with the smaller countries of Eastern Europe; an antiwar treaty with the United States would at least ensure American sympathy, if not involvement, in case of another European war. Kellogg delayed several months and then outmaneuvered Briand by proposing that the pledge against war not be confined just to France and the United States, but instead be extended to all nations. An unhappy Briand, who had wanted a bilateral treaty with the United States, had no choice but to agree, and so the diplomatic charade finally culminated in the elaborate signing ceremony in Paris.

Eventually the signers of the Kellogg-Briand Treaty included nearly every nation in the world, but the effect was negligible. All promised to renounce war as an instrument of national policy, except of course, as the British made clear in a reservation, in matters of self-defense. The treaty relied solely on the moral force of world opinion. The Pact of Paris was, as one senator shrewdly commented, only "an international kiss."

Unfortunately, the Kellogg-Briand Pact was symbolic of American foreign policy in the years after World War I. Instead of asserting the role of leadership its resources and power commanded, the United States kept aloof from other nations. America went its own way, extending trade and economic dominance but refusing to take the lead in maintaining world order. This retreat from responsibility seemed unimportant in the 1920s when the very exhaustion from World War I ensured relative peace and tranquillity. But in the '30s, when threats to world order arose in Europe and Asia, the American people retreated even deeper, searching for an isolationist policy that would spare them the agony of another great war.

■ "Married Again" is the caption of this 1928 cartoon depicting the hopeful promise of the Kellogg-Briand Treaty. This wicked world is once again pledging fidelity to peace "forever and ever and ever."

There was no place to hide in the modern world. The Nazi onslaught in Europe and the Japanese expansion in Asia finally led to American entry into World War II in late 1941, at a time when the chances for an Allied victory seemed most remote. With incredible swiftness, the nation mobilized its military and industrial strength. American armies were soon fighting on three continents, the U.S. Navy controlled the world's oceans, and the nation's factories were sending a vast stream of war supplies to more than twenty Allied countries.

When victory came in 1945, the United States was by far the most powerful nation in the world. But instead of the enduring peace that might have permitted a return to a less active foreign policy, the onset of the Cold War with the Soviet Union brought on a new era of tension and conflict. This time the United States could not retreat from responsibility. World War II was a coming of age for American foreign policy.

Retreat, Reversal, and Rivalry

"The day of the armistice America stood on the hilltops of glory, proud in her strength, invincible in her ideals, acclaimed and loved by a world free of an ancient fear at last," wrote journalist George Creel in 1920. "Today we writhe in a pit of our own digging, despising ourselves and despised by the betrayed peoples of earth." The bitter disillusionment Creel described ran through every aspect of American foreign policy in the 1920s. In contrast to Wilsonian idealism, American diplomats made loans, negotiated treaties and agreements, and pledged the nation's good faith, but they were careful not to make any binding commitments on behalf of world order. The result was neither isolation nor involvement but rather a cautious middle course that managed to alienate friends and encourage foes.

Retreat in Europe

The United States emerged from World War I as the richest nation on earth, displacing England from its prewar position of economic primacy.

The Allied governments owed the United States a staggering $10 billion in war debts, money they had borrowed during and right after the conflict. Each year of the 1920s saw the nation increase its economic lead as the balance of trade tipped heavily in America's favor. The war-ravaged countries of Europe borrowed enormous amounts from American bankers to rebuild their economies; Germany alone absorbed over $3 billion in American investments during the decade. By 1929, American exports totaled more than $7 billion a year, three times the prewar level, and American overseas investment had risen to $17.2 billion.

The European nations could no longer compete on equal terms. The high American tariff, first imposed in 1922 and then raised again in 1930, frustrated attempts by England, France, and a defeated Germany to earn the dollars necessary to meet their American financial obligations. The Allied partners in World War I asked Washington to cancel the $10 billion in war debts, particularly after they were forced to scale down their demands for German reparations payments. American leaders from Wilson to Hoover indignantly refused this request, claiming that the ungrateful Allies were trying to repudiate their sacred obligations.

Only a continuing flow of private American capital to Germany allowed the payment of reparations to the Allies and the partial repayment of the war debts in the 1920s. The financial crash of 1929 halted the flow of American dollars across the Atlantic and led to subsequent default on the debt payments, with accompanying bitterness on both sides of the ocean.

Political relations fared little better. The United States never joined the League of Nations, nor did it take part in the attempts by England and France to negotiate European security treaties. American observers attended League sessions and occasionally took part in economic and cultural missions in Geneva. But the Republican administrations of the twenties refused to compromise American freedom of action by embracing collective security, the principle on which the League was founded. And FDR, always realistic, made no effort to renew Wilson's futile quest. Thus the United States remained aloof from the European balance of power and refused to stand behind the increasingly shaky Versailles settlement.

The United States ignored the Soviet Union throughout the 1920s. American businessmen, however, wanted to sell their machinery and tools to Russia for that country's rapid industrialization. They began to press for diplomatic recognition of the Bolshevik regime which had come to power in the Russian Revolution of 1917. In 1933, Franklin Roosevelt finally ended the long estrangement by signing an agreement opening up diplomatic relations between the two countries. The Soviets soon went back on promises to stop all subversive activity in the United States and to settle prerevolutionary debts, but at least the two nations had opened a channel of communication, even if they rarely understood one another.

Reversal in Latin America

United States policy in the Western Hemisphere was both more active and more enlightened than in Europe. The State Department sought new ways in the 1920s to pursue traditional goals of political dominance and economic advantage in Latin America. The outcome of World War I lessened any fears of European threats to the area and thus enabled the United States to dismantle the interventions in the Caribbean carried out by Roosevelt, Taft, and Wilson (see chapter 24). At the same time, both Republican and Democratic administrations worked hard to extend American trade and investment in the nations to the south.

Under Harding, Coolidge, and Hoover, American marines were withdrawn from Haiti and the Dominican Republic, and in 1924 the last detachment left Nicaragua, ending a twelve-year occupation. Renewed unrest there the next year, however, led to a second intervention in Nicaragua, which did not end until the early 1930s.

Showing a new sensitivity, the State Department released the Clark Memorandum in 1930, a policy statement repudiating the controversial Roosevelt Corollary to the Monroe Doctrine. Under the Monroe Doctrine, the United States had no right to intervene in neighboring states, declared Undersecretary of State J. Reuben Clark, although he asserted a traditional claim to protect American lives and property under international law.

When FDR took office in 1933, relations with Latin America were far better than they had been

■ On his South American tour to promote the Good Neighbor policy, FDR greets the president of Uruguay.

under Wilson, but American trade in the hemisphere had fallen drastically as the Depression worsened. Roosevelt moved quickly to solidify the improved relations and gain economic benefits. With his usual flair for the dramatic, he proclaimed a policy of the "good neighbor" and then proceeded to win goodwill by renouncing the imperialism of the past.

In 1933, Secretary of State Cordell Hull signed a conditional pledge of nonintervention at a Pan-American conference in Montevideo, Uruguay. A year later, the United States renounced its right to intervene in Cuban affairs (the Platt Amendment) and loosened its grip on Panama. By 1936, American troops were no longer occupying any Latin American nation. FDR personally cemented the new policy by traveling to Buenos Aires to sign an agreement that forbade intervention "directly or indirectly, and for whatever reason" in the internal affairs of an American state.

The United States had not changed its basic goal of political and economic dominance in the hemisphere; rather, the new policy of benevolence reflected Roosevelt's belief that cooperation and friendship were more effective tactics than threats and armed intervention. Mexico tried his patience in 1938 by nationalizing its oil resources; with admirable restraint, the President finally negotiated a settlement in 1941 on terms favorable to Mexico. Yet this economic loss was more than offset by the new trade opportunities opened up by the Good Neighbor policy. American commerce with Latin America increased fourfold in the 1930s, and investment rose substantially from its Depression low. Most important, FDR succeeded in forging a new policy of regional collective security. As the ominous events leading to World War II unfolded in Europe and Asia, the nations of the Western Hemisphere looked to the United States for protection against external danger.

Rivalry in Asia

In the years following World War I, the United States and Japan were on a collision course in the Pacific. The Japanese, lacking the raw materials to sustain their developing industrial economy, were determined to expand onto the Asian mainland. They had taken Korea by 1905 and during World War I had extended their control over the mines, harbors, and railroads of Manchuria, the industrial region of northeast China. The American Open Door policy remained the primary obstacle to complete Japanese dominion over China. The United States thus faced the clear-cut choice of either abandoning China or forcefully opposing Japan's expansion. American efforts to avoid making this painful decision postponed the eventual showdown but not the growing rivalry.

The first attempt at a solution came in 1921 when the United States convened the Washington Conference. The major objective was a political settlement of the tense Asian situation, but the most pressing issue was a dangerous naval race between Japan and the United States. Both nations were engaged in extensive shipbuilding programs begun during the war. Great Britain was forced to compete in order to preserve its traditional control of the sea; even so, projected construction indicated that both the United States and Japan would overtake the British navy by the end of the decade. Japan, spending nearly one third of its budget on naval construction, was eager for an agreement; in the United States, growing congressional concern over appropriations suggested the need for slowing the naval buildup.

In his welcoming address at the Washington Conference, Secretary of State Charles Evans Hughes outlined a specific plan for naval disarmament, calling for the scrapping of sixty-six battleships—thirty American, nineteen British, and seventeen Japanese. Three months later, delegates signed a Five Power Treaty embodying the main elements of Hughes' proposal: limitation of capital ships (battleships and aircraft carriers) in a ratio of 5–5–3 for the United States, Britain, and Japan respectively and 1.75–1.75 for France and Italy. England reluctantly accepted equality with the United States, while Japan agreed to the lower ratio only in return for an American pledge not to fortify Pacific bases such as the Philippines and Guam. The treaty cooled off the naval race even though it did not include cruisers, destroyers, or submarines.

The Washington Conference produced two other major agreements, the Nine Power Treaty and the Four Power Treaty. The first simply pledged everyone to uphold the Open Door policy, while the other compact replaced the old Anglo-Japanese alliance with a new Pacific security pact signed by the United States, Great Britain, Japan, and France. Neither document contained any enforcement provision beyond a promise to consult in case of a violation. In essence, the Washington treaties formed a parchment peace, a pious set of pledges that attempted to freeze the status quo in the Pacific.

This compromise lasted less than a decade. In September 1931, Japanese forces overran Manchuria, violating the Nine Power Treaty and the Kellogg-Briand Pact in a brutal act of aggression. The United States, paralyzed by the Depression, responded feebly. Secretary of State Henry L. Stimson sent an observer to Geneva to assure cooperation with the League of Nations, which was content to investigate the "incident." In January 1932, Stimson fell back on moral force, issuing notes vowing that the United States would not recognize the legality of the Japanese seizure of Manchuria. Despite ultimate concurrence by the League on nonrecognition, the Japanese ignored the American moral sanction and incorporated the former Chinese province, now renamed Manchukuo, into their expanding empire.

Aside from the good-neighbor approach in the Western Hemisphere, American foreign policy faithfully reflected the prevailing disillusionment with world power that gripped the country after World War I. The United States avoided taking any constructive steps toward preserving world order, preferring instead the empty symbolism of the Washington treaties and the Kellogg-Briand Pact.

Isolationism

The retreat from an active world policy in the 1920s turned into a headlong flight back to isolationism in the '30s. Two factors were responsible. First, the Depression made foreign policy seem remote and unimportant to most Americans. As unemployment increased and the economic crisis intensified after 1929, many people grew apathetic about events abroad. Second, the danger of war abroad, when it did finally penetrate the American consciousness, served only to strengthen the desire to escape involvement.

Three powerful and discontented nations were on the march in the 1930s—Germany, Italy, and Japan. In Germany, Adolf Hitler came to power in 1933 as the head of a National Socialist, or Nazi, movement. A shrewd, charismatic, and eloquent leader, Hitler capitalized on both domestic discontent and bitterness over World War I. Blaming the Jews for all of Germany's ills, he quickly imposed a totalitarian dictatorship in which the Nazi party ruled and the führer was supreme. At first, his foreign policy seemed harmless, but as he consolidated his power, the ultimate threat to world peace became clearer. Hitler took Germany out of the League of Nations, reoccupied the Rhineland, and formally denounced the Treaty of Versailles. His boasts of uniting all Germans into a Greater Third Reich that would last a thousand years filled his European opponents with terror, blocking any effective challenge to his regime.

In Italy, another dictator, Benito Mussolini, had come to power in 1922. Emboldened by Hitler's success, he embarked on an aggressive foreign policy in 1935. His invasion of the independent African nation of Ethiopia led its emperor, Haile Selassie, to call upon the League of Nations for support. With England and France far more concerned about Hitler, the League's halfway measures utterly failed to halt Mussolini's conquest. "Fifty-two nations had combined to resist aggres-

Captured German painting. Millions of Germans idolized Adolph Hitler, portrayed here as a white knight. After the painting came into American hands, a GI slashed Hitler's face to indicate his displeasure with the mystique of the Führer.

sion," commented historian A. J. P. Taylor; "all they accomplished was that Haile Selassie lost all his country instead of only half." Collective security had failed its most important test.

Japan formed the third element in the threat to world peace. Militarists began to dominate the government in Tokyo by the mid-1930s, using tactics of fear and even assassination against their liberal opponents. By 1936, Japan had left the League of Nations and had repudiated the Washington treaties. A year later, its armies began an invasion of China that marked the beginning of the Pacific phase of World War II.

The resurgence of militarism in Germany, Italy, and Japan undermined the Versailles settlement and threatened to destroy the existing balance of power. England and France in Europe proved as powerless as China in Asia to stop the tide of aggression. In 1937, the three totalitarian nations signed an anti-Comintern pact completing a Berlin-Rome-Tokyo axis. Their alliance ostensibly was aimed at the Soviet Union, but in fact it threatened the entire world. Only a determined American response could unite the other nations against this Axis threat. Unfortunately,

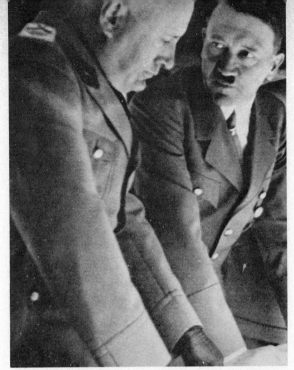

■ *Benito Mussolini, dictator of Italy, shown conferring with his partner in the Rome-Berlin axis. Mussolini, sometimes called the "sawdust Caesar," was clearly subordinate to Hitler, who dominated the partnership.*

the United States deliberately abstained from assuming this role of leadership until it was nearly too late.

The Lure of Pacifism and Neutrality

The growing danger of war abroad led to a rising American desire for peace and noninvolvement. Memories of World War I contributed heavily. The novel *All Quiet on the Western Front*, as well as the movie based on it, reminded people of the brutal trench warfare. Historians began to treat the Great War as a mistake, criticizing Wilson for failing to preserve American neutrality and claiming that the clever British had duped the United States into entering the war. Walter Millis advanced this thesis in a popular book, *America's Road to War, 1914–1917*, published in 1935. It was hailed as a vivid description of the process by which "a peace-loving democracy, muddled but excited, misinformed and whipped to a frenzy, embarked upon its greatest foreign war."

American youth made clear their determina-

tion not to repeat the mistakes of their elders. Pacifism swept across college campuses. A Brown University poll indicated 72 percent of the students opposed military service in wartime. At Princeton, undergraduates formed the Veterans of Future Wars, a parody on veterans' groups, to demand a bonus of $1000 apiece before they marched off to a foreign war! In April 1934, students and professors alike walked out of class to attend massive antiwar rallies, which became an annual rite of spring in the 1930s. Amid demonstrators carrying signs reading "Abolish the R.O.T.C." and "Build Schools—Not Battleships," pacifist orators urged students to sign a pledge not to support their country "in any war it might conduct."

The pacifist surge found a scapegoat in the munitions industry. The publication of several books exposing the unsavory business tactics of large arms dealers such as Krupps in Germany and Vickers in Britain led to a demand to curb these "merchants of death." Senator Gerald Nye of North Dakota headed a special Senate committee which spent two years investigating American munitions dealers. The committee revealed the enormous profits such firms as Du Pont reaped from World War I, but Nye went further, charging that bankers and munitions makers were responsible for American intervention in 1917. No proof was forthcoming, but the public—prepared to believe the worst of businessmen during the Depression—accepted the "merchants-of-death" thesis.

The Nye Committee's revelations culminated in neutrality legislation. In 1935, Senator Nye and another Senate colleague introduced measures to ban arms sales and loans to belligerents and to prevent Americans from traveling on belligerent ships. By outlawing the activities that led to World War I, they hoped the United States could avoid involvement in the new conflict. This "never-again" philosophy proved irresistible. In August 1935, Congress passed the first of three neutrality acts. The 1935 law banned the sale of arms to nations at war and warned American citizens not to sail on belligerent ships. In 1936, a second act added a ban on loans, and in 1937, a third neutrality act made these prohibitions permanent and required, on a two-year trial basis, that all trade other than munitions be conducted on a cash-and-carry basis.

President Roosevelt played a passive role in the adoption of the neutrality legislation. At first opposed to the arms embargo, he finally approved it for six months in 1935 in a compromise designed to save important New Deal legislation in Congress. Yet he also appeared to share the isolationist assumption that a European war would have no impact on vital national interests. He termed the first neutrality act "entirely satisfactory" when he signed it. Others in the administration criticized the mandatory nature of the new law, pointing out that it prevented the United States from distinguishing between aggressors and their victims. Privately, Roosevelt expressed some of the same reservations, but publicly he bowed to the prevailing isolationism. He signed the subsequent neutrality acts without protest, and during the 1936 election he delivered an impassioned denunciation of war. "I hate war," he told an audience in Chautauqua, New York. "I have passed unnumbered hours, I shall pass unnumbered hours, thinking and planning how war may be kept from this nation."

Yet FDR did take a few steps to try to limit the nation's retreat into isolationism. His failure to invoke the neutrality act after the Japanese invasion of China in 1937 enabled the hard-pressed Chinese to continue buying arms from the United States. A year later, he used his influence to block a proposal by Indiana Congressman Louis Ludlow to require a nationwide referendum before Congress could declare war. FDR's strongest public statement came in Chicago in October 1937 when he denounced "the epidemic of world lawlessness" and called for an international effort to "quarantine" this disease. When reporters asked him if his call for "positive efforts to preserve peace" signaled a repeal of the neutrality acts, however, Roosevelt quickly reaffirmed this isolationist legislation. Whatever his private yearning for cooperation against aggressors, the President had no intention of challenging the prevailing public mood of the 1930s.

War in Europe

The neutrality legislation played directly into the hands of Adolf Hitler. Bent on the conquest of Europe, he could now proceed without worrying about American interference. In March 1938, he seized Austria in a bloodless coup. Six months later, he was demanding the Sudetenland, a province of Czechoslovakia with a large German population. When the British and French leaders agreed to meet with Hitler at Munich, FDR voiced his approval. Roosevelt carefully kept the United States aloof from the subsequent surrender of the Sudetenland. At the same time, he gave his tacit approval of the Munich agreement by telling the British prime minister that he shared his "hope and belief that there exists today the greatest opportunity in years for the establishment of a new order based on justice and on law."

Six months after the meeting at Munich, Hitler violated his promises by seizing nearly all of Czechoslovakia. In the United States, Roosevelt permitted the State Department to press for neutrality revision. An administration proposal to repeal the arms embargo and place *all* trade with belligerents, including munitions, on a cash-and-carry basis soon met stubborn resistance from isolationists. They argued that cash-and-carry would favor England and France, who controlled the sea. The House rejected the measure by a narrow margin, and the Senate's Foreign Relations Committee voted 12 to 11 to postpone any action on neutrality revision.

In July 1939, Roosevelt finally abandoned his aloof position and held a meeting with Senate leaders to plead for reconsideration. Warnings of the imminence of war in Europe by both the President and the secretary of state failed to impress the isolationists. Senator William Borah, who had led the fight against the League of Nations in 1919, responded that he felt the chances for war in Europe were remote. After canvassing the senators present, Vice-President John Nance Garner bluntly told FDR that neutrality revision was dead. "You haven't got the votes," Garner commented, "and that's all there is to it."

On September 1, 1939, Hitler began World War II by invading Poland. England and France responded two days later by declaring war, although there was no way they could prevent the German conquest of Poland. Russia had played a key role, refusing Western overtures for a common front against Germany and finally signing a nonaggression treaty with Hitler in late August. The Nazi-Soviet Pact enabled Germany to avoid a two-front war; the Russians were rewarded with a generous slice of eastern Poland.

Hitler sent his armies into Poland with tremendous force and firepower, devastating the country. Below, a motorized division drives through a town battered by repeated bombings. When Jews, such as these residents of the Warsaw Ghetto (right), fell into the hands of the Nazi occupiers, they were deported to slave labor camps that soon turned into mass extermination camps.

President Roosevelt reacted to the outbreak of war by proclaiming American neutrality, but the successful aggression by Nazi Germany brought into question the isolationist assumption that American well-being did not depend upon the European balance of power. Strategic as well as ideological considerations began to undermine the earlier belief that the United States could safely pursue a policy of neutrality and noninvolvement. The long retreat from responsibility was about to end as Americans came to realize that their own democracy and security were at stake in the European war.

The Road to War

For two years the United States tried to remain at peace while war raged in Europe and Asia. In contrast to Wilson's attempt to be impartial during most of World War I, however, the American people displayed an overwhelming sympathy for the Allies and total distaste for Germany and Japan. Roosevelt made no secret of his preference for an Allied victory, but a fear of isolationist criticism compelled him to move slowly, and often deviously, in adopting a policy of aid for England and France—short of actually entering the war.

Two weeks after the outbreak of war in Europe, Roosevelt called Congress into special session to revise the neutrality legislation. He wanted to repeal the arms embargo in order to supply weapons to England and France, but he refused to state this aim openly. Instead he asked Congress to replace the arms embargo with cash-and-carry regulations. Belligerents would be able to purchase war supplies in the United States, but they would have to pay cash and transport the goods in their own ships. Public opinion strongly supported the President, and Congress passed the revised neutrality policy by heavy margins in early November 1939.

A series of dramatic German victories had a profound impact on American opinion. Quiet during the winter of 1939–1940, the Germans struck with lightning speed and devastating effect in the spring. In April, they seized Denmark and Norway, and on May 10, 1940, they unleashed the *blitzkreig* (lightning war) on the western front. Using tanks, armored columns, and dive bombers in close coordination, the Germany army cut deep into the Allied lines, dividing the British and French forces. Within three weeks, the British were driven off the continent. In another three weeks, France fell to Hitler's victorious armies.

Americans were stunned. Hitler had taken only six weeks to achieve what Germany had failed to do in four years of fighting in World War I. Suddenly they realized that they did have a stake in the outcome; if England fell, Hitler might well gain control of the British navy. The Atlantic would no longer be a barrier; instead, it would be a highway for German penetration of the New World.

Roosevelt responded by invoking a policy of all-out aid to the Allies short of war. In a speech at Charlottesville, Virginia, in June (just after Italy entered the war by invading France), he denounced Germany and Italy as representing "the gods of force and hate" and vowed that "the whole of our sympathies lies with those nations that are giving their life blood in combat against these forces." It was too late to help France, but in early September, FDR announced the transfer of fifty old destroyers to England in exchange for rights to build air and naval bases on eight British possessions in the Western Hemisphere. Giving warships to a belligerent nation was clearly a

A hastily organized flotilla of privately owned small boats chugged across the Channel from England at the end of May 1940 and performed the miracle of Dunkirk—rescuing a third of a million British troops trapped on the beach at the French Channel port, under heavy bombardment from German planes. A supreme effort by the Royal Air Force won superiority in the sky over the evacuation area.

breach of neutrality, but Roosevelt stressed the importance of guarding the Atlantic approaches, calling the destroyers-for-bases deal "the most important action in the reinforcement of our national defense that has been taken since the Louisiana Purchase."

Isolationists cried out against this departure from neutrality. A headline in the *Saint Louis Post-Dispatch* read, "Dictator Roosevelt Commits Act of War." A group of Roosevelt's opponents in the Midwest formed the America First Committee to protest the drift toward war. Such diverse individuals as aviator-hero Charles Lindbergh, conservative Senator Robert A. Taft of Ohio, socialist leader Norman Thomas, and liberal educator Robert M. Hutchins condemned FDR for involving the United States in a foreign conflict. Voicing belief in a "Fortress America," they denied that Hitler threatened American security and claimed that the nation had the strength to defend itself regardless of what happened in Europe.

To support the administration's policies, opponents of the isolationists organized the Committee to Defend America by Aiding the Allies. Eastern Anglophiles, moderate New Dealers, and liberal Republicans made up the bulk of the membership, with Kansas newspaper editor William Allen White serving as chairman. The White Committee, as it became known, advocated unlimited assistance to England short of war, although some of its members privately favored entry into the conflict. Above all, the interventionists challenged the isolationist premise that events in Europe did not affect American security. "The future of western civilization is being decided upon the battlefield of Europe," White declared.

In the ensuing debate, the American people gradually came to agree with the interventionists. The battle of Britain helped. "Every time Hitler bombed London, we got a couple of votes," noted one interventionist. Frightened by the events in Europe, Congress approved large sums for preparedness, increasing the defense budget from $2 billion to $10 billion during 1940. Roosevelt courageously asked for a peacetime draft, the first in American history, to build up the army; in September, Congress agreed.

The sense of crisis affected domestic politics. Roosevelt ran for an unprecedented third term in

		The Election of 1940	
Candidate	Party	Popular Vote	Electoral Vote
Roosevelt	Democrat	27,263,448	449
Willkie	Republican	22,336,260	82

1940 because of the European war; the Republicans nominated Wendell Willkie, a former Democratic businessman who shared FDR's commitment to aid for England. Both candidates made appeals to peace sentiment during the campaign, but Roosevelt's decisive victory made it clear that the nation supported his increasing departure from neutrality.

After the election, FDR took his boldest step. Responding to British Prime Minister Winston Churchill's warning that England was running out of money, the President asked Congress to approve a new program to lend and lease goods and weapons to countries fighting against aggressors. Roosevelt's call for America to become "the great arsenal of democracy" seemed straightforward enough, but he acted somewhat deviously by naming the program Lend-Lease and by comparing it to loaning a neighbor a garden hose to put out a fire.

Isolationists angrily denounced Lend-Lease as both unnecessary and untruthful. "Lending war equipment is a good deal like lending chewing gum," commented Senator Taft. "You don't want it back." In March 1941, however, Congress voted by substantial margins to authorize the President to "sell, transfer title to, exchange, lease, lend, or otherwise dispose of" war supplies to "any country the President deems vital to the defense of the United States." The accompanying $7-billion appropriation ended the "cash" part of cash-and-carry and ensured Britain full access to American war supplies.

The "carry" problem still remained. German submarines were sinking over five hundred thousand tons of shipping a month. England desperately needed the help of the American navy in escorting convoys across the U-boat-infested waters of the North Atlantic. Roosevelt, fearful of

Kneeling at the Capitol Plaza in Washington, women from various mothers' groups conduct a pray-in to protest the passage of the lend-lease bill.

In leading the nation to the brink of war in Europe, Roosevelt opened himself to criticism from both sides in the domestic debate. Interventionists felt that he had been too cautious in dealing with the danger to the nation from Nazi Germany. Isolationists were equally critical of the President, claiming that he had misled the American people by professing peace while plotting for war. Roosevelt was certainly less than candid, relying on executive discretion to engage in highly provocative acts in the North Atlantic. He agreed with the interventionists that in the long run American security would be threatened by a German victory in Europe. But he also was aware that a poll taken in September 1941 showed that nearly 80 percent of the American people wanted to stay out of World War II. Realizing that leading a divided nation into war would be disastrous, FDR played for time, inching the country toward war while waiting for the Axis nations to make the ultimate move. Japan finally obliged at Pearl Harbor.

Showdown in the Pacific

Japan had taken advantage of the war in Europe to expand further in Asia. Although successful after 1937 in conquering the populous coastal areas of China, the Japanese had been unable to defeat Chiang Kai-shek, whose forces retreated into the vast interior of the country. The German defeat of France and the Netherlands in 1940, however, left their colonial possessions in the East Indies and Indochina vulnerable and defenseless. Japan now set out to incorporate these territories—rich in oil, tin, and rubber—into a Greater East Asia Co-Prosperity Sphere.

isolationist reaction, responded with naval patrols in the eastern half of the ocean. Hitler placed his submarine commanders under strict restraints to avoid drawing America into the European war. Nevertheless, incidents were bound to occur. In September 1941, after a U-boat narrowly missed torpedoing an American destroyer pursuing it, Roosevelt denounced the German submarines as the "rattlesnakes of the Atlantic" and issued orders for the navy to convey British ships halfway across the ocean.

Undeclared naval war quickly followed. On October 17, 1941, a German submarine damaged the U.S. destroyer *Kearney;* ten days later, another U-boat sank the *Reuben James,* killing over one hundred American sailors. FDR issued orders for the destroyers to shoot U-boats on sight. He also asked Congress to repeal the "carry" section of the neutrality laws and permit American ships to deliver supplies to England. In mid-November, Congress approved these moves by slim margins. Now American merchant ships as well as destroyers would become targets for German attacks. By December, it seemed only a matter of weeks—or months at most—until repeated sinkings would lead to a formal declaration of war against Germany.

The Roosevelt administration countered with economic pressure. Japan was heavily dependent upon the United States for shipments of petroleum and scrap iron and steel. In July 1940, President Roosevelt signed an order setting up a licensing and quota system for the export of these crucial materials to Japan and banned the sale of aviation gasoline altogether. With Britain fighting for survival and France and the Netherlands occupied by Germany, the United States was now employing economic sanctions to defend Southeast Asia against Japanese expansion.

Tokyo appeared not to be impressed. In early

September, Japanese troops occupied strategic bases in the northern part of French Indochina. Later in the month, Japan signed the Tripartite Pact with Germany and Italy, a defensive treaty that confronted the United States with a possible two-ocean war. The new Axis alignment confirmed American suspicions that Japan was part of a worldwide totalitarian threat. Roosevelt and his advisers, however, saw Germany as the primary danger; thus they pursued a policy of all-out aid to England while hoping that economic measures alone would deter Japan.

The embargo on aviation gasoline, extended to include scrap iron and steel in late September 1940, was a burden Japan could bear, but a possible ban on all oil shipments was a different matter. Japan lacked petroleum reserves of its own and was entirely dependent on imports from the United States and the Dutch East Indies. In an attempt to ease the economic pressure through negotiation, Japan sent a new envoy to Washington in the spring of 1941. But these talks quickly broke down. Tokyo wanted nothing less than a free hand in China and an end to American sanctions, while the United States insisted on an eventual Japanese evacuation of all China.

In July 1941, Japan invaded southern Indochina, beginning the chain of events that led to war. Washington knew of this aggression before it occurred. Naval intelligence experts had broken the Japanese diplomatic code and were intercepting and reading all messages between Tokyo and the Japanese embassy in Washington. President Roosevelt responded on July 25, 1941, with an order freezing all Japanese assets in the United States. This step, initially intended only as a temporary warning to Japan, soon became a permanent embargo due to positive public reaction and State Department zeal. Trade with Japan, including the vital oil shipments, came to a complete halt. When the Dutch government-in-exile took similar action, Japan faced a dilemma: in order to have oil shipments resumed, Tokyo would have to end its aggression; the alternative would be to seize the needed petroleum supplies in the Dutch East Indies, an action that would mean war.

After one final diplomatic effort failed, General Hideki Tojo, an army militant, became the new premier of Japan. To mask its war preparations, Tokyo sent yet another envoy to Washington with new peace proposals. Code-breaking enabled American diplomats to learn that the Japanese terms were unacceptable even before they were formally presented. Army and navy leaders urged President Roosevelt to seek at least a temporary settlement with Japan to give them time to prepare American defenses in the Pacific. Secretary of State Cordell Hull, however, refused to allow any concession; on November 20, he sent a stiff ten-point reply to Tokyo that included a demand for Japanese withdrawal from China.

The Japanese response came two weeks later. On the evening of December 6, 1941, the first thirteen parts of the reply to Hull's note arrived in Washington, with the fourteenth part to follow the next morning. Naval intelligence actually decoded the message faster than the Japanese embassy clerks. A messenger delivered the text to President Roosevelt late that night; after glancing at it, he commented, "This means war." The next day, December 7, the fourteenth part arrived, revealing that Japan totally rejected the American position.

Officials in Washington immediately sent warning messages to American bases in the Pacific, but they failed to arrive in time. At 7:55 in the morning, just before 1 P.M. in Washington, squadrons of Japanese carrier-based planes caught the American fleet at Pearl Harbor totally by surprise. In little more than an hour, they crippled the American Pacific fleet and its major base, sinking eight battleships and killing more than twenty-four hundred American sailors.

In Washington, the Japanese envoys had requested a meeting with Secretary Hull at 1 P.M. Just before the meeting news arrived of the attack on Pearl Harbor. An irate Cordell Hull read the note the Japanese handed him and then, unable to restrain himself any longer, burst out, "In all my fifty years of public service, I have never seen a document that was more crowded with infamous falsehoods and distortions—on a scale so huge that I never imagined until today that any government was capable of uttering them."

The next day, President Roosevelt termed December 7 "a date which will live in infamy" and asked Congress to declare war against Japan. With only one dissenting vote, both houses did so. On December 11, Germany and Italy declared war against the United States; the nation was now fully involved in World War II.

Naval air installation at Pearl Harbor, *December 7, 1941, during the surprise attack. Stunned servicemen watch the raging fires.*

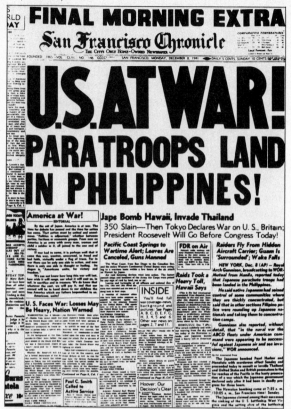

■ *War headline in extra editions, December 8 (top). Congress declared war on Japan that afternoon after FDR addressed the nation (bottom).*

The whole country united behind Roosevelt's leadership to seek revenge for Pearl Harbor and to defeat the Axis threat to American security. After the war, however, critics charged that FDR had entered the conflict by a back door, claiming that the President had deliberately exposed the Pacific fleet to attack. Subsequent investigations uncovered negligence in both Hawaii and Washington but no evidence to support the conspiracy charge. Commanders in Hawaii, like most military experts, believed that the Japanese would not launch an attack on a base four thousand miles away from Japan. FDR, like too many Americans, had badly underestimated the daring and skill of the Japanese; he and the nation alike paid a heavy price for this cultural and racial prejudice. But there was no plot. Roosevelt could not have known that Hitler, so restrained in the Atlantic, would reverse his policy and declare war against the United States after Pearl Harbor. Perhaps the most frightening aspect of the whole episode is that it took the shock of the Japanese sneak attack to make the American people aware of the full extent of the Axis threat to their well-being and lead them to end the long retreat from responsibility.

Turning the Tide Against the Axis

In the first few months after the United States entered the war, the outlook for victory was bleak. In Europe, Hitler's armies controlled virtually the entire continent, from Norway in the north to Greece in the south. Despite the non-aggression pact, German armies had penetrated deep into Russia after an initial invasion in June 1941. Although they had failed to capture either Moscow or Leningrad, the Nazi forces had conquered the Ukraine and by the spring of 1942 were threatening to sweep across the Volga and seize the oil fields in the Caucasus. In North Africa, General Erwin Rommel's Afrika Korps had pushed the British back into Egypt and threatened the Suez Canal (see the map on p. 788).

The situation was no better in Asia. The Pearl Harbor attack had enabled the Japanese to move unopposed across Southeast Asia. Within three months they had conquered Malaya and the Dutch East Indies, with its valuable oil fields, and were pressing the British back both in Burma and New Guinea. American forces under General Douglas MacArthur had tried vainly to block the Japanese conquest of the Philippines. MacArthur finally escaped by torpedo boat to Australia; the American garrison at Corregidor surrendered after a long siege, the survivors then enduring the cruel death march across the Bataan peninsula. With the American navy still recovering from the devastation at Pearl Harbor, Japan controlled the western half of the Pacific (see the map on p. 790).

Over the next two years, the United States and its allies would finally halt the German and Japanese offensives in Europe and Asia. But then they faced the difficult process of driving back the enemy, freeing the vast conquered areas, and finally defeating the Axis powers on their home territory. It would be a difficult and costly struggle that would require great sacrifice and heavy losses; World War II would test American will and resourcefulness to the hilt.

Wartime Partnerships

The greatest single advantage that the United States and its partners possessed was their willingness to form a genuine coalition to bring about the defeat of the Axis powers. Although there were many strains within the wartime alliance, it did permit a high degree of coordination. In striking contrast was the behavior of Germany and Japan, each fighting a separate war without any attempt at cooperation.

The United States and Britain achieved a complete wartime partnership. Prewar military talks led to the formation of a Combined Chiefs of Staff, headquartered in Washington, which directed Anglo-American military operations. The close cooperation between President Roosevelt and Prime Minister Churchill ensured a common strategy. The leaders decided at the outset that a Germany victory posed the greater danger and thus gave priority to the European theater in the conduct of the war. In a series of meetings in December 1941, Roosevelt and Churchill signed a Declaration of the United Nations, eventually subscribed to by twenty-six countries, that pledged them to fight together until the Axis powers were defeated.

Relations with the other members of the United Nations coalition in World War II were not quite so harmonious. The decision to defeat Germany first displeased the Chinese, who had been at war with Japan since 1937. Roosevelt tried to appease Chiang Kai-shek with a trickle of supplies, flown in at great risk by American airmen over the Himalayas from India. France posed a more delicate problem. FDR virtually ignored the Free French government in exile under General Charles de Gaulle. Roosevelt preferred to deal with the Vichy regime, despite its collaboration with Germany, because it still controlled the French fleet and retained France's overseas territories.

The greatest strain of all within the wartime coalition was with the Soviet Union. Although Roosevelt had ended the long period of nonrecognition in 1933, close ties had failed to develop. The Russian refusal to pay prerevolutionary debts, together with continued Soviet support of domestic Communist activity in the United States in the 1930s, intensified American distaste for Stalin's regime. The great Russian purge trials and the temporary Nazi-Soviet alliance from 1939 to 1941, along with deep-seated cultural and ideological differences, made wartime cooperation difficult.

World War II in Europe and North Africa

The tide of battle shifted in this theater during the winter of 1942–1943. The massive German assault on the eastern front was turned back by the Russians at Stalingrad, and the Allied forces recaptured North Africa.

Axis Powers
before World War II

Extent of Axis control
early Nov. 1942

Allies

Neutral nations

Allied troop
movements

Major battles

ICELAND

NORWAY

SWEDEN

FINLAND

Leningrad
besieged
Sept. 1941–
Jan. 19, 1944

EST.

LAT.   Sept. 1944

Moscow

LITH.

SOVIET UNION

Northern
Ireland

North
Sea

DEN.

East
Prussia
(Ger.)

Warsaw

Stalingrad
Aug. 21, 1942–
Jan. 31, 1943

Volga R.

GREAT
BRITAIN

IRELAND

Berlin
surrendered
May 2, 1945

July 1944

Aug. 1943

POLAND

London

NETH.

Elbe R.

Rhine

BELG.

Apr. 1945

Oder R.

Ukraine

March 1944

Caucasus

ATLANTIC
OCEAN

D-Day
June 6, 1944

FRANCE

Battle of the Bulge
Dec. 16, 1944–
Jan. 31, 1945

GERMANY

Czechoslovakia

Normandy

Paris
liberated
Aug. 1944

SWITZ.

Austria

HUNG.

Dec.
1944

ROM.

Aug. 1944

Black Sea

VICHY
FRANCE
occupied
Nov. 1942

Aug. 1944

ITALY

YUGO.

Danube R.

BULG.

TURKEY

PORT.

SPAIN

Rome
liberated
June 4, 1944

ALB.
(It.)

GREECE

SYRIA

Nov. 1942

Sp.
Morocco

July 1943

Sicily

Rhodes
(It.)

Crete
(Greece)

Cyprus
(Br.)

LEB.

PALESTINE
(Br.)

ALGERIA

Kasserine Pass
Feb. 14–22, 1943

Mediterranean   Sea

Suez
Canal

TRANSJORDAN

MOROCCO

FRENCH NORTH AFRICA
(Vichy France)
Joined Allies Nov. 1942

TUNISIA

Nov. 1942

El Alamein
Oct. 23–Nov. 5, 1942

Nile R.

| 0 | 200 | 400 Miles |
| 0 | 200 | 400 Kilometers |

LIBYA (It.)

EGYPT

Ever the pragmatist, Roosevelt tried hard to break down the old hostility and establish a more cordial relationship with Russia during the war. Even before Pearl Harbor, he extended Lend-Lease aid, and after American entry into the war, this economic assistance grew rapidly, limited only by the difficulty in delivering the supplies. Eager to keep Russia in the war, the President promised a visiting Russian diplomat in May 1942 that the United States would create a second front in Europe by the end of that year, a pledge he could not fulfill. In January 1943, Roosevelt joined with

Churchill at the Casablanca conference to declare a policy of unconditional surrender, vowing that the Western Allies would fight on until the Axis nations were completedly defeated.

Despite these promises, the Soviet Union bore the brunt of battle against Hitler in the early years of the war, fighting alone against more than two hundred German divisions. The United States and England, grateful for the respite to build up their forces, could do little more than offer promises of future help and send Lend-Lease supplies. The result was a rift that never fully healed—one that did not prevent the defeat of Germany but did ensure future tensions and uncertainties between the Soviet Union and the Western nations.

Halting the German Blitz

From the outset, the United States favored an invasion across the English Channel as the key to victory in Europe. Army planners, led by Chief of Staff George C. Marshall and his protégé, Dwight D. Eisenhower, were convinced that such a frontal assault would be the quickest way to win the war. Roosevelt concurred, in part because it fulfilled his second-front commitment to the Soviets.

The initial plan, drawn up by Eisenhower, called for a full-scale invasion of Europe in the spring of 1943, with provision for a temporary beachhead in France in the fall of 1942 if necessary to keep Russia in the war. Marshall surprised everyone by placing Eisenhower, until then a relatively junior general, in charge of implementing the plan.

But the British, remembering the heavy casualties of trench warfare in World War I, preferred a perimeter approach, with air and naval attacks around the edge of the continent, until Germany was properly softened up for the final invasion. Their strategists assented to the basic plan but strongly urged that a preliminary invasion of North Africa be launched in the fall of 1942. Roosevelt, too, wanted American troops engaged in combat against Germany before the end of 1942 to offset growing pressure at home to concentrate on the Pacific; hence, after he overruled objections from his military advisers, American and British troops landed on the Atlantic and Mediterranean coasts of Morocco and Algeria in November 1942.

The British launched an attack against Rommel at El Alamein in Egypt and soon forced the Afrika Korps to retreat across Libya to Tunisia. Eisenhower, delayed by poor roads and bad weather, was slow in bringing up his forces, and in their first encounter with Rommel at the Kasserine Pass in the desert south of Tunis, inexperienced American troops suffered a humiliating defeat. General George Patton quickly rallied the demoralized soldiers, and by May 1943, Germany had been driven from Africa, leaving behind nearly three hundred thousand troops.

During these same months, the Red Army had broken the back of German military power in the battle of Stalingrad. Turned back at the critical bend in the Volga, Hitler had poured in division after division in what was ultimately a losing cause; never again would Germany be able to take the offensive in Europe.

At Churchill's insistence, FDR agreed to follow up the North African victory with the invasion first of Sicily and then Italy in the summer of 1943. Italy dropped out of the war when Mussolini fled to Germany, but the Italian campaign

■ *American troops entering Palermo, Sicily, on July 23, 1943. Italy soon capitulated, but the Italian campaign bogged down under fierce German resistance.*

proved to be a strategic dead end. Germany sent in enough divisions to establish a strong defensive line in the mountains south of Rome; American and British troops were forced to fight their way slowly up the peninsula, suffering heavy casualties.

More important, these Mediterranean operations delayed the second front, postponing it eventually to the spring of 1944. Meanwhile, the Soviets began to push the Germans out of Russia and looked forward to the liberation of Poland, Hungary, and Romania, where they could establish "friendly" Communist regimes. Having borne the brunt of the fighting against Nazi Germany, Russia was ready to claim its reward— the postwar domination of Eastern Europe.

Checking Japan in the Pacific

The decision to defeat Germany first and the vast expanses of the Pacific dictated the nature of the war against Japan—amphibious, island-hopping campaigns rather than any attempt to reconquer the Dutch East Indies, Southeast Asia, and China. There would be two separate American operations. One, led by Douglas MacArthur based in Australia, would move from New Guinea back to the Philippines, while the other, commanded by Admiral Chester Nimitz from Hawaii, was directed at key Japanese islands in the Central Pacific. The original plan called for the two offensives to come together for the final invasion of the Japanese home islands.

World War II in the Pacific

The tide of battle turned in the Pacific the same year as in Europe. The balance of sea power shifted back to the United States from Japan after the naval victories of 1942.

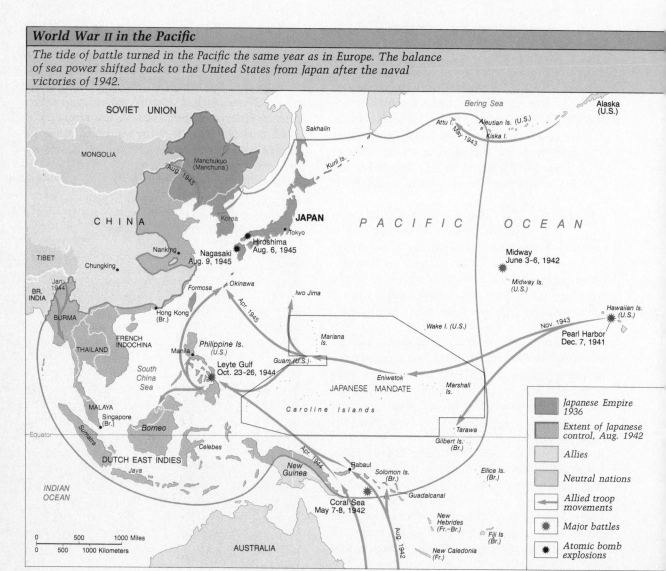

790

America and the World, 1921-1945

Success in the Pacific depended above all else on control of the sea. The devastation at Pearl Harbor gave Japan the initial edge, but fortunately the United States had not lost any of its four aircraft carriers. In the battle of the Coral Sea in May 1942, American naval forces blocked a Japanese thrust to outflank Australia. The turning point came one month later at Midway. A powerful Japanese task force threatened to seize this remote American outpost, over a thousand miles west of Pearl Harbor; Japan's real objective was the destruction of what remained of the American Pacific fleet. Superior American air power enabled Nimitz's forces to engage the enemy at long range. Japanese fighters shot down thirty-five of forty-one attacking torpedo bombers, but a second wave of dive bombers scored hits on three Japanese carriers. The battle of Midway ended with the loss of four Japanese aircraft carriers compared to just one American. It was the first defeat the modern Japanese navy had ever suffered, and it left the United States in control of the Central Pacific.

Encouraged by this victory, American forces launched their first Pacific offensive in the Solomon Islands, east of New Guinea, in August 1942. Both sides suffered heavy losses, but six months later the last Japanese were driven from the key island of Guadalcanal. At the same time, MacArthur began the long, slow, and bloody job of driving the Japanese back along the north coast of New Guinea.

By early 1943, the defensive phase of the war with Japan was over. The enemy surge had been halted in both the Central and the Southwest Pacific, and the United States was preparing to penetrate the Gilbert, Marshall, and Caroline islands and recapture the Philippines. Just as Russia had broken German power in Europe, so the United States, fighting alone except for Australia and New Zealand, had halted the Japanese. And, like the Soviet plans for Eastern Europe, America expected to reap the rewards of victory by dominating the Pacific in the future.

The Home Front

World War II had a greater impact than the Depression on the future of American life. While American soldiers and sailors fought abroad, the nation

■ *American war production was twice that of all Axis countries. Here, Boeing aircraft workers celebrate the completion of their five-thousandth bomber.*

underwent sweeping social and economic changes at home.

American industry made the nation's single most important contribution to victory. Even though over fifteen million Americans served in the armed forces, it was the nearly sixty million who worked on farms and factories who achieved the miracle of production that ensured the defeat of Germany and Japan. The manufacturing plants that had run at half-capacity through the 1930s now hummed with activity. In Detroit, automobile assembly lines were converted to produce tanks and airplanes; Henry Ford built the giant Willow Run factory, covering sixty-seven acres, where forty-two thousand workers turned out a B-24 bomber every hour. Henry J. Kaiser, a California industrialist who constructed huge West Coast shipyards to meet the demand for cargo vessels and landing craft, operated on an equally large scale. His Richmond, California, plant lowered the time to build a merchant ship from 105 to 14 days. In part, America won the battle of the Atlantic by building ships faster than German U-boats could sink them.

This vast industrial expansion, however, created many problems. In 1942, President Roosevelt appointed Donald Nelson, a Sears, Roebuck executive, to head a War Production Board (WPB). A jovial, easy-going man, Nelson soon was outmaneuvered by the army and the navy, which preferred to negotiate directly with large corporations. The WPB allowed business rapid depreciation, and thus huge tax credits, for new plants and awarded lucrative cost-plus contracts for urgently needed goods. Shortages of such critical materials as steel, aluminum, and copper led to an allocation system based on military priorities. Rubber, cut off by the Japanese conquest of Southeast Asia, was particularly scarce; the administration finally began gasoline-rationing in 1943 to curb pleasure-driving and prolong tire life. The government itself built fifty-one synthetic rubber plants which by 1944 were producing.nearly one million tons for the tires of American airplanes and military vehicles. All in all, the nation's factories turned out twice as many goods as did German and Japanese industry combined.

Roosevelt revealed the same tendency toward compromise in directing the economic mobilization as he did in shaping the New Deal. When the Office of Price Administration—which tried to curb inflation by controlling prices and rationing scarce goods like sugar, canned food, and shoes—clashed with the WPB, FDR appointed James Byrnes to head an Office of Economic Stabilization. Byrnes, a former South Carolina senator and Supreme Court justice, used political judgment to settle disputes between agencies and keep all groups happy. The President was also forced to compromise with Congress, which pared down the administration's requests for large tax increases. Half the cost of the war was financed by borrowing; the other half came from revenues. A $7-billion revenue increase in 1942 included so many first-time taxpayers that in the following year the Treasury Department instituted a new practice—withholding income taxes from workers' wages.

The result of this wartime economic explosion was a growing affluence. Despite the federal incentives to business, heavy excess-profit taxes and a 94 percent tax rate for the very rich kept the wealthy from benefiting unduly. The huge increase in federal spending, from $9 billion in 1940 to $98 billion in 1944, spread through American society. A government agreement with labor unions in 1943 held wage rates to a 15 percent increase, but the long hours of overtime resulted in doubling and sometimes tripling the weekly paychecks of factory workers. Farmers shared in the new prosperity as their incomes quadrupled

■ *During and immediately after the war, ration stamps were issued for scarce food items, shoes, tires, and gasoline.*

between 1940 and 1945. For the first time in the twentieth century, the lowest fifth of wage earners increased their share of the national income in relation to the more affluent; their income rose by 68 percent between 1941 and 1945, compared to a 20 percent increase for the well-to-do. Most important, this rising income ensured postwar prosperity. Workers and farmers saved their money, channeling much of it into government war bonds, waiting for the day when they could buy the cars and home appliances they had done without during the long years of depression and war.

A Nation on the Move

The war led to a vast migration of the American population. Young men left their homes for training camps and then for service overseas. Defense workers and their families, some nine million people in all, moved to the new booming shipyards, munitions factories, and aircraft plants. Norfolk, Virginia; San Diego, California; Mobile, Alabama, and other centers of defense production grew by more than 50 percent in just a year or two. Rural areas lost population while coastal regions, especially along the Pacific and Gulf of Mexico, drew millions of people. The location of army camps in the South and West created boom conditions in the future Sunbelt, as did the concentration of aircraft factories and shipyards in this region. California had the greatest gains, adding nearly two million to its population in less than five years.

This movement of people caused severe social problems. Housing was in short supply. Migrating workers crowded into house trailers and boardinghouses, bringing unexpected windfalls to landlords. In one boom town, a reporter described an old Victorian house that had five bedrooms on the second floor. "Three of them," he wrote, "held two cots apiece, the two others held three cots." But the owner revealed that "the third floor is where we pick up the velvet. . . . We rent to workers in different shifts . . . three shifts a day . . . seven bucks a week apiece."

Family life suffered under these crowded living conditions. An increase in the number of marriages, as young people searched for something to hang on to in the midst of wartime turmoil, was offset by a rising divorce rate. The baby boom that would peak in the 1950s began during the war, but children suffered. There were few day-care centers for working women to use; "latch-key children" and "eight-hour orphans" were all too common. Schools in the boom areas were unable to cope with the influx of new students; a teacher shortage, intensified by the lure of higher wages in war industries, compounded the educational crisis.

Despite these problems, women found the war a time of economic opportunity. The demand for workers led to a dramatic rise in female employment, from fourteen million working women in 1940 to nineteen million by 1945. Women entered industries once viewed as exclusively male; by the end of the war, they worked alongside men tending blast furnaces in steel mills and welding hulls in shipyards. Few challenged the traditional view of sex roles, yet the wartime experience helped undermine the concept that woman's only proper place was in the home. Women enjoyed the hefty weekly paychecks, which rose by 50 percent from 1941 to 1943, and they took pride in their contributions to the war effort. "To hell with the life I have had," commented a former fashion designer. "This war is too damn serious, and it is too damn important to win it."

Blacks shared in the wartime migration, but their social and economic gains were limited by

■ "Rosie the Riveter," a song extolling women workers, was very popular during the war. This photograph from Life is by Margaret Bourke-White.

racial prejudice. Nearly one million served in the armed forces, but relatively few saw combat. The army placed blacks in segregated units, usually led by white officers, and used them for service and construction tasks. The navy was even worse, relegating them to menial jobs until late in the war. Blacks were denied the chance to become petty officers, Secretary of the Navy Frank Knox explained, because experience had shown that "men of the colored race . . . cannot maintain discipline among men of the white race."

Black civilians fared a little better. In 1941, black labor leader A. Philip Randolph threatened a massive march on Washington to force President Roosevelt to end racial discrimination in defense industries and government employment and to integrate the armed forces. FDR compromised, persuading Randolph to call off the march and drop his integration demand in return for an executive order creating a Fair Employment Practices Committee (FEPC) to ban racial discrimination in war industries. As a result, black employment by the federal government rose from sixty thousand in 1941 to two hundred thousand by the end of the war, but the FEPC proved less successful in the private sector. Weak in funding and staff, the FEPC was able to act on only one third of the eight thousand complaints it received. The nationwide shortage of labor was more influential than the FEPC in accounting for the rise in black employment during wartime. Blacks moved from the rural South to northern and western cities, finding jobs in the automobile, aircraft, and ship-building industries.

This movement of an estimated seven hundred thousand people helped transform the race problem from a regional issue into a national concern that could no longer be ignored. The limited housing and recreational facilities for both black and white war workers created tensions that led to urban race riots. On a hot Sunday evening in June 1943, blacks and whites began exchanging insults and then blows near Belle Island recreation park in Detroit. The next day, a full-scale riot broke out in which twenty-three blacks and nine whites died. The fighting raged for twenty-four hours until National Guard troops were

Black Migration from the South, 1940–1950

Movement was from the Southeast to the Mid-Atlantic and New England states and from the south central states to the Midwest and Far West.

The migration of blacks from the South to northern cities was recorded in a series of sixty tempora panels by Jacob Lawrence, a black artist. The paintings are done in sharp primary colors and a forceful but simple design. They form a continuous narrative of visual history and black experience.

brought in to restore order. Later that summer, only personal intervention by New York Mayor Fiorello LaGuardia quelled a Harlem riot that took the lives of six blacks.

These outbursts of racial violence fueled the resentments that would grow into the postwar civil-rights movement. For most blacks, despite the economic gain, World War II was a reminder of the inequality of American life. "Just carve on my tombstone," remarked one black soldier in the Pacific, "here lies a black man killed fighting a yellow man for the protection of a white man."

One third of a million Mexican-Americans served in the armed forces and shared some of the same experiences as blacks. Although they were not as completely segregated, many served in the Eighty-eighth Division, made up largely of Mexican-American officers and troops, which earned the nickname "Blue Devils" in the Italian campaign. At home, Spanish-speaking people left the rural areas of Texas, New Mexico, and California for jobs in the cities, especially in aircraft plants and petroleum refineries. Despite low wages and union resistance, they improved their economic position substantially. But they still faced discrimination based both on skin color and language, most notably in the Los Angeles "zoot-suit" riots in 1943 when white sailors attacked Mexican-American youths dressed in their distinctive long jackets and flared pants tightly pegged at the ankles. The racial prejudice heightened feelings of ethnic identity and led returning Mexican-American veterans to form organizations such as the American G.I. Forum to press for equal rights in the future.

A tragic counterpoint to the voluntary movement of American workers in search of jobs was the forced relocation of 112,000 Japanese-Americans from the West Coast. Responding to racial fears in California after Pearl Harbor, President Roosevelt approved an army order in February 1942 to move both the Issei (Japanese-Americans who had emigrated from Japan) and the Nisei (people of Japanese ancestry born in the United States and therefore American citizens) to concentration camps in the interior. Forced to sell their farms and businesses at distress prices, the Japanese-Americans lost not only their liberty but also most of their worldly goods. Herded into ten hastily built detention centers in seven western states, they lived as prisoners in tar-papered

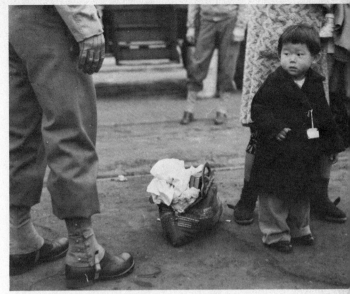

■ *A bewildered Nisei toddler, tagged like a piece of luggage and guarded by a GI, waits to be taken to a detention camp.*

barracks behind barbed wire, guarded by armed troops.

Appeals to the Supreme Court proved fruitless; in 1944, six justices upheld relocation on grounds of national security in wartime. Beginning in 1943, individual Japanese-Americans could win release by pledging their loyalty and finding a job away from the West Coast; some thirty-five thousand left the camps during the next two years. The government finally closed the detention centers in January 1945, but nearly five thousand former prisoners chose to return to Japan at the war's end. The Japanese-Americans never experienced the torture and mass death of the German concentration camps, but their treatment was a disgrace to a nation fighting for freedom and democracy.

Win-the-War Politics

Franklin Roosevelt used World War II to strengthen his leadership and maintain Democratic political dominance. As war brought about prosperity and removed the economic discontent that had sustained the New Deal, FDR announced that "Dr. New Deal" had given way to "Dr. Win-the-War." Congress, already controlled by a conservative coalition of southern Democrats and northern Republicans, had almost slipped into GOP hands in 1942. With a very low voter turnout, due in part to the large numbers of men in service and uprooted workers who failed to establish residency requirements for voting, the Republicans won forty-four new seats in the House and nine in the Senate and elected governors in New York and California as well.

In 1944, Roosevelt responded to the Democratic slippage by dropping Henry Wallace, his liberal and visionary vice-president, for Harry Truman, a moderate and down-to-earth Missouri senator who was acceptable to all factions of the Democratic party. Equally important, FDR received increased political support from organized labor, which had grown in membership during the war from ten to fifteen million. The newly organized Political Action Committee (PAC) of the CIO, headed by Sidney Hillman, conducted massive door-to-door drives to register millions of workers and their families.

The Republicans nominated Thomas E. Dewey, who had been elected governor of New York after gaining fame as a prosecutor of organized crime. Dewey, moderate in his views, played down opposition to the New Deal and instead tried to make Roosevelt's age and health the primary issues, along with the charge that the Democrats were soft on communism. Referring to Hillman's role in the campaign and Communist leader Earl Browder's endorsement of FDR, a GOP poster proclaimed, "YOU don't have to 'clear everything with Sidney.' Vote Republican and keep the Communists, Hillman and Browder from running your country and your life."

Despite his abrasive campaign style, Dewey did not advocate a return to isolationism. The Republican party was trying hard to shake the obstructionist image it had gained during the League of Nations fight in 1919; it went on record in 1943 as favoring American postwar cooperation for world peace. Indeed, Dewey pioneered a bipartisan approach to foreign policy. He accepted wartime planning for the future United Nations and kept the issue of an international organization out of the campaign.

Reacting to the issues of his age and health, especially after a long bout with influenza in the spring, FDR disregarded the advice of his doctors

■ *The most controversial of the Big Three wartime conferences was the February 1945 meeting at the Russian Black Sea resort of Yalta.*

and took a five-hour, rain-soaked drive through the streets of New York City in an open car just before the election. His vitality impressed the voters, and in November 1944 he swept back into office for a fourth term, although the margin of 3.6 million votes was his smallest yet. But the vigorous campaign had taken its toll. Suffering from high blood pressure and congestive heart disease, the President was thin and pale, tiring easily after only a few hours of work. He rallied his waning energy to attend the Yalta Conference in Russia with Churchill and Stalin, but his health continued to fail after his return in mid-February.

In early April, FDR left Washington for Warm

		The Election of 1944	
Candidate	Party	Popular Vote	Electoral Vote
Roosevelt	Democrat	25,611,936	432
Dewey	Republican	22,013,372	99

Springs, Georgia, where he had always been able to relax. He was sitting for his portrait at midday on April 12, 1945, when he suddenly complained of a "terrific headache," then slumped forward and died. The nation mourned a man who had gallantly met the challenges of depression and global war. Many grieved that FDR did not live to see the final triumph over the Axis powers, but he must have known that victory was at hand. Unfortunately, he had taken no steps to prepare his successor, the inexperienced Harry Truman, for the difficult problems that lay ahead.

Victory

World War II ended with surprising swiftness. Once the Axis tide had been turned by 1943 in Europe and Asia, it did not take long for Russia, the United States, and England to mount the offensives that drove Germany and Japan back across the vast areas they had conquered and set the stage for their final defeat.

The long-awaited second front finally came on June 6, 1944. For two years, the United States and England concentrated on building up an invasion force of nearly three million troops and a vast armada of ships and landing craft to carry them across the English Channel. In hopes of catching Hitler by surprise, Eisenhower chose the Normandy peninsula, where the absence of good harbors had led to lighter German fortifications. Allied aircraft bombed the roads, bridges, and rail lines of northern France for six weeks preceding the assault in order to block the movement of German reinforcements once the invasion began.

D-day was originally set for June 5, but bad weather forced a delay. Relying on a forecast of a break in the storm, Eisenhower gambled on going ahead on June 6. During the night, three divisions parachuted down behind the German defenses; at dawn, the British and American troops fought their way ashore along a forty-mile stretch of beach, encountering stiff German resistance at several points. By the end of the day, however, Eisenhower had won his beachhead; a week later, more than a third of a million men were slowly pushing back the German forces through the hedgerows of Normandy. The breakthrough came

■ *The nation's grief at FDR's death is mirrored in the face of this serviceman as the President's funeral cortege passes.*

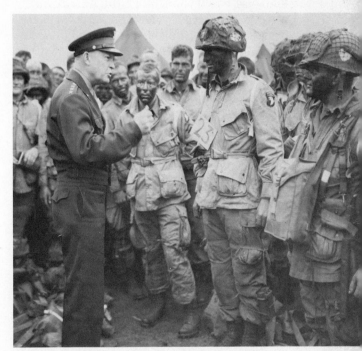

■ *Before the D-Day takeoff, General Eisenhower, the Supreme Allied Commander, offers a last word to paratroopers who will be dropped behind German lines.*

on July 25 when General Omar Bradley decimated the enemy with a massive artillery and aerial bombardment at Saint-Lô, opening a gap for General George Patton's Third Army. American tanks raced across the French countryside, trapping thousands of Germans and liberating Paris by August 25. Allied troops reached the Rhine River by September, but a shortage of supplies, especially gasoline, forced a three-month halt.

Hitler took advantage of this breathing spell to deliver a daring counterattack. In mid-December, the remaining German armored divisions burst through a weak point in the Allied lines in the Ardennes Forest, planning a breakout to the coast that would have cut off nearly one third of Eisenhower's forces. A combination of tactical surprise and bad weather, which prevented Allied air support, led to a huge bulge in the American lines. But an airborne division dug in at the key crossroads of Bastogne, in Belgium, and held off a much larger German force. Allied reinforcements and clearing weather then combined to end the attack. By committing nearly all his reserves to the Battle of the Bulge, Hitler delayed Eisenhower's advance into Germany, but he had fatally weakened German resistance in the West.

The end came quickly. A massive Russian offensive began in mid-January and swept across the Oder River toward Berlin. General Bradley's troops, finding a bridge left virtually intact by the retreating Germans, crossed the Rhine on March 7. Eisenhower overruled the British, who favored one concentrated drive on Berlin. Instead the Allied forces advanced on a broad front, capturing the industrial Ruhr basin and meeting the Russians at the Elbe by the last week in April. With the Red Army already in the suburbs of Berlin, Adolf Hitler committed suicide on April 30. A week later, on May 7, 1945, Eisenhower accepted the unconditional surrender of all German forces. Just eleven months and a day after the landings in Normandy, the Allied forces had brought the war in Europe to a successful end.

War Aims and Wartime Diplomacy

The American contribution to Hitler's defeat was relatively minor compared to the damage inflicted by the Soviet Union. At the height of the German invasion of Russia, more than 300 Soviet divisions had been locked in battle with 250 German ones, a striking contrast to the 58 divisions the United States and Britain used in the Normandy invasion. As his armies overran Poland and the Balkan countries, Joseph Stalin was determined to retain control over this region, which had been the historic pathway for Western invasion into Russia. Delay in opening the second front and an innate distrust of the West convinced the Soviets that they should maximize their territorial gains by imposing Communist regimes on Eastern Europe.

American postwar goals were quite different. Now believing that the failure to join the League of Nations in 1919 had led to the coming of World War II, the American people and their leaders vowed to put their faith in a new attempt at collective security. At Moscow in 1943, Secretary of State Cordell Hull won Russian agreement to participate in a future world organization at the war's end. In the first wartime Big Three conference, held at Teheran, Iran, in late 1943, Stalin reaffirmed this commitment and also indicated to President Roosevelt that Russia would enter the war against Japan once Germany was defeated.

By the time the Big Three met again at Yalta, in February 1945, the military situation favored the Russians. While British and American forces were still recovering from the Battle of the Bulge, the Red Army was advancing to within fifty miles of Berlin. Stalin drove a series of hard bargains. He refused to give up his plans for Communist domination of Poland and the Balkans, although he did agree to Roosevelt's request for a Declaration of Liberated Europe, which called for free elections without providing for any method of enforcement or supervision. More important for the United States, Stalin promised to enter the Pacific war three months after Germany surrendered. In return, Roosevelt offered extensive concessions in Asia, including Russian control over Manchuria. While neither a sellout nor a betrayal, as some critics have charged, Yalta was a diplomatic victory for the Soviets—one that reflected Russia's major contribution to a victory in Europe.

The defeat of Nazi Germany dissolved the bond between the United States and the Soviet Union in World War II. With very different histories, cultures, and ideologies, the two nations had little in common beyond their enmity toward

Hitler. At the Potsdam Conference in July 1945, the growing rift between the former allies became apparent. The United States condemned the Soviet insistence on control of Poland and the Balkans; the Russians were equally adamant in their demands for German reparations. The seeds of the future cold war were beginning to sprout even before the Second World War had ended.

Triumph and Tragedy in the Pacific

The total defeat of Germany in May 1945 turned all eyes toward Japan. Although the Combined Chiefs of Staff had originally estimated that it would take eighteen months after Germany's surrender to conquer Japan, American forces moved with surprising speed. Admiral Nimitz swept through the Gilbert, Caroline, and Marshall islands in 1944, securing bases for further advances and building airfields for American B-29s to begin a deadly bombardment of the Japanese home islands. General MacArthur cleared New Guinea of the last Japanese defender in early 1944 and began planning his long-heralded return to the Philippines. American troops landed on the island of Leyte on October 20, 1944, and Manila fell by the end of the year. The Japanese navy, in a Pacific version of the Battle of the Bulge, launched a daring three-pronged attack on the American invasion fleet in Leyte Gulf. The U.S. Navy rallied to blunt all three Japanese thrusts, sinking four carriers and ending any further Japanese naval threat.

The defeat of Japan was now only a matter of time. The United States had three possible ways to proceed. The military favored a full-scale invasion, beginning on the southernmost island of Kyushu in November 1945 and culminating with an assault on Honshu (the main island of Japan) and a climactic battle for Tokyo in 1946, with casualties expected to run into the hundreds of thousands. Diplomats suggested a negotiated peace, urging that the United States modify the unconditional-surrender formula to permit Japan to retain the institution of the emperor. At Potsdam, Churchill and Truman did issue a call for surrender, warning Japan it faced utter destruction, but they made no mention of the emperor.

The third possibility involved the highly secret

Chronology	
1922	Washington Naval Conference limits tonnage
1926	World Court rejects qualified U.S. entry
1928	Kellogg-Briand Pact outlaws war (August) Clark Memorandum repudiates Roosevelt Corollary (December)
1931	Japan occupies China's Manchurian province
1933	FDR extends diplomatic recognition to USSR
1936	Hitler's troops reoccupy Rhineland
1937	FDR signs permanent Neutrality Act (May) FDR urges quarantine of aggressor nations (October) Japanese planes sink U.S.S. *Panay* in China (December)
1938	Ludlow war referendum buried in Congress (January) Munich Conference appeases Hitler (September)
1939	Germany invades Poland; World War II begins
1941	Japanese attack Pearl Harbor; United States enters World War II
1942	U.S. defeats Japanese at battle of Midway (June) Allies land in North Africa (November)
1943	Soviets smash Nazis at Stalingrad
1944	Allies land on Normandy beachheads
1945	Big Three met at Yalta (February) FDR dies; Harry Truman becomes president (April) Germany surrenders unconditionally (May) U.S. drops atomic bombs on Hiroshima and Nagasaki; Japan surrenders (August)

Manhattan Project. Since 1939, the United States had spent $2 billion to develop an atomic bomb based on the fission of radioactive uranium and plutonium. On July 16, 1945, they successfully tested their handiwork at Alamogordo, New Mexico (see the special feature in this chapter).

Informed of this achievement upon his arrival at Potsdam, President Truman authorized the

Scientists and the Atomic Bomb

The years between World Wars I and II saw great progress in the study of atomic physics as scientists throughout Europe and America sought to unlock the secrets of the atom. These scientists considered themselves to be members of an international community of scholars, sharing their discoveries irrespective of nationality. But the rise of Nazi Germany threatened this free exchange of ideas, leading many of the great physicists from Europe to seek refuge in England and the United States.

Many physicists thought atomic energy had little application, but others feared even the slightest possibility of such awesome power in the hands of Hitler. The best safeguard, they reasoned, would be to keep secret all progress in atomic research. Leo Szilard, for example, a Hungarian-born physicist who had studied with Albert Einstein at the University of Berlin and emigrated to the United States in 1933, even tried to prevail upon his colleagues not to publish their findings. When Szilard's plan for self-censorship failed, he and several of his fellow émigrés decided to warn the American government of the possible military uses of atomic fission.

After an unsuccessful attempt to interest the Department of the Navy in atomic energy, Szilard decided to appeal directly to President Roosevelt. First he went to Einstein (pictured in photo above) for assistance, and his old mentor lent his name and prestige to Szilard's endeavor. Szilard probably penned the "Einstein Letter"; nonetheless, it represented Einstein's deep concern about the state of atomic research and the growing German threat. Upon reading the letter, FDR turned to his attaché, General Edwin "Pa" Watson, and said, "Pa, this requires action."

The President soon assembled an advisory group known as the Uranium Committee to determine the feasibility of atomic weapons. Although it had been émigré scientists who brought the possibility of an atomic bomb to the attention of the American government, they were excluded from the deliberations of the Uranium Committee. Foreign-born scientists were not considered a good security risk.

Ironically, these security measures contributed to the ultimate benefit of Allied atomic research. In America and Britain, foreign scientists—barred from participating in high-priority military projects such as the development of radar—devoted themselves single-mindedly to atomic energy. When Otto Frisch and Rudolph Pierels, two German refugees who fled to England, developed a theoretical design for an atomic bomb, the British government decided to pursue further research. Upon reading the British report, Vannevar Bush, chairman of the newly created National Defense Research Committee, recommended that the U.S. government take steps to ascertain the possible applications of atomic energy. Though still cautious in his projection of its military potential, he suggested that "if such an explosive were made, it would be thousands of times more powerful than existing explosives and its use might be determining."

In 1942, after the United States had joined the war against the Axis powers, research on atomic energy entered a new phase. Roosevelt and Churchill agreed to a joint atomic research program, based in America where it could be insulated from the European war. Control of the project was transferred from civilian committees to the War Department. By the fall of 1942, the atomic bomb project, code-named the Manhattan Engineering District, was under way, and General Leslie R. Groves of the Army Corps of Engineers was in command.

The scientists on the Manhattan Project feared that they were lagging behind Germany in the race to harness atomic power. Everyone on the project felt that speed was of the utmost importance. But the desire to proceed quickly brought the scientists into conflict with their military partners. The Manhattan Project was compartmentalized. Communication between labs as well as individuals was limited to designated channels. Mail was scrutinized by military censors. Knowledge of the overall progress of the project was kept on a "need-to-know" basis. The military considered such security measures necessary to prevent information leaks; the scientists objected to their isolation within the project. Most of the researchers who joined the operation did so for the intellectual challenge as well as for patriotic reasons. In recruiting personnel for the Los Alamos lab, Robert Oppenheimer found that the greatest attraction was the opportunity to participate in the world's most advanced atomic physics program. Once in the project, however, scientists found themselves cut off from their colleagues working in other areas and unable to ascertain where their work fit in the larger design. The Manhattan Project was not the intellectually free atmosphere that many of the scientists desired; neither was it the all-military operation preferred by General Groves.

But security regulations and academic freedom were not the only issues creating tensions within the project. Enrico Fermi and his team of theoretical physicists at the Chicago Metallurgical Laboratory overcame the first and greatest obstacle in December 1942, creating a self-sustaining chain reaction. The most important activities then shifted to the other labs. As one scientist observed, it became "a question of development and the solving of a multitude of mechanical problems."

These physicists now had time to reflect on the actual use of the atomic bomb and its postwar implications. As the German collapse drew ever nearer and military intelligence discovered that the Nazis were in fact years behind the Allies in atomic research, the Chicago scientists began to raise questions: when and how the atomic bomb should be deployed; the likelihood of a postwar arms race; and the possibilities for international control of atomic energy. Recognizing clearly that the atomic bomb could not long remain a secret, members of the Manhattan Project appealed to Roosevelt, and later to President Truman, to take steps to ensure a peaceful postwar world. But after several years of work and the signs of expenditure of $2 billion, the atomic bomb had developed its own momentum. Few outside the project's labs considered forswearing its use, and the signs of deterioration in the wartime alliance with the Soviet Union did not bode well for international control.

Those working at the Los Alamos lab had the least time to ruminate about their work, for theirs was the final step in the development of the atomic bomb. Throughout 1944 and early 1945, they worked feverishly to complete their task before the war's end. On July 16, 1945, after several delays, the first atomic bomb was tested in a remote section of desert near Alamogordo, New Mexico. The blast created a fireball brighter than several suns; a mushroom cloud rose 40,000 feet into the sky; windows were broken 125 miles away; a blind woman saw the light. In General Groves' assessment, "The test was successful beyond the most optimistic expectations." From the control bunker in the New Mexico desert, Oppenheimer was reminded of a passage from the Hindu *Bhagavad-Gita* as he witnessed the explosion. "I am become death, destroyer of worlds."

These traumatized victims of the first A-bomb blast August 6, 1945, over Hiroshima are seeking first aid a few hours after the explosion.

army air force to use the atomic bomb against Japan. Truman had been unaware of the existence of the Manhattan Project before he became president on April 12. Now he simply followed the recommendation of a committee headed by Secretary of War Henry L. Stimson to drop the bomb on a Japanese city without any prior warning. Neither Truman nor Stimson had any qualms about this momentous decision. They viewed it as a legitimate wartime measure, one designed to save the lives of hundreds of thousands of Americans and Japanese that would be lost in a full-scale invasion.

Weather conditions on the morning of August 6 dictated the choice of Hiroshima as the bomb's target. The explosion incinerated four square miles of the city, instantly killing more than sixty thousand. Two days later, Russia entered the war against Japan, and the next day, August 9, the United States dropped a second bomb on Nagasaki. There were no more atomic bombs available, but no more were needed. The emperor personally broke a deadlock in the Japanese cabinet and persuaded his ministers to surrender unconditionally on August 14, 1945. Three weeks

later, Japan signed a formal capitulation agreement on the decks of the battleship *Missouri* in Tokyo Bay to bring World War II to its official close.

The second great war of the twentieth century has had a lasting impact on American life. For the first time, the nation's military potential had been reached. In 1945, the United States was unquestionably the strongest country on the earth, with eleven million men and women in uniform, a vast array of shipyards, aircraft plants, and munitions factories in full production, and a monopoly over the atomic bomb. For better or worse, the nation was now launched on a global career. In the future, the United States would be involved in all parts of the world, from Western Europe to remote jungles in Asia, from the nearby Caribbean to the distant Persian Gulf. And despite its enormous strength in 1945, the nation's new world role would encompass failure and frustration as well as power and dominion.

The legacy of war was equally strong at home. Four years of fighting brought about industrial recovery and unparalleled prosperity. The old pattern of unregulated free enterprise was as much a victim of the war as of the New Deal; big government and huge deficits had now become the norm as economic control passed from New York and Wall Street to Washington and Pennsylvania Avenue. The war led to far-reaching changes in American society that would only become apparent decades later. Such distinctive patterns of recent American life as the baby boom and the growth of the Sun belt can be traced back to wartime origins. The Second World War was a watershed in twentieth-century America, ushering in a new age of global concerns and domestic upheaval.

Recommended Reading

The best general account of American attitudes toward the world in the 1920s can be found in Selig Adler, *The Isolationist Impulse* (1957). Robert Dallek provides a thorough account of FDR's diplomacy in *Franklin D. Roosevelt and American Foreign Policy, 1932–1934* (1979). For a more critical view, see Robert A. Divine, *Roosevelt and World War II* (1969).

Two good books on the continuing controversy over Pearl Harbor are Roberta Wohlstetter, *Pearl Harbor: Warning and Decision* (1962), and Gordon W. Prange, *At Dawn We Slept* (1981). Both authors deny the charge that Roosevelt deliberately exposed the naval base to attack.

In his brief overview of wartime diplomacy, *American Diplomacy During the Second World War* (1964), Gaddis Smith stresses the tensions within the victorious coalition. The two best accounts of the home front are Richard Polenberg, *War and Society* (1972) and John W. Blum, *V Was for Victory* (1976).

Additional Bibliography

On American foreign policy in the period between the wars, see Selig Adler, *The Uncertain Giant, 1921–1941* (1965); Arnold A. Offner, *The Origins of the Second World War* (1975); L. Ethan Ellis, *Republican Foreign Policy, 1921–1933* (1971); Robert H. Ferrell, *Peace in Their Time* (1952); Charles Chatfield, *For Peace and Justice* (1971); Charles DeBenedetti, *Origins of the Modern American Peace Movement, 1915–1929* (1978); Michael J. Hogan, *Informal Entente* (1977); Melvin P. Leffler, *The Elusive Quest* (1978); Akira Iriye, *After Imperialism* (1965); Roger Dingman, *Power in the Pacific* (1976); Thomas H. Buckley, *The United States and the Washington Conference, 1921–1922* (1970); Dorothy Borg, *The United States and the Far Eastern Crisis of 1933–38* (1964); and Robert F. Smith, *The United States and Revolutionary Nationalism in Mexico, 1916–1932* (1972).

For foreign policy during the Hoover years, see Robert

H. Ferrell, *American Diplomacy in the Great Depression* (1957); Alexander DeConde, *Herbert Hoover's Latin American Policy* (1951); and Armin Rappaport, *Henry L. Stimson and Japan* (1963). Diplomatic developments in the 1930s under FDR are covered in Dorothy Borg, *The United States and the Far Eastern Crisis of 1933–1938* (1964); Stephen E. Pelz, *Race to Pearl Harbor* (1974); Bryce Wood, *The Making of the Good Neighbor Policy* (1961); Irwin F. Gellman, *Good Neighbor Diplomacy* (1979); Dick Steward, *Trade and Hemisphere* (1979); Manfred Jonas, *Isolationism in America, 1935–1941* (1966); Robert A. Divine, *The Illusion of Neutrality* (1962); and Wayne A. Cole, *Senator Gerald Nye and American Foreign Relations* (1963).

Examinations of Roosevelt's policies during World War II include Robert Sherwood, *Roosevelt and Hopkins* (1948); James M. Burns, *Roosevelt: Soldier of Freedom* (1970); and Lloyd Gardner, *Economic Aspects of New Deal Diplomacy* (1964). For details of the American entry into the war, see William L. Langer and S. Everett Gleason, *The Challenge to Isolation* (1950) and *The Undeclared War* (1953); Robert A. Divine, *The Reluctant Belligerent*, 2d ed. (1979); Bruce Russett, *No Clear and Present Danger* (1972); Wayne S. Cole, *America First* (1953); Warren F. Kimball, *The Most Unsordid Act: Lend-Lease, 1939–1941* (1969); David Reynolds, *The Creation of the Anglo-American Alliance, 1937–1941* (1982); Saul Friedlander, *Prelude to Downfall: Hitler and the United States* (1967); Herbert Feis, *The Road to Pearl Harbor* (1950); Paul W. Schroeder, *The Axis Alliance and Japanese-American Relations: 1941* (1958); Dorothy Borg and Shumpei Okamoto, eds., *Pearl Harbor as History* (1973); and Harry Elmer Barnes, ed., *Perpetual War for Perpetual Peace* (1953).

Military and strategic aspects of World War II are covered in A. Russell Buchanan, *The United States and World War II*, 2 vols. (1964); Chester Wilmot, *The Struggle for Europe* (1952); Kent Roberts Greenfield, *American Strategy in World War II* (1963); and Mark A. Stoller, *The Politics at the Second Front, 1941–1943* (1977). For wartime diplomacy, see Herbert Feis, *Churchill, Roosevelt and Stalin* (1957); William H. McNeill, *America, Britain, and Russia, 1941–1946* (1953); Tang Tsou, *America's Failure in China* (1963); Michael Schaller, *The U.S. Crusade in China, 1936–1945* (1979); Akira Iriye, *Power and Culture* (1981); Diane Clemens, *Yalta* (1970); and Ralph B. Levering, *American Opinion and the Russian Alliance, 1939–1945* (1976).

On the atomic bomb, see Richard G. Hewlett and Oscar E. Anderson, *The New World, 1939–1946* (1962); Gar Alperovitz, *Atomic Diplomacy* (1965); Martin Sherwin, *A World Destroyed* (1975); Herbert Feis, *The Atomic Bomb and the End of World War II* (1966); and Robert J. C. Butow, *Japan's Decision to Surrender* (1954). Social developments during World War II are examined in Roger Daniels, *Concentration Camps, USA* (1971); Karen Anderson, *Wartime Women* (1981); Neil A. Wynn, *The Afro-Americans and the Second World War* (1976); and A. Russell Buchanan, *Black Americans in World War II* (1977).

chapter 28

THE
ONSET OF
THE COLD WAR

"I am getting ready to go see Stalin and Churchill," President Truman wrote to his mother in July 1945, "and it is a chore." On board the cruiser *Augusta*, the new President continued to complain about the upcoming Potsdam Conference in his diary. "How I hate this trip!" he confided. "But I have to make it—win, lose or draw—and we must win. . . . I [am] giving nothing away except to save starving people and even then I hope we can only help them to help themselves."

Halfway around the world, Joseph Stalin left Moscow a day late because of a slight heart attack. The Russian leader hated to fly, so he traveled by rail. He ordered the heavily guarded train to detour around Poland for fear of an ambush, further delaying his arrival. When he made his entrance into Potsdam, a suburb of Berlin miraculously spared the total destruction that his forces had created in the German capital, he was ready to claim the spoils of war.

These two men, one the veteran revolutionary who had been in power for two decades, the other an untested leader in office for barely three months, symbolized the enormous differences that now separated the wartime allies. Stalin was above all the realist. Brutal in securing total control at home, he was more flexible in his foreign policy, bent on exploiting Russia's victory in World War II rather than aiming at world domination. Cunning and caution were the hallmarks of his diplomatic style. Small in stature, ungainly in build, he radiated a catlike quality as he waited behind his unassuming façade, ready to dazzle an opponent with his "brilliant, terrifying tactical mastery." Truman, in contrast, personified traditional Wilsonian idealism. Lacking Roosevelt's guile, the new President placed his faith in international cooperation. Like many Americans, he believed implicitly in his country's innate goodness. Self-assured to the point of cockiness, he came to Potsdam clothed in the armor of self-righteousness.

The two men met for the first time on July 17, 1945. "I told Stalin that I am no diplomat," the President recorded in his diary, "but usually said yes and no to questions after hearing all the argument." The Russian dictator's reaction remains a mystery, but Truman felt that the first encounter went well. "I can deal with Stalin," he wrote. "He is honest—but smart as hell."

Together with Winston Churchill and his replacement, Clement Attlee, whose Labour party had just triumphed in British elections, Truman and Stalin clashed for the next ten days over such difficult issues as reparations, the Polish border, and the fate of Eastern Europe. Truman presented the ideas and proposals formulated by his advisers; he saw his task as essentially procedural, and when he presided, he moved the agenda along in brisk fashion. After he had "banged through" three items one day, he commented, "I am not going to stay around this terrible place all summer, just to listen to speeches. I'll go home to the Senate for that." In an indirect, roundabout way, he informed Stalin of the existence of the atomic bomb, tested successfully in the New Mexico desert just before the conference began. Truman offered no details, and the impassive Stalin asked for none, commenting only that he hoped the United States would make "good use of it against the Japanese."

Reparations proved to be the crucial issue at Potsdam. The Russians wanted to rebuild their war-ravaged economy with German industry; the United States feared it would be saddled with the entire cost of caring for the defeated Germans. A compromise was finally reached. Each side would take reparations primarily from its own occupation zone, a solution that foreshadowed the future division of Germany. "Because they could not agree on 'how to govern Europe,'" wrote historian Daniel Yergin, Truman and Stalin "began to divide it." The other issues were referred to the newly created Council of Foreign Ministers, which would meet in the fall in London.

The conference thus ended on an apparent note of harmony; beneath the surface, however, the bitter antagonism of the Cold War was festering. America and Russia, each distrustful of the other, were preparing for a long and bitter confrontation.

President Truman, Churchill, and Stalin relax in the palace garden before the meeting at Potsdam, July 25, 1945. The conference dealt with the division of Germany into four occupation zones and recognized Soviet occupation of German territory east of the Oder River, but the mutual suspicion apparent at Potsdam soon crystallized as the Cold War.

A dozen years later, Truman reminisced to an old associate about Potsdam. "What a show that was!" Describing himself as "an innocent idealist" surrounded by wolves, he claimed that all the agreements reached there were "broken as soon as the unconscionable Russian Dictator returned to Mosow!" And then he added ruefully, "And I liked the little son of a bitch. . . ."

The Cold War Begins

The conflict between the United States and the Soviet Union began gradually. For two years, the nations tried to adjust their differences, primarily over three crucial issues, through discussion and negotiation. The Council of Foreign Ministers provided the forum. Beginning in London during the fall of 1945 and meeting with their Russian counterparts in Paris, New York, and Moscow, American diplomats searched for a way to live in peace with a suspicious Soviet Union.

The Division of Europe

The fundamental disagreement was over who would control postwar Europe. In the east, the Red Army had swept over Poland and the Bal-

kans, laying the basis for Soviet domination there. American and British forces had liberated Western Europe from Scandinavia to Italy. The Russians, mindful of past invasions from the west across the plains of Poland, were intent on imposing Communist governments loyal to Moscow in the Soviet sphere. The United States, on the other hand, upheld the principle of national self-determination, insisting that the people in each country should freely choose their postwar rulers. The Soviets saw this demand for free elections as subversive, since they knew that popularly chosen regimes would be unfriendly to Russia. Suspecting American duplicity, Stalin brought down an "Iron Curtain" (Churchill's phrase) from the Baltic to the Adriatic as he created a series of satellite governments.

Germany was the key. The temporary zones of occupation gradually hardened into permanent lines of division. Ignoring the Potsdam Conference agreement that the country be treated as an economic unit, the United States and Great Britain were by 1946 refusing to permit the Russians to take reparations from the industrial Western zones. The initial harsh occupation policy gave way to more humane treatment of the German people and a slow but steady economic recovery. The United States and England merged their zones and championed the idea of the unification of all Germany. Russia, fearing a resurgence of

German military power, responded by intensifying the communization of its zone, which included the jointly occupied city of Berlin. By 1947, England, France, and the United States were laying plans to transfer their authority to an independent West Germany.

The Soviet Union consolidated its grip on Eastern Europe in 1946 and 1947. One by one, Communist regimes replaced coalition governments in Poland, Hungary, Rumania, and Bulgaria. Moving cautiously to avoid provoking the West, Stalin used communism as a means to dominate half of Europe, both to protect the security of the Soviet state and to advance its international power. The climax came in March 1948 when a coup in

Czechoslovakia overthrew a democratic government and gave the Soviets a strategic foothold in Central Europe.

The division of Europe was an inevitable outgrowth of World War II. Both sides were intent on imposing their values in the areas liberated by their troops. The Russians were no more likely to withdraw from Eastern Europe than the United States and Britain were from Germany, France, and Italy. A frank recognition of competing spheres of influence might have avoided further escalation of tension. But the Western nations, remembering Hitler's aggression in the 1930s, began to see Stalin as an equally dangerous threat to their well-being. Instead of accepting him as a

Europe After World War II

The heavy black line splitting Germany shows in graphic form the division of Europe between the Western and Soviet spheres of influence. The two power blocs faced each other across an "iron curtain."

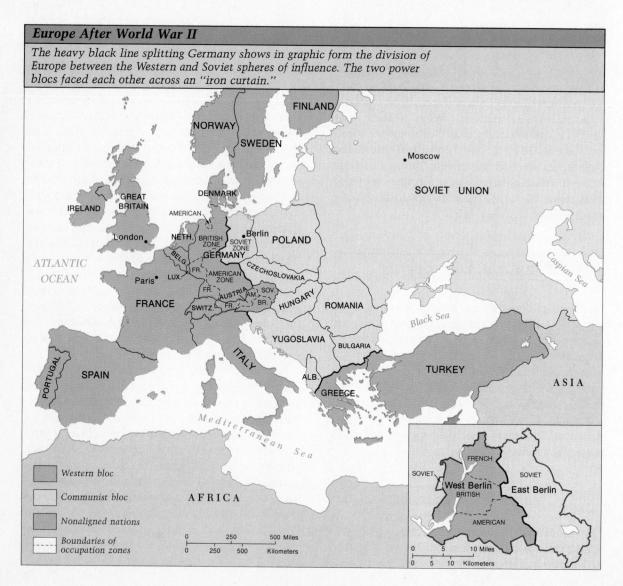

cautious leader bent on protecting Russian security, they perceived him as an aggressive dictator leading a Communist drive for world domination.

Withholding Economic Aid

The Second World War had inflicted enormous damage on Russia. The brutal fighting had taken between fifteen and twenty million Russian lives, destroyed over thirty thousand factories, and torn up forty thousand miles of railroad track. The industrialization that Stalin had achieved at such great sacrifice in the 1930s had been badly set back; even agricultural production had fallen by half during the war. Outside aid and assistance were vital for the reconstruction of the Soviet Union.

American leaders knew of Russia's plight and hoped to use it to good advantage. Wartime ambassador Averell Harriman wrote in 1944 that economic aid was "one of the most effective weapons at our disposal" in dealing with Russia. President Truman was convinced that economically "we held all the cards and the Russians had to come to us."

There were two possible forms of postwar assistance—loans and Lend-Lease. In January 1945, the Soviets requested a $6-billion loan to finance postwar reconstruction. Despite initial American encouragement, President Roosevelt deferred action on this request; as relations with Russia cooled, the chances for action dimmed. "Our experience," commented Harriman in April 1945, had "incontrovertibly proved it was not possible to bank goodwill in Moscow." By the war's end, the loan request, though never formally turned down, was dead.

Lend-Lease proved no more successful. In the spring of 1945, Congress instructed the administration not to use Lend-Lease for postwar reconstruction. President Truman went further, however, by signing an order on May 11, 1945, terminating all shipments to Russia, including those already at sea. The State Department saw the action as applying "leverage against the Soviet Union"; Stalin termed it "brutal." Heeding Russian protests, Truman resumed Lend-Lease shipments, but only until the war was over in August. After that, all Lend-Lease ended.

Deprived of American assistance, the Russians were forced to rebuild their economy through reparations. American and British resistance prevented them taking reparations in Western Germany, but the Soviets systematically removed factories and plants from other areas they controlled, including their zone of Germany, Eastern Europe, and Manchuria. Slowly the Russian economy recovered from the war, but the bitterness over the American refusal to extend aid convinced Stalin of Western hostility and thus deepened the growing antagonism.

The Atomic Dilemma

Overshadowing all else was the atomic bomb. Used by the United States with deadly success at Hiroshima and Nagasaki, the new weapon raised problems that would have been difficult for friendly nations to resolve. Given the uneasy state of Russian-American relations, the effect was disastrous.

The wartime policy followed by Roosevelt and Churchill ensured a postwar nuclear arms race. Instead of informing their major ally of the developing atomic bomb, they kept it a closely guarded secret. Stalin learned of the Manhattan Project through espionage and responded by starting a Soviet atomic program in 1943. By the time Truman informed Stalin of the weapon's existence at Potsdam, the Russians were well on the way to making their own bomb.

After the war, the United States developed a disarmament plan based on turning control of fissionable material, then the processing plants, and ultimately its stockpile of bombs over to an international agency. When President Truman appointed financier Bernard Baruch to present this proposal to the United Nations, Baruch insisted on changing it in several important ways, adding sanctions against violators and exempting the international agency from the UN veto. Ignoring scientists who pleaded for a more cooperative position, Baruch followed instead the advice of Army Chief of Staff Dwight D. Eisenhower, who cited the rapid demobilization of American armed forces (from nearly twelve million in 1945 to less than two million in 1947) to argue that "we cannot at this time limit our capability to produce or use this weapon." In effect, the Baruch Plan, with its multiple stages and emphasis on inspection, would preserve the American atomic monopoly for the indefinite future.

The Soviets responded predictably. Diplomat Andrei Gromyko presented a simple plan calling for a total ban on the production and use of the new weapon as well as the destruction of all existing bombs. The Russian proposal was founded on the same perception of national self-interest as the Baruch Plan. Though Russia had also demobilized rapidly, it still had nearly three million men under arms in 1947 and wished to use its conventional strength to the utmost by outlawing the atomic bomb.

No agreement was possible. Neither the United States nor the Soviet Union could abandon its position without surrendering a vital national interest. Wanting to preserve its monopoly, America stressed inspection and control; hoping to neutralize the U.S. advantage, Russia advocated immediate disarmament. The nuclear dilemma, inherent in the Soviet-American rivalry, blocked any national settlement. Instead, the two superpowers agreed to disagree. Trusting neither each other nor any form of international cooperation, each concentrated on taking maximum advantage of its wartime gains. Thus the Russians exploited the territory they had conquered in Europe while the United States retained its economic and strategic advantages over the Soviet Union. The result was the Cold War.

Containment

A major departure in American foreign policy occurred in January 1947 when General George C. Marshall, the wartime army chief of staff, became secretary of state. Calm, mature, and orderly of mind, Marshall had the ability—honed in World War II—to think in broad, strategic terms. An extraordinarily good judge of ability, he relied on gifted subordinates to handle the day-by-day implementation of his policies. In the months after taking office, he came to rely on two men in particular: Dean Acheson and George Kennan.

Acheson, an experienced Washington lawyer and bureaucrat, was appointed undersecretary of state and given free rein by Marshall to conduct American diplomacy. In appearance, he seemed

■ *Dean Acheson helped formulate the Truman doctrine for aid to Greece and Turkey and was one of the principal architects of the Marshall Plan for assistance to wartorn Europe.*

more British than American, with his impeccable Ivy League clothes and bushy mustache. A man of keen intelligence, he had a carefully cultivated reputation for arrogance and a low tolerance for mediocrity. As an ardent Anglophile, he wanted to see the United States take over a faltering Britain's role as the supreme arbiter of world affairs. Recalling the lesson taught by the Munich Conference of September 1938, he opposed appeasement and advocated a policy of negotiating only from strength.

Marshall's other mainstay was George Kennan, who headed the newly created Policy Planning Staff. A career foreign-service officer, Kennan had become a Soviet expert, mastering Russian history and culture as well as speaking the language fluently. He served in Moscow after U.S. recognition in 1933 and again during World War II, developing there a profound distrust for the Soviet regime. In a crucial telegram in 1946, he warned that the Kremlin believed "that there can be no compromise with rival power" and advocated a policy of containment, arguing that only strong and sustained resistance could halt the outward flow of Russian power. As self-assured as Acheson, Kennan believed that neither Congress nor public opinion should interfere with the conduct of foreign policy by the experts.

In the spring of 1947, a sense of crisis impelled Marshall, Acheson, and Kennan to set out on a new course in American diplomacy. Dubbed "containment," after an article by Kennan in *Foreign Affairs*, the new policy both consolidated the evolving postwar anticommunism and established guidelines that would shape America's role in the world for the next two decades.

The Truman Doctrine

The initial step came in response to an urgent British request. Since March 1946, England had been supporting the Greek government in a bitter civil war against Communist guerrillas. On February 21, 1947, the British informed the United States that they could no longer afford to aid Greece or Turkey, the latter under heavy pressure from the Soviets for access to the Mediterranean. Believing that the Russians were responsible for the strife in Greece (in fact, they were not), Marshall, Acheson, and Kennan quickly decided that the United States would have to take over Britain's role in the eastern Mediterranean.

Worried about congressional support, especially since the Republicans had gained control of Congress in 1946, Marshall called a meeting with the legislative leadership in late February. He outlined the problem, and then Acheson took over to describe "a highly possible Soviet breakthrough" that "might open three continents to Soviet penetration." Comparing the situation in Greece to one rotten apple spoiling an entire barrel, Acheson warned that "the corruption of Greece would infect Iran and all to the East . . . Africa . . . Italy and France." Claiming that the Soviets were "playing one of the greatest gambles in history," Acheson concluded that "we and we alone were in a position to break up the play."

The awed congressional leaders were deeply impressed. Finally, Republican Senator Arthur M. Vandenberg spoke up, saying he would support the President, but adding that to ensure public backing, Truman would have to "scare hell" out of the American people.

The President followed the senator's advice. On March 12, 1947, he asked Congress for $400 million for military and economic assistance to

Courtesy of Richmond Times-Dispatch

■ *Critics expressed doubts about the Truman Doctrine, as in this cartoon, but the national mood was shifting toward approval of the containment policy.*

Greece and Turkey. He made clear that more was involved than just these two countries—the stakes in fact were far higher. "It must be the policy of the United States," Truman told the Congress, "to support free peoples who are resisting attempted subjugation by armed minorities or by outside pressure." After a brief debate, both the House and the Senate approved the program by margins of better than three to one.

The Truman Doctrine marked a formal declaration of cold war against the Soviet Union. Truman used the crisis in Greece to secure congressional approval and build a national consensus for the policy of containment. In less than two years, the civil war in Greece ended, but the American commitment to oppose Communist expansion, whether by internal subversion or external aggression, placed the United States on a collision course with the Soviet Union around the globe.

The Marshall Plan

Western Europe was far more vital to U.S interests than was the eastern Mediterranean, yet by 1947 many Americans felt the area was open to

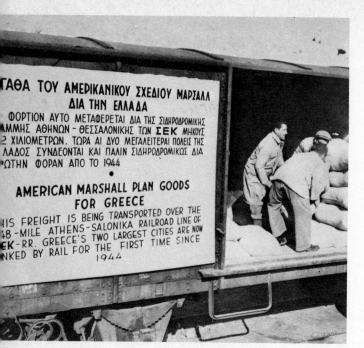

ΤΑΘΑ ΤΟΥ ΑΜΕΡΙΚΑΝΙΚΟΥ ΣΧΕΔΙΟΥ ΜΑΡΣΑΛΛ
ΔΙΑ ΤΗΝ ΕΛΛΑΔΑ

ΦΟΡΤΙΟΝ ΑΥΤΟ ΜΕΤΑΦΕΡΕΤΑΙ ΔΙΑ ΤΗΣ ΣΙΔΗΡΟΔΡΟΜΙΚΗΣ
ΜΜΗΣ ΑΘΗΝΩΝ - ΘΕΣΣΑΛΟΝΙΚΗΣ ΤΩΝ ΣΕΚ ΜΗΚΟΥΣ
2 ΧΙΛΙΟΜΕΤΡΩΝ. ΤΩΡΑ ΑΙ ΔΥΟ ΜΕΓΑΛΕΙΤΕΡΑΙ ΠΟΛΕΙΣ ΤΗΣ
ΛΑΔΟΣ ΣΥΝΔΕΟΝΤΑΙ ΚΑΙ ΠΑΛΙΝ ΣΙΔΗΡΟΔΡΟΜΙΚΩΣ ΔΙΑ
ΡΩΤΗΝ ΦΟΡΑΝ ΑΠΟ ΤΟ 1944

**AMERICAN MARSHALL PLAN GOODS
FOR GREECE**

HIS FREIGHT IS BEING TRANSPORTED OVER THE
48-MILE ATHENS-SALONIKA RAILROAD LINE OF
EK-RR. GREECE'S TWO LARGEST CITIES ARE NOW
NKED BY RAIL FOR THE FIRST TIME SINCE
1944

■ *The European Recovery Program (Marshall Plan) created for the United States an enormous reservoir of good will in Europe.*

Soviet penetration. The problem was economic in nature. Despite $9 billion in piecemeal American loans, England, France, Italy, and the other European countries had great difficulty in recovering from World War II. Food was scarce, with millions existing on less than fifteen hundred calories a day; industrial machinery was broken down and obsolete; and workers were demoralized by years of depression and war. The cruel winter of 1947, the worst in fifty years, compounded the problem. Resentment and discontent led to growing Communist voting strength, especially in Italy and France. Unless the United States could do something to reverse the process, it seemed as though all Europe might drift into the Communist orbit.

In the weeks following proclamation of the Truman Doctrine, American officials dealt with this problem. Secretary of State Marshall, returning from a frustrating Council of Foreign Ministers meeting in Moscow, warned that "the patient is sinking while the doctors deliberate." Acheson believed that it was time to extend American "economic power" in Europe both "to call an

effective halt to the Soviet Union's expansionism" and "to create a basis for political stability and economic well-being." The experts drew up a plan for the massive infusion of American capital to finance the economic recovery of Europe. Speaking at a Harvard commencement on June 5, 1947, Marshall presented the broad outline. He offered extensive economic aid to all the nations of Europe if they could reach agreement on ways to achieve "the revival of a working economy in the world so as to permit the emergence of political and social conditions in which free institutions can exist."

The fate of the Marshall Plan depended on the reaction of the Soviet Union and the U.S. Congress. Marshall had taken, in the words of one American diplomat, "a hell of a gamble" by including Russia in his offer of aid. At a meeting of the European nations in Paris in July 1947, the Soviet foreign minister ended the suspense by abruptly withdrawing. Neither Russia nor its satellites would take part, apparently because Moscow saw the Marshall Plan as an American attempt to weaken Soviet control over Eastern Europe. The other European countries then made a formal request for $17 billion over the next four years.

Congress responded cautiously to this proposal, appointing a special joint committee to investigate. The administration lobbied vigorously, pointing out that the Marshall Plan would help the United States by stimulating trade with Europe as well as checking Soviet expansion. It was the latter argument, however, that proved decisive. When the Czech coup touched off a war scare in March 1948, Congress quickly approved the Marshall Plan by heavy majorities. Over the next four years, the huge American investment paid rich dividends, generating a broad industrial revival in Western Europe that became self-sustaining by the 1950s. The threat of Communist domination faded, and a prosperous Europe proved to be a bonanza for American farmers, miners, and manufacturers.

The Western Military Alliance

The third and final phase of containment came in 1949 with the establishment of the North Atlantic Treaty Organization (NATO). NATO grew out of European fears of Russian military aggression. Recalling Hitler's tactics in the 1930s, the people of Western Europe wanted assurance that the United States would protect them from attack as they began to achieve economic recovery. American diplomats were sympathetic. "People could not go ahead and make investments for the future," commented Averell Harriman, "without some sense of security."

England, France, and the Low Countries (Belgium, the Netherlands, and Luxembourg) began the process in March 1948 when they signed the Brussels Treaty, providing for collective self-defense. In January 1949, President Truman called for a broader defense pact including the United States; ten European nations, from Norway in the North to Italy in the south, joined the United States and Canada in signing the North Atlantic Treaty in Washington on April 4, 1949. This historic departure from the traditional policy of isolation—the United States had not signed such a treaty since the French alliance in the eighteenth century—caused extensive debate, but the Senate ratified it in July by a vote of 82 to 13.

There were two main features of NATO. First, the United States committed itself to the defense of Europe in the key clause which stated that "an armed attack against one or more . . . shall be considered an attack against them all." In effect, the United States was extending its atomic shield over Europe. The second feature was designed to reassure worried Europeans that the United States would honor this commitment. In late 1950, President Truman appointed General Dwight D. Eisenhower to the post of NATO supreme commander and authorized the stationing of four American divisions in Europe to serve as the nucleus of the NATO army. Now any Russian assault would automatically involve American troops and thus deter the Soviet Union.

The Western military alliance escalated the developing Cold War. Whatever its advantage in building a sense of security among worried Europeans, it represented an overreaction to the Soviet danger. Americans and Europeans alike were attempting to apply the lesson of Munich to the Cold War. But Stalin was not Hitler, and the Soviets were not the Nazis. There was no evidence of any Russian plan to invade Western Europe, and in the face of the American atomic bomb, none was likely. All NATO did was to intensify Russian fears of the West and thus increase the level of international tension.

The Berlin Blockade

The main Russian response to containment came in 1948 at the West's most vulnerable point. American, British, French, and Soviet troops each occupied a sector of Berlin, but the city was located over one hundred miles within the Russian zone of Germany (see the map of postwar Europe on p. 808). Stalin decided to test his opponents' resolve by cutting off all rail and highway traffic to Berlin on June 20, 1948.

The timing was very awkward for Harry Truman. He had his hands full resisting efforts to force him off the Democratic ticket, and he faced a difficult reelection effort against a strong Republican candidate, Governor Thomas E. Dewey of New York. Immersed in election-year politics, Truman was caught unprepared by the Berlin blockade. The alternatives were not very appealing. The United States could withdraw its forces and lose not just a city, but the confidence of all Europe; it could try to send in reinforcements and fight for Berlin; or it could sit tight and attempt to find a diplomatic solution. Truman made the basic decision in characteristic fashion, telling the military that there would be no thought of pulling out. "We were going to stay, period," an aide reported Truman as saying.

In the next few weeks, the President and his advisers developed ways to implement this decision. Rejecting proposals for provoking a showdown by sending an armored column down the main highway, the administration adopted a two-phase policy. The first part was a massive airlift of food, fuel, and supplies for both the ten thousand troops and the two million civilians in Berlin. A fleet of fifty-two C-54s and eighty C-47s began making two daily round-trip flights to Berlin, carrying 2500 tons every twenty-four hours. Then, to guard against Soviet interruption of the airlift, Truman transferred sixty American B-29s, planes capable of delivering atomic bombs, to bases in England. The President was bluffing; the B-29s were not equipped with atomic bombs, but at the time the threat was effective.

For a few weeks, the world teetered on the edge

of war. Stalin did not attempt to disrupt the flights to Berlin, but he rejected all American diplomatic initiatives. The airlift gradually increased to more than four thousand tons a day, but at any time the Russians could have halted it by jamming radar or shooting down the defenseless cargo planes. Governor Dewey patriotically supported the President's policy, thus removing foreign policy from the presidential campaign. Yet for Truman the tension was fierce. In early September he asked his advisers to brief him "on bases, bombs, Moscow, Leningrad, etc." "I have a terrible feeling afterward that we are very close to war," he confided in his diary. "I hope not."

Slowly the tension eased. The Russians did not shoot down any planes, and the daily airlift climbed to nearly seven thousand tons. Truman, a decided underdog, won a surprising second term in November over a complacent Dewey (see the map of the 1948 election on p. 839), in part because the Berlin crisis had rallied the nation behind his leadership. In early 1949, the Soviets gave in, ending the blockade in return for another meeting of the Council of Foreign Ministers on Germany—a conclave that proved as unproductive as all the earlier ones.

The Berlin crisis marked the end of the initial phase of the Cold War. The airlift had given the United States a striking political victory, showing the world the triumph of American ingenuity over Russian stubbornness. Yet it could not disguise the fact that the Cold War had cut Europe in two. Behind the Iron Curtain, the Russians had consolidated control over the areas won by their troops in the war. The United States had used the Marshall Plan to revitalize Western Europe, but a divided continent was a far cry from the wartime hopes for a peaceful world. And the rivalry that began in Europe would soon spread into a worldwide contest between the superpowers. Such was the bitter legacy of World War II.

The Cold War Expands

The rivalry between the United States and the Soviet Union grew in the late 1940s and early 1950s. Both sides ended the postwar demobilization and began to rebuild their military forces with new methods and new weapons. Equally significant, the diplomatic competition spread from Europe to Asia as each of the superpowers sought to enhance its influence in the Orient. By the time Truman left office in early 1953, the Cold War had taken on global proportions.

The Military Dimension

After World War II, American leaders were intent on reforming the nation's military system in light of the wartime experience. Two goals were uppermost. First, nearly everyone agreed in the aftermath of Pearl Harbor that the armed services should be unified into an integrated military system. The developing Cold War reinforced this decision. Without unification, declared George Marshall in 1945, "there can be little hope that we will be able to maintain through the years a military posture that will secure for us a lasting peace." Equally important, planners realized the need for new institutions to coordinate military and diplomatic strategy so that the nation could cope effectively with threats to its security.

In 1947, Congress responded by passing the National Security Act. It established a Department of Defense, headed by a civilian secretary of cabinet rank presiding over three separate services—the army, the navy, and the new air force. In addition, the act created the Central Intelligence Agency (CIA) to coordinate the intelligence-gathering activities of various government agencies. Finally, the act provided for a National Security Council (NSC)—composed of the service secretaries, the secretary of defense, and the secretary of state—to advise the president on all matters regarding the nation's security.

Despite the appearance of equality among the services, the air force quickly emerged as the dominant power in the atomic age, both to deter an enemy from attacking the nation's vital interests and to wage war if deterrence failed. President Truman, intent on cutting back defense expenditures, favored the air force in his 1949 military budget, allotting this branch over one half the total sum. After the Czech coup and the resulting war scare, Congress granted an additional $3 billion, much of it earmarked for the air force. The appropriation included funds for a new B-36 to replace the B-29 as the nation's primary strategic bomber.

American military planners received an even greater boost in the fall of 1949 when the Soviet Union exploded its first atomic bomb. President Truman appointed a high-level committee to explore mounting an all-out effort to build a hydrogen bomb to maintain American nuclear supremacy.

Some scientists had technical objections to the H-bomb, which was still far from being perfected, while others opposed the new weapon on moral grounds, claiming that its enormous destructive power (intended to be one thousand times greater than the atomic bomb) made it unthinkable. George Kennan suggested a new effort at international arms control with the Soviets, but Dean Acheson—who succeeded Marshall as secretary of state in early 1949—felt it was imperative that the United States develop the hydrogen bomb before the Soviet Union. When Acheson presented the committee's favorable report to the President in January 1950, Truman took only seven minutes to decide to go ahead with the awesome new weapon.

At the same time, Acheson ordered the Policy Planning Staff, now headed by Paul Nitze after Kennan resigned in protest, to draw up a new statement of national defense policy. NSC-68, as the document eventually became known, was based on the premise that the Soviet Union sought "to impose its absolute authority over the rest of the world" and thus "mortally challenged" the United States. Rejecting such options as appeasement or a return to isolation, Nitze advocated a massive expansion of American military power so that the United States could halt and overcome the Soviet threat. Contending that the nation could afford to spend "upward of 50 percent of its gross national product" for security, NSC-68 proposed increasing defense spending from $13 to $45 billion annually. Approved in principle by the National Security Council in April 1950, NSC-68 stood as a symbol of the Truman administration's determination to win the Cold War regardless of cost.

The Cold War in Asia

The Soviet-American conflict developed more slowly in Asia. At Yalta, the two superpowers had agreed to a Far Eastern balance of power, with the Russians dominating Northeast Asia and the Americans in control of the Pacific, including both Japan and its former island empire.

The United States moved quickly to consolidate its sphere of influence. General Douglas MacArthur, in charge of Japanese occupation, denied the Soviet Union any role in the recon-

Views of the Cold War:
The Debate Among Historians

The outbreak of the Cold War between the United States and the Soviet Union led to an intense and bitter controversy among American historians. One group blamed the conflict solely on the Soviet Union, claiming that the Russians were bent on world domination; opponents argued that the United States had provoked the Cold War through attempts to establish a Pax Americana after World War II.

The scholarly debate followed the course of the Cold War itself. When the diplomatic contest between the United States and Russia was at its height in the 1950s, American historians maintained that the Cold War was clearly the result of Soviet aggression. This orthodox view stemmed from an attempt to absorb the lessons of the 1930s, when the Western democracies had failed to halt the aggression of Germany and Japan until it was almost too late. Citing Munich and the folly of appeasement, historians asserted that Stalin and the Soviet Union were pursuing the same kind of expansionist policies in Europe that Hitler and Nazi Germany had been guilty of in the 1930s. Some saw the Russians as aiming at dominance in Europe; others believed the Soviets desired world domination. The most influential of these writers, former State Department official Herbert Feis, found the origin of the Cold War in the failure of Franklin D. Roosevelt to prepare the American people for the postwar expansion of the Soviet Union.

According to this orthodox view, the Russians nearly achieved their aggressive plan. Weak American diplomacy enabled Stalin to establish an Iron Curtain over Eastern Europe, and by 1947 there was a growing danger of Communist penetration into such Western European countries as Italy and France. Then in the spring of 1947, American policy suddenly met the challenge. According to Joseph Jones in *The Fifteen Weeks*, the President and the secretary of state reversed American policy at the last minute with the Truman Doctrine and the Marshall Plan. These two measures, along with NATO in 1949, formed the essence of containment, the American determination to preserve a favorable balance of power in Europe to check the Russian drive for world control.

This highly nationalistic view of how the Cold War began prevailed through the early 1960s. It justified heavy American military expenditures by portraying the United States as the protector of the free world. The belated and defensive American response to Soviet aggression also fitted neatly into a familiar pattern. Three times in the twentieth century—in 1917, in 1941, and again in 1947—the United States had reluctantly acted to preserve a decent and civilized world.

In the next decade, however, two developments undermined this complacent explanation. First, the escalation of the Vietnam War in 1965 led to a new mood of doubt and dissent over American foreign policy. As the wisdom of U.S. intervention in Vietnam came into question, historians began to probe the roots of the Cold War to find out why Americans had ended up fighting an unpopular war in Southeast Asia. Second, the State Department archives and the private papers of American diplomats were opened for historical research in the 1960s, providing scholars with a behind-the-scenes view of policymaking that often contradicted the accepted version.

The early revisionists, notably Denna F. Fleming and Gar Alperovitz, tended to blame the Cold War on the transfer of power from Roosevelt to Truman and particularly on the decision to drop the atomic bomb. According to this view, Roosevelt tried hard to cooperate with the Soviets, relying on his personal ties with Stalin to ensure postwar cooperation. FDR understood the historic Russian concern over security, which led to an insistence on friendly regimes in Eastern Europe. Truman, however, lacking Roosevelt's experience in foreign policy, immediately antagonized the Russians by challenging their control over Poland and the Balkans. According to Alperovitz, Truman even tried to use the atomic bomb to force a Russian retreat in Eastern Europe, and his decision to use this dread weapon was based as much on a desire to overwhelm the Soviets as to defeat Japan.

Later revisionists gave greater weight to economic factors in accusing the United States of starting the Cold War. Writers such as Gabriel Kolko argued that it was an American need to dominate world markets that lay behind the refusal to accept Soviet control of Eastern Europe. A capitalist system that needed to expand overseas to overcome its own inherent weaknesses prevented the United States from reaching a territorial settlement with Russia that could have led to a peaceful world. Thus a powerful and expansionist United States, not an insecure Soviet Union, was responsible for the Cold War.

In the 1970s, as détente mellowed Soviet-American relations, a more balanced view of the origins of the diplomatic conflict emerged. Writers like John Lewis Gaddis and Daniel Yergin, who became known as postrevisionists, began to treat the Cold War as a historical event that transcended simple accusations of national guilt. Rather than challenging the revisionists completely, they tried to incorporate their views into a broader explanation that stressed the inevitability of the Cold War.

The postrevisionists based their explanation on the confusion and misunderstanding prevalent at the end of World War II. The United States, misled by the experience with Hitler in the 1930s, mistook Stalin's attempt to bolster Russian security in Eastern Europe for a design for world conquest. When Truman responded with containment, which was essentially an effort to preserve the balance of power in postwar Europe, the Russians thought that America and its allies were bent on encircling and eventually destroying the Soviet Union. A vicious cycle then began, with each nation perceiving every step taken by the other as a threat to its existence. Neither the United States nor the Soviet Union alone was guilty of beginning the Cold War; both must share responsibility for this tragedy.

The postrevisionist explanation is very close to an early explanation for the Cold War advanced by historian William H. McNeill. Writing in 1950, McNeill pointed out that throughout history victorious coalitions had split apart as soon as the common enemy was overcome. The defeat of the Axis had created a vacuum of power in which the United States and the Soviet Union were bound to clash to determine who would control the future of Europe.

Yet even this view does not explain why the competition between the two nations became so intense. Other wartime alliances have dissolved without creating such a fierce rivalry. Here is where the atomic bomb played a key role. The existence of a new weapon of vast destructive power added an unknown element to the international arena, one that was beyond all previous experience. The very survival of the two antagonists became a genuine matter of concern in the nuclear age. Thus Hiroshima not only ended the Second World War; it also created the unstable diplomatic climate that gave rise to the Cold War.

struction of Japan. Instead he supervised the transition of the Japanese government into a constitutional democracy, shaped along Western lines, in which Communists were barred from all government posts. The Japanese willingly renounced war in their new constitution, relying instead on American forces to protect their security. American policy was equally nationalistic in the Pacific. A trusteeship arrangement with the United Nations merely disguised the fact that the United States held full control over the Marshall, Mariana, and Caroline islands. American scientists conducted atomic bomb tests at Bikini atoll in 1946, and by 1949, MacArthur was declaring that the entire Pacific "had become an Anglo-Saxon lake and our line of defense runs through the chain of islands fringing the coast of Asia."

As defined at Yalta, China lay between the Soviet and American spheres. When World War II ended, the country was torn between Chiang Kai-shek's Nationalists in the South and Mao Tse-tung's Communists in the North. Chiang had many advantages, including American political and economic backing and official Soviet recognition. But corruption was widespread among the Nationalist leaders, and a raging inflation that soon reached 100 percent a year devastated the Chinese middle classes and thus eroded Chiang's base of power. Mao used tight discipline and patriotic appeals to strengthen his hold on the peasantry and extend his influence. When the Soviets abruptly vacated Manchuria in 1946, after stripping it of virtually all the industrial machinery Japan had installed, Mao inherited control of this rich northern province. Ignoring American advice, Chiang rushed north to occupy Manchurian cities, overextending his supply lines and exposing his forces to Communist counterattack.

American policy aimed at averting a Chinese civil war. Before he became secretary of state, George Marshall undertook the difficult task of forming a coalition government between Chiang and Mao. For a few months in early 1946, Marshall appeared to have succeeded, but Chiang's attempts to gain control of Manchuria doomed the agreement. In reality, there was no basis for compromise. Chiang insisted he "was going to liquidate Communists," while Mao was trying to play off the United States against Russia in his bid for power. By 1947, as China plunged into full-scale civil war, the Truman administration had

During World War II Mao Tse-tung, leader of the Communist forces in China, fought the Japanese, sometimes alongside American GIs. Later, Mao triumphed over the Nationalists and created a Marxist China.

given up any meaningful effort to influence the outcome. Political mediation had failed, military intervention was out of the question, and a policy of continued American economic aid served only to appease domestic supporters of Chiang Kai-shek; 80 percent of the military supplies ended up in Communist hands.

The climax came at the end of the decade. Mao's forces drove the Nationalists out of Manchuria in late 1948 and advanced across the Yangtze by mid-1949. Acheson released a lengthy White Paper justifying American policy in China on the grounds that the civil war there "was beyond the control of the government of the United States." An American military adviser concurred, telling Congress that the Nationalist defeat was due to "the world's worst leadership" and "a complete loss of will to fight." Republican senators, however, disagreed, blaming American diplomats for sabotaging the Nationalists and terming the White Paper "a 1054-page whitewash of a wishful, do-nothing policy." While the domestic debate raged over responsibility for the loss of China, Chiang's forces fled the mainland for sanctuary on Formosa (Taiwan) in December 1949. Two months later, Mao and Stalin signed a Sino-Soviet treaty of mutual assistance that clearly placed China in the Russian orbit.

The American response to the Communist triumph in China was twofold. First, the State Department refused to recognize the legitimacy of the new regime in Peking, maintaining instead formal diplomatic relations with the Nationalists on Formosa. Citing the Sino-Soviet alliance, Assistant Secretary of State Dean Rusk called the Peking regime "a colonial Russian government" and declared, "It is not the Government of China. It does not pass the first test. It is not Chinese." Then, to compensate for the loss of China, the United States focused on Japan as its main ally in Asia. The State Department encouraged the buildup of Japanese industry, and the Pentagon expanded American bases on the Japanese home islands and Okinawa. A Japanese-American security pact led to the end of American occupation by 1952. The Cold War had now split Asia in two.

The Korean War

The showdown between the United States and the Soviet Union in Asia came in Korea. Traditionally the cockpit of international rivalry in Northeast Asia, Korea had been divided at the thirty-eighth parallel in 1945. The Russians occupied the industrial North, installing a Communist government under the leadership of Kim Il-Sung. In the agrarian South, Syngman Rhee, a conservative nationalist, emerged as the American-sponsored ruler. Neither regime heeded a UN call for elections to unify the country. The two superpowers pulled out most of their occupation forces by 1949. The Russians, however, helped train a well-equipped army in the North, while the United States—fearful that Rhee would seek unification through armed conquest—gave much more limited military assistance to South Korea.

On June 25, 1950, the North Korean army suddenly crossed the thirty-eighth parallel in great strength. The Soviet role in this act of aggression is shrouded in mystery. Presumably Stalin ordered the attack in an attempt to expand the Soviet sphere in Asia and to counter the American buildup of Japan. Yet there is also evidence to suggest that Kim Il-Sung acted on his own, confident that the Russians would have no choice but to back his move.

There was nothing ambiguous about the American response. President Truman saw the invasion as a clear-cut case of Soviet aggression reminiscent of the 1930s. "Communism was acting in Korea just as Hitler, Mussolini, and the Japanese had acted ten, fifteen, and twenty years earlier," he commented in his memoirs. Following the advice of Acheson, the President convened the UN Security Council and, taking advantage of a temporary Soviet boycott, secured a resolution condemning North Korea as an aggressor and

The Korean War, 1950–1953

After a year of seesawing battle lines, the fighting stalled around the truce line shown; this became the armistice line in July 1953.

SOVIET UNION

CHINA

Yalu R.

Furthest UN advance Nov. 1950

Sea of Japan

NORTH KOREA

Pyongyang

Truce Line 1953

Panmunjom

38th Parallel

Inchon Landing Sept. 15, 1950

Seoul

SOUTH KOREA

Yellow Sea

Pusan Perimeter Furthest North Korean advance Sept. 1950

Pusan

0   100 Miles

0   100 Kilometers

International boundaries, 1950

North Korean invasion June-Sept. 1950

UN offensive Sept.-Nov. 1950

Communist Chinese offensive Nov. 1950-Jan. 1951.

calling on the member nations to engage in a collective-security action. Within a few days, American troops from Japan were in combat in South Korea. The conflict, which would last for more than three years, was technically a police action fought under UN auspices; in reality, the United States was at war with a Soviet satellite in Asia.

In the beginning, the fighting went badly as the North Koreans continued to drive down the peninsula. But by August, American forces had halted the Communist advance near Pusan. In September, General MacArthur changed the whole complexion of the war by carrying out a brilliant amphibious assault at Inchon, on the waist of Korea, cutting off and destroying most of the North Korean army in the South. Encouraged by this victory, Truman began to shift from his original goal of restoring the thirty-eighth parallel to a new one, the unification of Korea by military force.

The administration ignored warnings from Peking, sent by way of India, against an American invasion of North Korea; "I should think it would be sheer madness for the Chinese to intervene," commented Dean Acheson. MacArthur was even more confident. "We are no longer fearful of their intervention," he told Truman at a Wake Island conference in mid-October. Noting that the Chinese had no air force, the general prophesied that if they crossed the Yalu River into Korea, "there would be the greatest slaughter."

Rarely has an American president received worse advice than Truman did from Acheson and MacArthur. The UN forces crossed the thirty-eighth parallel in October, advanced confidently to the Yalu in November, and then were completely routed by a massive Chinese counterattack that drove them out of all North Korea by December. MacArthur finally stabilized the fighting near the thirty-eighth parallel, but when Truman decided to give up his attempt to unify Korea, the general protested to Congress, calling for a renewed offensive and proclaiming, "There is no substitute for victory."

Truman courageously relieved the popular hero of the Pacific of his command on April 11, 1951. At first, MacArthur seemed likely to force the President to back down. Huge crowds came forward to welcome him home and hear him call for victory over the Communists in Asia. At a special congressional hearing, the administration struck back effectively by warning that MacArthur's strategy would expose all Europe to Soviet attack. General Omar Bradley, Truman's chief military adviser, succinctly pointed out that a "showdown" with communism in Asia would be "the wrong war, at the wrong place, at the wrong time, and with the wrong enemy."

Congress and the American people came to accept MacArthur's recall. The Korean War settled into a stalemate near the thirty-eighth parallel as truce talks with the Communists bogged down for the rest of Truman's term in office. The President could take heart from the fact that he had achieved his primary goal, defense of South Korea and the principle of collective security. Yet by taking the gamble to unify Korea by force, he had confused the American people and humiliated the United States in the eyes of the world.

In the last analysis, the most significant result of the Korean conflict was the massive American rearmament it brought about. The war led to the implementation of NSC-68—the army expanded to 3.5 million troops, the defense budget increased to $50 billion a year by 1952, and the United States acquired military bases in distant quarters of the world, ranging from Saudi Arabia to Morocco. America was now committed to waging a global contest against the Soviet Union with arms as well as words.

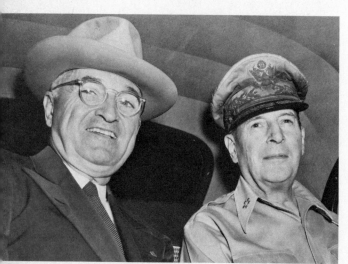

■ *President Truman and General MacArthur at Wake Island in October 1950 when hopes were high for total victory in Korea.*

After the Chinese onslaught of November 1950, U.S. Marines retreated to the sea along icy roads in near-zero weather. They faced three Chinese divisions in the bloody struggle but managed to bring out their wounded and their equipment.

Eisenhower and the Cold War

Significant changes took place in American foreign policy with the election of Dwight D. Eisenhower in 1952. Unlike 1948, when bipartisan agreement over containment and the Berlin blockade prevailed, in 1952 the Cold War was a primary issue in the presidential campaign. After defeating Ohio Senator Robert A. Taft for the GOP nomination, General Eisenhower ran against Democratic candidate Adlai E. Stevenson, the governor of Illinois, on a platform condemning containment as "futile" and "immoral." Instead of abandoning the captive peoples of Eastern Europe to Communist enslavement, the Republicans promised their liberation. Eisenhower backed away from these vague words during the campaign, however, preferring to focus on the stalemated Korean War. Criticizing the Truman administration for failing either to win a victory or negotiate a truce, Eisenhower promised that if elected, he would go to Korea personally to work out a solution. A grateful nation responded by choosing him over Stevenson by a margin of 55 to 45 percent.

Despite his lack of experience in American domestic politics, Eisenhower was unusually well prepared to lead the nation at the height of the Cold War. His long years of military service had exposed him to a wide variety of international issues, both in Asia and in Europe, and to an even broader array of world leaders, such as Douglas MacArthur, Winston Churchill, and Charles de Gaulle. His gifts were primarily political and diplomatic rather than strictly military. He was blessed with a sharp, pragmatic mind and organizational genius that enabled him to plan and carry out large enterprises, grasping the precise relationship between the parts and the whole. Above all, he had a serene confidence in his own ability. At the end of his first day in the White House, he confided in his diary: "Plenty of worries and difficult problems. But such has been my portion for a long time—the result is that this just seems like a continuation of all I've been doing since July 1941. . . . "

Eisenhower chose John Foster Dulles as his secretary of state. The myth soon developed that Ike gave Dulles free rein to conduct American diplomacy. Appearances were deceptive. Eisenhower preferred to work behind the scenes. He let Dulles make the public speeches and appearances before congressional committees, where his hardline views placated GOP extremists. But Dulles carefully consulted with the President before every appearance, meeting frequently with Eisen-

From Herblock's Special For Today (Simon & Schuster, 1958)

■ *(Above) Secretary of State John Foster Dulles shown reporting to President Eisenhower and the nation after a European tour in 1955. (Right) Cartoonist Herblock, a sharp critic of Dulles' hard line, depicts him in a Superman suit pushing Uncle Sam to the brink of nuclear war.*

hower at the White House and telephoning him several times a day. Ike respected his secretary of state's broad knowledge of foreign policy and his skill in conducting American diplomacy, but he made all the major decisions himself. "There's only one man I know who has seen *more* of the world and talked with more people and *knows* more than he does," Ike said of Dulles, "and that's me."

From the outset, Eisenhower was determined to bring the Cold War under control. Ideally, he wanted to end it, but as a realist, he would settle for a relaxation of tensions with the Soviet Union. In part, he was motivated by a deeply held budgetary concern. Defense spending had increased from $15 billion to $50 billion under Truman; Ike was convinced that the nation was in danger of going bankrupt unless military spending was reduced. As president, he inaugurated a "new look" for American defense, cutting back on the army and navy and relying even more heavily than Truman had on the air force and its nuclear striking power. As a result, the defense budget dropped to $40 billion annually. In 1954, Dulles announced reliance on massive retaliation —in fact a continuation of Truman's policy of deterrence. Rather than becoming involved in limited wars such as Korea, the United States

would consider the possibility of using nuclear weapons to halt any Communist aggression which threatened vital U.S. interests anywhere in the world.

While he permitted Dulles to make his veiled nuclear threats, Eisenhower's fondest dream was to end the arms race. Sobered by the development of the hydrogen bomb, successfully tested by the United States in November 1952 and by the Soviet Union in August 1953, the President began a new effort at disarmament with the Russians. Yet before this initiative could take effect, Ike had to weather a series of crises around the world that tested his skill and patience to the utmost.

Confrontations in Asia

The first task facing the new president was to end the Korean War. Before taking office, Eisenhower fulfilled his campaign promise to travel to Korea. Once there, he quickly ruled out a military offensive as too costly in lives and money. Despite objections from Dulles, who wanted to give "the Chinese one hell of a licking," Ike preferred the path of diplomacy. In the spring of 1953, he had Dulles deliver a secret warning to China by way of India: Unless the Chinese agreed to a truce, the

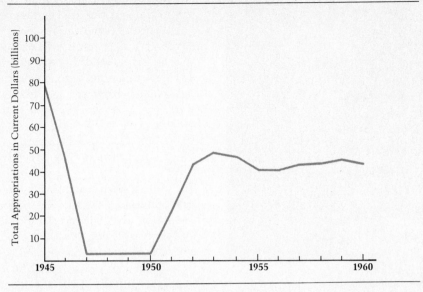

Source: Compiled from *U.S. Bureau of the Census,* Historical Statistics of the United States, Colonial Times to 1970, *Bicentennial Edition, Washington, D.C., 1975.*

United States would use its nuclear weapons to break the stalemate. Mao, impressed by Ike's threat and shaken by the death of Stalin in March, agreed to negotiate. American and Communist diplomats signed a truce agreement on July 2, 1953, which ended the fighting but left Korea divided—as it had been before the war—near the thirty-eighth parallel.

The President was not as successful in dealing with Indochina, another trouble spot he inherited from Truman. Since 1950 the United States had been giving the French economic and military aid in their civil war against Communist guerrillas led by Ho Chi Minh. The Chinese increased their support to Ho's forces after the Korean War ended, until by the spring of 1954 the French were on the brink of defeat. The Viet Minh had trapped nearly ten thousand French troops at Dien Bien Phu deep in the interior of northern Indochina; in desperation France turned to the United States for help. Admiral Arthur Radford, chairman of the Joint Chiefs of Staff, proposed an American air strike to lift the siege. Although the other Joint Chiefs had doubts about this plan, hawkish Republican senators were clamoring for action.

Eisenhower decided against Radford's proposal, but he killed it in his typically indirect fashion. Fearful that an air attack would lead to an inter-vention by ground forces, Ike insisted that both Congress and American allies in Europe approve the policy in advance. Congressional leaders, recalling the recent Korean debacle, were reluctant; the British were appalled and ruled out any joint action. The President used these objections to turn down intervention in Indochina in 1954. Much later, just before the American involvement in the Vietnam War in the 1960s, he stated his reasons more candidly. "The jungles of Indochina would have swallowed up division after division of United States troops," he explained. Equally important, he believed that U.S. involvement in France's war would have compromised the American "tradition of anti-colonialism." "The standing of the United States as the most powerful of the anti-colonial powers is an asset of incalculable value to the Free World," he concluded.

Dien Bien Phu fell to the Communists in May 1954. At an international conference held in Geneva during the following summer, Indochina was divided at the seventeenth parallel. Ho gained control of North Vietnam, while the French continued to rule in the South, with provision for a general election within two years to unify the country. The election was never held, largely because the United States feared it

823
Eisenhower and the Cold War

Ho Chi Minh, a dedicated Vietnamese nationalist and founder of that country's Communist party, led the movement that drove the French from Indochina in 1954.

would result in an overwhelming mandate for Ho Chi Minh. In the fall of 1954, the United States replaced France as the major supporter of the new government of South Vietnam led by Ngo Dinh Diem. Vietnam, like Korea, was split in two, but unfortunately this solution was only temporary.

Communist China posed an even graver problem for the Eisenhower administration. In the fall of 1954, the mainland government threatened to seize islands off the coast of China, notably Quemoy and Matsu, occupied by the Nationalists. Fearful that this would be the first step toward an invasion of Formosa, Eisenhower permitted Dulles to sign a security treaty with Chiang Kai-shek committing the United States to defend Formosa. When the Communists began shelling the offshore islands, Eisenhower persuaded Congress to pass a resolution authorizing him to use force to defend Formosa and "closely related localities."

Despite repeated requests, however, the President refused to say whether he would use force to repel a Chinese attack on Quemoy or Matsu. Instead he and Dulles hinted at the use of nuclear weapons, but they carefully stated that their action would depend on whether they considered an attack on the offshore islands part of a larger offensive aimed at Formosa. The Chinese leaders, unsure whether Eisenhower was bluffing, decided

not to test American resolve. The shelling stopped in 1955, and though the Communists resumed it again in 1958, another firm but equally ambiguous American response forced them to desist. In his memoirs, Eisenhower took pride that he had threaded his way "with watchfulness and determination, through narrow and dangerous waters between appeasement and global war."

Turmoil in the Middle East

The gravest crisis came in the Middle East when Egyptian leader Gamal Nasser seized the Suez Canal in July 1956. England and France were ready to use force immediately; their citizens owned the canal company, and their economies were dependent on the canal for the flow of oil from the Persian Gulf. President Eisenhower, however, was staunchly opposed to intervention, preferring to seek a diplomatic solution with Nasser, who kept the canal running smoothly. For three months, Dulles did everything possible to restrain the European allies, but finally they decided to take a desperate gamble—invade Egypt and seize the canal while relying on the United States to prevent any Russian interference.

Eisenhower was furious when England and France launched their attack in early November. Campaigning for reelection against Adlai Stevenson on the slogan of keeping the peace, Ike had to abandon domestic politics to deal with the threat of war. "The White House crackled with barracks-room language," reported one observer; the President told an aide that the Western allies had made "a complete *mess* and *botch* of things." Unhesitatingly, he instructed Dulles to sponsor a UN resolution calling for British and French withdrawal from Egypt. Yet when the Russians supported the American proposal and went further, threatening rocket attacks on British and French cities and even offering to send "volunteers" to fight in Egypt, Eisenhower made it clear that he would not tolerate Soviet interference. He put the Strategic Air Command on alert and said of the Russians, "If those fellows start something, we may have to hit 'em—and, if necessary, with everything in the bucket."

Just after noon on election day, November 6, 1956, British Prime Minister Anthony Eden

■ *The first wave of U.S. Marines splashed ashore on the beach near Beirut, Lebanon, in July 1958. Sent to avert a Christian-Moslem civil war, they stayed only one hundred days.*

some fourteen thousand troops airlifted from bases in Germany. The military wanted to occupy the entire country, but Eisenhower insisted on limiting American forces to the area of Beirut. The mission of the troops, he argued, was "not primarily to fight," but simply to show the flag. Lebanese political leaders quickly agreed on a successor to Chamoun, and American soldiers left the country before the end of October. This restrained use of force achieved Eisenhower's primary goal of quieting the explosive Middle East. It also served, as Secretary of State Dulles pointed out, "to reassure many small nations that they could call on us in a time of crisis."

Covert Actions

In addition to keeping the peace amid these dangerous crises, the Eisenhower administration worked behind the scenes in the 1950s to expand the nation's global influence. In 1953, the CIA was instrumental in overthrowing a popularly elected government in Iran and placing the Shah in full control of that country. American oil companies were rewarded with lucrative concessions, and Eisenhower felt that he had gained a valuable ally on the Russian border. But these short-run gains created a deep-seated animosity among Iranians that would haunt the United States in the future.

Closer to home, in Latin America, Eisenhower once again relied on covert action. In 1954, the CIA masterminded the overthrow of a leftist regime in Guatemala. The immediate advantage was in denying the Soviets a possible foothold in the Western Hemisphere, but Latin Americans resented the thinly disguised interference of the United States in their internal affairs. More important, when Fidel Castro came to power in Cuba in 1959, the Eisenhower administration— after a brief effort at conciliation—adopted a hard line that helped drive Cuba into the Soviet orbit and led to new attempts at covert action.

Eisenhower's record as a Cold Warrior was thus mixed. His successful ending of the Korean War and his peacekeeping efforts in Indochina and Formosa and in the Suez crisis are all to his credit. Yet his reliance on coups and subversion directed by the CIA in Iran and Guatemala reveal Ike's corrupting belief that the ends justified the

called the President to inform him that England and France were ending their invasion. Eisenhower breathed a sigh of relief. American voters rallied behind Ike, electing him to a second term by a near landslide. As a result of the Suez crisis, the United States replaced England and France as the main Western influence in the Middle East. With Russia strongly backing Egypt and Syria, the Cold War had found yet another battleground.

Two years later, Eisenhower found it necessary to intervene in the strategic Middle Eastern country of Lebanon. Political power in this neutral nation was divided between Christian and Moslem elements. When the outgoing Christian president, Camille Chamoun, broke with tradition by seeking a second term, Moslem groups (aided by Egypt and Syria) threatened to launch a rebellion. At first, Eisenhower turned down Chamoun's request for American intervention to avert a civil war, but after an unexpected nationalist coup overthrew the pro-Western government of Iraq, Ike decided to act in order to uphold the U.S. commitment to political stability in the Middle East.

American marines from the Sixth Fleet moved swiftly ashore on July 15, 1958, securing the Beirut airport and preparing the way for a force of means. Nevertheless, Eisenhower did display an admirable ability to stay calm and unruffled in moments of great tension, reassuring the nation and the world. And above all, he could boast, as he did in 1962, of his ability to keep the peace. "In those eight years," he reminded the nation, "we lost no inch of ground to tyranny . . . . One war was ended and incipient wars were blocked."

Waging Peace

Eisenhower hoped to ease Cold War tensions by ending the nuclear arms race. The advent of the hydrogen bomb intensified his concern over nuclear warfare; by 1955, both the United States and the Soviet Union had added this dread new weapon to their arsenals. With new long-range ballistic missiles being perfected, it was only a matter of time before Russia and the United States would be capable of destroying each other completely. Peace, as Winston Churchill noted, now depended on a balance of terror.

Throughout the fifties, Eisenhower sought a way out of the nuclear dilemma. In April 1953, shortly after Stalin's death, he gave a speech in which he called on the Russians to join him in a new effort at disarmament, pointing out that "every warship launched, every rocket fired signifies, in the final sense, a theft from those who hunger and are not fed, those who are cold and are not clothed." When the Soviets ignored this appeal, the President tried again in December 1953. Addressing the UN General Assembly, he outlined an "atoms-for-peace" plan whereby the United States and the Soviet Union would donate fissionable material to a new UN agency to be used for peaceful purposes. Despite Ike's appeal "to serve the needs rather than the fears of mankind," the Russians again rebuffed him. Undaunted, Eisenhower tried once more. At the Geneva summit conference in 1955, Ike proposed to Nikita Khrushchev, just emerging as Stalin's successor after a two-year struggle for power, a way to break the disarmament deadlock. "Open skies," as reporters dubbed the plan, would overcome the traditional Russian objection to on-site inspection by having both superpowers open their territory to mutual aerial surveillance. Unfortunately, Khrushchev dismissed open skies as "a very transparent espionage device," and the Geneva Conference ended without any significant breakthrough in the Cold War.

After his reelection in 1956, the President made a new effort to initiate nuclear-arms control. Concern over atmospheric fallout from nuclear testing had led presidential candidate Adlai Stevenson to propose a mutual ban on such experiments. At first Eisenhower rejected the test-ban idea, arguing it could be effective only as part of a comprehensive disarmament agreement, but the Russians supported it. Finally, in 1958, the President changed his mind after American and Soviet scientists developed a system to detect nuclear testing in the atmosphere without on-site inspection. In October 1958, Eisenhower and Khrushchev each voluntarily suspended further weapons tests pending the outcome of a conference held at Geneva to work out a test-ban treaty. Although the Geneva Conference failed to make progress, neither the United States nor the Soviet Union resumed testing for the remainder of Ike's term in office.

The suspension of testing halted the pollution of the world's atmosphere, but it did not lead to the improvement in Russian-American relations that Eisenhower sought. In the late 1950s, Khrushchev took advantage of the Soviet feat in

■ *Eisenhower talking to Soviet leader Khrushchev during Khrushchev's American tour in 1959.*

from Straight Herblock (Simon & Schuster, 1964)

■ *Cartoonist Herblock's view of the Khrushchev-Eisenhower meetings.*

■ *The capture of U-2 pilot Gary Powers, shot down over Russia, put an end to Soviet-American plans for a Paris summit meeting in 1960.*

launching Sputnik, the first artificial satellite to orbit the earth, to intensify the Cold War. Playing on Western fears that the Soviets had made a breakthrough in missile technology, the Russian leader began to issue threats, proclaiming, "We will bury capitalism," and telling Americans, "Your grandchildren will live under Communism." The most serious threat of all came in November 1958 when Khrushchev declared that within six months he would sign a separate peace treaty with East Germany, thereby ending American, British, and French occupation rights in Berlin.

Eisenhower met the second Berlin crisis as firmly as Truman had the first. He refused to abandon the city, but he also tried to avoid a military showdown. Prudent diplomacy forced Khrushchev to extend his ultimatum indefinitely. After a trip to the United States, culminating in a personal meeting with Eisenhower at Camp David, the Russian leader agreed to attend a summit conference in Paris in May 1960.

This much-heralded meeting never took place. On May 1, two weeks before the leaders were to convene in Paris, the Soviets shot down an American U-2 plane piloted by Francis Gary Powers. The United States had been overflying Russia since 1956 in these high-altitude spy planes,

gaining vital information about the Soviet missile program. When Eisenhower belatedly took full responsibility for the Powers' overflight, Khrushchev responded with a scathing personal denunciation and a refusal to meet with the American president.

Eisenhower deeply regretted the breakup of the Paris summit, telling an aide that "the stupid U-2 mess" had destroyed all his efforts for peace. Sadly he concluded that "he saw nothing worthwhile left for him to do now until the end of his presidency." Khrushchev marked time for the next nine months, waiting for the American people to choose a new president. Eisenhower did make a final effort at peace, however. Three days

Chronology

1945 Truman meets Stalin at Potsdam Conference (July)
World War II ends with Japanese surrender (August)

1946 Winston Churchill gives "Iron Curtain" speech

1947 Truman Doctrine announced to Congress (March)
George Marshall outlines Marshall Plan (June)

1948 Soviets begin blockade of Berlin (June); U.S. begins airlift of supplies to Berlin civilians

1949 NATO treaty signed in Washington (April)
Soviet Union tests its first atomic bomb (August)

1950 Truman authorizes building of hydrogen bomb (January)
North Korea invades South Korea (June)

1951 Truman recalls MacArthur from Korea

1952 Dwight D. Eisenhower elected president

1953 Stalin dies (March)
Korean War truce signed at Panmunjon (July)

1954 Fall of Dien Bien Phu to Viet Minh ends French control of Indochina

1955 Eisenhower meets Krushchev at Geneva summit

1956 England and France touch off Suez crisis

1957 Russia launches Sputnik satellite

1958 United States and Russia halt nuclear testing

1959 Fidel Castro takes power in Cuba

1960 American U-2 plane shot down over Russia

---

before leaving office, he delivered a farewell address in which he gave a somber warning about the danger of massive military spending. "In the councils of government, we must guard against the acquisition of unwarranted influence, whether sought or unsought, by the military-industrial complex," he declared. "The potential for the disastrous rise of misplaced power exists and will persist."

Rarely has an American president been more

prophetic. In the next few years, the level of defense spending would skyrocket as the Cold War escalated under his successors in the White House. The military-industrial complex reached its acme of power in the 1960s when the United States realized the full implications of Truman's doctrine of containment. Eisenhower had succeeded in keeping the peace for eight years, but he had failed to halt the momentum of the Cold War he had inherited from Harry Truman. Ike's efforts to ease tension with the Soviet Union were dashed by his own distrust of communism and by Khrushchev's belligerent rhetoric and behavior. Still, he had begun the process of relaxing tensions that would survive the troubled sixties, flourish briefly under the name of détente in the next decade, and then become yet another casualty of the continuing Cold War.

Recommended Reading

The Cold War has spawned a vast array of books, some enduring in nature and many that are already outdated. The best general guide to American diplomacy since World War II is Walter LaFeber, *America, Russia and the Cold War, 1945–1980*, 4th ed. (1980). LaFeber, who writes from a moderately revisionist perspective, is more concerned with explaining the course of American foreign policy than in criticizing it. On the much-debated question of the origins of the Cold War, the best balanced account is Daniel Yergin, *Shattered Peace* (1977), a book which characterizes American policy as flawed by misunderstanding rather than by ill will.

The classic account of containment is still the lucid recollection of its chief architect, George Kennan, *Memoirs, 1925–1950* (1967). John L. Gaddis uses Kennan's ideas as a point of departure for his account of the changing nature of American Cold War policy in *Strategies of Containment* (1982). For developments in the Far East, consult the perceptive book by Akira Iriye, *The Cold War in Asia* (1974).

The groundwork for the recent reevaluation of Dwight D. Eisenhower as an effective leader in foreign policy was laid by Emmet J. Hughes in his memoir *The Ordeal of Power* (1962). Hughes, a speechwriter for Eisenhower, was the first to play down the influence of John Foster Dulles. For a more recent examination of Ike's achievements in foreign policy, see Robert A. Divine, *Eisenhower and the Cold War* (1981).

Additional Bibliography

Surveys of American foreign policy since 1945 include Stephen Ambrose, *Rise to Globalism*, 2d ed. (1980); John Spanier, *American Foreign Policy Since World War II*, 8th ed. (1980); Ralph Levering, *The Cold War, 1945–*

1972 (1982); and James A. Nathan and James K. Oliver, *United States Foreign Policy and World Order*, 2d ed. (1981). Adam B. Ulam provides a perceptive summary of Soviet-American relations for this period in *The Rivals* (1971). For a good critique, see John C. Donovan, *The Cold Warriors* (1974).

Gar Alperovitz began the revisionist controversy over the origins of the Cold War in *Atomic Diplomacy* (1965), which focuses on Truman's use of the atomic bomb as a veiled diplomatic weapon. Other revisionist accounts include Lloyd Gardner, *Architects of Illusion* (1970); Joyce Kolko and Gabriel Kolko, *The Limits of Power* (1972); Thomas G. Paterson, *Soviet-American Confrontation* (1973); and Lawrence Wittner, *American Intervention in Greece, 1943–1949* (1982). For a brief, moderate revisionist view, see Thomas G. Paterson, *On Every Front* (1979). Robert Tucker offers a shrewd assessment of revisionism in *The Radical Left and American Foreign Policy* (1971). Post revisionist studies include John L. Gaddis, *The United States and the Origins of the Cold War* (1972); Vojtech Mastny, *Russia's Road to the Cold War* (1979); and Robert L. Messer, *The End of an Alliance* (1982). For a lively account of the Potsdam Conference, see Charles L. Mee, *Meeting at Potsdam* (1975).

The foreign policy of the Truman administration is covered in Harry S. Truman, *Memoirs*, 2 vols. (1955, 1956) and two works by Robert J. Donovan: *Conflict and Crisis* (1977) and *Tumultuous Years* (1982). See also Robert H. Ferrell, *George C. Marshall* (1966); Gaddis Smith, *Dean Acheson* (1972); David S. McLellan, *Dean Acheson* (1976); and Dean Acheson, *Present at the Creation* (1969). For military policy, see Walter Millis, ed., *The Forrestal Diaries* (1951); Richard F. Haynes, *The Awesome Power* (1973); Warner R. Schilling et al., *Strategy, Politics and Defense Budgets* (1962); and Thomas H. Etzold and John L. Gaddis, eds., *Containment* (1976). Studies of special interest include Gregg

Herken, *The Winning Weapon* (1980) on atomic diplomacy under Truman; Joseph Jones, *The Fifteen Weeks* (1955), a classic Cold Warrior account of the Truman Doctrine; and Jean Edward Smith, *The Defense of Berlin* (1964) on the two Berlin crises.

For the Cold War in the Far East, consult Tang Tsou, *America's Failure in China, 1941–1950* (1963); Herbert Feis, *Contest Over Japan* (1968); Dorothy Borg and Waldo Heinrichs, eds., *The Uncertain Years: Chinese-American Relations, 1947–1950* (1980); Russell D. Buhite, *Soviet-American Relations in Asia, 1945–1954* (1982); William W. Strueck, *The Road to Confrontation* (1981); and Robert M. Blum, *Drawing the Line* (1982). Books on the Korean War include David Rees, *Korea: The Limited War and American Politics* (1968); Charles W. Dobbs, *The Unwanted Symbol* (1981); Bruce Cumings, *The Origins of the Korean War* (1981); and John W. Spanier, *The Truman-MacArthur Controversy and the Korean War* (1959). For Indochina, see Ellen J. Hammer, *The Struggle for Indochina, 1940–1955* (1966) and Melvin Gurtov, *The First Vietnamese Crisis* (1967).

The most fully detailed biography of Eisenhower is the critical one by Peter Lyon, *Eisenhower: Portrait of the Hero* (1974). For a more sympathetic yet fragmentary account, see William B. Ewald, *Eisenhower the President* (1981). Blanche W. Cook uses recently available materials to offer a critique of Ike's diplomacy in *The Declassified Eisenhower* (1981). Eisenhower's two volumes of memoirs, *Mandate for Change* (1963) and *Waging Peace* (1966), are full and revealing accounts. For information on specific topics, see Richard Immerman, *The CIA in Guatemala* (1982); Chester Cooper, *The Lion's Last Roar* (1978) on the Suez crisis; Robert W. Stookey, *America and the Arab States* (1975) on the Middle East; Robert A. Divine, *Blowing on the Wind* (1978) on the nuclear test-ban issue; and Burton Kaufman, *Trade and Aid* (1982) on foreign economic policy.

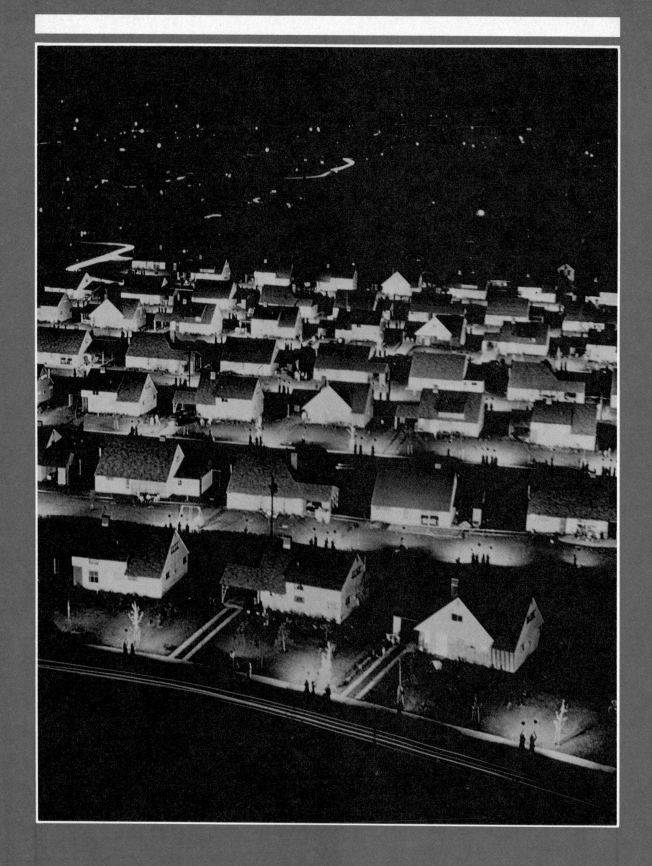

chapter 29

AFFLUENCE
AND ANXIETY

On May 7, 1947, William Levitt announced plans to build two thousand rental houses in a former potato field on Long Island, thirty miles from midtown Manhattan. Using mass production techniques he had learned while erecting navy housing during the war, Levitt quickly built four thousand homes and rented them to young veterans. A change in government financing regulations led him to begin offering his houses for sale in 1948 for a small amount down and a low monthly payment. Young couples, crowded in city apartments or still living with their parents, rushed out to buy Levitt's houses. By 1949, he had sold the four thousand, and by the time Levittown—as he called the new community— was completed in 1951, it contained over seventeen thousand homes.

Levitt eventually built two more Levittowns, one in Pennsylvania and one in New Jersey; each contained the same curving streets, neighborhood parks and playgrounds, and community swimming pools as did the first development. Some observers denounced Levittown, seeing it as the symbol of conformity and materialism, but William Levitt had tapped the postwar desire of young Americans to move to the suburbs and raise their children outside the central city.

The secret of Levittown's appeal was the basic house, a 720-square-foot Cape Cod design built on a concrete slab. It had a kitchen, two bedrooms and bath, a living room complete with a fireplace and sixteen-foot picture window, and an expansion attic with room for two more bedrooms. Levitt built only one interior, but there were four different facades to break the monotony. The original house sold for $6990 in 1948; even the improved model, a ranch-style house, sold for less than $10,000 in 1951.

Levitt's houses were ideal for young people just starting out in life. They were cheap, comfortable, and efficient, and each home came with a refrigerator, cooking range, and washing machine. Despite the conformity of the houses, the three Levittowns were surprisingly diverse communities; residents had a wide variety of religious, ethnic, and occupational backgrounds. Blacks, however, were rigidly excluded. In time, as the more successful families moved on to larger homes in more expensive neighborhoods, the Levittowns became enclaves for lower-middle-class families.

Levittown symbolized the most significant social trend of the postwar era in the United States —the flight to the suburbs. The residential areas surrounding cities like New York and Chicago nearly doubled in the 1950s. While central cities remained relatively stagnant during the decade, suburbs grew by 46 percent; by 1960 some sixty million people, one third of the nation, lived in suburban rings around the cities. This massive shift in population from the central city was accompanied by a baby boom that started during World War II. Young married couples began to have three, four, or even five children (compared with only one or two children in American families during the 1930s). These larger families led to a 19 percent growth in the nation's population

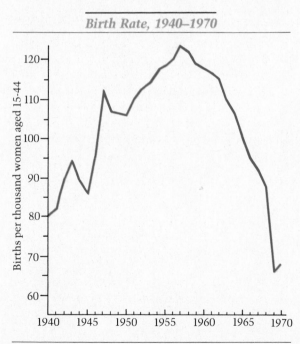

Birth Rate, 1940–1970

Births per thousand women aged 15-44

Source: *U.S. Bureau of the Census,* Historical Statistics of the United States, Colonial Times to 1970, *Bicentennial Edition, Washington, D.C., 1975.*

Shoppers in a New York City department store in 1951 besiege the salesclerks at the electric mixer counter. Consumers were starved for home appliances, which had been unaffordable before the war and unavailable during the war.

between 1950 and 1960, the greatest increase in growth rate since 1910.

The economy boomed as residential construction soared. By 1960, one fourth of all existing homes were less than ten years old and factories were turning out large quantities of appliances and television sets for the new households. A multitude of new consumer products—ranging from frozen foods to filter cigarettes, from high fidelity phonographs to cars equipped with automatic transmissions and tubeless tires—appeared in stores and showrooms. In the suburbs, the supermarket replaced the corner grocer, carrying a vast array of items that enabled homemakers to provide their families with a more varied diet.

A new affluence replaced the poverty and hunger of the Great Depression, but many Americans could not forget the haunting memories of the thirties. The absorption with material goods took on an almost desperate quality, as if a profusion of houses, cars, and home appliances could guarantee that the nightmare of depression would never return. Critics were quick to disparage the quality of life in suburban society. They condemned the conformity, charging the newly affluent with forsaking traditional American individualism to live in identical houses, drive look-alike cars, and accumulate the same material possessions. Folk-

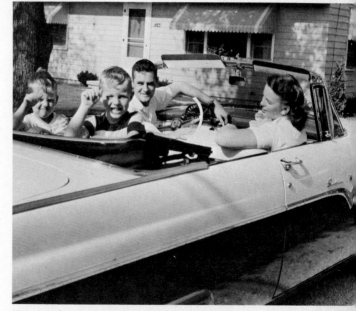

A Sunday outing in the 1950s. The family car was embellished with much shiny chrome and elongated tailfins.

singer Malvina Reynolds caught the essence of postwar suburbia in her 1963 song:

Little boxes on the hillside,
Little boxes made of ticky tacky
Little boxes on the hillside,
Little boxes all the same.
There's a green one and a pink one
And a blue one and a yellow one
And they're all made out of ticky tacky
And they all look just the same.

("Little Boxes," words and music by Malvina Reynolds. Copyright © 1962 Schroder Music Co. (ASCAP) Used by permission. All rights reserved.)

Events abroad added to the feeling of anxiety in the postwar years. Nuclear war became a frighteningly real possibility. The rivalry with the Soviet Union led to a new red scare, resulting in charges of treason and betrayal being leveled at loyal Americans. Frustrated by the stalemate with

■ *A suburban development in the Bay area of California, perceived as a study in patterned uniformity. It features upgraded "ticky-tacky" houses.*

Russia, many Americans cheered demagogues like Senator Joseph McCarthy, who looked for the Communist enemy at home rather than abroad. Loyalty oaths and book-burning revealed how insecure Americans had become in the era of the Cold War. Thus beneath the bland surface of suburban affluence, a dark current of distrust and insecurity marred the picture of a nation fulfilling its economic destiny.

The Postwar Boom

For fifteen years following World War II, the nation witnessed a period of unparalleled economic growth. A pent-up demand for consumer goods fueled a steady industrial expansion. And heavy government spending during the Cold War added an extra stimulus to the economy, offsetting brief recessions in 1949 and 1953 and moderating a steeper one in 1957–1958. By the end of the decade, the American people had achieved an affluence that finally erased the lingering memories of the Great Depression.

The Stress of Reconversion

The task of reconverting American industry from its wartime production of guns, tanks, and bombers back to the creation of consumer goods led to considerable stress and tension. Prices and wages caused most of the concern. Congress, responding to the public's distaste for continuing wartime regulations, voted in 1946 to weaken price controls. With returning servicemen and affluent civilians vying for scarce goods, prices rose 25 percent in less than two years. Workers, accustomed to wartime paychecks heavy with overtime, began to demand higher wages and shorter hours. A wave of labor unrest swept over the country in the spring of 1946, culminating in two critical strikes: a walkout by coal miners that threatened to close down much of American industry and a paralyzing strike by railroad workers.

President Truman was caught in the middle. Sensitive to union demands, he permitted businessmen to negotiate large pay increases and then pass on the cost to consumers in the form of higher prices. He criticized Congress for weakening wartime price controls, but he failed to insist that the controls be retained, and he offered nothing else to curb inflation. Housewives blamed him for the rising price of food, while organized labor condemned Truman as the country's "No. 1 Strikebreaker" when he asked Congress for power to draft striking railway workers into the army.

The Republicans seized on the nation's economic woes to attack the Democrats, declaring "To err is Truman" and adopting a very effective slogan in the 1946 congressional elections: "Had enough?" The American people, weary of inflation and labor unrest, responded by electing a majority of Republicans to both the House and the Senate for the first time since 1930.

Postwar Prosperity

Although the GOP-dominated Eightieth Congress had little to do with it, the economy began to move forward as the result of two long-term factors. First, American consumers—after being held in check by depression and then by wartime scarcities—finally had a chance to indulge their suppressed appetites for material goods. At the war's end, personal savings stood at more than $37 billion, providing a powerful stimulus to consumption. Initially, American factories could not turn out enough automobiles and appliances to satisfy the horde of buyers. By 1950, however, production lines had finally caught up with the demand. In that year, Americans bought more than six million cars, and the gross national product (GNP) reached $318 billion (50 percent higher than in 1940).

The Cold War provided the additional stimulus the economy needed when postwar expansion slowed. The Marshall Plan and other foreign-aid programs financed a heavy export trade. Then the outbreak of the Korean War helped overcome a brief recession and ensure continued prosperity as the government spent massive amounts on guns, planes, and munitions. In 1952, the nation spent $44 billion, two thirds of the federal budget, on national defense. Although Eisenhower managed to bring about some modest reductions, defense spending continued at a level of $40 billion throughout the decade.

■ *The deluge of advertising images of the 1950s was transformed into the "pop" art of the 1960s, using such popular and commonplace objects as these Coke bottles, painted by Andy Warhol.*

It was in the 1950s that the nation achieved a level of affluence that erased the persisting fear of another Great Depression. The baby boom and the spectacular growth of suburbia served as great stimulants to the consumer-goods industries. Manufacturers turned out an ever increasing number of refrigerators, washing machines, and dishwashers to equip the kitchens of Levittown and its many imitators across the country. The automobile industry thrived with suburban expansion as two-car families became more and more common. In 1955, in an era when oil was abundant and gasoline sold for less than 30¢ a gallon, Detroit sold a record 8 million cars. The electronics industry boomed. Consumers were eager to acquire the latest marvel of home entertainment—the television set.

In addition, commercial enterprises snapped up office machines and the first generation of computers; industry installed electronic sensors and processors as it underwent extensive automation, and the military displayed an insatiable appetite for electronic devices for its planes and ships. As a result, American industry averaged more than $10 billion a year in capital investment, and employment rose above the long-sought goal of sixty million.

Yet the economic abundance of the 1950s was not without its problems. While some sections of the nation (notably the emerging Sunbelt areas of the South and West) benefited enormously from the growth of the aircraft and electronics industries, older manufacturing regions, such as New England, did not fare as well. The steel industry increased its capacity during the decade, but it began to fall behind the rate of national growth. Agriculture continued to experience bumper crops and low prices so that rural regions, like the vast areas of the Plains States, failed to share in the general affluence. Unemployment persisted despite the boom, rising to over 7 percent in a sharp recession that hit the country in the fall of 1957 and lasted through the summer of 1958. The rate of economic growth slowed in the second half of the decade, causing concern about the continuing vitality of the American economy.

None of these flaws, however, could disguise the fact that the nation was prospering to an extent no one dreamed possible in the 1930s. The GNP grew to $440 billion by 1960, more than double the 1940 level. More important, workers now labored fewer than forty hours a week; they rarely worked on Saturdays, and nearly all enjoyed a two-week paid vacation each year. By the mid-1950s, the average American family had twice as much real income to spend as its counterpart had possessed in the boom years of the 1920s. From 1945 to 1960, per-capita disposable income rose by $500—to $1845—for every man, woman, and child in the country. The American people, in one generation, had moved from poverty and depression to the highest standard of living the world had ever known.

Life in the Suburbs

Sociologists had difficulty describing the nature of suburban society in the fifties. Some saw it as classless, while others noted the absence of both the very rich and the very poor and consequently labeled it "middle class." Rather than forming a homogenous social group, though, the suburbs contained a surprising variety of people, whether classified as "upper lower," "lower middle," and "upper middle" or simply as blue collar, white collar, and professional. Doctors and lawyers often lived in the same developments as shoe salesmen and master plumbers. The traditional

In the early 1950s television viewing at home became a significant leisure-time pursuit. It was a group activity that involved the whole family. Evenings out at the movies became less and less frequent.

distinctions of ancestry, education, and size of residence no longer differentiated people so easily.

Yet suburbs could vary widely, from working-class communities clustered near factories built in the countryside to old, elitist areas like Scarsdale, New York, and Shaker Heights, Ohio. Most were almost exclusively white and Christian, but suburbs like Great Neck on Long Island and Richmond Heights outside Miami enabled Jews and blacks to take part in the flight from the inner city.

Life in all these suburban communities depended on the automobile. Highways and expressways allowed husbands to commute to jobs in the cities, often an hour or more away. The car was equally essential for wives. They shopped at the stores that first grew up in "miracle miles" along the highways and later at the shopping centers that began to dot the countryside by the mid-1950s. Children rode buses to school, then were driven to piano lessons and Little League ball games. Two cars became a necessity for almost every suburban family, thus helping to spur the boom in automobile production.

The home became the focus for activities and aspirations. The postwar shortage of housing which often forced young couples to live with their parents or in-laws created an intense de-

mand for new homes in the suburbs. When questioned, prospective buyers expressed a desire for "more space," for "comfort and roominess," and for "privacy and freedom of action" in their new residences. Men and women who moved to the suburbs prized the new kitchens with their built-in dishwashers, electric ovens, and gleaming counters; the extra bedrooms that ensured privacy from and for the children; the large garages that could be converted into recreation rooms; and the small, neat lawns that gave them an area for outdoor activities as well as a new way to compete with their neighbors. "Togetherness" became the code word of the fifties. Families did things together, whether gathering around the TV sets that dominated living rooms, attending community activities, or taking vacations in the huge station wagons of the era.

The emphasis on family life did not encourage the development of feminism. The end of the war saw many women who had entered the work force return to the home, where the role of wife and mother continued to be viewed as the ideal one for women in the 1950s. Trends toward getting married earlier and having larger families reinforced the tendency of women to devote all their efforts to housework and childraising rather than acquiring professional skills and pursuing careers outside the home. Adlai Stevenson, ex-

Percentage of Wives in the Labor Force

Year	Percentage
1950	24.8
1951	26.7
1952	26.8
1953	27.7
1954	28.1
1955	29.4
1956	30.2
1957	30.8
1958	31.4
1959	32.3
1960	31.7

Source: Compiled from U.S. Bureau of the Census, Historical Statistics of the United States, Colonial Times to 1970, Bicentennial Edition, Washington, D.C., 1975.

tolling "the humble role of housewife," told Smith College graduates that there was much they could do "in the living room with a baby in your lap or in the kitchen with a can opener in your hand." Dr. Benjamin Spock's 1946 best-seller, *Baby and Child Care*, became a fixture in millions of homes, while the traditional women's magazines like *McCall's* and *Good Housekeeping* thrived by featuring articles on natural childbirth and inspirational pieces such as "Homemaking Is My Vocation."

Nonetheless, the number of working wives doubled between 1940 and 1960. By the end of the fifties, 40 percent of American women had jobs outside the home. The heavy expenses involved in rearing and educating children led wives and mothers to seek ways to augment the family income, inadvertently preparing the way for a new demand for equality in the 1960s.

Farewell to Reform

It is not surprising that the spirit of reform underlying the New Deal failed to flourish in the postwar years. Growing affluence took away the sense of grievance and the cry for change that was so strong in the thirties. Eager to enjoy the new prosperity after years of want and sacrifice, the American people turned away from federal regulation and welfare programs.

Truman and the Fair Deal

Harry S. Truman attempted to carry on the New Deal tradition of Franklin D. Roosevelt. For ten years, he had been a loyal Democratic senator, faithfully supporting Roosevelt's recovery and reform measures in Congress. He was a respected legislator, with a reputation for being hard-working, reliable, and intensely partisan. But he was relatively unknown to the public, and his background as a Missouri county judge associated with Kansas City machine politics did little to inspire confidence in his ability to lead the nation. Surprisingly well read—especially in history and biography—Truman possessed sound judgment, the ability to reach decisions quickly, and a fierce and uncompromising sense of right and wrong.

Two weaknesses marred his performance in the White House. One was a fondness for old friends, which resulted in the appointment of many Missouri and Senate cronies to high office. Men like Attorney General Tom Clark, Secretary of the Treasury Charles Snyder and White House military aide Harry Vaughn brought little credit to the Truman administration, while the loss of such effective public servants as Secretary of the Interior Harold Ickes and Labor Secretary Frances Perkins hurt. Truman's other serious limitation was his lack of political vision. He tried to perpetuate FDR's New Deal, but he engaged in a running battle with Congress rather than pursuing a coherent legislative program.

The fact that the postwar mood was not conducive to a new outburst of reform, of course, handicapped Truman's performance. Not only were the American people enjoying material prosperity, but also the Cold War diverted attention from domestic problems. In September 1945, the President outlined a broad program designed to ensure economic security, but his proposal soon dropped out of sight as the nation became distracted by labor unrest and inflation. Congress did pass the Employment Act of 1946, which asserted the principle that the government was responsible for the state of the economy. One of the provisions of the act was the creation of a Council of Economic Advisers to guide the president, but the original goal of mandatory federal planning to achieve full employment failed to survive the legislative process.

After the Republican victory in 1946, relations between the President and Congress became increasingly stormy. Truman successfully vetoed two GOP measures to give large tax cuts to the wealthy, but Congress overrode his veto of the Taft-Hartley Act in 1947. Designed to redress the imbalance in labor-management relations created by the Wagner Act, the Taft-Hartley Act outlawed specific unfair labor union practices—including the closed shop and secondary boycotts—and it permitted the president to invoke an eighty-day cooling-off period to delay strikes that might endanger national health or safety. Despite Truman's claim that it was a "slave-labor" bill, American unions were able to survive its provisions.

President Truman's political fortunes reached their lowest ebb in early 1948. Former Vice-President Henry A. Wallace, claiming to represent the New Deal, announced his third-party (Progressive) candidacy in the presidential contest that year. Worried Democratic party leaders sought to persuade Truman to step aside and allow General Dwight D. Eisenhower to become the Democratic candidate. When Eisenhower turned down bids from both parties, the Democrats reluctantly renominated Truman. The prospects for victory in the fall, however, looked very dim—especially after disgruntled Southerners bolted the Democratic party to nominate Strom Thurmond, the governor of South Carolina, on a States' Rights party ticket.

The defection of the Dixiecrats in the South and Wallace's liberal followers in the North led political experts to predict an almost certain Republican victory. Governor Thomas E. Dewey of New York, the GOP candidate, was so certain of winning that he waged a cautious and bland campaign designed to give him a free hand once he was in the White House. With nothing to lose, Truman barnstormed around the country denouncing the "do-nothing" Republican Eightieth Congress. The President's "give-'em-hell" tactics reminded voters of how much they owed the Democrats for helping them survive the Depression. To the amazement of the pollsters, Truman won a narrow but decisive victory in November. The old Roosevelt coalition—farmers, organized labor, urban ethnic groups, and blacks—had held together, enabling Truman to remain in the White House and the Democrats to gain control of Congress.

A triumphant Truman announced his legislative program on January 5, 1949. Venturing beyond an extension of FDR's proposals to increase the minimum wage and broaden Social Security

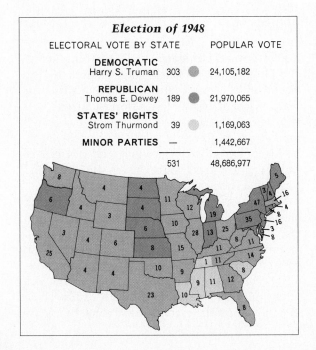

Election of 1948

ELECTORAL VOTE BY STATE		POPULAR VOTE
DEMOCRATIC Harry S. Truman	303	24,105,182
REPUBLICAN Thomas E. Dewey	189	21,970,065
STATES' RIGHTS Strom Thurmond	39	1,169,063
MINOR PARTIES	—	1,442,667
	531	48,686,977

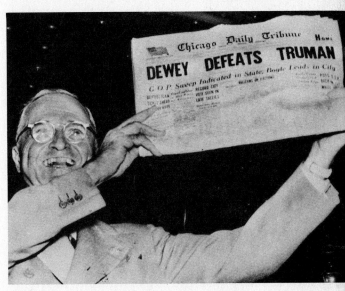

■ A jubilant Harry Truman, on the morning after his 1948 election win, displays the headline blazoned on the front page of the Chicago Tribune—a newspaper that believed the pollsters.

coverage, he called for a "Fair Deal," a reform package that comprised a new program of national medical insurance, federal aid to education, enactment of a Fair Employment Practices Commission (FEPC) to prevent economic discrimination against blacks, and an overhaul of the farm subsidy program.

The Fair Deal was never enacted. Except for raising the minimum wage to seventy-five cents an hour and broadening Social Security to cover ten million more Americans, Congress refused to pass any of Truman's health, education, or civil-rights measures. The nation's doctors waged an effective campaign against the President's health-insurance plan, and southern senators blocked any action of FEPC. Aid to education, repeal of Taft-Hartley, and the new farm program all failed to win congressional approval. In part, Truman was to blame for trying to secure too much too soon; if he had selected one or two measures and given them priority, he might have been more successful. More important, however, was the fact that despite the Democratic victory in 1948, Congress remained under the control of a bipartisan conservative coalition of northern Republicans and southern Democrats, the same alignment that had halted Roosevelt's reforms after 1938.

Although his legislative failure became certain in 1950 when war once again subordinated domestic issues to foreign policy, President Truman deserves credit for maintaining and consolidating the New Deal. His spirited leadership prevented any Republican effort to repeal the gains of the 1930s. Moreover, even though he failed to get any new measures enacted, he broadened the reform agenda and laid the groundwork for future advances in health care, aid to education, and civil rights.

Eisenhower's Modern Republicanism

In 1952, the American people turned to Dwight D. Eisenhower, the hero of World War II, to restore their sense of national self-confidence. Truman's second term had witnessed increasing bitterness and frustration. Senator Joseph McCarthy had exploited a developing red scare (see pp. 842–45), the Korean War had settled into a bloody

Eisenhower accepting the Republican nomination in 1952. Ike possessed a forceful personality and had the knack of dealing successfully with difficult people.

stalemate, and several of Truman's aides had been caught in scandals involving personal gifts.

Eisenhower seemed to be the perfect man to clean up "the mess in Washington." Immensely popular because of his amiable manner, winning smile, and heroic stature, he alone appeared to have the ability to unite a divided nation. In the 1952 campaign, Ike displayed hidden gifts as a politician in running against Adlai Stevenson, the eloquent Illinois governor whose appeal was limited to diehard Democrats and liberal intellectuals. Despite the embarrassment caused by the disclosure of a secret fund benefiting his running mate, Richard Nixon of California, Eisenhower won easily. He carried thirty-nine states, including four in the formerly solid Democratic South. The Republican party, however, did not fare as well; it gained just a slight edge in the House and controlled the Senate by only one seat.

Moderation was the keynote of the Eisenhower presidency. His major goal from the outset was to restore calm and tranquillity to a badly divided nation. Unlike FDR and Truman, he had no commitment to social change or economic reform. Ike was a fiscal conservative who was intent on balancing the budget. Yet unlike some Republicans of the extreme right wing, he had no

The Election of 1952			
Candidate	Party	Popular Vote	Electoral Vote
Eisenhower	Republican	33,936,137	442
Stevenson	Democrat	27,314,649	89

plans to dismantle the social programs of the New Deal. He sought instead to keep military spending in check, to encourage as much private initiative as possible, and to reduce federal activities to the bare minimum. Defining his position as "Modern Republicanism," he claimed that he was "conservative when it comes to money and liberal when it comes to human beings."

On domestic issues, Eisenhower elected to delegate authority and to play a passive role. He concentrated his own efforts on the Cold War abroad. The men he chose to run the nation reflected his preference for successful corporation executives. Thus George Humphrey, an Ohio industrialist, carried out a policy of fiscal stringency as secretary of the treasury, while Charles E. Wilson (the former head of General Motors) sought to keep the Pentagon budget under control as secretary of defense. Neither man was wholly successful, and both were guilty of tactless public statements. Humphrey warned that unless Congress showed budgetary restraint "we're gonna have a depression which will curl your hair," and Wilson gained notoriety by proclaiming "what was good for our country was good for General Motors, and vice versa."

Eisenhower was equally reluctant to play an active role in dealing with Congress. A fervent believer in the separation of powers, Ike did not wish to engage in intensive lobbying. He left congressional relations to aides such as Sherman Adams, a former New Hampshire governor who served as White House chief of staff. Adams' skill at resolving problems at lower levels insulated Eisenhower from many of the nation's pressing domestic problems.

The Election of 1956			
Candidate	Party	Popular Vote	Electoral Vote
Eisenhower	Republican	35,585,245	457
Stevenson	Democrat	26,030,172	73

Relations with Congress were weakened further by Republican losses in the midterm election of 1954. The Democrats regained control of both houses and kept it throughout the 1950s. The President had to rely on two Texas Democrats, Senate Majority Leader Lyndon B. Johnson and House Speaker Sam Rayburn, for legislative action; at best, it was an awkward and uneasy relationship.

The result was a very modest legislative record. Eisenhower did continue the basic social measures of the New Deal. In 1954, he signed bills extending Social Security benefits to more than seven million Americans, raising the minimum wage to $1 an hour, and adding four million workers to those eligible for unemployment benefits. He consolidated the administration of welfare programs by creating the Department of Health, Education and Welfare in 1953. Oveta Culp Hobby, the first woman to hold a cabinet post in a Republican administration, headed the new department. But Ike steadfastly opposed Democratic plans for compulsory health insurance—which he condemned as the "socialization of medicine"—and comprehensive federal aid to education, preferring to leave everything except school construction in the hands of local and state authorities. This lack of presidential support and the continuing grip of the conservative coalition in Congress blocked any further reform in the 1950s.

The one significant legislative achievement of the Eisenhower years came with the passage of the Highway Act of 1956. After a twelve-year delay, Congress appropriated funds for a 41,000-mile interstate highway system consisting of multilane divided expressways that would connect all the nation's major cities. Justified on grounds of national defense, the 1956 act pleased a variety of highway users: the trucking industry, automobile clubs, organized labor (eager for construction jobs), farmers (needing to speed their crops to market), and state highway officials (anxious for the 90 percent of the funding contributed by the federal government). Eisenhower's insistence that general revenue funds not be used to provide the federal share—estimated at $25 billion—of the total cost led to the creation of a highway trust fund raised by taxes on fuel, tires, and new cars and trucks. Built over the next twenty years, the interstate highway system had a profound influence on American life. It stimulated the economy and shortened travel time dramatically, while intensifying the nation's dependence on the automobile and distorting metropolitan growth patterns into long strips paralleling the new expressways.

The Interstate Highway System

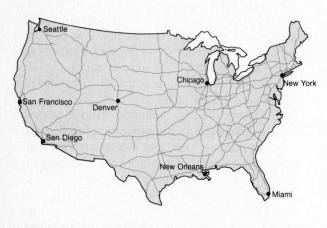

Overall, the Eisenhower years marked an era of political moderation. The American people, enjoying the abundance of the 1950s, seemed quite content with legislative inaction. The President was sensitive to the nation's economic health; when recessions developed in 1953 and again in 1957 after his landslide reelection victory, he quickly abandoned his goal of a balanced budget in favor of a policy advocating government spending to restore prosperity. These steps, along with modest increases in New Deal welfare programs, led to a steady growth in the federal budget from $29.5 billion in 1950 to $76.5 in 1960. Eisenhower was able to balance the budget in only three of his eight years in office, and the $12-billion deficit in 1959 was larger than any ever before recorded in peacetime. Thus Eisenhower maintained the New Deal legacy of federal responsibility for social welfare and the state of the economy while successfully resisting demands for more extensive government involvement in American life.

The Second Red Scare

In the midst of the affluence and apathy of postwar American life, one issue stirred up deep passion—a blind, unreasoning fear of communism. Locked in the Cold War with the Soviet Union, the American people began to look for the enemy at home as well as abroad. The result was a prolonged emotional outburst that led to an oppressive conformity in thought and belief.

The Loyalty Issue

Fear of radicalism had been a recurrent feature of American life since the early days of the Republic. Federalists had tried to suppress dissent with the Alien and Sedition Acts in the 1790s; the Know Nothings had campaigned against foreigners and Catholics in the 1850s, and the first red scare after World War I had been directed against both aliens and radicals. The Cold War heightened the traditional belief that subversion from abroad endangered the Republic. Bold rhetoric from members of the Truman administration, portraying the men in the Kremlin as inspired revolutionaries bent on world conquest, frightened the American people. They viewed the Soviet Union as a successor to Nazi Germany—a totalitarian police state that threatened the basic liberties of a free people.

A series of revelations of Communist espionage activities reinforced these fears. Canadian officials uncovered a Soviet spy ring in 1946, and the House Un-American Activities Committee held hearings indicating that Communist agents had flourished in the Agriculture and Treasury departments in the 1930s.

The most famous disclosure came in August 1948, however, when Whittaker Chambers, a repentant Communist, accused Alger Hiss of having been a Soviet spy in the 1930s. When Hiss, who had been a prominent State Department official, denied the charges, Chambers led investigators to a hollowed-out pumpkin on his Maryland farm. Inside the pumpkin were microfilms of confidential government documents. Chambers claimed that Hiss had passed these State Department materials to him in the late 1930s. Although the statute of limitations prevented a

■ *The conviction of Alger Hiss, shown here on his way to prison, convinced many Americans that internal subversion threatened the nation's survival.*

charge of treason against Hiss, he was convicted of perjury in January 1950 and sentenced to a five-year prison term.

Although Truman tried to dismiss the loyalty issue as a "red herring," he felt compelled to take protective measures, thus lending substance to the charges of subversion. In March 1947, he began a loyalty program, instituting security checks of government employees in order to root out Communists. Originally intended to remove subversives for whom "reasonable grounds exist for belief that the person involved is disloyal," within four years the Loyalty Review Board was dismissing workers as security risks if there was "reasonable doubt" of their loyalty. Thousands of government workers lost their jobs, charged with guilt by association with radicals or with membership in left-wing organizations. Often those charged had no chance to face their accusers.

In 1948, the Justice Department further heightened fears of subversion. It charged eleven officials of the Communist party with advocating the violent overthrow of the government. After a long trial, the jury found them guilty, and the party officials received prison sentences and heavy fines; in 1951, the Supreme Court upheld these convictions as constitutional.

Such repressive measures failed, however, to reassure the nation. Events abroad intensified the sense of danger. The Communist triumph in China in the fall of 1949 came as a shock; soon there were charges that "fellow travelers" in the State Department were responsible for "the loss of China." In September 1949, when the Truman administration announced that the Russians had detonated their first atomic bomb, the ending of America's nuclear monopoly was blamed on Soviet espionage. In early 1950, Klaus Fuchs—a British scientist who had worked on the wartime Manhattan Project—admitted giving the Russians vital information about the A-bomb.

A few months later, the government charged American Communists Ethel and Julius Rosenberg with conspiracy to transmit atomic secrets to the Soviet Union. In 1951, a jury found the Rosenbergs guilty of treason, and Judge Irving Kaufman sentenced them to die for what he termed their "loathsome offense." Despite their insistent claims of innocence and worldwide appeals on their behalf, the Rosenbergs were electrocuted on June 19, 1953. Thus by the early 1950s, nearly all the ingredients were at hand for

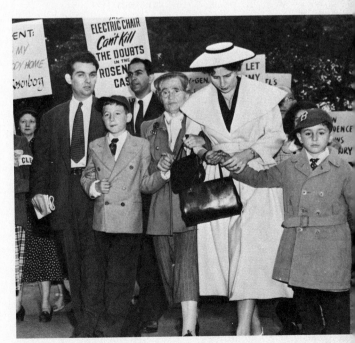

■ *Three days before Julius and Ethel Rosenberg were executed for treason, their two young sons, ten and six years old, marched to the White House to plead executive clemency for their parents.*

a new outburst of hysteria—fear of Russia, evidence of espionage, and a belief in a vast unseen conspiracy. The only element missing was a leader to release this new outburst of intolerance.

McCarthyism in Action

On February 12, 1950, Senator Joseph R. McCarthy of Wisconsin delivered a routine Lincoln's Birthday speech in Wheeling, West Virginia. This little known Republican suddenly attracted national attention when he declared, "I have here in my hand a list of 205—a list of names that were made known to the Secretary of State as being members of the Communist Party and who nevertheless are still working and shaping policy in the State Department." The charge that there were Communists in the State Department—repeated in different places with the number changed to 57, then 81—was never substantiated. But McCarthy's Wheeling speech triggered a four-and-a-half-year crusade to hunt down alleged Communists in government. The stridency and sensationalism of the senator's accusations soon won the name "McCarthyism."

McCarthy's basic technique was the multiple untruth. He leveled a bevy of charges of treasonable activities in government. While officials were refuting his initial accusations, he brought forth a steady stream of new ones, so that the corrections never caught up with the latest blast. He failed to unearth a single confirmed Communist in government, but he kept the Truman administration in turmoil. Drawing on an army of informers, primarily disgruntled federal workers with grievances against their colleagues and superiors, he charged government agencies with harboring and protecting Communist agents, and he accused the State Department of deliberately losing the Cold War. His briefcase bulged with documents, but he did very little actual research, relying instead on reports (often outdated) from earlier congressional investigations. He exploited the press with great skill, combining current accusations with promises of future disclosures to guarantee headlines.

The secret of McCarthy's power was the fear he engendered among his Senate colleagues. In 1950, Maryland Senator Millard Tydings, who headed a committee critical of McCarthy's activities, failed to win reelection when McCarthy opposed him; after that, other senators ran scared. McCarthy delighted in making sweeping, startling charges of Communist sympathies against prominent public figures. A favorite target was aristocratic Secretary of State Dean Acheson, whom he ridiculed as the "Red Dean," with his "cane, spats and tea-sipping little finger"; he even went after General George Marshall, claiming that the wartime army chief of staff was an agent of the Communist conspiracy. Nor were fellow Republicans immune. One GOP senator was described as "a living miracle in that he is without question the only man who has lived so long with neither brains nor guts."

These attacks on the wealthy, famous, and privileged won McCarthy a devoted national following. Even though at the height of his influence in early 1954 he gained the approval of only 50 percent of the respondents in a Gallup poll. McCarthy drew a disproportionate backing from working-class Catholics and ethnic groups, especially the Irish, Poles, and Italians, who normally voted Democratic. He offered a simple solution to the complicated Cold War: defeat the enemy at home rather than continue to engage in costly foreign-aid programs and entangling alliances abroad. Above all, McCarthy appealed to conservative Republicans in the Midwest who shared his right-wing views and felt cheated by Truman's upset victory in 1948. Even GOP leaders who viewed McCarthy's tactics with distaste, such as Robert A. Taft of Ohio, quietly encouraged him to attack the vulnerable Democrats.

The Legacy of McCarthyism

McCarthy did not end his crusade with the Republican victory in 1952. Instead, he used his new position as chairman of the Senate Committee on Government Operations as a base for ferreting out Communists on the federal payroll. He made a series of charges against the foreign-affairs agencies and demanded that certain books be purged from American information libraries overseas. Eisenhower's advisors urged the President to use his own great prestige to stop McCarthy. But Ike refused such a confrontation, saying, "I will not get into a pissing contest with that skunk."

The Wisconsin senator finally overreached

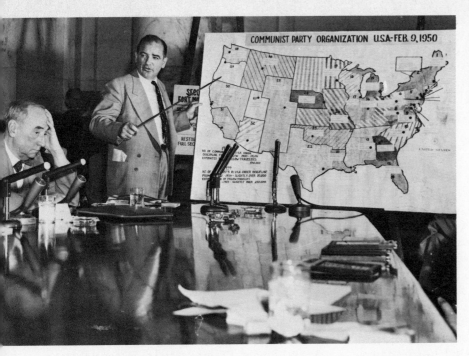

COMMUNIST PARTY ORGANIZATION U.S.A-FEB. 9, 1950

■ Senator Joseph McCarthy's unsubstantiated charges of Communist infiltration of the army led to his downfall. Army counsel Joseph Welch (left) listens wearily to McCarthy's rambling diatribe.

himself. In early 1954, he uncovered a suspected Communist dentist in the military and proceeded to attack the upper echelons of the United States Army, telling one much-decorated general that he was "not fit to wear the uniform." The controversy culminated in the televised Army-McCarthy hearings. For six weeks, the senator revealed his crude, bullying behavior to the American people. Viewers were repelled by his frequent outbursts that began with the insistent cry, "Point of order, Mr. Chairman, point of order," and by his attempt to slur the reputation of a young lawyer associated with army counsel Joseph Welch. This last maneuver led Welch to condemn McCarthy for his "reckless cruelty" and ask rhetorically, as millions watched on television, "Have you no sense of decency, sir . . . ?"

Courageous Republicans, led by George Aiken of Vermont and Margaret Chase Smith of Maine, joined with Democrats to bring about the Senate's censure of McCarthy in December 1954, by a vote of 67 to 22. Once rebuked, McCarthy fell quickly from prominence. He died three years later virtually unnoticed and unmourned.

Yet his influence was profound. Not only did he paralyze national life with what a Senate subcommittee described as "the most nefarious campaign of half-truth and untruth in the history of the Republic," but he also helped impose a political and cultural conformity that froze dissent for the rest of the 1950s. Long after McCarthy's passing, the nation tolerated loyalty oaths for teachers, the banning of left-wing books in public libraries, and the blacklisting of entertainers in radio, television, and films. Freedom of expression was inhibited, and the opportunity to try out new ideas and approaches was lost as the United States settled into a sterile Cold War consensus.

The Struggle over Civil Rights

Although the Cold War gave birth to the ugly loyalty issue, it had a more positive effect on another social problem—the denial of civil rights to black Americans. The contradiction between the denunciation of the Soviet Union for its human-rights violations and the second-class status of Afro-Americans began to arouse the national conscience. Fighting for freedom against Communist tyranny abroad, Americans had to face the reality of the continued denial of freedom to a submerged minority at home.

Blacks had benefited economically from World War II, but they were still a seriously disadvantaged group. Those who had left the South for better opportunities in northern and western cities were concentrated in blighted and segregated neighborhoods, working at low-paying jobs, suffering economic and social discrimination, and failing to share fully in the postwar prosperity.

In the South, conditions were much worse. State laws forced blacks to live almost totally segregated from white society. Not only did blacks attend separate (and almost always inferior) schools, but they also were rigidly excluded from all public facilities. They were forced to use separate waiting rooms in train stations, separate seats on all forms of transportation, separate drinking fountains, and even separate telephone booths. "Segregation was enforced at all places of public entertainment, including libraries, auditoriums, and circuses," Chief Justice Earl Warren noted. "There was segregation in the hospitals, prisons, mental institutions, and nursing homes. Even ambulance service was segregated."

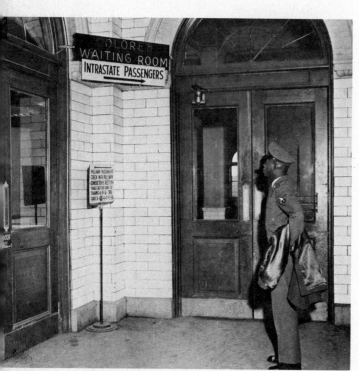

■ *Train station in Atlanta, 1956. By this time the armed forces were desegregated, but this black airman was required by Georgia law to sit in a "Colored Waiting Room."*

Civil Rights as a Political Issue

Truman was the first president to attempt to alter the historic pattern of racial discrimination in the United States. In 1946 he appointed a presidential commission on civil rights. A year later, in a sweeping report entitled "To Secure These Rights" the commission recommended the reinstatement of the wartime Fair Employment Practices Committee (FEPC), the establishment of a permanent civil-rights commission, and the denial of federal aid to any state that condoned segregation in schools and public facilities. The President's ten-point legislative program in 1948 included some of these measures, notably a new FEPC and a civil-rights commission. But southern resistance blocked any action by Congress, and the inclusion of a strong civil-rights plank in the 1948 Democratic platform led to the walkout of some southern delegations and a separate States'-Rights (Dixiecrat) ticket in several states of the South that fall.

Black voters in the North responded by backing Truman overwhelmingly over Dewey in the 1948 election. In key states—California, Ohio, and Illinois—it was the black voters in Los Angeles, Cleveland, and Chicago that ensured the Democratic victory. Truman responded by including civil-rights legislation in his Fair Deal program in 1949. Once again, however, determined southern opposition blocked congressional action on a permanent FEPC and an antilynching measure.

Even though President Truman had been unable to secure any significant legislation, he had succeeded in adding civil rights to the liberal agenda. From this time forward, it would be an integral part of the Democratic reform program. And Truman was able to use his executive power to assist blacks. He strengthened the civil-rights division of the Justice Department, which aided black groups in their efforts to challenge school segregation and restrictive housing covenants in the courts. Most important, in 1948 Truman issued an order calling for the desegregation of the armed forces. The navy and the air force quickly complied, but the army resisted until the manpower needs of the Korean War finally overcame the military's objections. By the end of the 1950s, the armed forces had become far more integrated than American society at large.

The nation's schools soon became the primary target of civil-rights advocates. The NAACP concentrated first on universities, successfully waging an intensive legal battle to win admission for qualified blacks to graduate and professional schools. Led by Thurgood Marshall, NAACP lawyers then took on the broader issue of segregation in the country's public schools. Challenging the 1896 Supreme Court decision (*Plessy* v. *Ferguson*) which upheld the constitutionality of separate but equal public facilities, Marshall argued that even substantially equal but separate schools did profound psychological damage to black children and thus violated the Fourteenth Amendment.

A unanimous Supreme Court agreed in its 1954 decision in the case of *Brown* v. *Board of Education of Topeka*. Chief Justice Earl Warren, recently appointed by President Eisenhower, wrote the landmark opinion which flatly declared that "separate educational facilities are inherently un-equal." To divide grade-school children "solely because of their race," Warren argued, "generates a feeling of inferiority as to their status in the community that may affect their hearts and minds in a way unlikely ever to be undone." Despite this sweeping language, Warren realized that it would be difficult to change historic patterns of segregation quickly. Accordingly, in 1955 the Court ruled that implementation should proceed "with all deliberate speed" and left the details to the lower federal courts.

The process of desegregating the schools proved to be agonizingly slow. Officials in the border states quickly complied with the Court's ruling, but states deeper in the South responded with a policy of massive resistance. Local White Citizens' Councils organized to fight for retention of racial separation; 101 congressmen and senators signed a Southern Manifesto in 1956 which denounced the *Brown* decision as "a clear abuse of judicial power." School boards, encouraged by this show of defiance, found a variety of ways to evade the Court's ruling. The most successful

■ *Linda Brown (left). Her parents were the plaintiffs in the* Brown v. Board of Education of Topeka *landmark Supreme Court case. Thurgood Marshall (above), a leading black activist, was chief counsel for the Browns.*

was the passage of pupil-placement laws. These laws enabled local officials to assign individual students to schools on the basis of scholastic aptitude, ability to adjust, and "morals, conduct, health and personal standards." These stalling tactics led to long disputes in the federal courts; by the end of the decade, less than 1 percent of the black children in the Deep South attended school with whites.

A conspicuous lack of presidential support further weakened the desegregation effort. Dwight Eisenhower was not a racist, but he believed that people's attitudes could not be changed by "cold lawmaking"—only "by appealing to reason, by prayer, and by constantly working at it through our own efforts." Quietly and unobtrusively, he worked to achieve desegregation in federal facilities, particularly in veterans' hospitals, navy yards, and the District of Columbia school system. Yet he refrained from endorsing the *Brown* decision, which he told an aide he believed had "*set back* progress in the South *at least fifteen years*."

Southern leaders mistook Ike's silence for tacit support of segregation. In 1957, Governor Orville Faubus of Arkansas called out the national guard to prevent the integration of Little Rock's Central High School on grounds of a threat to public order. After 270 armed troops turned back 9 young black students, a federal judge ordered the guardsmen removed; but when the blacks entered the school, a mob of 500 jeering whites surrounded the building. Eisenhower, who had told Faubus that "the Federal Constitution will be upheld by me by every legal means at my command," sent in 1000 paratroopers to ensure the rights of the 9 blacks to attend Central High. The children finished the school year under armed guard. Then Little Rock authorities closed Central High School for the next two years; when it reopened, there were only 3 blacks in attendance.

Despite the snail's pace of school desegregation, the *Brown* decision led to other advances. In 1957, the Eisenhower administration proposed the first general civil-rights legislation since Reconstruction. Strong southern resistance and compromise by both the administration and Senate Democratic leader Lyndon B. Johnson of Texas weakened the bill considerably. The final act, however, did create a permanent Commission for Civil Rights, one of Truman's original

■ *Angry whites taunt one of the black students trying to pass through the lines of Arkansas National Guardsmen to enroll in Little Rock's Central High School in 1957.*

goals. It also provided for federal efforts aimed at "securing and protecting the right to vote." A second civil-rights act in 1960 slightly strengthened the voting-rights section.

Like the desegregation effort, the attempt to ensure black voting rights in the South was still largely symbolic. Southern registrars used a variety of devices, ranging from intimidation to unfair tests, to deny blacks the suffrage. Yet the actions of Congress and the Supreme Court marked a vital turning point in national policy toward racial justice.

The Beginnings of Black Activism

The most dynamic force for change came from blacks themselves. The shift from legal struggles in the courts to black protest in the streets began with an incident in Montgomery, Alabama. On December 1, 1955, Rosa Parks—a black seamstress who had been active in the local NAACP chapter—violated a city ordinance by refusing to give up her seat to a white person on a local bus.

■ *Rosa Parks' refusal to move to the back of the bus in Montgomery led to a citywide bus boycott in 1955 organized by Rev. Martin Luther King, Jr., who soon came to the attention of the police (bottom left). Lunch counter sit-ins were another effective protest tactic (top right).*

After her arrest, blacks gathered to protest and found a young, eloquent leader in Martin Luther King, Jr. The son of a successful Atlanta preacher, King had studied theology at Boston University and only recently had taken his first church in Montgomery. He agreed to lead a massive boycott of the city's bus system, which depended heavily on black patronage.

The Montgomery bus boycott started out with a modest goal. Instead of challenging the legality of segregated seating, King simply asked that seats be taken on a first-come, first-served basis, with blacks being seated from the back and the whites from the front of each bus. As the protest continued, however, and as they endured both legal harassment and sporadic acts of violence, the blacks began to be more assertive. An effective system of car pools enabled the protesters to avoid using the city buses. Soon they were insisting on a complete end to segregated seating as they sang their new song of protest:

Ain't gonna ride them buses no more
Ain't gonna ride no more
Why in the hell don't the white folk know
That I ain't gonna ride no more.

The Struggle over Civil Rights

The boycott ended in victory a year later when the Supreme Court ruled the Alabama segregated-seating law unconstitutional. King had won far more than this limited dent in the wall of segregation, however. He had provided blacks with a new weapon to fight racial oppression. Drawing on his study of Mahatma Gandhi's techniques of peaceful opposition to imperial authority in India, King worked out a philosophy of passive resistance that stressed nonviolence and love. "Blood may flow in the streets of Montgomery, before we receive our freedom," he told his followers at the height of the boycott, "but it must be our blood and not that of the white man. We must not harm a single hair on the head of our white brothers." The ultimate goal for King was to reunite the broken community through bonds of Christian love. The result, he prophesied, would be to enable future historians to say of the effort, "There lived a great people—a black people—who injected new meaning and dignity into the veins of civilization."

A year after the successful bus boycott, King founded the Southern Christian Leadership Conference (SCLC) to direct the crusade against segregation. Then in February 1960 another spontaneous event sparked a further advance for passive resistance. Four black students from North Carolina Agricultural and Technical College sat down at a dime-store lunch counter in Greensboro, North Carolina, and refused to move after being denied service. Other students, both whites and blacks, joined in similar "sit-ins" across the South, as well as "kneel-ins" at churches and "wade-ins" at swimming pools. By the end of the year, some fifty thousand young people had succeeded in desegregating public facilities in over a hundred southern cities. Several thousand of the demonstrators were arrested and put in jail, but the movement gained strength, leading to the formation of the Student Nonviolent Coordinating Committee (SNCC) in April 1960. From this time on, SCLC and SNCC, with their tactic of direct, though peaceful, confrontation, would replace the NAACP and its reliance on court action in the forefront of the civil-rights movement. The change would eventually lead to dramatic success for the movement, but it also ushered in a period of heightened tension and social turmoil in the 1960s.

The Good Life?

Despite the second red scare and the civil-rights movement, the consumer culture remained the dominant social theme of the 1950s. Yet even with an abundance of creature comforts and added hours of leisure time, the quality of life left many Americans anxious and dissatisfied.

Areas of Greatest Growth

Organized religion flourished in the climate of the 1950s. Ministers, priests, and rabbis all commented on the rise in church and synagogue attendance in the new communities. Will Herberg claimed that religious affiliation had become the primary identifying feature of modern American life, dividing the nation into three separate segments—Protestant, Catholic, and Jewish.

Some observers condemned the bland, secular nature of suburban churches, which seemed to be an integral part of the consumer society. "On weekdays one shops for food," wrote one critic, "on Saturdays one shops for recreation, and on Sundays one shops for the Holy Ghost." But the popularity of religious writer Norman Vincent Peale, with his positive gospel that urged people to "start thinking faith, enthusiasm and joy," suggested that the new churches filled a genuine if shallow human need. At the same time, the emergence of neo-orthodoxy in Protestant seminaries (notably through the ideas of Reinhold Niebuhr) and the rapid spread of radical forms of fundamentalism (such as the Assemblies of God) indicated that millions of Americans still were searching for a more personal religious faith.

Schools provided an immediate growth problem for the new suburban communities. The unprecedented increase in the number of school-age children, from twenty to thirty million in the first eight grades, overwhelmed the resources of many local districts, leading to demands for federal aid. Congress granted limited help for areas affected by defense plants and military bases, but Eisenhower's reluctance to unbalance the budget —along with traditional adherence to state control over public education—blocked further federal assistance.

Equally important, a controversy arose over the nature of education in the 1950s. Critics of "progressive" education called for sweeping educational reforms and a new stress on traditional academic subjects. Suburban communities often had bitter fights; affluent parents demanded kindergarten enrichment programs and grade-school foreign-language instruction while working-class people resisted such costly innovations. The one thing all seemed to agree on was the desirability of a college education. The number of young people attending colleges increased from 1.5 million in 1940 to 3.6 million by 1960, leading to a rapid expansion of universities.

College Student Enrollment, 1940–1960
(in millions)

1940	1950	1960
1.5	2.2	3.6

■ *In this scene from* Marty, *a memorable TV play performed live in 1953, Marty (Rod Steiger) and his newfound friend (Nancy Marchand) try to break through the barriers of shyness.*

The largest growth area was the exciting new medium of television. From a shaky start just after the war, TV boomed in the fifties, pushing radio aside and even undermining many of the nation's mass-circulation magazines. By 1957, the three networks controlled the airwaves, reaching forty million sets over nearly five hundred stations. Advertisers soon took charge of the new medium, using many of the techniques first pioneered in radio—including pretaped commercials, quiz shows, and soap operas.

At first, the insatiable demand for programs encouraged a burst of creativity. Playwrights such as Reginald Rose, Rod Serling, and Paddy Chayefsky wrote a series of notable dramas for *Play-house 90, Studio One,* and the *Goodyear Television Playhouse.* Broadcast live from cramped studios, these productions thrived on tight dramatic structures, movable scenery, and frequent close-ups of the actors. *Marty,* Paddy Chayefsky's deceptively simple story of a Bronx butcher's decision to marry, epitomized the golden age of television. Later made into a successful movie, *Marty* reflected its author's belief that "there is far more exciting drama in the reasons why a man gets married than in why he murders someone."

Advertisers, however, quickly became disillusioned with the live anthology programs, which usually dealt with controversial subjects or focused on ordinary people and events. In contrast, sponsors wanted shows that stressed excitement, glamour, and instant success. Westerns and situation comedies soon prevailed after a fling with quiz shows ended in scandal.

The Kinsey Reports: Exploring Human Sexual Behavior

"Kinsey brought sex out of the bedroom and into the world's parlor." So said a colleague of Alfred Kinsey (see photo above), a scholar who achieved national prominence as an expert on sex. Kinsey was thrust into the public eye by the publication of his two studies: *Sexual Behavior in the Human Male* (1948) and its sequel *Sexual Behavior in the Human Female* (1953). When he died in 1956, he was one of the best-known research scientists in the United States.

Kinsey's road to fame as an authority on human sexual behavior was not a straight path. He was the eldest child of uneducated parents. His father, a self-taught engineer, was determined that his son would follow in his footsteps. But at the end of his sophomore year in college, Kinsey decided to study biology instead; his angry father then cut off his financial support. Undeterred, he pursued his interest in biology and zoology, completed his doctorate at Harvard in 1920, and received an assistant professorship in zoology at Indiana University.

Kinsey's early years in Bloomington were productive. He married and raised a family, published a biology textbook, and wrote two major studies of the gall wasp—an insect on which he was an international authority. In 1938, when a new course on marriage was offered at the University, Kinsey turned his attention to human sexual behavior. Taking an interdisciplinary approach, the new class drew lecturers from biology, medicine, sociology, law, economics, and ethics. Kinsey was chosen to chair the faculty committee in charge of the curriculum.

The course was a great success, but Kinsey was distressed by the lack of scientific literature on human sexual behavior. He found that there was no reliable body of statistics describing sexual activity among humans. To provide such information, Kinsey began interviewing his students, recording their sexual histories much as he would thousands of others later in his large-scale studies.

Over the next sixteen years, Kinsey and his colleagues conducted over 18,000 interviews while compiling data for his studies. In 1947, he founded the Institute for Sex Research at Indiana University. A total of 5300 males were interviewed for *Sexual Behavior in the Human Male*; the responses of 5940 women were used in *Sexual Behavior in the Human Female*. Though some racial minorities were interviewed, only whites were used in the publications. Even among whites, the sample was haphazard but not random, a fact that the statisticians among his critics were quick to point out.

While some social scientists found Kinsey's sampling techniques questionable, his interviewing techniques were highly regarded. Kinsey created an immediate rapport with his subjects and treated all reports with matter-of-fact detachment. Questions were phrased to encourage honesty and openness. Reports of married couples were checked against one another to ensure honesty, and selected respondents were reinterviewed to verify the accuracy of their recollections. All responses were anonymous; they were recorded on IBM cards according to a secret numerical code. Kinsey even had plans for the destruction of the data in case law-enforcement officials demanded access to the records.

Kinsey tried to present his findings on human sexual behavior with the same empirical objectivity that he used in his zoological studies. He considered himself a scientist, not a moralist. But amid the charts, graphs, and statistics, there was a message in Kinsey's reports: toleration. He wrote in the introduction to his volume on men, "This is first of all a report on what people do which raises no question of what they should do." Sex was "a normal biologic function, acceptable in whatever form it is manifested."

In 1948, after the publication of *Sexual Behavior in the Human Male*, George Gallup asked Americans, "Do you think it is a good thing or a bad thing to have this information on sex available?" Of those polled, 57 percent thought it was a good thing, 11 percent thought it was bad, 4 percent thought it acceptable "if properly presented" and kept from children, and 28 percent had no opinion. When Gallup asked the same question about Kinsey's study of women in 1953, 49 percent favored it, 19 percent opposed it, 4 percent gave it qualified approval, and 28 percent still had no opinion. Part of the decline in Kinsey's positive rating can be attributed to his assault on sexual stereotypes. Challenging popular belief, Kinsey showed that women possessed the same sexual needs and desires as men and were not motivated solely by any maternal instinct. But the lower rating also represented the growing force of a vocal minority opposed to Kinsey's research.

Despite the general interest in Kinsey's studies and the popularity of his books, many segments of American society attacked his work. His fellow academics criticized him for engaging in research which was beyond his competence as a zoologist. Statisticians, psychologists, and sociologists reacted against his invasion of their academic domains. Freudian psychiatrists criticized his departure from psychoanalytical orthodoxy, while humanists objected to the impersonalization and quantification of this most intimate aspect of human behavior. But the most vociferous attacks came from the Christian clergy.

Spanning the spectrum from Reinhold Niebuhr to Billy Graham, they denounced Kinsey for his biological approach to sex and his failure to address its moral and religious aspects. Graham went so far as to suggest that "it is impossible to estimate the damage this book will do to the already deteriorating morals of America." And in Kinsey's home state, the Indiana chapter of the National Council of Catholic Women demanded "some reassurance that Indiana University is still a place fit for the educating of youth of our state." A Presbyterian minister in Indianapolis even saw "a kinship" between the Kinsey Reports and communism.

Indiana University remained staunch in its support of Kinsey. The Rockefeller Foundation, however—the source of a large percentage of Kinsey's funds—was not so steadfast. At the urging of Representative B. C. Reece, a conservative Tennessee Republican, Congress formed a committee to investigate tax-exempt foundations. Reece admitted to the press that the real reason for the committee was to investigate the financial backing of the Kinsey Reports. The Rockefeller Foundation, worried about a congressional investigation and the bad publicity it might create, turned down the Kinsey Institute's request for continued support in 1954. Two years later Alfred Kinsey died, his work, in his own opinion, still largely incomplete.

In retrospect, the objections to the Kinsey Reports do not seem credible. Kinsey did not advocate premarital or extramarital sex, homosexuality, promiscuity, or communism. He merely showed America its sexual habits, in all their infinite variety. Although many of his critics accused him of trivializing sex, reducing it to bar graphs and statistics, he can be more accurately credited with demystifying human sexual behavior.

Aware that audiences were fascinated by contestants with unusual expertise (a shoemaker answering tough questions on operas, a grandmother stumping experts on baseball), producers began giving away huge cash prizes on *The $64,000 Question* and *Twenty-one*. In 1959, the nation was shocked when Charles Van Doren, a Columbia University professor, confessed that he had been given the answers in advance to win $129,000 on *Twenty-one*. The three networks quickly dropped all the big-prize quiz programs, replacing them with comedy, action, and adventure shows such as *The Untouchables* and *Bonanza*. Despite its early promise of artistic innovation, television had become a technologically sophisticated but safe conveyor of the consumer culture.

Critics of the Consumer Society

One striking feature of the 1950s was the abundance of self-criticism. A number of widely read books explored the flaws in the new suburbia. John Keats' *The Crack in the Picture Window* described the endless rows of tract houses "vomited up" by developers as "identical boxes spreading like gangrene." Their occupants—whom he dubbed the Drones, the Amiables, and the Fecunds—lost any sense of individuality in their obsession with material goods.

Richard and Katherine Gordon were more concerned about the psychological toll of suburban life in their 1960 book *The Split Level Trap*. They labeled the new life-style "Disturbia" and bemoaned the "haggard" men, "tense and anxious" women, and the "gimme" kids it produced. The most sweeping indictment came in William H. Whyte's *The Organization Man* (1956), based on a study of the Chicago suburb of Park Forest. Whyte perceived a change from the old Protestant ethic, with its emphasis on hard work and personal responsibility, to a new social ethic, where everything centered on "the team" and the ultimate goal was "belongingness." The result was a stifling conformity and the loss of personal identity.

The most influential social critic of the fifties was Harvard sociologist David Riesman. His book *The Lonely Crowd* appeared in 1950 and set the tone for intellectual commentary about suburbia for the rest of the decade. Riesman described the

shift from the "inner-directed" American of the past who had relied on such traditional values as self-denial and frugality to the "other-directed" American of the consumer society who constantly adapted his behavior to conform to social pressures. The consequence—a decline in individualism and a tendency for people to become acutely sensitive to the expectations of others—produced a bland and tolerant society of consumers lacking creative and adventurous people.

C. Wright Mills was a far more caustic, though less popular, commentator on American society in the 1950s. Anticipating government statistics that revealed that white-collar workers (sales clerks, office workers, bank tellers) now outnumbered blue-collar workers (miners, factory workers, millhands), Mills described the new middle class in ominous terms in his books *White Collar* (1951) and *Power Elite* (1956). The corporation was the villain for Mills, depriving office workers of their own identities and imposing an impersonal discipline through manipulation and propaganda. The industrial assembly line had given way to an even more dehumanizing workplace, the modern office. "At rows of blank-looking counters sat rows of blank-looking girls with blank, white folders in their blank hands, all blankly folding blank papers."

This disenchantment with the consumer culture reached its most eloquent expression with the "beats," a literary group that rebelled against the materialistic society of the 1950s. Jack Kerouac's novel *On the Road*, published in 1957, set the tone for the new movement. The name came from the quest for beatitude, a state of inner grace that is sought in Zen Buddhism. Flouting the respectability of suburbia, the "beatniks"—as middle-class America termed them—were easily identified by their long hair, bizarre clothing, and penchant for sexual promiscuity and drug experimentation. They were conspicuous dropouts from a society they found senseless. Poet Lawrence Ferlinghetti, who held forth in the City Lights Bookshop in San Francisco (a favorite resort of the beats), summed it up this way: "I was a wind-up toy someone had dropped wound up into a world already running down."

Despite the disapproval they evoked from mainstream Americans, the beat generation had only compassion for their detractors. "We love everything," Kerouac proclaimed, "—Bill Gra-

■ *"Beat" writers like Jack Kerouac bemoaned the conformity and staleness of the 1950s. Kerouac's cross-country wanderings provided the material for his novel,* On the Road, *written in 1957.*

ham, the Big Ten, Rock and Roll, Zen, apple pie, Eisenhower—we dig it all." Yet as highly visible nonconformists in an era of stifling conformity, the beats demonstrated a style of social protest that would flower into the counterculture of the sixties.

The Reaction to Sputnik

The profound insecurity that underlay American life throughout the fifties burst into view in October 1957, when the Soviets sent the satellite Sputnik into orbit around the earth. The public's reaction to this impressive scientific feat was panic. The declining rate of economic growth; the recession of 1957–1958; the growing concern that American schools, with their frills and frivolities and their emphasis on social adjustment, were lagging behind their Russian counterparts—all contributed to a conviction that the nation had

somehow lost its previously unquestioned primacy in the eyes of the world.

In the late 1950s, the President and Congress moved to restore national confidence. Eisenhower appointed James R. Killian, president of the Massachusetts Institute of Technology, as his special assistant for science and technology and to oversee a crash program in missile development. The House and Senate followed by creating the National Aeronautics and Space Administration (NASA) in 1958. Congress appropriated vast sums to allow the agency to compete with the Russians in the space race. Soon a new group of heroes, the astronauts, began the training that led to suborbital flights and eventually to John Glenn's five-hour flight around the globe in 1962. (See the picture essay on the space program following p.864.)

Congress also sought to match the Soviet educational advances by passing the National Defense Education Act (NDEA). This legislation authorized federal financing of scientific and foreign-language programs in the nation's schools and colleges. Soon American students were hard at work mastering the "new physics" and the "new math."

The belief persisted, however, that the faults lay deeper, that in the midst of affluence and abundance Americans had lost their competitive edge. Economists pointed to the higher rate of Soviet economic growth, and social critics bemoaned a supermarket culture that stressed consumption over production, comfort over hard work. Disturbed by the charge that the nation had lost its sense of purpose, President Eisenhower finally appointed a Commission on National Goals "to develop a broad outline of national objectives for the next decade and longer." Ten prominent citizens from all walks of life, led by Henry W. Wriston of Brown University, issued a report which called for increased military spending abroad, greater economic growth at home, broader educational opportunities, and more government support for both scientific research and the advancement of the arts. The consensus seemed to be that rather than a change of direction, all the United States needed was a renewed commitment to the pursuit of excellence.

The fifties ended on a mixed note. The temporary despair engendered by Sputnik had led to a healthy, if excessive, national self-assessment.

ment, the sense of stagnation, even decline, lingered on through Eisenhower's second term, offering the Democrats a tempting issue to exploit in the 1960 election.

Recommended Reading

Two excellent books survey the social, cultural, and political trends in the United States during the postwar period. In *One Nation Divisible* (1980), Richard Polenberg analyzes class, ethnic, and racial changes, while William Leuchtenburg offers a fine overview of American life since 1945 in *A Troubled Feast*, updated ed. (1983).

The best book on the Truman period is Alonzo L. Hamby, *Beyond the New Deal* (1973), which focuses on Truman's attempts to preserve and extend the liberal reform tradition. Charles Alexander provides a balanced view of the Eisenhower years in *Holding the Line* (1975), portraying the Republican president as an able chief executive who was well suited to the times.

Of the many books on the postwar red scare, Earl Latham's *The Communist Controversy in Washington* (1966) is the most thorough and reliable. There is no single volume that deals with all aspects of the civil-rights movement, but two fine biographies—David L. Lewis' *King* (1970) and Stephen B. Oates' *Let the Trumpet Sound* (1982)—present perceptive portraits of Martin Luther King, Jr., the movement's most influential leader.

Douglas Miller and Marian Novak offer a comprehensive catalogue of social and cultural developments in *The Fifties: The Way We Really Were* (1977). The most incisive account of suburban life is Scott Donaldson's *The Suburban Myth* (1969), which rebuts many of the contemporary critiques.

Additional Bibliography

Biographies of Truman include Merle Miller, *Plain Speaking* (1973); Margaret Truman, *Harry S. Truman* (1973); Robert H. Ferrell, *Harry S. Truman and the Modern American Presidency* (1982); and two volumes by Robert J. Donovan: *Conflict and Crisis* (1977) and *Tumultuous Years* (1982). Studies of specific policies include Barton J. Bernstein, ed., *Politics and Policies of the Truman Administration* (1970); R. Alton Lee, *Truman and Taft-Hartley* (1966); Susan M. Hartmann, *Truman and the 80th Congress* (1971); Allen J. Matusow, *Farm Policies and Politics in the Truman Administration* (1966); and Monte M. Poen, *Harry S. Truman and the Medical Lobby* (1979).

Three studies of the 1948 election are Irwin Ross, *The Loneliest Campaign* (1968); Norman D. Markowitz, *The Rise and Fall of the People's Century: Henry A. Wallace and American Liberalism, 1941–1948* (1973); and Allen Yarnell, *Democrats and Progressives* (1973). John Blum offers an interesting selection from

Amid the self-criticism, there was much that Americans of the fifties could point to with pride. They had created a booming consumer society which provided the great majority with an opportunity for a rich and full life and banished fears of another Great Depression. The standard of living Americans achieved in the 1950s would become the aspiration of most of the world's population in the decades to come. Yet despite this achieve-

Henry Wallace's diary in *The Price of Vision* (1973), while James T. Patterson gives an excellent portrait of Senator Robert A. Taft in *Mr. Republican* (1968).

Herbert Parmet began the scholarly reappraisal of Dwight Eisenhower in *Eisenhower and the American Crusades* (1973). Other useful books on the Eisenhower years include Fred Greenstein, *The Hidden Hand Presidency* (1982); Elmo Richardson, *The Presidency of Dwight D. Eisenhower* (1979); Samuel Lubell, *The Future of American Politics* (1952); Garry Wills, *Nixon Agonistes* (1971); John Bartlow Martin, *Adlai Stevenson and the World* (1977); James L. Sundquist, *Politics and Policy: The Eisenhower, Kennedy and Johnson Years* (1968); Gary W. Reichard, *The Reaffirmation of Republicanism: Eisenhower and the 83rd Congress* (1975); and Mark Rose, *Interstate* (1979). For economic developments during the 1950s, consult Edward S. Flash, *Economic Advice and Presidential Leadership* (1965); Harold G. Vatter, *The U.S. Economy in the 1950's* (1962); and two books by John Kenneth Galbraith: *American Capitalism* (1952) and *The Affluent Society* (1958).

The relationship of the Truman administration to the Communist issue is covered in Allan D. Harper, *The Politics of Loyalty* (1970); Athan G. Theoharis, *Seeds of Repression* (1971); and Richard Freeland, *The Truman Doctrine and the Origins of McCarthyism* (1972). Other works on the second red scare are Walter Goodman, *The Committee* (1968); Victor Navasky, *Naming Names* (1980); Allen Weinstein, *Perjury: The Hiss-Chambers Case* (1978); and William L. O'Neill, *A Better World* (1982), which examines its impact on American intellectuals. Among the many books on McCarthyism, the best are Thomas C. Reeves, *The Life and Times of Joe McCarthy* (1982); Richard H. Rovere, *Senator Joe McCarthy* (1959); Michael P. Rogin, *The Intellectuals and McCarthy* (1967); Robert Griffith, *The Politics of Fear* (1970); Richard M. Fried, *Men Against McCarthy* (1976); Edwin R. Bagley, *Joe McCarthy and the Press* (1981); and David Oshinski, *A Conspiracy So Immense: The World of Joe McCarthy* (1983).

Truman's contributions to the civil-rights movement are surveyed critically in Harry C. Berman, *The Politics of Civil Rights in the Truman Administration* (1970) and more sympathetically in Donald R. McCoy and Richard T. Ruetten, *Quest and Response* (1973). Other important books on civil rights are Richard Dalfiume, *Desegregation of the U.S. Armed Forces* (1969); Richard Kluger, *Simple Justice* (1975) on the *Brown* decision; Benjamin Muse, *Ten Years of Prelude* (1964); Steven Lawson, *Black Ballots* (1977) on the voting rights issue; and Numan V. Bartley, *The Rise of Massive Resistance* (1969) on the southern reaction.

Bernard Rosenberg and D. M. White, eds., *Mass Culture* (1957) is a useful anthology of cultural trends. Other significant books on social and intellectual themes in the 1950s include David Potter, *People of Plenty* (1954), a perceptive analysis of abundance; William Dobriner, ed., *The Suburban Community* (1958), a helpful collection of scholarly essays; Herbert Gans, *The Levittowners* (1967); Will Herberg, *Protestant, Catholic, Jew* (1955); Lawrence Lipton, *The Holy Barbarians* (1959) on the "beat generation"; Eric Barnouw, *The Image Empire* (1970), a critical view of television; Kent Anderson, *Television Fraud* (1978) on the rigged TV quiz shows; Lloyd Swenson et al., *This New Ocean* (1966) on the early space program; and Barbara B. Clowse, *Brainpower and the Cold War* (1981) about the impact of Sputnik on the educational controversy.

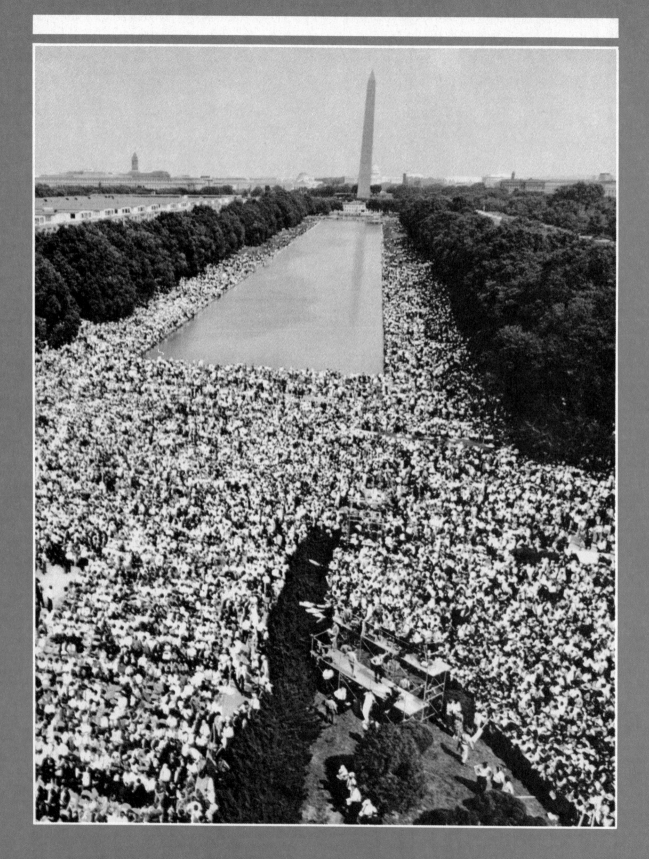

chapter 30

THE CLIMAX
OF LIBERALISM

On Monday evening, September 26, 1960, John F. Kennedy and Richard M. Nixon faced each other in the nation's first televised debate between two presidential candidates. Kennedy, as the relatively unknown Democratic challenger, had proposed the debates; Nixon, confident of his mastery of television, had accepted even though as Eisenhower's vice-president and the early front-runner in the election he had more to lose and less to gain. In the Chicago studios of CBS, technicians worked all day adjusting the lights, arranging the cameras, and making technical changes to satisfy the two candidates' media advisers.

Richard Nixon arrived an hour early, looking tired and ill at ease. He was still recuperating from a knee injury which had slowed his campaign and left him pale and weak as he pursued a hectic catch-up schedule. Makeup experts offered to hide Nixon's heavy beard and soften his prominent jowls, but the GOP candidate declined, preferring to let an aide apply a light coat of Max Factor's "Lazy Shave," a pancake cosmetic. John Kennedy, tanned from open-air campaigning in

California and rested by a day spent nearly free of distracting activity, refused to wear any makeup. He did, however, change from a gray to a dark blue suit better adapted to the intense lighting on the set.

At 8:30 P.M. central time, moderator Howard K. Smith welcomed an audience estimated at seventy-seven million to this historic event. Kennedy led off, echoing Abraham Lincoln by saying that the nation faced the question of "whether the world will exist half-slave and half-free." Although the ground rules limited the first debate to domestic issues, Kennedy argued that foreign and domestic policy were inseparable. He accused the Republicans of letting the country drift at home and abroad. "I think it's time America started moving again," he concluded. Nixon, caught off-guard, seemed to agree with Kennedy's assessment of the nation's problems, but he contended that he had better solutions. "Our disagreement," the vice-president pointed out, "is not about the goals for America but only about the means to reach those goals."

Nearly 110 million viewers watched the four televised debates between presidential candidates John F. Kennedy and Richard Nixon. Kennedy's polished performance helped dispel fears that he was too young and inexperienced for the job.

For the rest of the hour, the two candidates answered questions from a panel of journalists. Radiating confidence and self-assurance, Kennedy used a flow of statistics and details to create the image of a man deeply knowledgeable about all aspects of government. Nixon fought back with a defense of the Eisenhower record, but he seemed nervous and unsure of himself. The reaction shots of each candidate listening to the other's remarks showed Kennedy calm and serene, Nixon tense and uncomfortable.

Polls taken over the next few weeks revealed a sharp swing to Kennedy. Many Democrats and independents who had thought him too young or too inexperienced were impressed by his performance. Nixon suffered more from his unattractive image than from what he said; those who heard the debate on radio thought that the Republican candidate more than held his own. In the three additional debates held during the campaign, Nixon improved his performance notably by wearing makeup to soften his appearance and by taking the offensive from Kennedy on the issues. But the damage had been done. A postelection poll revealed that of four million voters who were influenced by the debates, three million voted for Kennedy.

The televised debates were only one of many factors influencing the outcome of the 1960 election. In essence, Kennedy won because he took full advantage of all his opportunities. Lightly regarded by Democratic leaders, he won the nomination by appealing to the rank-and-file in the primaries, but then astutely chose Lyndon Johnson of Texas as his running mate to blunt Nixon's southern strategy.

During the fall campaign, Kennedy exploited the national mood of frustration that had followed Sputnik. At home, he promised to stimulate the lagging economy and carry forward long-overdue reforms in education, health care, and civil rights under the banner of the "New Frontier." Abroad, he pledged a renewed commitment to the Cold War, vowing that he would lead the nation to victory over the Soviet Union. He met the issue of his Catholicism head on, telling a group of Protestant ministers in Houston that as president he would always place country above religion. In the shrewdest move of all, he won over black voters by helping to secure the release of Martin Luther King, Jr., from a Georgia jail

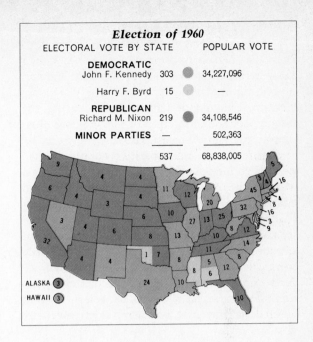

where the civil-rights leader was being held on a trumped-up charge.

The Democratic victory in 1960 was paper-thin. Kennedy's edge in the popular vote was only two tenths of 1 percent, and his wide margin in the electoral college (303 to 219) was tainted by voting irregularities in several states—notably Illinois and Texas—which went Democratic by very slender majorities. Yet even though he had no mandate, Kennedy's triumph did mark a sharp political shift. In contrast to the aging Eisenhower, Kennedy symbolized youth, energy, and ambition. His mastery of the new medium of television reflected his sensitivity to the changes taking place in American life in the sixties. He came to office promising reform at home and advance abroad. Over the next five years, he and Lyndon Johnson achieved many of their goals only to find the nation caught up in new and even greater dilemmas.

Waging the Cold War

From the day he took office, John F. Kennedy gave foreign policy top priority. In part, this decision reflected the perilous world situation, the immediate dangers ranging from a developing civil war in Vietnam to the emergence of Fidel Castro as a Soviet ally in Cuba. But it also corresponded to Kennedy's personal priorities. As a congressman and senator, he had been an intense Cold Warrior, supporting containment after World War II, lamenting the loss of China, and accusing the Eisenhower administration of allowing the Russians to open up a dangerous missile gap. Bored by committee work and legislative details, he had focused on foreign policy in the Senate, gaining a seat on the Foreign Relations Committee and publishing a book of speeches, *The Strategy of Peace*, in early 1960.

In his inaugural address, Kennedy indicated an intense concern with the Cold War. Ignoring the domestic issues aired during the campaign, he dealt exclusively with the world. "Let every nation know, whether it wishes us well or ill, that we shall pay any price, bear any burden, meet any hardship, support any friend, oppose any foe," the new President declared, "to assure the survival and success of liberty. We will do all this and more."

His appointments reflected his determination to win the Cold War. His choice of Dean Rusk, an experienced but unassertive diplomat, to head the State Department indicated that Kennedy planned to be his own secretary of state. He surrounded himself with young, pragmatic advisers who prided themselves on toughness: McGeorge Bundy, dean of Harvard College, became national security adviser; Walt W. Rostow, an MIT economist, was Bundy's deputy; and Robert McNamara, the youthful president of the Ford Motor Company, took over as secretary of defense.

These New Frontiersmen, later dubbed "the best and the brightest" by journalist David Halberstam, all shared a hard-line view of the Soviet Union and the belief that American security depended upon superior force and the willingness to use it. Walt Rostow summed up their view of the contest with Russia best when he wrote, "The cold war comes down to this test of whether we and the democratic world are fundamentally tougher and more purposeful in the defense of our vital interests than they are in the pursuit of their global ambitions."

Flexible Response

The first goal of the Kennedy administration was to build up the nation's armed forces. During the 1960 campaign, Kennedy had warned that the Soviets were opening a missile gap. In fact, the United States had a significant lead in nuclear striking power by early 1961, with a fleet of over 600 B-52 bombers, 2 Polaris submarines, and 16 Atlas ICBMs capable of delivering more than 2000 warheads against Russian targets. Nevertheless, the new administration, intent on putting the Soviets on the defensive, authorized the construction of an awesome nuclear arsenal that included 1000 Minuteman solid-fuel ICBMs (five times the number Eisenhower had felt necessary) and 32 Polaris submarines carrying 656 missiles. The United States thus opened a missile gap in reverse, creating the possibility of a successful American first strike.

■ In his inaugural address, Kennedy challenged young people to ask "what you can do for your country?"

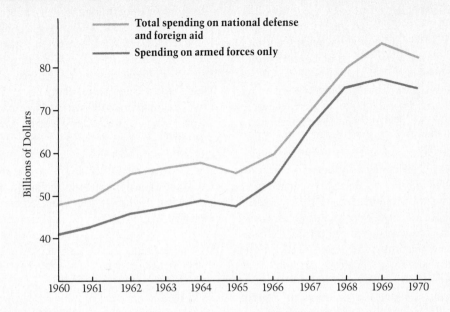

U.S. Government Spending on National Defense and Foreign Aid, 1960–1970

Total spending on national defense and foreign aid

Spending on armed forces only

Source: Compiled from U.S. Bureau of the Census, Historical Statistics of the United States, Colonial Times to 1970, Bicentennial Edition, Washington, D.C., 1975.

At the same time, the Kennedy administration augmented conventional military strength. Secretary of Defense McNamara developed plans to add five combat-ready army divisions, three tactical air wings and a ten-division strategic reserve. These vast increases led to a $6-billion jump in the defense budget in 1961 alone. The President took a personal interest in counterinsurgency. He expanded the Special Forces unit at Fort Bragg, North Carolina, and insisted, over army objections, that it adopt a distinctive green beret as a symbol of its elite status.

The purpose of this buildup was to create an alternative to Eisenhower's policy of massive retaliation. Instead of responding to Communist moves with nuclear threats, the United States could now call on a wide spectrum of force—ranging from ICBMs to Green Berets. Thus, as Robert McNamara explained, the new strategy of flexible response meant that the United States could "choose among several operational plans. . . . We shall be committed only to a system that gives us the ability to use our forces in a controlled and deliberate way." The danger, how-

ever, was that the existence of such a powerful arsenal would tempt the new administration to test its strength against the Soviet Union.

Crisis over Berlin

The first confrontation came in Germany. Since 1958, Soviet Premier Khrushchev had been threatening to sign a peace treaty that would put access to the isolated western zones of Berlin under the control of East Germany. The steady flight of skilled workers to the West through the Berlin escape route weakened the East German regime dangerously, and the Soviets felt they had to resolve this issue quickly.

At a summit meeting in Vienna in June 1961, Kennedy and Khrushchev focused on Berlin as the key issue. Pointing out that sixteen years had passed since the end of World War II, the Russian leader called the current situation "intolerable" and announced that the Soviet Union would proceed with an East German peace treaty. Kennedy was equally adamant, defending the American presence in Berlin and refusing to give up occupation rights which he considered crucial to the defense of Western Europe. In their last session, the failure to reach agreement took on an ominous tone. "I want peace," Khrushchev declared, "but, if you want war, that is your problem." "It is you, not I," the young President replied, "who wants to force a change." When the Soviet leader said he would sign a German peace treaty by December, Kennedy added, "It will be a cold winter."

The climax came sooner than either man expected. On July 25, Kennedy delivered an impassioned televised address to the American people in which he called the defense of Berlin "essential" to "the entire Free World." Announcing a series of arms increases, including $3 billion more in defense spending and a nationwide program of fallout shelters, the President took the unprecedented step of calling more than 150,000 reservists and National Guardsmen to active duty. Above all, he sought to convince Khrushchev of his determination and resolve. "I hear it said that West Berlin is militarily untenable," he commented. "And so was Bastogne. And so, in

fact, was Stalingrad. Any dangerous spot is tenable if men—brave men—will make it so."

Aware of superior American nuclear striking power, Khrushchev settled for a stalemate. On August 13, the Soviets sealed off their zone of the city. They began the construction of the Berlin Wall to stop the flow of brains and talent to the West. For a brief time, Russian and American tanks maneuvered within sight of each other at Checkpoint Charlie, but by fall the tension gradually eased. The Soviets signed the separate peace treaty; Berlin—like Germany and, indeed, all Europe—remained divided between the East and the West. Neither side could claim a victory, but Kennedy felt that at least he had proved America's willingness to honor its commitments.

Containment in Southeast Asia

Two weeks before Kennedy's inaugural, Nikita Khrushchev gave a speech in Moscow in which he declared Soviet support for "wars of national liberation." The Russian leader's words were actually aimed more at China than the United

A grim symbol of the Cold War, the brick and barbed-wire Berlin Wall forms a solid barrier in front of the Brandenburg Gate, a historic Prussian war monument.

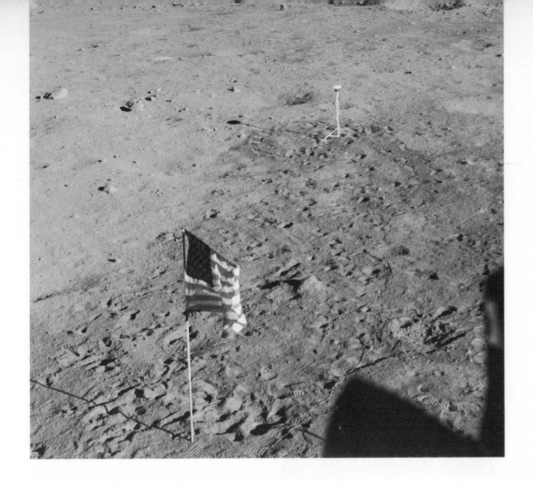

THE SPACE PROGRAM
COMMITMENT TO THE FUTURE

"These are extraordinary times," said President John F. Kennedy in a special message to Congress on May 25, 1961, "and we face an extraordinary challenge." The contest was with the Soviet Union, and outer space was the field of honor. Russia had stolen a march on the United States, sending a man into orbit before an American had even reached outer space. "Now is the time," Kennedy observed, "time for this nation to take a clearly leading role in space achievements." Project Apollo, a manned lunar landing within the decade, was our answer to the challenge.

Man had always looked to the heavens with awe and wonder, but the American space program was not the product of romantic or scientific curiosity. Clearly, there was a race, a "space race," and America's preeminence in world affairs was at stake.

Russia and the United States had been competing in rocket technology since World War II. As the disaffected allies marched into Germany, each sought to gain the secrets of the German V-2, the first supersonic ballistic missile. Although the Soviet Zone of occupation contained the primary V-2 plant, the U.S. Army's *Operation Paperclip* brought to the United States most of the top personnel of the German Rocket program. Werner Von Braun and more than one hundred other German scientists and engineers were recruited for the army missile program. American military rocketry continued to receive priority over civilian space projects. President Eisenhower's fiscal conservatism and his low estimate of the significance of space exploration prevailed until the successful launch of the Soviet satellite *Sputnik I* on October 4, 1957.

The flag of the United States on lunar soil, amid the footprints of Neil Armstrong and Edwin Aldrin, astronauts on the Apollo 11 *moon trip.*

While Eisenhower publicly dismissed *Sputnik* as an event of only "scientific interest" and denied the existence of a "space race," American confidence was shaken. Both houses of Congress established Space Committees; Eisenhower created the National Aeronautics and Space Administration (NASA); and the satellite program planned new *Explorers*, *Pioneers*, and other unmanned experiments. In the fall of 1958, Project Mercury, the United States' first manned space program, was announced.

Meanwhile, the Soviets pursued a variety of outer space objectives. Soviet spacecraft hit the moon and photographed its dark side. *Sputnik V* launched two dogs into orbit and returned them safely to earth. But despite these Soviet successes, Eisenhower rejected NASA's proposed lunar mission, judging its benefits too narrowly scientific and its cost far too high. He continued to advocate a slow and steady program, with little sense of urgency.

John Kennedy pointed to Eisenhower's lack of initiative in space programs in his 1960 presidential campaign. "We are in a strategic space race with the Russians," he said in a campaign statement, "and we are losing." Referring to space as America's New Frontier, Kennedy created a slogan for his administration. But it took two unsettling events in April 1961 to gain his endorsement of Project Apollo.

Sputnik I on its support stand before launching. The first news of Sputnik *was not carried in Soviet newspapers until two days after the launch.*

The Mercury-Redstone rocket fails its first test, November 21, 1960. It later successfully carried astronauts Alan B. Shepard, Jr., and Virgil I. (Gus) Grissom into space.

On April 12, Soviet Cosmonaut Yuri Gagarin's first successful manned orbit of the earth put America even further behind in the space race. Despite the Kennedy rhetoric about closing the gap, the Soviet lead seemed greater than ever. Then, less than one week after the Gagarin flight, the American-sponsored invasion of Cuba at the Bay of Pigs collapsed in humiliating failure. Just as the Soviets gained worldwide acclaim in space, the United States was humiliated in Cuba, and—as Kennedy well knew—prestige is not merely a matter of public relations but a real factor in world affairs. The combination of these events led the President, already predisposed toward space exploration, to look to NASA for a way to redeem America's tarnished image. Kennedy had three criteria in mind: the project would have to be spectacular, achievable within the decade, and a guaranteed American "first." Project Apollo fit the bill. "If we can get to the moon before the Russians," said Kennedy, "then we should." Eight years and nearly $24 billion later, on July 20, 1969, the Kennedy program came to fruition. Astronaut Neil Armstrong stepped out onto the surface of the moon and uttered the first words ever spoken on earth's natural satellite. "That's one small step for a man," he said, "one giant leap for mankind."

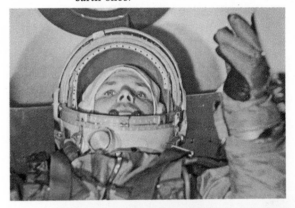

Twenty-three days before astronaut Alan B. Shepard, Jr., rode into space on the Mercury-Redstone rocket, Soviet cosmonaut Yuri A. Gagarin orbited the earth once.

Tethered to a twenty-five-foot umbilical cord, astronaut Edward H. White II "walks" in space on June 3, 1965. By the end of 1966 the United States had flown ten manned missions; the Soviets had flown none.

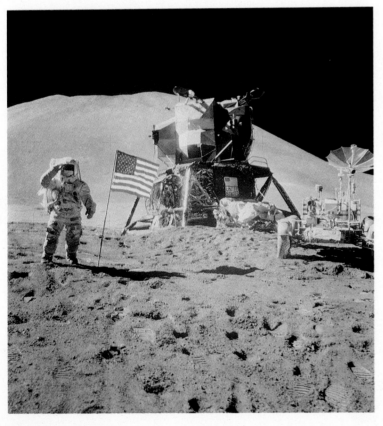

The historic first walk by Apollo 11 astronauts Neil A. Armstrong and Edwin E. Aldrin, Jr., on July 20, 1969. Shown here is the Lunar Landing Module and Roving Vehicle (moon buggy) at Hadley Base.

Although the American space program was active before 1961, the Kennedy decision to send men to the moon marked the beginning of its heyday. Gemini, Apollo, Skylab, and the Space Shuttle are all products of the space race. Tremendously successful, American space projects have nonetheless had their detractors. Even at the time, many questioned the wisdom of spending billions on space when millions of Americans were ill-fed, ill-housed, and under-educated. While more time must pass before an even-handed assessment of the American space program is possible, it is evident today that there was not much of a contest; the United States won handily. Whether those feats of technological prowess enhanced American prestige and strengthened the United States international position is more problematic. The space program did, however, provide Americans with a renewed sense of pride and accomplishment.

President John F. Kennedy and Dr. Wernher von Braun. After World War II, German engineer von Braun was instrumental in developing the rocketry that launched the space and moon missions.

Despite the controversy over the billions of dollars spent on the race to the moon, Americans have always gathered to watch rocket launchings. Through television coverage, millions of other people worldwide have followed the American space program.

On March 1, 1962, New York City sponsored a traditional ticker-tape parade for astronaut John H. Glenn, Jr., the first American to orbit the earth. After leaving the space program, Glenn was elected to the U.S. Senate.

States; the two powerful Communist nations were now rivals for influence in the Third World. But the new American President, ignoring the growing Sino-Soviet split, concluded that the United States and Russia were locked in struggle for the hearts and minds of the uncommitted in Asia, Africa, and Latin America.

Calling for a new policy of nation-building, Kennedy advocated financial and technical assistance designed to help Third World nations achieve economic modernization and stable, pro-Western governments. Measures ranging from the formation of the idealistic Peace Corps to the creation of the ambitious Alliance for Progress—a massive economic aid program for Latin America—were part of this effort. Unfortunately, Kennedy relied even more on counterinsurgency and the Green Berets to beat back the Communist challenge.

Southeast Asia offered the gravest test. In landlocked Laos, the Pathet Lao, a pro-Communist rebel group, overthrew an American-backed government in early 1961. In response, the President sent a regiment of marines to nearby Thailand and beefed up the team of 500 military advisers in Laos. But when the Joint Chiefs of Staff warned that American intervention might require as many as 250,000 troops and that they could guarantee victory only "if we are given the right to use nuclear weapons," Kennedy decided to accept a Soviet offer to negotiate. A year later, Russian and American diplomats in Geneva signed an agreement to neutralize Laos.

In nearby South Vietnam, however, Kennedy became involved in a deepening civil conflict. The insurgency began as a spontaneous protest against the repressive policies of Premier Ngo Dinh Diem, who had come to power in 1955 in Saigon with American support. In March 1960, the Communist government of North Vietnam, led by the venerable Ho Chi Minh, began directing efforts of the Viet Cong rebels in the South. As the guerrilla war intensified in the fall of 1961, the President sent two trusted advisers, Walt Rostow and General Maxwell Taylor, to South Vietnam. They returned favoring the dispatch of eight thousand American combat troops. "As an area for the operation of U.S. troops," reported General Taylor, "SVN [South Vietnam] is not an excessively difficult or unpleasant place to operate. . . . The risks of backing into a major

Protesting the policies of the Diem government, a Buddhist monk sets himself aflame in a ritual suicide.

Asian war by way of SVN," he concluded, "are present but are not impressive."

The President decided against sending in combat troops in 1961, but he authorized substantial increases in economic aid to Diem and in the size of the military mission in Saigon. The number of American advisers grew from fewer than a thousand in 1961 to over sixteen thousand by late 1963. The flow of supplies and the creation of "strategic hamlets," fortified villages designed to protect the peasantry from the Viet Cong, slowed the Communist momentum. American helicopters gave government forces mobility against the Viet Cong for the first time, but by 1963 the situation had again become critical. Diem had failed to win the support of his own people; Buddhist monks set themselves aflame in public protests; and even Diem's own generals plotted his overthrow.

President Kennedy was in a quandary. He realized that the fate of South Vietnam would be determined not by America but by the Vietnamese. "In the final analysis," he said in September 1963, "it is their war. They are the ones who have to win it or lose it." But at the same time,

Kennedy was not prepared to accept the possible loss of all Southeast Asia. Saying it would be "a great mistake" to withdraw from South Vietnam, he told reporters, "Strongly on our mind is what happened in the case of China at the end of World War II, where China was lost. . . . We don't want that." Although aides later claimed he planned to pull out after the 1964 election, Kennedy raised the stakes by tacitly approving a coup that led to Diem's overthrow and death on November 1, 1963. The resulting power vacuum in Saigon made further American involvement in Vietnam almost certain.

Containing Fidel Castro

Kennedy's determination to check global Communist expansion reached a peak of intensity in Cuba. In the 1960 campaign, pointing to the growing ties between the Soviet Union and Fidel Castro's regime, he had accused the Republicans of permitting a "Communist satellite" to arise on "our very doorstep." Kennedy had even issued a statement backing "anti-Castro forces in exile," calling them "fighters for freedom" who held out hope for "overthrowing Castro."

In reality, the Eisenhower administration had been training a group of Cuban exiles in Guatemala since March 1960 as part of a CIA plan to topple the Castro regime. Many of the new President's advisers had doubts about the proposed invasion. Some saw little chance for success because the operation depended heavily on a broad uprising of the Cuban people. Others—notably Senator William Fulbright of Arkansas, chairman of the Foreign Relations Committee—viewed it as an immoral act that would discredit the United States. "The Castro regime is a thorn in the flesh," Fulbright argued, "but it is not a dagger in the heart." The President, however, committed by his own campaign rhetoric and assured of success by the military, decided to go ahead.

On April 17, 1961, fourteen hundred Cuban exiles moved ashore at the Bay of Pigs on the southern coast of Cuba. Even though the United States had masterminded the entire operation, Kennedy insisted on covert action, even canceling at the last minute a planned American air strike on the beachhead. With air superiority, Castro's well-trained forces had no difficulty in quashing the invasion. They killed nearly five hundred exiles and forced the rest to surrender within forty-eight hours.

■ *Like the exploding Cuban cigar, Kennedy's plan for the Bay of Pigs backfired.*

Courtesy The National Library of Wales

■ *Cold War allies: Cuban premier Fidel Castro (right) and Soviet premier Nikita Khrushchev (left).*

Aghast at the swiftness of the defeat, President Kennedy took personal responsibility for the failure. In his address to the American people, however, he showed no remorse for arranging the violation of a neighboring country's sovereignty, only regret at the outcome. Above all, he expressed renewed defiance, warning the Soviets that "our restraint is not inexhaustible." He went on to assert that the United States would resist "Communist penetration" in the Western Hemisphere, terming it part of the "primary obligations . . . to the security of our nation." For the remainder of his presidency, Kennedy continued to harass the Castro regime, imposing an economic blockade on Cuba, supporting a continuing series of raids by exile groups operating out of Florida, and failing to stop the CIA from experimenting with bizarre plots to assassinate Fidel Castro.

At the Brink

The climax of Kennedy's crusade came in October 1962 with the Cuban missile crisis. Throughout the summer and early fall, the Soviets engaged in a massive arms buildup in Cuba, ostensibly to protect Castro from an American invasion. In the United States, Republican candidates in the 1962 congressional elections called for a firm American response; Kennedy contented himself with a stern warning against the introduction of any offensive weapons, which he believed would directly threaten American security. Khrushchev publicly denied any such intent, but secretly he took a daring gamble, building twenty-four medium-range (one thousand mile) and eighteen intermediate-range (two thousand mile) missile sites in Cuba. Later he claimed his purpose was purely defensive, but most likely he was responding to the pressures from his own military to close the enormous strategic gap in nuclear striking power that Kennedy had opened.

On October 14, 1962, American U-2 planes finally discovered the missile sites that were nearing completion. As soon as he learned of the Russian action, Kennedy decided to seek a showdown with Khrushchev. Insisting on absolute secrecy, he convened a special group of advisers to consider how to respond.

An initial preference for an immediate air strike gradually gave way to discussion of either a full-scale invasion or a naval blockade. The President and his advisers ruled out diplomacy, rejecting a proposal to offer the withdrawal of obsolete American missiles from Turkey in return for a similar Russian pullout in Cuba. Kennedy finally agreed to a two-step procedure. He would proclaim a quarantine of Cuba to prevent the arrival of new missiles and threaten a nuclear strike to force the removal of those already there. If the Russians did not cooperate, then the United States would invade Cuba and dismantle the missiles by force.

On the evening of October 22, the President informed the nation of the existence of the Soviet missiles and his plans to remove them. He spared no words in blaming Khrushchev for "this clandestine, reckless and provocative threat to world peace," and he made it clear that any missile attack from Cuba would lead to "a full retaliatory response upon the Soviet Union."

For the next six days, the world hovered on the brink of nuclear catastrophe. Khrushchev replied defiantly, accusing Kennedy of pushing mankind "to the abyss of a world nuclear-missile war." In the Atlantic, some sixteen Soviet ships continued on course toward Cuba, while the American navy was deployed to intercept them five hundred miles from the island. In Florida, nearly a quarter of a million men were being concentrated in the largest invasion force ever assembled in the continental United States.

The first break came at midweek when the Soviet ships suddenly halted to avert a confrontation at sea. "We're eyeball to eyeball," commented Secretary of State Dean Rusk, "and I think the other fellow just blinked." Kennedy felt better on Friday when Khrushchev sent him a long, rambling letter offering a face-saving way out—Russia would remove the missiles in return for an American promise never to invade Cuba. The President was ready to accept when a second Russian message raised the stakes by insisting that the American missiles be withdrawn from Turkey. Kennedy refused to bargain; Khrushchev had endangered world peace by putting the missiles in Cuba secretly, and he must take them out immediately. Nevertheless, while the military went ahead with plans for the invasion of Cuba, the President, heeding his brother's advice, decided to make one last appeal for peace. Ignoring the second Russian message, he sent a cable to Khrushchev accepting his original offer.

On Saturday night, October 27, Robert Kennedy—the President's brother and most trusted adviser—met with Soviet ambassador Anatoly Dobrynin to make it clear that this was the last chance to avert nuclear confrontation. "We had to have a commitment by tomorrow that those bases would be removed," Robert Kennedy recalled telling him. "He should understand that if they did not remove those bases, we would remove them." Then the President's brother calmly remarked that if Khrushchev did not back down, "there would be not only dead Americans but dead Russians as well."

At nine the next morning, Khrushchev agreed to remove the missiles in return for Kennedy's promise not to invade Cuba. The crisis was over.

On the surface, Kennedy appeared to have won a striking personal and political victory. His party successfully overcame the Republican challenge in the November elections and his own popularity reached new heights in the Gallup poll. The American people, on the defensive since Sputnik, suddenly felt that they had proved their superiority over the Russians; they were bursting with national pride. Arthur Schlesinger, Kennedy's confidant and later his biographer, claimed that the Cuban crisis showed the "whole world . . . the ripening of an American leadership unsurpassed in the responsible management of power. . . . It was this combination of toughness and restraint, of will, nerve and wisdom, so brilliantly controlled, so matchlessly calibrated, that dazzled the world."

The Cuban missile crisis had more substantial results as well. Shaken by their close call, Kennedy and Khrushchev agreed to install a "hot line" to speed direct communication between Washington and Moscow in an emergency. Long-stalled negotiations over the reduction of nuclear testing suddenly resumed, leading to the limited test ban treaty of 1963, which outlawed tests in the atmosphere while still permitting them underground. Above all, Kennedy displayed a new maturity as a result of the crisis. In a speech at American University in June 1963, he shifted from the rhetoric of confrontation to that of conciliation. Speaking of the Russians, he said, "Our most basic common link is the fact that we all inhabit this planet. We all breathe the same air. We all cherish our children's future. And we are all mortal."

Despite these hopeful words, the missile crisis also had an unfortunate consequence. Those who believed that the Russians understood only the language of force were confirmed in their penchant for a hard line. Hawks who had backed Kennedy's military buildup felt that events had justified a policy of nuclear superiority. The Russian leaders drew similar conclusions. Aware that the United States had a four-to-one advantage in nuclear striking power during the Cuban crisis, one Soviet official told his American counterpart, "Never will we be caught like this again." After 1962, the Soviets embarked on a crash program to build up their navy and to overtake the American lead in nuclear missiles. Within five years, they had the nucleus of a modern fleet and had surpassed the United States in ICBMs. Kennedy's fleeting moment of triumph thus ensured the escalation of the arms race. His legacy was a bittersweet one of short-term success and long-term anxiety.

The New Frontier at Home

Kennedy hoped to change the course of history at home as well as abroad. In the 1960 campaign, he had accused the Republicans of letting the nation drift, pointing to high unemployment, the low rate of economic growth, and the failure to act on such serious national problems as health care and education. His call to get the nation moving again promised a bold new effort at economic stimulation and legislative reform. This appeal was particularly attractive to young people, who had shunned political involvement during the Eisenhower years.

The new administration reflected Kennedy's aura of youth and energy. Major cabinet appointments went to activists—notably Connecticut Governor Abraham Ribicoff as secretary of health, education and welfare; labor lawyer Arthur J. Goldberg as secretary of labor; and Arizona Congressman Stuart Udall as secretary of the interior. The most controversial choice was Robert F. Kennedy, the President's brother, as attorney general. Critics scoffed at his lack of legal experience, leading JFK to note jokingly that he wanted to give Bobby "a little experience before he goes out to practice law." In fact, the President prized his brother's loyalty and shrewd political advice.

Equally important were the members of the White House staff who handled domestic affairs. Like their counterparts in foreign policy, these New Frontiersmen—Kenneth O'Donnell, Theodore Sorenson, Richard Goodwin, and Walter Heller—prided themselves on being tough-minded and pragmatic. In contrast to Eisenhower, Kennedy relied heavily on academics and intellectuals to help him infuse the nation with energy and a new sense of direction.

Kennedy's greatest asset was his own personality. A cool, attractive, and intelligent man, he possessed a sense of style that endeared him to the American public. He invited artists and musicians as well as corporate executives to White House entertainments; and his speeches were filled with references to Emerson and Shakespeare. He seemed to be a new Lancelot, bent on calling forth the best in national life; admirers likened his inner circle to King Arthur's court at Camelot. Reporters loved him, both for his fact-filled and candid press conferences and for his witty comments. Thus, after the Bay of Pigs fiasco, when his standing in the polls actually went up, he remarked, "It's just like Eisenhower. The worse I do, the more popular I get."

■ With their gala dinners and balls, the Kennedys brought a glamorous tone to the White House. Here, at an April 1962 party for Nobel Prize laureates, poet Robert Frost greets the couple.

The Congressional Obstacle

Neither Kennedy's wit nor charm proved strong enough to break the logjam in Congress. Since the late 1940s, a series of reform bills ranging from health care to federal aid to education had been stalled on Capitol Hill. Kennedy had embraced these traditional Democratic measures in his campaign, labeling them the New Frontier and promising their adoption. Despite his triumph in 1960, however, the election complicated his task. The Democrats lost twenty seats in the House and two in the Senate; even though they retained majorities in both branches, a conservative coalition of northern Republicans and southern Democrats opposed all efforts at reform.

The situation was especially critical in the House, where 101 southern representatives held the balance of power between 160 northern Democrats and 174 Republicans. Aided by Speaker Sam Rayburn, Kennedy was able to enlarge the Rules Committee and overcome a traditional conservative roadblock, but the narrowness of the vote, 217 to 212, revealed how difficult it would be to enact reform measures. "There is no sense in raising hell and then not being successful," JFK noted ruefully after Catholic objections to his aid to education bill—which excluded federal money for church schools—led to its defeat in the House. Discouraged, the President gave up the fight for health care in the Senate; he settled instead for a modest increase in the minimum wage and the passage of manpower training and area-redevelopment legislation.

Kennedy had no more success in enacting his program in 1962 and 1963. The conservative coalition stood firmly against education and health-care proposals. Shifting ground, the President did win approval for a trade-expansion act in 1962 designed to lower tariff barriers, but no significant reform legislation was passed. Although the composition of Congress was the main obstacle, Kennedy's greater interest in foreign policy and his distaste for legislative infighting contributed to the outcome. JFK did not enjoy "blarneying with pompous congressmen and simply would not take the time to do it," one observer noted. As a result, the New Frontier languished in Congress.

Economic Advance

Kennedy gave a higher priority to the sluggish American economy. During the last years of Eisenhower's administration, the rate of growth had slowed to just over 2 percent annually, while unemployment rose to new heights with each recession. JFK was determined to recover quickly from the recession he had inherited and to stimulate the economy to achieve a much higher rate of long-term growth. In part, he wanted to redeem his campaign pledge to get the nation moving again; he also felt that the United States had to surpass the Soviet Union in economic vitality.

Kennedy received conflicting advice from the experts. Those who claimed the problem was essentially technological urged manpower-training and area-redevelopment programs to modernize American industry. Others called for long-overdue federal spending to rebuild the nation's public facilities—from parks and playgrounds to decaying bridges and courthouses in the cities. Kennedy sided with the first group, largely because Congress was opposed to massive spending on public works.

The actual stimulation of the economy, however, came not from social programs but from greatly increased appropriations for defense and space. The $6-billion increase in the arms budget in 1961 gave the economy a great lift, and Kennedy's decision to send a man to the moon (a decision made only a week after the Bay of Pigs debacle) eventually cost $25 billion. By 1962, over half the federal budget was devoted to space and defense; aircraft and computer companies in the South and West benefited, but unemployment remained uncomfortably high in the older industrial areas of the Northeast and Midwest.

The administration's desire to keep the inflation rate low led to a serious confrontation with the business community. Kennedy relied on informal wage and price guidelines to hold down the cost of living. But in April 1962, just after the President had persuaded the steelworkers' union to accept a new contract with no wage increases and only a few additional benefits, U.S. Steel head

Roger Blough informed Kennedy that his company was raising steel prices by $6 a ton. Outraged, the President publicly called the increase "a wholly unjustifiable and irresponsible defiance of the public interest" and accused Blough of displaying "contempt for the interests of 185 million Americans." Privately, Kennedy was even blunter. He confided to aides, "My father always told me that all businessmen were sons-of-bitches, but I never believed it till now."

Roger Blough soon gave way. The President's tongue-lashing, along with a cutoff in Pentagon steel orders and the threat of an antitrust suit, forced him to reconsider. When several smaller steel companies refused to raise their prices in hopes of expanding their share of the market, U.S. Steel rolled back its prices. The business community deeply resented the President's action, and when the stock market, which had been rising steadily since 1960, suddenly fell sharply in late May 1962, analysts were quick to label the decline "the Kennedy market."

Troubled by his strained relations with business and by the continued lag in economic growth, the President decided to adopt a more unorthodox approach in 1963. Walter Heller, chairman of the Council of Economic Advisers, had been arguing for a major cut in taxes since 1961 in the belief that it would stimulate consumer spending and give the economy the jolt it needed. The idea of a tax cut and resulting deficits

Unemployment, 1960–1969

Source: Compiled from U.S. Bureau of the Census, Historical Statistics of the United States, Colonial Times to 1970, *Bicentennial Edition, Washington, D.C., 1975.*

during a period of prosperity went against economic orthodoxy, but Kennedy finally gave his approval. In January 1963, the President proposed a tax reduction of $13.5 billion, asserting that "the unrealistically heavy drag of Federal income taxes on private purchasing power" was the "largest single barrier to full employment." When finally enacted by Congress in 1964, the massive tax cut led to the longest sustained economic advance in American history.

Kennedy's economic policy was far more successful than his legislative efforts. Although the rate of economic growth doubled to 4.5 percent by the end of 1963 and unemployment was reduced substantially, the cost of living rose only 1.3 percent a year. Personal income went up 13 percent in the early 1960s, but the greatest gains came in corporate profits—up 67 percent in this period. Yet critics pointed out that the Kennedy administration failed to close the glaring loopholes in the tax laws that benefited the rich and that it did not make any effort to help those at the bottom by forcing a redistribution of national wealth. And despite the overall economic growth, the public sector continued to be neglected. "I am not sure what the advantage is," complained economist John Kenneth Galbraith, "in having a few more dollars to spend if the air is too dirty to breathe, the water too polluted to drink, the commuters are losing out in the struggle to get in and out of the cities, the streets are filthy, and the schools so bad that the young, perhaps wisely, stay away."

Moving Slowly on Civil Rights

Kennedy faced a genuine dilemma over the issue of civil rights. Despite his own lack of a strong record while in the Senate, he had portrayed himself during the 1960 campaign as a crusader for black rights. He had promised to launch an attack on segregation in the Deep South and had endeared himself to blacks across the nation when he helped win Martin Luther King's release from a Georgia jail. Fear of alienating the large bloc of southern Democrats, however, forced him to play down civil-rights legislation.

The President's solution was to defer congressional action in favor of executive leadership in this area. He directed his brother, Attorney General Robert Kennedy, to continue and expand the Eisenhower administration's efforts to achieve voting rights for southern blacks. To register previously disfranchised blacks, the Justice Department worked with the civil-rights movement —notably the Student Non-Violent Coordinating Committee (SNCC)—in the Deep South. In two years, the Kennedy administration increased the number of voting-rights suits fivefold, but the attorney general could not force the FBI to provide protection for the civil-rights volunteers who risked their lives by encouraging blacks to register. "SNCC's only contact with federal authority," noted one observer, "consisted of the FBI agents who stood by taking notes while local policemen beat up SNCC members."

Other efforts had equally mixed results. Vice-President Lyndon Johnson headed a presidential Commission on Equal Employment Opportunities that worked with defense industries and other government contractors to increase jobs for blacks. But a limited budget and a reliance on voluntary cooperation prevented any dramatic gains; black employment improved only in direct proportion to economic growth in the early 1960s.

Kennedy did succeed in appointing a number of blacks to high government positions: Robert Weaver became chief of the federal housing agency, and Thurgood Marshall, who pleaded the *Brown* v. *Topeka* school desegregation case before the Supreme Court, was named to the United States Circuit Court. On the other hand, among his judicial appointments, Kennedy included one Mississippi jurist who referred to blacks in court as "niggers" and once compared them to "a bunch of chimpanzees."

The civil-rights movement refused to accept Kennedy's indirect approach. In May 1961, the Congress of Racial Equality (CORE) sponsored a "freedom ride" in which a biracial group attempted to test a 1960 Supreme Court decision outlawing segregation in all bus and train stations used in interstate commerce. When they arrived in Birmingham, Alabama, the freedom riders were attacked by a mob of angry whites. "It's the most horrible thing I've ever seen," a Justice Department official reported. "It's terrible, terrible." The attorney general quickly dispatched several hundred federal marshals to protect the freedom riders, but the President was more upset at the

■ *With his diploma in hand, James Meredith leaves the podium after receiving his degree in graduation exercises at the University of Mississippi, September 18, 1963.*

on September 25 indicates the attorney general's concern for the legal, rather than the moral issues involved:

RFK: *I think the problem is that the federal courts have acted and when there is a conflict between your state and the federal courts under arrangements made some years ago—*

BARNETT: *The institution is supported by the taxpayers of this state and controlled by the Trustees.*

RFK: *Governor, you are a part of the United States.*

BARNETT: *. . . I am going to treat you with every courtesy, but I won't agree to let that boy get to Ole Miss. I will never agree to that. I would rather spend my whole life in a penitentiary than do that.*

RFK: *I have a responsibility to enforce the laws of the United States.*

BARNETT: *I appreciate that. You have a responsibility. Why don't you let the NAACP run their own affairs and quit cooperating with that crowd? . . .*

Despite Barnett's later promise of cooperation, the night before Meredith enrolled at the University of Mississippi, a mob attacked the federal marshals and National Guard troops sent to protect him. The violence left 2 dead and 375 injured, including 166 marshals and 12 guardsmen, but Meredith attended the university and eventually graduated.

In 1963, Kennedy sent the deputy attorney general to face down Governor George C. Wallace, an avowed racist who had promised "to stand in the schoolhouse door" to prevent the integration of the University of Alabama. After a brief confrontation, Wallace yielded to federal authority, and two black students peacefully desegregated the state university.

"I Have a Dream"

Martin Luther King, Jr., finally forced Kennedy to abandon his cautious tactics and come out openly in behalf of racial justice. In the spring of 1963, King began a massive protest in Birmingham, one

distraction the protestors created. Deeply involved in the Berlin crisis, Kennedy directed one of his aides to get in touch with the leaders of CORE. "Tell them to call it off," he demanded. "Stop them."

In September, after the attorney general finally convinced the Interstate Commerce Commission to issue an order banning segregation in interstate terminals and buses, the freedom rides ended. The Kennedy administration then sought to prevent further confrontations by involving civil-rights activists in its voting drive.

A pattern of belated reaction to southern racism marked the basic approach of the Kennedys. When James Meredith courageously sought admission to the all-white University of Mississippi in 1962, the President and the attorney general worked closely with Mississippi Governor Ross Barnett to avoid violence. A transcript of Robert Kennedy's conversation with Governor Barnett of the South's most segregated cities. Public marches and demonstrations aimed at integrating public facilities and opening up jobs for blacks quickly led to police harassment and many arrests, including that of King himself. Police Commissioner Eugene "Bull" Connor was determined to crush the civil-rights movement; King was equally determined to prevail. Writing from his cell in Birmingham, he vowed an active campaign to bring the issue of racial injustice to national attention (see the special feature in this chapter).

Bull Connor played directly into King's hands. On May 3, as six thousand children marched in place of the jailed protesters, authorities broke up a demonstration with clubs, snarling police dogs, and high-pressure water hoses strong enough to take the bark off a tree. With a horrified nation watching scene after scene of this brutality on television, the Kennedy administration quickly intevened to arrange a settlement with the Birmingham civic leaders that ended the violence and granted the blacks most of their demands.

More important, Kennedy finally ended his long hesitation and sounded the call for action. "We are confronted primarily with a moral issue," he told the nation on June 11. "It is as old as the Scriptures and is as clear as the American Constitution. . . ." Eight days later, the adminis-

tration sponsored civil-rights legislation providing equal access to all public accommodations as well as an extension of voting rights for blacks.

Despite pleas from the government for an end to demonstrations and protests, the movement's leaders decided to keep pressure on the administration. They scheduled a massive march on Washington for August 1963. The President and the attorney general persuaded the sponsors to tone down their rhetoric—notably one speech by a SNCC leader which termed the Kennedy legislation "too little, too late." On August 28, more than two hundred thousand marchers gathered for a day-long rally in front of the Lincoln Memorial where they listened to hymns, speeches, and prayers for racial justice (see the chapter opening photo on p. 858). The climax of the event was Martin Luther King's eloquent description of his dream for America. It concluded:

> When we let freedom ring, when we let it ring from every village and every hamlet, from every state and every city, we will be able to speed up that day when all God's children, black men and white men, Jews and Gentiles, Protestants and Catholics, will be able to join hands and sing, in the words of that old Negro spiritual. "Free at last! Free at last! Thank God almighty, we are free at last!"

■ The attempts of blacks to end discrimination and secure their civil rights met violent resistance in Birmingham, Alabama, where police used snarling dogs, fire hoses, clubs, and electric cattle prods to turn back the unarmed demonstrators.

By the time of Kennedy's death in November 1963, his civil-rights legislation was well on its way to passage in Congress. Yet even this achievement did not fully satisfy his critics. For two years, they had waited for him to deliver on his campaign promise to wipe out housing discrimination "with a stroke of the pen." When the executive order on housing was finally issued in November 1962, it proved disappointing; it ignored all past discrimination and applied only to homes and apartments financed by the federal government. For many, Kennedy had raised hopes for racial equality that he never fulfilled.

But unlike Eisenhower, he had provided presidential leadership for the civil-rights movement. His emphasis on executive action gradually paid off, especially in extending voting rights. By early 1964, 40 percent of southern blacks had the franchise, compared to only 28 percent in 1960. Moreover, Kennedy's sense of caution and restraint, painful and frustrating as it was to black activists, had proved well founded. Avoiding an early, and possibly fatal, defeat in Congress, he had waited until a national consensus emerged and then had carefully channeled it behind effective legislation. Behaving very much the way Franklin Roosevelt did in guiding the nation into World War II, Kennedy chose to be a fox rather than a lion on civil rights.

The Supreme Court and Reform

The most active impulse for social change in the early 1960s came from a surprising source: the usually staid and conservative Supreme Court. Under the leadership of Earl Warren, a pragmatic jurist more noted for his political astuteness than his legal scholarship, the Court ventured into new areas. A group of liberal judges—especially William O. Douglas, Hugo Black, and William J. Brennan, Jr.—argued for social reform, while advocates of judicial restraint (such as John Marshall Harlan and Felix Frankfurter) fought stubbornly against the new activism.

In addition to ruling against segregation, the Warren Court in the Eisenhower years had angered conservatives by protecting the constitutional rights of victims of McCarthyism. In *Yates* v. *U.S.* (1956), the judges reversed the conviction of fourteen Communist leaders, claiming that government prosecutors had failed to prove that the accused had actually organized a plot to overthrow the government. Mere advocacy of

Black Voter Registration Before and After the Voting Rights Act of 1965

State	1960	1966	Increase	Percentage of Increase over 1960
Alabama	66,000	250,000	184,000	278.8
Arkansas	73,000	115,000	42,000	57.5
Florida	183,000	303,000	120,000	65.6
Georgia	180,000	300,000	120,000	66.7
Louisiana	159,000	243,000	84,000	52.8
Mississippi	22,000	175,000	153,000	695.4
North Carolina	210,000	282,000	72,000	34.3
South Carolina	58,000	191,000	133,000	229.3
Tennessee	185,000	225,000	40,000	21.6
Texas	227,000	400,000	173,000	76.2
Virginia	100,000	205,000	105,000	105.0

Source: Compiled from U.S. Bureau of the Census, Statistical Abstract of the United States: 1982–83 *(103d edition) Washington, D.C., 1982.*

The liberal political activism of the Supreme Court during the 1960s drew sharp criticism and led to demands for the impeachment of Chief Justice Earl Warren. This billboard was erected on a highway near Decatur, Illinois, in 1963.

revolution, the Court said, did not justify conviction. In 1957, the Court issued a series of rulings that led dissenting Justice Tom Clark to protest what he saw as giving defendants "a Roman holiday for rummaging through confidential information as well as vital national secrets."

The resignation of Felix Frankfurter in 1962 enabled President Kennedy to appoint Secretary of Labor Arthur Goldberg, a committed liberal, to the Supreme Court. With a clear majority now favoring judicial intervention, the Warren Court issued a series of landmark decisions designed to extend to state and local jurisdictions the traditional rights afforded the accused in federal courts. Thus, in *Gideon* v. *Wainwright* (1963), *Escobedo* v. *Illinois* (1964), and *Miranda* v. *Arizona* (1966), the majority decreed that defendants had to be provided lawyers, had to be informed of their constitutional rights, and could not be interrogated or induced to confess to a crime without defense counsel being present. In effect, the Court extended to the poor and the ignorant those constitutional guarantees that had always been available to the rich and to persons aware of their rights—notably hardened criminals.

The most far-reaching Warren Court decisions came in the area of legislative reapportionment— a "political thicket" that Justice Frankfurter had always refused to enter. In 1962, the Court ruled in *Baker* v. *Carr* that Tennessee had to redistribute its legislative seats to give citizens in Mem-

phis equal representation. Subsequent decisions reinforced the ban on rural overrepresentation as the Court proclaimed that places in all legislative bodies, including the House of Representatives, be allocated on the basis of "people, not land or trees or pastures." The principle of "one man, one vote" greatly increased the political power of cities at the expense of rural areas; it also involved the Court directly in the reapportionment process, frequently forcing judges to draw up new legislative and congressional districts.

The activism of the Supreme Court stirred up a storm of criticism. The rulings that extended protection to criminals and those accused of subversive activity led some Americans to charge that the court was encouraging crime and weakening national security. The John Birch Society, an extreme anti-Communist group, demanded the impeachment of Earl Warren. Decisions banning school prayers and permitting pornography incensed many conservative Americans, who saw the Court as undermining moral values. "They've put the Negroes in the schools," complained one southern congressman, "and now they've driven God out." Legal scholars worried more about the weakening of the Court's prestige as it became more directly involved in the political process. On balance, however, the Warren Court helped achieve greater social justice by protecting the rights of the underprivileged and by permitting dissent and free expression to flourish.

Letter from Birmingham Jail

April 16, 1963

On Good Friday in the spring of 1963, the Reverend Dr. Martin Luther King, Jr., was arrested during a civil-rights parade in Birmingham, Alabama. King, in Birmingham at the request of the local chapter of his Southern Christian Leadership Conference, was held incommunicado for twenty-four hours in solitary confinement and barred from seeing even his lawyer. During his eight days in jail, several Alabama priests, rabbis, and ministers wrote to the local newspaper, asking blacks not to support King's civil-rights efforts. In reply, Dr. King wrote a nine-thousand-word statement, "begun on the margins of the newspaper [and] continued on scraps of writing paper supplied by a friendly Negro trusty, and concluded on a pad my attorneys were eventually permitted to leave me."

My Dear Fellow Clergymen:

While confined here in the Birmingham city jail, I came across your recent statement calling my present activities "unwise and untimely."

. . . I am cognizant of the interrelatedness of all communities and states. I cannot sit idly by in Atlanta and not be concerned about what happens in Birmingham. Injustice anywhere is a threat to justice everywhere. We are caught in an inescapable network of mutuality, tied in a single garment of destiny. Whatever affects one directly, affects all indirectly.

. . . There can be no gainsaying the fact that racial injustice engulfs this community. Birmingham is probably the most thoroughly segregated city in the United States. Its ugly record of brutality is widely known. Negroes have experienced grossly unjust treatment in the courts. There have been more unsolved bombings of Negro homes and churches in Birmingham than in any other city in the nation. . . .

You may well ask "Why direct action? Why sit-ins, marches and so forth? Isn't negotiation a better path?" You are quite right in calling for negotiation. Indeed, this is the very purpose of direct action. Nonviolent direct action seeks to create such a crisis and foster such a tension that a community which has constantly refused to negotiate is forced to confront the issue. . . .

For years now I have heard the word "Wait!" It rings in the ear of every Negro with piercing familiarity. . . .

We have waited for more than 340 years for our constitutional and God-given rights . . . . But when you have seen vicious mobs lynch your mothers and fathers at will and drown your sisters and brothers at whim; when you have seen hate-filled policemen curse, kick and even kill your black brothers and sisters; when you see the vast majority of your twenty million Negro brothers smothering in an airtight cage of poverty in the midst of an affluent society; when you suddenly find your tongue twisted and your speech stammering as you seek to explain to your six-year-old daughter why she can't go to the public amusement park that has just been advertised on television, and see tears welling up in her eyes when she is told that Funtown is closed to colored children; . . . when you have to concoct an answer for a five-year-old son who is asking "Daddy, why do white people treat colored people so mean?"; when you take a cross-country drive and find it necessary to sleep night after night in the uncomfortable corners of your automobile because no motel will accept you; when you are humiliated day in and day out by nagging signs reading "white" and "colored"; when your first name becomes "nigger," and your middle name becomes "boy" (however old you are) and your last name becomes "John," and your wife and mother are never given the respected title "Mrs."; . . . when you are forever fighting a degenerating sense of "nobodiness"— then you will understand why we find it difficult to wait. . . .

I must make two honest confessions to you, my Christian and Jewish brothers. First, I must confess that over the past few years I have been gravely disappointed with the white moderate. I have almost reached the regrettable conclusion that the Negro's great stumbling block in his stride toward freedom is not the White Citizen's Counciler or the Ku Klux Klanner, but the white moderate, who is more devoted to "order" than to justice; who prefers a negative peace which is the absence of tension to a positive peace which is the presence of justice; who constantly says: "I agree with you in the goal you seek, but I cannot agree with your methods of direct action"; who paternalistically believes he can set the timetable for another man's freedom; who lives by a mythical concept of time and who constantly advises the Negro to wait for a "more convenient season." Shallow understanding from people of good will is more frustrating than absolute misunderstanding from people of ill will. Lukewarm acceptance is much more bewildering than outright rejection . . . .

Let me take note of my other major disap-pointment. I have been so greatly disappointed with the white church and its leadership. Of course, there are some notable exceptions. . . .

. . . But even if the church does not come to the aid of justice, I have no despair about the future. . . . We will reach the goal of freedom in Birmingham and all over the nation, because the goal of America is freedom. Abused and scorned though we may be, our destiny is tied up with America's destiny. Before the pilgrims landed at Plymouth, we were here. Before the pen of Jefferson etched the majestic words of the Declaration of Independence across the pages of History, we were here. For more than two centuries our forebears labored in this country without wages; they made cotton king. . . . If the inexpressible cruelties of slavery could not stop us, the opposition we now face will surely fail. . . .

One day the South will recognize its real heroes. They will be the James Merediths. . . . They will be old, oppressed, battered Negro women, symbolized in a seventy-two-year-old woman in Montgomery, Alabama, who rose up with a sense of dignity and with her people decided not to ride segregated buses, and who responded with ungrammatical profundity to one who inquired about her weariness "My feets is tired, but my soul is at rest." They will be the young high school and college students, the young ministers of the gospel and a host of their elders, courageously and nonviolently sitting in at lunch counters and willingly going to jail for conscience' sake. One day the South will know that when these disinherited children of God sat down at lunch counters, they were in reality standing up for what is best in the American dream and for the most sacred values in our Judeo-Christian heritage. . . .

. . . Let us all hope that the dark clouds of racial prejudice will soon pass away and the deep fog of misunderstanding will be lifted from our fear-drenched communities, and in some not too distant tomorrow the radiant stars of love and brotherhood will shine over our great nation with all their scintillating beauty.

Yours for the cause of Peace and Brotherhood,
Martin Luther King, Jr.

"Let Us Continue"

The New Frontier came to a sudden and violent end on November 22, 1963, when Lee Harvey Oswald assassinated John F. Kennedy during a motorcade in downtown Dallas. The shock of losing the young President, who had become a symbol of hope and promise for a whole generation, stunned the entire world. The American people were bewildered by the rapid sequence of events: the brutal killing of their beloved President; the televised slaying of Oswald by Jack Ruby in the basement of the Dallas police station; the heroic behavior of Kennedy's widow, Jacqueline, at the ensuing state funeral; and the hurried Warren Commission report, which identified Oswald as the lone assassin. Afterward critics would charge that Oswald had been part of a vast conspiracy, but at the time the prevailing national reaction was a numbing sense of loss.

Vice-President Lyndon B. Johnson moved quickly to fill the vacuum left by Kennedy's death. Sworn in on board Air Force One as he returned to Washington, he soon met with a stream of world leaders to reassure them of American political stability. Five days after the tragedy in Dallas, Johnson spoke eloquently to a special joint session of Congress. Recalling JFK's summons in his inaugural address, "Let us begin," the new President declared. "Today in the moment of new resolve, I would say to all my fellow Americans, 'let us continue.'" Asking Congress to enact Kennedy's tax and civil-rights bills as a tribute to the fallen leader, LBJ concluded, "Let us here highly resolve that John Fitzgerald Kennedy did not live or die in vain."

Johnson in Action

Lyndon Johnson suffered from the inevitable comparison with his young and stylish predecessor. LBJ was acutely aware of his own lack of education and polish; he sought to surround himself with Kennedy advisers and insiders, hoping that their learning and sophistication would rub off on him. Johnson's assets were very real—an intimate knowledge of Congress, an incredible energy and determination to succeed, and a fierce ego. When a young marine officer tried to direct him to the proper helicopter, saying, "This one is

■ *Aboard Air Force One on the return from Dallas to Washington, D.C., Judge Sarah Hughes administers the presidential oath of office to Lyndon Johnson. His wife and JFK's widow look on.*

■ *Moments after this photograph was taken in the Dallas police headquarters, accused presidential assassin Lee Harvey Oswald was fatally shot.*

yours," Johnson replied, "Son, they are all my helicopters."

LBJ's height and intensity gave him a powerful presence; he dominated any room he entered, and he delighted in using his physical power of persuasion. One Texas politician explained why he had given in to Johnson: "Lyndon got me by the lapels and put his face on top of mine and he talked and talked and talked. I figured it was either getting drowned or joining."

Yet LBJ found it impossible to project his intelligence and vitality to large audiences. Unlike Kennedy, he wilted before the camera, turning his televised speeches into stilted and awkward performances. Trying to belie his reputation as a riverboat gambler, he came across like a foxy grandpa, clever and calculating and not to be trusted. He lacked Kennedy's wit and charm, and reporters delighted in describing the way he berated his aides or shocked the nation by baring his belly to show the scar from a recent operation.

Whatever his shortcomings in style, however, Johnson possessed far greater ability than Kennedy in dealing with Congress. He entered the White House with more than thirty years experience in Washington as legislative aide, congressman, and senator. His encyclopedic knowledge of the legislative process and his shrewd manipulation of individual senators had enabled him to become the most influential Senate majority leader in history. Famed for "the Johnson treatment," a legendary ability to use personal persuasion to gain his goals, Johnson in fact relied more on his close ties with the Senate's power brokers —or "whales," as he called them—than on his exploitation of the "minnows."

Above all, Johnson sought consensus. Indifferent to ideology, he had moved easily from New Deal liberalism to oil-and-gas conservatism as his career advanced. He had carefully cultivated Richard Russell of Georgia, leader of the Dixie bloc, but he also had taken Hubert Humphrey, a Minnesota liberal, under his wing. He had performed a balancing act on civil rights, working with the Eisenhower administration on behalf of the 1957 Voting Rights Act, yet carefully weakening it to avoid alienating southern Democrats. When Kennedy dashed Johnson's own intense presidential ambitions in 1960, LBJ had gracefully agreed to be his running mate and had endured the humiliation of the vice-presidency loyally

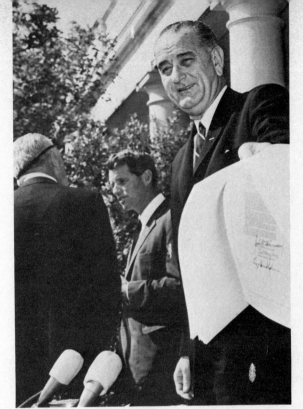

■ *LBJ was very successful at persuading Congress to enact the legislation he favored. Here he holds the signed bill authorizing his "war on poverty."*

and silently. Suddenly thrust into power, Johnson used his gifts wisely. Citing his favorite scriptural passage from Isaiah, "Come now, and let us reason together, saith the Lord," he concentrated on securing passage of Kennedy's tax and civil-rights bills in 1964.

The tax cut came first. Aware of the power wielded by Senate Finance Committee Chairman Harry Byrd, a Virginia conservative, Johnson astutely lowered Kennedy's projected $101.5-billion budget for 1965 to $97.9 billion. Although Byrd voted against the tax cut, he let the measure out of his committee, telling Johnson, "I'll be working for you behind the scenes." In February, Congress reduced personal income taxes by more than $10 billion, touching off a sustained economic boom. Consumer spending increased by an impressive $43 billion in the next eighteen months, and new jobs opened up at the rate of one million a year.

Johnson was even more influential in passing the Kennedy civil-rights measure. Staying in the background, he encouraged liberal amendments that strengthened the bill in the House. With Hubert Humphrey leading the floor fight in the Senate, Johnson refused all efforts at compromise, counting on growing public pressure to force northern Republicans to abandon their traditional alliance with southern Democrats. Everett M. Dirksen of Illinois, the GOP leader in the Senate, met repeatedly with Johnson at the White House. When LBJ refused to yield, Dirksen finally announced, "The time has come for equality of opportunity in sharing in government, in education, and in employment," and led a Republican vote to end a fifty-seven-day filibuster.

The 1964 Civil Rights Act, signed on July 2, made illegal the segregation of blacks in public facilities, established a Fair Employment Practices Committee to lessen racial discrimination in employment, and protected the voting rights of blacks. An amendment sponsored by segregationists in an effort to weaken the bill added sex to the prohibition of discrimination in Title VII of the act; in the future, women's groups would use this clause to secure government support for greater equality in employment and education.

The Election of 1964

Passage of two key Kennedy measures within six months did not satisfy Johnson. Having established the theme of continuity, he now set out to win the presidency in his own right. Eager to surpass Kennedy's narrow victory in 1960, he hoped to win by a great landslide.

Searching for a cause of his own, LBJ found one in the issue of poverty. Beginning in the late 1950s, economists had warned that the prevailing affluence only disguised a persistent and deep-seated problem of poverty. John Kenneth Galbraith had urged a policy of increased public spending to help the poor, but Kennedy ignored Galbraith's advice. In 1962, however, Michael Harrington's book *The Other America* attracted national attention. Writing with passion and eloquence, Harrington claimed that nearly one fifth of the nation, some thirty-five million Americans, lived in poverty.

Three groups predominated among the poor—blacks, the aged, and households headed by women. The problem, Harrington contended, was that the poor were invisible, living in slums or

depressed areas like Appalachia and cut off from the educational facilities, medical care, and employment opportunities afforded more affluent Americans. Moreover, poverty was a vicious cycle. The children of the poor were trapped in the same culture of poverty as their parents, living without hope or knowledge of how to enter the mainstream of American life.

Johnson quickly took over proposals that Kennedy had been developing and made them his own. In his State of the Union address in January 1964, LBJ announced, "This administration, today, here and now, declares unconditional war on poverty in America." Over the next eight months, Johnson fashioned a comprehensive poverty program under the direction of R. Sargent Shriver, Kennedy's brother-in-law. The President added $500 million to existing programs to come up with a $1-billion effort which Congress passed in August 1964.

The new Office of Economic Opportunity (OEO) set up a wide variety of programs, ranging from Head Start for preschoolers to the Job Corps for high-school dropouts in need of vocational training. The emphasis was on self-help, with the government providing money and know-how so that the poor could reap the benefits of neighborhood day-care centers, consumer-education classes, legal-aid services, and adult remedial-reading programs. The level of funding was never high enough to meet the OEO's ambitious goals, and a controversial attempt to include representatives of the poor in the Community Action Program led to bitter political feuding with city and state officials. Nonetheless, the war on poverty, along with the economic growth provided by the tax cut, helped reduce the ranks of the poor by nearly ten million between 1964 and 1967.

For Johnson, the new program established his reputation as a reformer in an election year. He still faced two obstacles. The first was Robert F. Kennedy, the late president's brother who continued as attorney general but who wanted to become vice-president and Johnson's eventual successor in the White House. Desperate to prove his ability to succeed without Kennedy help, LBJ commented, "I don't need that little runt to win," and chose Hubert Humphrey as his running mate.

The other hurdle was the Republican candidate, Senator Barry Goldwater, an outspoken con-

Among those whom LBJ hoped would benefit from the war on poverty were people like Tom Fletcher, an unemployed sawmill worker, and his eight children, shown here (left) greeting the President and Lady Bird. LBJ's declaration of war on poverty soon turned into a blueprint for the "Great Society," an ambitious plan for social improvement that included such projects as the Head Start program (bottom left) and the Job Corps (below).

servative from Arizona. An attractive and articulate man, Goldwater openly advocated a rejection of the welfare state and a return to unregulated free enterprise. To Johnson's delight, Goldwater chose to place ideology ahead of political expediency. The senator spoke out boldly against the Tennessee Valley Authority, denounced Social Security, and advocated a hawkish foreign policy. "In Your Heart, You Know He's Right," read the Republican slogan, leading the Democrats to reply, "Yes, Far Right," and in reference to a careless Goldwater comment about using nuclear weapons, Johnson backers punned, "In Your Heart, You Know He Might."

Johnson stuck carefully to the middle of the road, embracing the liberal reform program—which he now called "The Great Society"—while stressing his concern for balanced budgets and fiscal orthodoxy. The more Goldwater sagged in the polls, the harder Johnson campaigned, determined to achieve his treasured landslide. On election day, LBJ did even better than FDR had in 1936, taking 61.1 percent of the popular vote and sweeping the electoral college; Goldwater carried only Arizona and five states of the Deep South.

first year," he told an aide. "Doesn't matter what kind of majority you come in with. You've got just one year when they treat you right, and before they start worrying about themselves."

Johnson gave two traditional Democratic reforms—health care and education—top priority. Aware of strong opposition to a comprehensive medical program, LBJ settled for Medicare, which mandated health insurance under the Social Security program for Americans over age sixty-five, with a supplementary Medicaid program for the indigent. To symbolize the end of a long struggle, Johnson flew to Independence, Missouri, so that Truman could witness the ceremonial signing of the Medicare law.

LBJ overcame the religious hurdle on education by supporting a child-benefit approach, allocating federal money to advance the education of students in parochial as well as public schools. The Elementary and Secondary Education Act of 1965 provided over $1 billion in federal aid, with the largest share going to school districts with the highest percentage of impoverished pupils. During his administration, federal aid to education increased sharply.

The Election of 1964

Candidate	Party	Popular Vote	Electoral Vote
Johnson	Democrat	43,126,584	486
Goldwater	Republican	27,177,838	52

Equally important, the Democrats achieved huge gains in Congress, controlling the House by a margin of 295 to 140 and the Senate by 68 to 32. Kennedy's legacy and Goldwater's candor had enabled Johnson to break the conservative grip on Congress for the first time in a quarter of a century.

The Triumph of Reform

LBJ moved quickly to secure his legislative goals. Despite solid majorities in both Houses, including seventy freshman Democrats who had ridden into office on his coattails, Johnson knew he would have to enact the Great Society as swiftly as possible. "You've got to give it all you can, that

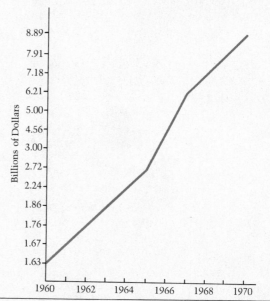

Federal Aid to Education, 1960–1970

Source: Compiled from U.S. Bureau of the Census, Historical Statistics of the United States, Colonial Times to 1970, Bicentennial Edition, Washington, D.C., 1975.

Civil rights proved to be the most difficult test of Johnson's leadership. Martin Luther King, concerned that three million southern blacks were still denied the right to vote, in early 1965 chose Selma, Alabama, as a test case. The white authorities in Selma, led by Sheriff James Clark, used cattle prods and bullwhips to break up the demonstrations and jailed over two thousand blacks. Johnson intervened in March, after TV cameras showed Sheriff Clark's deputies brutally halting a march from Selma to Montgomery. The President ordered the Alabama National Guard to federal duty to protect the demonstrators, had the Justice Department draw up a new voting-rights bill, and personally addressed the Congress on civil rights. "I speak tonight for the dignity of man and the destiny of democracy," he began. Calling the denial of the right to vote "deadly wrong," LBJ issued a compelling call to action. "Their cause must be our cause too. Because it is not just Negroes, but really it is all of us who must overcome the crippling legacy of bigotry and injustice."

Five months later, Congress passed the Voting Rights Act of 1965. Once again Johnson had worked with Senate Republican leader Dirksen to break a southern filibuster and assure passage of a measure. The act banned literacy tests in states and counties in which less than half the population had voted in 1964 and provided for federal registrars in these areas to assure blacks the franchise.

The results were dramatic. In less than a year, 166,000 blacks were added to the voting rolls in Alabama, while black registration went up 400 percent in Mississippi. By the end of the decade, the percentage of eligible black voters who had registered had risen from 40 to 65 percent. For the first time since Reconstruction, blacks were playing an active and effective role in southern politics.

Before the Eighty-ninth Congress ended its first session in the fall of 1965, it had passed eighty-nine bills. These included measures to create two new cabinet departments (Transportation, and Housing and Urban Affairs); acts to provide for highway safety and to ensure clean air and water; and large appropriations for higher education, public housing, and the continuing war on poverty. In nine months, Johnson had enacted the entire Democratic reform agenda, moving the nation beyond the New Deal by mandating federal concern for health, education, and the quality of life in both city and countryside.

The man responsible for this great leap forward, however, had failed to win the public adulation he so deeply desired. His legislative skills had made the most of the opportunities offered by the 1964 Democratic landslide, but the people did not respond to Johnson's leadership with the warmth and praise they had showered on Kennedy. Reporters continued to portray him as a crude wheeler-dealer; as a maniac who drove around Texas back roads at ninety miles an hour, one hand on the wheel and the other holding a glass of beer; or as a bully who picked up his dog by the ears. No one was more aware of this lack of affection than LBJ himself. His public support, he told an aide, is "like a Western river, broad but not deep." Tragically, Johnson was right. When foreign-policy problems soon eroded his popularity, few remembered his remarkable legislative achievements. Yet in one brief outburst of reform, he had accomplished more than any president since FDR.

All the Way with LBJ

Lyndon Johnson's strengths as a legislative leader were offset by his liabilities in foreign policy. LBJ had no background or feeling for international affairs. Even more than in domestic policy, he relied heavily on Kennedy's advisers—notably Secretary of State Rusk, Secretary of Defense McNamara, and McGeorge Bundy (the national security adviser until he was replaced in 1966 by the even more hawkish Walt Rostow).

Despite his lack of experience in world affairs, Johnson brought deeply held beliefs to bear on diplomatic problems. "What I learned as a boy in my teens and in college about World War I was that it was our lack of strength and failure to show stamina," he told biographer Doris Kearns, "that got us into that war." Watching the failure of isolation and appeasement in the 1930s only reinforced his conviction—shared by his generation—that war came from weakness, not from strength. He had also seen the devastating political impact of the Communist triumph in China on the Democratic party in the 1940s. "I am not going to lose Vietnam," he told the American ambassador to Saigon just after taking office in 1963. "I am not going to be the President who saw Southeast Asia go the way China went."

Aware of the problem Castro had caused John Kennedy, LBJ moved firmly to contain communism in the Western Hemisphere. When a military junta overthrew a leftist regime in Brazil, Johnson offered covert aid and open encouragement. He was equally forceful in compelling Panama to restrain rioting aimed at the continued American presence in the Canal Zone.

In 1965, to block the possible emergence of a Castro-type government, LBJ sent twenty thousand American troops to the Dominican Republic. Johnson's flimsy justification—ranging from the need to protect American tourists to a dubious list of suspected Communists among the rebel leaders—served only to alienate liberal critics in the United States, particularly Senate Foreign Relations Committee Chairman William Fulbright, a former Johnson favorite. The intervention ended in 1966 with the election of a conservative government. Senator Fulbright, however, continued his criticism of Johnson's foreign policy by publishing *The Arrogance of Power*, a biting analysis of the fallacies of containment. Fulbright's defection symbolized a growing gap between the President and liberal intellectuals; the more LBJ struggled to uphold the traditional Cold War policies he had inherited from Kennedy, the more he found himself under attack from Congress, the media, and the universities.

The Vietnam Dilemma

The situation in Vietnam plagued Johnson from the outset. He took office only three weeks after the coup that had removed Diem and left a vacuum of power. In 1964, seven different governments ruled South Vietnam; there were three governments within one month. According to an American officer, the atmosphere in Saigon "fairly smelled of discontent," with "workers on strike, students demonstrating, [and] the local press pursuing a persistent campaign of criticism of the new government." Resisting pressure from the Joint Chiefs of Staff for direct American military involvement, LBJ simply continued Kennedy's policy of economic and technical assistance. He sent in seven thousand more military

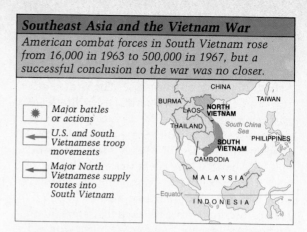

Southeast Asia and the Vietnam War

American combat forces in South Vietnam rose from 16,000 in 1963 to 500,000 in 1967, but a successful conclusion to the war was no closer.

* Major battles or actions
* U.S. and South Vietnamese troop movements
* Major North Vietnamese supply routes into South Vietnam

advisers and an additional $50 million in aid, but he insisted it was still up to the Vietnamese themselves to win the war. At the same time, he expanded American support for covert operations, including amphibious raids on the North.

These undercover activities led directly to the

Gulf of Tonkin affair. On August 2, 1964, North Vietnamese torpedo boats attacked the *Maddox*, an American destroyer engaged in electronic intelligence-gathering in the Gulf of Tonkin, in the mistaken belief that the American ship had been involved in a South Vietnamese raid nearby. The *Maddox* escaped unscathed, but to show American resolve, the navy sent in another destroyer, the *C. Turner Joy*. On the evening of August 4, the two destroyers, responding to sonar and radar contacts, opened fire on North Vietnamese gunboats in the area. Later investigation suggested that the North Vietnamese gunboats had not attacked the American ships, but Johnson ordered retaliatory air strikes on North Vietnamese naval bases.

The next day the President asked Congress to pass a resolution authorizing him to take "all necessary measures to repel any armed attack against the forces of the United States and to prevent further aggression." He did not in fact need this authority; he had already ordered the retaliatory air strike without it. Later, critics charged that LBJ wanted a blank check from Congress to carry out the future escalation of the Vietnam War, but such a motive is unlikely. He had already rejected immediate military intervention. In part, he wanted the Gulf of Tonkin Resolution to demonstrate to North Vietnam the American determination to defend South Vietnam at any cost. "The challenge we face in Southeast Asia today," he told Congress, "is the same challenge that we have faced with courage and that we have met with strength in Greece and Turkey, in Berlin and Korea . . . ." He also wanted to preempt the Vietnam issue from his Republican opponent, Barry Goldwater, who had been advocating a tougher policy. By taking a firm stand on the Gulf of Tonkin incident, Johnson could both impress the North Vietnamese and outmaneuver a political rival at home.

Congress responded with alacrity. The House acted unanimously, while only two senators (Wayne Morse of Oregon and Ernest Gruening of Alaska) voted against the Gulf of Tonkin Resolution. Johnson appeared to have won a spectacular victory. His standing in the Gallup poll shot up from 42 to 72 percent, and he had effectively blocked Goldwater from exploiting Vietnam as a campaign issue.

In the long run, however, this easy victory

"Only Thing We're Sure Of—There Is a Tonkin Gulf!"

Courtesy Bill Canfield-Star Ledger (Newark) 1968

■ *Although the Gulf of Tonkin Resolution won the nearly unanimous approval of Congress, Johnson's action drew harsh criticism later.*

proved very costly. Once having used force against North Vietnam, LBJ was more likely to do so in the future. And although he apparently had no intention of widening the conflict in August 1964, the congressional resolution was phrased broadly enough to enable him to use whatever level of force he wished—including unlimited military intervention. Above all, when he did wage war in Vietnam, he left himself open to the charge of deliberately misleading Congress. Presidential credibility proved to be Johnson's ultimate Achilles' heel; in that sense, his political downfall began with the Gulf of Tonkin Resolution.

Escalation

The full-scale American involvement in Vietnam began in 1965 in a series of steps designed primarily to prevent a North Vietnamese victory. With the political situation in Saigon growing more hopeless every day, the President's advisers urged

Although the United States conducted thousands of air strikes over North Vietnam and committed half a million troops to the South, it failed to win the advantage. North Vietnamese and Viet Cong continued to disappear silently into the dense foliage of the jungle after surprise attacks. Bill Mauldin depicts Johnson's two options—all-out war or complete pullout—as equally precarious.

the bombing of the North as the only conceivable solution. American air attacks would serve several purposes: they would block North Vietnamese infiltration routes, make Hanoi pay a heavy price for its role, and lift the sagging morale of the South Vietnamese. But most important, as Mc-George Bundy reported after a visit to Pleiku (site of a Viet Cong attack on an American base which took nine lives), "Without new U.S. action defeat appears inevitable—probably not in a matter of weeks or perhaps even months, but within the next year or so." Johnson responded in February 1965 by ordering a long-planned aerial bombardment of selected North Vietnamese targets.

The air strikes, aimed at impeding the Communist supply line and damaging Hanoi's economy, proved ineffective. In April, Johnson authorized the use of American ground forces in South Vietnam, but he restricted them to defensive operations intended to protect American air bases. The Joint Chiefs, as well as civilian advisers like Walt Rostow, then pressed the President for both unlimited bombing and an invasion of the North. Rejecting the clear-cut alternatives of withdrawal or the massive use of force, LBJ settled for a steady military escalation designed to compel Hanoi to accept a diplomatic solution. In July, the President permitted a gradual increase in

The Strategists

Bill Mauldin, The Sun Times. © 1966, Chicago Sun Times. Reproduced Courtesy of Wil-Jo Associates, Inc. & Bill Mauldin

the bombing of North Vietnam and allowed American ground commanders to conduct combat operations in the South. Most ominously, he approved the immediate dispatch of fifty thousand troops to Vietnam and the future commitment of fifty thousand more.

These July decisions formed "an open-ended commitment to employ American military forces as the situation demanded," writes historian George Herring, and they were "the closest thing to a formal decision for war in Vietnam." Convinced that withdrawal would destroy American credibility before the world and that an invasion of the North would lead to World War III, Johnson opted for large-scale but limited military intervention. Moreover, LBJ feared the domestic consequences of either extreme. A pullout could cause a massive political backlash at home, as conservatives condemned him for betraying South Vietnam to communism. All-out war, however, would mean the end of his social programs. Once Congress focused on the conflict, he explained to biographer Doris Kearns, "that bitch of a war" would destroy "the woman I really loved—the Great Society." So he settled for a limited war, committing a half-million American troops to battle in Southeast Asia, all the while pretending it was a minor engagement and refusing to ask the American people for the support and sacrifice required for victory.

Lyndon Johnson was not solely responsible for the Vietnam War. He inherited both a policy that assumed that Vietnam was a vital national interest and a deteriorating situation in Saigon that demanded a more active American role. Truman, Eisenhower, and Kennedy had taken the United States deep into the Vietnam maze; it was Johnson's fate to have to find a way out. But LBJ must bear full responsibility for the way he tried to resolve his dilemma. The failure to confront the people with the stark choices they faced, the insistence on secrecy and deceit, the refusal to acknowledge that he had committed the nation to a dangerous military involvement—these were Johnson's sins in Vietnam. His own lack of self-confidence in foreign policy and his fear of domestic reaction led directly to his undoing.

In retrospect, 1965 marks a watershed in recent American history. It was the year that saw the culmination of the reform impulse with the

Chronology

1960 John F. Kennedy narrowly wins presidential election

1961 JFK establishes Peace Corps (March)
U.S.-backed Bay of Pigs invasion crushed by Cubans (April)
JFK commits U.S. to landing a man on the moon by 1969 (May)

1962 James Meredith is first black to enroll at University of Mississippi (September)
Cuban missile crisis takes world to brink of nuclear war (October)

1963 United States, Great Britain, and USSR sign Limited Nuclear Test Ban Treaty (August)
JFK assassinated; Lyndon B. Johnson sworn in as president (November)

1964 President Johnson declares war on poverty (January)
Congress passes Civil Rights Act (July)
Congress overwhelmingly passes Gulf of Tonkin Resolution (August)
Johnson wins presidency in landslide victory (November)

1965 Martin Luther King, Jr., leads Selma-Montgomery march (March)
Medicare legislation provides aged with medical care (July)
LBJ commits 50,000 American troops to combat in Vietnam (July)
Johnson signs Voting Rights Act (August)
184,300 U.S. troops fighting in Vietnam (December)

greatest outpouring of welfare legislation since the New Deal. But it was also the year which saw the policy of global containment reach its fullest expression in the jungles of Southeast Asia. Lyndon Johnson set out to fulfill the mandate he had inherited from John Kennedy—to enact a stalled reform program and halt any Communist advance abroad. The tragedy of Lyndon Johnson was not that he ignored his obligations, but that he attempted to carry them out, only to find that his efforts did not bring him the acclaim and stature that he so desperately wanted.

For the American people, 1965 ushered in a new era of turmoil and unrest. The traditional reliance on government action to achieve greater affluence and wider opportunities for all Americans gave way to a rejection of liberalism by both the left and the right. The search for order abroad provoked an even angrier reaction, and Vietnam became a symbol of national humiliation and shame. The years after 1965 would find the nation seeking new political values to replace those shattered under Kennedy and Johnson. It would prove to be a long and difficult quest.

Recommended Reading

The best general treatment of the political and diplomatic trends of the 1960s is Jim F. Heath, *Decade of Disillusionment* (1975), which stresses the continuity in policy between the Kennedy and Johnson administrations. The debate over the merits of Kennedy's performance in the White House is reflected in Arthur M. Schlesinger, Jr., *A Thousand Days* (1965), a highly laudatory view by a JFK partisan, and in Bruce Miroff, *Pragmatic Illusions* (1976), which offers a radical critique of both foreign and domestic aspects of the New Frontier. By far the most complete and analytical study of Kennedy's foreign policy is Roger Hilsman, *To Move a Nation* (1967), which is particularly strong on Vietnam and the Cuban missile crisis.

Eric Goldman has provided the most comprehensive account of the Johnson administration in *The Tragedy of Lyndon Johnson* (1969). Like Schlesinger, Goldman writes both as historian and White House insider, but he balances his sympathetic treatment of the Great Society with a critical view of LBJ's foreign policy. Another insider, Harry McPherson, offers a candid portrait of Johnson both as Senate majority leader and president in *A Political Education* (1972). For the Vietnam War, the most balanced and reliable survey is George Herring, *America's Longest War* (1979).

Additional Bibliography

Kennedy's career before he became president is discussed in James MacGregor Burns, *John Kennedy*, 2d ed. (1961); Joan Blair and Clay Blair, Jr., *The Search for JFK* (1976); and Herbert Parmet, *Jack* (1980). Favorable evaluations of the Kennedy presidency include Theodore Sorenson, *Kennedy* (1965); Benjamin Bradlee, *Conversations with Kennedy* (1975); and Lewis J. Paper, *The Promise and the Performance* (1975). For a more critical view, see Henry Fairlie, *The Kennedy Promise* (1973) and Garry Wills, *The Kennedy Imprisonment* (1981), the latter dealing with Robert and Edward Kennedy as well. The best-balanced account is Herbert Parmet, *JFK: The Presidency of John F. Kennedy* (1983). William Manchester, *Death of a President* (1967), gives the standard view of JFK's assassination; the best of the many dissenting accounts is Edward J. Epstein, *Inquest* (1966).

British journalist Louis Heren offers an objective and lucid survey of the Johnson presidency in *No Hail, No Farewell* (1970). Other books on LBJ include the president's memoirs, *The Vantage Point* (1971); Robert Novak and Rowland Evans, *Lyndon B. Johnson* (1966); Doris Kearns, *Lyndon Johnson and the American Dream* (1976); Merle Miller, *Lyndon* (1980); and two books that focus on his Texas background, Alfred Steinberg, *Sam Johnson's Boy* (1965) and Ronnie Dugger, *The Politician* (1982). The most detailed account of Johnson's early career is Robert Caro's critical volume *The Path to Power* (1982); for a briefer but more astute assessment of Johnson's complex character, see George Reedy, *Lyndon Johnson: A Memoir* (1982). Robert A. Divine, ed., *Exploring the Johnson Years* (1981) contains seven essays surveying major themes of the Johnson administration.

For political developments in the first half of the sixties, see Theodore White, *The Making of the President* (1961), the first in a series of election books; Sidney Kraus, *The Great Debates* (1962) on the Nixon-Kennedy TV debates; and two memoirs by prominent Democrats, Larry O'Brien, *No Final Victories* (1974) and Hubert H. Humphrey, *The Education of a Public Man* (1976).

Books on economic developments include Seymour Harris, *Economics of the Kennedy Years* (1964); Hobart Rowen, *The Free Enterprisers* (1964); and Jim F. Heath, *John F. Kennedy and the Business Community* (1969). Among studies of the Supreme Court are Alexander Bickel, *Politics and the Warren Court* (1965); Richard C. Cortner, *The Apportionment Cases* (1970); Anthony Lewis, *Gideon's Trumpet* (1965); and G. Edward White, *Earl Warren* (1982).

Victor S. Navasky's account of Robert Kennedy as attorney general, *Kennedy Justice* (1971) is quite critical. More sympathetic books on the same topic are Arthur Schlesinger, Jr., *Robert Kennedy and His Times* (1976); Carl Brauer, *John F. Kennedy and the Second Reconstruction* (1977); and Harris Wofford, *Of Kennedys and Kings* (1980). For civil-rights developments under Johnson, consult Benjamin Muse, *The American Negro Revolution* (1969) and David Garrow, *Protest at Selma* (1976).

The Great Society, particularly in regard to welfare and the war on poverty, can be traced in John C. Donovan, *The Politics of Poverty* (1973); Gilbert Steiner, *The State of Welfare* (1971); Sar Levitan, *The Great Society's Poor Law* (1969); James T. Patterson, *America's Struggle Against Poverty* (1982); and Julie Roy Jeffrey, *Education for the Children of the Poor* (1976).

Kennedy's foreign policy is subjected to critical scrutiny in Richard J. Walton, *Cold War and Counterrevolution* (1972) and Louise FitzSimmons, *The Kennedy Doctrine* (1972). Philip Geyelin analyzes LBJ's foreign-policy weaknesses in *Lyndon B. Johnson and the World* (1966), while Walt W. Rostow defends both the Kennedy and Johnson records in *The Diffusion of Power* (1972). Concerning nuclear weapons in the 1960s, consult Michael Mandelbaum, *The Nuclear*

Question (1979); Desmond Ball, *Politics and Force Levels* (1981); and Harland B. Moulton, *Nuclear Superiority and Parity* (1972).

On Latin America, Theodore Draper, *Castro's Revolution* (1962); Peter Wyden, *The Bay of Pigs* (1979); Elie Abel, *The Missile Crisis* (1966); Robert F. Kennedy, *Thirteen Days* (1968); Graham Allison, *The Essence of Decision* (1971); and Herbert Dinerstein, *The Making of the Missile Crisis* (1976) all deal with aspects of the Cuban problem. Books on Johnson's intervention in the Dominican Republic include John B. Martin, *Overtaken by Events* (1966); Jerome Slater, *Intervention and Negotiation* (1970); Abraham Lowenthal, *The Dominican Intervention* (1972); and Piero Gleijeses, *The Dominican Crisis* (1976).

David Halberstam, *The Best and the Brightest* (1972) focuses on decision-making in Washington in regard to the Vietnam War. Other books on Vietnam are Neil Sheehan, ed., *The Pentagon Papers* (1971); Chester Cooper, *The Lost Crusade* (1970); Robert Shaplen, *The Lost Revolution* (1965); Leslie H. Gelb and Richard K. Betts, *The Irony of Vietnam* (1979); and two works on the Gulf of Tonkin incident, Joseph C. Goulden, *Truth Is the First Casualty* (1969) and Anthony Austin, *The President's War* (1971).

Biographies and memoirs relating to foreign policy include Warren Cohen, *Dean Rusk* (1980); Chester Bowles, *Promises to Keep* (1971); Glen T. Seaborg, *Kennedy, Khrushchev and the Test Ban* (1982); and Thomas Powers, *The Man Who Kept the Secrets* (1979), which uses the career of Richard Helms to illuminate the history of the CIA.

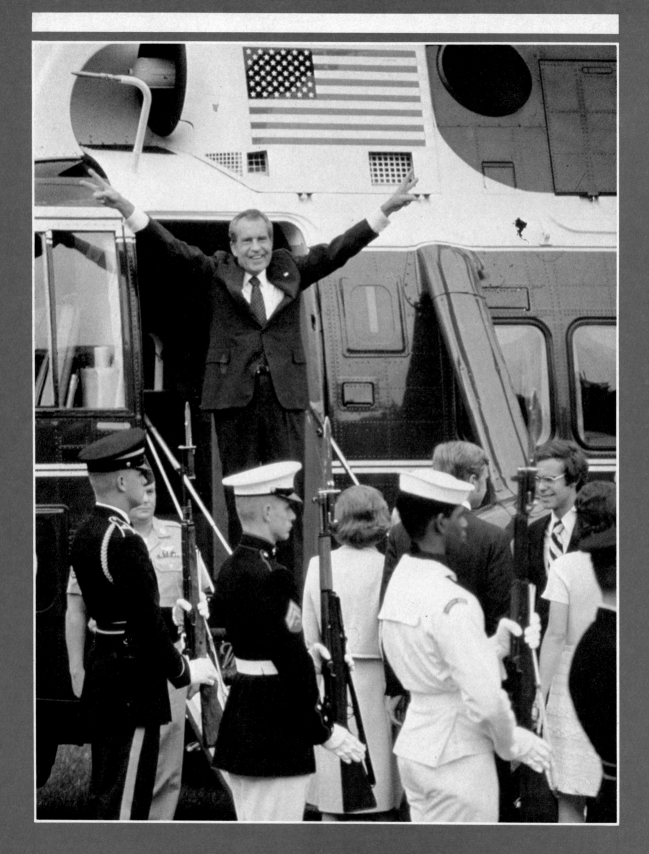

chapter 31

PROTEST AND REACTION: FROM VIETNAM TO WATERGATE

"We are the people of this generation, bred in at least modest comfort, housed now in universities, looking uncomfortably to the world we inherit." So began the preamble to the Port Huron Statement, a manifesto of the newly reorganized Students for a Democratic Society (SDS) that became the call to arms for an entire generation. Like most revolutions, this one began small. Only fifty-nine delegates attended the convention held at a union summer camp in Port Huron, Michigan, in June 1962. The two main organizers, Al Haber and Tom Hayden, recent graduates of the University of Michigan, hoped to transform their small student-protest group into the vehicle that would rid American society of poverty, racism, and violence.

Their timing was perfect. College enrollments were climbing rapidly as a result of the post-World War II baby boom and growing affluence. There were twenty-seven million young people between the ages of fourteen and twenty-four in 1960; before the end of the decade, more than half the American population would be under age thirty. And many, repelled by the crass materialism of American life—with its endless suburbs and shopping centers—were ready to embrace a new life-style based on the belief that "man is sensitive, searching, poetic, and capable of love." They were ready to create what Jack Newfield called "a new adversary culture based on community and psychic liberation. Drugs, rock music, underground papers, long hair, colorful dress and liberated sex," he explained, "are all part of it."

In some ways, the sixty-six-page proposal adopted at Port Huron was prosaic, repeating many conventional liberal reforms, such as expanded public housing and broader health-insurance programs. But it offered a startling new approach by advocating "participatory democracy" as its main tactic for social change. "We seek the establishment of a democracy of individual participation" in order to achieve two goals: "that the individual share in those social decisions determining the quality and direction of his life" and "that society be organized to encourage independence in men." In contrast to both traditional liberalism and old-fashioned socialism, the SDS sought salvation through the individual rather than the group. Personal control of one's life and destiny, not simply the creation of new bureaucracies, became the hallmark of the New Left.

In the next few years, the SDS grew phenomenally. The 10 original campus chapters swelled to 151 by 1966; the Port Huron Statement, despite its length, was distributed across the nation—20,000 copies by 1964; 40,000 two years later. Spurred on by the Vietnam War and massive campus unrest, the SDS could count more than 100,000 followers and was responsible for disruptions at nearly 1000 colleges in 1968. Yet its very emphasis on the individual and its fear of bureaucracy left it leaderless and subject to division and disunity. By 1970 a split between factions, some of which were given to violence, led to its complete demise.

The meteoric career of the SDS symbolized the turbulence of the 1960s. For a brief time, it seemed as though the nation's youth had gone berserk, indulging in a wave of experimentation with drugs, sex, and rock music. Older Americans felt that all the nation's traditional values, from the Puritan work ethic to the family, were under attack. In fact, only a minority of American youth joined in the cultural insurgency.

In small towns and among blue-collar workers in the cities, young people went to Friday-night high-school football games, cheered John Wayne as he wiped out the Viet Cong in the movie, *The Green Berets*, and attended church with their parents on Sunday. The rebellion was generally limited to children of the upper middle class, products of "economic surplus and spiritual starvation." But like the flappers of the 1920s, they set the tone for an entire era and left a lasting impression on American society.

Years of Turmoil

The agitation of the 1960s was at its height from 1965 to 1968, the years that marked the escalation of the Vietnam War. Disturbances that began on college campuses quickly spread to infect the entire society, from the ghettos of the cities to the lettuce fields of the Southwest. All who felt disadvantaged—students, blacks, browns, women, hippies—took to the streets to give vent to their feelings.

The Student Revolt

The first sign of student rebellion came in the fall of 1964 at the prestigious University of California at Berkeley. A small group of radical students resisted university efforts to deny them a place to solicit volunteers and funds for off-campus causes. Forming the Free Speech Movement (FSM), they struck back by occupying administration buildings and blocking the arrest of a nonstudent protester. For the next two months, the campus was in turmoil. The administration overreacted, calling in the police; the faculty, predictably, condemned the radicals' tactics but supported their goals; the rest of the student body, distraught at the size, complexity, and impersonality of the university, rallied behind the FSM.

In the end, the protesters won the rights of free speech and association that they championed, and youth everywhere had a new model for effective direct action. The hero was Mario Savio, a student who had eloquently summed up the cause by likening the university to a great machine and telling others "you've got to put your bodies upon the gears, and upon the wheels, upon the levers, upon all the apparatus, and you've got to make it stop."

The Free Speech Movement at Berkeley offered many insights into the causes of campus unrest. It was fueled in part by student suspicion of an older, Depression-born generation that viewed affluence as the answer to all problems. The catchword of the movement was coined by activist Jack Weinberg in the midst of the turmoil: "Don't trust anyone over thirty." Unable to exert much influence on the power structure that directed the consumer society, the students turned on the university, which they viewed as the faithful servant of the corporate and political elite as it trained hordes of technicians to operate the new computers, harbored the research laboratories that perfected dreadful weapons, and regimented its students with IBM punch cards. The feeling of powerlessness that underlay the Berkeley riots were best revealed by the protester carrying the sign that read, "I am a UC student. Please don't bend, fold, spindle or mutilate me."

War, racism, and poverty were the three great evils that student radicals addressed. Many were involved first in the civil-rights cause, but after

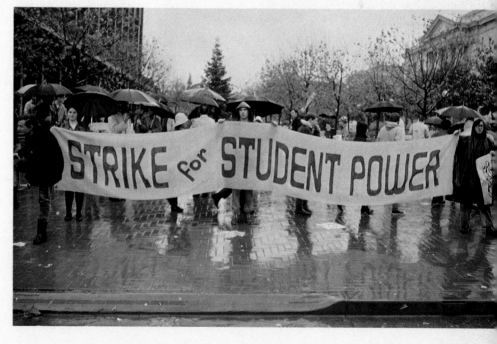

Powerless but determined to gain the "Establishment's" attention, the children of the upper middle class began their crusade against poverty, racism, and war by "taking it to the streets."

As outrage about Vietnam grew, the SDS was able to enlist the support of prominent entertainers like Joan Baez, shown here at a protest rally in Texas.

In a scene that was to be repeated countless times across the nation, unarmed protestors faced a cordon of army troops. This confrontation took place at the Pentagon in October 1967.

blacks began to take over the leadership in this area by 1965, white militants found a new issue—the Vietnam War. The first student teach-ins began at the University of Michigan in March 1965; soon they spread to campuses across the nation. More than twenty thousand protesters, under SDS auspices, gathered in Washington in April to listen to entertainers Joan Baez and Judy Collins sing antiwar songs and hear journalist I. F. Stone and Senator Ernest Gruening of Alaska, who voted against the Gulf of Tonkin Resolution, denounce Johnson's war. "End the War in Vietnam Now, Stop the Killing," read the signs.

As the fighting in Southeast Asia intensified in 1966 and 1967, the protests grew larger and the slogans more extreme. "Hey, Hey, LBJ, How Many Kids Have You Killed Today?" chanted students as they proclaimed, "Hell, No, We Won't Go!" At the Pentagon in October 1967, over one hundred thousand demonstrators—mainly students, but housewives, teachers, and young professionals as well—confronted a cordon of military policemen guarding the heart of the nation's war machine. From the windows above, Secretary of Defense McNamara and his generals looked down on the protesters. "The troops you employ belong to us and not to you," an SDS leader shouted up to them through his bullhorn. "They don't belong to the generals."

The climax came in the spring of 1968. Driven both by opposition to the war and concern for social justice, the SDS and black radicals at Columbia University joined forces in April. They seized five buildings, effectively paralyzing one of the country's leading colleges. After eight days of tension, the New York City police regained control. In the melee more than two hundred students were injured and seven hundred were arrested. The brutal repression quickened the pace of protest elsewhere. Students held sit-ins at more than forty colleges, ranging from Cheyney State in Pennsylvania to Northwestern in Illinois. Violent marches and arrests took place at sixty others.

The students failed to stop the war, but they did succeed in gaining a voice in their education. University administrations allowed undergraduates to sit on faculty committees to plan the curriculum and gave up their once rigid control of dormitory and social life. But the students' greatest impact lay outside politics and the campus.

They spawned a cultural uprising that transformed the manners and morals of America.

The Cultural Revolution

In contrast to the political revolt of the elitist SDS, the cultural rebellion by youth in the sixties was pervasive. Led by college students, young people challenged the prevailing adult values, in clothing, hairstyles, sexual conduct, work habits, and music. Blue jeans and love beads took the place of business suits and wristwatches; long hair and unkempt beards for men, bare feet and bralessness for women became the new uniform of protest. Families gave way to communes; once quiet and conservative neighborhoods like San Francisco's Haight-Ashbury district became havens for runaways and drug users, the "flower children" of the sixties.

Theorists quickly emerged to extol the new way of life. Theodore Roszak gloried in the rejection of modern science and technology in his influential book, *The Making of a Counter Culture* (1969). "In its place," he wrote, "there must be a new culture in which the non-intellective capacities of personality . . . become the arbiters of the true, the good and the beautiful." Yale law school professor Charles Reich portrayed the emergence of a new world of love, beauty, and racial harmony in his rhapsodic work, *The Greening of America* (1970). He dubbed the new society "Consciousness III." Herbert Marcuse, the visionary Marxist who became the guru of the new culture, called for people to overcome capitalist repression and live by an "aesthetic ethos."

Music became the touchstone of the new departure. Folk singers like Joan Baez and Bob Dylan, popular for their songs of social protest in the mid-sixties, gave way to rock groups such as the Beatles, whose lyrics were often suggestive of drug use, and finally to "acid rock" as symbolized by the Grateful Dead. The climactic event of the decade came at the Woodstock concert at Bethel in upstate New York when four hundred thousand young people indulged in a three-day orgy of rock music, drug experimentation, and public sexual activity.

Former Harvard psychology professor Timothy Leary encouraged youth to join him in trying out the drug scene. Millions accepted his invitation, "Tune in, turn on, drop out," literally, as they

The cultural revolution—and the challenge to adult values, life-styles, and standards of living—climaxed in August 1969 at the Woodstock music festival, billed as "Three Days of Peace and Music." Despite rainy weather, extreme shortages of food and water, and massive traffic jams, the three-day happening inspired idealistic visions of a "Woodstock nation."

experimented with marijuana and with LSD—a new and dangerous chemical hallucinogen. Yippie leader Jerry Rubin praised drugs for leading to "the total end of the Protestant ethic: screw work, we want to know ourselves."

The Yippies, led by Rubin and Abbie Hoffman, represented the ultimate expression of cultural insurgency. Shrewd buffoons who mocked the consumer culture, they delighted in capitalizing on the mood of social protest to win attention. Once, when testifying before a congressional committee investigating internal subversion, Rubin dressed as a revolutionary war soldier; Hoffman appeared in the gallery of the New York Stock Exchange in 1967, raining money down on the cheering brokers below. The Yippies succeeded in revealing the hypocrisy of American society, but in the process they fragmented the protest movement; serious radicals dismissed these so-called flower children as parasites.

Black Power

The civil-rights movement, which had spawned the mood of protest in the sixties, fell on hard times. The legislative triumphs of 1964 and 1965 were relatively easy victories over southern bigotry; now the movement faced the far more complex problem of achieving economic equality in the cities of the North, where more than half of the nation's blacks lived. Mired in poverty, crowded into ghettos from Harlem in New York City to Watts in Los Angeles, blacks had actually fallen further behind whites in disposable income since the beginning of the integration effort. The civil-rights movement had raised the expectations of urban blacks for improvement; frustration mounted as they failed to experience any significant economic gain.

The first sign of trouble came in the summer of 1964, when black teen-agers in Harlem and Rochester, New York, rioted. The next summer, a massive outburst of rage and destruction swept over Watts as the inhabitants burned buildings and looted stores. Riots in the summer of 1966 were less destructive, but in 1967 the worst ones yet took place in Newark and Detroit, where forty-three were killed and hundreds injured. The mobs attacked the shops and stores, expressing a burning grievance against a consumer society from which they were excluded by their poverty. One participant in the Detroit mayhem likened it to "an outing," with the whole family taking part. "The rebellion—it was caused by the commercials," he explained. "I mean you saw all those things you'd never been able to get—go out and get 'em. Men's clothing, furniture, appliances, color TV. All that crummy TV glamour just hanging out there."

The civil-rights coalition fell apart, a victim of both its legislative success and economic failure. Black militants took over the leadership of SNCC; they disdained white help and even reversed Martin Luther King's insistence on nonviolence. The split over tactics became public during a Mississippi Freedom March in 1966 in which King pleaded for a continuation of peaceful protest. SNCC's new leader, Stokely Carmichael, disagreed, telling blacks that they should seize power in those parts of the South where they outnumbered whites. "I am not going to beg the white man for anything I deserve," he said, "I'm going to take it." A few days later, in Greenwood, Mississippi, Carmichael raised the cry of "black power" to the cheers of six hundred marchers.

The slogan, which marked a radical change from King's call for peaceful integration of the races, caught on quickly. SNCC spoke of the need for blacks to form "our own institutions, credit unions, co-ops, political parties" and even write "our own history." Others went further than calls for ethnic separation. H. Rap Brown, who replaced Carmichael as the leader of SNCC in 1967, told a black crowd in Cambridge, Maryland, to "get your guns" and "burn this town down," while Huey Newton, one of the founders of the militant Black Panther party, proclaimed, "We make the statement, quoting from Chairman Mao, that Political Power comes through the Barrel of a Gun."

King suffered the most from this extremism. He tried to keep control of the civil-rights movement by leading a campaign for better housing for blacks in Chicago, only to meet with indifference from the ghetto-dwellers and bitter hostility from the city's political machine and working-class whites. His denunciation of the Vietnam War cost him the support of the Johnson administration and alienated him from the more conservative civil-rights groups like the NAACP and the Urban League. He finally seized on poverty as the proper

Summer in Detroit in 1967 was marred by violent riots, as black frustration peaked and looters grabbed the consumer goods they could not afford to buy.

enemy for attack, but before he could lead his Poor People's March on Washington in 1968, he was assassinated in Memphis in early April.

Both blacks and whites realized that the nation had lost its most eloquent spokesman for racial harmony. His tragic death elevated King to the status of a martyr, but it also led to one last outbreak of urban violence, as blacks exploded in Washington, D.C., burning buildings within a few blocks of the White House. "It was as if the city were being abandoned to an invading army," wrote a British journalist. "Clouds of smoke hung over the Potomac, evoking memories of the London blitz. . . ."

Yet there was a positive side to the emotions engendered by black nationalism. Spokesmen began to urge blacks to take pride in their ethnic heritage, to embrace their blackness as a positive value. Sales of hair-straighteners, long a staple in black barber and beauty shops, plummeted; blacks began to wear Afro hairstyles and dress in dashikis, stressing their African roots. Students began to demand new black-studies programs in the colleges; the word Negro—identified with white supremacy of the past—virtually disappeared from usage overnight, replaced by the favored Afro-American" or "black." Singer James Brown best expressed the sense of racial identity: "Say It Loud—I'm Black and I'm Proud."

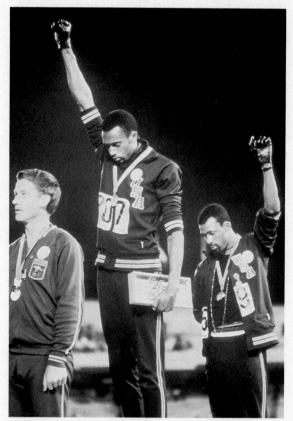

The world witnessed both pride and protest when 1968 Olympic medalists Tommie Smith (center) and John Carlos raised the black power salute during the national anthem.

897
Years of Turmoil

Ethnic Nationalism

Other groups quickly emulated the black phenomenon. American Indians decried the callous use of their identity as football mascots; in response, universities such as Stanford changed their symbols. Puerto Ricans demanded that their history be included in school and college texts. Polish, Italian, and Czech groups insisted on respect for their nationalities. Congress acknowledged these demands with passage of the Ethnic Heritage Studies Act of 1972. Instead of trying to melt all groups down into a standard American type, Congress now gave what one sponsor of the measure called "official recognition to ethnicity as a positive constructive force in our society today." Some $15 million was appropriated to subsidize ethnic-studies courses in schools and colleges across the nation.

Mexican-Americans were in the forefront of the ethnic groups that became active in the 1970s. The primary impulse came from the efforts of César Chávez to organize the poorly paid grape pickers and lettuce workers in California into the National Farm Workers Association (NFWA). Building on the earlier efforts of Filipinos, who had organized some field workers,

Chávez appealed to ethnic nationalism in mobilizing Mexican-American field hands to strike against grape growers in the San Joaquin Valley in 1965. The NFWA's main demand, a wage of $1.40 an hour, was relatively modest, but Chávez's techniques were more radical. Rallying Mexican farm workers with a red flag featuring a bold thunderbird (a cultural symbol), he soon won the attention of the media. A national boycott of grapes by Mexican-Americans and their sympathizers among the young people of the counterculture led to a series of hard-fought victories over the growers. The five-year struggle resulted in a union victory in 1970, but at an enormous cost—95 percent of the farm workers involved had lost their homes and their cars. Undaunted, Chávez turned next to the lettuce fields, and although he met with resistance from both the growers and the Teamster's Union, he succeeded in raising the hourly wage of farm workers in California to $3.53 by 1977 (it had been $1.20 in 1965).

Chávez's efforts helped spark an outburst of ethnic consciousness among Mexican-Americans that swept through the urban barrios of the Southwest. Aware that a majority of their compatriots were functionally illiterate as a result of language difficulties and inferior schools, Mexi-

Ethnic Identities

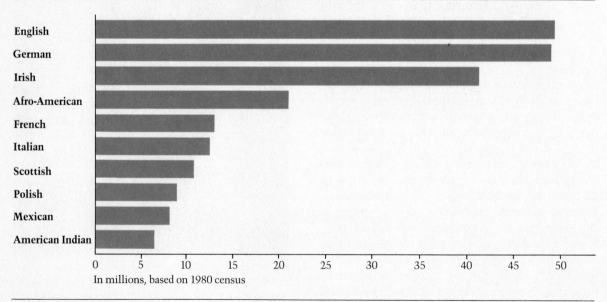

In millions, based on 1980 census

Source: U.S. Bureau of the Census

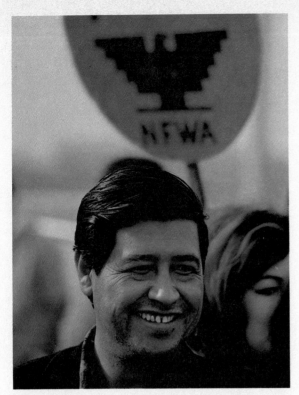

■ *By organizing successful strikes among the poorly paid grape and lettuce pickers in California, César Chávez sparked pride among Mexican-Americans.*

The Chicano movement had a broad cultural impact. In California and Texas, Mexican-Americans began forming paramilitary organizations known as the Brown Berets. This militancy led inevitably to suspicion and hostility on the part of whites as well as to police harassment, which served only to intensify the Brown Berets' radical stance. At the same time, other Chicanos succeeded in compelling the Frito-Lay Company to replace their Frito Bandito, a threatening cartoon character who stole corn chips, with Frito Amigo, who gave them away to children. A more significant cultural milestone came in 1967 with the founding of *El Grito: A Journal of Contemporary Mexican-American Thought* which published scholarly articles on Chicano history and culture.

Women's Liberation

Active as they were in the civil-rights and anti-war movements, women soon learned that the male leaders of these causes were little different from corporate executives—they expected women to fix the food and type the communiqués while the men made the decisions. Or as a protest leader once said in jest, "The position of women in our movement should be prone." Understandably, women soon realized that they could only achieve respect and equality by mounting their own protest.

In some ways, the position of women in American society was worse in the 1960s than it had been in the '20s. After forty years, there was a lower percentage of women enrolled in the nation's colleges and professional schools. There had been a great upsurge in female employment (nearly two thirds of all new jobs in the sixties went to women), but women with college degrees earned only half as much as similarly trained men. Women were still relegated to stereotyped occupations like nursing and teaching; there were few female lawyers and even fewer women doctors. And sex roles, as portrayed on television commercials, continued to call for the husband to be the breadwinner and the wife to be the homemaker.

Betty Friedan was the first to seize upon the sense of grievance and discrimination that developed among women in the 1960s. The beginning

can-American leaders campaigned for bilingual programs and improved educational opportunities. Young activists began to call themselves Chicanos, which had previously been a derogatory term, and to take pride in their cultural heritage; in 1968, they succeeded in establishing the first Mexican-American studies program at California State College at Los Angeles. Campus leaders called for reform, urging high-school students to insist on improvements. "If you are a student at Lincoln [high school] you should be angry!" declared activist Raúl Ruiz in 1967. "You should demand! You should protest! You should organize for better education! This is your right! This is your life!" Heeding such appeals, nearly ten thousand students at East Los Angeles high schools walked out of class in March 1968. These walkouts sparked similar movements in San Antonio, Texas, and Phoenix, Arizona, and led to significant reforms, such as the introduction of bilingual programs in grade schools and the hiring of more Chicano teachers at all levels.

of the effort to raise women's consciousness was her 1963 book, *The Feminine Mystique*. Calling the American home "a comfortable concentration camp," she attacked the prevailing view that women were completely contented with their housekeeping and child-rearing tasks, claiming that housewives had no self-esteem and no sense of identity. "I'm a server of food and putter on of pants and a bedmaker," a mother of four told Friedan, "somebody who can be called on when you want something. But who am I?"

Working Wives, 1960–1969	
Year	Percent (as percentage of all married women)
1960	31.7
1961	34.0
1962	33.7
1963	34.6
1964	35.3
1965	35.7
1966	36.5
1967	37.8
1968	39.1
1969	40.4

Source: Compiled from U.S. Bureau of the Census, Historical Statistics of the United States, Colonial Times to 1970, Bicentennial Edition, *Washington, D.C., 1975.*

The 1964 Civil Rights Act helped women attack economic inequality head-on by making it illegal to discriminate in employment on the basis of sex. Women filed suit for equal wages, demanded that companies provide day care for their infants and preschool children, and entered politics to lobby against laws which—in the guise of protection of a weaker sex—were unfair to women. As the women's liberation movement grew, its advocates began to attack laws banning abortion and waged a campaign to toughen the enforcement of rape laws. They even attacked the hallowed Miss America contest for its sexist tone.

The women's movement met with many of the same obstacles as other protest groups in the '60s. The moderate leadership of the National Organization of Women (NOW), founded by Betty Friedan in 1966, soon was challenged by those with more extreme views. Ti-Grace Atkinson and Susan Brownmiller attacked revered institutions

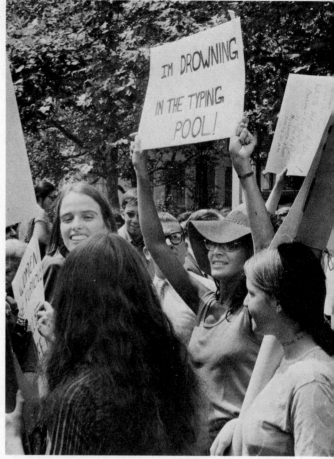

■ *In addition to real concerns about unequal wages and opportunities, many women felt suffocated and unfulfilled by their traditional roles in society.*

—the family and the home—and even denounced sexual intercourse with men because it is a method of male domination. Many women were repelled by the bra-burning and harsh rhetoric of the extremists and expressed satisfaction with their lives. "Where do they get the lunatic idea that women had rather work for a boss than stay home and run their own domain?" asked one female critic. But despite these disagreements, most women supported the effort to achieve equal status with men, and in 1972 Congress responded by approving the Equal Rights Amendment to the Constitution. This measure, first introduced in Congress in 1923, now could be voted on by state legislatures, the final step in the ratification process.

The Election of 1968

The turmoil of the sixties reached a crescendo in 1968 as the American people responded to the two dominant events of the decade—the war in Vietnam and the cultural insurgency at home. To add to the chaos, this election year witnessed a series of bizarre events, including two assassinations, the withdrawal from the race of an incumbent president, and the emergence of the most effective third-party candidate in fifty years.

Stalemate in Vietnam

The war in Southeast Asia cast a long shadow over the election of 1968. The escalation begun in 1965 had failed to produce the expected American victory. Bombing of the North proved ineffective, failing either to damage an essentially agrarian economy or to block the flow of supplies southward through Laos and Cambodia. In fact, the American air attacks, with their inadvertent civilian casualties, gave North Vietnam a powerful propaganda weapon which it used to sway world opinion against the United States.

The war in the South went no better. Despite the steady increase in American ground forces, from 184,000 in late 1965 to more than 500,000 by early 1968, the Viet Cong still controlled much of the countryside. The search-and-destroy tactics employed by the American commander, General William Westmoreland, proved ill-suited. The Viet Cong, aided by North Vietnamese regulars, were waging a war of insurgency, avoiding fixed positions and striking from ambush. In a vain effort to destroy the enemy, Westmoreland used superior American firepower wantonly, devastating the countryside, causing many civilian casualties, and driving the peasantry into the arms of the guerrillas.

The climax came in late January 1968 when the Viet Cong launched the Tet offensive. To mark the lunar New Year, the VC recklessly attacked the South Vietnamese cities and provincial capitals. American and government troops quickly beat back this bold assault, but at home television viewers were shocked by scenes of Viet Cong guerrillas fighting within the walls of the American embassy compound in Saigon. The outcome

■ *Despite LBJ's optimistic predictions that victory was at hand, by early 1968 it became apparent that American troops were trapped in a bloody stalemate.*

was a tactical defeat for the Communists but a decided political setback for the United States. President Johnson had been hammering away at the idea that the war was almost over; suddenly it appeared to be nearly lost. CBS-TV newscaster Walter Cronkite took a quick trip to Saigon to find out what had happened. Horrified at what he saw, he exclaimed to his guides, "What the hell is going on? I thought we were winning the war." He returned home to tell his audience, "It seems now more certain than ever that the bloody experience of Vietnam is to end in a stalemate."

President Johnson reluctantly came to the same conclusion after the Joint Chiefs of Staff requested an additional 205,000 men to achieve victory in Vietnam following the Tet offensive. He began to listen to his new secretary of defense, Clark Clifford, who replaced Robert McNamara in January 1968. In mid-March, after receiving advice from a group of experienced Cold Warriors, including such illustrious figures as Dean Acheson and McGeorge Bundy, the President decided to limit the bombing of North Vietnam in an effort to open up peace negotiations with Hanoi. In a speech to the nation on Sunday evening,

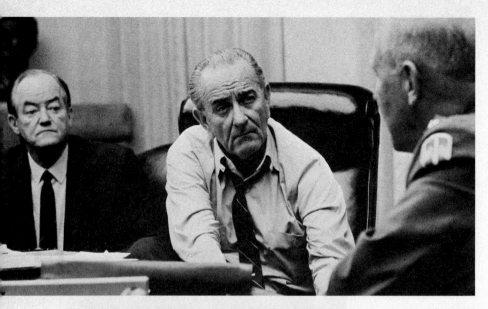

Besieged by the relentless hounding of demonstrators and respected commentators, the eroding support of political colleagues, and his personal agony over the continuing loss of American troops, a grim and exhausted LBJ meets with Westmoreland (right) and Hubert Humphrey, who remained publicly loyal despite his private misgivings.

■ In 1967 British cartoonist Leslie Illingworth showed LBJ caught in "The Time Machine," in which LBJ was fated to be ground down, despite his panic-striken and exhausting scramble.

March 31, 1968, Johnson outlined his plans for a new effort at ending the war peacefully, and then concluded by saying, as proof of his sincerity, "I shall not seek, and I will not accept, the nomination of my party for another term as your President." Thus a stunned nation learned that Lyndon Johnson had become the first major political casualty of the Vietnam War.

The Democrats Divide

Johnson's withdrawal had come in response to political as well as military realities. By 1966, the antiwar movement had spread from the college campuses to Capitol Hill. Former supporters such as Senator William Fulbright now began to question the conflict. Housewives and middle-class professionals began attending the antiwar rallies; respected commentators such as Walter Lippmann and Professor Hans Morgenthau came out against the Vietnam War as foolish and unproductive. Johnson began to feel like a prisoner in the White House, since in his infrequent public appearances he was hounded by larger and larger groups of antiwar demonstrators, whose taunts and jeers wounded him deeply.

The essentially leaderless protest against the war took on a new quality on January 3, 1968, when Senator Eugene McCarthy, a Democrat from Minnesota, announced that he was challenging LBJ for the party's presidential nomination. McCarthy at first seemed an unlikely candidate. A cool, aloof, almost arrogant intellectual, he was motivated primarily by a belief that Kennedy and Johnson had abused the power of the presidency. A devout Catholic, he raised the banner of idealism, telling audiences, "Whatever is morally necessary must be made politically possible."

It was his stance against the war, however, that attracted the support of American youth. College students flocked to his support, shaving their beards and cutting their hair to be "clean for Gene." In the New Hampshire primary in early March, the nation's earliest political test, McCarthy shocked the political experts by coming within a few thousand votes of defeating President Johnson.

McCarthy's strong showing in New Hampshire led Robert Kennedy, who had been weighing the risks in challenging Johnson, to enter the presidential race. Despite the obvious charge of opportunism he faced, Kennedy had a much better chance than did McCarthy to defeat LBJ and win in the fall. Elected senator from New York in 1964, Bobby Kennedy had become an effective spokesman for the disadvantaged, as well as an increasingly severe critic of the Vietnam War. Unlike McCarthy, whose appeal was largely limited to upper-middle-class whites and college students, Kennedy attracted strong support among blue-collar workers, blacks, Chicanos and other minorities who formed the nucleus of the continuing New Deal coalition. Moreover, in contrast to McCarthy, whose cool wit and lack of

passion bothered even his staunchest admirers, Kennedy provoked an intense emotional loyalty among his followers.

Lyndon Johnson's dramatic withdrawal caused an uproar in the Democratic party. With Johnson's tacit backing and strong support from party regulars and organized labor, Vice-President Hubert H. Humphrey immediately declared his candidacy. Humphrey, a classic Cold War liberal who had worked equally hard for social reform at home and American expansion abroad, was totally unacceptable to the antiwar movement. Accordingly, he decided to avoid the primaries and work for the nomination within the framework of the party.

Kennedy and McCarthy, the two antiwar candidates, were thus left to contest the spring primaries, causing agonizing choices among those who stood for change. Kennedy won everywhere except in Oregon, but his narrow victory in California ended in tragedy when a Palestinian immigrant, Sirhan Sirhan, assassinated him in a Los Angeles hotel.

With his strongest opponent struck down, Hubert Humphrey had little difficulty turning back the challenges from Eugene McCarthy and

■ *Alarmed by the militant antiwar demonstrators drawn to the Democratic convention, Chicago Mayor Daley erected barbed wire fences around the convention hall.*

■ *McCarthy's antiwar stance won the support of thousands of college students who went "clean for Gene."*

■ *Frustrated by the outcome of the Democratic convention, thousands of unarmed, middle-class antiwar college students gathered for an evening rally in Chicago's Grant Park. Within hours, thousands would be gassed and clubbed in what was later termed a "police riot."*

George McGovern, a last-minute replacement for Kennedy, at the Chicago convention. Backed by that city's political boss, Mayor Richard Daley, the vice-president relied on party leaders to defeat an antiwar resolution and win the nomination on the first ballot by a margin of more than two to one. Those hoping for change had to be content with one small victory—the abolition of the unit rule among state delegations, which would make open conventions possible in the future.

Humphrey's triumph was marred by violence outside the heavily guarded convention hall. Radical groups had urged their members to come to Chicago to agitate; the turnout was relatively small but included many who were ready to provoke the authorities in their despair over the convention's outcome. Epithets and cries of "pigs" brought about a savage response from Daley's police, who shared their mayor's contempt for the protesters. "The cops had one thing on their mind," commented journalist Jimmy Breslin. "Club and then gas, club and then gas, club and then gas."

The bitter fumes of tear gas hung in the streets for days afterward; the battered heads and bodies

of demonstrators and innocent bystanders alike flooded the city's hospital emergency rooms. What an official investigation later termed a "police riot" marred Humphrey's nomination and made a sad mockery out of his call for "the politics of joy." The Democratic party itself had become the next victim of the Vietnam War.

The Republican Resurgence

The primary beneficiary of the Democratic debacle was Richard Nixon. Written off as politically dead after his unsuccessful race for governor of California in 1962, Nixon had slowly rebuilt his place within the party by working loyally for Barry Goldwater in 1964 and for GOP congressional candidates two years later. Positioning himself squarely in the middle, with Governor Nelson Rockefeller of New York to his left and Governor Ronald Reagan, who had inherited Goldwater's following, to his right, he quickly became the front-runner for the Republican nomination. At the GOP convention in Miami Beach —blissfully tranquil compared to the Democrats'

■ *By positioning himself politically between Rockefeller on the left and Reagan on the right, Nixon easily won the Republican presidential nomination.*

dicapped by LBJ's stubborn refusal to speed up the diplomatic preliminaries to full-scale peace talks and to end all bombing of North Vietnam. His campaign gradually gained momentum, however, as he picked up support from union leaders and from blacks who remembered his strong stand on civil rights. When he broke with Johnson in late September by announcing in Salt Lake City that if elected he would "stop the bombing of North Vietnam as an acceptable risk for peace," he began to overtake Nixon.

Unfortunately for Humphrey, a third-party candidate cut deeply into the normal Democratic majority. George Wallace had first gained national attention as the racist governor of Alabama whose motto was, "Segregation now . . . segregation tomorrow . . . segregation forever." In 1964, he had shown surprising strength in Democratic primaries in northern states. His appeal was to blue-collar workers and white ethnics—Poles, Italians, Greeks—who believed that many of the gains made by blacks during the 1960s had come at their expense.

experience in Chicago—Nixon won an easy first-ballot nomination and chose Maryland Governor Spiro Agnew as his running mate. Agnew, little-known on the national scene, was a former Rockefeller backer who had won the support of conservatives by taking a strong stand against black rioters.

In the fall campaign, Nixon opened up a wide lead by avoiding controversy and reaping the benefit of discontent with the Vietnam War. He exploited television skillfully, appearing before carefully arranged panels to answer friendly questions. He played the peace issue shrewdly, appearing to advocate an end to the conflict without ever taking a definite stand. The United States should "end the war and win the peace," he declared, hinting that he had a secret formula for peace but never revealing what it was. Above all, he chose the role of reconciler for a nation torn by emotion, a leader who promised to bring a divided country together again.

Humphrey, in contrast, found himself hounded by antiwar demonstrators who heckled him constantly. He walked a tightwire, desperate for the continued support of President Johnson but han-

■ *By appealing to the urban working classes who felt threatened by black gains, third-party candidate George Wallace cut deeply into the Democratic majority that might have supported Humphrey.*

By attacking both black spokesmen and their liberal white allies, Wallace appealed to the sense of powerlessness among the urban working classes. "Liberals, intellectuals and long hairs have run the country for too long," Wallace told his followers. "When I get to Washington," he promised, "I'll throw all these phonies and their briefcases into the Potomac."

Running on the ticket of the American Independence Party with General Curtis LeMay—whose solution to the Vietnam War was to "nuke 'em back to the Stone Age"—as his running mate, Wallace was a close third in the September polls, gaining support from more than 20 percent of the electorate. But as the election neared, his following declined. Humphrey continued to gain, especially after Johnson agreed in late October to end all bombing of North Vietnam. By the first week in November, the outcome was too close for the experts to call.

Nixon won the election with the smallest share of the popular vote of any winning candidate since 1916. But he swept a broad band of states from Virginia and the Carolinas through the Midwest to the Pacific for a clear-cut victory in the electoral college. Humphrey held on to the urban Northeast, scoring well only among blacks and manual laborers. Wallace took just five states in the Deep South, but his heavy inroads into blue-collar districts in the North shattered the New Deal coalition.

The election marked a repudiation of the politics of protest and the cultural insurgency of the mid-sixties. The combined popular vote for Nixon and Wallace, 56.5 percent of the electorate, signified that there was a silent majority that was fed up with violence and confrontation. The "social issue"—a growing concern over psychedelic drugs, rock music, lack of decorum in dress and behavior, and sexual permissiveness—had replaced the traditional economic issue to erode the normal Democratic majority and elect a Republican president. Or as Richard Scammon put it, most of the voters were made up of "the unyoung, the unblack, and the unpoor." By voting for Nixon and Wallace, the American people were sending out a message: they wanted a return to traditional values and an end to the war in Vietnam.

Nixon in Power

The man who took office as the thirty-sixth president of the United States on January 20, 1969, seemed to be a new Nixon. Gone was the fiery rhetoric and the penchant for making enemies. In their place, observers found an air of moderation and restraint. He appeared to have his emotions under firm control. The scars of too many political battles had given him a veneer of toughness, even of indifference. But beneath the surface, he remained bitter, hurt, and sensitive to criticism.

An innately shy man, Nixon hoped to enjoy the power of the presidency in splendid solitude. Described by Barry Goldwater as "the most complete loner I've ever known," Nixon assembled a powerful White House staff whose main task was to isolate him from Congress, the press, and even his own cabinet. Loyal subordinates like H. R. Haldeman and John Ehrlichman took charge of domestic issues, often making decisions without even consulting Nixon, who once said that "the country could run itself domestically without a President." Foreign policy was Nixon's great passion, and here he relied heavily on Henry Kissinger, his national security adviser, to formulate

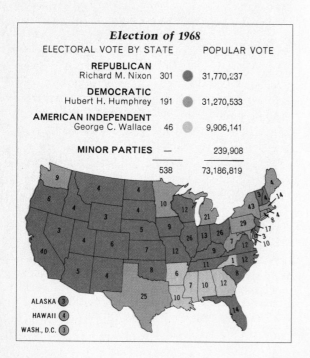

Election of 1968

ELECTORAL VOTE BY STATE		POPULAR VOTE
REPUBLICAN Richard M. Nixon	301	31,770,237
DEMOCRATIC Hubert H. Humphrey	191	31,270,533
AMERICAN INDEPENDENT George C. Wallace	46	9,906,141
MINOR PARTIES	—	239,908
	538	73,186,819

ALASKA ③
HAWAII ④
WASH., D.C. ③

■ *For their roles in the Watergate cover-up, Nixon aides Jeb Stuart Magruder,*
H. R. Haldeman, and John Ehrlichman served time in federal prison. Nixon
was granted a "full, free, and absolute pardon" by his successor, Gerald Ford.

policy, leaving Secretary of State William Rogers to keep the State Department bureaucrats busy with minor details.

The Nixon White House soon could be likened to a fortress under siege. Distrusting everyone, from the media to members of his own party, the President sought to rule the nation without help from either Congress or his cabinet. An almost paranoid belief that he was surrounded by enemies led Nixon to authorize wiretapping and covert surveillance to plug news leaks to the press and to preserve secrecy. In his quest for privacy, the President cut himself off from the nation and thus sowed the seeds of his downfall.

Reshaping the Great Society

Nixon began his first term on a hopeful note, promising the nation peace and respite from the chaos of the sixties. Rejecting the divisions that had split Americans apart, he promised in his inaugural address to "bring us together." "We cannot learn from one another until we stop shouting at one another—until we speak quietly enough so that our words can be heard as well as our voices."

Nixon's moderation promised a return to the politics of accommodation that had characterized the Eisenhower era. Faced with a Democratic Congress, Nixon, like Ike, appeared ready to accept the main outlines of the welfare state. Instead of any massive overthrow of the Great Society, he focused on making the federal bureaucracy function more efficiently.

Daniel Patrick Moynihan, a Democrat who had helped LBJ design his reforms, joined the White House staff as urban affairs adviser and came up with the Family Assistance Plan as a way to overhaul the clumsy welfare system. Instead of piecemeal handouts, each poor family would receive an annual payment of $1600, a variation of a guaranteed annual wage, which had long been a goal of liberals. Democrats, however, quickly criticized Moynihan's plan for the low level of payments and a provision requiring heads of poor households to register for employment as a condition for receiving the annual payment. Despite its many attractive features, including substantial aid to the working poor, the Family Assistance Plan failed to win congressional approval.

Nixon was more successful with his effort to shift responsibility for social problems from Washington to state and local authorities. He developed the concept of revenue sharing, by which federal funds would be dispersed to state, county, and city agencies to meet local needs. Conservatives, who objected to separating the pain of collecting public funds from the pleasure of disbursing them, opposed the plan, but in 1972 Congress finally approved a measure to share $30.1 billion with local governments over a five-year period. An accompanying ceiling of $2.5 billion a year on federal welfare payments, however, meant that much of the revenue-sharing payments had to be allocated by cities and states to programs previously paid for by the federal government.

In the area of civil rights Nixon made a shrewd political move. Action by Congress and the outgoing Johnson administration had ensured that massive desegregation of southern schools, delayed for over a decade by legal action, would finally begin just as Nixon took office. Nixon and his attorney general, John Mitchell, decided to shift the responsibility for this process to the courts. In the summer of 1969, the Justice Department asked a federal judge to delay the integration of thirty-three school districts in Mississippi. The Supreme Court quickly ruled against the Justice Department, declaring that "the obligation of every school district is to terminate dual school systems at once." Thus, in the minds of southern white voters, it was the hated Supreme Court, not Richard Nixon, who had forced them to integrate their schools.

Nixon used similar tactics in his attempt to reshape the Supreme Court along more conservative lines. His appointment of Warren Burger, an experienced federal judge with moderate views to replace the retiring Earl Warren as Chief Justice, met with little objection. But when the President nominated Clement Haynesworth of South Carolina to fill another vacancy on the Court, liberal Democrats led an all-out attack. The Senate, troubled by conflict-of-interest charges against Haynesworth, who in fact had a sound record as a federal judge, rejected the appointment. Seventeen Republicans voted with the majority.

Nixon then responded by offering the name of G. Harrold Carswell, a Florida jurist whose legal record was so bad that one senator finally defended him on the dubious grounds that "there are lots of mediocre judges." When the senators rejected Carswell by a narrow margin, Nixon de-

nounced them for insulting "millions of Americans who live in the South." Once again, the President had used the Supreme Court to enhance his political appeal to Southerners.

Nixon finally filled the Court position with Harry Blackmun, a reputable conservative from Minnesota, who easily won confirmation. Subsequently, the President appointed Lewis Powell, a distinguished Virginia lawyer, and William Rehnquist, a rigidly conservative Justice Department attorney from Arizona, to the Supreme Court. Surprisingly, the Burger Court, despite its more conservative make-up, did not engage in any massive overturn of the Warren Court's decisions. It continued to uphold the legality of desegregation, ruling in 1971 that busing was a necessary and proper way of achieving integrated schools. In other rulings, it restricted the government's right to wiretap suspected subversives, overturned state laws prohibiting abortion, and insisted that the death penalty only be invoked under very limited and precise circumstances.

The moderation of the Supreme Court and the legislative record of the Nixon administration indicated that the nation was not yet ready to abandon the reforms adopted in the 1960s. The pace of change slowed down in areas such as civil rights and welfare, but the commitment to social justice was still clear.

Nixonomics

The economy posed a more severe test for Richard Nixon. He inherited a growing inflation that accompanied the Vietnam War, the product of Lyndon Johnson's unsuccessful attempt to wage the war without raising taxes. The budget deficit was a staggering $25 billion in 1968 and the inflation rate had risen to 5 percent. Strongly opposed to the idea of federal controls, Nixon rejected suggestions of national guideposts to hold down wages and prices. Instead, he opted for a reduction in government spending while encouraging the Federal Reserve Board to curtail the money supply, forcing up interest rates and slowing the rate of business expansion.

The result was disastrous. Inflation continued, reaching nearly 6 percent by the end of 1970, the highest rate since the Korean War. At the same time the economy underwent its first major recession since 1958. The stock market tumbled; the Dow-Jones average fell from over 900 to just above 600, the sharpest drop in thirty years. Unemployment rose to 6 percent by the end of 1970, and business failures jumped alarmingly.

The collapse of the Penn Central Railroad was the most spectacular bankruptcy in the nation's history. Democrats quickly coined a new word, "Nixonomics," to describe the disaster. According to Democratic Chairman Larry O'Brien, it meant that "all the things that should go up—the stock market, corporate profits, real spendable income, productivity—go down, and all the things that should go down—unemployment, prices, interest rates—go up."

Conditions seemed to worsen in 1971. Inflation continued unabated, and the nation's balance of trade became negative as imports exceeded exports by a substantial margin, leading to a weakening of the dollar abroad.

In mid-August, Nixon acted suddenly and boldly to halt the economic decline. Abandoning his earlier resistance to controls, he announced a ninety-day freeze on wages and prices to be followed by federally imposed guidelines in both areas. The new secretary of the treasury, Democrat John Connally, carried out a devaluation of the dollar which, along with a 10 percent surtax on all imports, led to a greatly improved balance of trade. The sudden Nixon economic reversal quickly ended the recession. Industrial production increased by over 5 percent in the first quarter of 1972 and the Dow-Jones average broke the 1000 barrier for the first time.

Building a Republican Majority

"The Great Nixon Turnaround," as historian Lloyd Gardner termed it, came too late to help the Republicans in the 1970 congressional elections. From the time he took office in 1969, the President was obsessed with the fact that he had received only 43 percent of the popular vote in 1968. He owed his election to the third-party candidacy of George Wallace. The Republicans were still a minority party, and to be reelected in 1972, Nixon would need to win over southern whites and blue-collar workers who had followed Wallace out of the Democratic Party.

Attorney General John Mitchell, who had been Nixon's campaign manager in 1968, had devised a southern strategy to help achieve a Republican majority by 1972. The administration's well-publicized objection to school desegregation in the South and the attempt to put Haynesworth and Carswell on the Court were part of this design. Kevin Phillips, one of Mitchell's aides, urged the Nixon administration to direct its appeal to "middle Americans"—southern whites, Catholic ethnic groups, blue-collar workers, and, above all, the new suburbanites of the South and West. In his 1969 book, *The Emerging Republican Majority*, Phillips argued that the GOP's future lay in the Sunbelt. "From space-center Florida across the booming Texas plains to the Los Angeles-San Diego suburban corridor," he contended, "the nation's fastest-growing areas are strongly Republican and conservative."

Nixon unleashed his vice-president, Spiro Agnew, the former governor of Maryland, in an attempt to exploit the social issue in the 1970 election. Blaming all national problems—from drug abuse and sexual permissiveness to crime in the streets—on Democratic liberals and their allies in the media, Agnew delivered a series of scathing speeches. He denounced intellectuals as "an effete corps of impudent snobs," branded television commentators as "a tiny and closed fraternity of privileged men," and damned the press in general as "nattering nabobs of negativism." Despite howls of protest, Agnew proved to be an effective political weapon, as blue-collar workers began displaying on their cars bumper stickers with the proud assertion, "Spiro Is My Hero."

The Democrats struck back by changing their tactics. Warned by Richard Scammon and Ben Wattenberg in *The Real Majority* (1970) that most voters were not young, black, or poor, Democratic candidates were careful to stress economic issues, blaming the Republicans for both inflation and recession. On the social issue, they joined in the chorus against crime, pornography, and drugs. Running for the Senate in Minnesota, Hubert Humphrey reversed his previous stand and came out against gun control; in Illinois, Adlai Stevenson III campaigned for reelection wearing an American flag in his lapel.

The outcome was a standoff. Agnew's attacks helped the GOP to limit the usual off-year losses in the House to nine seats, while the Republicans actually gained two votes in the Senate. But the Democrats did well in state elections and proved once again that economic issues were crucial in American politics. Nixon and the Republicans still did not command a national majority.

In Search of Détente

Richard Nixon gave foreign policy top priority, and he proved surprisingly adept at it. In Kissinger, he had a White House specialist who had devoted his life to the study of diplomacy. A refugee from Nazi Germany, Kissinger had become a professor of government at Harvard, the author of several influential books, and an acknowledged authority on international affairs. Nixon and Kissinger approached foreign policy from a similar realistic perspective. "They recognized a cold and logical world without fated allies or enemies—only interested parties," comment-

ed one close observer. Instead of viewing the Cold War as an ideological struggle for survival with communism, they saw it as a traditional great-power rivalry, one to be managed and controlled rather than to be won.

Kissinger had a grand design. Realizing that recent events, especially the Vietnam War and the rapid Soviet arms buildup of the 1960s, had eroded America's position of primacy in the world, he planned a strategic retreat. There were five major centers of power by the 1970s—the United States, Russia, China, Japan, and the NATO countries of Western Europe. Russia had great military strength, but its economy was weak and it had a dangerous rival in China. Kissinger planned to use American trade—notably grain and high technology—to induce Soviet cooperation, while at the same time improving U.S. relations with China. With Russia neutralized, the United States would then focus on its economic rivalry with Japan and the countries of Western Europe.

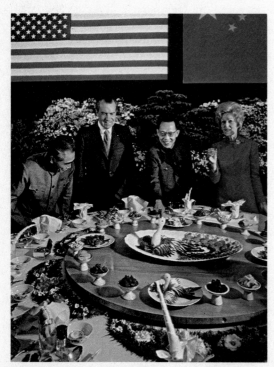

■ *Kissinger's search for détente began with a calculated decision to improve relations with China, the USSR's next-door rival. In a highly publicized state visit, Nixon and Chinese leaders were seen sharing banquets and touring the Great Wall of China.*

Nixon and Kissinger shrewdly played the China card as their first step toward achieving détente—that is, a relaxation of tension—with the Soviet Union. In the summer of 1971, the administration revealed that Kissinger had secretly gone to China and had made the arrangements for a state visit by President Nixon. The following February, accompanied by a planeload of reporters and television camera crews, Nixon made a triumphal tour of China, meeting with the Communist leaders and ending more than two decades of Sino-American hostility. The problem of Taiwan prevented full-scale diplomatic relations, but Nixon agreed to establish an American liaison mission in Peking as a first step toward ultimate recognition.

The Soviets, who viewed China as a dangerous adversary along a two-thousand-mile frontier in Asia, responded by agreeing to reach an arms-control pact with the United States. The Strategic Arms Limitation Talks (SALT) had been underway since 1969. During a visit to Moscow in May 1972, President Nixon signed two vital documents with Soviet leader Leonid Brezhnev. The first limited the two superpowers to two hundred antiballistic missiles (ABMs) apiece; the second froze the number of offensive ballistic missiles for a five-year period. SALT I recognized the existing Soviet lead in missiles, but the American deployment of multiple warheads that could each be individually targeted (MIRV), ensured a continuing American strategic advantage.

The SALT I agreements were most important as a symbolic first step toward control of the nuclear-arms race. They signified that the United States and Russia were trying to achieve a settlement of their differences by peaceful means. The sale of American grain to Russia, along with proposed trade agreements to share more advanced American computer technology with the Soviets, seemed to promise a genuine relaxation of the dangerous tensions of the Cold War.

A triumphant Kissinger (left) and Nixon (right) clink glasses to celebrate the signing of two vital arms agreements with Soviet leader Leonid Breshnev (center) in Moscow on May 26, 1972.

"Do Me A Favor—Help Me Drop It!"

SALT I achieved what this 1970 cartoon had portrayed as a staggering if not impossible task.

Ending the Vietnam War

Vietnam remained the one foreign-policy challenge that Nixon could not overcome. He had a three-part plan to end the conflict—renewed bombing, a hard line in negotiations with Hanoi, and the gradual withdrawal of American troops. The last tactic, known as Vietnamization, proved the most successful. The plan involved training the troops of South Vietnam to take over the American combat role. The number of American soldiers in Vietnam dropped from 543,000 in 1968 to 39,000 by 1972; domestic opposition to the war declined sharply with the accompanying drop in casualties and reductions in the draft call.

By John Fischetti, Chicago Daily News, 1970, Courtesy of Field Newspaper Syndicate

"I NEVER DID SAY HOW, BUT I TOLD YOU I'D GET YOU OUT OF VIETNAM"

■ Trying to "get out" of Vietnam by expanding the war into neutral Cambodia incensed both political cartoonists and antiwar demonstrators.

U.S. Troop Levels in Vietnam
(as of Dec. 31 of each year)

Year	Number of Troops (in thousands)
1960	900
1961	3,200
1962	11,300
1963	16,300
1964	23,300
1965	184,300
1966	385,300
1967	485,600
1968	536,100
1969	475,200
1970	334,600
1971	156,800
1972	24,200

Source: U.S. Department of Defense.

The call for renewed bombing proved the most controversial part of the plan. As early as the spring of 1969, Nixon secretly ordered raids on Communist supply lines in neutral Cambodia. Then in April 1970, he ordered both air and ground strikes into Cambodia. These relieved pressure on hard-pressed South Vietnamese forces but caused a massive outburst of antiwar protests at home. Students demonstrated against the invasion of Cambodia on campuses across the nation. Tragedy struck at Kent State University in Ohio in early May. After rioters had fire-bombed an ROTC building, the governor sent in national guard troops who were taunted and harassed by irate students. The guardsmen then opened fire, killing four students and wounding eleven more. The victims were innocent bystanders; two were young women caught in the fusillade on their way between classes. A week later two black students were killed at Jackson State College in Mississippi; soon there were riots and protests on nearly every campus in the country in what one educator called "the most disastrous month of May in the history of American higher education."

Nixon had little sympathy for the demonstrators, telling aides that they were "bums" who were intent on "blowing up the campuses." The "silent majority" to whom he appealed seemed to agree; one poll showed that most Americans blamed the students, not the national guard, for the deaths at Kent State. Construction workers showed their support for the President by attacking student protesters in New York City and then marching on City Hall shouting, "All the way, U.S.A." An "Honor America Day" program, held in Washington, D.C., on July 4 attracted 250,000 people who heard Billy Graham and Bob Hope endorse the President's policies. Nixon's Cambodian invasion did little to shorten the Vietnam War, but the public reaction reinforced the President's resolve not to surrender.

The third tactic, negotiation with Hanoi, finally proved successful. Beginning in the summer

By May of 1970, the antiwar movement threatened to divide the nation. At Kent State, unarmed and innocent bystanders were shot. Members of the "silent majority" (below) took to the streets in anti-antiwar protests.

of 1969, Kissinger held a series of secret meetings with North Vietnam's foreign minister, Le Duc Tho. In the summer and fall of 1972, after heavy American B-52 raids on North Vietnam had halted a Communist thrust into the South, the two sides were near agreement. South Vietnamese objections blocked a settlement before the 1972 election. When Hanoi tried to make last-minute changes, Nixon ordered a series of savage B-52 raids on Hanoi that finally led to the signing of a truce on January 27, 1973. In return for the release of all American prisoners of war, the United States agreed to remove its troops from South Vietnam within sixty days. The political clauses allowed the North Vietnamese to keep their troops in the South, thus virtually guaranteeing future control of all Vietnam by the Communists.

The agreement was, in fact, a disguised surrender, but finally the American combat role in the Vietnam War was over. After eight years of fighting, the loss of more than fifty-six thousand American lives, and the expenditure of over $100 billion, the United States had emerged from the quagmire in Southeast Asia. Yet known only to a few insiders around the President, the nation was already deeply enmeshed in another dilemma— what Gerald R. Ford termed "the long national nightmare" of Watergate.

■ Through four years of secret meetings, Kissinger and Hanoi's Le Duc Tho finally negotiated an end to the American combat role in Vietnam.

Surviving in Vietnam

Vietnam ranks after World War II as America's second most expensive war. Between 1950 and 1975, the United States spent $123 billion on combat in Southeast Asia. More importantly, Vietnam ranks—after our Civil War and World Wars I and II—as the nation's fourth deadliest war, with 57,661 Americans killed in action.

Yet, when the last U.S. helicopter left Saigon, Americans suffered what historian George Herring terms "collective amnesia." Everyone, even those who had fought in 'Nam,' seemed to want to forget Southeast Asia. It took nearly ten years for the government to erect a national monument to honor those who served in Vietnam. The Vietnam Veterans Memorial in Washington, D.C., (see photo above) was dedicated in November 1982; on its polished black granite walls are carved the names of the dead and missing in action. And only in 1981 did collections of oral histories of some of those who served in Vietnam appear: Al Santoli's well-documented *Everything We Had: An Oral History of the Vietnam War by Thirty-three American Soldiers Who Fought It*, and Mark Baker's *Nam: The Vietnam War in the Words of the Men and Women Who Fought There*. Both books demonstrate that in the steaming jungles of Vietnam one thing mattered most: survival.

One Vietnam veteran expressed the general feeling of men in combat: "War is not killing. Killing is the easiest part. . . . Sweating twenty-four hours a day, seeing guys drop all around you from heatstroke, not having food, not having water, sleeping only three hours a night for weeks at a time, that's what war is. Survival."

During his term President Kennedy ordered a more than tenfold increase in the number of U.S. advisers in Vietnam. Yet, for the ten to twelve thousand predominantly career soldiers there by December of 1962, Vietnam seemed a nice little nine-to-five war. Recalls radio technician Jan Barry of the army's 18th Aviation Company, "If we wanted to go out and chase people around and shoot at them . . . we had a war going. If we didn't . . . they left us alone." In those early days, even the Special Forces Green Berets "used to stop at four-thirty and have a happy hour and get drunk," says Barry, adding that "there was no war after four-thirty. On Saturdays, no war. On Sundays, no war. On holidays, no war. That's right, a nine-to-five war."

Within two years, however, the Joint Chiefs of Staff and President Johnson committed fifty thousand American troops to combat in Vietnam, and the nice little war turned grim. By mid-1967, in fact, more than four hundred thousand Americans were fighting in Vietnam. As many as three hundred died each week. Combat, recalls 26th

Marine Division scout-sniper James Hebron, turned out "totally different" from what he had expected when he had joined the corps at age seventeen early in 1967. "There was no romance at all," says Hebron. During one combat period, Hebron's Bravo Company went without a hot meal for seven months. During that same operation, he notes, "I didn't brush my teeth for two months," explaining that "they sent toothbrushes . . . we had to use them to clean our rifles."

The Screaming Eagles of the elite 101st Airborne Division arrived in Vietnam shortly before the Tet offensive of January 1968. Lieutenant Robert Santos, destined to become one of the division's most decorated men, told his platoon, "two things can happen to you. You can get wounded and go home early. Or you can die." He added that the "best way to go home is whole. If you stick with me . . . and learn from the [more experienced men] you won't get wounded. You won't die." Santos and his men earned a basketful of medals for valor in combat. Lieutenant Santos explains those medals in grim terms: "My responsibility was to kill and in the process of killing to be so good at it that I indirectly saved my men's lives." So, notes Santos, "You come home with the high body count, high kill ratio," but, he concludes, "there's nothing, nothing, that's very satisfying about that."

Few who served in Vietnam survived unscathed, whether psychologically or physically. One of the 303,600 Americans wounded during the long war was 101st Airborne platoon leader James Bombard, first shot and then blown up by a mortar round during the bitter Tet fighting at Hue in February 1968. He describes his traumatic experience as

feeling the bullet rip into your flesh, the shrapnel tear the flesh from your bones and the blood run down your leg. . . . To put your hand on your chest and to come away with your hand red with your own blood, and to feel it running out of your eyes and out of your mouth, and seeing it spurt out of your guts, realizing you were dying. . . . I was ripped open from the top of my head to the tip of my toes. I had forty-five holes in me.

Somehow Bombard survived Vietnam.

The fighting continued for four years after President Nixon took office. Robert Rawls served as a rifleman with the 1st Cavalry Division from early 1969 to early 1970. He recalls:

We got fire fights after fire fights. My first taste of death. After fire fights you could smell it. They brought the [dead men] back wrapped in ponchos. . . . they just threw them up on the helicopter and [piled empty, reusable supply cases] on top of them. You could see the guys' feet hanging out. . . . I had nightmares. . . . I can still see those guys.

As the war dragged on, pacifist frustration at home paralleled the bitterness of those who had fought in Vietnam. John Muir's experience is typical. Early in the war, Muir had served as a rifleman with the 1st Marine Division during the battle of Dong Ha. Muir's single company fought continuously for four days and four nights, frequently in hand-to-hand combat, against two divisions of the North Vietnamese Army. When the marines were relieved, only ninety-one men —all wounded—were still able to fight at all. Muir's squad, however, had been wiped out: he had ended up throwing rocks at his attackers.

"It was a major battle," recalls Muir. "We did a fine job there. If it had happened in World War II, they still would be telling stories about it. But it happened in Vietnam, so nobody knows about it."

Withdrawing U.S. forces from Vietnam ended only the combat. Returning veterans fought government disclaimers concerning the toxicity of the defoliant Agent Orange. VA hospitals across the nation still contain thousands of para- and quadriplegic Vietnam veterans, as well as the maimed from earlier wars. Throughout America the "walking wounded" find themselves still embroiled in the psychological aftermath of Vietnam. To this day, says former 1st Infantry Division combat medic David Ross, "If I'm walking someplace and there's grass, I find myself sometimes doing a shuffle and looking down at the ground. . . . I'm looking for a wire or a piece of vine that looks too straight, might be a [land mine] trip wire. Some of the survival habits you pick up stay residual for a long time."

The Crisis of Democracy

"The illegal we do immediately; the unconstitutional takes a little longer," Henry Kissinger once said jokingly of the Nixon administration. Unfortunately, he was far closer to the truth than anyone realized.

The Politics of Deceit

Richard Nixon's consuming distrust of even his own associates quickly led to a series of underhanded and illegal activities. In the spring of 1969, he ordered the bombing of Cambodia without informing Congress. When details began to leak to the press, the President ordered wiretaps on the telephones of both reporters and members of Kissinger's National Security Council staff. A year later, White House aide Tom Charles Huston drew up a proposal for a new secret committee of FBI and CIA officials to coordinate undercover federal operations. The Huston plan contemplated—in the name of national security—wiretapping, electronic eavesdropping, and "surreptitious entries"—a bureaucratic euphemism for burglaries and break-ins. Only the opposition of FBI director J. Edgar Hoover, who feared a threat to his own agency's independence, blocked implementation of this illegal scheme.

When the *New York Times* and the *Washington Post* began publishing the Pentagon Papers, a classified Defense Department study of the Vietnam War, Nixon decided to take drastic measures to plug any further leaks of secret documents. His aides created a self-styled "plumbers" unit within the White House directed by G. Gordon Liddy, a former FBI agent, and E. Howard Hunt, a veteran of the CIA. Charged with preserving secrecy and discrediting those who kept the press informed, Hunt and Liddy set out to embarrass Daniel Ellsberg, the Defense Department official who had leaked the Pentagon Papers. In a vain effort to find damaging information, they went so far as to break into the office of Ellsberg's psychiatrist in Los Angeles.

Elsewhere in the White House, aides John Dean and Charles Colson were busy preparing an enemies list, which contained the names of several hundred prominent Americans, ranging from movie stars like Jane Fonda and Paul Newman to journalists and educators such as columnist James Reston and Kingman Brewster, president of Yale University. The White House labored under a siege mentality that seemed to justify any and all measures necessary to defeat its opponents, who were thought to include the media, the intellectual community, and virtually all minority groups.

Nixon went to great lengths to guarantee his reelection in 1972. A Committee to Re-elect the President (CREEP) was formed, headed by Attorney General John Mitchell. Specialists in dirty tricks, notably Donald Segretti, harassed Democratic contenders, while G. Gordon Liddy, of the White House "plumbers," developed an elaborate plan to spy on the opposition. Liddy's scheme included bugging the Democratic national headquarters in the Watergate complex in Washington. In the early morning hours of June 17, James McCord and four other men working under the direction of Hunt and Liddy were caught by police during a break-in at Watergate. The continuing abuse of power had finally culminated in an illegal act which soon threatened to bring down the entire Nixon administration.

The Election of 1972

The irony of the Watergate break-in was that by the time it occurred, Nixon's election was assured. Aided by Segretti's dirty tricks, which included issuing phony press releases and campaign documents to embarrass such prominent contenders as Edmund Muskie and Hubert Humphrey, the Democrats destroyed themselves. First Muskie, the front-runner, replying in the New Hampshire primary to a Segretti-inspired letter accusing him of prejudice against French Canadians, lost his composure. Then a lone assassin, Arthur Bremer, shot and seriously wounded George Wallace, who was succeeding in his promise to "rattle the eye teeth of the Democratic party" in the spring primaries. Paralyzed, Wallace was forced to drop out of the race, leaving Nixon with a complete monopoly over the political right.

Senator George McGovern of South Dakota then became the leading Democratic candidate. Aided by rules that he had helped write

■ *The unceremonious dumping of vice-presidential nominee Thomas Eagleton (left) tarnished McGovern's image and cost him critical support.*

manner appealed only to those already committed to his cause.

Richard Nixon shrewdly let McGovern's apparent extremism and New Left support become the main issue in the campaign, rather than the President's own record in office. Staying carefully aloof from partisanship, Nixon let others campaign for him, relying heavily on the recent improvement in the economy and his foreign-policy triumphs with China and Russia to sway the nation's voters.

The result was a stunning victory. Nixon won a popular landslide with 60.8 percent of the vote—second only to Lyndon Johnson's record in 1964—and an even more decisive sweep of the electoral college, taking every state but Massachusetts. The very low turnout and Democratic control of both Houses of Congress suggests that the election was primarily a repudiation of McGovern and the radicalism he appeared to stand for, rather than an endorsement of Richard Nixon. The voting patterns did suggest, however, the beginning of a major political realignment, as only blacks, Jews, and low-income voters continued to vote overwhelmingly Democratic. The GOP made significant gains in the South and West, thus giving substance to Kevin Phillips' prediction of an emerging Republican majority based in the Sunbelt.

which opened up the party convention to women, youth, and minorities, McGovern emerged as the Democratic nominee. He ran on a platform that advocated a negotiated settlement in Vietnam, the right to abortion, and tolerance of diverse life-styles. The South Dakota senator hoped to unite the New Left with traditional Democratic voters, but his strong stand against the Vietnam War and in favor of social reform was perceived as "anti-establishment" by middle-class America and greatly strengthened Nixon's appeal.

McGovern quickly lost what little strength he had by his inept handling of the vice-presidential nomination. Originally selecting Missouri Senator Thomas Eagleton, McGovern dumped him for R. Sargent Shriver of Maryland when it was disclosed that Eagleton had undergone psychiatric treatment for depression. Integrity had been McGovern's strongest point; when he dropped Eagleton from the ticket despite a promise to stand behind him "1000 percent," that quality was called into question. Under the slogan, "Come Home, America," McGovern attempted to wage a crusade against the war and on behalf of reform, but his stiff speaking style (which one commentator said sounded like a minister saying grace at a Rotary lunch) and his self-righteous

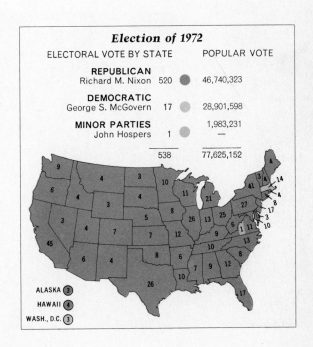

Election of 1972

ELECTORAL VOTE BY STATE		POPULAR VOTE
REPUBLICAN Richard M. Nixon	520	46,740,323
DEMOCRATIC George S. McGovern	17	28,901,598
MINOR PARTIES John Hospers	1	1,983,231 —
	538	77,625,152

ALASKA ③
HAWAII ④
WASH., D.C. ③

The Watergate Scandal

Only Richard Nixon knew how fragile his victory was in 1972. The President apparently had no foreknowledge of the Watergate break-in, but he was deeply implicated in the attempt to cover up the involvement of White House aides in the original burglary. On June 23, only six days after the crime, he ordered the CIA to keep the FBI off the case, on the specious grounds that it involved national security. The President even urged his aides to lie under oath, if necessary. "I don't give a [expletive deleted] what happens," Nixon said to John Mitchell. "I want you all to stonewall it, let them plead the Fifth Amendment, cover-up, or anything else. . . ."

In the short run, the cover-up, directed by White House counsel John Dean, worked. Hunt and Liddy were convicted for their roles in the Watergate break-in, but they carefully avoided implicating either CREEP or Nixon's inner circle of advisers. Despite some very revealing stories by reporters Bob Woodward and Carl Bernstein in the *Washington Post*, the public was kept ignorant of the true dimensions of the Watergate affair.

The first thread unraveled when federal judge John Sirica, known for his firmness toward criminals, sentenced the burglars to long jail terms. James McCord was the first to crack, informing Sirica that he had received money from the White House and had been promised a future pardon in return for his silence. By April 1973, Nixon was forced to fire John Dean, who refused to become the scapegoat for the cover-up, and to allow Haldeman and Ehrlichman, who were deeply implicated, to resign. The Senate then appointed a special committee to investigate the Watergate episode, with North Carolina Democrat Sam Ervin as chairman. In a week of dramatic testimony, John Dean revealed the President's personal involvement in the cover-up. Still Nixon hoped to weather the storm, since it was basically a matter of whose word was to be believed, that of the President or of a discredited aide.

The existence of tapes of conversations in the Oval Office, recorded regularly since 1970, finally brought Nixon down. At first the President tried to invoke executive privilege to withhold the tapes. When Archibald Cox, appointed as Watergate special prosecutor, demanded the release of the tapes, Nixon responded by firing Cox. When Attorney General Eliot Richardson refused to remove Cox, Nixon fired him too. But the new Watergate prosecutor, Leon Jaworski, continued

The faces of Senators Howard Baker (left) and Sam Ervin (center) became familiar to a large television audience, who daily watched them uncover new and alarming dimensions of the Watergate scandal.

Threatened by the release of his secret tapes and facing three articles of impeachment, an embattled Richard Nixon resigned the presidency on August 9, 1974, as his loyal family watched.

to press for the tapes. Nixon tried to release only a few of the less damaging ones, but the Supreme Court ruled unanimously in June 1974 that the tapes had to be turned over to Judge Sirica.

By that time the House Judiciary Committee, acting on evidence compiled by the staff of the Ervin committee, voted three articles of impeachment, charging Nixon with obstruction of justice, abuse of power, and contempt of Congress. Faced with the release of tapes which directly implicated him in the cover-up, the President finally chose to resign on August 9, 1974.

Nixon's resignation proved to be the culmination of the Watergate scandal. The entire episode revealed both the weaknesses and strengths of the American political system. Most regrettable was the abuse of presidential authority—a reflection both of the growing power of the modern presidency and of the fatal flaws in Richard Nixon's character. Unlike such previous executive-branch scandals as the Whiskey Ring and Teapot Dome, Watergate involved a lust for power rather than for money. Realizing that he had reached the White House almost by accident, Nixon did everything possible to retain his hold on his office. He used the "plumbers" to maintain executive secrecy, he directed the Internal Revenue

Service and the Justice Department to punish his enemies and reward his friends, and he created CREEP to free himself from dependency on the Republican Party in his quest for reelection.

But Watergate also demonstrated the vitality of a democratic society. The press, particularly Woodward and Bernstein, showed how investigative reporting could unlock even the most closely guarded executive secrets. Judge Sirica proved that an independent judiciary was still the best bulwark for individual freedom. And Congress rose to the occasion, both by carrying out a successful investigation of executive misconduct and by following a scrupulous and nonpartisan impeachment process that left Nixon with no chance to escape his ultimate fate.

The nation survived the shock of Watergate with its institutions intact. The presidency was shorn of its excessive power. Attorney General John Mitchell and twenty-five presidential aides were sentenced to jail terms. Future occupants of the White House would never again feel that they were above the law. Congress, in decline since Lyndon Johnson's exercise of executive dominance, was rejuvenated, with its members now intent on extending congressional authority into all areas of American life.

Chronology

1963 Betty Friedan publishes *The Feminine Mystique*

1966 National Organization for Women (NOW) formed

1967 Riots in Detroit kill 43, injure 2000, leave 5000 homeless

1968 Viet Cong launch Tet offensive (January)
Johnson announces he will not seek reelection (March)
Martin Luther King, Jr., assassinated in Memphis, Tennessee (April)
Robert F. Kennedy assassinated in Los Angeles, California (June)

1970 U.S. forces invade Cambodia (April)
Ohio National Guardsmen kill four students at Kent State University (May)

1971 *New York Times* publishes the Pentagon Papers (June)
Nixon announces wage-and-price freeze (August)

1972 President Nixon visits China (February)
U.S. and USSR sign SALT I accords in Moscow (May)
White House "Plumbers" unit breaks into Democratic headquarters in Watergate complex (June)
Richard Nixon wins reelection in landslide victory over McGovern

1973 U.S. and North Vietnam sign truce ending Vietnam War (January)

1974 Supreme Court orders Nixon to surrender White House tapes (June)
Richard M. Nixon resigns presidency (August)

There was, however, one lasting casualty. The people's faith in politicians was severely shaken. The events of the 1960s and the early '70s, ranging from the Vietnam War to Watergate, from ghetto riots to violent antiwar demonstrations, had left the American people in a mood of cynicism and despair. Nixon had broken the slender bond of trust between those who govern and those who are governed. After the Watergate experience, the ultimate challenge facing presidential aspirants was to offer the kind of inspired leadership that would rekindle the flagging democratic spirit.

Recommended Reading

The most penetrating analysis of the youthful protesters of the 1960s is Kenneth Keniston, *Young Radicals* (1968). Keniston, a social psychologist, interviewed a group of antiwar activists in 1967 to arrive at a detailed assessment of their motives and aspirations. For a broader picture of the New Left and the SDS in particular, see Irwin Unger, *The Movement* (1974).

Garry Wills provides the most revealing portrait of the career and character of Richard Nixon in *Nixon Agonistes* (1970). Wills concentrates on the prepresidential years; for Nixon in office, the best accounts are two memoirs: William Safire, *Before the Fall* (1975), a speechwriter's account that focuses on domestic policy; and Henry Kissinger, *The White House Years* (1979), the national security adviser's view of Nixon's foreign policy.

The best books on Watergate are still the two contemporary accounts by Bob Woodward and Carl Bernstein. *All the President's Men* (1974) tells how these two reporters penetrated the cover-up; in *The Final Days* (1976), they detail Nixon's fall from power.

Additional Bibliography

Books on the New Left include S. Kirkpatrick Sale, *SDS* (1973); Jack Newfield, *A Prophetic Minority* (1966); Christopher Lasch, *The Agony of the American Left* (1969); Edward J. Bacciocco, *The New Left in America* (1974); and Todd Gitlin, *The Whole World Is Watching* (1981), a scholary account by a former SDS leader that blames the media for the New Left's downfall. For other aspects of the youth rebellion, see Paul Goodman, *Growing Up Absurd* (1960) and Lewis Feuer, *The Conflict of Generations* (1972). Representative books reflecting the views of the counterculture are Charles Reich, *The Greening of America* (1970); Herbert Marcuse, *An Essay on Liberation* (1969); and Theodore Roszak, *The Making of a Counter Culture* (1969).

The transition from the quest for integration to the assertion of black power is traced in James C. Harvey, *Black Civil Rights During the Johnson Administration* (1973); Clayborne Carson, *In Struggle* (1981); and Stokely Carmichael and C. V. Hamilton, *Black Power* (1967). For the urban riots of the sixties, see Robert Conot, *Rivers of Blood, Years of Darkness* (1967) on Watts; John Hersey, *The Algiers Hotel Incident* (1968) on Detroit; and James W. Button, *Black Violence* (1978), which shows the impact of the riots on federal policy. The growing self-consciousness of other minorities is described in Michael Novak, *The Rise of the Unmeltable Ethnics* (1973); Matt Meier and Feliciano Rivera, *The Chicanos* (1972); and Rodolfo Acuña, *Occupied America: A History of Chicanos*, 2d ed. (1981). For the emerging feminist movement, see two books by William Chafe, *The American Woman* (1972) and *Women and Equality* (1977); and Sara Evans, *Personal Politics* (1979).

The tumultuous election of 1968 is described in Theodore White, *The Making of the President, 1968* (1969) and Lewis Chester, Godfrey Hodgson, and Bruce Page, *American Melodrama* (1969). For Wallace's role, see Jody Carlson, *George C. Wallace and the Politics of Powerlessness, 1964–1976* (1981). Fawn Brodie traces Nixon's prepresidential career critically in *Richard Nixon* (1981); Earl Mazo and Stephen Hess are more sympathetic in *Nixon* (1968). Other important books on Nixon include Jules Witcover, *The Resurrection of Richard Nixon* (1970); Rowland Evans and Robert Novak, *Nixon in the White House* (1971); and the President's own memoir, *RN* (1978). For Nixon's domestic policies, see Leonard Silk, *Nixonomics* (1972); Daniel Moynihan, *Politics of a Guaranteed National Income* (1973); and two books on the Supreme Court nomination controversies by Richard Harris, *Justice* (1970) and *Decision* (1971).

The major shifts in American politics in the late 1960s are described in Richard N. Scammon and Ben J. Wattenberg, *The Real Majority* (1970); S. Kirkpatrick Sale, *Power Shift* (1975); David L. Broder, *The Party's Over* (1971); Samuel Lubell, *The Hidden Crisis in American Politics* (1970); and Frederick G. Dutton, *The Changing Sources of Power* (1971).

Henry Brandon, *The Retreat of American Power* (1973); Tad Szulc, *The Illusion of Peace* (1978); and Stanley Hoffman, *Primacy or World Order* (1978) all describe Nixon's foreign policy and the search for détente. Books that focus on Kissinger's role include Marvin Kalb and Bernard Kalb, *Kissinger* (1974), a sympathetic view; Roger Morris, *Uncertain Greatness* (1977), a critical analysis; and Seyom Brown, *The Crisis of Power* (1979), a balanced account. For SALT, see John Newhouse, *Cold Dawn* (1973). William Shawcross, a British journalist, blames Kissinger for the secret bombing of Cambodia in *Sideshow* (1979).

Books on the antiwar movement and the violent protests in 1970 include Alexander Kendrick, *The Wound Within* (1974); Thomas Powers, *The War at Home* (1973); John Mueller, *War, Presidents and Public Opinion* (1973); I. F. Stone, *The Killings at Kent State* (1971); Noam Chomsky, *American Power and the New Mandarins* (1977); and Lawrence M. Baskir and William A. Strauss, *Chance and Circumstance* (1978), a study of the impact of the draft on American youth. The different lessons drawn from the Vietnam experience are expounded in Earl C. Ravenal, *Never Again* (1978), a plea for nonintervention, and Norman Podhoretz, *Why We Were in Vietnam* (1982), a defense of the war.

The election of 1972 is dealt with uncritically by Theodore White in *The Making of the President, 1972* (1973) and entertainingly by Hunter S. Thompson in *Fear and Loathing: On the Campaign Trail '72* (1973).

General accounts of Watergate include Theodore White, *Breach of Faith* (1975); Jonathan Schell, *Time of Illusion* (1976); and J. Anthony Lukas, *Nightmare* (1976). For the abuse of power that reached its culmination in the Watergate affair, see Arthur M. Schlesinger, Jr., *The Imperial Presidency* (1973); David Wise, *The American Police State* (1976); and Athan Theoharis, *Spying on Americans* (1978). Among the many memoirs by Watergate participants, the most revealing is John Dean, *Blind Ambition* (1976).

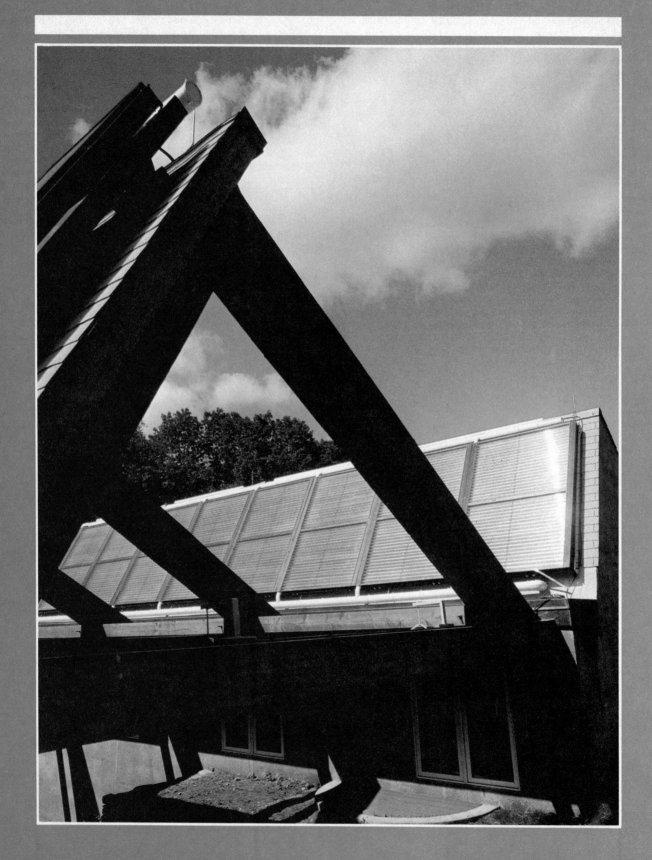

chapter 32

THE
AGE OF
SCARCITY

On October 6, 1973, Egypt and Syria launched a surprise attack on Israel. The invasion, which came while the Israelis were observing the Jewish holy day of atonement, Yom Kippur, caught American leaders completely off-guard. After recovering from the initial shock, President Nixon and Henry Kissinger, who had become secretary of state in September, expected Israel to repel the Arab invaders and display the same military dominance it had used to win the Six Day War in 1967. In that conflict, Israel had devastated its Arab neighbors, taking possession of the Golan Heights from Syria, the Sinai peninsula from Egypt, and Jerusalem and the West Bank from Jordan. Instead of increasing Israeli security, however, these conquests had only added to Middle East tensions. They unified the Arab countries, who now called for the return of their lands, and increased Egyptian and Syrian dependence on the Soviet Union for arms and political support.

Henry Kissinger saw the outbreak of the Yom Kippur War as an opportunity to shift American policy from its traditional pro-Israeli position to a more neutral stance. The secretary of state wanted the United States to play the role of honest broker between Israel and its Arab neighbors. To achieve that position, he was hoping that the Yom Kippur War would end without a clear-cut victory for either side, permitting the United States to step in and arrange a diplomatic settlement.

Events nearly betrayed Kissinger's strategy. The initial Egyptian and Syrian attacks proved surprisingly successful, finally leading Nixon and Kissinger to approve a massive resupply of Israel in mid-October. But when the Israeli counterattack drove the Syrians back toward Damascus and trapped an entire Egyptian army near the Suez Canal, the secretary intervened diplomatically to prevent a victory for Israel that would preclude American mediation. Joint Soviet-American efforts to arrange a cease-fire nearly broke down in the face of Israeli militancy. Kissinger then ordered a worldwide nuclear alert that persuaded both the Soviets and the Israelis that the United States was intent on imposing a political settlement. Finally, the fighting ended in late October.

Kissinger's apparent diplomatic triumph, however, was offset by an unforeseen consequence of

Egyptian and Israeli tanks fight it out on the sands of the Sinai peninsula during the Yom Kippur War of 1973. With the help of Henry Kissinger's shuttle diplomacy the combatants disengaged and an uneasy truce was established.

the Yom Kippur War. On October 17, the Arab members of the Organization of Petroleum Exporting Countries (OPEC) announced a 5 percent cut in oil production, with additional cuts of 5 percent each month until Israel gave up the lands it had seized in 1967. President Nixon announced a $2.2 billion aid package for Israel on October 19, and the next day Saudi Arabia cut off oil shipments to the United States and to the Netherlands, the European nation that had most strongly supported American policy in the Middle East.

The Arab oil embargo had a disastrous impact on the American economy. First, it produced a worldwide shortage of oil. Arab producers cut production by 25 percent from the September 1973 level, leading to a curtailment of 10 percent in the world supply. For the United States, which imported one third of its daily consumption, it meant a loss of nearly two million barrels a day. Increased imports from Iran, Libya, and Nigeria helped offset the Arab embargo, but American consumers began to panic. Long lines formed at automobile service stations as motorists kept filling their tanks in fear of running out of gas.

A dramatic increase in oil prices proved to be a far more significant result of the embargo. The relatively low price of oil had been creeping upward in the early 1970s as demand began to match supply; after the Arab embargo began, OPEC, led by the Shah of Iran, raised crude oil prices fourfold. In the United States, gasoline prices at the pumps nearly doubled in a few weeks time, while the cost of home heating fuel rose even more sharply.

President Nixon responded with a series of temporary measures, including pleas to turn down thermostats in homes and offices, close service stations on weekends to curb pleasure driving, and reduce automobile speed limits to fifty miles per hour. He also outlined a plan for American energy independence. Designed to end reliance on imported oil, the plan encouraged conservation and the use of alternative sources of energy, such as coal and nuclear power. When the Arab oil embargo ended in March, after Kissinger negotiated an Israeli pullback in the Sinai, the American public relaxed. Gasoline once again became plentiful, thermostats were raised, and people rekindled their love affair with the automobile.

But the energy crisis did not end with the

Editorial cartoon by Lou Grant of the Oakland Tribune, © Los Angeles Times Syndicate, Reprinted by permission.

■ *"Hat in Hand" shows a new and unaccustomed posture for Uncle Sam following the Arab oil embargo.*

lifting of the embargo. The Arab action marked the beginning of a new era in American history. The United States, with only 6 percent of the world's population, had been using nearly 40 percent of the earth's energy supplies. The vast reserves of petroleum and natural gas had fueled American economic expansion down through World War II, and then oil imports had sustained postwar growth with artificially low energy costs. In 1970, domestic oil production began to decline; the embargo served only to highlight the fact that the nation was now dependent on other countries, notably those in the Persian Gulf, for its economic well-being.

The consequences soon became clear. The growing shortage of oil and natural gas led to a steady increase in energy costs which contributed heavily to inflation. The revenues sent to OPEC members further weakened the American economy, leading to periodic recessions, higher interest rates, and the slowing of economic growth. A nation that based its way of life on abundance and expansion suddenly was faced with the reality of limited resources and economic stagnation. A land of plenty now had to face the challenge of scarcity.

Energy and the Economy

The energy crisis that began with the Arab oil embargo in 1973 had a profound impact. The price American consumers paid for oil went up sixfold during the 1970s. The result was rampant inflation, rising unemployment, and an end to the postwar era of rapid economic growth.

The Oil Shocks

Cheap energy had been the underlying force behind the amazing expansion of the American economy after World War II. The world price of oil had actually declined in the 1950s and '60s as huge new fields in the Middle East and North Africa came into production. The GNP had more than doubled between 1950 and 1973; the American people had come to base their way of life on gasoline prices that averaged about $.35 a gallon. The huge gas-guzzling cars, the flight to the suburbs, the long drive to work each day, the detached houses heated by fuel oil and natural gas and cooled by central air conditioning represented a dependence on inexpensive energy that everyone took for granted.

The first great oil shock of the '70s came with the Yom Kippur War and the resulting Arab oil embargo. Few had noticed a gradual increase in OPEC prices in the early 1970s; the world level had risen from $1.80 a barrel to $3.07 by mid-1973, but the regulated domestic price had remained stable at the $3.00 mark. Global demand for oil, intensified by the explosive economic development of Western Europe and Japan as well as the United States, had now caught up with oil production. In the ensuing shortfall, the OPEC nations quickly raised prices, first to over $5.00 a barrel, then to $11.65.

The effect on the American economy was devastating. In 1979, consumers had to pay an additional $16.4 billion to cover the cost of imported oil. Gasoline prices jumped from $.35 to $.65 a gallon; the cost of manufacturing went up proportionately, while utility rates rose sharply as a result of the higher cost of fuel oil and natural gas. Suddenly the American people faced drastic and unexpected increases in such everyday expenses as driving to work and heating their homes.

The result was a sharp decline in consumer spending and the worst recession since World War II. The GNP dropped by 6 percent in 1974 and unemployment rose to over 9 percent, the highest level since the Great Depression of the 1930s. Detroit was hit the hardest. Buyers shied away from big cars with their low gas mileage, but many were skeptical of the first generation of American-made small cars, notably the Ford Pinto and the Chevrolet Vega. Sales declined by 20 percent, and by the fall of 1974, Detroit's big three automakers had laid off more than 225,000 workers.

President Gerald R. Ford, who followed Richard Nixon into the White House, was concerned at first with inflation; he responded belatedly to the economic crisis by proposing a tax cut to stimulate consumer spending. Congress passed a $22.8 billion reduction in taxes in early 1975 which included rebates averaging $130 for each individual taxpayer, an across-the-board cut in personal income tax rates, and an increase in investment tax credits for business. With this stimulus, the economy gradually recovered by 1976, but the resulting budget deficits helped keep inflation above 5 percent and prevented a return to full economic health.

American Oil Imports, 1966–1979

The next administration, headed by Jimmy Carter of Georgia, had little more success in achieving a rapid rate of economic growth. Continued federal deficits and relatively high interest rates kept the economy sluggish throughout 1977 and '78. Then in 1979 the outbreak of the Iranian Revolution and the overthrow of the shah touched off another oil shock. Although the cut-off of Iranian oil led to a shortfall of only 3 percent of the world's oil supply, the members of the OPEC cartel took advantage of the situation to raise prices by a staggering $21 a barrel over the next eighteen months. The price of oil, which had actually declined in relation to industrial prices in the mid-1970s, now shot up to over $30 a barrel. Gasoline prices climbed to more than $1 a gallon at American service stations, and an even greater wave of inflation than the 1973 increase occurred.

The American people panicked. When lines began to form at gas stations in California and Florida in early May 1979, drivers started filling their tanks every day or two. Soon stations were jammed and supplies ran short as the nation's normal inventory shifted from underground storage reservoirs to motorists' gas tanks. Service stations began closing on weekends, and in state after state governors experimented with plans regulating gasoline purchases. The long lines frustrated American drivers; incidents of violence began to mount and the public took out its fury on the Carter administration. In June, the President's staff warned him of the danger in the "worsening short-term energy crisis." "Nothing else has so frustrated, confused, angered the American people," Carter was told, "or so targeted their distress at you personally."

By the fall of 1979, world supply had caught up with demand, and the oil scare ended. But the price of gasoline remained at over a dollar a gallon, and the inflation rate began to reach double-digit levels again. The twin oil shocks of the seventies had left the economy battered and had undermined the average American's faith in the future.

The Search for an Energy Policy

The oil shocks of 1973 and 1979 were but two symptoms of a much deeper energy crisis. Put

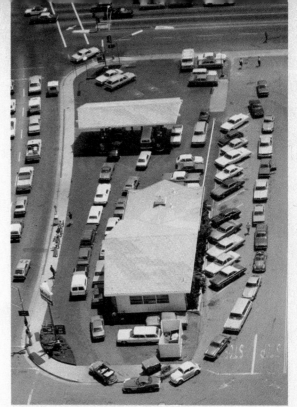

■ *The age of cheap and abundant oil was ending. As prices climbed and supplies dwindled, Americans found themselves waiting in long gas lines.*

simply, the United States was running out of the fossil fuels on which it had relied for its economic growth in the past. Domestic oil production peaked in 1970 and declined every year thereafter; there were more ample reserves of natural gas, but both fuels were nonrenewable sources of energy that would eventually be exhausted. American political leaders had to devise a national policy to meet not only the temporary shortfalls of the seventies but also the long-term energy problem inherent in past reliance on fossil fuels.

The success of the environmental movement in the late 1960s and early '70s compounded the problem. Efforts to protect the environment and curtail pollution of the nation's air and water had led to significant legislative restrictions on American industry. Congress created the Environmental Protection Agency in 1970 to monitor industry and passed a Clean Air Act that encouraged public utilities to shift from using coal, which polluted the atmosphere, to clean-burning fuel oil and natural gas to generate electricity. The observance of Earth Day in April 1970, complete with a

■ (Top) Earth Day protestors dramatize the dangers of environmental pollution. (Bottom) Santa Barbara sea birds trapped in oil slicks.

massive parade up New York City's Fifth Avenue, and outrage over an oil spill in the Santa Barbara channel, reflected the national consensus behind the environmental movement.

The energy crunch pitted the environmentalists and advocates of economic growth in direct confrontation. Those who put ecology first lost out. In the mid-1970s, Congress authorized construction of the Alaskan pipeline over environmentalists' objections and ordered public utilities to resume burning coal to produce electricity. By the end of the decade, groups such as the Sierra Club and Friends of the Earth had failed in their efforts to halt the gradual relaxation of environmental regulations to permit strip-mining of coal and offshore drilling for oil.

The nation's leaders had an even more difficult time devising a coherent and workable long-term national energy policy. Gerald Ford placed a high premium on expanding production as a means of overcoming the shortage. The Republicans advocated removing price controls on oil and natural gas to give wildcatters the incentive to bring in new supplies of these fuels. Greater production of coal, expanded nuclear power plants, and new technology to explore the possibilities of synthetic fuels and solar energy were all parts of the Republican approach to the energy problem.

The Democrats, in contrast, stressed price controls and conservation. In Congress, Democratic leaders were intent on shielding American consumers from the full brunt of the world price increase. They wanted to continue an elaborate system of price controls instituted by Nixon in 1973, and they favored stand-by plans for gas rationing as a better way to allocate scarce supplies than relying on the marketplace. Democratic conservation measures included plans for tax breaks for those who insulated their homes, pressure on automakers to improve gas mileage for cars, and large appropriations for mass-transit systems for American cities.

The nation failed to adopt either the Republican or the Democratic energy plans; instead, Congress tried to muddle through with elements of both approaches. Thus, on the production front, Ford was able to win approval for building the Alaskan pipeline, which made an additional 1.5 million barrels of oil a day available to American consumers. Carter placed a strong emphasis on reviving the lagging American coal industry. Congress continued the price controls on domestic oil for another forty months in late 1975, and in its most significant step toward conservation, mandated annual increases in gasoline mileage that forced Detroit to produce more fuel-efficient cars. Since nearly 10 percent of the world's oil production was burned up every day on American highways, this one congressional act would result eventually in substantial gasoline savings.

The overall outcome, however, was a patchwork that fell far short of a coherent national strategy for solving the energy problem. Neither Ford's appeal for decontrol nor Carter's call for a national conservation effort that would be "the moral equivalent of war" worked. Oil imports actually increased by 50 percent between 1973 and 1979, rising from 6 million to 9 million barrels a day, nearly half of the nation's daily petroleum usage. When the oil shock of 1979–1980 revealed how vulnerable the American economy was to OPEC, Carter reversed his policy and asked Congress to decontrol the price of domestic oil.

The Great Inflation

The gravest consequence of the oil shocks was inflation. The startling increase in price levels in the 1970s stemmed from many causes. The Vietnam War, particularly Johnson's early attempts to avoid a tax increase to pay for the fighting, created budget deficits that grew from $63 billion for the entire decade of the sixties to a total of $420 billion in the seventies. A worldwide shortage of food, resulting from both rapid population increases and poor harvests around the globe in the mid-1970s, triggered a 20 percent rise in American food prices in 1973 alone. But above all else, it was the sixfold increase in petroleum prices that raised the cost of every economic

activity, from transportation to farming, from manufacturing to mining, that was the primary source of the great inflation of the 1970s.

The impact on consumers was staggering. The price of an automobile jumped 72 percent between 1973 and 1978, while the cost of new homes went up 67 percent in the same period. During the decade, the price of a hamburger doubled, milk went from $.28 to $.59 a quart, and the cost of a loaf of bread—the proverbial staff of life—rose from $.24 to $.89. Corresponding wage increases failed to do more than keep most Americans even; for the first time since World War II, real wages did not increase in the 1970s, and in 1980 the real income of the average American family fell by 5.5 percent.

Curbing inflation proved to be beyond the power of the federal government. President Ford's early efforts to roll back prices by rhetoric—including the WIN (Whip Inflation Now) buttons—were a casualty of the 1974 recession. President Carter proved equally powerless. His attempts to cut back on government spending in order to balance the budget were more than offset by the price rises of 1979 and 1980 that followed the second oil shock. Finally, in October 1979, the Federal Reserve Board, led by Carter appointee Paul Volcker, began a sustained effort to halt inflation by mandating increased bank reserves to curtail the supply of money in circulation. The

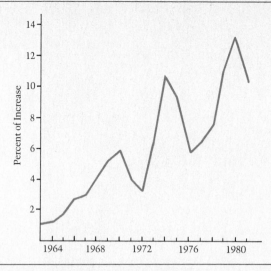

Annual Increase in Consumer Price Index, 1962–1981

Source: U.S. Bureau of the Census, Statistical Abstract of the United States: 1982–83 *(103d edition) Washington, D.C., 1982.*

new tight money policy served only to heighten inflation in the short run by driving interest rates up to record levels. By the spring of 1980, the prime interest rate reached 20 percent.

The Shifting American Economy

Inflation and the oil shocks helped bring about significant changes in American business and industry in the 1970s. The most obvious result was the slowing of the rate of economic growth, with the GNP advancing only 3.2 percent for the decade, compared to 3.7 percent in the 1960s. More important, American industry began to lose its position of primacy in world markets. In 1959, U.S. firms had been the leaders in eleven of thirteen major industrial sectors, ranging from manufacturing to banking. By 1976, American companies led in only seven areas, and in all but one category—aerospace—U.S. corporations had declined in relation to Japanese and Western European competitors.

The most serious losses came in the heavy industries where the United States had once led the world. In 1946, American firms had produced 60 percent of the world's iron and steel; by 1978, they accounted for only 16 percent. New steel producers in Western Europe, Japan, and the Third World, using more advanced technology and aided by government subsidies, were producing steel far more efficiently than their American counterparts. As a result, by the end of the 1970s, fully 20 percent of all iron and steel used in the United States was imported, and American firms were closing down their obsolete mills in the East and Midwest, idling thousands of workers.

Foreign competition did even more damage in the automobile industry. The oil shocks led to a consumer demand for small, efficient cars. German and Japanese automakers seized the opportunity to expand their once small volume of sales in the United States. By 1977, imported cars had captured 18.3 percent of the American market, with Japan leading the way with its well-built and fuel-saving Toyotas, Datsuns, and Hondas. In response, Detroit spent $70 billion retooling to produce a new fleet of smaller, lighter, front-wheel-drive cars, but American manufacturers barely survived the foreign invasion. Only government-backed loans helped the Chrysler Corporation stave off bankruptcy.

In other areas, American corporations fared much better. The multinationals that had emerged in the boom years of the 1960s continued to thrive. IBM sold computers all over the globe, while Pepsi-Cola outmaneuvered its traditional rival to penetrate the Iron Curtain. The growth of conglomerates—huge corporations that combined many dissimilar industrial concerns—

In their battle for survival, American automakers sought to reduce labor costs and improve quality by exploiting technical advances in the use of robots.

■ Electronics firms clustered around California's San Jose area, nicknamed the "silicon valley," like microchips in a computer.

accelerated as companies like Gulf & Western and the Transamerica Corporation diversified by buying up Hollywood studios, insurance companies, and recreational-equipment manufacturers. The growth of high-technology industries proved to be the most profitable new trend of the 1970s. Computer companies and electronics firms grew at a rapid rate, especially after the development of the silicon chip, a small, wafer-thin microprocessor that can perform complex calculations almost instantly. Video games, automated cash registers, and home computers were but a few of the new products made possible by the technological revolution.

The result was a geographic shift of American industry from the East and Midwest to the Sunbelt. Electronics manufacturers flourished in California, Texas, and North Carolina, where they grew up around major universities. The absence of well-entrenched labor unions, the availability of skilled labor, and the warm, attractive climate of the southern and western states lured many new concerns to the Sunbelt. At the same time, the decline of the steel and auto industries was leading to massive unemployment and economic stagnation in the northern industrial heartland. The one exception was New England, where the rise of new scientific companies around Boston helped offset the earlier decline of the textile industry.

The overall pattern was one of an economy in transition. The oil shocks had caused serious problems of inflation, slower economic growth, and rising unemployment rates. But American business still displayed the enterprise and the ability to develop new technologies that gave promise of continued economic vitality in the 1980s.

Politics After Watergate

The energy crisis and the economic dislocations of the mid-1970s could not have come at a worse time. Watergate had a paralyzing impact on the American political system. An awareness that the Cold War had led to an imperial presidency created a growing demand to weaken the power of the president and strengthen congressional authority. The result was an increasing tension between the White House and Capitol Hill which prevented the kind of strong, effective leadership needed to meet the unprecedented problems of the 1970s.

The Ford Administration

Gerald R. Ford had the distinction of being the first president who had not been elected to national office. Richard Nixon had appointed him to the vice-presidency to succeed Spiro Agnew, who had been forced to resign in order to avoid prosecution for accepting bribes while he was governor of Maryland. Ford, a longtime Michigan congressman who had risen to the post of House minority leader, was a popular choice. Amiable and unpre-

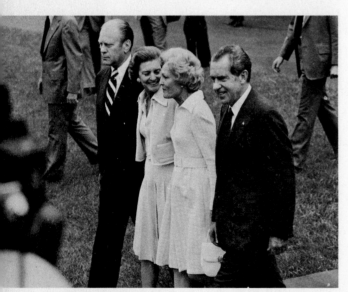

■ The transfer of presidential power from Richard Nixon to Gerald Ford took place on August 9, 1974, shortly after this photo was taken.

tentious, he seemed ready to restore public confidence in the presidency when he replaced Nixon in August 1974.

Ford's honeymoon lasted only a month. On September 8, 1974, he shocked the nation by announcing that he had granted Richard Nixon a full and unconditional pardon for all federal crimes he "committed or may have committed or taken part in" during his presidency. Some critics charged darkly that Nixon and Ford had made a secret bargain; others pointed out how unfair it was for Nixon's aides to serve their prison terms while the chief criminal went free. Ford apparently acted in an effort to end the bitterness over Watergate, but his attempt backfired, eroding public confidence in his leadership and linking him indelibly with the scandal.

Ford proved equally inept in his relations with Congress. Though he prided himself on his good relations with members of both houses, he opposed such Democratic measures as federal aid to education and control over strip-mining. In a little more than a year, he vetoed thirty-nine separate bills. In fact, Ford, who as a congressman had opposed virtually every Great Society measure, proved far more conservative than Nixon in the White House. He urged federal agencies to do nothing to disturb "maximum freedom for private enterprise," and he openly opposed school busing, to the dismay of civil-rights advocates.

The 1976 Campaign

Ford's weak record and the legacy of Watergate made the Democratic nomination a prize worth fighting for in 1976. A large field of candidates entered the contest, but a virtual unknown, former Georgia Governor Jimmy Carter, quickly became the front-runner. Aware of the voters' disgust with politicans of both parties, Carter ran as an outsider, portraying himself as a Southerner who had no experience in Washington and one who could thus give the nation fresh and untainted leadership. As one astonished Democrat, Averell Harriman, exclaimed, "Carter? How can Carter be nominated? I don't know him and don't know anyone who does."

Appearing refreshingly candid, Carter claimed to be an honest man, ready to deal fairly with the American people. On television the basic Carter commercial showed him sitting on a rail at his Georgia peanut farm, dressed in blue jeans, looking directly into the camera and saying, "I'll never tell a lie."

Carter swept through the primaries and won the Democratic nomination easily, naming Senator Walter Mondale of Minnesota as his running mate. Victory in November seemed assured. Ford had barely beaten back a determined challenge from former California Governor Ronald Reagan, who was the idol of the right wing. The polls gave Carter a thirty-three-point lead when the campaign began, but he quickly lost ground as he began to hedge on the issues. President Ford counterattacked, saying of his Democratic opponent, "he wavers, he wanders, he wiggles and he waffles." But Ford, who had developed a reputation as a bumbler from both his uninspired leadership and occasional physical stumbles on golf courses and airport ramps, reinforced his own image of ineptitude. In a televised debate, responding to a question about Iron Curtain countries, he declared that "there is no Soviet domination of Eastern Europe."

Carter won an extremely narrow victory in 1976. Despite Watergate and Ford's weak record, the Democratic candidate took only 49.98 percent of the popular vote. Ford swept nearly the entire West, but Carter carried the South and key northern industrial states like New York and Ohio. Far more than most recent elections, the

The Election of 1976

Candidate	Party	Popular Vote	Electoral Vote
Carter	Democrat	40,830,763	297
Ford	Republican	39,147,793	240
McCarthy	Independent	756,631	

outcome turned on class and racial factors. "The affluent, the well-educated, the suburbanites largely went for Ford," commented one observer, "the socially and economically disadvantaged for Carter." The black vote clinched the victory for the Democrats. Carter received over 90 percent of the votes of blacks, and their ballots provided the margin of victory in Ohio, Pennsylvania, and seven southern states.

Disenchantment with Carter

The new President, described by an associate as "superficially self-effacing but intensely shrewd," was an ambitious and intelligent politician. He had a rare gift for sensing what people wanted and appearing to give it to them. Liberals thought he clearly stood with them; conservatives were equally convinced that he was on their side. He was especially adept at utilizing symbols. He emerged from airplanes carrying his own garment bag; after his inauguration he walked up Pennsylvania Avenue hand-in-hand with his wife Rosalynn and daughter Amy. "Look," he seemed to be saying, "I am just an ordinary citizen who happens to be in the White House."

The substance, however, failed to match the style. He had no discernible political philosophy, no clear sense of direction. He sought the White House convinced that he was brighter and better than his competitors, but once there he had no cause or mission to fulfill. He called himself a populist, but that label meant little more than an appeal to the common man, a somewhat ironic appeal, given Carter's personal wealth.

■ Despite his intelligence and hard work, Jimmy Carter's policies seemed to lack vision, and the public began to question his ability to lead.

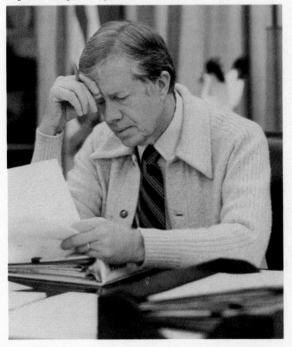

"The idea of a millionaire populist has always amused me," commented his attorney general, fellow Georgian Griffin Bell, "since the two persuasions seem contradictory."

The makeup of his administration reflected the conflicting tendencies that would eventually destroy the Carter administration. In the White House, he surrounded himself with close associates from Georgia, fellow outsiders like presidential adviser Hamilton Jordan and press secretary Jody Powell. Yet he picked established Democrats for key cabinet positions; Cyrus Vance, a New York lawyer, as secretary of state; Joseph Califano, a former aide to Lyndon Johnson, to head HEW; and Michael Blumenthal, the president of the Bendix Corporation, as secretary of the treasury. In the lower ranks, however, he selected liberal activists, followers of George McGovern, Ted Kennedy, and Ralph Nader, people who were intent on regulating business and preserving the environment. The result was bound to be tension and conflict, as the White House staff and the federal bureaucracy worked at cross purposes, one group seeking change while the other attempted to protect the President.

Lacking both a clear set of priorities and a coherent political philosophy, the Carter administration was doomed to fail. The President strove hard for a balanced budget but was forced to accept mounting deficits. Federal agencies fought to save the environment and help consumers but served only to anger industry. For example, head of the highway safety program Joan Claybrook, a former associate of Ralph Nader, recalled 12.9 million automobiles in 1977. Her predecessor in 1976 had recalled only 3.4 million.

In the crucial area of social services, Joseph Califano failed repeatedly in his efforts to carry out long-overdue reforms. His attempt to overhaul the nation's welfare program, which had become a $30-billion annual operation serving some thirty million Americans, won little support from the White House. Carter's unwillingness to take the political risks involved in revamping the overburdened Social Security system by reducing benefits and raising the retirement age blocked Califano's efforts. And the HEW secretary finally gave up his attempt to draw up a workable National Health Insurance plan when he was caught in the crossfire between President Carter and Senator Kennedy.

Informed by his pollsters in 1979 that he was losing the nation's confidence, Carter sought desperately to redeem himself. After a series of meetings at Camp David with a wide variety of advisers, he gave a speech in which he attributed the blame for his failure to the American people, accusing them of creating "a crisis of confidence . . . that strikes at the very heart and soul and spirit of our national will." Then a week after what his critics termed the "national malaise" speech, he requested the resignation of Califano and Treasury Secretary Blumenthal. But neither the attempt to pin responsibility on the American people nor the firing of cabinet members could hide the fact that Carter, despite his good intentions and hard work, had failed to provide the bold leadership the nation needed.

From Détente to Renewed Cold War

America's position in the world declined sharply in the 1970s. In part, the fault was internal. The Vietnam War left the American people convinced that the nation should never again intervene abroad and Watergate discredited strong presidential leadership, shifting power over foreign policy to Congress. The new national consensus was symbolized by the War Powers Act, passed in 1973, which required the President to consult with Congress before sending American troops into action overseas. At the same time, external events and developments, notably the control over oil exercised by OPEC and the threats posed by revolutionary nationalism in the Middle East and Latin America, further weakened American foreign policy. No longer able to dominate the international scene, the United States began to play the role of spectator, and at times even of victim.

American diplomats tried three different strategies in the '70s in an effort to adjust to the new realities of power. During the Ford presidency, Secretary of State Kissinger continued the policy of détente. Aware that the Soviet Union had neutralized America's traditional nuclear advantage, Kissinger sought to use both economic incentives and Russian fear of China to moderate Soviet policy. In the Carter administration,

Estimated Total Costs of U.S. Wars, 1775–1980
(in millions of dollars)

	Wartime Costs	Veterans' Benefit Costs	Interest Payments on War Loans	Estimated Long-term Costs
American Revolution	100	28	20	148
War of 1812	93	20	14	127
Mexican War	73	26	10	109
Civil War (Union side only)*	3,200	3,289	1,200	7,689
Spanish-American War	400	2,096	60	2,556
World War I	26,000	13,383	11,100	50,383
World War II	288,000	57,565	200,000	545,565
Korean Conflict	54,000	9,564	7,500	71,064
Vietnam Conflict	111,000	9,330	3,000	123,330

Costs to the Confederate side are estimated at $1 billion.
Source: U.S. Bureau of the Census, Statistical Abstract of the United States: 1982–83
(103d edition) Washington, D.C., 1982.

American foreign policy oscillated between two poles. Although Secretary of State Cyrus Vance tried to maintain elements of détente, President Carter called for an American crusade on behalf of human rights in the world. At the same time, National Security Adviser Zbigniew Brzezinski advocated more hawkish policies which stressed the Soviet arms buildup and the need for confrontation. By the late 1970s, Brzezinski's hard line had triumphed over both Vance's version of détente and Carter's concern for human rights.

Retreat in Asia and Africa

It was Gerald Ford's fate to reap where Nixon had sown. In 1974, Congress cut in half the administration's request for $1.4 billion in military aid to South Vietnam. A year later, when a North Vietnamese offensive proved surprisingly successful, Ford was unable to get Congress to grant any additional aid. Bereft of American assistance and weakened by internal corruption, the South Vietnamese government was unable to stop the advance on Saigon in April 1975. American forces concentrated on evacuating 150,000 loyal South Vietnamese, but many more were left behind when the last helicopter left the roof of the embassy in Saigon. Bitter and humiliated, the American people dejectedly watched the televised scene as the North Vietnamese celebrated their conquest of the South.

■ *Through television, millions of Americans watched the fall of Saigon. Thousands of South Vietnamese sought refuge in the U.S. embassy compound.*

Less than a month later, Ford had a chance to remind the world of American power. The Khmer Rouge government of Cambodia seized an American freighter, the *Mayaguez*, and imprisoned its crew. When the Communists ignored the initial American protest, Ford authorized an armed attack on Cambodia by two thousand marines from bases in Thailand. By the time the American forces landed on a small offshore island, Cambodia had freed the crewmen. The nation took pride in the President's resort to force, but forty Americans paid for his decision with their lives.

Events in Africa, however, proved that caution and restraint were still the hallmark of American foreign policy in the 1970s. The new nation of Angola had won its independence from Portugal in 1974, only to be caught up in a civil war between rival forces. The United States and China backed one group in this small country, but the Soviet Union, using several thousand Cuban troops, helped put a rival faction in power.

Despite repeated pleas from Ford and Kissinger, Congress refused to sanction American interven-

tion. Covert action by the CIA proved ineffective, but the government of Angola turned out to be neutral, relying on technical assistance from the United States to offset military aid from Russia. Most Americans were relieved by the outcome in Angola, not sharing Kissinger's belief that the nation had been "traumatized by Vietnam as we were by Munich."

Accommodation in Latin America

President Carter was more successful than Ford in adjusting to the growing nationalism in the world, particularly in Central America, where the United States had imposed order for most of the twentieth century by backing reactionary regimes.

The first test came in Panama. Resentment over American ownership of the Panama Canal had led Lyndon Johnson to enter into negotiations aimed at the eventual return of the waterway to Panama. Carter completed the long diplo-

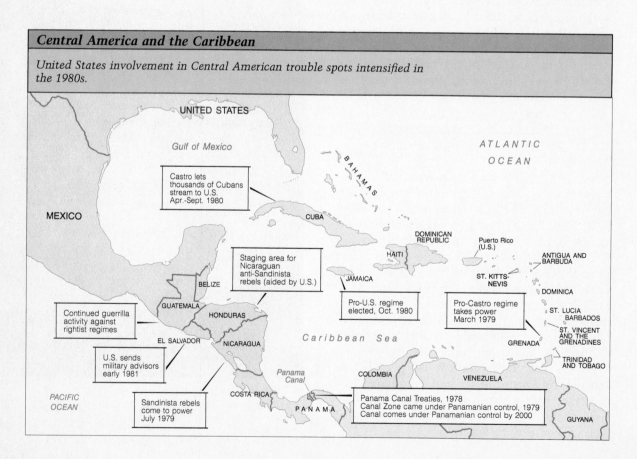

Central America and the Caribbean

United States involvement in Central American trouble spots intensified in the 1980s.

An eighteen-year-old guerrilla fighter at a rebel camp in El Salvador. Known as "Claudia," which is not her real name, she is part of a rebel group battling the Salvadoran military forces.

encouraged left-wing guerrillas to step up attacks on the governments of Guatemala and El Salvador. Carter hoped to find responsible democratic leaders to support in these countries, but both situations quickly deteriorated into classic struggles between the conservative elite, who controlled the land and the army, and radicals who rallied the peasantry to their side. The situation was most critical in El Salvador, where Carter decided to back the government against the rebels, authorizing increased American military aid just before he left office in January 1981. Carter was unable to find a workable alternative between the extremes of reactionary dictatorship and radical revolution in Central America. His successor in the White House faced a dangerous situation in the hemisphere.

The Quest for Peace in the Middle East

The inconclusive results of the Yom Kippur War gave Henry Kissinger the opportunity to play the role of peacemaker in the troubled Middle East. Shuttling back and forth between Cairo and Jerusalem, and then to Damascus, the secretary of state finally succeeded in arranging a pullback of Israeli forces in both the Sinai and the Golan Heights. Although he failed to achieve his goal of an Arab-Israeli settlement, Kissinger had succeeded in demonstrating that the United States could play the role of neutral mediator between the Israelis and Arabs. And equally important, he had detached Egypt from dependence on the Soviet Union, thereby weakening Russian influence in the Middle East.

Jimmy Carter tried at first to bring the Soviets back into the Middle Eastern peacemaking process by proposing a big power settlement. In November 1977, however, Egyptian President Anwar Sadat stunned the world by traveling to Jerusalem in an effort to reach agreement directly with Israel. The next year, Carter abandoned his efforts to work with the Russians and instead invited both Sadat and Israeli Prime Minister Menachem Begin to negotiate under his guidance at Camp David. For thirteen days, President Carter met with Sadat and Begin, finally emerging with the ambiguous Camp David accords. A framework for negotiations, rather than an actual

matic process in 1977 by signing two treaties. One restored sovereignty in the 500-square-mile canal zone to Panama, while the other provided for gradual Panamanian responsibility for operating the canal, with appropriate safeguards for its use and defense by the United States. Despite the intense opposition of right-wing Republicans, who charged Carter with "giving away" the Panama Canal, the Senate ratified the treaties in 1978, and thus paved the way for the return of the canal to Panama by the year 2000.

Carter tried to be equally understanding when a group of Nicaraguan leftists known as the Sandinistas began a revolt against dictator Anastasio Somoza, who fell from power in 1979. The United States had withheld support from Somoza and worked with several Latin American nations, notably Venezuela and Mexico, to establish a new Nicaraguan government that included both rebel and business leaders. Congressional reluctance to extend economic aid, however, and the regime's gradual shift to the left, including closer ties with Castro's Cuba, created a widening rift between the United States and Nicaragua by the end of the 1970s.

The success of the Sandinistas in Nicaragua

■ *The Camp David accords in 1978 set the stage for a peace treaty between Egypt and Israel. Here a beaming Jimmy Carter watches as Prime Minister Begin embraces President Sadat. But this personal triumph for Carter was short-lived.*

peace settlement, the Camp David agreements dealt gingerly with the problem of Palestinian autonomy in the West Bank and Gaza Strip areas.

In 1979, Israel and Egypt signed a peace treaty which provided for the gradual return of the entire Sinai to Egypt but left the fate of the Palestine Arabs vague and unsettled. By excluding both the Palestine Liberation Organization (PLO) and the Soviet Union from the negotiations, the United States alienated Egypt from the other Arab nations and drove the more radical states closer to the Soviet Union.

Any sense of progress in the Middle East as a result of Camp David was quickly offset in 1979 with the outbreak of the Iranian Revolution. Under Nixon and Kissinger, the United States had come to depend heavily on the shah and his powerful army for defense of the vital Persian Gulf. Carter continued the close relationship with the shah, despite growing signs of domestic discontent with his leadership. In a visit to Teheran in late 1977, the President praised the shah for making Iran "an island of stability" and for per-

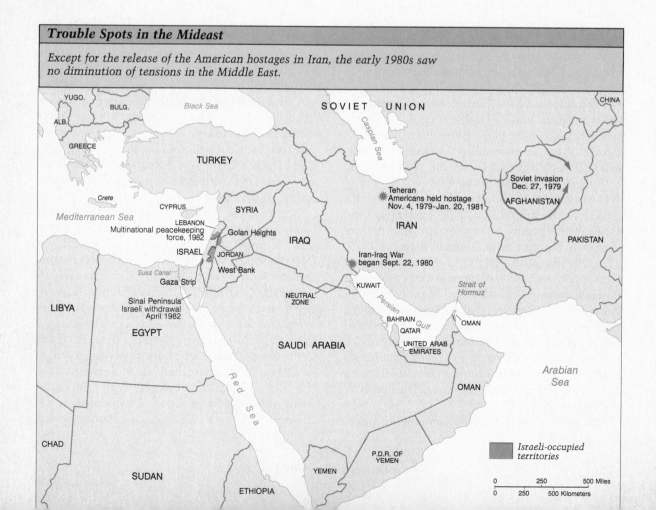

Trouble Spots in the Mideast

Except for the release of the American hostages in Iran, the early 1980s saw no diminution of tensions in the Middle East.

sonally deserving "the respect and the admiration and love which your people give to you." Yet little more than a year later Iran was in chaos as the exiled Ayatollah Ruhollah Khomeini led a fundamentalist Moslem revolt against the shah.

Unaware of the deep resentment most Iranians felt toward the shah—a resentment based both on dislike of sweeping modernization programs and police-state rule—the Carter administration misjudged the nature of the Iranian Revolution. At first the United States encouraged the shah to remain in Iran, but when he decided to leave the country in January 1979, Carter tried to work with a moderate regime rather than encourage an army coup. With Khomeini's return from exile, Moslem militants quickly came to power in Teheran. In October 1979, Carter permitted the exiled shah to enter the United States for medical treatment. Irate mobs in Iran denounced the United States and on November 4, militant students seized the U.S. embassy in Teheran and took fifty-eight Americans prisoner.

The prolonged hostage crisis revealed the extent to which American power had declined in the 1970s. Carter relied first on diplomacy and economic reprisals in a vain attempt to free the hostages. American allies in Western Europe and Japan, dependent on Middle Eastern oil, quickly disassociated themselves from the United States, while Khomeini offset the American economic embargo by signing trade agreements with the Soviet Union. In an attempt to impress the Iranians, the United States concentrated its naval forces in the Indian Ocean. In his State of the Union message in January 1980, the president enunciated a new Carter Doctrine, telling the world that the United States would fight to protect the vital oil supplies of the Persian Gulf. "Twin threats to the flow of oil—from regional instability and now potentially from the Soviet Union—require that we firmly defend our vital interest when threatened."

Carter was unable to back up these brave words with meaningful action. Plans for a rapid deployment force were prepared, but it would be several years before these mobile troops could be deployed. In April 1980, the President authorized a desperate rescue mission that ended in failure when several helicopters broke down in the Iranian desert. The mission was aborted, an accident cost the lives of eight crewmen, and Secretary of

Americans were shocked by the deep anger Iranian mobs directed toward the Americans staffing the U.S. embassy in Teheran.

The burnt helicopters in the Iranian desert emphasized America's frustration and its inability to rescue the hostages.

State Cyrus Vance—who had opposed the rescue attempt—resigned in protest. The hostage crisis dragged on through the summer and fall of 1980, a symbol of American weakness that proved to be a powerful political handicap to Carter in the upcoming presidential election.

The End of Détente

The policy of détente was already in trouble when Carter took office in 1977. Congressional refusal to relax trade restrictions on the Soviet Union had doomed Kissinger's attempts to win political concessions from the Soviets through economic incentives. The Kremlin's repression of the growing dissident movement, led by nuclear physicist Andrei Sakharov, and its harsh policy restricting the emigration of Soviet Jews had caused many Americans to doubt the wisdom of seeking accommodation with the Soviet Union.

President Carter's emphasis on human rights appeared to the Russians to be a direct repudiation of détente. In his inaugural address, Carter reaffirmed his concern over the mistreatment of human beings anywhere in the world, declaring "our commitment to human rights must be absolute." It was easier said than done. Carter did withhold aid from authoritarian governments in Chile and Argentina, but equally repressive regimes in South Korea and the Philippines continued to receive generous American support. Human rights proved, in the words of one presidential aide, "absolute in principle but flexible in application." The Soviets, however, were disturbed by the principle, particularly after Carter received Soviet exiles in the White House.

Secretary of State Vance concentrated on continuing the main pillar of détente, the strategic arms limitation talks (SALT). In 1974, President Ford had met with Brezhnev in Vladivostok and reached tentative agreement on the outline of SALT II. The chief provision was for a ceiling of 2400 nuclear launchers by each side, a level which would not require either Russia or the United States to give up any existing delivery vehicles. In March 1977, Vance went to Moscow to propose a drastic reduction in this level; the Soviets, already angry over human rights, rejected the American proposal as an attempt to overcome the Russian lead in land-based ICBMs.

Zbigniew Brzezinski, Carter's national security adviser, worked from the outset to reverse the policy of détente. Commenting that he was "the first Pole in 300 years in a position to really stick it to the Russians," he favored confrontation with the Kremlin. Although Carter signed a SALT II treaty with Russia in 1978 which lowered the ceiling on nuclear delivery systems to 2250, growing opposition in the Senate played directly into Brzezinski's hand. He prevailed on the President to advocate adoption of a new MX missile to replace the existing Minuteman ICBMs, which some experts thought were now vulnerable to a Soviet first strike. This new weapons system, together with the planned Trident submarine, ensured that regardless of SALT, the nuclear arms race would be speeded up in the 1980s.

Brzezinski also was successful in persuading the President to use China to outmaneuver the Soviets. After a trip to China in 1978, Brzezinski arranged for the sale of advanced technology to China (including items denied the Russians), and the possibility of resuming full diplomatic relations was explored. Finally, on January 1, 1979, the United States and China exchanged ambassa-

■ *Soviet tanks rolled into Afghanistan in December 1979, dealing a near-mortal blow to East-West détente.*

Military Power: United States vs. USSR, 1980–1981

	United States	Soviet Union
Intercontinental Ballistic Missiles (ICBMs)	1,052[a]	1,398
Submarine-launched Ballistic Missiles (SLBMs)	576[b]	950
Long-Range Strategic Bombers	348[c]	156
Total Delivery Vehicles (ICBMs, SLBMs, Bombers)	1,976	2,504
Nuclear Warheads	9,200	6,000
European Nuclear Forces[d]	924	2,537
Anti-Ballistic Missile Launchers (ABM)	0	32
Aircraft Carriers	12	1
Armed Forces Personnel	2,050,000 (plus 2,768,000 NATO forces)	4,822,000 (plus 1,122,000 Warsaw Pact forces)

*Although the United States lagged behind the Soviet Union in certain categories, the U.S. Department of Defense and other government sources explained that the figures revealed a basic equivalence in strategic nuclear power. Moreover, in measuring the fighting abilities of both sides, technological skills, qualities of leadership, and economic strength must be considered. Also, some of the Soviet military power was deployed, not against Western Europe or the United States, but against China.

[a]Fifty-two single-warhead Titan-IIs (two others were out of commission and not counted); 450 single-warhead Minuteman IIs; and 550 MIRVed Minuteman IIIs.

[b]80 Polaris; 304 Poseidon; 192 Trident.

[c]B-52s

[d]Total launchers for Western allies (NATO and France) and Warsaw Pact. Figures represent bombers and missiles. The Soviets disputed the figures (disagreeing on which weapons should be counted) and offered instead: 1,031 for the Western allies and 1.055 for the Warsaw Pact. Under NATO auspices, the United States set 1983 for deployment of 108 Pershing missiles and 464 ground-launched cruise missiles in Europe.

Source: Thomas G. Paterson, J. Garry Clifford, and Kenneth J. Hagan, American Foreign Policy: A History (Lexington, Mass.: D. C. Heath, 1983).

dors, thereby completing the reconciliation that Nixon had begun in 1971. The new relationship between China and the United States presented the Soviet Union with the problem of defending itself against two distinct enemies.

The Cold War, in abeyance for nearly a decade, resumed with full fury in December 1979 when the Soviet Union invaded Afghanistan. Although this move was apparently defensive in nature, designed to ensure a regime friendly to the Soviet Union, it appeared to many as the beginning of a Soviet thrust toward the Indian Ocean and the Persian Gulf. Carter responded to this aggression with a series of stern acts: the United States banned the sale of high technology to Russia, embargoed the export of grain, resumed draft registration, and even boycotted the 1980 Mos-

cow Olympics. These American moves did not halt the invasion of Afghanistan; instead, they put the United States and Russia back on a collision course.

The results doomed détente. Aware that he could not get a two-thirds vote in the Senate, Carter withdrew the SALT II treaty. Right-wing groups in the United States began to warn of Soviet military superiority and call for a massive American arms build-up. The hopeful phrases of détente gave way to belligerent rhetoric as groups like the Committee on the Present Danger called for an all-out effort against the Soviet Union. Jimmy Carter, who had come into office hoping to advance human rights and control the nuclear arms race, now found himself a victim of the renewed Cold War.

Cycles in History

Most historians believe that the events and trends they describe are unique, reflecting a variety of individual characteristics that make each war, each election, and each era different. Yet some scholars have noticed that certain trends tend to recur over long periods of time; others go even further, suggesting that there are cyclical rhythms in American history that make it possible to predict the future.

The two most plausible cycles relate to political behavior and to foreign policy. In 1949, Arthur M. Schlesinger, Sr., a noted cultural historian, described an oscillation between liberalism and conservatism in American politics from the Revolution through World War II (see Table 1). Periods of liberal reform alternated with eras of conservatism in approximately sixteen-year cycles. Presenting his findings at the end of a liberal era, Schlesinger prophesied that the conservative swing would last until 1962, and then would give way to a new surge of liberalism, that would continue until about 1978. The election of John F. Kennedy and the adoption of Lyndon Johnson's Great Society program in the mid-1960s fits in neatly with Schlesinger's prediction, as does Ronald Reagan's conservative triumph in 1980, which was foreshadowed by Republican gains in the 1978 congressional elections.

Political scientist Frank L. Klingberg, writing in 1952, offered an equally persuasive explanation of the fluctuation between isolation and internationalism in American foreign policy. Periods of introversion, Klingberg argued, alternated about every twenty-five years with eras of an active world policy throughout American history (see Table 2). Klingberg's forecast for the future proved nearly as accurate as Schlesinger's. The shift to an active world policy which began in 1940, would continue until the late 1960s, he claimed, and then would give way to a period of relative withdrawal through the early 1990s. The Vietnam War triggered a strong protest movement which forced Lyndon Johnson to begin winding down the conflict in 1968, and led to a policy of détente in the 1970s under Nixon and Ford.

---

1. Schlesinger's Political Periods

Liberal	Conservative
1765–1787	1787–1801
1801–1816	1816–1829
1829–1841	1841–1861
1861–1869	1869–1901
1901–1919	1919–1931
1931–1947	(1947–1962)*
(1962–1978)*	(1978–1993)*

Arthur M. Schlesinger, Paths to the Present,
p. 81. Copyright 1949, by the Macmillan Company.
*projected

2. Klingberg's Foreign Policy Moods

Isolation	Participation
1776–1798	1798–1824
1824–1844	1844–1871
1871–1891	1891–1919
1919–1940	(1940–1967)*
(1967–1988)*	(1988–2015)*

Frank L. Klingberg, "The Historical Alternation of Moods in American Foreign Policy," World Politics *(1952): 250.*
*projected

Both scholars see the cycles as reflecting a deep-seated and natural rhythm comparable to the tides that ebb and flow in the world's oceans. Neither war nor depression seems to alter the pattern, and even strong leaders such as Abraham Lincoln and Franklin Roosevelt had to adapt themselves to this basic law of American life. Both authors see the pendulum-like swing between opposite poles as a healthy mechanism, which enables the nation to adapt to change while holding on to inherited values. Schlesinger calls it a "balance wheel of orderly evolution," which ensures "a fair field" for both liberals and conservatives over time. Klingberg is slightly less enthusiastic, but he still feels that the alternating pattern holds promise of continued American leadership in world affairs.

In addition to predicting future trends, the Schlesinger and Klingberg cycles reveal a significant correlation between domestic politics and foreign policy. During periods of conservative control, the nation has tended toward isolation, while during liberal eras, a more active foreign policy has prevailed. From 1776 to 1947, the span covered by both authors, liberalism was in vogue eighty years and conservatism ninety-one. For forty-eight of the eighty liberal years, the nation pursued an active world policy. The link between isolationism and conservatism is not quite as strong; for fifty-one of the ninety-one years of conservative dominance, the United States was in a stage of withdrawal from world affairs (see Table 3).

What do these cycles tell us of the future? Schlesinger's pattern suggests that we can expect the current era of Reaganism to persist through the decade of the 1980s, with a shift back to liberalism likely around 1993. Klingberg's analysis forecasts a continued passive world role until about 1988, when we can expect a return to a more active foreign policy. And in keeping with the nation's historic tendencies, the liberal administrations of the final decade of the twentieth century and the early years of the twenty-first will be extending American power and influence once again on a global basis.

A Decade of Social Change

The 1970s witnessed a series of significant shifts in American society that paralleled the economic changes brought about by inflation and the oil shocks. The nation's population in 1980 stood at just over 226 million, a gain of 11.4 percent from 1970, the smallest rate of increase since the census of 1940. The vast majority—nearly 186 million—were white, while blacks still formed the largest ethnic minority—26.5 million.

A People on the Move

The most striking finding of the 1980 census was that for the first time in American history more than half of the population lived in the South and West. The states of the Northeast and Midwest had virtually stood still (New York had actually lost population in the 1970s), while the Sunbelt, notably Florida, California, and Texas, had boomed. This population shift reflected the changing economic realities of the decade. College-educated men and women, especially young professionals, and blue-collar workers with skills in demand gravitated to the Sunbelt, where more and more American corporations were moving their offices and factories.

The cities of the North suffered the most from this mass exodus. New York City, which almost went bankrupt midway through the decade, lost nearly a million people between 1970 and 1980. Midwestern cities like Cleveland and Saint Louis were equally hard hit, each losing a quarter of its population in just ten years as whites led the move either to the Sunbelt or to nearby suburbs. The central cities of the North and West lost many of their best-educated and most affluent citizens, leaving them with large low-income populations—mainly minority groups—with very expensive social needs.

Another striking population trend was the nationwide rise in the number of the elderly. At the beginning of the century, only 4.1 percent of the

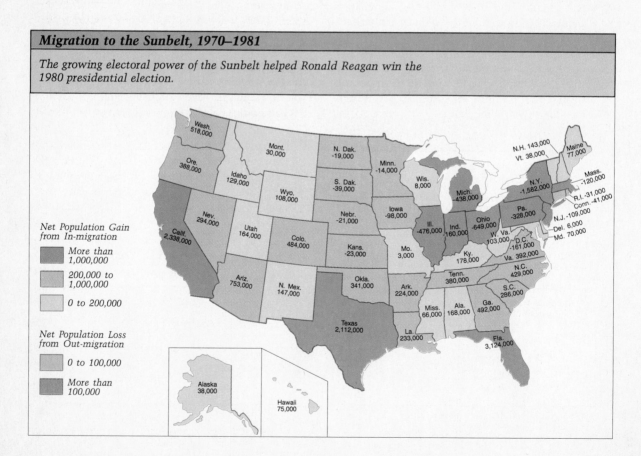

Migration to the Sunbelt, 1970–1981

The growing electoral power of the Sunbelt helped Ronald Reagan win the 1980 presidential election.

Net Population Gain from In-migration

- More than 1,000,000
- 200,000 to 1,000,000
- 0 to 200,000

Net Population Loss from Out-migration

- 0 to 100,000
- More than 100,000

Wash. 518,000
Ore. 388,000
Mont. 30,000
Idaho 129,000
N. Dak. -19,000
Minn. -14,000
Wis. 8,000
Mich. -438,000
N.H. 143,000
Vt. 38,000
Maine 77,000
Mass. -120,000
Nev. 294,000
Wyo. 108,000
S. Dak. -39,000
Iowa -98,000
Ohio -649,000
Pa. -328,000
N.Y. -1,582,000
R.I. -31,000
Conn. -41,000
Calif. 2,338,000
Utah 164,000
Colo. 484,000
Nebr. -21,000
Ill. -476,000
Ind. 160,000
W. Va. 103,000
D.C. -161,000
N.J. -109,000
Del. 6,000
Md. 70,000
Kans. -23,000
Mo. 3,000
Ky. 178,000
Va. 392,000
Ariz. 753,000
N. Mex. 147,000
Okla. 341,000
Ark. 224,000
Tenn. 380,000
N.C. 429,000
S.C. 286,000
Texas 2,112,000
La. 233,000
Miss. 66,000
Ala. 168,000
Ga. 492,000
Fla. 3,124,000
Alaska 38,000
Hawaii 75,000

Houston skyline. The growth and prosperity of the Sunbelt is reflected in the gleaming new skyscrapers erected in cities like Houston, Texas, during the 1970s and early '80s.

population was age sixty-five or older; by 1980, those over sixty-five made up 11.3 percent, and people over seventy-five were the single fastest growing group of all. Major advances in medicine had increased life expectancy from sixty-three in the 1930s to seventy-two by the mid-1970s. By 1980 American women could expect to live to age seventy-seven. There were a huge number of widows, many lonely and insecure, living on the edge of poverty. Yet thanks to the indexing of Social Security payments to inflation, the elderly fared relatively well economically during the decade.

A more traditional American process, that of immigration, underwent a surprising shift in the 1970s. A nation that had been built on a predominantly European influx suddenly found itself adding millions of Asians and Latin Americans to its population, with very few newcomers arriving from Europe. More than 5 million immigrants entered the United States in the 1970s, with the annual rate rising to over 700,000 by the end of the decade. In 1978, Mexico provided the most, 92,000 legal entrants and probably as many more illegal ones, with Vietnam close behind at 88,000 followed by the Philippines with 37,000 and Cuba with 30,000. In contrast, only 14,200 came from England, 7400 from Italy and a mere 982 from Ireland. The newcomers from Asia and Latin America filled the traditional economic role of

the immigrant, working at the dirty and difficult jobs that most Americans shunned, often for low wages and without receiving any government assistance. Their cultural, linguistic, and ethnic differences, however, created an assimilation problem at least as great as that of the "new" immigrants from southern and eastern Europe in the late nineteenth century.

Although the 1980 census revealed many departures from past experience, it also reaffirmed some traditional American patterns. In the face of inflation and unemployment, the American people continued to be prosperous. The median family income rose to $21,023, with just 11 percent of the population living below the government's official poverty line. Not only were Americans living longer, but thanks to Medicare, Medicaid, and private health plans, they were receiving better medical care than ever before, with health expenditures rising to $476 per person. A declining birthrate lowered enrollments in elementary and secondary schools, leading to better teacher-student ratios, while college attendance continued to climb. By 1981, there were nearly 12 million college students, compared to only a million and a half in 1941. Now more than 20 percent of the nation's young people received a college degree, compared to 12 percent of their parents' generation.

The overall picture was of a society in transition. The rising figures of crime, teen-age pregnancy, and drug use were balanced by better health and educational opportunities than any previous generation had enjoyed. Pockets of poverty, notably in the older industrial states, were matched by boom areas. America was still the land of opportunity for immigrants, even if they came now from Mexico and Vietnam, rather than Poland and Italy. And despite the ravages of inflation and the shock of the energy crunch, people continued to look to the future, aware of the new age of limitations in which they lived, but confident that they could still achieve the American dream.

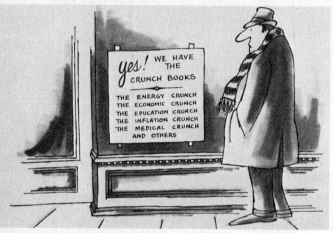

Drawing by H. Martin: © 1980
The New Yorker Magazine, Inc.

■ Naval cadets at Annapolis. Some women won admission to service academies during the 1970s, but most working women continued to face job discrimination.

The Changing Role of Women

The entry of women into the work force accelerated in the 1970s, climbing to a new high. Some 10 million women took jobs in the period from 1965 to 1975, compared to 7 million men. By the end of the decade, 52 percent of all adult women were working, and their ranks included 6 million more working wives than in 1970.

Women scored some impressive breakthroughs. They began to enter corporation boardrooms, became presidents of major universities, and were admitted to West Point and Annapolis. The appointment of Sandra Day O'Connor to the Supreme Court in 1981 marked a historic first. Yet despite the growing number of female elected officials, doctors, and lawyers, the vast majority of working women still suffered from economic discrimination. The Equal Pay Act, passed by Congress in 1972, and a number of lawsuits which forced corporations to pay women equal wages for equal work, helped close the gap, but the sex differential still remained. As late as 1980, the median pay for working women was only 60 percent of that for men.

Women had fewer children in the 1970s than in earlier decades. The birthrate, which had peaked at over 3.5 births for every woman of child-bearing age in the late 1950s, dropped to less than 2 by the mid-1970s. This trend toward smaller families was related to the great increase in working wives, an increase that was intensified by the economic pressures caused by inflation in the 1970s. Many women who pursued careers put off childbearing, waiting until they had established themselves professionally, while others simply decided to forgo children entirely. The drop in the birthrate also reflected the later age of marriage in the seventies, as well as the ever larger number of single women.

The postwar increase in the divorce rate continued unabated. Where marriages once outnumbered divorces by five to one in the 1950s, by 1980 the ratio was down to two to one. Marital breakup lost its stigma; for many, marriage ceased to be a sacred institution. The rise in the divorce rate resulted in a tremendous increase in what the census dubbed "one-parent households," reflecting a sharp decline in traditional family units. The number of one-parent families—nearly always a case of the mother rearing the children alone, rose by 79 percent during the decade. By the end of the 1970s, 22 percent of all American children were reared in homes with only one parent; in the case of blacks, the figure was 56 percent.

The women's movement sought two different but related objectives in the 1970s. The first was ratification of the Equal Rights Amendment. Approved by Congress in 1972, the amendment stated simply, "Equality of rights under the law shall not be denied or abridged by the United States or any state on account of sex." Within a year, twenty-two states had approved the amendment, but the efforts gradually faltered and finally stalled just three states short of ratification. The opposition came in part from working-class women who feared, as one union leader explained, that those employed as "maids, laundry workers, hospital cleaners, or dishwashers" would lose the protection of state laws that regulated wages and hours of work for women. Right-wing activist Phyllis Schlafly led an organized effort to defeat ERA, claiming that the amendment would lead to unisex toilets, homosexual marriages, and the drafting of women. The National Organization for Women (NOW) fought back, persuading Congress to extend the time for ratification by three years and waging intense campaigns for approval in Florida and Illinois. But the deadline for ratification finally passed on June 30, 1982, with the ERA forces still three states short. NOW leader Eleanor Smeal vowed a continuing struggle, declaring, "The crusade is not over. We know that we are the wave of the future."

The women's movement was more successful in its fight for reproductive rights. Heartened by the 1973 Supreme Court decision, *Roe* v. *Wade*, which struck down state laws banning abortions, feminists worked hard to extend the right of women to choose whether to have children. Right-to-life groups, backed by the Catholic

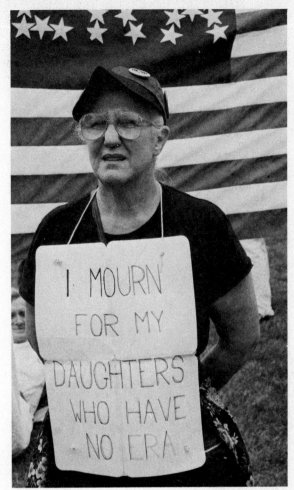

■ *Many women reasoned that rights granted by statute could easily be repealed in the future; therefore they embarked on a crusade to pass an equal rights amendment to the Constitution.*

church, fundamentalist Protestants, and extreme conservatives, sought to deny the use of public funds to pay for abortions, thereby limiting the exercise of this right to those women who could afford it. With the strong support of President Carter, Congress passed the Hyde amendment which forbade the use of federal money to pay for abortions, and in 1981 the Supreme Court upheld this legislation. Despite this setback, pro-choice groups organized privately funded family-planning agencies and abortion clinics to give poor women the opportunity to exercise control over their reproductive function.

Advance and Retreat for Blacks

For middle-class blacks, the 1970s were a decade of progress; they began to reap the gains of the affirmative-action programs spawned by LBJ's Great Society. By 1976, one third of all black workers held white-collar jobs, double the rate in 1960, and nearly 30 percent earned more than $12,000 a year. Education proved the key to black advances. With more than one million blacks enrolled in college by 1980, the opportunities for a middle-class style of life were greatly increased.

Many well-educated and affluent blacks tended to behave like whites in similar circumstances. Some joined the flight to the suburbs, leaving the central city in even larger proportions than whites. Others flocked to the Sunbelt, reversing the historic movement of rural blacks from the South to the North. In the 1970s, many young blacks, trained as doctors, lawyers, or business executives, returned to the cities of the South to pursue their careers. A 1978 survey by *Ebony* magazine identified Atlanta, Dallas, and Houston among the ten most attractive American cities for blacks. Atlanta and New Orleans both had black mayors by the end of the decade and, in fact, the South had become the most thoroughly integrated of all the nation's regions.

Occupations by Sex and Race, 1972 and 1980

Title of Occupation	Total Employed (millions) 1972	1980	1972 Percentage Female	Nonwhite	1980 Percentage Female	Nonwhite
Professional/Technical	11.4	15.6	39.3	7.2	44.3	8.9
Accountants	0.7	1.0	21.7	4.3	36.2	8.2
Computer specialists	0.2	0.5	16.8	5.5	25.7	8.0
Engineers	1.1	1.4	0.8	3.4	4.0	5.9
Lawyers and Judges	0.3	0.5	3.8	1.9	12.8	4.2
Life/Physical Scientists	0.2	0.3	10.0	7.8	20.3	9.6
Physicians/Dentists and related	0.6	0.7	9.3	6.3	12.9	8.2
Professors	0.4	0.5	28.0	7.2	33.9	7.1
Engineering/Science technicians	0.8	1.0	9.1	5.2	17.8	8.8
Writers/Artists/Entertainers	0.8	1.2	31.7	4.8	39.3	5.9
Sales	5.3	6.1	41.6	3.6	45.3	5.1
Real estate Agents/Brokers	0.3	0.5	36.7	2.6	50.7	2.1
Clerks-retail	2.3	2.3	68.9	5.0	71.1	7.2
Clerical	14.2	18.1	75.6	8.7	80.1	11.1
Bookkeepers	1.5	1.9	97.9	3.6	90.5	5.5
Clerical supervisors	0.1	0.2	57.8	10.1	70.5	12.0
Office machine operators	0.6	0.9	71.4	13.1	72.6	17.5
Secretaries	2.9	3.8	99.1	5.2	99.1	6.7
Crafts Workers	10.8	12.5	3.6	6.9	6.0	8.3
Blue-collar supervisors	1.4	1.7	6.9	6.0	10.8	7.8
Machinists and Jobsetters	0.4	0.6	0.6	6.2	4.0	8.7
Tool and die makers	0.1	0.1	0.5	2.2	2.8	2.3
Mechanics (except automobile)	1.7	2.1	1.0	5.3	2.6	7.5
Transport equipment operators	3.2	3.4	4.2	14.8	8.0	15.3
Laborers (nonfarm)	4.2	4.4	6.3	20.2	11.6	16.9
Farmers and Farm Managers	1.6	1.4	5.9	3.3	10.6	2.6
Farm Laborers/Supervisors	1.3	1.2	32.1	15.1	27.0	13.3
Service (non-private household)	9.5	11.9	57.0	10.5	58.9	18.2
Service (private household)	1.4	1.0	97.6	40.6	97.5	33.2

Source: U.S. Bureau of the Census, Statistical Abstract of the United States: 1982–83 (103d edition) Washington, D.C., 1982.

Yet despite these gains, there were also setbacks for blacks in the 1970s. The whole affirmative-action process was brought into question by the case of Allen Bakke, a white applicant to the medical school of the University of California at Davis. Bakke claimed that his rights had been violated when his application was rejected, because his credentials were better than those of several minority applicants who were awarded some of the 16 places reserved for "disadvantaged students" in the class of 100. When the highest state court in California ruled in favor of Bakke in 1976, the university appealed the verdict to the Supreme Court.

The Court issued its long-awaited ruling on June 28, 1978. By a five-to-four margin, the justices ruled in favor of Bakke, asserting that the use of "explicit racial classification" had denied him equal protection under the Fourteenth Amendment. At the same time, however, by a similar five-to-four vote, the Court upheld the principle of affirmative action, claiming that universities could make race "simply one element" in their effort to select a diverse student body.

In subsequent decisions, the Court upheld an affirmative-action program designed by Kaiser Aluminum to help advance minority workers and ordered American Telephone and Telegraph to hire more blacks and women to make up for past discrimination. It was Justice Harry A. Blackmun, a Nixon appointee, who explained the Court's position best by declaring, "in order to get beyond racism, we must first take account of race."

The plight of lower-class blacks, however, revealed that affirmative action had only a limited impact on their economic status. By the end of the seventies, fully one third of the nation's blacks lived below the poverty line, earning less than $8000 a year. In 1981, the median income for a black family was only $12,674, just over half of that of whites. Poor blacks, lacking education and job skills, could not join the migration to the Sunbelt and were stuck instead in the decaying central cities of the East and Midwest. Unemployment rates for blacks ran about 14 percent, twice that for whites, and among black teen-agers the level was a staggering 40 percent. As a result, most blacks did not share in the general affluence of the seventies.

■ *To minorities, the affirmative action guidelines set by the Supreme Court in the Alan Bakke case were too restrictive.*

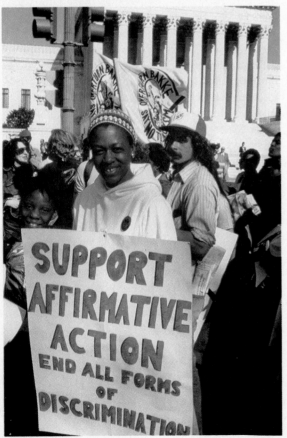

The Emerging Hispanics and Other Minorities

People with Spanish surnames, labeled Hispanics in the census, were the fastest growing of all ethnic groups in the United States in the 1970s. By 1980, there were over 14 million Hispanics in the country, an increase of more than 50 percent in ten years. The official statistics broke them down into four major categories: nearly 9 million Mexican-Americans, 2 million Puerto Ricans, 800,000 Cubans, and nearly 3 million more from other Latin countries.

Mexican-Americans, the largest group, were concentrated in the Southwest—3.6 million in California and 2.8 million in Texas. Cubans predominated in Florida, especially around Miami, and Puerto Ricans were centered in the North-

During the 1970s, Mexicans crossed the border in great numbers, hoping to better their lives. Many came without proper documentation. Here, border guards use a helicopter to spot people making an illegal entry.

east, particularly in New York City. These varied Hispanic groups had several features in common. All were relatively youthful, with a median age of twenty-two; most were relatively poor, with one fourth falling below the poverty line; and the great majority worked in either blue-collar or menial service jobs.

In the 1970s Chicanos, as Mexican-American activists preferred to call themselves, became vocal in expressing their grievances. They succeeded in winning a federal mandate for bilingual education, compelling elementary schools in states like Texas and California to teach Chicano schoolchildren in Spanish as well as in English. Mexican-American political leaders became active in local politics, leading the Democratic and Republican parties to bid for their votes. In Texas, José Angel Gutiérrez founded a third party, La Raza Unida. Although La Raza failed to win statewide influence, Gutiérrez succeeded in the early 1970s in gaining control of first the school board and then the city government of Crystal City, a South Texas community with a heavy Mexican population.

The entry of several million illegal immigrants from Mexico, once derisively called "wetbacks" and now known as "undocumented aliens," created a substantial social problem for the nation and especially for the Southwest. Critics charged that the flagrant violation of the nation's border with Mexico had led to an "invisible subculture outside the boundaries of law and legitimate institutions." They argued that these aliens took jobs away from American citizens, kept wages artificially low, and received extensive welfare benefits for which they were ineligible.

Defenders of the "illegals" contended that the nation gained from the abundant supply of workers who were willing to do the back-breaking jobs in fields and factories shunned by most Americans. Moreover, these illegal aliens usually paid sales and withholding taxes but rarely used government services for fear of being deported. Whichever view is correct, the fact remains that by 1980 there was an exploited class of illegal aliens living on the edge of poverty. The *Wall Street Journal* summed it up best by observing, "The people who benefit the most from this situation are certainly the employers, who have access to an underground market of cheap, productive labor, unencumbered by minimum wage laws, union restrictions or pension requirements."

The existence of several million illegal aliens from Mexico, along with the more than 14 million people with Spanish surnames counted in the 1980 census, meant that Hispanics were second only to the nation's 26.5 million blacks as a minority group. Other substantial ethnic groups included Chinese, bolstered by a steady flow of immigrants from Taiwan, who achieved higher educational levels and greater affluence than other minorities, and South Vietnamese, mainly refugees who came to the United States after the North Vietnamese conquest in 1975. Concentrated in coastal states, especially California and Texas, the Vietnamese immigrants gravitated toward commercial fishing and retail trade, sometimes coming into conflict with native-born Americans who resented the newcomers' competition. Like the blacks and Hispanics, the Asian immigrants—despite their educational advances —tended to form an underclass that did not share fully in the benefits of the American way of life. In the late twentieth century, as in the nineteenth, the "melting pot" was inadequate as a description of the nation's ethnic mosaic.

The Conservative Resurgence

The liberal Democratic political coalition first put together by Franklin D. Roosevelt in the early 1930s finally broke apart in the late 1970s. The Watergate scandal gave the Democrats a brief reprieve, but by the end of the decade the Republican party was taking advantage of a new conservative mood to make inroads into such traditionally Democratic voting groups as union members, Jews, and Southerners.

Thunder on the Right

During the 1970s, many signs pointed to growing public disenchantment both with liberal reliance on government to solve all the nation's problems and with increasing permissiveness in American society. In California, realtor Howard Jarvis led a popular rebellion against escalating property taxes; in 1978, the state's voters passed Proposition 13, which called for a 57 percent cut in taxes and resulted in a gradual reduction in social services. Concern over greater social acceptance of homosexuality and rising abortion and divorce rates impelled religious groups to engage in political activity to defend traditional family values. Jerry Falwell, a successful Virginia radio and television evangelist, founded the Moral Majority, a fundamentalist group dedicated to preserv-

■ *The growing political activism of religious conservatives, such as the Moral Majority led by Rev. Jerry Falwell, has been marked by successful campaigning for favored candidates.*

ing the American way of life. The Moral Majority held workshops and seminars to teach its followers how to become active in local politics, and it also issued "morality ratings" for congressmen and senators.

Conservatives proved far more skillful than liberals in mastering new political techniques. They developed direct-mail lists to elicit campaign contributions from millions of small givers; they used polls to single out the most effective issues to exploit; they perfected the system of telephone banks to get out the vote on behalf of conservative candidates on election day. Watergate induced reforms in campaign financing helped the right far more than they did liberals. Republicans especially benefited from a provision permitting PACs (political action committees) to raise and spend unlimited sums on behalf of favored candidates.

Conservatives also succeeded, for the first time since World War II, in making their cause intellectually respectable. Scholars and academics on the right flourished in new "think tanks," such as the American Enterprise Institute in Washington. William Buckley and Milton Friedman proved to be effective advocates of conservative causes in print and on television. Neo-conservatism, led by Norman Podheretz' *Commentary*, became fashionable among intellectuals, who denounced liberals for being too soft on the Communist threat abroad and too willing to compromise high standards at home in the face of demands for equality from blacks, women, and the disadvantaged. Scholars and political leaders—including such former liberal stalwarts as Daniel Patrick Moynihan, Nathan Glazer, and Daniel Bell—called for a reaffirmation of capitalism and a new emphasis on what was right about America rather than an obsessive concern with social ills.

By the end of the decade, Ronald Reagan had emerged as the most effective political spokesman for the conservative resurgence. A former movie actor and liberal Democrat, Reagan had embraced conservatism in the 1950s after a bitter fight against Communist influence in the Screen Actors Guild. As host of "General Electric Theater," a weekly television program, and then as a traveling lecturer for his sponsor, Reagan began to speak out in favor of business and against government regulation. In 1964, he scored a smashing success with a televised appeal for Barry Goldwater. Two years later, he easily won election as governor of California, terming himself a "citizen politician" to explain his qualifications and charming the voters with his magnetic smile.

■ *Ronald Reagan swept to victory in 1980. His great skill as a communicator was born of years as a sportscaster and movie actor.*

Reagan served two terms as governor of California. He delegated authority broadly to a small group of aides, preferring to play the role of "chairman of the board." Despite some initial difficulties, he proved to be an able administrator and effective political leader. But his sights were already set on Washington. As a selfmade man who had risen from humble origins, he believed in the traditional values of hard work and individualism and he felt it was his duty to "take government off the backs of the people." The man who had once called those on welfare "a faceless mass waiting for handouts" wanted to dismantle the elaborate Washington bureaucracy and return all social programs to the states. In 1976, he had barely lost out to Gerald Ford; he was now determined to win the presidency in 1980 and end the long period of rule by a liberal elite. "Are we going to have an elitist government that makes the decisions for people's lives," he asked, "or are we going to believe, as we had for so many decades, that the people can make decisions for themselves?"

The Reagan Victory

Jimmy Carter, the politician who had so skillfully used the Watergate trauma to win the presidency, now found himself on the defensive. Inflation, touched off by the second oil shock of the 1970s, reached double-digit figures—13.3 percent in 1979 and 12.4 percent in 1980. The Federal Reserve Board's effort to shrink the money supply had led to a recession, with unemployment reaching 7.8 percent by July 1980. What Ronald Reagan dubbed the "misery index," the combined rate of inflation and unemployment, hit 28 percent early in 1980 and stayed higher than 20 percent throughout the year.

Foreign policy proved almost as damaging to Carter. The Soviet invasion of Afghanistan eroded hopes for continued détente; the hostage crisis in Iran highlighted the nation's sense of helplessness in the face of flagrant violations of its sovereignty. In the short run, Carter used that crisis to beat back the challenge to his renomination by fellow Democrat Edward Kennedy. The President stayed in the White House during the spring primaries, reminding the voters of his devotion to duty, while the Massachusetts senator campaigned amid continuing questions about his behavior a decade earlier at Chappaquiddick, where a young woman had drowned in the car he drove off a bridge. His explanations failed to allay suspicions about the incident. The Democrats rallied behind Carter, although the convention delegates displayed a notable lack of enthusiasm in renominating him.

Ronald Reagan, meanwhile, recovered from a brief stumble to sweep aside his Republican challengers and win the nomination easily, naming George Bush as his running mate. In the fall campaign, Reagan hammered away at the state of the economy and of the world. He blamed Carter for inflation, which robbed workers of any gain in real wages, and scored heavily among traditionally Democratic blue-collar groups. Reagan also accused Carter of allowing the Soviets to outstrip the United States militarily and promised a massive buildup of American forces if he were elected. Although Republican strategists thought that Carter might attempt an "October surprise"—a negotiated release of the American hostages at the height of the campaign—the Iranian situation actually helped Reagan by accentuating U.S. weakness in the world.

Carter struck back by claiming that Reagan was too reckless to conduct American foreign policy in the nuclear age. Charging that this election would decide "whether we have peace or war," the President tried to portray his Republican challenger as a warmonger. The attack backfired. In a televised debate arranged late in the campaign, Reagan reassured the American people of his devotion to peace, leaving Carter with the onus of trying to land a low blow. At the end of the confrontation, Reagan scored impressively when he ended a summation of the country's dire economic condition by suggesting voters ask themselves simply, "Are you better off now than you were four years ago? Is it easier for you to go and buy things in the stores than it was four years ago?"

On election day, the American people answered with a resounding no. Reagan carried forty-four states and gained 51 percent of the popular vote. Carter won only six states and 41 percent of the popular vote, while liberal John Anderson, running as an independent candidate, received the remaining 8 percent but failed to carry a single state. Reagan clearly benefited from

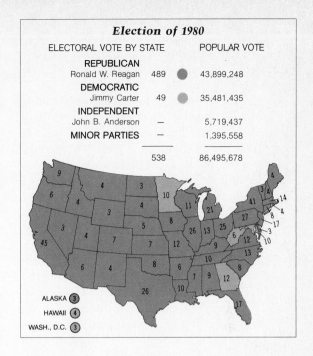

the growing political power of the Sunbelt; he carried every state west of the Mississippi and in the South lost only Georgia, Carter's home state. Even more impressive were his inroads into the old New Deal coalition. Reagan received 50.5 percent of the blue-collar vote and 46 percent of the Jewish vote, the best showing by a Republican since 1928. Only one group remained loyal to Carter; black voters gave him 85 percent of their ballots.

Even more surprising was the sweeping nature of the Republican victory. For the first time since 1954, the GOP gained control of the Senate, 53 to 46, and the party picked up 33 seats in the House to narrow the Democratic margin from 114 to 50. Liberals were the chief losers in Congress, many of them victims of a vendetta waged by the Moral Majority.

The meaning of the election was less clear than the outcome. Nearly all observers agreed that the voters had rendered a judgment on the Carter administration. "The most important issue of this campaign," commented pollster Robert Teeter, "was Jimmy Carter's record." But most experts did not feel that the outcome reflected a major realignment in American politics equivalent to the Democratic victory of FDR in 1932. Voters were expressing a distaste for current economic conditions, not a strongly held ideological preference. Political scientist Walter Dean Burnham termed the result "a conservative revitalization," but one which stopped short of making the Republicans the dominant party.

Journalist Theodore White disagreed, calling the outcome "a rejection of an entire system of ideas, those framed by the Great Society, perhaps even those rooted in the New Deal." White may well be right. In the eight presidential elections since 1952, Republican candidates have received 52.3 percent of the popular vote, compared to 47.7 percent for the Democrats; they won four elections (1952, 1956, 1972, and 1980) by landslides, one (1968) narrowly, and lost two close ones (1960 and 1976). Only in 1964 did the Republicans lose by a wide margin. The movement of the population from the Northeast and Midwest to the South and West, along with the flight from the city, helped the Republicans far more than the Democrats. Thus Reagan's victory in 1980 could signal a momentous shift in American party fortunes, marking the beginning of GOP dominance to rival the Democratic control of the previous half century.

Reaganomics

Reagan viewed his election as a mandate to achieve two goals: end inflation and regain American military parity with Russia. He hoped to conquer inflation by cutting back on government spending, especially on social programs. At the same time he would continue to support the Federal Reserve's policy, begun by Chairman Paul Volcker in 1979, of slowing the growth of the money supply. His determination to increase defense spending sharply in order to catch up with the Soviets, however, ran directly counter to his budget-cutting proposals. Moreover, Reagan's commitment to supply-side economics—the idea that lowering taxes would stimulate private investment and increase productivity—was bound to lead to large federal deficits, which in turn would fuel inflation and high interest rates.

Undaunted, Reagan unveiled his plans for economic revitalization in two televised speeches in February 1981. "I regret to say that we are in the worst economic mess since the Great Depres-

sion," he informed the nation. The President's solution was to depart from the conventional economic wisdom and enact deep cuts in spending and in taxes simultaneously. He called upon Congress to reduce income taxes by 10 percent a year for three years and then proposed a cut of $41.4 billion in the 1982 federal budget. Sparing only the military and what Reagan called the "truly deserving needy," the spending reductions cut heavily into social programs such as food stamps and Medicaid, with the main burden falling on lower-income groups.

Despite nominal Democratic control of the House, Congress quickly approved the new program, dubbed "Reaganomics" by the press. A group of conservative Democrats led by Congressman Phil Gramm of Texas, mainly from the South and hence dubbed "boll weevils," joined with Republicans in passing a budget resolution in May 1981 that cut $35 billion from 175 domestic programs. Two months later Congress enacted the largest tax cut in American history. Reagan accepted a change which limited the reduction in the first year to 5 percent, but full 10 percent cuts in 1982 and 1983 meant that personal income taxes would be reduced by 25 percent, a change that greatly benefited those with high incomes. At the same time, military spending increased from $165 billion to nearly $200 billion.

■ *After 444 days in captivity, the Americans held hostage in Iran were released on January 20, 1981, the day of Ronald Reagan's inauguration as president.*

■ *Reagonomics did succeed in bringing down inflation to less than 7 percent by mid-1982, but at a heavy social cost. Tax cuts and higher military spending led to a major recession in which 10 percent of the work force stood in lines for unemployment compensation over many months. Even so-called recession-proof jobs were adversely affected.*

Financial experts who warned that the large deficits caused by the combination of tax cuts and heavy military spending would lead to recession proved correct. The huge government borrowing forced the interest rate to rise in financial markets; the prime climbed back to over 18 percent by the end of the year, and mortgage rates reached 17 percent. The result was a drastic slowdown in business expansion and a sharp decline in sales of cars and houses. By 1982, the nation was in the throes of a major recession, with unemployment reaching a postwar high of 10 percent in October.

The voters finally had a chance to express their disenchantment with Reaganomics in the 1982 congressional elections. The Republicans lost twenty-six seats in the House, ending conservative control of that body, and barely held on to a four-seat majority in the Senate. Democrats gained seven governorships, five in the Midwest, traditionally a Republican stronghold. The largest

voter turnout in an off-year election since 1962, and a particularly heavy black vote, helped the Democrats, who won back many of the blue-collar workers who had been wooed by Reagan in 1980.

The 1982 elections revealed the contradictory nature of the national mood. Apparently, the voters were displeased with the massive unemployment and deepening recession, which they attributed to Reaganomics. "To put it bluntly," commented pollster Louis Harris, "people have had the daylights scared out of them in terms of the economy." But still they expressed considerable doubt that the Democrats, who failed to offer an alternative remedy, could do better in restoring economic health. In fact, Reagan had accomplished his major campaign promise of stemming inflation; the rate dropped to just over 10 percent in 1981 and down to less than 7 percent in 1982. Yet the cost the nation had to pay for price stability—10 percent unemployment and one third of factory capacity idle—proved politically damaging to the Republicans.

Unfortunately, the economic future of the United States in the 1980s lay beyond the simple slogans of partisan political debate. The era of abundance touched off by World War II had come to an end in the 1970s. The period of rapid industrial growth and consumer prosperity, made possible by artificially low energy costs and the absence of foreign competition, had become a victim of the energy crisis and the industrial advances in Western Europe and Japan. The easy solutions of the past, notably a reliance on government spending made possible by a steadily expanding economy, would no longer be possible. The true test facing the American democratic system was to produce leaders and programs that could reconcile the people to the new age of scarcity in which they now lived.

Recommended Reading

The best account of the impact of the Yom Kippur War on American foreign policy is the second volume of Henry Kissinger's memoirs, *Years of Upheaval* (1982). The secretary of state describes the course of American foreign policy during Nixon's abbreviated second term.

Richard Barnet gives a thorough description of the impact of the energy crisis and foreign industrial competition on the American economy in the 1970s in *The Lean Years* (1980). Two superior collections of essays on the impact of the oil shocks are Robert Stobaugh and Daniel Yergin, eds., *Energy Future* (1980) and Daniel Yergin and Martin Hillenbrand, eds., *Global Insecurity* (1982).

The most satisfactory account of political developments in the 1970s, culminating in the election of Ronald Reagan, is the last of Theodore White's chronicles of presidential politics, *America in Search of Itself* (1982).

Additional Bibliography

For the Ford administration, the most useful books are Richard Reeves, *A Ford, Not a Lincoln* (1975); Clark Mollenhoff, *The Man Who Pardoned Nixon* (1976); Robert Hartmann, *Palace Politics* (1980), an insider's account by a disgruntled aide; and the President's own memoir, Gerald R. Ford, *A Time to Heal* (1979). On the election of 1976, see Jules Witcover, *Marathon* (1977) and Elizabeth Drew, *American Journal* (1977).

Books on the Carter administration include James Wooten, *Dasher* (1978) and Betty Glad, *Jimmy Carter* (1980), which focus on Carter's political career; Haynes Johnson, *In the Absence of Power* (1980), a journalist's view of the Carter presidency; and five memoirs: Joseph Califano, *On Governing America* (1981), which is critical of the President; Griffin Bell, *Taking Care of the Law* (1982), a defensive view by the attorney general; Jimmy Carter, *Keeping Faith* (1982), a sketchy and disappointing account; Zbigniew Brzezinski, *Power and Principle* (1983), a candid critique of Carter's foreign policy; and Cyrus Vance, *Hard Choices* (1983), which defends his record as secretary of state.

The major developments in the Middle East are traced in Edward R. F. Sheehan, *The Arabs, Israelis and Kissinger* (1976) and William B. Quandt, *Decade of*

Decisions (1977). Other books on foreign-policy issues of the 1970s are Strobe Talbot, *Endgame* (1979), on the negotiation of SALT II; Roy Rowan, *The Four Days of the Mayaguez* (1975); John Stockwell, *In Search of Enemies* (1976), an exposé of CIA activities in Angola; Barry Rubin, *Paved with Good Intentions* (1980), on U.S. policy in Iran; and Michael Ledeen and William Lewis, *Debacle* (1981), on the Iranian hostage crisis. Jonathan Schell, *The Fate of the Earth* (1982) is a frightening description of the danger of nuclear war.

For additional information on economic themes, see John Blair, *The Control of Oil* (1976); Peter R. Odell, *Oil and World Power*, 5th ed. (1979); and Richard Barnet and Ronald Muller, *Global Reach* (1974), on the rise of the multinationals. The fate of affirmative action in the 1970s is traced in Allan P. Sindler, *Bakke, DeFunis, and Minority Admissions* (1978) and J. Harvie Wilkinson, III, *From Brown to Bakke* (1979). Arthur Corwin examines problems of Mexican immigration critically in *Immigrants—and Immigrants* (1978). For the women's movement in the seventies, see Jo Freeman, *The Politics of Women's Liberation* (1979).

Good accounts of the resurgence of conservative thought are Peter Steinfels, *The Neo-Conservatives* (1979) and Norman Podheretz, *Breaking Ranks* (1979). On Reagan's political career, see Lou Cannon, *Reagan* (1982); Bill Boyarsky, *Ronald Reagan* (1981); and Rowland Evans and Robert Novak, *The Reagan Revolution* (1981). The election of 1980 is dealt with in Thomas Ferguson and Joel Rogers, eds., *The Hidden Election of 1980* (1981); Jack W. Germond and Jules Witcover, *Blue Smoke and Mirrors* (1981); Elizabeth Drew, *Portrait of an Election* (1981); and John F. Stacks, *Watershed* (1982).

The Declaration of Independence

In Congress, July 4, 1776

The Unanimous Declaration
of the thirteen United States of America,

When in the Course of human events, it becomes necessary for one people to dissolve the political bands which have connected them with another, and to assume among the Powers of the earth, the separate and equal station to which the Laws of Nature and of Nature's God entitle them, a decent respect to the opinions of mankind requires that they should declare the causes which impel them to the separation.

We hold these truths to be self-evident, that all men are created equal, that they are endowed by their Creator with certain unalienable Rights, that among these are Life, Liberty and the pursuit of Happiness. That to secure these rights, Governments are instituted among Men, deriving their just powers from the consent of the governed, That whenever any Form of Government becomes destructive of these ends, it is the Right of the People to alter or to abolish it, and to institute new Government, laying its foundation on such principles and organizing its powers in such form, as to them shall seem most likely to effect their Safety and Happiness. Prudence, indeed, will dictate that Governments long established should not be changed for light and transient causes; and accordingly all experience hath shown, that mankind are more disposed to suffer, while evils are sufferable, than to right themselves by abolishing the forms to which they are accustomed. But when a long train of abuses and usurpations, pursuing invariably the same Object evinces a design to reduce them under absolute Despotism, it is their right, it is their duty, to throw off such Government, and to provide new Guards for their future security.—Such has been the patient sufferance of these Colonies; and such is now the necessity which constrains them to alter their former Systems of Government. The history of the present King of Great Britain is a history of repeated injuries and usurpations, all having in direct object the establishment of an absolute Tyranny over these States. To prove this, let Facts be submitted to a candid world.

He has refused his Assent to Laws, the most wholesome and necessary for the public good.

He has forbidden his Governors to pass Laws of immediate and pressing importance, unless suspended in their operation till his Assent should be obtained; and when so suspended, he has utterly neglected to attend to them.

He has refused to pass other Laws for the accommodation of large districts of people, unless those people would relinquish the right of Representation in the Legislature, a right inestimable to them and formidable to tyrants only.

He has called together legislative bodies at places unusual, uncomfortable, and distant from the depository of their Public Records, for the sole purpose of fatiguing them into compliance with his measures.

He has dissolved Representative Houses repeatedly, for opposing with manly firmness his invasions on the rights of the people.

He has refused for a long time, after such dissolutions, to cause others to be elected; whereby the Legislative Powers, incapable of Annihilation, have returned to the People at large for their exercise; the State remaining in the mean time exposed to all the dangers of invasion from without, and convulsions within.

He has endeavoured to prevent the population of these States; for that purpose obstructing the Laws for Naturalization of Foreigners; refusing to pass others to encourage their migrations hither, and raising the conditions of new Appropriations of Lands.

He has obstructed the Administration of Justice, by refusing his Assent to Laws for establishing Judiciary Powers.

He has made Judges dependent on his Will alone, for the tenure of their offices, and the amount and payment of their salaries.

He has erected a multitude of New Offices, and sent hither swarms of Officers to harass our people, and eat out their substance.

He has kept among us, in times of peace, Standing Armies without the Consent of our legislatures.

He has affected to render the Military independent of and superior to the Civil Power.

He has combined with others to subject us to a jurisdiction foreign to our constitution, and unacknowledged by our laws; giving his Assent to their acts of pretended Legislation:

For quartering large bodies of armed troops among us:

For protecting them, by a mock Trial, from Punishment for any Murders which they should commit on the Inhabitants of these States:

For cutting off our Trade with all parts of the world:

For imposing taxes on us without our Consent:

For depriving us in many cases, of the benefits of Trial by Jury:

For transporting us beyond Seas to be tried for pretended offences:

For abolishing the free System of English Laws in a neighbouring Province, establishing therein an Arbitrary government, and enlarging its Boundaries so as to render it at once an example and fit instrument for introducing the same absolute rule into these Colonies:

For taking away our Charters, abolishing our most valuable Laws, and altering fundamentally the Forms of our Governments:

For suspending our own Legislatures, and declaring themselves invested with Power to legislate for us in all cases whatsoever.

He has abdicated Government here, by declaring us out of his Protection and waging War against us.

He has plundered our seas, ravaged our Coasts, burnt our towns, and destroyed the lives of our people.

He is at this time transporting large armies of foreign mercenaries to compleat the works of death, desolation and tyranny, already begun with circumstances of Cruelty & perfidy scarcely paralleled in the most barbarous ages, and totally unworthy the Head of a civilized nation.

He has constrained our fellow Citizens taken Captive on the high Seas to bear Arms against their Country, to become the executioners of their friends and Brethren, or to fall themselves by their Hands.

He has excited domestic insurrections amongst us, and has endeavoured to bring on the inhabitants of our frontiers, the merciless Indian Savages, whose known rule of warfare, is an undistinguished destruction of all ages, sexes and conditions.

In every stage of these Oppressions We have Petitioned for Redress in the most humble terms: Our repeated Petitions have been answered only by repeated injury. A Prince, whose character is thus marked by every act which may define a Tyrant, is unfit to be the ruler of a free people.

Nor have We been wanting in attentions to our British brethren. We have warned them from time to time of attempts by their legislature to extend an unwarrantable jurisdiction over us. We have reminded them of the circumstances of our emigration and settlement here. We have appealed to their native justice and magnanimity, and we have conjured them by the ties of our common kindred to disavow these usurpations, which would inevitably interrupt our connections and correspondence. They too have been deaf to the voice of justice and of consanguinity. We must, therefore, acquiesce in the necessity, which denounces our Separation, and hold them, as we hold the rest of mankind, Enemies in War, in Peace Friends.

We, therefore, the Representatives of the united States of America, in General Congress, Assembled, appealing to the Supreme Judge of the world for the rectitude of our intentions, do, in the Name, and by authority of the good People of these Colonies, solemnly publish and declare, That these United Colonies are, and of Right ought to be Free and Independent States; that they are Absolved from all Allegiance to the British Crown, and that all political connection between them and the State of Great Britain, is and ought to be totally dissolved; and that as Free and Independent States, they have full power to levy War, conclude Peace, contract Alliances, establish Commerce, and to do all other Acts and Things which Independent States may of right do. And for the support of this Declaration, with a firm reliance on the Protection of Divine Providence, we mutually pledge to each other our Lives, our Fortunes and our sacred Honor.

JOHN HANCOCK

BUTTON GWINNETT
LYMAN HALL
GEO. WALTON
WM. HOOPER
JOSEPH HEWES
JOHN PENN
EDWARD RUTLEDGE
THOS. HEYWARD, JUNR.
THOMAS LYNCH, JUNR.
ARTHUR MIDDLETON
SAMUEL CHASE
WM. PACA
THOS. STONE
CHARLES CARROLL OF CARROLLTON
GEORGE WYTHE
RICHARD HENRY LEE
TH. JEFFERSON
BENJ. HARRISON

THOS. NELSON, JR.
FRANCIS LIGHTFOOT LEE
CARTER BRAXTON
ROBT. MORRIS
BENJAMIN RUSH
BENJA. FRANKLIN
JOHN MORTON
GEO. CLYMER
JAS. SMITH
GEO. TAYLOR
JAMES WILSON
GEO. ROSS
CAESAR RODNEY
GEO. READ
THO. M'KEAN
WM. FLOYD
PHIL. LIVINGSTON
FRANS. LEWIS
LEWIS MORRIS

RICHD. STOCKTON
JNO. WITHERSPOON
FRAS. HOPKINSON
JOHN HART
ABRA. CLARK
JOSIAH BARTLETT
WM. WHIPPLE
SAML. ADAMS
JOHN ADAMS
ROBT. TREAT PAINE
ELBRIDGE GERRY
STEP. HOPKINS
WILLIAM ELLERY
ROGER SHERMAN
SAM'EL. HUNTINGTON
WM. WILLIAMS
OLIVER WOLCOTT
MATTHEW THORNTON

The Constitution of the United States of America

We the People of the United States, in Order to form a more perfect Union, establish Justice, insure domestic Tranquility, provide for the common defence, promote the general Welfare, and secure the Blessings of Liberty to ourselves and our Posterity, do ordain and establish this Constitution for the United States of America.

Article I.

Section 1

All legislative Powers herein granted shall be vested in a Congress of the United States, which shall consist of a Senate and House of Representatives.

Section 2

The House of Representatives shall be composed of Members chosen every second Year by the People of the several States, and the Electors in each State shall have the Qualifications requisite for Electors of the most numerous Branch of the State Legislature.

No Person shall be a Representative who shall not have attained to the Age of twenty five Years, and been seven Years a Citizen of the United States, and who shall not, when elected, be an Inhabitant of that State in which he shall be chosen.

Representatives and direct Taxes shall be apportioned among the several States which may be included within this Union, according to their respective Numbers, which shall be determined by adding to the whole Number of free Persons, including those bound to Service for a Term of Years, and excluding Indians not taxed, three fifths of all other Persons.[1] The actual Enumeration shall be made within three Years after the first Meeting of the Congress of the United States, and within every subsequent Term of ten Years, in such Manner as they shall by Law direct. The Number of Representatives shall not exceed one for every thirty Thousand, but each State shall have at Least one Representative; and until such enumeration shall be made, the State of New Hampshire shall be entitled to chuse three, Massachusetts eight, Rhode-Island and Providence Plantations one, Connecticut five, New-York six, New Jersey four, Pennsylvania eight, Delaware one, Maryland six, Virginia ten, North Carolina five, South Carolina five, and Georgia three.

When vacancies happen in the Representation from any State, the Executive Authority thereof shall issue Writs of Election to fill such Vacancies.

The House of Representatives shall chuse their Speaker and other Officers; and shall have the sole Power of Impeachment.

Section 3

The Senate of the United States shall be composed of two Senators from each State, chosen by the Legislature thereof, for six Years; and each Senator shall have one Vote.

Immediately after they shall be assembled in Consequence of the first Election, they shall be divided as equally as may be into three Classes. The Seats of the Senators of the first Class shall be vacated at the Expiration of the second Year, of the second Class at the Expiration of the fourth Year, and of the third Class at the Expiration of the sixth Year, so that one third may be chosen every second Year; and if Vacancies happen by Resignation, or otherwise, during the Recess of the Legislature of any state, the Executive thereof may make temporary Appointments until the next Meeting of the Legislature, which shall then fill such Vacancies.[2]

No Person shall be a Senator who shall not have attained to the Age of thirty Years, and been nine Years a Citizen of the United States, and who shall not, when elected, be an Inhabitant of that State for which he shall be chosen.

The Vice President of the United States shall be President of the Senate, but shall have no Vote, unless they be equally divided.

The Senate shall chuse their other Officers, and also a President pro tempore, in the Absence of the Vice President, or when he shall exercise the Office of President of the United States.

The Senate shall have the sole Power to try all Impeachments. When sitting for that Purpose, they shall be on Oath or Affirmation. When the President of the United States is tried the Chief Justice shall preside: And no Person shall be convicted whithout the Concurrence of two thirds of the Members present.

Judgment in Cases of Impeachment shall not extend further than to removal from Office, and disqualification to hold and enjoy any Office of honor, Trust or

---

[1] "Other Persons" being black slaves. Modified by Amendment XIV, Section 2.

[2] Provisions changed by Amendment XVII.

Profit under the United States: but the Party convicted shall nevertheless be liable and subject to Indictment, Trial, Judgment and Punishment, according to Law.

Section 4
The Times, Places and Manner of holding Elections for Senators and Representatives, shall be prescribed in each State by the Legislature thereof; but the Congress may at any time by Law make or alter such Regulations, except as to the Places of chusing Senators.

The Congress shall assemble at least once in every Year, and such Meeting shall be on the first Monday in December, unless they shall by Law appoint a different Day.[3]

Section 5
Each House shall be the Judge of the Elections, Returns and Qualifications of its own Members, and a Majority of each shall constitute a Quorum to do Business; but a smaller Number may adjourn from day to day, and may be authorized to compel the Attendance of absent Members, in such Manner, and under such Penalties as each House may provide.

Each House may determine the Rules of its Proceedings, punish its Members for disorderly Behaviour, and, with the Concurrence of two thirds, expel a Member.

Each House shall keep a Journal of its Proceedings, and from time to time publish the same, excepting such Parts as may in their Judgment require Secrecy; and the Yeas and Nays of the Members of either House on any question shall, at the Desire of one fifth of those Present, be entered on the Journal.

Neither House, during the Session of Congress, shall, without the Consent of the other, adjourn for more than three days, nor to any other Place than that in which the two Houses shall be sitting.

Section 6
The Senators and Representatives shall receive a Compensation for their Services, to be ascertained by Law, and paid out of the Treasury of the United States. They shall in all Cases, except Treason, Felony and Breach of the Peace, be privileged from Arrest during their Attendance at the Session of their respective Houses, and in going to and returning from the same; and for any Speech or Debate in either House, they shall not be questioned in any other Place.

No Senator or Representative shall, during the Time for which he was elected, be appointed to any civil Office under the Authority of the United States, which shall have been created, or the Emoluments whereof shall have been encreased during such time; and no Person holding any Office under the United States, shall be a Member of either House during his Continuance in Office.

---

[3]Provision changed by Amendment XX, Section 2.

Section 7
All Bills for raising Revenue shall originate in the House of Representatives; but the Senate may propose or concur with Amendments as on other Bills.

Every Bill which shall have passed the House of Representatives and the Senate, shall, before it become a Law, be presented to the President of the United States; If he approve he shall sign it, but if not he shall return it, with his Objections to that House in which it shall have originated, who shall enter the Objections at large on their Journal, and proceed to reconsider it. If after such Reconsideration two thirds of that House shall agree to pass the Bill, it shall be sent, together with the Objections, to the other House, by which it shall likewise be reconsidered, and if approved by two thirds of that House, it shall become a Law. But in all such Cases the Votes of both Houses shall be determined by yeas and Nays, and the Names of the Persons voting for and against the Bill shall be entered on the Journal of each House respectively. If any Bill shall not be returned by the President within ten Days (Sundays excepted) after it shall have been presented to him, the Same shall be a Law, in like Manner as if he had signed it, unless the Congress by their Adjournment prevent its Return, in which Case it shall not be a Law.

Every Order, Resolution, or Vote to which the Concurrence of the Senate and House of Representatives may be necessary (except on a question of Adjournment) shall be presented to the President of the United States; and before the Same shall take Effect, shall be approved by him, or being disapproved by him, shall be repassed by two thirds of the Senate and House of Representatives, according to the Rules and Limitations prescribed in the Case of a Bill.

Section 8
The Congress shall have Power To lay and collect Taxes, Duties, Imposts and Excises, to pay the Debts and provide for the common Defence and general Welfare of the United States; but all Duties, Imposts and Excises shall be uniform throughout the United States;

To borrow Money on the credit of the United States;

To regulate Commerce with foreign Nations, and among the several States, and with the Indian Tribes;

To establish an uniform Rule of Naturalization, and uniform Laws on the subject of Bankruptcies throughout the United States;

To coin Money, regulate the Value thereof, and of foreign Coin, and fix the Standard of Weights and Measures;

To provide for the Punishment of counterfeiting the Securities and current Coin of the United States;

To establish Post Offices and post Roads;

To promote the Progress of Science and useful Arts, by securing for limited Times to Authors and Inventors the exclusive Right to their respective Writings and Discoveries;

To constitute Tribunals inferior to the supreme Court;

To define and punish Piracies and Felonies committed on the high Seas, and Offences against the Law of Nations;

To declare War, grant Letters of Marque and Reprisal, and make Rules concerning Captures on Land and Water;

To raise and support Armies, but no Appropriation of Money to that Use shall be for a longer Term than two Years;

To provide and maintain a Navy;

To make Rules for the Government and Regulation of the land and naval Forces;

To provide for calling forth the Militia to execute the Laws of the Union, suppress Insurrections and repel Invasions;

To provide for organizing. arming, and disciplining, the Militia, and for governing such Part of them as may be employed in the Service of the United States, reserving to the States respectively, the Appointment of the Officers, and the Authority of training the Militia according to the discipline prescribed by Congress;

To exercise exclusive Legislation in all Cases whatsoever, over such District (not exceeding ten Miles square) as may, by Cession of particular States, and the Acceptance of Congress, become the Seat of the Government of the United States, and to exercise like Authority over all Places purchased by the Consent of the Legislature of the State in which the Same shall be, for the Erection of Forts, Magazines, Arsenals, dock-Yards, and other needful Buildings;—And

To make all Laws which shall be necessary and proper for carrying into Execution the foregoing Powers, and all other Powers vested by this Constitution in the Government of the United States, or in any Department or Officer thereof.

Section 9

The Migration or Importation of such Persons as any of the States now existing shall think proper to admit, shall not be prohibited by the Congress prior to the Year one thousand eight hundred and eight, but a Tax or duty may be imposed on such Importation, not exceeding ten dollars for each Person.

The Privilege of the Writ of Habeas Corpus shall not be suspended, unless when in Cases of Rebellion or Invasion the public Safety may require it.

No Bill of Attainder or ex post facto Law shall be passed.

No Capitation, or other direct, Tax shall be laid, unless in Proportion to the Census or Enumeration herein before directed to be taken.

No Tax or Duty shall be laid on Articles exported from any State.

No Preference shall be given by any Regulation of Commerce or Revenue to the Ports of one State over those of another: nor shall Vessels bound to, or from, one State, be obliged to enter, clear, or pay Duties in another.

No Money shall be drawn from the Treasury, but in Consequence of Appropriations made by Law; and a regular Statement and Account of the Receipts and Expenditures of all public Money shall be published from time to time.

No Title of Nobility shall be granted by the United States: And no Person holding any Office of Profit or Trust under them, shall, without the Consent of the Congress, accept of any present, Emolument, Office, or Title, of any kind whatever, from any King, Prince, or foreign State.

Section 10

No State shall enter into any Treaty, Alliance, or Confederation; grant Letters of Marque and Reprisal; coin Money; emit Bills of Credit; make any Thing but gold and silver Coin a Tender in Payment of Debts; pass any Bill of Attainder, ex post facto Law, or Law impairing the obligation of Contracts, or grant any Title of Nobility.

No State shall, without the Consent of the Congress, lay any Imposts or Duties on Imports or Exports, except what may be absolutely necessary for executing its inspection Laws: and the net Produce of all Duties and Imposts, laid by any State on Imports or Exports, shall be for the Use of the Treasury of the United States; and all such Laws shall be subject to the Revision and Controul of the Congress.

No State shall, without the Consent of Congress, lay any Duty of Tonnage, keep Troops, or Ships of War in time of Peace, enter into any Agreement or Compact with another State, or with a foreign Power, or engage in War, unless actually invaded, or in such imminent Danger as will not admit of delay.

Article II.

Section 1

The executive Power shall be vested in a President of the United States of America. He shall hold his Office during the Term of four Years, and, together with the Vice President, chosen for the same Term, be elected, as follows:

Each State shall appoint, in such Manner as the Legislature thereof may direct, a Number of Electors, equal to the whole Number of Senators and Representatives to which the State may be entitled in the Congress: but no Senator or Representative, or Person holding an Office of Trust or Profit under the United States, shall be appointed an Elector.

The Electors shall meet in their respective States, and vote by Ballot for two Persons, of whom one at least shall not be an Inhabitant of the same State with themselves. And they shall make a List of all the Persons voted for, and of the Number of Votes for each; which List they shall sign and certify, and transmit sealed to the Seat of the Government of the United States, directed to the President of the Senate. The President of the Senate shall, in the Presence of the Senate and House of Representatives, open all the

Certificates, and the Votes shall then be counted. The Person having the greatest Number of Votes shall be the President, if such Number be a Majority of the whole Number of Electors appointed; and if there be more than one who have such Majority, and have an equal Number of Votes, then the House of Representatives shall immediately chuse by Ballot one of them for President; and if no Person have a Majority, then from the five highest on the List the said House shall in like Manner chuse the President. But in chusing the President, the Votes shall be taken by States, the Representation from each State having one Vote; A quorum for this Purpose shall consist of a Member or Members from two thirds of the States, and a Majority of all the States shall be necessary to a Choice. In every Case, after the Choice of the President, the Person having the greatest Number of Votes of the Electors shall be the Vice President. But if there should remain two or more who have equal Votes, the Senate shall chuse from them by Ballot the Vice President.[4]

The Congress may determine the Time of chusing the Electors, and the Day on which they shall give their Votes; which Day shall be the same throughout the United States.

No person except a natural born Citizen, or a Citizen of the United States, at the time of the Adoption of this Constitution, shall be eligible to the Office of President; neither shall any Person be eligible to that Office who shall not have attained to the Age of thirty five Years, and been fourteen Years a Resident within the United States.

In Case of the Removal of the President from Office, or of his Death, Resignation, or Inability to discharge the Powers and Duties of the said Office, the Same shall devolve on the Vice President, and the Congress may by Law provide for the Case of Removal, Death, Resignation or Inability, both of the President and Vice President, declaring what Officer shall then act as President, and such Officer shall act accordingly, until the Disability be removed, or a President shall be elected.

The President shall, at stated Times, receive for his Services, a Compensation, which shall neither be encreased nor diminished during the Period for which he shall have been elected, and he shall not receive within that Period any other Emolument from the United States, or any of them.

Before he enter on the Execution of his Office, he shall take the following Oath or Affirmation:—"I do solemnly swear (or affirm) that I will faithfully execute the Office of President of the United States, and will to the best of my Ability, preserve, protect and defend the Constitution of the United States."

Section 2

The President shall be Commander in Chief of the Army and Navy of the United States, and of the Militia of the several States, when called into the actual Service of the United States; he may require the Opinion, in writing, of the principal Officer in each of the executive Departments, upon any Subject relating to the Duties of their respective Offices, and he shall have Power to grant Reprieves and Pardons for Offences against the United States, except in Cases of Impeachment.

He shall have Power, by and with the Advice and Consent of the Senate, to make Treaties, provided two thirds of the Senators present concur; and he shall nominate, and by and with the Advice and Consent of the Senate, shall apppoint Ambassadors, other public Ministers and Consuls, Judges of the supreme Court, and all other Officers of the United States, whose Appointments are not herein otherwise provided for, and which shall be established by Law: but the Congress may by Law vest the Appointment of such inferior Officers, as they think proper in the President alone, in the Courts of Law, or in the Heads of Departments.

The President shall have Power to fill up all Vacancies that may happen during the Recess of the Senate, by granting Commissions which shall expire at the End of their next Session.

Section 3

He shall from time to time give to the Congress Information of the State of the Union, and recommend to their Consideration such Measures as he shall judge necessary and expedient; he may, on extraordinary Occasions, convene both Houses, or either of them, and in Case of Disagreement between them, with Respect to the Time of Adjournment, he may adjourn them to such Time as he shall think proper; he shall receive Ambassadors and other public Ministers; he shall take Care that the Laws be faithfully executed, and shall Commission all the Officers of the United States.

Section 4

The President, Vice President and all civil Officers of the United States, shall be removed from Office on Impeachment for, and Conviction of, Treason, Bribery, or other high Crimes and Misdemeanors.

Article III.

Section 1

The judicial Power of the United States, shall be vested in one supreme Court, and in such inferior Courts as the Congress may from time to time ordain and establish. The Judges, both of the supreme and inferior Courts, shall hold their offices during good Behaviour, and shall, at stated Times, receive for their Services, a Compensation, which shall not be diminished during their Continuance in Office.

Section 2

The judicial Power shall extend to all Cases, in Law

[4]Provisions superseded by Amendment XII.

and Equity, arising under this Constitution, the Laws of the United States, and Treaties made, or which shall be made, under their Authority;—to all Cases affecting Ambassadors, other public Ministers and Consuls;—to all Cases of admiralty and maritime Jurisdiction;—to Controversies to which the United States shall be a Party;—to Controversies between two or more States;—between a State and Citizens of another State;—between Citizens of different States,—between Citizens of the same State claiming Lands under Grants of different States, and between a State, or the Citizens thereof, and foreign States, Citizens or Subjects.[5]

In all Cases affecting Ambassadors, other public Ministers and Consuls, and those in which a State shall be Party, the supreme Court shall have original Jurisdiction. In all the other Cases before mentioned, the supreme Court shall have appellate Jurisdiction, both as to Law and Fact, with such Exceptions, and under such Regulations as the Congress shall make.

The Trial of all Crimes, except in Cases of Impeachment, shall be by Jury; and such Trial shall be held in the State where the said Crimes shall have been committed, but when not committed within any State, the Trial shall be at such Place or Places as the Congress may by Law have directed.

Section 3

Treason against the United States, shall consist only in levying War against them, or in adhering to their Enemies, giving them Aid and Comfort. No person shall be convicted of Treason unless on the Testimony of two Witnesses to the same overt Act, or on Confession in open Court.

The Congress shall have Power to declare the Punishment of Treason, but no Attainder of Treason shall work Corruption of Blood, or Forfeiture except during the Life of the Person attainted.

Article IV.

Section 1

Full Faith and Credit shall be given in each State to the public Acts, Records, and judicial Proceedings of every other State. And the Congress may by general Laws prescribe the Manner in which such Acts, Records and Proceedings shall be proved, and the Effect thereof.

Section 2

The Citizens of each State shall be entitled to all Privileges and Immunities of Citizens in the several States.

A Person charged in any State with Treason, Felony, or other Crime, who shall flee from Justice, and be found in another State, shall on Demand of the executive Authority of the State from which he fled, be

[5]Clause changed by Amendment XI.

delivered up, to be removed to the State having Jurisdiction of the Crime.

No Person held to Service or Labour in one State, under the Laws thereof, escaping into another, shall, in Consequence of any Law or Regulation therein, be discharged from such Service or Labour, but shall be delivered up on Claim of the Party to whom such Service or Labour may be due.

Section 3

New States may be admitted by the Congress into this Union; but no new State shall be formed or erected within the Jurisdiction of any other State; nor any State be formed by the Junction of two or more States, or Parts of States, without the Consent of the Legislatures of the States concerned as well as of the Congress.

The Congress shall have Power to dispose of and make all needful Rules and Regulations respecting the Territory or other Property belonging to the United States; and nothing in this Constitution shall be so construed as to Prejudice any Claims of the United States, or of any particular States.

Section 4

The United States shall guarantee to every State in this Union a Republican Form of Government, and shall protect each of them against Invasion; and on Application of the Legislature, or of the Executive (when the Legislature cannot be convened) against domestic violence.

Article V.

The Congress, whenever two thirds of both Houses shall deem it necessary, shall propose Amendments to this Constitution, or, on the Application of the Legislatures of two thirds of the several States, shall call a Convention for proposing Amendments, which, in either Case, shall be valid to all Intents and Purposes, as Part of this Constitution, when ratified by the Legislatures of three fourths of the several States, or by Conventions in three fourths thereof, as the one or the other Mode of Ratification may be proposed by the Congress; Provided that no Amendment which may be made prior to the Year One thousand eight hundred and eight shall in any Manner affect the first and fourth Clauses in the Ninth Section of the first Article; and that no State without its Consent, shall be deprived of its equal Suffrage in the Senate.

Article VI.

All Debts contracted and Engagements entered into, before the Adoption of this Constitution, shall be as valid against the United States under this Constitution, as under the Confederation.

This Constitution, and the Laws of the United States which shall be made in Pursuance thereof; and all Treaties made, or which shall be made, under the Authority of the United States, shall be the supreme Law of the Land; and the Judges in every State shall be bound thereby, any Thing in the Constitution or Laws of any State to the Contrary notwithstanding.

The Senators and Representatives before mentioned, and the Members of the several State Legislatures, and all executive and Judicial Officers, both of the United States and of the several States, shall be bound by Oath or Affirmation, to support this Constitution; but no religious Test shall ever be required as a Qualification to any Office of public Trust under the United States.

Article VII.

The Ratification of the Conventions of nine States, shall be sufficient for the Establishment of this Constitution between the States so ratifying the Same.

done in Convention by the Unanimous Consent of the States present the Seventeenth Day of September in the Year of our Lord one thousand seven hundred and Eighty seven and of the Independence of the United states of America the Twelfth[6] IN WITNESS whereof We have hereunto subscribed our Names,

[6]The Constitution was submitted on September 17, 1787, by the Constitutional Convention, was ratified by the conventions of several states at various dates up to May 29, 1790, and became effective on March 4, 1789.

GEORGE WASHINGTON,
President and Deputy from Virginia

New Hampshire
JOHN LANGDON
NICHOLAS GILMAN

Massachusetts
NATHANIEL GORHAM
RUFUS KING

Connecticut
WILLIAM S. JOHNSON
ROGER SHERMAN

New York
ALEXANDER HAMILTON

New Jersey
WILLIAM LIVINGSTON
DAVID BREARLEY
WILLIAM PATERSON
JONATHAN DAYTON

Pennsylvania
BENJAMIN FRANKLIN
THOMAS MIFFLIN
ROBERT MORRIS
GEORGE CLYMER
THOMAS FITZSIMONS
JARED INGERSOLL
JAMES WILSON
GOUVERNEUR MORRIS

Delaware
GEORGE READ
GUNNING BEDFORD, JR.
JOHN DICKINSON
RICHARD BASSETT
JACOB BROOM

Maryland
JAMES McHENRY
DANIEL OF ST. THOMAS JENIFER
DANIEL CARROLL

Virginia
JOHN BLAIR
JAMES MADISON, JR.

North Carolina
WILLIAM BLOUNT
RICHARD DOBBS SPRAIGHT
HU WILLIAMSON

South Carolina
J. RUTLEDGE
CHARLES C. PINCKNEY
PIERCE BUTLER

Georgia
WILLIAM FEW
ABRAHAM BALDWIN

Amendments to the Constitution

Amendment I

Congress shall make no law respecting an establishment of religion, or prohibiting the free exercise thereof; or abridging the freedom of speech, or of the press; or the right of the people peaceably to assemble, and to petition the Government for a redress of grievances.

Amendment II

A well regulated Militia being necessary to the security of a free State, the right of the people to keep and bear Arms, shall not be infringed.

Amendment III

No Soldier shall, in time of peace be quartered in any house, without the consent of the Owner, nor in time of war, but in a manner to be prescribed by law.

Amendment IV

The right of the people to be secure in their persons, houses, papers, and effects, against unreasonable searches and seizures, shall not be violated, and no Warrants shall issue, but upon probable cause, supported by Oath or affirmation, and particularly describing the place to be searched, and the persons or things to be seized.

Amendment V

No person shall be held to answer for a capital, or otherwise infamous crime, unless on a presentment or indictment of a Grand Jury, except in cases arising in the land or naval forces, or in the Militia, when in actual service in time of War or public danger; nor shall any person be subject for the same offense to be twice put in jeopardy of life or limb; nor shall be compelled in any criminal case to be a witness against himself, nor be deprived of life, liberty, or property, without due process of law; nor shall private property be taken for public use, without just compensation.

Amendment VI

In all criminal prosecutions, the accused shall enjoy the right to a speedy and public trial, by an impartial jury of the State and district wherein the crime shall have been committed, which district shall have been previously ascertained by law, and to be informed of the nature and cause of the accusation; to be confronted with the witnesses against him; to have compulsory process for obtaining witnesses in his favor, and to have the Assistance of Counsel for his defence.

Amendment VII

In Suits at common law, where the value in controversy shall exceed twenty dollars, the right of trial by jury shall be preserved, and no fact tried by a jury, shall be otherwise re-examined in any Court of the United States, than according to the rules of the common law.

Amendment VIII

Excessive bail shall not be required, nor excessive fines imposed, nor cruel and unusual punishments inflicted.

Amendment IX

The enumeration in the Constitution, of certain rights, shall not be construed to deny or disparage others retained by the people.

Amendment X

The powers not delegated to the United States by the Constitution, nor prohibited by it to the States, are reserved to the States respectively, or the people.[7]

Amendment XI

The Judicial power of the United States shall not be construed to extend to any suit in law or equity, commenced or prosecuted against one of the United States by Citizens of another State, or by Citizens or Subjects of any Foreign State.[8]

[7]The first ten amendments were all proposed by Congress on September 25, 1789, and were ratified and adoption certified on December 15, 1791.
[8]Proposed by Congress on March 4, 1794, and declared ratified on January 8, 1798.

The Electors shall meet in their respective states, and vote by ballot for President and Vice-President, one of whom, at least, shall not be an inhabitant of the same state with themselves; they shall name in their ballots the person voted for as President, and in distinct ballots the person voted for as Vice-President, and they shall make distinct lists of all persons voted for as President, and of all persons voted for as Vice-President, and of the number of votes for each, which lists they shall sign and certify, and transmit sealed to the seat of the government of the United States, directed to the President of the Senate;—The President of the Senate shall, in the presence of the Senate and House of Representatives, open all the certificates and the votes shall then be counted;—The person having the greatest number of votes for President, shall be the President, if such number be a majority of the whole number of Electors appointed; and if no person have such majority, then from the persons having the highest numbers not exceeding three on the list of those voted for as President, the House of Representatives shall choose immediately, by ballot, the President. But in choosing the President, the votes shall be taken by states, the representation from each state having one vote; a quorum for this purpose shall consist of a member or members from two-thirds of the states, and a majority of all the states shall be necessary to a choice. And if the House of Representatives shall not choose a President whenever the right of choice shall devolve upon them, before the fourth day of March next following, then the Vice-President shall act as President, as in the case of the death or other constitutional disability of the President.—The person having the greatest number of votes as Vice-President, shall be the Vice-President, if such number be a majority of the whole number of Electors appointed, and if no person have a majority, then from the two highest numbers on the list, the Senate shall choose the Vice-President; a quorum for the purpose shall consist of two-thirds of the whole number of Senators, and a majority of the whole number shall be necessary to a choice. But no person constitutionally ineligible to the office of President shall be eligible to that of Vice President of the United States.[9]

Amendment XIII

Section 1

Neither slavery nor involuntary servitude, except as a punishment for crime whereof the party shall have been duly convicted, shall exist within the United States, or any place subject to their jurisdiction.

Section 2

Congress shall have power to enforce this article by appropriate legislation.[10]

[9]Proposed by Congress on December 9, 1803; declared ratified on September 25, 1804; supplemented by Amendments XX and XXIII.
[10]Proposed by Congress on January 31, 1865; declared ratified on December 18, 1865.

Section 1

All persons born or naturalized in the United States, and subject to the jurisdiction thereof, are citizens of the United States and of the State wherein they reside. No State shall make or enforce any law which shall abridge the privileges or immunities of citizens of the United States; nor shall any State deprive any person of life, liberty, or property, without due process of law; nor deny to any person within its jurisdiction the equal protection of the laws.

Section 2

Representatives shall be apportioned among the several States according to their respective numbers, counting the whole number of persons in each State, excluding Indians not taxed. But when the right to vote at any election for the choice of electors for President and Vice-President of the United States, Representatives in Congress, the Executive and Judicial officers of a State, or the members of the Legislature thereof, is denied to any of the male inhabitants of such State, being twenty-one years of age, and citizens of the United States, or in any way abridged, except for participation in rebellion, or other crime, the basis of representation therein shall be reduced in the proportion which the number of such male citizens shall bear to the whole number of male citizens twenty-one years of age in such State.

Section 3

No person shall be a Senator or Representative in Congress, or elector of President and Vice President, or hold any office, civil or military, under the United States, or under any State, who, having previously taken an oath, as a member of Congress, or as an officer of the United States, or as a member of any State legislature, or as an executive or judicial officer of any State, to support the Constitution of the United States, shall have engaged in insurrection or rebellion against the same, or given aid or comfort to the enemies thereof. But Congress may by a vote of two-thirds of each House, remove such disability.

Section 4

The validity of the public debt of the United States, authorized by law, including debts incurred for payment of pensions and bounties for services in suppressing insurrection or rebellion, shall not be questioned. But neither the United States nor any State shall assume or pay any debt or obligation incurred in aid of insurrection or rebellion against the United States, or any claim for the loss or emancipation of any slave; but all such debts, obligations and claims shall be held illegal and void.

Section 5

The Congress shall have power to enforce, by appropriate legislation, the provisions of this article.[11]

[11]Proposed by Congress on June 13, 1866; declared ratified on July 28, 1868.

Amendment XV

Section 1

The right of citizens of the United States to vote shall not be denied or abridged by the United States or by any State on account of race, color, or previous condition of servitude.

Section 2

The Congress shall have power to enforce this article by appropriate legislation.[12]

Amendment XVI

The Congress shall have power to lay and collect taxes on incomes, from whatever source derived, without apportionment among the several States, and without regard to any census or enumeration.[13]

Amendment XVII

The Senate of the United States shall be composed of two Senators from each State, elected by the people thereof, for six years; and each Senator shall have one vote. The electors in each State shall have the qualifications requisite for electors of the most numerous branch of the State legislatures.

When vacancies happen in the representation of any State in the Senate, the executive authority of such State shall issue writs of election to fill such vacancies: *Provided,* That the legislature of any State may empower the executive thereof to make temporary appointments until the people fill the vacancies by election as the legislature may direct.

This amendment shall not be so construed as to affect the election or term of any Senator chosen before it becomes valid as part of the Constitution.[14]

Amendment XVIII

Section 1

After one year from the ratification of this article the manufacturer, sale, or transportation of intoxicating liquors within, the importation thereof into, or the exportation thereof from the United States and all territory subject to the jurisdiction thereof for beverage purposes is hereby prohibited.

Section 2

The Congress and the several States shall have concurrent power to enforce this article by appropriate legislation.

[12]Proposed by Congress on February 26, 1869; declared ratified on March 30, 1870.
[13]Proposed by Congress on July 12, 1909; declared ratified on February 25, 1913.
[14]Proposed by Congress on May 13, 1912; declared ratified on May 31, 1913.

Section 3

This article shall be inoperative unless it shall have been ratified as an amendment to the Constitution by the legislatures of the several States, as provided in the Constitution, within seven years from the date of the submission hereof to the States by the Congress.[15]

Amendment XIX

The right of citizens of the United States to vote shall not be denied or abridged by the United States or by any State on account of sex.

Congress shall have power to enforce this article by appropriate legislation.[16]

Amendment XX

Section 1

The terms of the President and Vice President shall end at noon on the 20th day of January, and the terms of Senators and Representatives at noon on the 3d day of January, of the years in which such terms would have ended if this article had not been ratified; and the terms of their successors shall then begin.

Section 2

The Congress shall assemble at least once in every year, and such meeting shall begin at noon on the 3d day of January, unless they shall by law appoint a different day.

Section 3

If, at the time fixed for the beginning of the term of the President, the President elect shall have died, the Vice President elect shall become President. If a President shall not have been chosen before the time fixed for the beginning of his term, or if the President elect shall have failed to qualify, then the Vice President elect shall act as President until a President shall have qualified; and the Congress may by law provide for the case wherein neither a President elect nor a Vice President elect shall have qualified, declaring who shall then act as President, or the manner in which one who is to act shall be selected, and such person shall act accordingly until a President or Vice President shall have qualified.

Section 4

The Congress may by law provide for the case of the death of any of the persons from whom the House of Representatives may choose a President whenever the right of choice shall have devolved upon them, and for the case of the death of any of the persons from whom the Senate may choose a Vice President whenever the right of choice shall have devolved upon them.

[15]Proposed by Congress on December 18, 1917; declared ratified on January 29, 1919; repealed by Amendment XXI.
[16]Proposed by Congress on June 4, 1919; declared ratified on August 26, 1920.

Section 5

Sections 1 and 2 shall take effect on the 15th day of October following the ratification of this article.

Section 6

This article shall be inoperative unless it shall have been ratified as an amendment to the Constitution by the legislatures of three-fourths of the several States within seven years from the date of its submission.[17]

Amendment XXI

Section 1

The eighteenth article of amendment to the Constitution of the United States is hereby repealed.

Section 2

The transportation or importation into any States, Territory, or possession of the United States for delivery or use therein of intoxicating liquors, in violation of the laws thereof, is hereby prohibited.

Section 3

This article shall be inoperative unless it shall have been ratified as an amendment to the Constitution by conventions in the several States, as provided in the Constitution, within seven years from the date of the submission hereof to the States by the Congress.[18]

Amendment XXII

Section 1

No person shall be elected to the office of the President more than twice, and no person who has held the office of President, or acted as President, for more than two years of a term to which some other person was elected President shall be elected to the office of the President more than once. But this Article shall not apply to any person holding the office of President when this Article was proposed by the Congress, and shall not prevent any person who may be holding the office of President, or acting as President, during the term within which this Article becomes operative from holding the office of President or acting as President during the remainder of such term.

Section 2

This article shall be inoperative unless it shall have been ratified as an amendment to the Constitution by the legislatures of three-fourths of the several States within seven years from the date of its submission to the States by the Congress.[19]

Amendment XXIII

Section 1

The District constituting the seat of Government of the United States shall appoint in such manner as the Congress shall direct:

A number of electors of President and Vice President equal to the whole number of Senators and Representatives in Congress to which the District would be entitled if it were a State, but in no event more than the least populous State; they shall be in addition to those appointed by the States, but they shall be considered, for the purposes of the election of President and Vice President, to be electors appointed by a State; and they shall meet in the District and perform such duties as provided by the twelfth article of amendment.

Section 2

The Congress shall have power to enforce this article by appropriate legislation.[20]

Amendment XXIV

Section 1

The right of citizens of the United States to vote in any primary or other election for President or Vice President, for electors for President or Vice President, or for Senator or Representative in Congress, shall not be denied or abridged by the United States or any state by reason of failure to pay any poll tax or other tax.

Section 2

The Congress shall have the power to enforce this article by appropriate legislation.[21]

Amendment XXV

Section 1

In case of the removal of the President from office or his death or resignation, the Vice President shall become President.

Section 2

Whenever there is a vacancy in the office of the Vice President, the President shall nominate a Vice President who shall take the office upon confirmation by a majority vote of both houses of Congress.

Section 3

Whenever the President transmits to the President pro tempore of the Senate and the Speaker of the House of Representatives his written declaration that he is unable to discharge the powers and duties of his office,

[17]Proposed by Congress on March 2, 1932; declared ratified on February 6, 1933.
[18]Proposed by Congress on February 20, 1933; declared ratified on December 5, 1933.
[19]Proposed by Congress on March 24, 1947; declared ratified on March 1, 1951.

[20]Proposed by Congress on June 16, 1960; declared ratified on April 3, 1961.
[21]Proposed by Congress on August 27, 1962; declared ratified on January 23, 1963.

and until he transmits to them a written declaration to the contrary, such powers and duties shall be discharged by the Vice President as Acting President.

Section 4

Whenever the Vice President and a majority of either the principal officers of the executive departments or of such other body as Congress may by law provide, transmit to the President pro tempore of the Senate and the Speaker of the House of Representatives their written declaration that the President is unable to discharge the powers and duties of his office, the Vice President shall immediately assume the powers and duties of the office as Acting President.

Thereafter, when the President transmits to the President pro tempore of the Senate and the Speaker of the House of Representatives his written declaration that no inability exists, he shall resume the powers and duties of his office unless the Vice President and a majority of either the principal officers of the executive department or of such other body as Congress may by law provide, transmit within four days to the President pro tempore of the Senate and the Speaker of the House of Representatives their written declaration that the President is unable to discharge the powers and duties of his office. Thereupon Congress shall decide the issue, assembling within 48 hours for that purpose if not in session. If the Congress, within 21 days after receipt of the latter written declaration, or, if Congress is not in session, within 21 days after Congress is required to assemble, determines by two-thirds vote of both houses that the President is unable to discharge the powers and duties of his office, the Vice President shall continue to discharge the same as Acting President; otherwise, the President shall resume the powers and duties of his office.[22]

Amendment XXVI

Section 1

The right of citizens of the United States, who are 18 years of age or older, to vote shall not be denied or abridged by the United States or any state on account of age.

Section 2

The Congress shall have the power to enforce this article by appropriate legislation.[23]

---

[22]Proposed by Congress on July 6, 1965; declared ratified on February 10, 1967.
[23]Proposed by Congress on March 23, 1971; declared ratified on June 30, 1971.

Choosing the President

Presidential Election Year	Elected to Office			
	President	Party	Vice President	Party
1789	George Washington		John Adams	Parties not yet established
1792	George Washington		John Adams	Federalist
1796	John Adams	Federalist	Thomas Jefferson	Democratic-Republican
1800	Thomas Jefferson	Democratic-Republican	Aaron Burr	Democratic-Republican
1804	Thomas Jefferson	Democratic-Republican	George Clinton	Democratic-Republican
1808	James Madison	Democratic-Republican	George Clinton	Democratic-Republican
1812	James Madison	Democratic-Republican	Elbridge Gerry	Democratic-Republican
1816	James Monroe	Democratic-Republican	Daniel D. Tompkins	Democratic-Republican
1820	James Monroe	Democratic-Republican	Daniel D. Tompkins	Democratic-Republican
1824	John Quincy Adams	National Republican	John C. Calhoun Withdrew from the Presidential race to run for Vice President on both the Adams and the Jackson tickets.	Democratic
1828	Andrew Jackson	Democratic	John C. Calhoun	Democratic
1832	Andrew Jackson	Democratic	Martin Van Buren	Democratic
1836	Martin Van Buren	Democratic	Richard M. Johnson First and only Vice President elected by the Senate (1837), having failed to receive a majority of electoral votes.	Democratic
1840	William Henry Harrison	Whig	John Tyler	Whig

Major Opponents and Notable Contenders				Selection of Electors
For President	Party	For Vice President	Party	
				By state legislature
George Clinton	Democratic-Republican			By state legislature
Thomas Pinckney	Federalist			By state legislature
Aaron Burr	Democratic-Republican			
John Adams	Federalist			By state legislature
Charles Cotesworth Pinckney	Federalist			
Charles Cotesworth Pinckney	Federalist	Rufus King	Federalist	By state legislature
Charles Cotesworth Pinckney	Federalist	Rufus King	Federalist	By state legislature
George Clinton	Eastern Republican			
De Witt Clinton	Democratic-Republican/ Federalist	Charles Jared Ingersoll	Democratic-Republican/ Federalist	By state legislature
Rufus King	Federalist	John Eager Howard	Federalist	By state legislature
				By state legislature
Andrew Jackson	Democratic	Nathan Sanford	Democratic-Republican	By popular vote in 18 states
Henry Clay	Democratic-Republican	Nathaniel Macon	Democratic-Republican	
William H. Crawford	Democratic-Republican			
John Quincy Adams	National Republican	Richard Rush	National Republican	By popular vote
Henry Clay	National Republican	John Sergeant	National Republican	By popular vote
William Wirt	Anti-Masonic	Amos Ellmaker	Anti-Masonic	
Daniel Webster	Whig	John Tyler	Whig	By popular vote
Hugh L. White	Whig	Francis Granger	Anti-Masonic	
William Henry Harrison	Anti-Masonic			
Martin Van Buren	Democratic	Richard M. Johnson	Democratic	By popular vote
James G. Birney	Liberty	Thomas Earle	Liberty	

Presidential Election Year	Elected to Office			
	President	Party	Vice President	Party
1844	James K. Polk	Democratic	George M. Dallas	Democratic
1848	Zachary Taylor	Whig	Millard Fillmore	Whig
1852	Franklin Pierce	Democratic	William R. King	Democratic
1856	James Buchanan	Democratic	John C. Breckinridge	Democratic
1860	Abraham Lincoln	Republican	Hannibal Hamlin	Republican
1864	Abraham Lincoln	National Union/ Republican	Andrew Johnson	National Union/ Democratic
1868	Ulysses S. Grant	Republican	Schuyler Colfax	Republican
1872	Ulysses S. Grant	Republican	Henry Wilson	Republican
1876	Rutherford B. Hayes	Republican	William A. Wheeler	Republican
1880	James A. Garfield	Republican	Chester A. Arthur	Republican
1884	Grover Cleveland	Democratic	Thomas A. Hendricks	Democratic
1888	Benjamin Harrison	Republican	Levi P. Morton	Republican
1892	Grover Cleveland	Democratic	Adlai E. Stevenson	Democratic
1896	William McKinley	Republican	Garret A. Hobart	Republican
1900	William McKinley	Republican	Theodore Roosevelt	Republican
1904	Theodore Roosevelt	Republican	Charles W. Fairbanks	Republican

Major Opponents and Notable Contenders				Selection of Electors
For President	Party	For Vice President	Party	
Henry Clay	Whig	Theodore Frelinghuysen	Whig	By popular vote
James G. Birney	Liberty	Thomas Morris	Liberty	
Lewis Cass	Democratic	William O. Butler	Democratic	By popular vote
Martin Van Buren	Free-Soil	Charles F. Adams	Free-Soil	
Winfield Scott	Whig	William A. Graham	Whig	By popular vote
John P. Hale	Free-Soil	George W. Julian	Free-Soil	
John C. Frémont	Republican	William L. Dayton	Republican	By popular vote
Millard Fillmore	American	Andrew J. Donelson	American	
John Bell	Constitutional Union	Edward Everett	Constitutional Union	By popular vote
Stephen A. Douglas	Democratic	Herschel V. Johnson	Democratic	
John C. Breckinridge	Democratic	Joseph Lane	Democratic	
George B. McClennan	Democratic	George H. Pendleton	Democratic	By popular vote
Horatio Seymour	Democratic	Francis P. Blair	Democratic	By popular vote
Horace Greeley	Democratic and Liberal Republican	B. Gratz Brown	Democratic and Liberal Republican	By popular vote
Charles O'Conor	Democratic	John Quincy Adams II	Democratic	
James Black	Temperance	John Russell	Temperance	
Samuel J. Tilden	Democratic	Thomas A. Hendricks	Democratic	By popular vote
Peter Cooper	Greenback	Samuel F. Cary	Greenback	
Green Clay Smith	Prohibition	Gideon T. Stewart	Prohibition	
Winfield S. Hancock	Democratic	William H. English	Democratic	By popular vote
James B. Weaver	Greenback	B. J. Chambers	Greenback	
Neal Dow	Prohibition	H. A. Thompson	Prohibition	
James G. Blaine	Republican	John A. Logan	Republican	By popular vote
John P. St. John	Prohibition	William Daniel	Prohibition	
Benjamin F. Butler	Greenback	A. M. West	Greenback	
Grover Cleveland	Democratic	Allen G. Thurman	Democratic	By popular vote
Clinton B. Fisk	Prohibition	John A. Brooks	Prohibition	
Alson J. Streeter	Union Labor	C. E. Cunningham	Union Labor	
Benjamin Harrison	Republican	Whitelaw Reid	Republican	By popular vote
James B. Weaver	Populist	James G. Field	Populist	
John Bidwell	Prohibition	James B. Cranfill	Prohibition	
William Jennings Bryan	Democratic, Populist, and National Silver Republican	Arthur Sewall	Democratic and National Silver Republican	By popular vote
		Thomas E. Watson	Populist	
Joshua Levering	Prohibition	Hale Johnson	Prohibition	
John M. Palmer	National Democratic	Simon B. Buckner	National Democratic	
William Jennings Bryan	Democratic and Fusion Populist	Adlai E. Stevenson	Democratic and Fusion Populist	By popular vote
Wharton Barker	Anti-Fusion Populist	Ignatius Donnelly	Anti-Fusion Populist	
Eugene V. Debs	Social Democratic	Job Harriman	Social Democratic	
John G. Woolley	Prohibition	Henry B. Metcalf	Prohibition	
Alton B. Parker	Democratic	Henry G. Davis	Democratic	By popular vote
Eugene V. Debs	Socialist	Benjamin Hanford	Socialist	
Silas C. Swallow	Prohibition	George W. Carroll	Prohibition	

Presidential Election Year	Elected to Office			
	President	Party	Vice President	Party
1908	William Howard Taft	Republican	James S. Sherman	Republican
1912	Woodrow Wilson	Democratic	Thomas R. Marshall	Democratic
1916	Woodrow Wilson	Democratic	Thomas R. Marshall	Democratic
1920	Warren G. Harding	Republican	Calvin Coolidge	Republican
1924	Calvin Coolidge	Republican	Charles G. Dawes	Republican
1928	Herbert C. Hoover	Republican	Charles Curtis	Republican
1932	Franklin D. Roosevelt	Democratic	John N. Garner	Democratic
1936	Franklin D. Roosevelt	Democratic	John N. Garner	Democratic
1940	Franklin D. Roosevelt	Democratic	Henry A. Wallace	Democratic
1944	Franklin D. Roosevelt	Democratic	Harry S Truman	Democratic
1948	Harry S Truman	Democratic	Alben W. Barkley	Democratic
1952	Dwight D. Eisenhower	Republican	Richard M. Nixon	Republican
1956	Dwight D. Eisenhower	Republican	Richard M. Nixon	Republican
1960	John F. Kennedy	Democratic	Lyndon B. Johnson	Democratic
1964	Lyndon B. Johnson	Democratic	Hubert H. Humphrey	Democratic
1968	Richard M. Nixon	Republican	Spiro T. Agnew	Republican
1972	Richard M. Nixon	Republican	Spiro T. Agnew	Republican
1976	Jimmy Carter	Democratic	Walter Mondale	Democratic
1980	Ronald Reagan	Republican	George Bush	Republican

Major Opponents and Notable Contenders

For President	Party	For Vice President	Party	Selection of Electors
William Jennings Bryan	Democratic	John W. Kern	Democratic	By popular vote
		Benjamin Hanford		
Eugene V. Debs	Socialist	Aaron S. Watkins	Socialist	
Eugene W. Chafin	Prohibition		Prohibition	
William Howard Taft	Republican	James S. Sherman	Republican	By popular vote
Theodore Roosevelt	Progressive	Hiram W. Johnson	Progressive	
Eugene V. Debs	Socialist	Emil Seidel	Socialist	
Eugene W. Chafin	Prohibition	Aaron S. Watkins	Prohibition	
Charles E. Hughes	Republican	George R. Kirkpatrick	Socialist	By popular vote
Allen L. Benson	Socialist			
J. Frank Hanly	Prohibition	Ira D. Landrith	Prohibition	
Charles W. Fairbanks	Republican			
James M. Cox	Democratic	Franklin D. Roosevelt	Democratic	By popular vote
Eugene V. Debs	Socialist	Seymour Stedman	Socialist	
John W. Davis	Democratic	Charles W. Bryan	Democratic	By popular vote
Robert M. LaFollette	Progressive	Burton K. Wheeler	Progressive	
Alfred E. Smith	Democratic	Joseph T. Robinson	Democratic	By popular vote
Norman Thomas	Socialist	James H. Maurer	Socialist	
Herbert C. Hoover	Republican	Charles Curtis	Republican	By popular vote
Norman Thomas	Socialist	James H. Maurer	Socialist	
Alfred M. Landon	Republican	Frank Knox	Republican	By popular vote
William Lemke	Union	Thomas C. O'Brien	Union	
Wendell L. Willkie	Republican	Charles L. McNary	Republican	By popular vote
Thomas E. Dewey	Republican	John W. Bricker	Republican	By popular vote
Thomas E. Dewey	Republican	Earl Warren	Republican	By popular vote
J. Strom Thurmond	States' Rights Democratic	Fielding L. Wright	States' Rights Democratic	
Henry A. Wallace	Progressive	Glen H. Taylor	Progressive	
Adlai E. Stevenson	Democratic	John J. Sparkman	Democratic	By popular vote
Adlai E. Stevenson	Democratic	Estes Kefauver	Democratic	By popular vote
Richard M. Nixon	Republican	Henry Cabot Lodge	Republican	By popular vote
Barry M. Goldwater	Republican	William E. Miller	Republican	By popular vote
Hubert H. Humphrey	Democratic	Edmund S. Muskie	Democratic	By popular vote
George C. Wallace	American Independent	Curtis E. LeMay	American Independent	
George S. McGovern	Democratic	R. Sargent Shriver	Democratic	By popular vote
Gerald R. Ford	Republican	Robert J. Dole	Republican	By popular vote
Jimmy Carter	Democratic	Walter Mondale	Democratic	
John B. Anderson	Independent			
Ed Clark	Libertarian			

The Washington Administration

Secretary of State	Thomas Jefferson	1789–1793
	Edmund Randolph	1794–1795
	Timothy Pickering	1795–1797
Secretary of Treasury	Alexander Hamilton	1789–1795
	Oliver Wolcott	1795–1797
Secretary of War	Henry Knox	1789–1794
	Timothy Pickering	1795–1796
	James McHenry	1796–1797
Attorney General	Edmund Randolph	1789–1793
	William Bradford	1794–1795
	Charles Lee	1795–1797
Postmaster General	Samuel Osgood	1789–1791
	Timothy Pickering	1791–1794
	Joseph Habersham	1795–1797

The John Adams Administration

Secretary of State	Timothy Pickering	1797–1800
	John Marshall	1800–1801
Secretary of Treasury	Oliver Wolcott	1797–1800
	Samuel Dexter	1800–1801
Secretary of War	James McHenry	1797–1800
	Samuel Dexter	1800–1801
Attorney General	Charles Lee	1797–1801
Postmaster General	Joseph Habersham	1797–1801
Secretary of Navy	Benjamin Stoddert	1798–1801

The Jefferson Administration

Secretary of State	James Madison	1801–1809
Secretary of Treasury	Samuel Dexter	1801
	Albert Gallatin	1801–1809
Secretary of War	Henry Dearborn	1801–1809
Attorney General	Levi Lincoln	1801–1805
	Robert Smith	1805
	John Breckinridge	1805–1806
	Caesar Rodney	1807–1809
Postmaster General	Joseph Habersham	1801
	Gideon Granger	1801–1809
Secretary of Navy	Robert Smith	1801–1809

The Madison Administration

Secretary of State	Robert Smith	1809–1811
	James Monroe	1811–1817
Secretary of Treasury	Albert Gallatin	1809–1813
	George Campbell	1814
	Alexander Dallas	1814–1816
	William Crawford	1816–1817
Secretary of War	William Eustis	1809–1812
	John Armstrong	1813–1814
	James Monroe	1814–1815
	William Crawford	1815–1817
Attorney General	Caesar Rodney	1809–1811
	William Pinkney	1811–1814
	Richard Rush	1814–1817
Postmaster General	Gideon Granger	1809–1814
	Return Meigs	1814–1817
Secretary of Navy	Paul Hamilton	1809–1813
	William Jones	1813–1814
	Benjamin Crowninshield	1814–1817

The Monroe Administration

Secretary of State	John Quincy Adams	1817–1825
Secretary of Treasury	William Crawford	1817–1825
Secretary of War	George Graham	1817
	John C. Calhoun	1817–1825
Attorney General	Richard Rush	1817
	William Wirt	1817–1825
Postmaster General	Return Meigs	1817–1823
	John McLean	1823–1825
Secretary of Navy	Benjamin Crowninshield	1817–1818
	Smith Thompson	1818–1823
	Samuel Southard	1823–1825

The John Quincy Adams Administration

Secretary of State	Henry Clay	1825–1829
Secretary of Treasury	Richard Rush	1825–1829
Secretary of War	James Barbour Peter Porter	1825–1828 1828–1829
Attorney General	William Wirt	1825–1829
Postmaster General	John McLean	1825–1829
Secretary of Navy	Samuel Southard	1825–1829

The Jackson Administration

Secretary of State	Martin Van Buren Edward Livingston Louis McLane John Forsyth	1829–1831 1831–1833 1833–1834 1834–1837
Secretary of Treasury	Samuel Ingham Louis McLane William Duane Roger B. Taney Levi Woodbury	1829–1831 1831–1833 1833 1833–1834 1834–1837
Secretary of War	John H. Eaton Lewis Cass Benjamin Butler	1829–1831 1831–1837 1837
Attorney General	John M. Berrien Roger B. Taney Benjamin Butler	1829–1831 1831–1833 1833–1837
Postmaster General	William Barry Amos Kendall	1829–1835 1835–1837
Secretary of Navy	John Branch Levi Woodbury Mahlon Dickerson	1829–1831 1831–1834 1834–1837

The Van Buren Administration

Secretary of State	John Forsyth	1837–1841
Secretary of Treasury	Levi Woodbury	1837–1841
Secretary of War	Joel Poinsett	1837–1841
Attorney General	Benjamin Butler Felix Grundy Henry D. Gilpin	1837–1838 1838–1840 1840–1841
Postmaster General	Amos Kendall John M. Niles	1837–1840 1840–1841
Secretary of Navy	Mahlon Dickerson James Paulding	1837–1838 1838–1841

The William Harrison Administration

Secretary of State	Daniel Webster	1841
Secretary of Treasury	Thomas Ewing	1841
Secretary of War	John Bell	1841
Attorney General	John J. Crittenden	1841
Postmaster General	Francis Granger	1841
Secretary of Navy	George Badger	1841

The Tyler Administration

Secretary of State	Daniel Webster Hugh S. Legaré Abel P. Upshur John C. Calhoun	1841–1843 1843 1843–1844 1844–1845
Secretary of Treasury	Thomas Ewing Walter Forward John C. Spencer George Bibb	1841 1841–1843 1843–1844 1844–1845
Secretary of War	John Bell John C. Spencer James M. Porter William Wilkins	1841 1841–1843 1843–1844 1844–1845
Attorney General	John J. Crittenden Hugh S. Legaré John Nelson	1841 1841–1843 1843–1845
Postmaster General	Francis Granger Charles Wickliffe	1841 1841
Secretary of Navy	George Badger Abel P. Upshur David Henshaw Thomas Gilmer John Y. Mason	1841 1841 1843–1844 1844 1844–1845

The Polk Administration

Secretary of State	James Buchanan	1845–1849
Secretary of Treasury	Robert J. Walker	1845–1849
Secretary of War	William L. Marcy	1845–1849
Attorney General	John Y. Mason Nathan Clifford Isaac Toucey	1845–1846 1846–1848 1848–1849
Postmaster General	Cave Johnson	1845–1849
Secretary of Navy	George Bancroft John Y. Mason	1845–1846 1846–1849

The Taylor Administration

Secretary of State	John M. Clayton	1849–1850
Secretary of Treasury	William Meredith	1849–1850
Secretary of War	George Crawford	1849–1850
Attorney General	Reverdy Johnson	1849–1850
Postmaster General	Jacob Collamer	1849–1850
Secretary of Navy	William Preston	1849–1850
Secretary of Interior	Thomas Ewing	1849–1850

The Fillmore Administration

Secretary of State	Daniel Webster	1850–1852
	Edward Everett	1852–1853
Secretary of Treasury	Thomas Corwin	1850–1853
Secretary of War	Charles Conrad	1850–1853
Attorney General	John J. Crittenden	1850–1853
Postmaster General	Nathan Hall	1850–1852
	Sam D. Hubbard	1852–1853
Secretary of Navy	William A. Graham	1850–1852
	John P. Kennedy	1852–1853
Secretary of Interior	Thomas McKennan	1850
	Alexander Stuart	1850–1853

The Pierce Administration

Secretary of State	William L. Marcy	1853–1857
Secretary of Treasury	James Guthrie	1853–1857
Secretary of War	Jefferson Davis	1853–1857
Attorney General	Caleb Cushing	1853–1857
Postmaster General	James Campbell	1853–1857
Secretary of Navy	James C. Dobbin	1853–1857
Secretary of Interior	Robert McClelland	1853–1857

The Buchanan Administration

Secretary of State	Lewis Cass	1857–1860
	Jeremiah S. Black	1860–1861
Secretary of Treasury	Howell Cobb	1857–1860
	Philip Thomas	1860–1861
	John A. Dix	1861
Secretary of War	John B. Floyd	1857–1861
	Joseph Holt	1861
Attorney General	Jeremiah S. Black	1857–1860
	Edwin M. Stanton	1860–1861
Postmaster General	Aaron V. Brown	1857–1859
	Joseph Holt	1859–1861
	Horatio King	1861
Secretary of Navy	Isaac Toucey	1857–1861
Secretary of Interior	Jacob Thompson	1857–1861

The Lincoln Administration

Secretary of State	William H. Seward	1861–1865
Secretary of Treasury	Samuel P. Chase	1861–1864
	William P. Fessenden	1864–1865
	Hugh McCulloch	1865
Secretary of War	Simon Cameron	1861–1862
	Edwin M. Stanton	1862–1865
Attorney General	Edward Bates	1861–1864
	James Speed	1864–1865
Postmaster General	Horatio King	1861
	Montgomery Blair	1861–1864
	William Dennison	1864–1865
Secretary of Navy	Gideon Welles	1861–1865
Secretary of Interior	Caleb B. Smith	1861–1863
	John P. Usher	1863–1865

The Andrew Johnson Administration

Secretary of State	William H. Seward	1865–1869
Secretary of Treasury	Hugh McCulloch	1865–1869
Secretary of War	Edwin M. Stanton	1865–1867
	Ulysses S. Grant	1867–1868
	Lorenzo Thomas	1868
	John M. Schofield	1868–1869
Attorney General	James Speed	1865–1866
	Henry Stanbery	1866–1868
	William M. Evarts	1868–1869

Postmaster General	William Dennison	1865–1866
	Alexander Randall	1866–1869
Secretary of Navy	Gideon Welles	1865–1869
Secretary of Interior	John P. Usher	1865
	James Harlan	1865–1866
	Orville H. Browning	1866–1869

The Grant Administration

Secretary of State	Elihu B. Washburne	1869
	Hamilton Fish	1869–1877
Secretary of Treasury	George S. Boutwell	1869–1873
	William Richardson	1873–1874
	Benjamin Bristow	1874–1876
	Lot M. Morrill	1876–1877
Secretary of War	John A. Rawlins	1869
	William T. Sherman	1869
	William W. Belknap	1869–1876
	Alphonso Taft	1876
	James D. Cameron	1876–1877
Attorney General	Ebenezer Hoar	1869–1870
	Amos T. Ackerman	1870–1871
	G. H. Williams	1871–1875
	Edwards Pierrepont	1875–1876
	Alphonso Taft	1876–1877
Postmaster General	John A. J. Creswell	1869–1874
	James W. Marshall	1874
	Marshall Jewell	1874–1876
	James N. Tyner	1876–1877
Secretary of Navy	Adolph E. Borie	1869
	George M. Robeson	1869–1877
Secretary of Interior	Jacob D. Cox	1869–1870
	Columbus Delano	1870–1875
	Zachariah Chandler	1875–1877

The Hayes Administration

Secretary of State	William B. Evarts	1877–1881
Secretary of Treasury	John Sherman	1877–1881
Secretary of War	George W. McCrary	1877–1879
	Alex Ramsey	1879–1881
Attorney General	Charles Devens	1877–1881
Postmaster General	David M. Key	1877–1880
	Horace Maynard	1880–1881
Secretary of Navy	Richard W. Thompson	1877–1880
	Nathan Goff, Jr.	1881
Secretary of Interior	Carl Schurz	1877–1881

The Garfield Administration

Secretary of State	James G. Blaine	1881
Secretary of Treasury	William Windom	1881
Secretary of War	Robert T. Lincoln	1881
Attorney General	Wayne MacVeagh	1881
Postmaster General	Thomas L. James	1881
Secretary of Navy	William H. Hunt	1881
Secretary of Interior	Samuel J. Kirkwood	1881

The Arthur Administration

Secretary of State	F. T. Frelinghuysen	1881–1885
Secretary of Treasury	Charles J. Folger	1881–1884
	Walter Q. Gresham	1884
	Hugh McCulloch	1884–1885
Secretary of War	Robert T. Lincoln	1881–1885
Attorney General	Benjamin H. Brewster	1881–1885
Postmaster General	Timothy O. Howe	1881–1883
	Walter Q. Gresham	1883–1884
	Frank Hatton	1884–1885
Secretary of Navy	William H. Hunt	1881–1882
	William E. Chandler	1882–1885
Secretary of Interior	Samuel J. Kirkwood	1881–1882
	Henry M. Teller	1882–1885

The First Cleveland Administration

Secretary of State	Thomas F. Bayard	1885–1889
Secretary of Treasury	Daniel Manning	1885–1887
	Charles S. Fairchild	1887–1889
Secretary of War	William C. Endicott	1885–1889
Attorney General	Augustus H. Garland	1885–1889
Postmaster General	William F. Vilas	1885–1888
	Don M. Dickinson	1888–1889
Secretary of Navy	William C. Whitney	1885–1889
Secretary of Interior	Lucius Q. C. Lamar	1885–1888
	William F. Vilas	1888–1889
Secretary of Agriculture	Norman J. Colman	1889

The Benjamin Harrison Administration

Secretary of State	James G. Blaine	1889–1892
	John W. Foster	1892–1893
Secretary of Treasury	William Windom	1889–1891
	Charles Foster	1891–1893
Secretary of War	Redfield Proctor	1889–1891
	Stephen B. Elkins	1891–1893
Attorney General	William H. H. Miller	1889–1891
Postmaster General	John Wanamaker	1889–1893
Secretary of Navy	Benjamin F. Tracy	1889–1893
Secretary of Interior	John W. Noble	1889–1893
Secretary of Agriculture	Jeremiah M. Rusk	1889–1893

The Second Cleveland Administration

Secretary of State	Walter Q. Gresham	1893–1895
	Richard Olney	1895–1897
Secretary of Treasury	John G. Carlisle	1893–1897
Secretary of War	Daniel S. Lamont	1893–1897
Attorney General	Richard Olney	1893–1895
	James Harmon	1895–1897
Postmaster General	Wilson S. Bissell	1893–1895
	William L. Wilson	1895–1897
Secretary of Navy	Hilary A. Herbert	1893–1897
Secretary of Interior	Hoke Smith	1893–1896
	David R. Francis	1896–1897
Secretary of Agriculture	Julius S. Morton	1893–1897

The McKinley Administration

Secretary of State	John Sherman	1897–1898
	William R. Day	1898
	John Hay	1898–1901
Secretary of Treasury	Lyman J. Gage	1897–1901
Secretary of War	Russell A. Alger	1897–1899
	Elihu Root	1899–1901
Attorney General	Joseph McKenna	1897–1898
	John W. Griggs	1898–1901
	Philander C. Knox	1901
Postmaster General	James A. Gary	1897–1898
	Charles E. Smith	1898–1901

Secretary of Navy	John D. Long	1897–1901
Secretary of Interior	Cornelius N. Bliss	1897–1899
	Ethan A. Hitchcock	1899–1901
Secretary of Agriculture	James Wilson	1897–1901

The Theodore Roosevelt Administration

Secretary of State	John Hay	1901–1905
	Elihu Root	1905–1909
	Robert Bacon	1909
Secretary of Treasury	Lyman J. Gage	1901–1902
	Leslie M. Shaw	1902–1907
	George B. Cortelyou	1907–1909
Secretary of War	Elihu Root	1901–1904
	William H. Taft	1904–1908
	Luke E. Wright	1908–1909
Attorney General	Philander C. Knox	1901–1904
	William H. Moody	1904–1906
	Charles J. Bonaparte	1906–1909
Postmaster General	Charles E. Smith	1901–1902
	Henry C. Payne	1902–1904
	Robert J. Wynne	1904–1905
	George B. Cortelyou	1905–1907
	George von L. Meyer	1907–1909
Secretary of Navy	John D. Long	1901–1902
	William H. Moody	1902–1904
	Paul Morton	1904–1905
	Charles J. Bonaparte	1905–1906
	Victor H. Metcalf	1906–1908
	Truman H. Newberry	1908–1909
Secretary of Interior	Ethan A. Hitchcock	1901–1907
	James R. Garfield	1907–1909
Secretary of Agriculture	James Wilson	1901–1909
Secretary of Labor and Commerce	George B. Cortelyou	1903–1904
	Victor H. Metcalf	1904–1906
	Oscar S. Straus	1906–1909
	Charles Nagel	1909

The Taft Administration

Secretary of State	Philander C. Knox	1909–1913
Secretary of Treasury	Franklin MacVeagh	1909–1913
Secretary of War	Jacob M. Dickinson	1909–1911
	Henry L. Stimson	1911–1913
Attorney General	George W. Wickersham	1909–1913
Postmaster General	Frank H. Hitchcock	1909–1913

Secretary of Navy	George von L. Meyer	1909–1913
Secretary of Interior	Richard A. Ballinger	1909–1911
	Walter L. Fisher	1911–1913
Secretary of Agriculture	James Wilson	1909–1913
Secretary of Labor and Commerce	Charles Nagel	1909–1913

The Wilson Administration

Secretary of State	William J. Bryan	1913–1915
	Robert Lansing	1915–1920
	Bainbridge Colby	1920–1921
Secretary of Treasury	William G. McAdoo	1913–1918
	Carter Glass	1918–1920
	David F. Houston	1920–1921
Secretary of War	Lindley M. Garrison	1913–1916
	Newton D. Baker	1916–1921
Attorney General	James C. McReynolds	1913–1914
	Thomas W. Gregory	1914–1919
	A. Mitchell Palmer	1919–1921
Postmaster General	Albert S. Burleson	1913–1921
Secretary of Navy	Josephus Daniels	1913–1921
Secretary of Interior	Franklin K. Lane	1913–1920
	John B. Payne	1920–1921
Secretary of Agriculture	David F. Houston	1913–1920
	Edwin T. Meredith	1920–1921
Secretary of Commerce	William C. Redfield	1913–1919
	Joshua W. Alexander	1919–1921
Secretary of Labor	William B. Wilson	1913–1921

The Harding Administration

Secretary of State	Charles E. Hughes	1921–1923
Secretary of Treasury	Andrew Mellon	1921–1923
Secretary of War	John W. Weeks	1921–1923
Attorney General	Harry M. Daugherty	1921–1923
Postmaster General	Will H. Hays	1921–1922
	Hubert Work	1922–1923
	Harry S. New	1923
Secretary of Navy	Edwin Denby	1921–1923
Secretary of Interior	Albert B. Fall	1921–1923
	Hubert Work	1923

Secretary of Agriculture	Henry C. Wallace	1921–1923
Secretary of Commerce	Herbert C. Hoover	1921–1923
Secretary of Labor	James J. Davis	1921–1923

The Coolidge Administration

Secretary of State	Charles E. Hughes	1923–1925
	Frank B. Kellogg	1925–1929
Secretary of Treasury	Andrew Mellon	1923–1929
Secretary of War	John W. Weeks	1923–1925
	Dwight F. Davis	1925–1929
Attorney General	Henry M. Daugherty	1923–1924
	Harlan F. Stone	1924–1925
	John G. Sargent	1925–1929
Postmaster General	Harry S. New	1923–1929
Secretary of Navy	Edwin Denby	1923–1924
	Curtis D. Wilbur	1924–1929
Secretary of Interior	Hubert Work	1923–1928
	Roy O. West	1928–1929
Secretary of Agriculture	Henry C. Wallace	1923–1924
	Howard M. Gore	1924–1925
	William M. Jardine	1925–1929
Secretary of Commerce	Herbert C. Hoover	1923–1928
	William F. Whiting	1928–1929
Secretary of Labor	James J. Davis	1923–1929

The Hoover Administration

Secretary of State	Henry L. Stimson	1929–1933
Secretary of Treasury	Andrew Mellon	1929–1932
	Ogden L. Mills	1932–1933
Secretary of War	James W. Good	1929
	Patrick J. Hurley	1929–1933
Attorney General	William D. Mitchell	1929–1933
Postmaster General	Walter F. Brown	1929–1933
Secretary of Navy	Charles F. Adams	1929–1933
Secretary of Interior	Ray L. Wilbur	1929–1933
Secretary of Agriculture	Arthur M. Hyde	1929–1933

Secretary of Commerce	Robert P. Lamont	1929–1932
	Roy D. Chapin	1932–1933
Secretary of Labor	James J. Davis	1929–1930
	William N. Doak	1930–1933

The Franklin D. Roosevelt Administration

Secretary of State	Cordell Hull	1933–1944
	E. R. Stettinius, Jr.	1944–1945
Secretary of Treasury	William H. Woodin	1933–1934
	Henry Morgenthau, Jr.	1934–1945
Secretary of War	George H. Dern	1933–1936
	Henry A. Woodring	1936–1940
	Henry L. Stimson	1940–1945
Attorney General	Homer S. Cummings	1933–1939
	Frank Murphy	1939–1940
	Robert H. Jackson	1940–1941
	Francis Biddle	1941–1945
Postmaster General	James A. Farley	1933–1940
	Frank C. Walker	1940–1945
Secretary of Navy	Claude A. Swanson	1933–1940
	Charles Edison	1940
	Frank Knox	1940–1944
	James V. Forrestal	1944–1945
Secretary of Interior	Harold L. Ickes	1933–1945
Secretary of Agriculture	Henry A. Wallace	1933–1940
	Claude R. Wickard	1940–1945
Secretary of Commerce	Daniel C. Roper	1933–1939
	Harry L. Hopkins	1939–1940
	Jesse Jones	1940–1945
	Henry A. Wallace	1945
Secretary of Labor	Frances Perkins	1933–1945

The Truman Administration

Secretary of State	James F. Byrnes	1945–1947
	George C. Marshall	1947–1949
	Dean G. Acheson	1949–1953
Secretary of Treasury	Fred M. Vinson	1945–1946
	John W. Snyder	1946–1953
Secretary of War	Robert P. Patterson	1945–1947
	Kenneth C. Royall	1947
Attorney General	Tom C. Clark	1945–1949
	J. Howard McGrath	1949–1952
	James P. McGranery	1952–1953
Postmaster General	Frank C. Walker	1945
	Robert E. Hannegan	1945–1947
	Jesse M. Donaldson	1947–1953
Secretary of Navy	James V. Forrestal	1945–1947

Secretary of Interior	Harold L. Ickes	1945–1946
	Julius A. Krug	1946–1949
	Oscar L. Chapman	1949–1953
Secretary of Agriculture	Clinton P. Anderson	1945–1948
	Charles F. Brannan	1948–1953
Secretary of Commerce	Henry A. Wallace	1945–1946
	W. Averell Harriman	1946–1948
	Charles W. Sawyer	1948–1953
Secretary of Labor	Lewis B. Schwellenbach	1945–1948
	Maurice J. Tobin	1948–1953
Secretary of Defense	James V. Forrestal	1947–1949
	Louis A. Johnson	1949–1950
	George C. Marshall	1950–1951
	Robert A. Lovett	1951–1953

The Eisenhower Administration

Secretary of State	John Foster Dulles	1953–1959
	Christian A. Herter	1959–1961
Secretary of Treasury	George M. Humphrey	1953–1957
	Robert B. Anderson	1957–1961
Attorney General	Herbert Brownell, Jr.	1953–1958
	William P. Rogers	1958–1961
Postmaster General	Arthur E. Summerfield	1953–1961
Secretary of Interior	Douglas McKay	1953–1956
	Fred A. Seaton	1956–1961
Secretary of Agriculture	Ezra T. Benson	1953–1961
Secretary of Commerce	Sinclair Weeks	1953–1958
	Lewis L. Strauss	1958–1959
	Frederick H. Mueller	1959–1961
Secretary of Labor	Martin P. Durkin	1953
	James P. Mitchell	1953–1961
Secretary of Defense	Charles E. Wilson	1953–1957
	Neil H. McElroy	1957–1959
	Thomas S. Gates, Jr.	1959–1961
Secretary of Health, Education and Welfare	Oveta Culp Hobby	1953–1955
	Marion B. Folsom	1955–1958
	Arthur S. Flemming	1958–1961

The Kennedy Administration

Secretary of State	Dean Rusk	1961–1963
Secretary of Treasury	C. Douglas Dillon	1961–1963
Attorney General	Robert F. Kennedy	1961–1963
Postmaster General	J. Edward Day	1961–1963
	John A. Gronouski	1963

Secretary of Interior	Stewart L. Udall	1961–1963
Secretary of Agriculture	Orville L. Freeman	1961–1963
Secretary of Commerce	Luther H. Hodges	1961–1963
Secretary of Labor	Arthur J. Goldberg W. Willard Wirtz	1961–1962 1962–1963
Secretary of Defense	Robert S. McNamara	1961–1963
Secretary of Health, Education and Welfare	Abraham A. Ribicoff Anthony J. Celebrezze	1961–1962 1962–1963

The Lyndon Johnson Administration

Secretary of State	Dean Rusk	1963–1969
Secretary of Treasury	C. Douglas Dillon Henry H. Fowler	1963–1965 1965–1969
Attorney General	Robert F. Kennedy Nicholas Katzenbach Ramsey Clark	1963–1964 1965–1966 1967–1969
Postmaster General	John A. Gronouski Lawrence F. O'Brien Marvin Watson	1963–1965 1965–1968 1968–1969
Secretary of Interior	Stewart L. Udall	1963–1969
Secretary of Agriculture	Orville L. Freeman	1963–1969
Secretary of Commerce	Luther H. Hodges John T. Connor Alexander B. Trowbridge Cyrus R. Smith	1963–1964 1964–1967 1967–1968 1968–1969
Secretary of Labor	W. Willard Wirtz	1963–1969
Secretary of Defense	Robert F. McNamara Clark Clifford	1963–1968 1968–1969
Secretary of Health, Education and Welfare	Anthony J. Celebrezze John W. Gardner Wilbur J. Cohen	1963–1965 1965–1968 1968–1969
Secretary of Housing and Urban Development	Robert C. Weaver Robert C. Wood	1966–1969 1969
Secretary of Transportation	Alan S. Boyd	1967–1969

The Nixon Administration

Secretary of State	William P. Rogers Henry A. Kissinger	1969–1973 1973–1974
Secretary of Treasury	David M. Kennedy John B. Connally George P. Shultz William E. Simon	1969–1970 1971–1972 1972–1974 1974
Attorney General	John N. Mitchell Richard G. Kleindienst Elliot L. Richardson William B. Saxbe	1969–1972 1972–1973 1973 1973–1974
Postmaster General	Winton M. Blount	1969–1971
Secretary of Interior	Walter J. Hickel Rogers Morton	1969–1970 1971–1974
Secretary of Agriculture	Clifford M. Hardin Earl L. Butz	1969–1971 1971–1974
Secretary of Commerce	Maurice H. Stans Peter G. Peterson Frederick B. Dent	1969–1972 1972–1973 1973–1974
Secretary of Labor	George P. Shultz James D. Hodgson Peter J. Brennan	1969–1970 1970–1973 1973–1974
Secretary of Defense	Melvin R. Laird Elliot L. Richardson James R. Schlesinger	1969–1973 1973 1973–1974
Secretary of Health, Education and Welfare	Robert H. Finch Elliot L. Richardson Casper W. Weinberger	1969–1970 1970–1973 1973–1974
Secretary of Housing and Urban Development	George Romney James T. Lynn	1969–1973 1973–1974
Secretary of Transportation	John A. Volpe Claude S. Brinegar	1969–1973 1973–1974

The Ford Administration

Secretary of State	Henry A. Kissinger	1974–1977
Secretary of Treasury	William E. Simon	1974–1977
Attorney General	William Saxbe Edward Levi	1974–1975 1975–1977
Secretary of Interior	Rogers Morton Stanley K. Hathaway Thomas Kleppe	1974–1975 1975 1975–1977
Secretary of Agriculture	Earl L. Butz John A. Knebel	1974–1976 1976–1977
Secretary of Commerce	Frederick B. Dent Rogers Morton Elliot L. Richardson	1974–1975 1975–1976 1976–1977
Secretary of Labor	Peter J. Brennan John T. Dunlop W. J. Usery	1974–1975 1975–1976 1976–1977

Secretary of Defense	James R. Schlesinger Donald Rumsfeld	1974–1975 1975–1977
Secretary of Health, Education and Welfare	Casper Weinberger Forrest D. Mathews	1974–1975 1975–1977
Secretary of Housing and Urban Development	James T. Lynn Carla A. Hills	1974–1975 1975–1977
Secretary of Transportation	Claude Brinegar William T. Coleman	1974–1975 1975–1977

The Carter Administration

Secretary of State	Cyrus R. Vance Edmund Muskie	1977–1980 1980–1981
Secretary of Treasury	W. Michael Blumenthal G. William Miller	1977–1979 1979–1981
Attorney General	Griffin Bell Benjamin R. Civiletti	1977–1979 1979–1981
Secretary of Interior	Cecil D. Andrus	1977–1981
Secretary of Agriculture	Robert Bergland	1977–1981
Secretary of Commerce	Juanita M. Kreps Philip M. Klutznick	1977–1979 1979–1981
Secretary of Labor	F. Ray Marshall	1977–1981
Secretary of Defense	Harold Brown	1977–1981
Secretary of Health, Education and Welfare	Joseph A. Califano Patricia R. Harris	1977–1979 1979
Secretary of Health and Human Services	Patricia R. Harris	1979–1981
Secretary of Education	Shirley M. Hufstedler	1979–1981

Secretary of Housing and Urban Development	Patricia R. Harris Moon Landrieu	1977–1979 1979–1981
Secretary of Transportation	Brock Adams Neil E. Goldschmidt	1977–1979 1979–1981
Secretary of Energy	James R. Schlesinger Charles W. Duncan	1977–1979 1979–1981

The Reagan Administration

Secretary of State	Alexander M. Haig George Shultz	1981–1982 1982–
Secretary of Treasury	Donald Regan	1981–
Attorney General	William French Smith	1981–
Secretary of Interior	James Watt	1981–
Secretary of Agriculture	John Block	1981–
Secretary of Commerce	Malcolm Baldrige	1981–
Secretary of Labor	Raymond Donovan	1981–
Secretary of Defense	Casper Weinberger	1981–
Secretary of Health and Human Services	Richard Schweiker Margaret Heckler	1981–1983 1983–
Secretary of Education	Terrel Bell	1981–
Secretary of Housing and Urban Development	Samuel Pierce	1981–
Secretary of Transportation	Drew Lewis Elizabeth Dole	1981–1983 1983–
Secretary of Energy	James Edwards Donald Hodel	1981–1982 1982–

Supreme Court Justices

Name	Terms of Service[1]	Appointed by	Name	Terms of Service[1]	Appointed by
John Jay, N.Y.	1789–1795	Washington	George Shiras, Jr., Pa.	1892–1903	B. Harrison
James Wilson, Pa.	1789–1798	Washington	Howell E. Jackson, Tenn.	1893–1895	B. Harrison
John Rutledge, S.C.	1790–1791	Washington	Edward D. White, La.	1894–1910	Cleveland
William Cushing, Mass.	1790–1810	Washington	Rufus W. Peckham, N.Y.	1896–1909	Cleveland
John Blair, Va.	1790–1796	Washington	Joseph McKenna, Cal.	1898–1925	McKinley
James Iredell, N.C.	1790–1799	Washington	Oliver W. Holmes, Mass.	1902–1932	T. Roosevelt
Thomas Johnson, Md.	1792–1793	Washington	William R. Day, Ohio	1903–1922	T. Roosevelt
William Paterson, N.J.	1793–1806	Washington	William H. Moody, Mass.	1906–1910	T. Roosevelt
John Rutledge, S.C.[2]	1795	Washington	Horace H. Lurton, Tenn.	1910–1914	Taft
Samuel Chase, Md.	1796–1811	Washington	Charles E. Hughes, N.Y.	1910–1916	Taft
Oliver Ellsworth, Conn.	1796–1800	Washington	Willis Van Devanter, Wy.	1911–1937	Taft
Bushrod Washington, Va.	1799–1829	J. Adams	Joseph R. Lamar, Ga.	1911–1916	Taft
Alfred Moore, N.C.	1800–1804	J. Adams	**Edward D. White,** La.	1910–1921	Taft
John Marshall, Va.	1801–1835	J. Adams	Mahlon Pitney, N.J.	1912–1922	Taft
William Johnson, S.C.	1804–1834	Jefferson	James C. McReynolds, Tenn.	1914–1941	Wilson
Brockholst Livingston, N.Y.	1807–1823	Jefferson	Louis D. Brandeis, Mass.	1916–1939	Wilson
Thomas Todd, Ky.	1807–1826	Jefferson	John H. Clarke, Ohio	1916–1922	Wilson
Gabriel Duvall, Md.	1811–1835	Madison	**William H. Taft,** Conn.	1921–1930	Harding
Joseph Story, Mass.	1812–1845	Madison	George Sutherland, Utah	1922–1938	Harding
Smith Thompson, N.Y.	1823–1843	Monroe	Pierce Butler, Minn.	1923–1939	Harding
Robert Trimble, Ky.	1826–1828	J. Q. Adams	Edward T. Sanford, Tenn.	1923–1930	Harding
John McLean, Ohio	1830–1861	Jackson	Harlan F. Stone, N.Y.	1925–1941	Coolidge
Henry Baldwin, Pa.	1830–1844	Jackson	**Charles E. Hughes,** N.Y.	1930–1941	Hoover
James M. Wayne, Ga.	1835–1867	Jackson	Owen J. Roberts, Penn.	1930–1945	Hoover
Roger B. Taney, Md.	1836–1864	Jackson	Benjamin N. Cardozo, N.Y.	1932–1938	Hoover
Philip P. Barbour, Va.	1836–1841	Jackson	Hugo L. Black, Ala.	1937–1971	F. Roosevelt
John Cartron, Tenn.	1837–1865	Van Buren	Stanley F. Reed, Ky.	1938–1957	F. Roosevelt
John McKinley, Ala.	1838–1852	Van Buren	Felix Frankfurter, Mass.	1939–1962	F. Roosevelt
Peter V. Daniel, Va.	1842–1860	Van Buren	William O. Douglas, Conn.	1939–1975	F. Roosevelt
Samuel Nelson, N.Y.	1845–1872	Tyler	Frank Murphy, Mich.	1940–1949	F. Roosevelt
Levi Woodbury, N.H.	1845–1851	Polk	**Harlan F. Stone,** N.Y.	1941–1946	F. Roosevelt
Robert C. Grier, Pa.	1846–1870	Polk	James F. Byrnes, S.C.	1941–1942	F. Roosevelt
Benjamin R. Curtis, Mass.	1851–1857	Fillmore	Robert H. Jackson, N.Y.	1941–1954	F. Roosevelt
John A. Campbell, Ala.	1853–1861	Pierce	Wiley B. Rutledge, Iowa	1943–1949	F. Roosevelt
Nathan Clifford, Me.	1858–1881	Buchanan	Harold H. Burton, Ohio	1945–1958	Truman
Noah H. Swayne, Ohio	1862–1881	Lincoln	**Frederick M. Vinson,** Ky.	1946–1953	Truman
Samuel F. Miller, Iowa	1862–1890	Lincoln	Tom C. Clark, Texas	1949–1967	Truman
David Davis, Ill.	1862–1877	Lincoln	Sherman Minton, Ind.	1949–1956	Truman
Stephen J. Field, Cal.	1863–1897	Lincoln	**Earl Warren,** Cal.	1953–1969	Eisenhower
Salmon P. Chase, Ohio	1864–1873	Lincoln	John Marshall Harlan, N.Y.	1955–1971	Eisenhower
William Strong, Pa.	1870–1880	Grant	William J. Brennan, Jr., N.J.	1956–	Eisenhower
Joseph P. Bradley, N.J.	1870–1892	Grant	Charles E. Whittaker, Mo.	1957–1962	Eisenhower
Ward Hunt, N.Y.	1873–1882	Grant	Potter Stewart, Ohio	1958–1981	Eisenhower
Morrison R. Waite, Ohio	1874–1888	Grant	Byron R. White, Colo.	1962–	Kennedy
John M. Harlan, Ky.	1877–1911	Hayes	Arthur J. Goldberg, Ill.	1962–1965	Kennedy
William B. Woods, Ga.	1881–1887	Hayes	Abe Fortas, Tenn.	1965–1970	Johnson
Stanley Matthews, Ohio	1881–1889	Garfield	Thurgood Marshall, Md.	1967–	Johnson
Horace Gray, Mass.	1882–1902	Arthur	**Warren E. Burger,** Va.	1969–	Nixon
Samuel Blatchford, N.Y.	1882–1893	Arthur	Harry A. Blackmun, Minn.	1970–	Nixon
Lucius Q. C. Lamar, Miss.	1888–1893	Cleveland	Lewis F. Powell, Jr., Va.	1971–	Nixon
Melville W. Fuller, Ill.	1888–1910	Cleveland	William H. Rehnquist, Ariz.	1971–	Nixon
David J. Brewer, Kan.	1890–1910	B. Harrison	John Paul Stevens, Ill.	1975–	Ford
Henry B. Brown, Mich.	1891–1906	B. Harrison	Sandra Day O'Connor, Ariz.	1981–	Reagan

Chief Justices in bold type

[1] The date on which the justice took his judicial oath is here used as the date of the beginning of his service, for until that oath is taken he is not vested with the prerogatives of his office. Justices, however, receive their commissions ("letters patent") before taking their oath—in some instances, in the preceding year.

[2] Acting Chief Justice; Senate refused to confirm appointment.

Positions of the photographs are indicated in abbreviated form as follows: top (t), bottom (b), center (c), left (l), right (r). All photographs not credited are the property of Scott, Foresman.

Chapter Openers

Chapter 16, p. 448 *The First Vote. Harper's Weekly,* November 16, 1867. Newberry Library

Chapter 17, p. 480 *The Homesteader's Wife* (detail) by Harvey Dunn, 1916. South Dakota Memorial Art Center Collection, Brookings

Chapter 18, p. 514 A Bessemer convertor in a steel plant by S. B. Shiley, 1895. Courtesy Bethlehem Steel Corporation

Chapter 19, p. 544 *View Along Broadway from Maiden Lane* by J. J. Fogerty, *c.* 1885. The New-York Historical Society

Chapter 20, p. 572 *The Lost Bet* (detail) by Joseph Klir, 1892. Chicago's Twelfth Street celebrates Grover Cleveland's election. Chicago Historical Society

Chapter 21, p. 600 Rough Riders charge up San Juan Hill in *Bloody Ford* by Charles Johnson Post, 1898. Army Art Collection, U.S. Army Center of Military History

Chapter 22, p. 628 *Cliff Dwellers* (detail) by George Bellows, 1913. Los Angeles County Museum of Art, Los Angeles County Funds

Chapter 23, p. 656 Cover of *Puck,* August 1, 1906. Culver Pictures.

Chapter 24, p. 684 *The Machine Gunner* by Harvey Dunn, 1918. Smithsonian Institution

Chapter 25, p. 716 *Dance Hall* (detail from mural panel) by Thomas Hart Benton, 1930. Courtesy Maurice Segoura Gallery, New York, N.Y.

Chapter 26, p. 744 *Reading from Left to Right,* men huddling at a street corner by Raphael Soyer, 1938. Oil on canvas. 26¼ × 20½ inches. Collection Whitney Museum of American Art. Gift of Mrs. Emil J. Arnold in memory of Emil J. Arnold and in honor of Lloyd Goodrich

Chapter 27, p. 772 *United We Are Strong-United We Will Win.* World War II poster. West Point Museum Collections, United States Military Academy, West Point, N.Y.

Chapter 28, p. 804 Hydrogen bomb test over the Marshall Islands, 1952. UPI

Chapter 29, p. 830 Aerial view of Levittown, New Jersey. Leo Choplin/Black Star

Chapter 30, p. 890 200,000 people gathered at the Lincoln Memorial in Washington, D.C., to march for blacks' civil rights, August 1963. Robert W. Kelley, LIFE Magazine © 1970, TIME, Inc.

Chapter 31, p. 890 Ex-president Richard Nixon waving good-by as he leaves Washington, D.C., after his resignation, August 9, 1974. Roland Freeman/Magnum

Chapter 32, p. 922 A solar house. Arthur Tress/Magnum

Chapter 16

451 *Harper's Weekly.* Library of Congress   **453** Library of Congress   **455** *Frank Leslie's Illustrated Newspaper,* July 13, 1867   **457** Library of Congress   **458** National Archives   **459** *Harper's Weekly,* March 13, 1869. The Newberry Library, Chicago   **461** (l) Brown Brothers   **461** (r) Courtesy Jay P. Altmayer   **462** *Harper's Weekly,* June 23, 1866   **463** *Harper's Weekly*   **465** (l) Library of Congress   **465** (r)*Harper's Weekly,* July 25, 1868   **467** Maryland Historical Society, Baltimore   **468** (t) Giles County Historical Society, Pulaski, Tenn.   **468** (b) From *the Pictorial History of the Negro in America* by Langston Hughes and Milton Meltzer   **470** (both) The Sophia Smith Collection (Women's History Archive), Smith College, Northampton, MA   **472** Culver Pictures   **473** Rutherford B. Hayes Presidential Center   **475** The Historic New Orleans Collection   **476** Brown Brothers

Chapter 17

485 (t) Courtesy of The American Museum of Natural History   **485** (b) Courtesy Amon Carter Museum, Fort Worth   **488–89** (tl) Library of Congress   **488–89** (tr) U.S. Signal Corps in The National Archives   **488–89** (bl) From Amos Bad Heart Bull, *A Pictographic History of the Oglala Sioux,* University of Nebraska Press   **488–89** (br) Montana Historical Society, Helena   **490** (both) Arizona Historical Society   **491** Kansas State Historical Society, Topeka   **492** United States Military Academy, West Point, N.Y.   **493** Montana Historical Society, Helena   **496** Denver Public Library, Western Collection   **498** Baker Library, Harvard University Graduate School of Business Administration   **500** The New-York Historical Society   **501** California State Library   **502** Library of Congress   **504** Courtesy of the California Historical Society, San Francisco/Los Angeles   **505** Library of Congress   **506** Courtesy of Buffalo Bill Historical Center, Cody, Wyoming   **507** Solomon D. Butcher Collection, Nebraska State Historical Society   **509** Bettmann Archive

Chapter 18

517 Chicago Historical Society   **519** Coverdale and Colpitts Collection   **521** Coverdale and Colpitts Collection   **523** Union Pacific Railroad Museum Collection   **524** Library of Congress   **525** Library of Congress   **526** Culver Pictures   **527** Culver Pictures   **528** *Puck,* March 6, 1901   **530** (t) Brown Brothers   **530** (b) Thomas Alva Edison Foundation, Detroit   **532** Courtesy The Great Atlantic & Pacific Tea Co.   **534** (t) Library of Congress   **534** (b) The Byron Collection, Museum of the City of New York

535 Courtesy The Bancroft Library   537 Library of Congress
539 (b) *Harper's Weekly*, July 16, 1892   540 *Harper's Weekly*, 1877
541 Stefan Lorant Collection.

Chapter 19

547 The Huntington Library, San Marino, California   548 Missouri
Historical Society   550 (l) Culver Pictures   550 (r) Bettmann
Archive   551 Museum of the City of New York   552 American
Telephone & Telegraph Company   553 Brown Brothers   555 (tl)
The College Archive, Smith College, Northampton, MA   555 (tr)
Brown Brothers   555 (b) Bettmann Archive   558 Prints Division,
New York Public Library, Astor, Lenox and Tilden Foundations
560 Chicago Historical Society   562 (l) Brown Brothers   562 (tr)
Library of Congress   562 (br) *Harper's Weekly*   564 From Roger
Butterfield, *The American Past*, Simon & Schuster   567 (l) Museum
of the City of New York   567 (r) Photograph by Jessie Tarbox Beals,
Jacob A. Riis Collection, Museum of the City of New York   569 Jane
Addams Memorial Collection, The Library, University of Illinois at
Chicago

Chapter 20

574 (l) Culver Pictures   574 (r) Library of Congress   577 *Judge*,
The New-York Historical Society   582 Culver Pictures
583 Kansas State Historical Society, Topeka   585 Library of Con-
gress   586 (t) Free Library of Philadelphia   586 (b) Bettmann
Archive   589 (l) International Museum of Photography at George
Eastman House   589 (r) Valentine Museum, Richmond, Virginia
590 (t) By permission of the Trustees of the Estate of Samuel L. Clemens
(Mark Twain) deceased   590 (b) Illustration "The Whitewash Scene"
by Worth Brehm from *The Adventures of Tom Sawyer* by Mark Twain,
Illustrations copyright 1910 by Worth Brehm, Renewed 1937 by Mrs.
Worth Brehm, Reprinted by permission of Harper & Row, Publishers,
Inc.   591 (t) Culver Pictures   591 (b) Bettmann Archive
593 University of Hartford: J. Doyle DeWitt Collection   594 From L.
Frank Baum, *The Wizard of Oz*, Reilly & Lee Co.   596 Courtesy of
the Bancroft Library, University of California, Berkeley   599 *Puck*,
March 14, 1900

Chapter 21

604 The New-York Historical Society   605 Granger Collection
607 *Punch*, November 2, 1895   608 (t) Hawaii State Archives
608 (b) Culver Pictures   610 (l) *Puck*, March 2, 1881   610 (r)
Library of Congress   611 Bettmann Archive   612 (l) Granger
Collection   612 (r) *New York Journal*, January 15, 1897   613 *New
York Journal*, February 17, 1898   614 *New York Journal*, January 17,
1897   615 Culver Pictures   618 (l) Chicago Historical Society
618 (r) Courtesy of USMA Archives, West Point, N.Y.   621 New York
Public Library, Astor, Lenox and Tilden Foundations   622 (both)
Library of Congress   626 Culver Pictures

Chapter 22

631 (l) The Lawrence Lee Pelletier Library, Allegheny College   631 (r)
Culver Pictures   633 Chicago Historical Society   634 Culver Pictures   636 (l) Courtesy Mrs. Neill Whisnant, Portland, Oregon
636 (tr) Brown Brothers   636 (br) Brown Brothers   639 Brown
Brothers   642 Sears, Roebuck and Co.   643 Warshaw Collection
of Business Americana, Smithsonian Institution   644 (l) U.S. Department of Labor   644 (r) International Museum of Photography at
George Eastman House   645 (t) Schomberg Collection, New York
Public Library, Astor, Lenox and Tilden Foundations   645 (b) Bett-

mann Archive   646 The Sophia Smith Collection (Women's History
Archive), Smith College, Northampton, MA   647 The Sophia Smith
Collection (Women's History Archive), Smith College, Northampton, MA   649 The Jacob A. Riis Collection, Museum of the City of
New York   650 Bettmann Archive   651 A.B. Walker in LIFE
652 Wadsworth Atheneum, Hartford, Connecticut, Ella Gallup Sumner
and Mary Catlin Sumner Collection   653 Yale University Art Gallery, Gift of Collection Société Anonyme

---

Chapter 23

658 Brown Brothers   660 (t) Courtesy, Ford Archives, Henry Ford
Museum, Dearborn, Michigan   660 (c) Courtesy, Ford Archives,
Henry Ford Museum, Dearborn, Michigan   660 (r) The New York
Public Library   663 Brown Brothers   665 (both) Brown Brothers
666 Manchester (N.H.) Historic Association   667 Culver Pictures
669 *Puck*, Jan. 13, 1904   670 National Park Service   671 Brown
Brothers   672 Library of Congress   673 *Puck*, June 22, 1910
674 *Colliers*, 1905   675 Warshaw Collection of Business Americana,
Smithsonian Institution   677 *New York Herald*, July 1912
679 Brown Brothers   682 National Archives

Chapter 24

689 Library of Congress   690 *Puck*, 1901   693 (l) Library of Congress   693 (r) Brown Brothers   695 (t) *Puck*, Oct. 16, 1915
695 (b) West Point Museum   697 *Des Moines Register and Leader*,
July,   1915   699 (l)   UPI   702 National
Archives   703 National Archives   702–03 Smithsonian Institution   704 New York Public Library, Picture Collection
705 (both) National Archives   708 UPI   711 (tl) National Archives   711 (tr) Imperial War Museum   713 (t) Kirby in the *World
Journal Tribune*, 1920   713 (b) The Ohio Historical Society, Inc.

Chapter 25

718 Brown Brothers   720 *Vanity Fair* April, 1929   723 (l) Brown
Brothers   723 (r) *Frank Leslie's Illustrated Newspaper*, September 11,
1920   724 LIFE, June 3, 1926   725 (l) Drawing by Carl Rose; ©
1928, 1956. The New Yorker Magazine, Inc.   725 (r) *Dempsey and
Firpo*, 1924 by George Bellows. Oil on Canvas. 51 × 63¼ inches.
Collection of Whitney Museum of American Art. Acq. # 31.95
726 Brown Brothers   727 Brown Brothers   728 UPI   729 (t)
Brown Brothers   729 (b) Collection of American Literature, the
Beinecke Rare Book and Manuscript Library, Yale University   730 (l)
Des Moines Art Center, James D. Edmundson Fund, 1958   730 (r)
UPI   732 Chicago Historical Society   733 *The Passion of Sacco
and Vanzetti*, 1931–32 by Ben Shahn. From the Sacco and Vanzetti Series
of 23 paintings. Tempera. 84½ × 48 inches. Collection of Whitney
Museum of American Art. Gift of Edith and Milton Lowenthal in
memory of Juliana Force. Acq. # 49.22.   734 Smithers Collection.
Humanities Research Center. The University of Texas at Austin
735 Culver Pictures   736 Rollin Kirby, 1925   738 LIFE, 1922
739 From Stefan Lorant's *The Glorious Burden*. Authors Edition, Inc.,
Lenox, MA   741 (l) Museum of the City of New York   741 (r) UPI

Chapter 26

747 Library of Congress   749 (tl) Wide World   749 (tr) *The Detroit
News*   749 (bl) Collection of Nebraska Art Association, Courtesy of
Sheldon Memorial Art Gallery, University of Nebraska, Lincoln
749 (br) UPI   751 Brown Brothers   753 Franklin D. Roosevelt

Library, National Archives and Records Service   754 Culver Pictures
755 Franklin D. Roosevelt Library, National Archives and Records
Service   756 (l) Wide World   756 (r) Library of Congress
757 Library of Congress   759 Social Security Administration
761 (t) UPI   761 (c) Library of Congress   761 (b) Courtesy Mrs.
Philip Evergood   763 UPI   764 Brown Brothers   766 Franklin
D. Roosevelt Library, National Archives and Records Service   768 (l)
Daniel Robert Fitzpatrick, St. Louis *Post-Dispatch*   768 (r) Historical
Pictures Service, Chicago

Chapter 27

774 William A. Ireland, *The Columbus Dispatch*, 1928   776 Wide
World   778 U.S. Army/Center of Military History   779 National
Archives   781 (t) UPI   781 (b) H. Roger-Viollet   782 National
Maritime Museum, London   784 Wide World   786 (l) Navy
Department/National Archives   786 (r) Wide World   786 (b) *San
Francisco Chronicle*, December 8, 1941   789 U.S. Army
791 Vernon T. Manion. Courtesy Boeing Aircraft Corporation, Seattle
793 Margaret Bourke-White, LIFE Magazine © Time, Inc.   794 Jacob
Lawrence. "The migrants arrive in great numbers." No. 40 in the series
The Migration of the Negro. (1940–41) Tempera on composition board,
18 × 21". Collection, The Museum of Modern Art, New York. Gift of
Mrs. David M. Levy.   795 Library of Congress   796 Franklin D.
Roosevelt Library, National Archives and Records Service   797 (t)
Edward Clark, LIFE Magazine © 1945 Time, Inc.   797 (b) U. S. Army
800 Culver Pictures   802 Wide World

Chapter 28

807 Bettmann Archive   810 UPI   812 UPI   814 Bettmann Archive   818 © Bruce Barbey/Magnum Photos, Inc.   820 UPI
821 Bettmann Archive   822 (l) UPI   824 UPI   825 UPI
826 UPI   827 (r) UPI

Chapter 29

833 (t, b) Bettmann Archive   834 Robert Isaacs   835 Green Coca-
Cola Bottles, 1962. Oil on canvas. 82¼ × 57 inches. Collection of the
Whitney Museum of American Art.   836 Bettmann Archive
837 Bettmann Archive   839 UPI   840 Bob Henriques/Magnum
Photos, Inc.   843 (t, b) UPI   845 UPI   846 UPI   847 (l) Carl
Iwasaki, Life Magazine, Inc.   847 (r) Eve Arnold/Magnum Photos,
Inc.   848 UPI   849 (tl) UPI   849 (tr) © Bruce Roberts/Photo
Researchers, Inc.   849 (b) Charles Moore/Black Star   851 Culver
Pictures   852 Bettmann Archive   855 Fred DeWitt/TIME, Inc.

Chapter 30

860 UPI   862 Black Star   864 UPI   865 UPI   866 (l) UPI
869 UPI   872 Wide World   873 Charles Moore/Black Star
875 Wide World   876 Charles Moore/Black Star   878 (l) Jim
Murray/Black Star   878 (r) UPI   879 UPI   881 (t) UPI
881 (bl) Michael D. Sullivan   881 (br) Paul Conklin   886 (t)©
Philip Jones Griffiths/Magnum Photos, Inc.

Chapter 31

893 Wayne Miller/Magnum Photos, Inc.   894 (t) UPI   894 (b)
Peter A. Lake/Black Star   895 Burk Uzzle/Woodfin Camp and Associates   897 (t) Detroit Free Press/Black Star   897 (b) UPI   899 ©
Paul Fusco/ Magnum Photos, Inc.   900 © Betty Lane/Photo Re-
searchers, Inc.   901 Robert Ellison/Empire News/Black Star   902 (t)
Courtesy The Lyndon Baines Johnson Library   902 (b) *The Time
Machine*. Leslie Illingworth. Sept. 13, 1967, in *Punch*. Scratchboard.
15¼ × 12½ in. Courtesy The Lyndon Baines Johnson Library Collec-
tion, Austin, Tex.   903 (l) Charles Harbutt/Archive Pictures, Inc.
903 (r) UPI   904 Roger Malloch/Magnum Photos, Inc.   905 (t)
Elliott Erwitt/Magnum Photos, Inc.   905 (b) UPI   907 Courtesy
The White House   910 (l) Zoom/Magnum Distribution   910 (r)
Distributed by Magnum Photos, Inc.   911 (bl) UPI   913 (t) ©
Howard E. Ruffner/Black Star   913 (c) © Paul Fusco/Magnum Photos,
Inc.   913 (b) UPI   914 Susan Meiselas/Magnum Photos, Inc.
917 Leonard Freed/Magnum Photos, Inc.   918 Mark Godfrey/
Archive Pictures, Inc.   919 Mark Godfrey/Archive Pictures, Inc.

Chapter 32

924 Peter Arnold, Inc.   927 Tony Korody/Sygma   928 (t) UPI
928 (b) Peter Arnold, Inc.   929 © 1979 David Moore/Black Star
931 (t) Chuck O'Rear/West Light   931 (b) Jim Balog/Black Star
932 Wide World   933 Arthur Grace/Sygma   935 Nik Wheeler/
Black Star   937 UPI   938 D. B. Owen/Black Star © 1983
939 (t) P. Chauvel/Sygma   939 (b) J. L. Atlan/Sygma
940 SIPA/Black Star   945 Dan Connolly/Liaison Agency   946 (r)
Paul Conklin   947 Paul Conklin   949 Martin A. Levick/Black
Star   950 Alex Webb/Magnum Photos, Inc.   951 Dennis Brack/
Black Star   952 UPI   954 Mark Sherman/Bruce Coleman
955 Alex Webb/Magnum Photos, Inc.

Picture Essay 5
"White City":
The Columbian Exposition of 1893

1 At Night in the Grand Court. Culver Pictures

2 (t) A view southeast at the Agricultural Building. Courtesy Chicago
Historical Society
(c) A poster from the Exposition. Library of Congress
(b) Louis Sullivan's Transportation Building. Brown Brothers

3 (t) Interior of Electrical Building. Culver Pictures
(b) Machinery Hall. Brown Brothers

4 (t) Chairs being pushed along the Midway. Brown Brothers
(cl) Little Egypt performing. Brown Brothers
(cr) The ferris wheel. Courtesy Chicago Historical Society
(b) Japanese exhibit buildings. Culver Pictures

Picture Essay 6
Mexican-American Experience in the Southwest
following p. 704

1 Viceroy Jose de Iturrigaray and His Family, c. 1805. Museo Nacional de
Historia, Castillo de Chapultepec, Mexico City

2 (t) A chart defining racial mixtures, *Mestizo* + *Espanola* = *Castiza*. Museo Nacional de Historia, Castillo de Chapultepec, Mexico City

(c) *Charros at the Round-up*, by James Walker, 1877. The Dentzel Collection

(bl) A female torero from William H. Meyers' *Journals*, 1841–1844. Courtesy, The Bancroft Library

(br) From *Costumes Civils, Militaires et Religieux du Mexique*, by Claudio Linati, 1828. Prints Division, The New York Public Library, Astor, Lenox and Tilden Foundations

3 (t) *The Funeral of an Angel*

(b) *The Fandango*, Both by Theodore Gentilz (1819–1906). Courtesy, Library of the Daughters of the Republic of Texas at the Alamo, San Antonio, Texas

(c) *A Mexican Market in San Antonio*, by Theodore Gentilz. Courtesy, The San Antonio Museum Association, San Antonio, Texas

4 (tl) Threshing with goats, New Mexico, c. 1897. Photo by P.E. Harroun, Courtesy Museum of New Mexico

(tr) *Joaquin Murietta*, Artist unknown, undated. Courtesy, The Bancroft Library

(b) The Lugo family, Southern California, 1888. Natural History Museum of Los Angeles County

---

Picture Essay 7
The Automobile Culture: 1920–1939
following p. 768

1 Bettman Archive

2 (tl, r) Culver Pictures
(bl) Brown Brothers

3 (tl) Security Pacific National Bank Photograph Collection/Los Angeles Public Library
(tr) Culver Pictures
(bl) Minnesota Historical Society
(br) Library of Congress

4 (tl) Library of Congress
(bl) UPI
(br) Culver Pictures

Picture Essay 8
The Space Race: Commitment to the Future
following p. 864

1 NASA

2 (t) SOVFOTO
(bl) © 1957 by The New York Times Company. Reprinted by permission
(r) NASA

3 (l) NASA
(tr) TASS from SOVFOTO
(br) NASA

4 (l) Ralph Morse, LIFE Magazine © 1962, Time, Inc.
(tr) Wide World
(br) M. Naythons/Gamma-Liaison

In addition, the authors and publisher acknowledge with gratitude permission to reprint, quote form, or adapt the following materials. (The numbers shown below refer to pages of this text.)

509 Hamlin Garland, *A Son of the Middle Border*. P. F. Collier & Son, 1914. **533** Excerpt from *The Price* by Arthur Miller. Copyright © 1968, 1969 by Arthur Miller and Ingeborg M. Miller, Trustee. All rights reserved. Reprinted by permission of Viking Penguin Inc. and International Creative Management, Inc. **559** (Map) Adapted from *Historic City: The Settlement of Chicago*, City of Chicago, Department of Planning. **641** (Map) Adapted from *Historic City: The Settlement of Chicago*, City of Chicago, Department of Planning. **653** From "Chicago" in *Chicago Poems* by Carl Sandburg, copyright 1916 by Holt, Rinehart and Winston, Inc.; renewed 1944 by Carl Sandburg. Reprinted by permission of Harcourt Brace Jovanovich, Inc. **664** Joe Hill, "Workers of the World, Awaken!" cited in *American Folksongs of Protest* by John Greenway. University of Pennsylvania Press, 1953. **673** Upton Sinclair, *The Jungle*, 1906. **709** "The New Day" by Fenton Johnson cited in *The Book of American Negro Poetry*, ed. by James Weldon Johnson. New York: Harcourt, Brace and Company, 1931. **750** Studs Terkel, *Hard Times*. New York: Pantheon Books, 1970, p. 41. **876–77** From "Letter from Birmingham Jail—April 16, 1963" from *Why We Can't Wait* by Martin Luther King, Jr. Copyright © 1963 by Martin Luther King, Jr. Reprinted by permission of Harper & Row, Publishers, Inc. and Joan Daves.

Index

The letter *m* preceding a page number indicates that there is a map on that page.

McGuffey, William Holmes, 553
McGuffey's Readers, 553
McKay, Claude, 709, 730
Mackay, John W., 501
McKinley, William, 738; assassination of, 598, 615, 667; and Cuba, 612–613, 625; in election of 1896, 593, 596; in election of 1900, 598; Hawaii annexation by, 608–609; newspaper criticism of, 615; Open Door policy of, 625–626, 689–690, 777; and Philippines, 620–625; as president, 577, 597–598, 608–626; and Spanish-American War, 613, 616, 617, 619, 626
McKinley Tariff Act of 1890, 579, 588, 606, 607
McManes, James, 563
M'Naghten Rule, 565
McNamara, Robert, 862, 863, 883, 894, 901
McNeill, William H., 817
McPherson, Aimee Semple, 737
Macune, Dr. Charles W., 582
Macy, R. H., 532
Madero, Francisco I., 692
Magazines in early 1900s, 630–631. *See also* Newspapers
Mahan, Alfred Thayer, 610–611
Mail-order companies, 532
Maine battleship, sinking of, 613
Manhattan Project, 799–802, 809
Mann-Elkins Act of 1910, 676
Mansfield, Arabella, 534
Manufacturing. *See* Industrialization; Industry(ies); *entries beginning with* Industrial
Mao Tse-tung, 818, 819, 823
Marches on Washington: of black Americans in 1963, 874; of World War I veterans, 751
Marcuse, Herbert, 895
Marin, John, 653
Marriages during World War II, 793. *See also* Divorce; Families
Marshall, Alfred, 533
Marshall, George C., 789, 810–812, 815, 818, 844
Marshall, Thurgood, 847, 871
Marshall Plan, 811–812, 814, 816, 835
Mass entertainment, 1890–1920, 650–652. *See also* Entertainment
Mass production: of automobiles, 659–660, 662, 718–719 (*see also* Ford, Henry, as automaker); of clothing, 642; in industry, 662–663, 718–721
Mass society: education of, 1870–1900, 553–554; 1890s–1920, 639–645, 648–654
Masters, Edgar Lee, 653
Masterson, William B. (Bat), 505
Matisse, Henri, 902
Maximilian (emperor of Mexico), 605
Mayaguez incident, 936
Meat Inspection Act of 1906, 671
Medical care: in 1800s, 547–548; in 1960s, 882; in 1980, 945
Medicare and Medicaid programs, 882
Mellon, Andrew, 738–739
Mencken, H. L., 561, 724, 729, 736
Meredith, James, 872–873
Mergers in 1920s, 721
Mexican-Americans: in army, 795; as cowboys, 504–505; education of, 898–899; immigration of, 648, 736, 750, 950; nationalism of, 898–899; under New Deal, 763; time periods for: 1800s, 499, 504–505; 1900–1920, 648; 1930s, 763; World War II, 795; 1960s, 898–899; 1970s, 949–950

Mexico, relations with, under Wilson, 692–693
Middle class in 1920s, 722. *See also* Society, American, classes and ranking in
Middle East: in 1950s, 824–825; in 1970s and early 1980s, *m*938, 937–940. *See also* Arab oil embargo; Iran; Israel, wars in
Midway, battle of, 791
Migration: of black Americans, 708–709, *m*794, 948; to West, 494–499; during World War II, 792–795. *See also* Immigration; Population
Military alliance, Western, after World War II, 813
Military-industrial complex in 1960s, 828
Military power: of Soviet Union, 941; of U.S., 611–613, 616–620, 934. *See also specific wars*
Military spending, 835, 862–863, 870, 954–955
Military system. *See* Armed forces; Army; Navy
Miller, Arthur, 533
Millis, Walter, 777
Mills, C. Wright, 854
Minimum wage: under Eisenhower, 841; under Truman, 840
Mining: coal (*see entries beginning with* Coal); gold, *m*503, 500–503; safety laws for, 676
Minorities under New Deal, 762–763. *See also specific entries, for example:* Black Americans; Mexican-Americans
Minor v. *Happersett* (1875) case, 575
Miranda v. *Arizona* (1966) case, 875
Missionaries to civilize non–Anglo-Saxons, 604–605. *See also* Religion
Mitchell, John (attorney general), 908, 909, 916, 918, 919
Mitchell, John (labor leader), 669
Modernity, 1920s roots of, 717–723
Modern Republicanism of Eisenhower, 840–842
Mondale, Walter, 933
Money issued during Civil War, 465–466
Monopolies, 528
Monroe Doctrine, 605–607, 712; Lodge Corollary to, 689; Roosevelt Corollary to, 689, 776
Montgomery, Lucy M., 651
Montgomery bus boycott, 849–850
Moody, Dwight L., 548–549
Moore, Harriet, 653
Moral diplomacy of Woodrow Wilson, 691–692
Morality and manners, 1877–1890, 548–549
Moral Majority, 951
Morgan, Frank, 595
Morgan, J. Pierpont, 527, 658, 668–669, 739; as financier, 524, 526, 531, 588, 661, 676, 720
Morgenthau, Hans, 902
Morrill Land Grant Act of 1862, 554
Morse, Wayne, 885
Morton, Ferdinand (Jelly Roll), 651
Movies, 1900–1920, 450, 650
Moynihan, Daniel Patrick, 907, 952
Muck, Karl, 703
Muckraking era, 630–631
Mugwumps, 549
Muir, John, 915
Muller v. *Oregon* (1908) case, 636
Munn v. *Illinois* (1877) case, 577
Murphey, Charles F., 563
Murray, Phillip, 762
Music: 1860s–1890s, 549; 1900–1920, 650–651; 1920s, 729–730; 1960s, 895
Muskie, Edmund, 916
Mussolini, Benito, 778, 779, 789

■

Nader, Ralph, 934
Nagasaki bombing, 802
Napoleon III (emperor of France), 605
Nasser, Gamal, 824
Nast, Thomas, 549
National Aeronautics and Space Administration (NASA), 855
National American Woman Suffrage Association, 552, 634
National Association of Colored Women, 633–634
National Association for the Advancement of Colored People (NAACP), 648, 850
National Civic Federation, 570
National Conference of Social Work, 633
National Defense Education Act (NDEA) of 1958, 855
National Farmers' Alliance, 580–583
National Farmers' Alliance and Industrial Union, 580–583
National Farm Workers Association (NFWA), 898
National Grange of the Patrons of Husbandry, 509, 581, 582
National Health Insurance plan, 934
Nationalism: black, in 1960s, 896–897; ethnic, in 1960s, 898–899; New, of Theodore Roosevelt, 677–678
National Labor Relations Act of 1935, 759–762, 770, 839
National Labor Union, 536
National Municipal League, 637
National Organization for Women, 900, 947
National Origins Quota Act of 1924, 736
National Recovery Administration (NRA), 754, 762
National Security Act of 1947, 815
National Security Council (NSC), 815
National Union movement, 455
National Woman's party (NWP), 723–724
National Woman Suffrage Association, 471, 575
National Youth Administration (NYA), 756
Native Americans: education of, 490–491; land assigned to, 1800s, 491; under New Deal, 763; reservations of, 1800s, *m*487, 486–488; tribal lands of, *m*487, 484–487; tribal life of, end of, 490–491, 494; wars and battles of, *m*487, 486–490, 493; in West, crushing of, 484–491, 494
Naturalism in literature, 591–592
Natural selection and racial superiority theories, 604–605
Navy: expansion of, in 1880s, 609–611; increased strength of, in early 1900s, 688, 697; in Spanish-American War, 618–620. *See also* Armed forces; Army
Nazis, rise of, 1930s, 778. *See also* Germany, time periods for: 1930s; World War II
Nazi-Soviet alliance of 1939–1941, 780, 787
Neighborhood enclaves, 1900–1920, *m*641
Nelson, Donald, 791–792
Neo-conservatism in 1970s, 952. *See also* Conservatism
Neutrality: threats to, in World War I, 696; as Wilson foreign policy, 694–697
Neutrality acts of 1930s, 779–780; revision of, 782, 783
New Deal of Roosevelt, 752–757; under Eisenhower, 841, 842; end of, 764–765, 768–769; evaluation of, 769–770; under Johnson, 883; impact of, 760–764; minorities under, 762–